Letters of

Louis D. Brandeis

Letters of
Louis D. Brandeis

Volume III (1913–1915): *Progressive and Zionist*

EDITED BY MELVIN I. UROFSKY
AND DAVID W. LEVY

ALBANY, NEW YORK, 1973
STATE UNIVERSITY OF NEW YORK PRESS

First Edition

Published by State University of New York Press,
99 Washington Avenue, Albany, New York 12210
© 1973 State University of New York. All rights reserved.
Printed in the United States of America
Designed by P. J. Conkwright

Library of Congress Cataloging in Publication Data
Brandeis, Louis Dembitz, 1856–1941.

LETTERS OF LOUIS D. BRANDEIS.

CONTENTS:

Vol. I. 1870–1907: Urban reformer.
Vol. II. 1907–1912: People's attorney.
Vol. III. 1913–1915: Progressive and Zionist.

E664.B819A4   1971   347'.7326'34   73–129640
ISBN 0–87395–078–X (v. 1)

For our parents

Contents

Illustrations   xi

Acknowledgements   xiii

Note on Volume III   xv

Chronology, 1913–1915   xvii

Key to Letter Source Citations   xxi

Editorial Markings   xxiii

Letters of Louis D. Brandeis, 1913–1915   3

Index   685

Contents

Illustrations

Acknowledgements

Editor's volume III

War monetary policy

Keynes' measurement lecture

Editorial Matters

Index

Illustrations

Louis D. Brandeis in 1915 FRONTISPIECE
American Jewish Archives

ILLUSTRATION SECTION FOLLOWING PAGE 360

"Citizen Brandeis"
Boston Post

William Gibbs McAdoo
Library of Congress

Thomas Watt Gregory
Library of Congress

James Clark McReynolds
Library of Congress

Norman Hapgood
National Cyclopedia of American Biography

Cyrus Adler
American Jewish Archives

David Philipson
American Jewish Archives

Jacob Henry Schiff
American Jewish Archives

Louis Marshall
Zionist Archives and Library

Judah Leon Magnes
Zionist Archives and Library

Louis Lipsky
Zionist Archives and Library

Horace Meyer Kallen
YIVO Archives

Jacob deHaas
Zionist Archives and Library

Provisional Executive Committee for
General Zionist Affairs
Zionist Archives and Library

Acknowledgements

I N a project such this, debts are cumulative. Each volume not only adds new contributions but builds upon previous ones. To all the people mentioned in the first two volumes, we again acknowledge their help and generosity, and while it does not seem practical to mention each one again by name, we recognize the importance of their assistance in this work.

In the meantime, we have accumulated fresh debts which we are pleased to acknowledge here. In addition to the librarians, archivists, and scholars we have already thanked, we gratefully note the assistance we have received from Mrs. Sylvia Landress and Miss Esther Togman of the Zionist Archives and Library, New York; Miss Louise Calef, the Weizmann Archives, Rehovot, Israel; Mr. J.A. Monahan of the Microtext Division, Boston Public Library; Mrs. Eleanora M. Lynn, Maryland Department, Enoch Pratt Free Library, Baltimore; Miss Margaret Gleason, the Wisconsin State Historical Society, Madison; Mrs. Ann Prochaska, office of the president, Southwestern College, Winfield, Kansas; Mr. Roy P. Basler, chief of the Manuscript Division, and his staff at the Library of Congress; Mr. Martin F. Schmidt, Kentucky Division, Louisville Free Public Library; Ms. Joyce Giaquinta, Librarian, the State Historical Society of Iowa; Mrs. Patricia Harpole, Head and Reference Librarian, the Minnesota Historical Society; Mr. James E. Potter, State Archivist, Nebraska State Historical Society; Mrs. Fannie Zelcer, American Jewish Archives, Cincinnati; Ms. Judith A. Schiff, Chief Research Archivist, Yale University Library, New Haven; Mrs. Marion M. Branon, Texas Room, Houston Public Library; Mr. Henry Kapenstein, Chief of Central Public Services Division, Mr. William Felker, Head of General Information Department, Mr. Herbert Davis, Newspaper Division, and Ms. Marilyn S. Simon, Research Staff, all of the Free Library of Philadelphia. We owe special thanks to Mr. James R. Bentley of the Filson Club in Louisville for his assistance in matters relating to Kentucky. Much of our work has been done in our own university libraries, and we are especially grateful to the staffs of the libraries at the State University of New York at Albany and the University of Oklahoma.

The National Endowment for the Humanities has continued its generous support of this project, and we can only hope that the quality of our work justifies their faith both in the project and in the editors. Part of the work on this volume was begun under an interim grant from the National Historical Publications Commission, and additional assistance has been received from the Research Foundation of the State University of New York and the Faculty Research Committee of the University of Oklahoma. For administering our grants, we wish to thank Gloria Boyd of the University of Oklahoma and Frank Lucarelli and Joann Gallacchi of the Office of Sponsored Funds at Albany.

Mrs. Esther Maidenbaum cheerfully typed much of the manuscript; she was assisted by Laraine Rowe, Faye Moore, and Maryon Kaplan. Thomas L. Owen, Brian McMenamin, Gary C. Black, and Peter Jones assisted us in our research.

We are also grateful to the libraries, individuals, and publishers that have granted us permission to reprint these letters, or that have provided us with photographs.

Again we wish to record our thanks to Norman Mangouni, Director of the State University of New York Press, and the Editorial Board of the Press for their continuing support of the project. Thomas J. Davis, III, has again subjected our manuscript to a careful scrutiny, and the final work has been much improved by his labors. To our wives, Susan Linda Urofsky and Lynne Hunt Levy, our debt at this point goes beyond words.

A Note on Volume III

BETWEEN 1913 and 1915, Louis D. Brandeis was at the height of his career as a reformer, as indeed the progressive impulse itself reached its acme. As these letters show, the career and the impulse were closely related. A confidant of Woodrow Wilson, Brandeis was intimately involved in matters of patronage and policy, and he played a key role in the development of the Wilson administration's banking and antitrust programs. He continued his role as "people's attorney," defending wages and hours laws before the United States Supreme Court and assuming, under heavy criticism, the unique role of counsel for the public in the advanced rate hearings before the Interstate Commerce Commission. As usual, he was frequently consulted by various reform groups, and whenever possible he gave freely both of his time and advice. His views on numerous topics, but especially on the evils of the money trust, appeared regularly in *Harper's*, now edited by his close friend and ally Norman Hapgood, and in other reform journals as well. Despite his heavy involvement in national matters, he still kept a close watch on local Massachusetts affairs. His seven-year campaign against the Morgan-sponsored New England rail monopoly was finally won, and his early criticisms of New Haven finances justified. He helped to fight off efforts to undermine the sliding scale and campaigned for liberal politicians such as Governor David Walsh.

Yet the most important theme in these hectic years was Brandeis's sudden and explosive emergence as leader of the American Zionist movement, an activity that would claim his energies and attention the rest of his life. The letters dealing with Zionism in this volume are especially interesting for two reasons: First, they indicate a movement finding its metier, an organization lifted from obscurity to leadership of the world-wide effort to regain a Jewish homeland in Palestine. Second, they display in a microcosm, as it were, all of the different tendencies we have seen in Brandeis's other reform activities—the insistence on organization and accountability, the need to educate people in the basic tenets of the movement, the struggle against autocratic control, the selection of trusted lieutenants and the delegation of power and authority to them, and, underlying all of this, a commitment to moral uplift.

In December 1915, just a few weeks before the unanticipated announcement that President Wilson had nominated him to the Supreme Court, Brandeis could have looked back on a rich and rewarding sixty years. Yet within a few months he would begin his long and distinguished service on the nation's highest court, while at the same time becoming one of the two most powerful men in the international Zionist movement.

Chronology, 1913–1915

1913   January 28, Wilson discusses LDB's record with Norman Hapgood regarding possible Cabinet appointment
February, battle among Wilson's advisors regarding LDB in Cabinet
February 14, agreement reached with Thomas J. Lamont to sell *Harper's Weekly* to Hapgood
March 1, Wilson announces Cabinet without LDB
March 1, publication of Pujo Committee report
March 4, Wilson inaugurated as President
March 10, LDB makes first trip to Washington to consult with administration
March 20, LDB introduces Nahum Sokolow and makes first important Zionist speech
April 7, Wilson addresses special session of Congress on tariff reform
April 22, Interstate Commerce Commission reopens New Haven hearings, with LDB representing Boston Fruit and Produce Exchange
April 24, Wilson offers LDB chairmanship of United States Commission on Industrial Relations
April 25, LDB withdraws as counsel to Fruit and Produce Exchange and appears before the I.C.C. as private citizen
May 14, LDB addresses Association of National Advertising Managers on price maintenance
May 15, railroads submit new petition to I.C.C. for five per cent horizontal rate increase
May 19, LDB declines chairmanship of U.S. Commission on Industrial Relations
May 26, Supreme Court decides *Bauer* vs. *O'Donnell* (price maintenance case)
June, Norman Hapgood assumes editorial control of *Harper's Weekly*
June 11, LDB meets with Wilson to determine final shape of monetary reform
July 8, Mellen resigns as president of Boston & Maine Railroad
July 9, I.C.C. report castigates New Haven finances
July 17, Mellen resigns as president of New Haven Railroad

July 18, LDB joins associate executive committee of Federation of American Zionists

July 23, LDB declines election as American representative to World Zionist Congress

August 15, LDB invited to serve as counsel to I.C.C. in rate hearings

September 20, Massachusetts Public Service Commission opens hearings on New Haven request for $67,000,000 bond issue

September 25, I.C.C. report blasts New Haven safety record

October 3, Underwood-Simmons Tariff becomes law

October 14, Massachusetts P.S.C. approves New Haven bond request

November 22, LDB publishes first article on "Breaking the Money Trust" in *Harper's*

November 24, Advanced Rate hearings begin before I.C.C.

December 18, New Haven passes dividend

December 23, Federal Reserve Act becomes law

1914 January 3, J.P. Morgan Company resigns from thirty directorships

January 20, Wilson delivers antitrust message

January 30, LDB testifies before House Committee on Interstate Commerce

February 12–13, LDB testifies before I.C.C. on advanced rate request

February 16, LDB testifies before House Judiciary Committee on anti-trust legislation

February 24, Supreme Court upholds ten-hour law in *Hawley* vs. *Walker*

March 26, Savings Bank Insurance law amended to allow state-wide unification of certain procedures

April 16, LDB testifies before U.S. Commission on Industrial Relations

April 30–May 1, LDB makes final argument in advanced rate case

June 26–27, LDB testifies before Senate Committee on Interstate Commerce on antitrust legislation

July 13, final I.C.C. report on New Haven denounces Mellen administration

July 23, Justice Department files antitrust suit against New Haven

July 29, I.C.C. refuses rate increase

August 1, war breaks out in Europe

August 11, New Haven enters consent decree separating Boston & Maine from its control

August 30, LDB accepts chairmanship of Provisional Executive Committee on Zionist Affairs

August 31, LDB invites American Jewish Committee to cooperate in relief work

September 26, Federal Trade Commission bill becomes law

October 14, LDB cancels Zionist meeting in Cincinnati because of Rabbi Philipson's protest

October 15, Clayton Antitrust Act becomes law

October 19, I.C.C. reopens hearings on rate increase

October 25, American Jewish Relief Committee founded to coordinate relief work

November 3, progressives suffer defeats in state and congressional elections

December 16, I.C.C. grants general five percent rate increase

December 16–17, LDB argues Oregon minimum wage case before Supreme Court

December 30, Joseph Eastman appointed to Massachusetts Public Service Commission

1915 January 7, Governor Walsh recommends state support for savings bank life insurance publicity program

January 9, LDB testifies before House Committee on Interstate Commerce on price maintenance

January 12, LDB argues California eight-hour case before Supreme Court

January 22, LDB testifies before New York State Factory Investigating Committee

January 23, LDB testifies second time before U.S. Commission on Industrial Relations

January 28, Wilson vetoes literacy test for immigration restriction

February 22, Wilson nominates George Rublee to Federal Trade Commission

February 23, Supreme Court decides *Bosley* vs. *McLaughlin* confirming California eight-hour law

March 2, savings bank insurance law amended to allow policies of $1,000

March 4, Senate refuses to confirm Rublee nomination

March 6, Wilson names Rublee to F.T.C. on recess basis

March 14, relief ship *U.S.S. Vulcan* sails for Palestine

March 21, Jewish Congress Organizing Committee established

March–June, growing conflict between Provisional Committee and American Jewish Relief Committee

April 6, LDB gives speech on literacy test at New Century Club

April 12, LDB meets with McAdoo on Riggs Bank matter

April 16, Massachusetts legislature approves partial state subsidy for savings bank insurance program

April 21, Sullivan bill fixing gas prices killed in Massachusetts legislature

April 25, LDB talks at Eastern Council of Reform Rabbis on "The Jewish Problem: How to Solve It"

April 30, LDB testifies before Federal Trade Commission on procedures

May, garment industry protocol breaks down

June 24, Zionist convention opens in Boston; LDB begins move to consolidate various Zionist groups

June 30, Judah L. Magnes resigns from Provisional Committee

July 4, LDB gives speech at Faneuil Hall on "True Americanism"

July 12, LDB meets with Cyrus Adler regarding Jewish Congress

July 13–23, meetings of emergency council to save protocol and avert garment industry strike

July 28, LDB declines appointment to Pan-American Financial Conference Commission

August 4, garment industry contract signed

August 16, Leo Frank lynched

August 25, LDB accepts offer of B'nai Brith to mediate in congress dispute

October 3, mediation meeting over congress fails to reach compromise

October, Justice Department initiates antitrust suit against United Shoe Machinery Company

October 17, Julian Mack and Nathan Kaplan hold Zionist meeting in Cincinnati

November, Hapgood begins series of articles on Jews and Zionism in *Harper's*

November 3, David Walsh defeated in Massachusetts election

November 12, meeting with American Jewish Committee over congress again proves futile

November 14, American Jewish Committee begins retreat on congress issue

December 23, Jewish Congress Organizing Committee issues ultimatum on congress

Key to Letter Source Citations in this Volume

Berlin Office Records of the Central Zionist Office, Berlin (Zionistisches Zentralbureau), Central Zionist Archives, Jerusalem, Israel

Brandeis MSS Louis Dembitz Brandeis Papers, University of Louisville Law School Library, Louisville, Kentucky; letters and numbers refer to specific files

Commerce Dept. General Correspondence Files, Office of the Secretary, Department of Commerce Records, Record Group 40, National Archives, Washington, D.C.

Copenhagen Office Records of the Provisional Zionist Office at Copenhagen, Central Zionist Archives, Jerusalem, Israel

deHaas MSS Jacob deHaas Papers, Zionist Archives and Library, New York, New York

EBR Letters provided through the courtesy of Mrs. Elizabeth Brandeis Raushenbush

Filene MSS Edward Albert Filene Papers, Bergengren Memorial Museum Library, World Council of Credit Unions, Inc., Madison, Wisconsin

Frankfurter MSS–HLS Felix Frankfurter Papers, Harvard Law School Library, Cambridge, Massachusetts

Gottheil MSS Richard James Horatio Gottheil Papers, Central Zionist Archives, Jerusalem, Israel

Holmes MSS Oliver Wendell Holmes, Jr. Papers, Harvard Law School Library, Cambridge, Massachusetts

House MSS Edward Mandel House Papers, Sterling Library, Yale University, New Haven, Connecticut

Hurwitz MSS Henry Hurwitz Papers, YIVO Institute for Jewish Research, New York, New York

Kallen MSS Horace Meyer Kallen Papers, American Jewish Archives, Hebrew Union College—Jewish Institute of Religion, Cincinnati, Ohio

Kent MSS William Kent Papers, Sterling Library, Yale University, New Haven, Connecticut

LaFollette MSS Robert Marion LaFollette Papers, Manuscript Division, Library of Congress, Washington, D.C.

McAdoo MSS William Gibbs McAdoo Papers, Manuscript Division, Library of Congress, Washington, D.C.

McCarthy MSS   Charles McCarthy Papers, The State Historical Society of Wisconsin, Madison, Wisconsin

McReynolds MSS   James Clark McReynolds Papers, University of Virginia Library, Charlottesville, Virginia

Magnes MSS   Judah Leon Magnes Papers, Central Archives for the History of the Jewish People, Hebrew University Library, Jerusalem, Israel

Marshall MSS   Louis Marshall Papers, American Jewish Archives, Hebrew Union College—Jewish Institute of Religion, Cincinnati, Ohio

Mason, *Brandeis*   Alpheus Thomas Mason, *Brandeis: A Free Man's Life* (New York: Viking, 1946)

Middleton MSS   George Middleton Papers, Manuscript Division, Library of Congress, Washington, D.C.

Morgenthau MSS   Henry Morgenthau, Sr. Papers, Manuscript Division, Library of Congress, Washington, D.C.

Palestine Office   Records of the Palestina Amt at Jaffa, Central Zionist Archives, Jerusalem, Israel

G. Pinchot MSS   Gifford Pinchot Papers, Manuscript Division, Library of Congress, Washington, D.C.

Pound MSS   Roscoe Pound Papers, Harvard Law School Library, Cambridge, Massachusetts

Richards MSS   Bernard Gerson Richards Papers, Jewish Information Bureau, New York, New York

R. Szold MSS   Robert Szold Papers, Zionist Archives and Library, New York, New York

Wald MSS   Lillian D. Wald Papers, Special Collections, Columbia University Library, New York, New York

Wehle MSS   Louis Brandeis Wehle Papers, Franklin D. Roosevelt Library, Hyde Park, New York

Weizmann MSS   Chaim Weizmann Papers, Library of the Weizmann Institute, Rehovot, Israel

Wilson MSS   Woodrow Wilson Papers, Manuscript Division, Library of Congress, Washington, D.C.

EDITORIAL MARKINGS

[ ] Words, letters, or punctuation added by the
      editors. When brackets appear in the editorial
      heading, except for manuscript source, it
      signifies that the information enclosed
      is not certain, but merely the best estimate
      we can make.

[*] Indecipherable or illegible word; each asterisk
      indicates one word.

Letters of

Louis D. Brandeis

To Grenville Stanley MacFarland

January 1, 1913 Boston, Mass. [Brandeis Mss, NMF 1-M-2]

MY DEAR MR. MACFARLAND: [1] I have read with great satisfaction Mr. Hearst's [2] editorial "The Solution of the Problem of Oppressive Public Service Monopoly." [3] It is admirable and unanswerable. I should amend it only in one particular. Mr. Hearst says: "It is a case of 'Your money or your life'. Recent wrecks have proved that it is a case of 'Your money *and* your life.' "

Second: I have considered the draft of your interesting bill, and want to talk to you about it this morning.[4]

Third: I am enclosing the article by Carl Vrooman on "New England's Railroad Monopoly", which the American may care to print in connection with the discussion of your bill.[5]

Mr. Vrooman wrote the best book in the English language on government ownership of railroads.[6] He came to Boston recently to study our situation.   Cordially yours,

If the article is issued by the American, will you kindly send me twenty copies of it?

1. People identified in previous volumes are not again identified in this volume.

2. William Randolph Hearst (1863–1951) was the flamboyant newspaper editor and publisher who built up a large chain of papers by exploiting the public's insatiable desire for sensationalism. At one time he had political ambitions, and he was actually elected to Congress from a New York City district in 1902 and again in 1904; his bids for the mayoralty and the governorship were unsuccessful because of his involvement in voting scandals. The best biography is W. A. Swanberg, *Citizen Hearst* (New York, 1961).

3. The *Boston American* editorial was run on the front page of the 30 December 1912 issue and signed by Hearst himself. Claiming that the real culprit was not Charles S. Mellen, but J. P. Morgan, Hearst compared the New Haven to a highwayman standing at the crossroads and demanding the traveller's money or his life. The solution, he suggested, was the dissolution of the New Haven empire and closer governmental control of such natural monopolies as the railroads.

4. There is no copy of a bill from MacFarland in this file.

5. There is no article written by Vrooman in the *Boston American* during the next few weeks.

6. Carl S. Vrooman, *American Railway Problems in the Light of European Experience; or Government Regulation vs. Governmental Operation of Railways* (London and New York, 1910).

To Norman Hapgood

January 2, 1913 Boston, Mass. [Brandeis Mss, NMF 52-1]

MY DEAR NORMAN: I have yours of the 31st about Lamont.[1] It will be interesting to know what he proposes.

As I wrote you yesterday, I expect to leave for Chicago tomorrow noon.   Cordially yours,

P.S. Charles McCarthy was in Monday, and I asked him about the missing Anti-trust plank.[2] He said he had gotten no further in tracing it than O. K. Davis.[3] He also said that he had [George] Perkins in a position where through the "recall" in the Committee he could suppress him when necessary.

What you say about Morganthau [sic] is "important if true." [4]

1. Hapgood had met with Thomas Lamont who, according to Hapgood, had practically asked him to make an offer for *Harper's Monthly*. Although Hapgood had said "no," he admitted to LDB that perhaps something might develop out of the meeting.

2. See LDB to Frederick W. Mackenzie, 14 December 1912, n. 2.

3. Oscar King Davis (1866–1932), a leading progressive journalist, served as secretary of the Progressive Party, and had been involved in the plank mix-up. See his autobiography, *Released for Publication* (Boston, 1925).

4. At his meeting with Hapgood, Lamont had reported rumors that Henry Morgenthau would be head of either the Interior or the Treasury Departments. Actually, Wilson named Morgenthau ambassador to Turkey.

To John Foster Carr

January 3, 1913 Boston Mass. [Brandeis Mss, NMF 56-2]

DEAR SIR: [1] I am in receipt of yours of the 27th of the Guide to the United States for the Jewish Immigrant.[2]

I appreciate the important work which you are doing. I am so much engaged at present that it will be impossible now for me to aid in your work, but I hope at some later day to be able to arrange for the conference which you suggest.

With best wishes,   Yours very truly,

1. John Foster Carr (1869–1940) wrote and lectured extensively on the education and Americanization of immigrants.

2. Carr had enclosed a copy of his pamphlet, and asked LDB for an interview so that he might enlist his support in his work with immigrant groups.

To William C. Brown

January 20, 1913 Boston, Mass. [Brandeis Mss, NMF 1-M-2]

MY DEAR MR. BROWN: Upon my return to the City today I find your letter of the 6th concerning a purported letter of S. F. Miller to me dated December 11th.[1]

The so-called letter of S. F. Miller to me bears no signature in manuscript. It looks like one of many multigraph copies, and it seems as if some heading had been cut off from the sheet on which it comes to me. The letter was enclosed in the envelope which I send you herewith, which you will note is post-marked Chicago, December 28, 4 P.M., 1912, and is addressed to me, "Mr. Lewis D. Brandies, Attorney[,] Boston, Mass." There is an error both in the spelling of the first and the last name.

I, of course, paid no attention to this communication. I am extremely sorry that you have been subjected to this annoyance, and that my name has been used in this connection.

Yours very truly,

1. The Miller letter accused Brown and Charles E. Schaff (1856–1945), president of the Missouri, Kansas & Texas Railway Company, with dishonesty in purchasing. Brown offered to underwrite the expenses of an expert committee to go through the records of the New York Central purchasing office in order to disprove Miller's charges.

2. LDB received copies of the Miller letter from several sources, and similar letters were sent on this date to Frank Trumbull (1859–1920), chairman of the board of the Chesapeake & Ohio Railroad, and to Albert Hall Harris (1861–1931), vice-president of the New York Central and head of its legal department.

To Henry Carter Adams

January 21, 1913 Boston, Mass. [Brandeis Mss, NMF 1-M-2]

MY DEAR MR. ADAMS: I thank you for sending me your library copy of the "Digest of Senate Committee Hearings on Regulation of Railway Rates, 1905," and for the opportunity of examining your Appendix on the Prussian Railway Tariffs.[1] I am returning the volume to you by mail.

I wish some interested Congressman would have ordered another edition of these papers.

I have also received the paper from Mr. Lewis.[2]

The suggestions which you make are very interesting. An important advance in retail distribution is urgent. I don't know, however, that I could wholly assent to your suggestion, if it is to be taken literally, that our transportation facilities "are adjusted to the needs of the wholesale business." All industry and wholesale business demands regularity in deliveries, and the prevailing irregularities in deliveries seems to me almost intolerable. It certainly is not consistent with economic production, and seems almost absurd. Had we even a fair approach to regularity of deliveries, our railroads would find they had a huge surplus of freight cars, and the relief to shippers as well as railroads would be very great.   Yours very truly,

1. A conference report accompanying HR 12987, 59th Cong., 1st sess. (Washington, 1906).

2. James H. Lewis was a clerk in the Interstate Commerce Commission.

To Julius Henry Cohen

January 21, 1913 Boston, Mass. [Brandeis Mss, NMF 35-2]

MY DEAR MR. COHEN: Upon my return from the West I find your leaflet "Protocol of Peace in the Dress and Waist Industry."

I congratulate you upon the great public service that you have performed in this connection.

It must be a great satisfaction to all of us to find that work we did in 1910 is commending itself to others.[1]

Very cordially,

1. See LDB to Frederick W. Mackenzie, 22 January 1913.

To Ernest Parlin Jose

January 21, 1913 Boston, Mass. [Brandeis Mss, NMF 51-7]

MY DEAR MR. JOSE: Upon my return to the City I find your letter of the 17th in regard to water power charters in Vermont.

It seems to me clear that no absolute grants of water rights should be made by any state; that the state should grant the right or license to use; that the license should be subject to state regulation; and should pay a compensation; that the compensation should be in the form of annual rental, and that the rental should be subject to revision from time to time.

There has been so wide-spread an education of the public on this subject that it seems to me it should be possible to introduce this advanced policy in Vermont.

The general subject of water power grants has, as you know, been under very active consideration by the Secretary of the Interior recently, and through his initiative a conference upon the subject was held by State and Federal authorities and water users last November.[2]

I am enclosing you a clipping from the New York Evening Post of November 25, 1912, on this subject, which kindly return after perusal. I also enclose a memorandum of the National Conservation Association's outlines of public policy by Philip P. Wells.[3]

Mr. Wells, who is the legal adviser of the Department on this subject, was for many years associated with Mr. Gifford Pinchot. He has, no doubt, in conjunction with Mr. Pinchot and other conservationists, worked out the best plan for state, as well as federal action. I feel sure that he will be glad to send you any additional conclusions reached by him and his associates; and also give you more specific advice in reference to your local problem. I suggest, therefore, that you write to him, 1841 Lamont Street, N.W., Washington.   Yours very truly,

1. Ernest Parlin Jose (1869–1934) was a member of the Vermont legislature. He was opposing attempts by power companies to exploit the right of eminent domain and claimed that some of the proposed charters would deprive the citizens of Vermont of water rights for decades.

2. On November 18 and 19, 1912 a conference involving representatives of the Interior Department, the State of California, power companies, and other interested groups reached agreement on the need for federal regulation and on the general outlines of that regulation. The proposed regulation was much stricter than a plan the power companies had turned down five years earlier, in the belief that they could defeat regulatory legislation.

3. Wells had drafted a model charter which strictly protected the rights of the people as well as the natural resources in areas surrounding water-power sites. The model allowed the public, acting through the state government, to revoke the charter and take over the power plant should the private company fail to live up to its obligations.

To Gifford Pinchot

January 21, 1913 Boston, Mass. [G. Pinchot Mss]

MY DEAR GIFFORD: Upon my return from the West I find your letter of the 2nd about the Unity Life Insurance Company.[1]

The plan has in it some hopeful features, as well as elements of unsoundness. I think, therefore, that it is fortunate that you sternly rejected the proposals; but I am inclined to think that the situation is not such as to call for the issuing of a general warning note.

I think we shall get no satisfactory solution of life insurance except through such quasi-public institutions as our savings bank life insurance or full state insurance.

If you have not heard from Mr. Charles R. Crane as to arranging a meeting with Governor [Woodrow] Wilson, I think you had better write him on the subject.[2]

Very cordially yours,

1. Pinchot had written: "A gentleman blew into the office the other day with the moderate and wholly reasonable proposition that I should become President of the Unity Life Insurance Company, basing his request on the general proposition that it was not important whether I knew anything about life insurance and investments or not." Pinchot declined, but he wanted LDB's advice on whether the insurance scheme made any sense, or whether he should warn his friends against getting involved in it.

2. See next letter.

To William Kent

January 22, 1913 Boston, Mass. [Kent Mss]

MY DEAR KENT: Upon my return from the West I find yours of the 4th.[1]

I was with [Charles] Crane in Chicago, and I know that he is planning to arrange for you and Gifford to see Governor Wilson.

Crane expects to be able to arrange to come East next week.

I am tied up here at present, but hope to get to Washington before long and have a talk with you and [Walter L.] Fisher.

Most cordially yours,

P.S. I note what you say about the condition of the Atlantic Coast main Line. It is, as you say, Morganatic.[2]

1. Kent was upset over pending public land proposals in Congress as well as over the rumor that Albert Sidney Burleson (1863–1937), a reputed anticonservation congressman, would get the secretaryship of the Interior Department. Burleson, who had represented Texas since 1899, became Wilson's Postmaster-General and chief dispenser of patronage.

2. Kent wrote: "I wish that some one would lock Pierpont Morgan up for homicides already committed on his Southern roads or would put him under bonds as against homicides that he contemplates. One of my boys pulled out fourteen spikes with his fingers on a two mile stretch on the Atlantic Coast main line, in North Carolina. You are going after the New Haven people right."

To Frederick William Mackenzie

January 22, 1913 Boston, Mass. [Brandeis Mss, NMF 55-1]

MY DEAR MR. MACKENZIE: In the issue of December 2, 1911 LaFollette's discussed the report of the Joint Board of Sanitary Control of the Cloak, Suit and Skirt Industry.[1]

You have doubtless seen since then the report of the United States Bureau of Labor on the preferential union shop (January 1912). It is now nearly 2 ½ years since we established the protocol in the cloak, suit and skirt industry, and it has worked so well that it has recently been adopted as the basis of settlement in the shirt waist industry, which will probably result in bringing 20,000 or 30,000 more workers under the operation of the preferential union shop.

If you care to have the matter discussed fully in LaFollette's, I think it would be well to ask Dr. Henry Moscowitz [sic] 216 Madison Street, New York City, (who wrote the article in the January 1912 "Life & Labor") to write an article for you. Dr. Moscowitz had an important part in our original work of establishing the preferential union shop, and is one of the most competent of the social workers in New York.[2]

Very truly yours,

1. Belle Case LaFollette and Caroline L. Hunt, "An Epoch-Making Report," *LaFollette's Magazine* 3 (2 December 1911): 10–11.

2. Moskowitz did contribute an article to the magazine, "An Experiment in Industrial Control," *LaFollette's Magazine* 5 (19 April 1913): 5, 13–14.

To William J. O'Donnell

January 22, 1913 Boston, Mass. [Brandeis Mss, NMF 36-1]

MY DEAR SIR: [1] Prolonged absence from the city has delayed reply to your very courteous letter of the 8th.

I appreciate most highly the invitation to become the Vice-President of your Society, but feel compelled to decline as the work which I have on hand is such that I could not give to the Society the attention which it deserves, and I am loath to accept any position the duties of which I know in advance I should not be able to perform.

With thanks for your courtesy,

Yours very truly,

1. William J. O'Donnell was secretary of the American Society of Jurisprudence. He had invited LDB to be one of forty-eight vice-presidents, each one representing a state.

To Abraham Jacob Portenar

January 22, 1913 Boston, Mass. [Brandeis Mss, NMF 8-3]

MY DEAR MR. PORTENAR: [1] Frequent absences from the City and pressure of urgent work prevented my taking up, until now, your "Problems of Organized Labor." [2]

Your book is admirable, and I scarcely know whether to praise most its judicial temper, its breadth of view, the close reasoning, or the skill with which you have presented the subject. The Typographical Union may well feel some pride in the fact that it counts the author among its members.

You are entirely right in urging co-operation as the great plain on which the advance is to be made.

I hope some day to have the pleasure of meeting you and discussing some phases of the labor problems which are hardly touched upon in your book, including—

First: The question of the closed shop: It seems to me that neither the closed shop nor the open shop is tenable, and unless something better can be devised, we shall have to proceed upon the lines of the preferential union shop adopted by the cloak and suit makers, and more recently by the shirtwaist makers.

Second: You do not discuss specifically the question of efficiency: Great improvement in the condition of the working man can come only through lessening the cost of production and of distribution. The Union has been led partly by unfortunate experiences in the past and partly because of unsound economic views from doing as much as it should in the development of efficiency, fearing that the working man would not obtain his fair share of the increased profit. To my mind the unionist should join most heartily in advancing efficiency, and fight relentlessly for the greater share of the fruits of increased efficiency.

Third: The disciplining of members: The Union should be controlled largely by the rule of noblesse oblige. The ultimate success of unionism rests not alone upon its being an effective fighting body, but also that the issues raised should have full public support. Nothing would tend so effectively to give the unions public support as to have the unions honestly undertake to discipline their own members who are guilty of conduct unbecoming a union man, or improper or illegal acts like those of violence.

The above are only some of the questions I want to talk over with you when we meet.[3]   Very cordially yours,

1. Abraham Jacob Portenar (1864–19[?]) was a labor organizer and writer who lived in Brooklyn; he would later serve as acting director of the New York State Division of Industrial Relations.

2. *Organized Labor: Its Problems and How to Meet Them* (New York 1912).

3. Portenar asked LDB if the Macmillan Company, his publisher, could quote parts of this letter when advertising the book, and on 27 January LDB granted this permission.

To William Harrison Spring Stevens

January 22, 1913 Boston, Mass. [Brandeis Mss, NMF 53-1]

MY DEAR MR. STEVENS: [1] Prolonged absence from the City has delayed reply to your letter of the 11th.

You have performed a distinct public service in making available, through your "Industrial Combinations and Trusts", the most important material bearing upon the trust problem in America. These documents, with your excellent introductory notes, will prove a great aid to student, teacher and legislator; and the book should find many readers, also, among enlightened business men who are seeking to understand this urgent question.

Yours very truly,

1. William Harrison Spring Stevens (1885–19[?]) was on the faculty of Columbia University. He had recently published a volume of original documents entitled *Industrial Combinations and Trusts* (New York, 1913) which included parts of LDB's testimony before the Senate Interstate Commerce Committee. Stevens wanted LDB's opinion of the book and, if the opinion were favorable, permission to have his publishers quote it.

To Clinton Rogers Woodruff

January 22, 1913 Boston, Mass. [Brandeis Mss, NMF 21-3]

DEAR MR. WOODRUFF: Upon my return to the city I find yours of the 9th.

The calls upon me for contributions in connection with public work in which I am interested,—particularly those in which appeals can be made to only a few persons, are such that I feel unable to yield to your suggestion that I increase my contribution to the National Municipal League by becoming a contributing member.   Yours very truly,

To George H. Albee

January 23, 1913 Boston, Mass. [Brandeis Mss, NMF 1-M-2]

DEAR MR. ALBEE: I have yours of the 22nd relating to rates on boots and shoes between Boston, Brockton, Mass. and Augusta, Me. to New York City in 1907, 1909 and at the present time, and saying that the rates were the same then as now, you giving the rates December 11th as 25¢ from Boston and Brockton, and 30¢ from Augusta. Are you sure of this?

I was told by an Augusta manufacturer early in 1908 that the rate from Augusta, Maine, to New York City was 20¢ per 100#. That fact was published in the Anti-merger League circulars at that time and was, so far as I recollect, never denied.[1]

I assume that the Augusta rate was rail and water. Will you kindly look further into this and let me hear from you?

I was also told as to scrap leather rates from Boston to New

York, that they were 15¢ prior to April, 1907,—the time of the alleged agreement between Mellen and Morse [2]—that they were then raised to 20¢.

Please let me know whether this is correct and what they now are.[3]   Yours very truly,

1. See LDB to George L. Barnes, 10 April 1908.
2. See LDB to George L. Barnes, 15 April 1908, and to Theodore Roosevelt, 21 April 1908.
3. Albee replied on 1 February confirming LDB's information that the boot and shoe rate from Augusta had been 30¢ since January 1909; however, the scrap leather rate had been 15¢ per hundredweight since August 1902, and that rate was still in effect.

To Joseph Henry Beale

January 23, 1913 Boston, Mass. [Brandeis Mss, NMF 56-3]

MY DEAR BEALE: [1] I am greatly obliged to you for yours of the 22nd.[2]

The plan for your course for graduate students is fine. I hope that you will think it proper to make known through the Law Review promptly what you contemplate. Students will be making their plans soon, and faculties of other schools will be making their plans, and it is important that Harvard should be first in the field.[3]   Very cordially yours,

1. Joseph Henry Beale (1861–1943), former dean of the University of Chicago Law School, was Royall Professor of Law at the Harvard Law School. Among his many legal interests and writings was some work done on railroad legislation.
2. In a conversation with Roscoe Pound, LDB had suggested that the Law School should offer a course in criminal procedure and reform as part of its fourth-year graduate program. Beale was preparing to offer this course in the fall, and he wrote to inform LDB about some of the details as well as about some problems involving a library.
3. See LDB to Felix Frankfurter, 24 January 1913.

To Charles A. Lutz

January 23, 1913 Boston, Mass. [Brandeis Mss, NMF 1-M-2]

DEAR MR. LUTZ: [1] I am endeavoring to ascertain whether or not the New York, New Haven or [and] Hartford Railroad Company has during each of the five years ending June 30, 1912, made proper charges for depreciation of equipment, and with this in view I have endeavored from data available to determine the cost or value of the equipment on hand at the end of each year and the amounts charged either to Profit and Loss, Replacement of Equipment, Depreciation of Equipment, or Maintenance of Equipment.

The figures of book value June 30, 1907, I have assumed to be a correct statement of the value of the equipment at that time, since the New Haven had made about that date, through Vice President Stevens,[2] a careful appraisal of its equipment and adjusted the book value to the actual value then found.

The value of the equipment at the close of each year appears to be as follows (deducting in each instance amounts reserved for account "Reserve for Accrued Depreciation"):

1908	$47,284,637
1909	52,052,734
1910	54,089,359
1911	57,758,785
1912	62,507,140

The amount charged off either through Profit and Loss, Replacement of Equipment, or Depreciation during each of the years appears to be as follows:

1908	$2,576,679
1909	729,898
1910	817,948
1911	1,076,739
1912	1,416,248

The percentage of depreciation including replacement of profit and loss charges during each year figured on the value of the equipment at the end of the year appears to be as follows:

1908	5.575%
1909	1.402
1910	1.512
1911	1.769
1912	2.265

It is of course clear that these depreciation percentages (1908—5.575, 1909, 1.402, 1910—1.512, 1911—1.769, and 1912—2.265) would be wholly inadequate to cover the depreciation of equipment. I have examined similar charges on the Pennsylvania and the Louisville & Nashville, and find them to be as follows:

	1908	1909	1910	1911	1912
Pa	7.648	8.8407	5.664	3.874	3.967
L. & N.	5.348	4.691	16.881	6.901	6.925

For the purpose of determining the complete charges for depreciation and renewals on the New Haven I have consolidated the specific maintenance of Equipment and Depreciation charges and the Profit and Loss charges as follows:

1908	$8,492,432
1909	5,906,356
1910	6,461,772
1911	7,193,424
1912	8,046,991

and it thus appears that the percentage of these consolidated Maintenance, Depreciation, Replacement and Profit and Loss charges for each of these years is as follows:

1908	18.376
1909	11.35
1910	11.9
1911	12.4
1912	12.8

It would seem that the combined charges of maintenance given by the New Haven would be wholly inadequate to cover the equipment, that is, to keep it in repair and to provide for depreciation including obsolescence, and with that in view I have made a similar calculation as to the combined Maintenance of Equipment and Depreciation charges of the Pennsylvania and the Louisville and Nashville for several years, with the following result:

	1906	1909	1910	1911	1912
Pa	37.080	37.966	24.560	22.956	No report
L. & N.	25.051	20.517	43.866	36.051	37.277

I have no data which would enable me to determine whether the cost or book value on June 30, 1907, of the Pennsylvania and the Louisville & Nashville were correct, but if they are approximately correct, there is obviously an extraordinary disparity between the percentage of Maintenance of Equipment and Depreciation charges of the Pennsylvania and the Louisville & Nashville as compared with the New Haven. It is of course possible that the allowances of these roads are very much greater than is proper.

I should be greatly obliged if you would examine the above calculations and let me know whether the figures given appear to you to be correct, and also let me have as far as possible any explanation of this disparity in the charges between the New Haven and the other companies.

I should also be glad if you would let me know how the New Haven's Maintenance and Depreciation charges compare with those of other companies.

I should also be glad to have you let me have your opinion (as roads are generally operated) whether book value of the equipment assuming it to be also the actual, is a fair or the best basis on which to figure the proper maintenance or depreciation charges, or whether you think other data, like the number of miles run, should be taken into consideration.[3]   Very truly yours,

1. Charles A. Lutz was chief examiner of accounts for the Interstate Commerce Commission.

2. John Frank Stevens (1853–1943), an experienced consulting engineer, had served as vice-president in charge of operations for the New Haven from 1907 to 1909. He then became president of the Pacific & Eastern Railroad.

3. Lutz did not reply until 1 March and only then after a prodding telegram from LDB. He declared that it was impossible to answer LDB's questions in a specific manner, since there was a great deal of confusion regarding depreciation, and rates varied according to carrier.

To John Appleton Stewart

January 23, 1913 Boston, Mass. [Brandeis Mss, NMF 36-1]

MY DEAR MR. STEWART: [1] Upon my return to the city I find your courteous letter of the 15th inviting me to become a member of your National Committee.

I am, as you assume, heartily in sympathy with the general purposes of the organization, and if becoming a member of the committee will be treated merely as testifying to that sympathy, as you indicate, I shall be glad to accept, but my time is so fully occupied at present that I should not dare to assume additional obligations.

With best wishes,   Very truly yours,

1. John Appleton Stewart (1865–1928), a New York manufacturer, was chairman of the executive committee for the Celebration of the One Hundredth Anniversary of Peace Among English Speaking Peoples.

To Walker Whiting Vick

January 23, 1913 Boston, Mass. [Brandeis Mss, NMF 52-2]

MY DEAR SIR: [1] Upon my return to the city I find your letter of the 18th.

I desire through you to thank Mr. Thomas Nelson Page [2] for the honor of the appointment as a member of the Committee on Reception.[3]

Yours very truly,

1. Walker Whiting Vick (1878–1926), after careers in mining and journalism, had joined Woodrow Wilson's campaign as manager of the New York headquarters. In 1913 he was secretary of the Inaugural Committee, and Wilson later rewarded him with the post of customs receiver during the occupation of Santo Domingo.
2. Thomas Nelson Page (1853–1922) wrote a number of popular novels about the Old South in general and Virginia in particular. In order to appease Virginia's two senators, Wilson named him ambassador to Italy. At Wilson's inauguration he served as chairman of the Committee on Reception. See Theodore L. Gross, *Thomas Nelson Page* (New York, 1967).
3. Brandeis decided not to attend the inauguration, although, as he wrote to a friend: "I feel very lonesome in our little provincial town and long to see my good friends in the Capital."

To Daniel Willard

January 23, 1913 Boston, Mass. [Brandeis Mss, NMF 1-M-2]

MY DEAR MR. WILLARD: When I saw you in New York on December 17th I expected to be in New York soon, and promised to let you know so that we might continue our discussion.[1] Lest you might suppose that I had forgotten my promise, I write to say that I have been in the West most of the time since, and have not spent any day in New York except a Sunday with my family.

The date of my next trip to New York has not yet been fixed, but I will endeavor to let you know when I am to be there; and of course shall be glad to see you here if you chance to be in Boston.   Yours very truly,

1. Probably LDB wanted to discuss railroad efficiency with Willard, who had been the most responsive of all railroad presidents to LDB's scientific management appeals. See LDB to Felix Frankfurter, 27 February 1911, n.2.

To Charles Richard Crane

January 24, 1913 Boston, Mass. [Brandeis Mss, NMF 52-2]

MY DEAR CHARLES: Since writing you this morning I have a letter from Gifford Pinchot, in which he says: —

"Charley Crane said he was going to get me a chance to talk with Governor Wilson. I wired him about it some time ago, but have heard nothing further. Of course, I am very keen to see the Governor, but I don't want to write to him direct."
I suppose you are bearing Gifford in mind.[1]

Yours very truly,

1. See LDB to William Kent, 22 January 1913.

To Felix Frankfurter

January 24, 1913 Boston, Mass. [Brandeis Mss, NMF 56-3]

MY DEAR FRANKFURTER: You have probably heard of the progressive law work which the Harvard Law School is undertaking, and in which Professor Pound is particularly interested.[1]

Professor Pound thinks there is an unusual opportunity to obtain what is perhaps the best criminal law library in the world, for about $5,000, and I want to help him raise that amount.

Professor Beale's letter to me of the 22nd, copy of which is enclosed, will give you some idea of what the library is. I, of course, have no personal opinion, but accept without hesitation Prof. Pound's and Prof. Beale's judgment, as well as their judgment that the possession of this library is important for the advanced work which they are undertaking.

It occurred to me that you might know of some New York (or other) lawyers, who would be glad to join in making this gift.[2]

I have just returned from the West where I have been for some weeks, and have not had an opportunity of seeing Walter E. Meyers [sic] [3] as I have not been in New York. I wrote him, however, on my return saying that I should be very glad to see him here. Of course I intend to see him when I am next in New York, but by reason of my prolonged absence from Boston, I am prevented from going just now.   Most cordially,

1. See LDB to Joseph Henry Beale, 23 January 1913.

2. On 27 January Frankfurter wrote back: "I have gladly written to several New York lawyers of the opportunity to ease their swollen fortunes. I should think enough men could be gotten to welcome the chance of enabling the School to do this kind of work. Judge Mack is in touch with people who want to spend some of their money wisely, and I sent him a copy of the correspondence. I hope you don't mind."

3. Possibly Walter E. Meyer (1882–1957), a New York attorney who later became a director of the St. Louis & Southwestern Railroad.

To Felix Frankfurter

January 28, 1913 Boston, Mass. [Frankfurter Mss—HLS]

MY DEAR FRANKFURTER: I did not have an opportunity until yesterday to examine the memorandum sent with yours of December 17th bearing upon the present unrest.[1]

I entirely agree with the memorandum in so far as it sets forth the difficulties which now confront the legislator, and the need of affording aid. I have, however, grave doubt whether the method suggested will be the most effective aid that could be afforded those seeking social advance.

My thought is this: —

To secure social advance we must regard the field of sociology and social legislation as a field for discovery and invention. Research is necessary as in the field of science and invention, as in the field of mechanical and other arts. In the field of mechanical invention, as in other fields of human enterprise, the successes are few and the failures are many. And the successes are rarely one man's work, or the work of a number of men consciously co-operating. The successes come very often by one man building upon another's apparent failure.

I should have little faith, therefore, in a small group of men evolving a social system or important elements of such a system. We must rely upon all America (and the rest of the world) for our social inventions and discoveries; and the value of the inventions and alleged discoveries can best be tested by current public discussion.

On the other hand, it seems to me that a small group of able, disinterested, well-equipped men, who could give their time to criticism and discussion of legislative proposals, discouraging those which appear to be unsound, and aiding those that appear to be sound, would be of great assistance in the forward movement.

I have not annotated the copy of the memorandum which you sent me as I have only the above suggestions to make. Shall I return the memorandum to the secretary?

Most cordially,

1. Unfortunately, there is no copy of this memorandum, written by Eustace Percy (see LDB to M. Hely-Hutchinson, 30 October 1914), in either the Brandeis Mss or the Frankfurter Mss. However, several newspaper clippings in the Brandeis Mss near a copy of this correspondence indicate that the subject involved the application of efficiency techniques to legislative drafting. The Efficiency Society of New York had announced plans to study the possibility of setting social goals and then designing the best ways of achieving those aims through efficient government.

To Norman Hapgood

January 28, 1913 Boston, Mass. [Brandeis Mss, NMF 52-1]

MY DEAR NORMAN: I received your two telegrams of yesterday and this morning your letter.[1]

We must, of course, let Charles [Crane] proceed in getting together the subscriptions in such way as he deems best, but it is important that the matter should be proceeded with as vigorously as possible.

I do not want to leave any stone unturned; and if and whenever it seems advisable for me to go to New York or to Washington, I hope to be able to arrange to do so. For the present,. however, I should not expect to go to Washington except on this matter.

When I last talked with Charles he seemed to have fair hope of [William] Kent's coming in, but not much of [Isaac Wayne] MacVeagh's.

My belief as to Charles' going to Richmond was based upon a communication I had from Rogers,[2] who then expected to meet Charles in New York on next Friday upon the former's return from Richmond. Do not fail to let me know the moment you think I can be of any service. I have an engagement here for Sunday evening which I should not like to break. My other engagements are more malleable, and I could arrange for an absence which would bring me back Sunday, or let me leave Sunday midnight.   Yours,

1. Although it was not until May 1913 that the arrangements were concluded, Hapgood by this time was definitely moving towards acquiring *Harper's Magazine*. A luncheon with Lamont in February brought agreement on a price of $100,000, which Charles R. Crane provided. Hapgood and LDB exchanged a number of letters and telegrams in the intervening weeks regarding details of the purchase and means to secure the financial backing.

2. Walter Stowell Rogers (1877–1965) was Charles Crane's assistant and later was publisher of the *Washington Herald*. Rogers was heavily involved in the financial negotiations for the purchase of *Harper's* and assisted Hapgood on questions involving financial management.

To David Otis Ives

January 28, 1913 Boston, Mass. [Brandeis Mss, NMF 1-M-2]

MY DEAR MR. IVES: As promised in our talk over the telephone last evening,—

First: I am sending you herewith Eastman's three reports on the interlocking directorates of the New Haven and supply companies, together with a copy of his letter to me of the 25th.[1]

It seems to me that the I.C.C. could do no more important work than to develop fully the extent to which railroad purchases are being controlled by insiders. You will recall the remark of Chairman Prouty during Codman's[2] testimony as to the impropriety of railroad directors dealing with concerns in which they are interested.

Second: I enclose herewith copy of my letter to Mr. Lutz of January 23rd., concerning the equipment charges of the New Haven.

It seems to me that the I.C.C. ought at once to investigate this matter thoroughly. If, as would appear, the New Haven has made grossly inadequate depreciation charges, it amounts to a falsification of the accounts, and the public, for obvious reasons, should know.

The facts set forth in my letter to Lutz indicate the necessity of the I.C.C. adopting some general rules covering depreciation of equipment also.

Third: Miss [Louise] Malloch has done much work on the Chicago & Alton matter, but has not as yet developed any facts which it seems worthwhile to telegraph you,

Yours very truly,

1. There are no copies of these reports in the Brandeis Mss.
2. Edmund Dwight Codman (1865–1947) was a Boston lawyer who served on a number of boards of directors of firms involved with railroads.

To Bernard Gerson Richards

January 28, 1913 Boston, Mass. [Richards Mss]

MY DEAR MR. RICHARDS: I thank you for your letter of the 27th and regret that the work I have on hand is such that I dare not accept your very kind invitation to take part in the meeting on March 15th.[1]

It is possible that I may be in New York while Mr. Nahum Sokolow [2] is here; and if so, I shall be very glad to meet him and you then.

With best wishes,   Very cordially,

1. A Zionist rally was held at Carnegie Hall in New York on 15 March, presided over by Dr. Solomon Schechter, president of the Jewish Theological Seminary; Sokolow delivered the main address.
2. Nahum Sokolow (1859–1936), a journalist and lecturer, was one of the first members of the Zionist movement and a leading figure in it until his death. Originally allied with David Wolfsohn, Sokolow by this time had become right-hand man to Dr. Chaim Weizmann (see LDB to Weiz-

mann, 11 October 1914). During World War I, Sokolow undertook a number of diplomatic missions for the Zionists and helped pave the way for the Balfour Declaration in 1917. In 1920 he was elected president of the Zionist Executive, and in 1931 became president of both the World Zionist Organization and the Jewish Agency for Palestine. His two-volume *History of Zionism, 1600–1918* (new edition, New York, 1969) is a standard work. There is no adequate biography, although basic information can be found in Simcha Kling, *Nachum Sokolow, Servant of His People* (New York, 1960); see also Arthur Hertzberg's introduction to Sokolow's *History*.

To Mitchell Oshkenaniew

January 30, 1913 Boston, Mass. [Brandeis Mss, NMF 45-3]

DEAR SIR: [1] I am in receipt of yours of the 27th, in which you ask whether I could act as your counsel in connection with the operations on the Menominee Indian Reservation.

My engagements are such that it would probably be impossible for me to undertake your case; but I venture to ask whether you have taken this matter up with Secretary [Walter L.] Fisher. I have a very high opinion of the Secretary, and believe that he would be specially interested in preventing any possible wrong to Indians; and would, therefore, give any complaints that you might make very careful consideration.   Yours very truly,

1. Mitchell Oshkenaniew was a Menominee Indian and a teacher living on a reservation in Neopit, Wisconsin. He wrote that the government had been carrying on logging operations on the reservation in violation of the treaty, and he wanted LDB's help in stopping this.

To Franklin Knight Lane

February 1, 1913 Boston, Mass. [Brandeis Mss, NMF 1-M-2]

MY DEAR MR. LANE: I have just read your report in the matter of "Express Rates, Practices, Accounts and Revenues".[1] It is the finest piece of work of its kind that I know.

You will doubtless recall the twenty-year contract between the Boston & Maine Railroad and the American Express Co. dated May 1, 1907, under which the Boston & Maine receives only 35 per cent. of the gross receipts of the Express Company. The contract was entered into obviously as a part of the transfer of the controlling interest in the Boston & Maine to the New Haven.

A statement concerning it is made in a recent report of the Public Service Commission of New Hampshire on an investigation of railroad rates, 216–17, copy of which I enclose. The New Hampshire Commission mentions the retirement of Mr. Ledyard [2] from the Boston & Maine Board of Directors, but fails to mention what your report shows,—that he became a Director of the New Haven; that the American Express Co. holds $5,132,400. of the New Haven's stock, and the Adams Express Co. $3,723,000.

First: In your report, page 456, in the "Schedule of Payment", you give the percentage of gross receipts—

Steam Railway
Mileage covered

15 or less	63.44
20 to 35	3570.68

Will you kindly let me have the several railroads which have the contracts for "15 or less" and "20 to 35" with the dates and duration of contract and mileage?

According to one statement of the mileage of the Boston & Maine system, including lines owned, leased, controlled and operated, it had itself a little over 3570 miles.

Second: Did your investigation develop any facts which you may properly communicate which would, in view of the general tendency to increase the proportion of gross receipts payable to the railroads, bear upon the propriety of the 35 per cent. contracts; and, particularly, did you collect any specific evidence bearing upon the making of that contract?

Third: Will you kindly send me a copy of the present Boston & Maine contract, and of the cancelled contract of July 1, 1904, if available; also, a copy of your report in the Express Case of June 8, 1912 and supplemental reports?

Fourth: Did you in your investigation concerning sleeping car rates collect any facts bearing upon the influence exerted to secure contracts by the relation of Mr. Pullman [3] or his associates with the railroads; and specifically get any information which you could properly communicate, concerning the contracts between the Pullman Company and the Boston & Maine. Mr. Pullman was elected a Director of the Boston & Maine December 14, 1892, and remained a Director until his death,—Oct. 19, 1897,

Yours very truly,

1. *Interstate Commerce Commission Reports* No. 4198, 24 (1912).

2. Henry Brockholst Ledyard (1844–1921), chairman of the board of the Michigan Central Railroad, was a director in several other lines. LDB is here making a case against interlocking directorates, an attack he would pursue vigorously in the struggles over the Federal Reserve Act and the Clayton Anti-trust Act.

3. George Mortimer Pullman (1831–1897) designed the first railroad sleeping car; the Pullman Palace Car Company, with the support of the Morgan interest, enjoyed a monopoly on the construction of sleepers. For details of Pullman's benevolently despotic attitude toward his workers, see Almont Lindsey, *The Pullman Strike* (Chicago, 1942), or Stanley Buder, *Pullman: An Experiment in Industrial Order and Community Planning, 1880–1930* (New York, 1967).

To Howard White

February 6, 1913 Boston, Mass. [Brandeis Mss, NMF 8-3]

MY DEAR MR. WHITE: [1] I have yours of the 4th in regard to arbitration.

In my opinion compulsory arbitration is thoroughly objectionable. Voluntary arbitration is, of course, often valuable and it seems indispensable; but my own experience has convinced me that most controversies between employer and employee can be settled by discussion; and insistance upon discussion,—that is upon ascertainment of facts,—is the most effective and satisfactory method of reaching a proper solution.

It seems to me that the Canadian act, which undertakes,—in the case of railroads and certain other interests—to compel an investigation into facts and full publicity, indicates a fruitful line of action.   Yours very truly,

1. Howard White was a freshman at Southwestern College in Winfield, Kansas.

To Augustus Owsley Stanley

February 8, 1913 Boston, Mass. [Brandeis Mss, NMF 53-1]

MY DEAR STANLEY: Upon my return to the city I find yours of January 30th in which you say that you are mailing me a bound set of the Steel investigation reports.[1] It has not yet come, and I am anxious to have it.

I note that you are trying to get a hearing on your bill. I hope you will succeed, and I shall be very glad to attend as you suggest.[2]   Most cordially,

1. U.S. Congress, House, Special Committee on the Investigation of the United States Steel Corporation, *United States Steel Corporation. Hearings* . . ., 62d Cong., 1st sess., 8 vols. (Washington, 1912).
2. Stanley had introduced anti-trust measures based upon the recommendations of his committee in the U.S. Steel investigation. These measures were eventually incorporated in the Clayton Anti-trust bill, and LDB testified on that proposal in January 1914.

To Alice Henry

February 10, 1913 Boston, Mass. [Brandeis Mss, NMF 8-3]

DEAR MISS HENRY: [1] Each issue of Life and Labor which comes to me confirms the conviction of the excellent work which it is doing. It has in a sense a field of its own, in presenting the story of the working woman, and in putting before the working woman and the general public the need of organization of the women workers.

Life and Labor should have the large circulation to which its merits entitle it.

With best wishes,   Very cordially yours,

1. Alice Henry was co-editor of *Life and Labor*, a monthly journal published by the National Women's Trade Union League.

To William Harrison Ingersoll

February 12, 1913 Boston, Mass. [Brandeis Mss, NMF 52-2]

DEAR MR. INGERSOLL: [1] Thank you for your letter of the 11th with enclosure.[2]

Your suggestion,—that the Government take up in the field of industry work similar to that of the Agricultural Experiment Stations,—has my most hearty approval; and I suggested such a course in respect to railroad work in my talk before the Railroad Securities Commission on March 6th, 1911, and discussed the idea in connection with industry somewhat in my testimony before

the Senate Committee on Interstate Commerce on December
14–16, 1911.

I think a very important field for Governmental action lies
there.   Yours very truly,

1. William Harrison Ingersoll (1880–1946) was a partner in the Ingersoll
Dollar Watch Company, and he later became involved in numerous other
business ventures. He and LDB worked together for many years on the
problems of fair pricing, and both men supported the idea that manufacturers of trademarked goods should be allowed to set a fair retail price that
could not be reduced by the retail seller. Ingersoll spent much of his life
working on fair pricing as a member of special committees of the United
States Chamber of Commerce, the American Marketing Association, and
other similar groups.

2. Ingersoll enclosed a letter he had written to Woodrow Wilson on 23
December 1912, proposing that the government apply scientific measures to
industry in order to help lower the cost of living. Moreover, he gently
chided LDB, together with other lawyers, for failing to distinguish between
price maintenance and price fixing; the one worked in favor of competition
and the other against it. LDB would soon utilize this argument and become
an advocate of price maintenance.

To Henry Moskowitz

February 12, 1913 Boston, Mass. [Brandeis Mss, NMF 35-2]

DEAR DR. MOSKOWITZ: I have a telegram from Mr. Harry A.
Gordon [1] as follows:

"I regret that the agreement between the White Goods Manufacturers and the Union which was made through your kind
offices has failed of consummation because of the breach of faith
on the part of the Union. My association refuses to further
treat with the irresponsible labor leaders."

I wish you would express to Mr. Gordon, whose address I have
not, my thanks for his courtesy in wiring me. I hope that the
rupture is not final, and that some arrangement may yet be put
through under which the community may have the benefit of the
working out under Mr. Gordon of satisfactory relations between
the Association's members and the white goods workers. [2]

Yours very truly,

1. Harry A. Gordon (1883–1947) was a New York attorney who served
as counsel to several employers' associations in the garment industry.

2. Although its demise would not come for another two years, the Protocol was beginning to founder. LDB's original arrangement depended upon the good faith of both parties, as well as relatively prosperous times in order to keep both employer and employee busy and satisfied. With the slackening of business, both sides became suspicious, and tended to see conspiratorial designs on the part of the other. See LDB to Charles Heineman, 1 June 1915.

To Frederic Allison Tupper

February 12, 1913 Boston, Mass. [Brandeis Mss, NMF 27-2]

MY DEAR MR. TUPPER: [1] I am very sorry that another engagement prevents my attending the hearing on Senate Bill #291 relating to teachers' pensions in the City of Boston, as I wish to urge strongly the passage of Section 3 of the Bill which removes the present maximum of $600.

To pay teachers whose salaries have been $1800 or less, a pension of one-third of their salaries, and to pay those whose salaries are over $1800, a pension of only $600, is obviously unjust, and it is an injustice particularly inexcusable since it is a discrimination without cause against ten per cent of our teaching force.

Surely the effort of the City should be to secure ever abler men and women as teachers, and to this end to offer as liberal salaries, including pensions, as the finances of Boston will premit. The present discrimination tends to defeat this purpose, and the end which our pension law was designed to secure.[2]

Very cordially yours,

1. Frederick Allison Tupper (1858–1951) had been headmaster of Brighton High School since 1899. He was also a trustee of the Teachers Pension Fund and a past president of the Massachusetts Teachers Association.
2. The bill ultimately passed the legislature and was enacted into law on 13 June 1913.

To Annie LePorte Diggs

February 13, 1913 Boston, Mass. [Brandeis Mss, NMF 44-6]

MY DEAR MRS. DIGGS: [1] I have not had until now an opportunity of reading your excellent little book, "Bedrock",[2] which you were good enough to send me in December. You have stated with great clearness some of our main social needs.

I am inclined to think that your "Agricultural Committee" might well adopt the expression *forward to the land* as a substitute for "back to the land". The new movement in connection with scientific agriculture makes farming something different in kind from what it has been in the past.

The organized effort for employment must ultimately be made to include continuity of employment; that is, elimination of the present irregularity of employment.

With best wishes,   Yours very truly,

1. Annie LePorte Diggs (1853–1916) was a Canadian-born reformer and reporter whose interests spanned Populism, women's suffrage, and the peace movement. During the 1890s she toured nearly every state west of the Mississippi in support of Populist candidates.

2. *Bedrock: Education and Employment, the Foundation of the Republic* (Detroit, 1912).

To Charles McCarthy

February 13, 1913 Boston, Mass. [McCarthy Mss]

MY DEAR MR. MCCARTHY: I have yours of the 11th.

First: I had not seen Senator LaFollette's bill nor the amendments to the Nelson Bill of which you speak. I assume that you have written or will write Senator LaFollette on the subject.[1]

Second: The New York organization to which you refer is probably the People's League—not the People's Lobby. A number of the social workers in New York, Boyd Fisher,[2] Mrs. J. Borden Harriman[3] and others, purposed forming an organization which would be an aid to progressive federal legislation. I attended at one informal meeting about the middle of December, when the organization was discussed in a general way, but have not been able to attend later meetings, and do not know definitely what plans have been worked out. Walsh[4] of Kansas City is much interested in the project.   Very cordially yours,

1. McCarthy had been requested by several congressmen to comment on two bills that aimed at providing a federal legislative reference department. One, sponsored by Senator Knute Nelson, provided for bipartisan appoint-

ments, and McCarthy condemned this approach as worse than no department at all. The other, introduced by LaFollette, while nonpartisan, paid too little in salaries, making it impossible, in McCarthy's opinion, to get good men.

2. Boyd Fisher was a progressive journalist.

3. Florence Jaffray Hurst Harriman (1870–1967) was the first woman ever to hold high appointive office in the United States government, when President Wilson named her a member of the Commission on Industrial Relations. An ardent Democrat, she served on the Party's national committee, and was appointed by Franklin Roosevelt as ambassador to Norway in 1937. Mrs. Harriman was a fine example of a person of wealth who was also attuned to social problems, and despite the ridicule heaped on her by extreme labor elements, was well thought of in progressive and reform circles.

4. Frank Patrick Walsh (1864–1949) was then a crusading Kansas City lawyer. Wilson named him chairman of the federal Commission on Industrial Relations, which Walsh used as a platform to attack John D. Rockefeller and other industrial barons who Walsh thought were mistreating labor. During World War I, he served as co-chairman with William Howard Taft of the War Labor Board; and, although supposedly representing the public, he consistently attacked employer interests.

To William Bayard Hale

February 14, 1913 Boston, Mass. [Brandeis Mss, NMF 52-2]

MY DEAR MR. HALE: [1] It hardly seems appropriate for me to say anything at present for publication, or to Mr. Wilson, about "The New Freedom",[2] which you were good enough to send me; but I want to say to you that your work as Editor has been performed admirably, and that Mr. Wilson's simple, convincing statement of fundamental principles on which his administration will proceed must prove of great educational value, and deepen our feeling of gratitude for his election.

Very cordially yours,

1. William Bayard Hale (1869–1924), after a short career as a clergyman, entered journalism in 1900; he edited *Cosmopolitan, Current Literature,* and *World's Work* between assignments for the *New York World* and *New York Times.* In 1913 he was working for Doubleday, Page and Company, the publishing house; but Woodrow Wilson sent him to Mexico later in the year as a special agent.

2. Woodrow Wilson, *The New Freedom* (Garden City, N.Y., 1913), which Hale edited, consisted of many of Wilson's 1912 campaign speeches.

To Charles Richard Crane

February 15, 1913 Boston, Mass. [Brandeis Mss, NMF 52-1]

MY DEAR CHARLES: I had your telegram yesterday saying that you expected to wire today, and not having heard from you yet, suppose that no information has come.

Please wire me in any event Monday morning what the situation appears to be, as I have asked Norman to defer saying anything to Collins [1] until I hear further from you.

Norman lunched with Lamont yesterday, who offered to sell him Harper's Weekly,—that is, the name and good will, for $100,000. The other assets of Harper's are insignificant. Norman has told Lamont that he would communicate with him sometime next week. This should, of course, be treated as confidential.

Most cordially,

P.S. I hope some satisfactory progress is being made in Crane matters.

1. Frederick Lewis Collins (1882–1950), president of McClure's Publications, had been negotiating with Hapgood about the possible sale of *McClure's Magazine*.

To William Ellsworth Smythe

February 15, 1913 Boston, Mass. [Brandeis Mss, NMF 52-2]

MY DEAR MR. SMYTHE: I have read with much interest your letter of January 22nd and the statement of Mr. Call, and have started it on its way to Governor Wilson; [1] but he is, of course, so much occupied with other matters at present that I think it doubtful whether he can give any attention to the Homestead Policy at this time.

The land question has undoubtedly become in America, as it has long been elsewhere, the fundamental problem; and I am sure that Governor Wilson realizes its importance. Indeed, nearly twenty years ago, when he wrote his essay on American history, published in the volume entitled, "Mere Literature", he showed a keen appreciation of the West and of its specific problem.[2]

Yours very truly,

1. Smythe had enclosed a statement by Joseph H. Call of Los Angeles, California, dealing with the disposal of remaining public lands in such a way as to foster individual as opposed to corporate ownership. LDB sent the two letters on to Norman Hapgood, who forwarded them to Congressman William Kent.

2. Wilson, in "The Course of American History," praised the men and the spirit which had opened the West, and he paid special attention to the need for land to which pioneers could go. See *Mere Literature, and Other Essays* (Boston, 1896), 213–47.

To Harry A. Bullock

February 25, 1913 Boston, Mass. [Brandeis Mss, NMF 52-2]

MY DEAR BULLOCK: Upon my return to the City I find yours of the 17th.

It cannot be necessary to tell an old newspaper man not to believe all that he hears, but I am glad of any excuse which brings me a letter from you.[1]

I trust that all goes well with you in the B.R.T., but I must confess to a feeling of considerable jealousy at having you engaged in transportation instead of journalism.[2] The press of the Country needs such men as you, and I hope that things will go so well with you in railroading that you will feel yourself able to return to newspaper work soon.   Very cordially yours,

1. Believing that LDB would be the next Secretary of Commerce, Bullock had urged the appointment of Walter Meriwether, an experienced and able shipping news reporter, to be the next shipping commissioner for the Port of New York.

2. Bullock had left the *New York Times* to work for the Brooklyn Rapid Transit Company.

To Ella A. Knapp

February 25, 1913 Boston, Mass. [Brandeis Mss, NMF 47-3]

DEAR MISS KNAPP:[1] Upon my return to the City I find your letter of the 20th, in which you ask me to advise in relation to the course to be pursued in connection with proposed investigation in connection with the votes for equal suffrage.

The course to be pursued would depend so largely upon local regulations, practice and connections with which I am not familiar, that I feel unable to give you any advice. I should suppose, however, that as the Progressive party definitely committed itself to equal suffrage, it would be well to apply to some one of the leading Michigan lawyers who is actively known as affiliated with the progressive movement. I regret that my knowledge of the Michigan Bar is not such that I can make a more definite suggestion.

With best wishes,   Yours very truly,

1. Ella A. Knapp, of Kalamazoo, Michigan, had sought LDB's advice on the best way to secure women's suffrage in her state.

To Mark Sullivan

February 25, 1913 Boston, Mass. [Brandeis Mss, NMF 51-7]

MY DEAR SULLIVAN: Upon my return to the City I find your letters of the 20th and 21st about Glavis, with the clippings which I return herewith.

I had a talk with Heney about this matter recently. I don't believe that Glavis was conscious of doing anything improper, but he ought to have known better than to get into the position in which he did; and I don't think that his position with the public can be bettered by talking about it, at least at the present time.[1] I am inclined to think, also, that it is best for Collier's to bear the occasional prodding from subscribers in silence.

Yours very truly,

1. Shortly after the close of the Ballinger investigation, Glavis had been named secretary of the State Conservation Commission of California, at a monthly salary of $150; in March 1912 he also became secretary of the State Water Commission of California at an identical salary. In September 1912 the surveyor-general of California accused Glavis of using his prestige as secretary of the two commissions while acting for private interests as their attorney. To avoid a scandal, Glavis was allowed to resign in December 1912. The problem was complicated because Glavis was at the time opposing the vested land law of California regarding disposal of public land for support of schools. The entire episode is explored in James L. Penick, Jr., "Louis Russell Glavis: A Postscript to the Ballinger-Pinchot Controversy," *Pacific Northwest Quarterly*, 55 (April 1964): 67–75.

To Oscar Wilder Underwood

February 25, 1913 Boston, Mass. [Brandeis Mss, NMF 52-2]

MY DEAR MR. UNDERWOOD: [1] Mr. William Whitman of Boston tells me that he expects to see you this week, and wants you to know that when he makes a statement of fact his statement of fact can be relied upon.

I came in intimate relations with Mr. Whitman during the life insurance investigations of 1905,[2] and saw much of him for several years.

We disagree not only on the tariff,[3] but on many other economic, social, and political subjects, and I have had many occasions to challenge the correctness of his judgment in these respects, but I have a very high opinion of Mr. Whitman's integrity and of his public spirit, as he sees the public interest, and in all matters in which I have come into contact with him, I have found him careful and accurate in his statements of fact.

Very truly yours,

1. Oscar Wilder Underwood (1862–1929) represented the Ninth Alabama District in the House of Representatives from 1895 to 1915, after which he served in the Senate until 1927. From 1911 to 1915 he was chairman of the House Ways and Means Committee and led the fight to reduce tariff rates. Underwood was a favorite-son candidate whom the Southern states supported at Democratic presidential conventions from 1912 to 1924.

2. See LDB to Policy Holders, 22 July 1905.

3. For LDB's tariff views, see his letters to William C. Redfield and Woodrow Wilson, 1 August 1912.

To Robert Franz Foerster

February 27, 1913 Boston, Mass. [Brandeis Mss, NMF 46-4]

MY DEAR MR. FOERSTER: [1] I have your letter of the 25th.[2]

You will recall that I stated to your committee at our conference last fall that I was disposed to believe in the policy of making subsidies for the benefit of widows with dependent children, provided adequate administrative machinery could be devised; but that I considered the subject one which might result in serious harm if entered upon without due investigation, and without the invention of adequate administrative machinery.

It seemed to me impossible that with the short time and small appropriation granted to your Commission the necessary investigation could be made; and I am not satisfied that sufficient administrative machinery has been developed to make the experiment safe.

I regret of course that I have not the opportunity of studying your report. Under the circumstances I do not feel like expressing myself publicly in any way upon House Bill 1770.[3]

I am looking forward with interest to the reading of your report when it appears.   Very cordially yours,

1. Robert Franz Foerster (1883–1941), an economist, was professor of social ethics at Harvard University. He was director of the Boston Social Research Council and chairman of the special legislative commission to investigate support of dependent children of widows.

2. Foerster had written requesting LDB to support the commission's recommendation that the state provide some means of support to the dependent children of widows.

3. House bill 1770 ultimately was passed by the lower house on 5 June 1913 and the Massachusetts Senate the following day, when it was signed into law by the governor.

To Maurice Leon

February 28, 1913 Boston, Mass. [Brandeis Mss, NMF 52-2]

MY DEAR MR. LEON: [1] Replying to yours of the 27th.

I had the pleasure of meeting Mr. McReynolds [2] in connection with the Tobacco Trust Litigation, and know of his work in that and other connections. I have the highest opinion of his ability and character and should think the country would indeed be fortunate to have him fill the position of Attorney General.[3]

Please remember me most kindly to Mr. Davison,[4] who is an old friend. I hope to have the pleasure of meeting you soon.

Yours very truly,

1. Maurice Leon (1880–1952) was a New York lawyer and stepson of Richard Gottheil, with whom LDB was to work closely in Zionist affairs. During World War I he was instrumental in securing large loans for France.

2. James Clark McReynolds (1862–1946) first gained public attention as an assistant attorney-general during the Roosevelt administration when he resigned over what he considered ineffective enforcement of the anti-trust

law. This reputation for being a foe of monopoly led Woodrow Wilson to name McReynolds Attorney-General in 1913, and LDB worked closely with McReynolds on drafting a new anti-trust law and in prosecuting the New Haven. Aside from his passion against monopoly, McReynolds was extremely conservative, and to ease him out of the Cabinet, Wilson named him an associate justice of the United States Supreme Court in 1914. This was an appointment that Wilson frequently regretted, as McReynolds immediately became one of the most reactionary members of the high bench. In addition to his opposition to all social welfare measures, McReynolds was anti-Semitic, and he practically never spoke to LDB after the latter had joined the Court. When LDB resigned in 1939, McReynolds's name was conspicuously absent from the expected letter sent by the remaining justices to a departing member. In 1934, after the Court had upheld a Minnesota statute providing a moratorium on mortgages (*Home Building & Loan Association* v. *Blaisdell*) and a New York law which regulated milk prices (*Nebbia* v. *New York*), McReynolds told a friend that these two decisions meant "the end of the Constitution as you and I regarded it. An Alien influence has prevailed."

3. See LDB to Alfred Brandeis, 2 March 1913.

4. Charles Stewart Davison (1855–1942), the scion of an old Massachusetts family, had practiced law in New York since 1877; he served on numerous committees of legal and patriotic associations.

To Mary A. Swan

February 28, 1913 Boston, Mass. [Brandeis Mss, NMF 45-3]

DEAR MRS. SWAN: [1] Owing to absences from the City your letter of January 19th has remained unanswered, and I have been unable to give careful consideration to the questions raised by your article.[2]

My impressions are these:

First: As to suppressing court news involving boys and girls under 18: That seems to me clearly desirable.

Second: As to the destroying of court records, I have at present some doubt. I am not afraid of the truth; still I am not entirely convinced that you may not be right on this point also.

Yours very truly,

1. Mary A. Swan was the manager of the *Freeport* (Illinois) *Daily Standard*.

2. The *Daily Standard* had carried an article advocating suppressing news of juvenile courts and destroying records of juvenile arrests and convictions

once the child had made good, thus allowing them to enter adult life without a criminal record. Miss Swan was soliciting opinions on the article from prominent persons.

To Alfred Brandeis

March 2, 1913 Boston, Mass. [Brandeis Mss, unmarked folder]

MY DEAR AL: We are very happy over Amy's engagement.[1] It seems to me the two are unusually well mated, and it is fine to have the family supplemented by a son.

Madie's mind is thus turned to the contemplation of matrimony; and I cannot but think she will eventually yield.[2]

Today's papers will have removed the mystery as to the Cabinet.[3] As you know I had great doubts as for it's being desirable for me; so I concluded to literally let nature take its course and to do nothing either to get called or to stop the talk, although some of my friends were quite active. State Street, Wall Street and the local Democratic bosses did six months' unremitting work; but seem not to have prevailed until the last moment. The local Democratic bosses were swayed partly by their connections in the financial district, partly by the fear of being opposed in job-seeking. It is almost, indeed quite, amusing how much they fear me, attributing to me power and influence which I in no respect possess.

I shall know more when I go to New York and probably Washington the end of this week.

Do let me know, at once, about enclosed letter from Otto Fleishner. I can almost remember something about a Lederer somewhere: How else should Fleishner hit on the early seventies.

Madie will travel to N.Y. in Herbert White's company tomorrow.

1. Amy Brandeis had just become engaged to William Harold McCreary (1885–1946); McCreary taught English literature at the Louisville Male High School and published several volumes of poetry.

2. Adele Brandeis did not marry.

3. Rumors that LDB would receive a place in Wilson's cabinet had begun to circulate even before the election (see LDB to Alfred Brandeis, 15 September 1912), and indeed the president-elect had seriously considered LDB for the post of Attorney-General. Progressives of all types had inundated

Wilson with letters urging the appointment, and LaFollette sent word through Charles R. Crane that LDB could "pull together the progressives — whether LaFollette, Democratic or Bull Mooser—and harmonize progressive legislation." Similar sentiments reached Wilson from Felix Frankfurter, Benjamin B. Lindsey, William Jennings Bryan, and hundreds of other reformers. At the same time, financial interests began a vehement campaign to keep LDB out of any high federal position. Henry Lee Higginson utilized all of his many connections to bring pressure to bear upon Wilson, while the conservative press declared that LDB's appointment as Attorney-General would bring on a widespread depression (*Boston Journal*, 21 November 1912). Wilson wavered for a number of weeks, and finally yielded to the advice of E. M. House (see LDB to T. W. Gregory, 2 June 1913) that LDB's nomination would cause dissension among the Democrats and endanger the enactment of Wilson's program. The president-elect then considered LDB as a possible Secretary of Commerce, and discussed LDB's record with Norman Hapgood on 28 January 1912; rumors of this alternative, however, aroused the resentment of New England Democratic leaders, who had never been on good terms with LDB. Reluctantly, Wilson dropped the matter. Announcement of the Cabinet on 1 March, without LDB's name, brought cheer to the financiers, and one banker wrote to House: "You little know how much gratification is felt about the 'street' over the success of eliminating Brandeis from the Cabinet" (William A. Tucker to House, 4 March 1913, quoted in Link, *Wilson: The New Freedom*, 15). Reformers, on the other hand, were bitterly disappointed that Wilson had yielded to the "interests" in this fight. Some historians have suggested that anti-Semitism played a part in Wilson's rejection of LDB (see, for example, Yonathan Shapiro, *Leadership of the American Zionist Organization, 1897–1930* [Urbana, Ill., 1971], 63). Professor Link found no evidence for this charge in the Wilson Papers, and LDB does not mention it as a factor either. At this time, LDB had practically no identification with Jewish interests, and his involvement with Zionism would not become serious until later in 1913.

To John Hobart Marble

March 4, 1913 Boston, Mass. [Brandeis Mss, NMF 53-2]

My DEAR MARBLE: [1] Pursuant to your telephone I wired Mr. Wilson as follows, and confirmed the telegram by letter:

"If Mr. Lane [2] should retire from the Interstate Commerce Commission, I strongly recommend as his successor the present Secretary of the Commission, Mr. Marble, who is well qualified for the position by his character, experience and ability."

I assume that you and Mr. Lane thought a communication at

this time from me might be of service, and I hope that our sorrow in losing Mr. Lane from the Commission may be relieved by the joy of having you on it.[3]

With every good wish,   Most cordially yours,

1. John Hobart Marble (1869–1913) had worked for the Interstate Commerce Commission since 1906, first as an investigator and then as secretary of the agency.

2. Wilson had named Franklin K. Lane his Secretary of the Interior.

3. Wilson nominated Marble the next day, and the Senate confirmed him on 10 March; see LDB to Franklin Lane, 5 March 1913.

To Moses Edwin Clapp

March 5, 1913 Boston, Mass. [Brandeis Mss, NMF 53-2]

MY DEAR CLAPP: It was good to have your telegram, which should have been answered sooner.[1]

McReynolds will make an excellent Attorney General. You may remember what I said of his work when speaking of the tobacco trust prosecution.[2]

I expect to be in Washington soon, and want very much to have our long deferred talk on trusts and other matters.

Very cordially yours,

1. On 26 February, Clapp had wired: "Afternoon papers announce you have been selected for Attorney General. This seems almost too good to be true. If correct the country more than yourself is to be congratulated."

2. See LDB to James C. McReynolds, 5 March 1913.

To Gilson Gardner

March 5, 1913 Boston, Mass. [Brandeis Mss, NMF 53-2]

MY DEAR GARDNER: It was good to have your letter of the 1st.[1]

McReynolds will be a first rate Attorney General. His record in the trust prosecutions is excellent, and if Wickersham had not turned him down in the tobacco trust case, we should have had a real disintegration.[2]

I expect to see you soon in Washington.

Yours very truly,

1. Gardner wrote that he could not "wait for the official announcement to express my very great pleasure at the prospect that you are to be in the Wilson cabinet."

2. See LDB to Mark Sullivan, 9 October 1911, n. 1.

To Robert Marion LaFollette

March 5, 1913 Boston, Mass. [Brandeis Mss, SC 1-2]

MY DEAR BOB: Thank you for your night letter.[1]

I long to see all the LaFollettes, and plan to be in Washington soon.   Most Cordially,

1. LaFollette had wired: "Everybody understands you are now absolutely free to go forward using your great abilities for the public good as you have for so many years. I look forward to your cooperation in this independent work with high hopes. All join in sending you and Mrs. Brandeis all abiding love."

To Franklin Knight Lane

March 5, 1913 Boston, Mass. [Brandeis Mss, NMF 53-2]

MY DEAR MR. LANE: Our joy in having you in the Interior is lessened only by the sorrow of losing you from the Interstate Commerce Commission.

President Wilson, to do his utmost to repair this great loss, should appoint Marble as your successor.

I trust you will still find time to give some thought to our serious railroad problems.

With best wishes,   Most cordially yours,

To William Gibbs McAdoo

March 5, 1913 Boston, Mass. [Brandeis Mss, NMF 53-2]

MY DEAR MR. McADOO: It is fine to have you in the Treasury. Your inside knowledge of the financial world will be of inestimable service to the country, and we may look forward now to the "settlement" of the currency question with lessened anxiety.[1]

With every good wish,   Most cordially yours,

1. When Wilson first offered the Treasury secretaryship, McAdoo protested that he knew nothing about banking. Wilson declared that he considered that an asset since he wanted the Treasury run for the benefit of the people and not just for the bankers. The "settlement" of the currency problem, which vexed the nation for more than four decades, came with the passage of the Federal Reserve Act later that year. See LDB to Woodrow Wilson, 14 June 1913, and Link, *Wilson: The New Freedom*, ch. 7.

To James Clark McReynolds

March 5, 1913 Boston, Mass. [Brandeis Mss, NMF 53-2]

MY DEAR McREYNOLDS: In deciding upon you for Attorney General President Wilson has made the wisest possible choice.

Your record in trust prosecutions will assure the country that the President's trust policy will be carried out promptly and efficiently, and business be freed at last. We are indeed to be congratulated.

I intend to call upon you soon, and hope you will have time to talk over our special New England needs.[1]

With best wishes,   Very sincerely yours,

1. Under LDB's prodding, the Justice Department again began investigating the New Haven as a possible offender under the Sherman Act, ultimately filing a dissolution bill in 1914.

To William Cox Redfield

March 5, 1913 Boston, Mass. [Brandeis Mss, NMF 53-2]

MY DEAR MR. REDFIELD: It will indeed be a "new industrial day" when your wise and enlightened policies pervade business, and it is a great satisfaction to have you in a position which will so strongly reinforce your unanswerable arguments.[1]

There is much to talk over with you, and I hope to have the pleasure of calling on you soon.

With best wishes,   Most cordially yours,

1. Redfield had been named Secretary of Commerce. LDB refers to Redfield's recent book, *The New Industrial Day: A Book for Men Who Employ Men* (New York, 1912). Most historians feel that Redfield was not as effective or daring as LDB hoped he might be. For his side, see *With Congress and Cabinet* (New York, 1924).

To Alfred Brandeis

March 10, 1913 Washington, D.C.
[Brandeis Mss, unmarked folder]

DEAR AL: Louis Wehle has told you doubtless of our day together.

Since he left, I have been engaged largely in promoting the entent cordiale with the administration. Had a good private talk with the President this evening for an hour—and with Lane, Redfield, Bryan, and McReynolds today—inter alia pushing along New Haven and Shoe Machinery matters—& spent this morning at the I.C.C. on New Haven matters. There is no lack of occupation. Heard quite a little gossip about Charlie Nagel last evening.

He was as near the Supreme Court as this: Taft told the Chief Justice [1] Charlie would be appointed the next day. The C.J. called on Charlie 10 P.M. to welcome him for coming event. The next day another name was sent in. Taft also treated Charlie atrociously on dit.[2] in respect to O'Keefe's discharge.

Same inside source says Charlie had substantially no influence on Taft or the Administration. He is a great admirer of Charlie personally and intimate with him. Says Charlie was fearfully harried by his Chief's qualities.

1. Edward Douglass White (1845–1921), after a brief term as United States Senator from Louisiana, had been named to the Supreme Court by Grover Cleveland in 1894; Taft elevated him to Chief Justice in 1910.
2. "It is said."

To Seeber Edwards

March 12, 1913 Boston, Mass. [Brandeis Mss, NMF 53-2]

MY DEAR MR. EDWARDS: [1] Absence from the City has delayed reply to yours of the 5th in regard to the appointment of Judge Mumford to take Judge Brown's place.[2]

It is possible that the President or the Attorney General may consult me in regard to this appointment; and if so, I shall be only too glad to act on your suggestion.

Yours very truly,

1. Seeber Edwards (1869–1914), after graduation from the Harvard Law School, had entered practice in Providence, Rhode Island, as the partner of another of LDB's friends, Walter F. Angell.

2. Edwards had requested that LDB support the recommendation of a number of leading Rhode Island lawyers for President Wilson to nominate Charles Carney Mumford (1860–1918) to replace Arthur Lewis Brown (1854–1928) as United States District Judge for the district of Rhode Island. Taft had wanted to elevate Brown to the Court of Appeals, in which there was a vacancy, but the nomination was blocked by Democrats in the Senate who wanted to retain patronage appointments for the incoming Wilson administration. Although LDB did recommend Brown's promotion (see LDB to James C. McReynolds, 28 March 1913), the administration passed him over, and Brown continued as District Judge until his retirement in 1927. Mumford did not receive any judicial appointment.

To Lynn Haines

March 12, 1913 Boston, Mass. [Brandeis Mss, NMF 61-3]

DEAR MR. HAINES: [1] I thank you for yours of the 11th, and for "The Story of the Democratic House of Representatives".[2]

Upon further consideration I am confirmed in my impression that it would not be wise for me to become a member of the Executive Committee.

I shall be glad to send in my contribution of $500.00 as soon as you let me know that the League is organized for business.[3]

With best wishes.   Very cordially,

1. Lynn Haines (1876–1929) was a publicist whose books and pamphlets dealt primarily with legislative and congressional figures and problems. He wrote to LDB as executive secretary of the newly formed National Voters League. The League's purpose was to follow closely what actions were being considered by Congress, and to report to the public on those measures as well as on the positions taken by individual congressmen and senators.

2. The pamphlet, which was a chapter from Haines's book, *Law Making in America* (Bethesda, Md., 1912), discussed some of the problems which would be facing the newly-elected Congress.

3. See LDB to Haines, 10 May 1913.

To Norman Hapgood

March 12, 1913 Boston, Mass. [Brandeis Mss, NMF 53-2]

MY DEAR NORMAN: *First:* I saw Lane twice while in Washington. He is very much concerned about getting proper men to help him, and I should think it would be worth while for you to write him about C[hristopher]. P. Connelly. It didn't occur to me to mention Connelly when I talked with him, but strangely enough upon my return to the hotel I found that Connelly had called me up. You know so much more about Connelly than I do, and think so well of him, it seems to me in any event it would be better for you to write Lane about him.[1]

Second: I was in Washington until Monday night. Besides Lane [I] had a talk with Bryan, Redfield, and the Attorney General. McAdoo was not in when I called, but I saw his secretary,— Newton.[2] I also had an hour's talk with the President Monday evening. All were extremely cordial, and expressed themselves as eager for all help which can be given them.

Each of them, except Bryan,[3] impressed me as feeling deeply what Walter Fisher suffered from,—the need of good assistants, or, as the President and Lane put it,—"associates". I think Lane particularly is anxious to build up for himself a cabinet made up of the heads of his leading departments.

Of the final stage of making up the cabinet, with the ultimate selection of Redfield, I heard a good deal of gossip of one kind and another, much of it conflicting and none of it particularly illuminating. [Rudolph] Spreckels, whom I saw yesterday at breakfast in New York, had a long talk with the President, and expressed to him very emphatically his disappointment; and he thought the West would share his belief that the President had made a great mistake. He pressed the President pretty hard as to his reasons for action. I hope to see you soon, and until then will endeavor to carry in my memory all that I have heard.

Yours,

1. Connelly did not receive any federal appointment.

2. Byron R. Newton (1862–1938) had been a reporter on the New York *Herald* before joining McAdoo as his secretary.

3. LDB's analysis of Bryan was correct; the Great Commoner saw the State Department primarily as a vehicle for rewarding deserving Democrats. For commentary on his poor appointments, see Link, *Wilson: The New Freedom,* 95–114. See also Richard Challener's critical essay, "William Jennings Bryan," in Norman Graebner, ed., *An Uncertain Tradition* (New York, 1961). The most exhaustive examination of Bryan as Secretary of State is Paolo E. Coletta's second volume, *William Jennings Bryan: Progressive Politician and Moral Statesman, 1909–1915* (Lincoln, Neb., 1969), chs. 4–12.

To George Middleton

March 12, 1913 Boston, Mass. [Middleton Mss]

MY DEAR MIDDLETON: Thank you for yours of the 7th which reaches me upon my return from Washington.

I am inclined to think that so far as I personally am concerned the disposition which has been made of the Cabinet matter is best.

The Senator [1] and I are planning to do some legislative work together, of which we are very hopeful.

It was a great pleasure to have the evening with you and Fola.
Most cordially yours,

1. Robert M. LaFollette, Middleton's father-in-law.

To Raymond Wellington Pullman

March 12, 1913 Boston, Mass. [Brandeis Mss, NMF 53-2]

MY DEAR MR. PULLMAN: Replying to yours of the 11th.

I am glad you called my attention to the Railroad Scales matter. I had noticed that the investigation had been ordered.[1]

Do not believe anything you hear about my accepting an office.[2] I am convinced my best usefulness will be as a public private citizen.

I expect to be in Washington soon and hope to see my good friends to whom you refer.   Very cordially yours,

1. Pullman had written asking LDB if he had any comment on Congress's authorizing an investigation of railroad scales and if he had run into any problems concerning scales in his previous dealings with shippers.
2. After it was official that LDB would not be in the Cabinet, rumors abounded that Wilson had offered him other positions. Pullman had heard that one offer was for Commissioner of Indian Affairs, and he urged LDB not to take that office.

To David Stern

March 13, 1913 Boston, Mass. [Brandeis Mss, NMF 60-2]

DEAR SIR: [1] Replying to yours of the 11th.

With a view to determining the reasonableness of the rates

being charged by your local Public Service Company, I should suggest the following:

First: Ascertain the actual cost of the property of the Company; i.e., what actual money of the investor has been put into the property; and how far the capitalization really represents actual cost, if not value.

Second: If possible, also obtain actual value. To do this would probably be difficult, requiring expert services which may not be available; but an ascertainment of the actual value is certainly desirable if possible.

Third: Make careful inquiry into net income and operating costs, and determine, among other things, to what extent the operating costs, as reported, are actual; i.e., whether any amounts are charged up as costs which are not actual.

Fourth: Get comparative data as to charges in other cities similarly situated.

As bearing on value and costs, you will find instructive the report of the Committee on Interstate Commerce of the United States presented by Senator LaFollette, February 21, 1913 (report #1290) on the valuation of several classes of property of common carriers.[2] This report deals with railroads, but you will find it suggestive.*

You will also find of value the published reports of the Public Service Commission of Wisconsin in cases involving the fixing of rates. Yours very truly,

* Your Senator can get this for you.

1. David Stern, a lawyer in Greensboro, North Carolina, had written to LDB asking how he could determine if the local traction rates were equitable.

2. U.S. Senate, Committee on Interstate Commerce, *Valuation of Several Classes of Property of Common Carriers,* Senate Report 1290 to accompany H.R. 22593, 62d Cong., 3d sess. (Washington, 1913).

To Norman Hapgood

March 15, 1913 Boston, Mass. [Brandeis Mss, NMF 52-1]

MY DEAR NORMAN: I have yours of the 14th about Harper's.[1]

First: When I am next in New York, which ought to be soon,

I want to talk over with Collins broadly the question of magazine finances. The statement seems to be made recurrently that last year was a very bad year for magazines. I should like to know specifically why such has been the fact. Business was good. In most concerns the gross sales were probably larger than ever before. The question arises if magazines have had a particularly bad year, has it been due to conditions external to the magazine, which may be expected to change, or was it due to the fact that magazines are doing business on the wrong basis? [2]

Second: You asked me for "an account of the railroad inefficiency evidence before the Interstate Commerce Commission". Are you referring to the general railroad inefficiency evidence in the Advance Rate Case, or to evidence recently introduced with reference to the New Haven in the hearings before Commissioner Prouty?

You probably recall my discussion on scientific management which formed a part of the brief in the Advance Rate Case, and my closing oral argument in that case. These appear in Senate Document No. 725, 1911, Volume 8, page 4752, and Vol. 9, page 5251. A part of my brief on scientific management has been reprinted.[3]   Yours cordially,

1. Hapgood had written that Thomas W. Lamont mentioned the possibility that Willard Straight (1880–1918) and another banker would underwrite *Harper's Magazine,* with Hapgood as the editor.
2. See LDB to Horace W. Paine, 20 January 1914.
3. *Scientific Management and Railroads* (New York, 1912).

To Norman Hapgood (Telegram)

March 17, 1913 Boston, Mass. [Brandeis Mss, NMF 53-2]

He [1] tries to be on good terms with all elements of his party. Long had general retainers from railroads; made [may] not have any now. Eminently respectable but spineless, and could never be induced to take part in any of the fights to protect the people.

1. Hapgood had telegraphed for LDB's opinion of Charles S. Hamlin, whom McAdoo had just named as assistant secretary of the Treasury.

To Caroline I. Hibbard[1]   (Telegram)

March 18, 1913 Boston, Mass. [Brandeis Mss, NMF 37-3]

Woman's suffrage must be generally adopted, because the participation of women in political affairs will promote social efficiency. Much that is required to be done to improve social and industrial conditions can be done only with women's aid. We cannot relieve them from the duty of taking part in public affairs.[2]

1. Caroline I. Hibbard, a staff writer for *Strauss Magazine*, had solicited LDB's views on women's suffrage.

2. Cf. LDB to Alfred Brandeis, 30 January 1884, n. 1 and to Amy F. Acton, 1 February 1905.

To Samuel Untermyer

March 18, 1913 Boston, Mass. [Brandeis Mss, NMF 58-3]

MY DEAR MR. UNTERMYER: [1] I thank you for your letter of the 17th and for the copy of the report of the Pujo Committee.[2] It is admirable, and most of your recommendations I should heartily approve. In some respects it seems to me that the recommendations do not go far enough, and I should not be surprised to find that in those instances your Committee failed to follow your advice.

I want very much to have at least a few hours with you on my next visit to New York. I may find tomorrow that I must be there on Thursday, and if so, I shall wire you tomorrow hoping that you will have some time, preferably in the evening, free.

I am afraid that I cannot arrange now for the day in the country with you which you so kindly suggest.

Most cordially yours,

1. Samuel Untermyer (1858–1940) was one of the most successful attorneys in the country, and his firm handled many important cases from the 1870s on. Untermyer represented the Morgan and Rockefeller interests on occasion, but he also defended labor unions against company coercion. In 1912 and 1913 he served as counsel to the Pujo Committee (see next note), and in the debate over the Federal Reserve Act he argued along with William Jennings Bryan for complete federal control of the banking and currency system.

2. Spurred on by the muckrakers' accounts of misdeeds in the world of high finance, the Democrats in the 62d Congress secured approval for an

investigation into the control of money and credit. The investigating committee was chaired by Representative Arsene Paulin Pujo (1861–1939) of Louisiana, head of the House Banking Committee. Focussing especially on the Morgan interests, the committee showed how a small coterie of banking and investment houses controlled a large percentage of American business. The report swung popular opinion into favor of strict reform of the currency system. See U.S. House of Representatives, *Report of Committee Appointed Pursuant to H.R. 429 and 594 . . .* , 62d Cong., 3d sess. (Washington, 1913). LDB summarized and popularized the committee's findings in a series of articles for *Harper's* which were published as *Other People's Money and How the Bankers Use It* (New York, 1914).

To Frederick Haynes Newell

March 19, 1913 Boston, Mass. [Brandeis Mss, NMF 53-2]

MY DEAR DR. NEWELL: [1] Replying to yours of the 17th.

First: I believe that your opinion that the Government work is done at least as efficiently as the railroad work is well founded. My own study in connection with railroads, particularly in the Advance Rate Case, convinced me that much of the work in connection with railroads was very inefficient, and I have little doubt that the Government work is on the whole conducted far more honestly than railroad work. The effect of the interlocking directorates, and the huge commissions of controlling bankers, have certainly had a very demoralizing effect upon railroad subordinates. Of course I have no detailed knowledge as to relative honesty.

Second: As to definite examples of railroad extravagance:

I doubt whether I have any examples which would be of great value to you in publicly combatting Mr. Hill's contention,[2] but the operations of our New Haven system are developing a crop of instances of waste, the like of which I should suppose does not exist in any important Government Bureau. The Boston & Maine — American Express Company contract unearthed by the Public Service Commission of New Hampshire, is described in the enclosed extract from that Commission's report filed in November 1912.

Other instances are shown by the facts reported in the so-called Massachusetts Validation Report on the New Haven Railroad, 1911. The Committee was very favorable to the New Haven, but it was constrained to find that trolley properties purchased at a cost of $108,677,512 were worth no more than $57,471,635. The instance in respect to the purchase of interests in the Rhode Island trolleys for $24,000,000, which were not worth more than $6,000,000, is a startling example.

The Interstate Commerce Commission is now making its own examination into the New Haven's finances and accounting. The result is soon to be made public, and I have no doubt you will find there most abundant evidence of the case of one of the great railroad corporations which is controlled by Mr. Hill's great friend, J. P. Morgan.

There is of course also very great waste in railroad operation. One of the flagrant instances of this is the waste of fuel. You will find in the "Railway Age Gazette" of November 24, 1911 an article by L. C. Fritch, Chief Engineer of the Chicago Great Western,[3] on this subject which shows the waste of fifty per cent, and the easily preventable waste of twenty-five per cent, of the railroads, and some instances are being mentioned in connection with our New Haven system at present, but the data are not in form which would be useful to you in this connection.

With best wishes,   Cordially yours,

1. Frederick Haynes Newell (1862–1932) was director of the United States Reclamation Service and an expert on irrigation.

2. James J. Hill and his son Louis Warren Hill (1872–1948) were interested in investments in the Milk River irrigation project in Oregon. Currently, the Hills were feuding with Newell about delays in completing the project and in the process had accused the Reclamation Service of negligence and Newell of incompetence. For Newell's reply, see *New York Times,* 7 June 1913.

3. L. C. Fritch, "Opportunities for Economy on Railways," *Railway Age Gazette* 51 (24 November 1911): 1059–61. In addition to pointing out possible fuel economies, Fritch argued that every employee owed it to his employer to reduce waste.

To Roscoe Pound

March 19, 1913 Boston, Mass. [Pound Mss]

MY DEAR POUND: I have yours of the 18th about "The People's League".[1] I have no doubt that the League will be of service.

I have been consulted somewhat in regard to it, but am not sure whether I shall take an active part. I am quite sure, however, that with the great amount of work that you have on your hands in law reform, you might, and doubtless should, properly decline.

Very truly yours,

1. See LDB to Charles McCarthy, 13 February 1913, and to Mrs. J. Borden Harriman, 22 March 1913.

To Charles Richard Crane

March 22, 1913 Boston, Mass. [Brandeis Mss, NMF 52-1]

MY DEAR CHARLES: Norman tells me that Dodge [1] is expected back this week, and that you are expecting to be in New York next week. He has probably told you, also, that we may conclude it is wiser to try to get Harper's than to convert McClure's into a weekly.

You will know whether it is better to suggest to either Dodge or Jones [2] this possible change in our plans before getting a definite answer from them whether or not they wish to co-operate.

If you should find I am needed in New York next week, make the day next Thursday, as I shall have to be in Boston Friday and Saturday.

I hope matters are going well with you.

Most cordially,

1. Cleveland Hoadley Dodge (1860–1926) was a vice-president of the Phelps Dodge Corporation and a close friend of Woodrow Wilson.
2. Thomas Davies Jones (1851–1930), another close friend of Wilson's, was a director of the International Harvester Corporation and of the so-called Zinc Trust. Wilson nominated him to the Federal Reserve Board in 1914, but had to withdraw the name in the face of stiff opposition from anti-monopolist progressives.

To Florence Jaffray Hurst Harriman

March 22, 1913 Boston, Mass. [Brandeis Mss, NMF 59-5]

MY DEAR MRS. HARRIMAN: I am glad to accept the election as a member of the Executive Committee of the People's League, since it is to serve only until the first annual meeting. I fear that the duties of an efficient executive committee, as ours surely will be, may prove a little more onerous than I can bear in view of other work to which I am committed.

With best wishes,   Very cordially,

To Abraham Lincoln Filene

March 26, 1913 Boston, Mass. [Brandeis Mss, NMF 57-3]

MY DEAR FILENE: Thank you for yours of the 22nd enclosing a copy of Dr. Eliot's letter.[1] He is one who will, I think, never be converted to unionism despite his general openness of mind.

While in Washington yesterday I saw Dr. Charles P. Neill, and talked with him about publishing a supplement on the Protocol, which he is entirely disposed to do. I think he has a better opinion of it on the whole than [Charles H.] Winslow's remark led me to believe. His only criticism in our brief talk being that it is much more effective for unionism than the closed shop. I promised to see him again when I should have more time to talk with him.   Yours cordially,

1. Filene had sent Charles W. Eliot a copy of the *Protocol of Peace*. Eliot considered the Protocol an improvement over the strike, but condemned it in general because it supported the main tenets of unionism.

To Mary Alice Willcox

March 26, 1913 Boston, Mass. [Brandeis Mss, NMF 56-2]

MY DEAR PROFESSOR WILLCOX: [1] Repeated absences from the city have delayed a reply to your letter about the immigration Guide.

I received a copy of the Guide sometime ago, and have been waiting for an opportunity of studying it, and also studying certain problems in connection with immigration, which seem to me very important, but which it has been impossible for me to take up in view of other pressing public matters.

I shall hope before long to have time to do this, and then to have the pleasure of arranging to see you.

Very cordially yours,

1. Mary Alice Willcox (1856–1945[?]) had taught zoology at Wellesley College from 1883 until her retirement in 1910. She then turned her attention

to problems of immigration and served as chairman of the committee on naturalization of the Massachusetts Federation of Women's Clubs.

To Grenville Stanley MacFarland

March 27, 1913 Boston, Mass. [Brandeis Mss, NMF 1-M-2]

MY DEAR MR. MACFARLAND: I am amazed at the editorial in today's Boston American on the railroad situation entitled "The War is over; Lay Down Your Arms". It looks like a complete surrender to the New Haven's Interests.[1]

The war is not over; and I find it difficult to believe that Mr. Hearst has concluded to surrender.

Do read his signed editorial in the December 30, 1912 Boston American entitled "The Solution of the Problem of Oppressive Public Service Monopoly", and tell me how you can reconcile the two editorials.[2]   Very cordially yours,

1. The editorial praised the recent Chamber of Commerce recommendations which would have allowed the New Haven to continue its operations and status indefinitely, on the grounds that its leadership was now showing support for New England's economic growth. Urging all sides to bury past grievances, the paper contended that now "everybody concerned is to SHAKE HANDS. The slogan of the six States is to be 'BOOST, BROTHER, BOOST!'" If the New Haven was willing to let bygones be bygones, then so was the *American*, and all would work together in the future.

2. See LDB to MacFarland, 1 January 1913.

To James Clark McReynolds

March 28, 1913 Boston, Mass. [Brandeis Mss, NMF 53-2]

MY DEAR MR. MCREYNOLDS: As you requested I have made some further inquiries with reference to the appointment of a Circuit Judge in this Circuit.

Upon the whole I think the best course would be to promote Judge [Arthur L.] Brown.[1] All that I have heard about him confirms the good opinion which I had formed from my own experience with him.

Judge Bingham [2] of New Hampshire is well spoken of. He is

described as a fine Judge of the old type; but I think under the circumstances Judge Brown would be the better appointment.[3]

Very cordially yours,

1. See LDB to Seeber Edwards, 12 March 1913.
2. George Hutchins Bingham (1861–1949), after graduating from the Harvard Law School, had practiced in New Hampshire as an attorney until 1902, when he was named to the Supreme Court of that state.
3. The appointment went to Bingham.

To Joseph Bartlett Eastman

March 31, 1913 Boston, Mass. [Brandeis Mss, NMF 1-M-2]

MY DEAR MR. EASTMAN: I hope that with the assistance of Mr. Brown [1] you will be able to prepare before I reach Washington statements covering each year beginning July 1, 1907, of the corrected Income Account and the Profit and Loss of the New Haven in accordance with the actual facts,—for comparison with that rendered to the Commission and the stockholders of the Company.

This will involve among other things:

First: A determination of a proper depreciation charge on the equipment for each year and a charge as an additional operating expense of the difference between the amount which should have been charged and the amount which actually was charged against income.

In the year 1907–8 the aggregate charge on account of equipment depreciation and replacement was presumably adequate, but the greater part of that charge was made against Profit and Loss instead of against Income. In the later years the charges were made wholly against Income and appear to have been inadequate.

Second: A determination of the actual fixed or miscellaneous charges which do not appear as charges against the New Haven Income, but which were taken care of by some other means, for instance, the Providence Securities Company yielded a deficit in a single year rising above $700,000., yet it nowhere appears among the New Haven charges as having been paid for out of the reserve fund set aside to meet the deficit. Later when this reserve fund was exhausted, through other devices the actual liability on the New Haven's guaranty was met, without its appearing in the New Haven account.

Whether the liability upon the Boston Holding Company guaranty and the New York, Westchester & Boston guaranty appear in the accounts as charges against the New Haven I do not know.

Third: An estimate of what credits of dividends and so forth as "Other Income" are substantially fictitious. I have the impression that the amounts of "Other Income" have been determined in many instance[s] not by actual earnings of subsidiary companies but by the financial needs of the New Haven.

Fourth: A determination of the actual amounts improperly credited to Profit and Loss account, and of omissions of amounts which should have been charged to Profit and Loss Account.

Fifth: A determination of the amount actually paid out each year in excess of the earnings of such year.

Sixth: A statement showing the resources to be accounted for and resources accounted for.   Yours very cordially,

1. Possibly George N. Brown, Chief Examiner for the Interstate Commerce Commission.

To Roy Painter

March 31, 1913 Boston, Mass. [Brandeis Mss, NMF 55-1]

MY DEAR MR. PAINTER: [1] Replying to yours of the 26th:

I am disposed to think that compulsory arbitration of labor disputes would in most cases be mischievous—a possible exception in public service corporations.

The protocol and the preferential union shop seems to me full of promise. If you have not already done so, I suggest your reading Dr. Moskowitz' article in the January 1912 number of Life and Labor entitled "The Power for Constructive Reform in the Trade Union Movement", and Charles H. Winslow's report in the Bulletin of the Bureau of Labor No. 98, January 1912.

Yours very truly,

The former can be obtained from Women's Trade Union League, Chicago. The latter from U.S. Bureau of Labor, Washington.

1. Roy Painter was captain of the debating team of Washburn College in Topeka, Kansas. He wanted LDB's opinion of compulsory arbitration in labor disputes.

To Jesse Earl Thornton

March 31, 1913 Boston, Mass. [Brandeis Mss, NMF 69-2]

DEAR PROFESSOR THORNTON: [1] In reply to yours of the 24th, in which you ask whether in my opinion "a legal minimum wage in workshops, factories, and department stores include the workers in the sweated industries,—in other words home workers": —

I should suppose that any minimum wage law that is wisely drawn would probably include the sweated industries.

If you have not already done so, I suggest your getting from the Massachusetts Minimum Wage Commission a copy of its report.   Yours very truly,

1. Jesse Earl Thornton (1886–1965) was an Assistant Professor of English at Washington State College in Pullman, Washington and advisor to the college debating team. In 1914 he would begin his forty-year service at the University of Michigan.

To Garrett Droppers

April 1, 1913 Boston, Mass. [Brandeis Mss, NMF 58-1]

MY DEAR DROPPERS: Yours of the 29th has just reached me.[1]

It seems to me that the thing for you to do is to wire Secretary Bryan asking whether he will fix a time for seeing you and talk the matter over fully with him. I think you should do this at once.

Of course the President knows you, and I think both Mr. Bryan and the President will understand that you do not appear as an office seeker.

I should be glad to have you ask either of them to call upon me for an opinion about your qualifications for this position if you care to.[2]   Very cordially yours,

1. Droppers had written LDB that he thought himself qualified to do a creditable job as minister to Switzerland, especially since he had done considerable research on the Swiss tax system. He did not know how to repre-

sent himself to the administration, however, and did not want to appear an avid office-seeker.

2. Droppers did not receive the appointment to Switzerland; in 1914, however, Wilson named him minister to Greece and Montenegro.

To Marcus M. Marks

April 8, 1913 Boston, Mass. [Brandeis Mss, NMF 55-1]

MY DEAR MR. MARKS: [1] It would be a great pleasure to join you at the dinner on the 28th, if it should be possible for me to be in New York at that time, which now seems improbable.

I trust that the dinner signifies that you will not only suffer "punishment as an unbeliever", but that the punishment will fit the crime, and that you will declare your full adhesion to the preferential shop. Your conversion would undoubtedly lead to its adoption by the garment workers in the men's trade, which would be a vast step forward.   Yours very truly,

1. Marcus M. Marks (1858–1934) headed a large clothing firm in New York and was president of the National Association of Clothiers; later in the year he was elected Manhattan borough president on a fusion ticket. Marks eventually retired from business to devote himself to mediation work in labor disputes.

To Dickinson Sergeant Miller

April 8, 1913 Boston, Mass. [Brandeis Mss, NMF 58-1]

MY DEAR MILLER: Thank you for your letter which led me to make the call on Mr. Wayne MacVeagh, to which I had long looked forward. I saw him last Saturday, and had a most pleasant hour and a quarter with him.

You must be greatly pleased with the President's action in regard to China.[1] I trust the recognition of the Chinese Republic will come soon, and also a further declaration as to our relations to Mexico, Central and South America.[2]

Most cordially yours,

1. On 18 March, Wilson and Bryan, without informing the professional staff in the State Department or consulting with foreign governments, unilaterally repudiated American participation in the six-power loan agreement

with China. The President's reasoning, which found favor with most of the American people, was that the agreement violated China's integrity and took advantage of her weakness. In fact, the loan provided a stabilizing influence in erratic Far Eastern finances, and collapse of the agreement may have hurt China far more than it helped. See Tien-yi Li, *Woodrow Wilson's China Policy, 1913–1917* (New York, 1952).

2. The administration formally recognized the Chinese Republic on 2 May 1913; for Wilson's policy toward Latin America, see Arthur S. Link, *Woodrow Wilson and the Progressive Era, 1910–1917* (New York, 1954), chs. 4–5.

To Alfred Brandeis

April 9, 1913 Boston, Mass. [Brandeis Mss, M 3-3]

DEAR AL: Returned to Boston yesterday, having spent Monday in N.Y. on way from Washington. Nothing specially thrilling in W. Was there mainly on New Haven matters. The Co. & its backers are fighting hard—the inevitable & me—with increasing bitterness. But arithmetic must ultimately prevail, even over false accounting.

Everybody seems well satisfied with Wilson. Heard almost no criticism of him in W., but the talk about some members of the Cabinet has already begun & I guess no administration can escape without its trouble—particularly if we have a bit of hard times.

To Eugene Noble Foss

April 10, 1913 Boston, Mass. [Brandeis Mss, NMF 1-M-2]

MY DEAR GOVERNOR FOSS: I have, as you requested, examined Sections 15 and 16 of House Bill 229, relating to the issue of bonds, notes, and other indebtedness of railways, to give you my opinion in regard to same: [1]

I approve of the general principle of authorizing a railroad to incur indebtedness in an amount exceeding the capital stock and premium paid thereon; but the provisions of the Bill seem to me such as will leave the Commonwealth and the investors without adequate protection, for the following, among other reasons:

First: If the limit of indebtedness is to be increased it ought to be made clear that unsecured bonds or debentures now outstanding should be secured pro rata with any other bonds, notes, or other indebtedness hereafter issued and secured by mortgage or pledge, except, perhaps, of property to be hereafter acquired with the proceeds of the new issues.

Second: The consent of the Railroad Commission should be required for any proposed issue of notes or other evidences of indebtedness, whether payable at periods of more than twelve months after the date thereof, or payable within twelve months; otherwise the consent of the Commission becomes little more than a formality, as the right is given to issue bonds, notes, or other indebtedness for the purposes of funding its floating debt.

Third: The provision for application to the Commission for approval of the issue of capital stock, bonds, notes or other indebtedness, should extend to the issue of those securities regardless of whether or not the money is to be expended in this Commonwealth or in some other state or country, or to provide the means of paying the funded indebtedness for the expenditures made in this Commonwealth or in any other state or country.

Fourth: I do not see the justification for exempting from limitation all bonds, etc., to be issued "for the purpose of paying and refunding at maturity bonds lawfully issued prior to the second day of June 1897".   Yours very truly,

1. House bill 229, introduced by Representative Washburn, was an effort to clarify the rights of railroads to issue securities as well as the powers of the State to regulate the roads. With trouble mounting for the New Haven and B & M lines, it seemed as if they would soon have to resort to massive borrowing beyond the limits allowed under the old law. See LDB to Foss, 21 April 1913, and to Frederick J. MacLeod, 20 May 1913.

To Gifford Pinchot

April 10, 1913 Boston, Mass. [G. Pinchot Mss]

MY DEAR GIFFORD: It is very difficult to resist any opportunity of aiding your great work and of working with you.[1] Of course I am deeply interested in Conservation; and the special program which you outline as the immediate work of the Association, appeals to me strongly; but I feel that for the present there is greatest need for the little I can do in the industrial field, and that I ought to devote myself more particularly to the problems of labor and the trusts, including the Money Trust.

I know that very frequently the office of Director does not necessarily involve much work; but I feel sure that if I began seriously to deal with the problems of the Association, their importance and interest would compel more attention that [*sic*] it seems best for me to give at present.

I am very sorry I can't add yes to the thank you.[2]

With best wishes,　　Most cordially,

1. Pinchot had asked LDB to become a director of the National Conservation Association.
2. See LDB to Pinchot, 18 April 1913.

To Treadwell Cleveland, Jr.

April 14, 1913 Boston, Mass. [Brandeis Mss, NMF 58-1]

MY DEAR MR. CLEVELAND: Thank you for yours of the 12th and the enclosures. I also have yours of the 13th.[1]

I have been very much impressed with your good work and the service which you have been to the progressive cause. It would be a great satisfaction to me if opportunity offered to say a word in your behalf. Let me, however, say this to you now: that I feel that you are doing an extremely important work where you are, and that even if you are not able to accomplish all that you would like, there can be no doubt that you are accomplishing much and that your connection with so influential a paper as the News is of very great service to the public cause.

I hope you will not think of severing your connection with the News unless an exceptionally good opportunity should offer itself in a field that was either wider or could be worked more intensively.

With every good wish,　　Very cordially yours,

1. In his letter of the 12th Cleveland enclosed an interview he had conducted with LDB, which appeared in the *Newark* (N.J.) *Evening News* on 12 April 1913, in which LDB attacked court decisions that restricted unions from picketing and boycotting. The article was reprinted as "Brandeis on the

Labor Problem," *LaFollette's Magazine* 5 (24 May 1913): 5, 14; and it can also be found in *The Curse of Bigness*, 43–47. In his other letter, Cleveland modestly asked LDB if he knew of any newspapers in which he could gain complete control of the editorial policy; while he had no complaints about his treatment by the management of the *Evening News*, the paper's editorial policy was not as uncompromisingly progressive as he would wish.

To William Gibbs McAdoo

April 14, 1913 Boston, Mass. [McAdoo Mss]

MY DEAR MR. MCADOO: Replying to yours of the 11th:

First: Mr. E. A. Filene is eminently fitted by character, standing and qualifications for any of our Customs posts, or, indeed, for any other post in your Department; but I should not think there was the slightest possibility of his accepting any office. I may say that I consider Mr. Filene an ideal citizen, and one of the most useful men to the public in all New England.

Second: John A. Fahey would be an excellent appointment. Mr. Fahey was formerly a newspaper man, and was, until a few years ago, publisher of the Boston Evening Traveller. He exhibited a fine public spirit, and since retiring from the Traveller has given much of his time to public work, particularly as Director and member of the Executive Committee of the Boston Chamber of Commerce and in the National Chamber of Commerce. Mr. Fahey has for years been closely associated with Mr. E. A. Filene in public work; and Mr. Filene, who has known him intimately for many years, speaks of him habitually with great enthusiasm.

I do not think it at all probable that Mr. Fahey would be willing to accept an appointment to any of our Custom posts, but I have never spoken to him on the subject of holding office, and do not know.

Third: I am not able to give you any reliable information about Mr. Strecker.[1] I met him twice, but only for a few moments, and have never come into any contact with him either in business or public matters.

Fourth: I learn that Mr. Fahey excepts to be in Washington next week. I shall say nothing to him about your inquiry, but shall ask him to call and see you, as I know of no Democrat here who could give you a better picture of our political situation and the standing of the various leaders and factions in our community, (unless it be Grenville S. MacFarland, who, as a thorough Democrat, has been in close touch with the situation here), and I think it would be well for you to see them before you make any Massachusetts appointments.

As I told Mr. [Byron R.] Newton, I was merciful and refrained from calling upon you while in Washington last month, knowing how busy you have been. After this exercise of mercy I want to break in upon you when I am next in Washington, and have the pleasure of talking matters over with you.

Very cordially yours,

1. Charles Bren Strecker (1863–19[?]) was an assistant United States Treasurer in Boston. A newspaper publisher and printer, Strecker was also a director of the Boston Hebrew Benevolent Association.

To Jacob Meyer Rudy

April 14, 1913 Boston, Mass. [Brandeis Mss, NMF 48-2]

DEAR MR. RUDY: [1] I have considered most carefully your letter of the 8th and sympathize heartily with your desire to become a lawyer and a worthy one. I regret, therefore, that it is impossible to comply with your request to become an "apprentice" in our office. My partners and I agreed long ago to a rule which has been definitely applied,—not to take into our office anyone who is not a Law School graduate; and even if that rule did not exist, it would be impossible to add any to our office force as our rooms are now over full. I shall venture, however, in view of your letter, to give you some advice:

Don't imagine that the time that you spend in "a commercial house" is wasted. What a lawyer needs is knowledge, not only of law, but of affairs; and above all, of men and of human nature. The time that you spend in business may ultimately prove to be the most profitable preparation for an honorable and useful pursuit of your profession. Learn, above all things, to understand thoroughly business, business habit of mind, business practices, and business men; and treat every activity in life with which you come in contact as simply educating you to a better performance later of the specific duties of the profession which you are choosing for yourself. Remember every person you meet.[2]

In the next place, proper preparation for law involves good general education; and the education not only of books, but of life outside of business as well as in it.

In the third place, the best part of that education is the struggle,—the determination to overcome difficulties; and those difficulties with which you are now wrestling will probably do more to strengthen your will and your mind than conditions which might seem more favorable.

Be eager, but don't be impatient. Take time to do the thing that you have before you well.[3]

With best wishes,   Very cordially

1. Jacob Meyer Rudy (1892–[?]) was attending evening law school while working in a business office in Hartford, Connecticut. He wanted very much to be a lawyer but felt it hopeless to waste so much time in "business" when he wanted to use the law for reform work. He asked LDB to take him on as an apprentice.

2. See also LDB to William Harrison Dunbar, 2 February 1893.

3. See LDB to Rudy, 10 May 1913.

To Charles Warren

April 14, 1913 Boston, Mass. [Brandeis Mss, NMF 58-1]

MY DEAR WARREN: [1] Thank you for your article on "The Progressiveness of the United States Supreme Court." [2] You have performed a most laborious and useful task.

I long for the opportunity of taking up the study of the cases for which your article affords so excellent a guide.

There is one case which I should like to have had you discuss: Adair vs. United States, 208 U.S. 161.[3]

May I trouble you to send a copy of your article to Miss Josephine Goldmark, 270 W. 94th Street, New York City?
Yours very cordially

1. Charles Warren (1868–1954) was a distinguished Boston lawyer and legal historian. Warren practiced with Moorfield Storey and afterwards in a firm of his own until 1914, when he became assistant attorney-general of the United States. During the 1920s and 1930s he was frequently appointed special master by federal courts, and he represented the United States in

several international legal cases. At the same time, Warren wrote and lectured extensively on legal history. His most important work was the three-volume *The Supreme Court in United States History* (Boston, 1922); his earlier *History of the Harvard Law School and Early Legal Conditions in America* (3 vols., Boston, 1909) is considered a classic.

2. Warren attacked the notion that the Supreme Court was reactionary and placed the blame for much of the popular uneasiness with judicial decisions on the *Lochner* case (see LDB to Louis B. Wehle, 10 February 1908, n. 1). Reviewing the whole trend of cases from 1887 to 1911, however, Warren was able to list a long series of progressive state measures that had been upheld by the Court. "The Progressiveness of the United States Supreme Court," 13 *Columbia Law Review* 294 (1913).

3. In the *Adair* case (1908), the Court struck down a federal law which forbade employers from utilizing a so-called "yellow-dog" contract, in which the employee promised never to join a labor union. The case undercut organized labor's claim to legitimacy and was extremely reactionary. The most memorable part of the decision is Holmes's dissent, in which he charged his brethren with allowing their prejudices to take precedence over the will of the legislature.

To Oliver Wendell Holmes, Jr.

April 17, 1913 Boston, Mass. [Holmes Mss]

MY DEAR JUDGE HOLMES: Your little book of prose poems [1] has given me the joy of old friendships renewed and of new ones made; and has deepened my appreciation of the privilege of knowing you these many years.

Each address makes one feel that you have gone far in your striving: "To see so far as one may, and to feel the great forces that are behind every detail," and I am made to realize more clearly the volume of my "accepted truths" for which you are responsible.   Most cordially,

1. Oliver Wendell Holmes, *Speeches* (Boston, 1913).

To Louis Lipsky

April 17, 1913 Boston, Mass. [Brandeis Mss, Z 1-4]

DEAR MR. LIPSKY: [1] I have discussed yours of the 15th with Mr. DeHaas.[2]

I do not think that I have an opinion on the question which is entitled to great consideration, but I am inclined to think that it would on the whole be desirable to have Dr. Solis-Cohen[3] accompany Mr. Sokolow when he calls on Secretary Bryan, and that it would be best to call on Secretary Bryan first, and have him arrange, if he will, for Mr. Sokolow's meeting the President.

I enclose my check for $100. for the propaganda fund of the Federation.[4]   Cordially yours,

1. Louis Lipsky (1876–1963) devoted almost his entire life to the Zionist cause. As chairman of the executive committee of the Federation of American Zionists, Lipsky was one of a handful of men who held the young American Zionist movement together prior to 1914. From 1914 to 1920, he worked loyally for LDB but was never one of LDB's most trusted lieutenants. A brilliant journalist, Lipsky always identified with the Yiddish-speaking labor Zionists and by 1920 was edging away from Brandeis's group. At the 1921 Cleveland convention, Lipsky led the fight against LDB, and during the 1920's he headed the Zionist Organization. After the return to power of the Brandeis-Mack group in 1930, Lipsky was eased out of the organization, and he took up a career as an insurance executive. For his extremely critical view of LDB, see his *A Gallery of Zionist Profiles* (New York, 1956), 153–65.

2. Lipsky wanted to arrange a discussion between Nahum Sokolow, William Jennings Bryan, and possibly also President Wilson, leading to a more active American role in supporting and defending Zionist colonies in Palestine.

3. Solomon Solis-Cohen (1857–1948) was a Philadelphia physician and an active Zionist; he served on the Jewish Agency for Palestine from 1920 to 1940.

4. Prior to his total involvement after August 1914, LDB habitually sent unsolicited funds to the Zionists while evading their attempts to draw him into a more active commitment.

To Julius Meyer

April 17, 1913 Boston, Mass. [Brandeis Mss, Z 1-2]

DEAR MR. MEYER: [1] As requested in yours of the 16th I am enclosing herewith my application for membership in the Zion Association, and am also enclosing my check for $5.00, which Mr. DeHaas tells me is to be the annual fee.

I very much regret that my engagements for the rest of April are such that I dare not undertake to be present at the meeting arranged to perfect the permanent organization, but if you will send me notice of the meeting, I shall be glad to attend if I am free to do so.   Yours very truly,

1. Julius Meyer was chairman of the membership committee of the Zion Association of greater Boston.

To Edward George Lowry

April 18, 1913 Boston, Mass. [Brandeis Mss, NMF 1-N-2]

MY DEAR MR. LOWRY: [1] If the Post is still interested in New Haven matters, you may want to have a representative in Boston at the hearings which begin Monday next before Commissioner Prouty,[2] and may last throughout the week.[3]

The reports of the Interstate Commerce Commission's accountants, who have been at work on the New Haven books since October, will then be made public.   Yours very truly,

1. Edward George Lowry (1876–1943) was the managing editor of the *New York Evening Post*.

2. Charles Azro Prouty (1853–1921), after legal and political work in Vermont, was appointed to the Interstate Commerce Commission in 1896. He served on that body until 1914, the last two years of his term as chairman. After an unsuccessful attempt at the United States Senate seat from Vermont, in 1914, Prouty rejoined the I.C.C. as director of valuation. During the war he headed the public service and accounting division of the Railroad Administration.

3. Acting upon information supplied by LDB, the Interstate Commerce Commission opened new hearings on the New Haven on 22 April. With LDB acting as counsel to the Boston Fruit and Produce Exchange, the hearings elicited firm evidence to buttress many of LDB's accusations. Under close examination, New Haven officials admitted instances of improper transfer of accounts, juggling of real estate purchases and sales, phony transfers of stock, and many other items. Accounts of the hearings regularly made the front pages of the Boston newspapers, and many commentators who had previously attacked LDB now began to admit that he might have been right.

To Gifford Pinchot

April 18, 1913 Boston, Mass. [G. Pinchot Mss]

MY DEAR GIFFORD: Replying to yours of the 11th: [1]

I feel very strongly that I ought not to be a director when I know I shall not take part in directing; but if you have in your Association such a thing as an Advisory Board, I should be glad to appear on that.   Yours cordially,

1. Pinchot had renewed his request that LDB serve as a director of the National Conservation Association (see LDB to Pinchot, 10 April 1913). "I want it," he wrote, "not only because I want you but because I want the Association to keep in close touch through you with Wilson's Administration. . . . You can do as little work as you like personally. Your name will work for you while you sleep."

To Eugene Noble Foss

April 21, 1913 Boston, Mass. [Brandeis Mss, NMF 1-M-2]

MY DEAR GOVERNOR: Thank you for yours of the 18th enclosing copy of Chairman McCleod's [sic] very clear statement contained in his letter of the 17th.[1]

There is an additional point to which I think I should call attention: Railroad companies, besides issuing their own bonds, occasionally guarantee bonds of other companies; and at times these bonds of other companies create as extensive a liability as the liability of a bond issued directly. In other words, the maker of the bond contributes little or nothing to the security. For instance,—the New Haven is liable today on a guaranty of nearly $20,000,000 4% debentures issued by the Providence Securities Company. The Providence Securities Company was a $50,000 corporation. It has transferred all its assets, and has possibly been dissolved, and the value of the bond depended at all times upon the guaranty of the New Haven.

Why should not such guaranteed bonds be recognized by the law, as they are in fact, as much a part of the indebtedness as the direct debentures or mortgage bonds of the Railroad Company; that is, be counted in determining the limit of indebtedness, and be secured by any mortgage that is authorized?

Yours very truly,

1. In response to LDB's letter to Foss of 10 April, MacLeod noted that previous laws relating to railroad indebtedness would not be repealed by the proposed statute, so that the safeguards LDB sought would be in effect.

Moreover, since two members of the House Committee on Ways and Means had raised similar questions, the Committee adopted an amendment reaffirming previous limits on indebtedness. As to LDB's suggestion that all proposed note or bond issues should first be approved by the Railroad Commission, MacLeod objected that this would place an intolerable burden on the Commission. Railroads frequently issued short-term notes to meet temporary shortages, or in lieu of anticipated revenues, and to require Commission approval of these issues would be of benefit neither to the companies nor to the Commonwealth. MacLeod also disagreed with some other criticisms LDB had raised, and pointed out that they pertained to existing law rather than to the proposed statute. See LDB to MacLeod, 20 May 1913.

To Charles Culp Burlingham

April 23, 1913 Boston, Mass. [Brandeis Mss, NMF 1-M-2]

MY DEAR CHARLES: Replying to yours of the 22nd.[1]

What I wanted was not any definite reports of any particular company, but the conclusion which the steamship companies have reached as a matter of business experience as to:

First: What they ought to charge off each year for depreciation on their steamships, and

Second: What the average percentage of the cost of the steamship is which is expended for repairs.

In most branches of business experience develops an amount which ought to be charged off for depreciation, and what amount is ordinarily necessary for repairs; and I presume that steamship companies have reached something like a consensus of opinion on this point. What I want to know for my own information is what those percentages are.

I should be greatly obliged if you can get such information from your friends. I dare say that such of the companies as make public reports to their stockholders disclose in their accounts the charges which they themselves make as against operating revenues for these purposes.[2]   Very cordially yours,

1. In reply to an earlier request for information on steamship lines, Burlingham responded that the lines did not file reports with any commission and that several personal inquiries had not yielded any information.

2. On 30 April, Burlingham's son Charles informed LDB that three to five per cent was the range for annual depreciation, and the Cunard line considered twenty years the appropriate depreciation period for a steamship. As to

repairs, most lines set up separate funds based on prior experience and did not use any set percentage.

To Walter Ernest Clark

April 23, 1913 Boston, Mass. [Brandeis Mss, NMF 16-1]

MY DEAR MR. CLARK: [1] Replying to yours of the 20th:

Your recollection is substantially correct in regard to the Boston gas situation. You will find the information which you desire in my article in the American Review of Reviews for November 1907, Page 594, entitled "How Boston Solved the Gas Problem."

The five years which have elapsed since that article was written have confirmed to a most extraordinary degree the success of the experiment. The public is absolutely satisfied with the gas situation.

Before we introduced the sliding scale, our gas situation had been for nearly twenty years a stench in the nostrils of the community. Gas was the most hated of public service utilities. Since that time there has been universal satisfaction, heightened of course by very wise management on the part of Mr. [James L.] Richards.

The profit sharing with the public was supplemented by profit sharing with most of the employees, they receiving a dividend upon wages at the same rate as the dividend that is paid upon the stock, and the employees also obtain a representation upon the Board of Directors. The effect upon the Company has been equally as good as upon the public. The stock of the Gas Company is held, together with other properties, by the Massachusetts Gas Company, a voluntary association. Throughout the last six years there has probably been no stock on the market in which our community has shown such confidence as in this stock. Both stock and bonds sell upon an extraordinarily low basis of income return considering the nature of the concern. The Massachusetts Gas Company securities passed through the 1907 panic with less depression than any on our market.   Yours very truly,

1. Walter Ernest Clark (1873–1955) was professor of political science at the City College of New York; in 1917 he became president of the University of Nevada.

To Alton E. Briggs

April 25, 1913 Boston, Mass. [Brandeis Mss, NMF 1-M-2]

DEAR SIR: Your letter of yesterday is at hand.[1]

At the commencement of the session this morning, I shall formally withdraw my appearance as counsel for the Boston Fruit and Produce Exchange.

You will recall that at the opening hearing on July 1, 1912, Commissioner Prouty stated:

"The investigation which the Commission proposes to undertake will finally divide into three general heads. There will be:

First, the financial aspects of the subject. . . .

There is, second, what may be termed the traffic aspect of the question. . . .

There is, third and finally, the question of service."

Subsequently, Commissioner Prouty stated on several occasions that he deemed the financial inquiry the most important part of the investigation. In that view of Commisioner Prouty, I wholly concur.

The financial condition and practices of the railroads involve and underlie all other questions,—service and rates, safety of life and stability of investment and integrity of management. In these questions the people of all New England are vitally interested; not the shippers only, but the general travelling public, the employees of the railroads, and their stock and bond holders.

I have, therefore, arranged with Commissioner Prouty to continue to act in this investigation, but merely in the capacity of a citizen of Massachusetts.[2]

In a publication of yesterday one of the members of your Exchange is reported as saying that I "offered" my services to the Exchange. This you know is not true, as you and Mr. Mead called upon me and requested me to act, and after consideration, I assented, with the proviso that the matter being one of a public nature, I would not accept any compensation. What occurred is covered by the following correspondence:

"Boston, June 26, 1912

Boston Fruit & Produce Exchange,
  Alton E. Briggs, Esq., Secy.
  Over Faneuil Hall Market, Boston.

Dear Mr. Briggs:

Replying to yours and Mr. Mead's request of the 24th that I act as counsel for the Boston Fruit and Produce Exchange in the investigation to be commenced before Commissioner Prouty on the 1st:

I find it will be possible for me to act as your counsel and I shall be glad to do so.

Nothing was said at our conference about compensation. I prefer to treat this as a public service, and shall therefore not accept any compensation for my services in this connection.

Yours very truly,
(signed) Louis D. Brandeis."

"Boston Fruit and Produce Exchange,
Boston, June 27, 1912.

Mr. Louis D. Brandeis,
  161 Devonshire St.,
  Boston, Mass.
Dear Mr. Brandeis:

Your favorable decision in the matter of acting as counsel for the Boston Fruit and Produce Exchange in the investigation before Commissioner Prouty is accepted with much enthusiasm by our members.

That you will consider such service as a "public service" needs no comment on my part in attempting to express appreciation. When a man places himself as you have done in offering his service for the benefit of his fellow men without asking any pecuniary return, we can at least hope that the compensation of gratitude will exist in its highest degree, and we believe such gratitude does exist.

Kindly inform us in what way we can aid you, for our office, as well as myself, will be subject to your order in any matter pertaining to the hearing.

I am,

Very sincerely,
(signed) Alton E. Briggs
Executive Secretary."

May I trouble you to send a copy of these letters to the gentleman referred to in yesterday's publication so that he may be advised of the facts? [3]

Yours very truly,

1. Briggs had written that the Boston Fruit and Produce Exchange, when it had accepted LDB's offer of service the previous June, had only wanted him to represent them in that part of the hearings dealing with poor service, and had not expected him to get involved in questions of finance. When the hearings began to concentrate on finance, a number of members had objected to LDB's continued role, "and it is the expression of our Directors that further representation on your part for the Exchange not be continued." Briggs concluded the letter with a tender of thanks from the Exchange for LDB's services.

2. The following day LDB did appear as a "citizen" and was immediately challenged by the New Haven's chief attorney, Charles F. Choate. When LDB persisted, Choate informed the Commission that he, too, would "represent the people, the same as my dear brother, Mr. Brandeis." LDB then suggested that Choate had been continuously employed by the New Haven, and when Choate angrily responded that that was not true, LDB smilingly asked: "Well, then, you are counsel perhaps for the New England Navigation Company, subsidiary of the New Haven?" Amid muffled laughter, the Commission examiner read that Choate had received almost $14,000 from the New England company, of which half was marked for services to the New Haven. The following week Choate appeared as personal counsel to Charles Mellen. See *Boston American*, 25 April 1913 and Mason, *Brandeis*, 206–209.

3. The Exchange's firing of LDB had caused a sensation in the newspapers, and the general impression was that there had been widespread dissension between LDB and the directors of the Exchange. Briggs replied the same day that he regretted the distortion of the facts by the press. "If I did not appreciate that you were more familiar than I with press statements and comments, I should be tempted to write you and say 'I never said any such things', but I feel quite certain that no such statement is necessary from me." Briggs also assured LDB that he would forward the original exchange of letters to the unhappy member of the Exchange, and he would also offer it to anyone who wanted to know the truth. He hoped that LDB would not blame the entire Exchange for the actions of a few members. See next letter.

To *Boston American*

April 26, 1913 Boston, Mass. [Brandeis Mss, NMF 1-M-3]

DEAR SIRS: I think that some injustice has been done by the press in assuming that Mr. Briggs, the Executive Secretary of the Boston Fruit and Produce Exchange, was in some way responsible for the vote of the Board of Directors of that body on which comment has been made. Mr. Briggs is the Executive Secretary of the Exchange, and as such would necessarily be required to transmit any vote of his Board. As indicating the attitude of Mr. Briggs, and his belief as to the views of the other members of the Exchange, you may care to see his letter to me of April 25th, and also letter of Mr. E. J. Twombly of that date, copies of which are enclosed.[1]   Yours very truly

1. Twombly, a fruit and produce broker, had written to LDB that he considered the action of the Exchange directors very unjust, and that of the 800 members, he believed over 700 of them disagreed with the directors' discharge of LDB. "I think you are doing a splendid service for the New England public, and I believe the great majority of people appreciate it." This letter was published in the *American* on this date.

To E. Homer Marks

April 26, 1913 Boston, Mass. [Brandeis Mss, NMF 1-M-3]

MY DEAR MR. MARKS: [1] Thank you for your letter of the 22nd.
    As you may have seen from yesterday's reports as to my action in regard to the invitation to represent several Boston Merchants, it seems to me best to appear now merely as a citizen.
                                        Very truly yours,

1. E. Homer Marks was treasurer of the Legal Protection Federation, a cooperative agency consisting of ninety different organizations, many of which were labor unions. He asked LDB to represent the Federation before the Interstate Commerce Commission.

To William Cox Redfield

April 26, 1913 Boston, Mass. [Brandeis Mss, NMF 35-2]

MY DEAR MR. SECRETARY: You are of course familiar with the important advance in the women's garment industry which arose out of the settlement of the great New York strike of 1910, and resulted in the establishment of the Preferential Union Shop, and the Joint Board of Sanitary Control.
    The Bureau of Labor made a careful study of the Protocol which was published last year as Bulletin #68, and the Department of Labor is at present making a supplemental study, so rapid has been the advance of this "Protocol movement."

The extraordinary improvement in the sanitary condition prevailing in the garment industry under the protocol is due in large measure to the very efficient work of Dr. Geo. M. Price, Chairman of the Executive Committee.

The cloak and suit industry of New York is about to introduce a tuberculosis benefit for the trade of the city. The Joint Board of Sanitary Control is to administer such benefit, and Dr. Price is being sent by the Board to make a special study of the methods of tuberculosis control in Germany and other countries. He expects to leave on May 9th and to remain abroad four months.

I hope that you will agree with me that Dr. Price ought to be afforded all assistance possible to enable him to learn the utmost Europe has to teach on this subject, and will do what you can to aid in securing for him special facilities for investigation and study abroad.[1]   Very truly yours,

1. Price's observations were published in a lengthy Department of Labor document, *Administration of Labor Laws and Factory Inspection in Certain European Countries* (Washington, 1914).

To W. J. Van Camp

April 26, 1913 Boston, Mass. [Brandeis Mss, NMF 8-3]

DEAR SIR: [1] Replying to yours of April 16th.

First: I believe that the Industrial Commission, provided for by the last Congress, will, if its membership is adequate, do much toward increasing social and economic efficiency.

Second: The greatest need of unskilled labor is to reduce its quantity. There is little labor which could not be made more productive by greater skill. What is needed primarily is education and organization.

Third: The question as to the minimum wage would require at least an essay to answer and possibly a volume.

Very truly yours

1. Van Camp, a student at the State Normal School in Wayne, Nebraska, had asked LDB three questions, centering around the "Labor Problem." The third question was: "Do you believe a Minimum Wage should be established in all industries? Why or why not?"

To Norman Hapgood

April 28, 1913 Boston, Mass. [Brandeis Mss, NMF 52-1]

MY DEAR NORMAN: I have yours of the 27th.[1]

I think it would be well enough to call up Lamont sometime this week if he does not come forward. I should be very reluctant to create a bond issue, but if George Porter [2] and others were inclined to come in to provide the cash necessary for a settlement with Lamont of $100,000. or presumably less, I should not see any great objection to that, provided we retain control, with you and Charles [Crane] and others in a voting trust; although it would mean paying for Harper's probably more than it is worth on any fair basis.   Cordially,

P. S.   Our railroad hearings are continuing at least two days more, and possibly longer. I think that our Boston financiers and their friends are having their eyes opened,—a process painful to them and slow.

1. Hapgood had written that he was worried over Lamont's failure to come to terms in the negotiations for *Harper's* and he was wondering if they should try to raise the $100,000 Lamont wanted through a bond issue.

2. George French Porter (1881–1927) was involved in a number of midwestern financial enterprises and had been active in the Progressive Party.

To Charles Frederick Weed

April 28, 1913 Boston, Mass. [Brandeis Mss, NMF 63-2]

MY DEAR MR. WEED: I hear that Eastman's salary [1] is much in arrears. He has been doing excellent work, and I think his salary ought now to be paid. I am therefore enclosing my check for $500 to enable you to pay him.

Please credit this payment on my contribution for the year beginning May 1, 1913.   Yours very truly,

1. As secretary of the Public Franchise League.

To Robert Marion LaFollette

April 29, 1913 Boston, Mass. [La Follette Mss]

MY DEAR BOB: I was delighted to see in the April 26th Weekly your editorial "Commissions on Trial." [1]

I hope that you will follow this with another editorial bringing out the lines of legislation which we discussed last month, namely: the establishment of a Railroad Bureau of Costs and Experimental Station, and the abolition of interlocking directorates by the railroad companies, bankers' supply companies etc.[2]

In aid of that campaign I gave to the United Press representative last month a statement, of which I enclose a copy.[3]

Even LaFollette's would be satisfied with the volume of truth which we are disclosing in our hearings before Commissioner [Charles A.] Prouty and Examiner [W.] Prouty this week and last on the New Haven.[4]   Most cordially yours,

1. In a front-page editorial, LaFollette warned that regulatory commissions such as the Interstate Commerce Commission, unless closely watched and supported by the people, tend to become controlled by the very interests they are supposed to be regulating. "Commissions on Trial," *LaFollette's Weekly Magazine* 5 (26 April 1913): 1.

2. In another front-page article, the Senator called for increased prosecution of the New Haven, and cited its corruption and its interlocking directorates with other Morgan interests. "Prosecute the New Haven Merger," *LaFollette's Weekly Magazine* 5 (19 May 1913): 1, 3.

3. On 19 March 1913, LDB issued a statement upon passage of the La-Follette bill for the physical valuation of railroads by the I.C.C. He claimed that a true valuation was the only proper basis for rate-making, and now the public could have that information. The I.C.C. needed to know real costs, in order to judge if railroad expenses were just or wasteful. LDB also attacked interlocking directorates for creating unnecessary expenses.

4. W. Prouty was an examiner for the Interstate Commerce Commission.

To Woodrow Wilson

April 29, 1913 Boston, Mass. [Wilson Mss]

MY DEAR MR. PRESIDENT: With your permission, I will defer for about a week answering your most kind letter of the 24th tendering me the Chairmanship of the Commission on Industrial Relations;[1] as the Interstate Commerce Commission hearings on our New England transportation monopoly are absorbing my whole attention for the present.

Meanwhile I shall be glad to have Mr. Tumulty[2] send me a copy of the Act creating the Commission.[3]

Very cordially yours,

1. Wilson had written: "There is no one in the United States who could preside over and direct such an inquiry so well as you could, and I wonder if it is possible for you to strengthen the whole thing by assuming direction of it. It would gratify me very deeply if you could." For background of the Commission, see LDB to William Howard Taft, 30 December 1911; see also Graham Adams, Jr., *Age of Industrial Violence, 1910–1915* (New York, 1966).

2. Joseph Patrick Tumulty (1879–1954) was private secretary to Woodrow Wilson. Tumulty had met Wilson when the latter was seeking the New Jersey governorship and had played a major role in reconciling his progressive views with the sensitivities of the party bosses. As presidential secretary, Tumulty relieved Wilson of enormous administrative burdens and also served as liaison between the President on one hand and politicians and newsmen on the other. Unfortunately, Tumulty was often rash, and he was mistrusted by many progressives who saw him as an old line politico. In 1915 Colonel House started a movement to get rid of Tumulty but he was unable to do so; he did, however, undermine much of the trust that had existed between the President and his secretary. See Tumulty's *Woodrow Wilson As I Know Him* (Garden City, 1921) and John Morton Blum, *Joe Tumulty and the Wilson Era* (Boston, 1951).

3. See LDB to Woodrow Wilson, 19 May 1913.

To Joseph Shohan

April 30, 1913 Boston, Mass. [Brandeis Mss, Z 1–2]

DEAR DR. SHOHAN: [1] I am very sorry that the other calls upon me will not let me accept the position of President of the Zionists Association, which you so kindly suggest in your letter of yesterday, as I should feel that it involved a very distinct executive responsibility for which I have not the time at present.[2]

Many similar associations have provided an honorary president, like the National Conservation Association, of which Dr. Charles W. Eliot is Honorary President, and Gifford Pinchot, President. If your Association should see fit to create such an office, and you think my name would be of value to the cause, I should be very glad to appear in that capacity, but I do not think I ought to accept a position, the duties of which I have reason to think I cannot adequately perform.[3]   Cordially yours,

1. Joseph Shohan, a Roxbury physician, was secretary of the Zion Association of Greater Boston.

2. The Zion Association had asked LDB to be a member of its board of directors, and he had refused on 26 April; at that time he had offered to

join an advisory council. On 29 April Shohan wrote him a lengthy letter outlining the plans of the organization and tendering him the presidency, which he said involved no more than presiding over three yearly meetings.

3. On 3 May Shohan informed LDB that he had been elected Honorary President of the Zion Association of Greater Boston.

To Frederick Faber Forbes

May 1, 1913 Boston, Mass. [Brandeis Mss, NMF 1-M-3]

MY DEAR MR. FORBES: [1] Replying to yours of yesterday: [2]

I will endeavor to have a memorandum of the most salient points sent you as soon as possible. I cannot do so today as we are busy with the hearings which will continue today and probably tomorrow. I am writing, however, today because it seems to me important that the American should at once come out with a protest against advancing the freight rates,[3] until we get a united effort for greater efficiency and abolition of the interlocking directorates.

I am enclosing you a statement which I made in March with reference to covering proposed legislation on this subject,[4] and if available you may care to look at my article in the Engineering Magazine of October 1911, discussing the Bureau of Railroad Costs somewhat more fully.

There ought to be a very vigorous protest against this attempt to raise rates under present conditions. I hope you can write an editorial on this at once, and then follow it with another editorial outlining the New Haven disclosures, a memorandum as to which will follow.[5]   Yours very truly,

1. Frederick Faber Forbes (18[?]-1933) had just become managing editor of the *Philadelphia North American.*
2. Forbes had asked LDB to send him a memorandum about the New Haven investigation, since the wire service reports were too fragmentary to be of much help in writing editorials.
3. Eastern carriers had requested an increase in freight rates, and LDB, representing shippers, again accused the roads of inefficiency and misman-agement. In particular, LDB singled out the New Haven, which, he charged, was going bankrupt because of its greedy efforts to monopolize New England transportation. He compared the management of the line to that of a wildcat mining scheme and predicted that there would soon cease to be dividends, since the line had not earned its dividend in five of the last six

years. In conclusion, LDB argued that increasing freight rates to allow railroads to meet their problems was like giving a spendthrift more income to meet his debts at the end of the year. The real solution lay in proper management at all times. Supporting LDB's claims of poor service was Robert Homans, representing the Boston Chamber of Commerce. Charles F. Choate attempted to repudiate LDB's charges, but he limited himself principally to casting aspersions on the fairness of the Commission's examiner and the sources of LDB's information.

4. See LDB to Robert M. LaFollette, 29 April 1913, n. 3.

5. On 7 May, the *North American* carried a lengthy editorial attacking the railroad request for higher freight rates and citing statistics to show that the request was not justified. The editorial emphasized that the prime responsibility of the roads was to serve the public; while not denying the right to a profit, it noted that efficiency experts had argued that between one and two million dollars a day could be saved through the application of scientific management.

To Livy Strong Richard

May 1, 1913 Boston, Mass. [Brandeis Mss, LtB]

MY DEAR RICHARD: I see that the railroads are at last taking courage under the cover of recent floods to ask for a five per cent increase in freight rates.

No increase in freight rates ought to be allowed at the present moment, or so long as the vicious system of interlocking directorates make it impossible to know how much of the money is honestly and efficiently spent. We ought to have also, before raising the rates, the establishment of a Bureau of Railroad Costs. You may recall the statement I made on this subject to the United Press correspondent some six weeks ago, of which I enclose a copy.[1]   Yours very truly,

1. See LDB to Robert M. LaFollette, 29 April 1913, n.3.

To Charles Sumner Bird

May 10, 1913 Boston, Mass. [Brandeis Mss, NMF 32-2]

MY DEAR MR. BIRD: The New Haven hearings and my absence from the city delayed my seeing Mr. Fuller [1] and replying to yours of the 10th of April.

Upon careful consideration it seemed to me so improbable that the Boston Common could be put upon a permanent and paying basis, that I concluded it was not wise to become one of the subscribers of the sufficient fund to carry it for the next three or four months, as you suggested. Of course it is always a question which of the public causes in which one is interested is the more worth while, and I quite realize the fallibility of my own judgment in making such a decision.   Most cordially yours,

1. Frederick Timothy Fuller (1850–1942) was the editor of the *Boston Common*, and active in the Massachusetts Progressive Party. After the *Common* was discontinued, he joined the staff of the *Boston American*, and in 1919 he served as secretary to Senator David I. Walsh.

To Treadwell Cleveland, Jr.

May 10, 1913 Boston, Mass. [Brandeis Mss, NMF 1-M-3]

DEAR MR. CLEVELAND: Upon my return to the city I find yours of the 9th.[1]

It seems to me that before we become committed to higher rates, we should know that the money we now pay the railroads for passenger and freight service is properly applied. About two-thirds of all we pay goes to operating expenses. How do we know how much money is wasted through graft or inefficiency; and there is reason to believe that there is much of both, due in part to the interlocking directorates. It was important to get a physical railroad evaluation as bearing upon rates. It is far more important to do away with interlocking directorates, and establish a Bureau of Costs as an aid to efficient administration.

I enclose a copy of a brief statement I prepared sometime ago on this subject, which you may care to have.

Cordially yours,

P.S. I saw your friend [Raymond W.] Pullman in Washington yesterday.

1. Cleveland had wired: "Are shippers (yourself included) more inclined to agree that railroads are more entitled to higher rates than they were two years ago?"

To Lynn Haines

May 10, 1913 Boston, Mass. [Brandeis Mss, NMF 61-3]

MY DEAR MR. HAINES: I am glad to have yours of the 9th and the leaflet setting forth the plan and purpose of the National Voters' League and its officers.[1]

I have great faith in such work as your League is doing,—i.e., patiently ascertaining facts, and then making people understand what the facts are. This is the foundation of all progress, and I am inclined to think that when this task is faithfully performed, progress is easy. It is for this reason that I sent you my check for $500.00. I could think of no better use for the money.

With best wishes,   Very cordially yours,

1. See LDB to Haines, 12 March 1913. Haines had written to ask LDB for a letter suitable for publicity purposes.

To Henry Moskowitz

May 10, 1913 Boston, Mass. [Brandeis Mss, NMF 35-2]

MY DEAR DR. MOSKOWITZ: Supplementing my letter to you of yesterday from Washington:

Hourwitz [*sic*] appears considerably worked up, and it appears to me necessary to arrange for the conference on Wednesday.

I think you ought before that time to talk over this situation very fully with Hourwitz, and also with others, to get him into line. His main point seems to be that, without constant resort to the decisions of a court, the protocol will not work. I have considered the best feature of the protocol that we did not resort to Courts, and that we dealt by proper discussions of the questions as they arise.[2]

I expect to be at the Harvard Club on Wednesday morning, and think it would be well for me to see you before we go over to the meeting,—say, at 9:30.   Cordially yours,

1. Isaac A. Hourwich (1860–1924), a revisionist Marxist labor leader, was one of the more colorful socialists on New York's lower East Side. A founder of the Yiddish daily, *The Forward,* Hourwich was chief clerk of the International Ladies' Garment Workers Union. He had originally been

an admirer of LDB. See Melech Epstein, *Profiles of Eleven* (Detroit, 1965), ch. 8.

2. The cornerstone of the garment workers' Protocol was conciliation and mediation between the two sides, with a mechanism established to settle differences internally. The basic assumption was that both sides would give a little in order to reach a peaceful settlement, even though, at times, this might mean conceding some points. While the bulk of the employers and union officers subscribed to this principle, Hourwich objected that the union should never have to concede a point when it was in the right, and he proposed binding arbitration by the courts in place of the mediation of the Protocol. A stubborn man, he rallied dissident elements about him and almost killed the Protocol; finally, in 1914, with the threat of a general strike in the air, Hourwich resigned; later in the year, his chief opponent, John Dyche, was ousted from ILGWU leadership. See Mason, *Brandeis,* 306–10 for details.

To Jacob Meyer Rudy

May 10, 1913 Boston, Mass. [Brandeis Mss, NMF 48-2]

MY DEAR SIR: Absence from the city has delayed reply to your letter of the 29th.[1]

You, of course, must be careful, above all, of your health and no course of action should be pursued by you which menaces that.

I am sorry it is impossible for us to make a place for you in our office.

The rule to which I referred in my letter to you is not one to which exceptions can be made by any member of the firm; and I am quite sure that if any individual member of the firm undertook to make an exception there would very soon be no rule left.

Yours very truly,

1. Rudy had replied to LDB's earlier letter of 14 April (see above) that another reason he wished to leave his business job and become a lawyer was because the doctor had advised him that working and going to night law school was adversely affecting his health.

To Fred D. L. Squires

May 10, 1913 Boston, Mass. [Brandeis Mss, NMF 1-M-3]

DEAR SIR: [1] Yours of the 25th ult. reached me while I was in the midst of our hearings before the Interstate Commerce Commission, and answer has been since delayed by my absence in Washington in connection with the argument of the New England Railroad case before the Interstate Commerce Commission.

I hardly know how to answer your question as to where you can customarily find a fair presentation of the questions in which I am taking active interest. So far as concerns the recent railroad hearings, most of our Boston papers gave the news quite fully; particularly the Boston Post and the Globe. Frequently the press notices are not as adequate.

I shall be very glad to bear in mind your kindly interest, and will take the liberty of sending you from time to time some papers on matters which I think you may care for.

Yours very truly,

1. Fred D. L. Squires was editor of the *American Advance*, a newspaper devoted to prohibition; he wanted to know where he could get accurate accounts of LDB's activities, since, he felt, the daily papers and wire services distorted all the news.

To Mark Sullivan (Fragment)

May 10, 1913 Boston, Mass. [Mason, *Brandeis*, 206]

I determined many years ago not to make any denials of any kind or any explanation of any of the vile charges which the interests whom I am fighting put out. I did this partly because a denial would dignify the attack, and partly because if I once began to make denials or explanations, it would easily be in their power to occupy me in this way eight hours a day, and divert my attention from the more important business of attacking their methods.[1]

1. This letter was evidently written in response to a query from Sullivan as to why LDB did not respond to the attacks and charges made by the New Haven upon his character and motives during the Interstate Commerce Commission hearings.

To Oscar Wilder Underwood

May 10, 1913 Boston, Mass. [Brandeis Mss, NMF 58-1]

MY DEAR MR. UNDERWOOD: You doubtless have been too much occupied with tariff matters [1] to see much of the new members, but I hope when opportunity serves you will get acquainted with Mr. Raymond B. Stevens of New Hampshire,[2] who is one of the men who represents the best that there is in New England, and who is particularly familiar with our transportation problems.

Very truly yours,

1. President Wilson had made tariff reform the first order of business of his new administration. He delivered a special message to Congress on 8 April. Underwood was the chief author of the tariff bill and assumed the leadership of steering it through Congress. See Link, *Wilson: The New Freedom*, ch. 6.

2. In 1913 Raymond Bartlett Stevens (1874–1942) was serving his only term as representative from New Hampshire. Stevens served as LDB's chief congressional lieutenant in the battle over the Clayton Anti-trust Act, and he played a key role in the passage of the bill providing for the Federal Trade Commission. Wilson tried to appoint Stevens to the FTC, but state political biases led to his rejection by the Senate. Wilson later named him to the United States Shipping Board, and Franklin Roosevelt appointed him to the FTC and to the United States Tariff Commission, of which he was chairman after 1937.

To Samuel Untermyer

May 10, 1913 Boston, Mass. [Brandeis Mss, NMF 1-M-3]

MY DEAR MR. UNTERMYER: Thank you for yours of the 8th.

I was of course confident that the remark attributed to you was not authentic.[1]

I think matters are moving in the Department of Justice and that there is reason to expect that New Haven affairs will be taken up promptly. Very truly yours,

1. Untermyer had written protesting that he had had nothing to do with an article in the *Wall Street Journal* of 6 May 1913; in fact, he disagreed with it completely. The article, attributed to "one who knows whereof he speaks," compared LDB and Untermyer in their roles as counsel to investigating agencies. LDB, according to the writer, wanted to tear down the railroads of the country, and used the investigation to make vicious attacks on honorable businessmen. Untermyer, on the other hand, was said to have handled the Pujo investigation as a gentleman should, courteously questioning the great bankers and supporting the system of private enterprise. The article implied that Untermyer agreed with this comparison.

To Alfred Brandeis

May 12, 1913 Boston, Mass. [Brandeis Mss, Unmarked Folder]

DEAR AL: Yours of the 5th reached me *after* Friday. Guess we may as well omit the gift to the Louisville Y.M.H.A. I shall have so much more to donate to Boston Y.M.H.A. and Zionism.

I don't know whether I shall actively take part in Rate Advance matters but I have inspired some editorials the country over, demanding efficiency & abolishing interlocking directorates first.

The Mass. people are now talking Protective Com^tee for New Haven & B. & M. stockholders.

In Washington, [S. M.] Williams, N. Y. World correspondent, told me his first acquaintance with my name was at his birthplace, Portsmouth, O[hio]—seeing the Fanny Brandeis pass by.[1]

1. The "Fanny Brandeis" was the steamship operated by Adolph Brandeis's business.

To William Gibbs McAdoo

May 12, 1913 Boston, Mass. [McAdoo Mss]

MY DEAR MR. MCADOO: As requested by you at our conference on the 8th I have asked Mr. H. LaRue Brown of Boston to call on you on Thursday, the 15th, and have given him a letter of introduction.

Mr. Brown is 31 years old. He was born in Louisville, Kentucky, and attended the public schools there until 1896. Since that time he has lived in New England; first as a student at Phillips-Exeter Academy until 1900; than at Harvard College where he graduated in 1904, and later at the Harvard Law School, where he graduated in 1906.

Upon graduation he settled in Boston forming a co-partnership with two classmates under the name of Brown, Field and Murray; has practised continuously since, and has made very satisfactory progress at the Bar.

I first met Mr. Brown in 1908 when Mr. Swift,[1] the Reporter of Decisions at our Supreme Court was seeking a special assistant to bring up the arrears of work. I inquired at that time concerning

Mr. Brown of Prof. James Barr Ames, Dean of the Law School, and received a most favorable report upon his ability and character.

Mr. Brown served in 1908 as Special Assistant to the Reporter of Decisions. In 1909 he was selected by our Bureau of Statistics to prepare a somewhat elaborate report on Massachusetts decisions relating to injunctions in labor cases,—a very creditable piece of work, which was subsequently published by the State. In 1912 he was appointed, by Governor Foss, Chairman of the Minimum Wage Board. I am told that he could have had the position of Assistant Attorney General of Massachusetts made vacant by the appointment of Mr. Curtis [2] to the Assistant Secretaryship of the Treasury.

I have had occasion from time to time to recommend Mr. Brown in professional matters, involving both private and quasi-public work; among others, to one of the committees of the Boston Chamber of Commerce, and his performance seems always to have been of high order. I have been impressed with Mr. Brown's character and general ability. He is and has always been a Democrat.   Yours very truly,

1. Henry Walton Swift (1849–1925) had been a member of the Boston Common Council and of the Massachusetts House of Representatives before serving briefly as United States Marshall for Massachusetts in the late 1890s. In 1901 he began his service as reporter for the Supreme Judicial Court of Massachusetts.

2. James Freeman Curtis (1878–1952) had been assistant district attorney of Massachusetts from 1906 to 1909, and then served as assistant secretary of the treasury until 1913. In 1914 McAdoo named him counsel and deputy-governor of the Federal Reserve Bank of New York, a post he held until he returned to private law practice in 1919.

To Dudley E. Sicher

May 12, 1913 Boston, Mass. [Brandeis Mss, NMF 60-3]

DEAR MR. SICHER: [1] Absence from the city has delayed reply to your letter of the 25th of April, which brought me an interesting report of the plan of some leading members of the Cotton Garment Manufacturers' Association for promoting the education of workers in that trade.[2]

The experiment which you set forth seems to me important and hopeful. Undoubtedly, the welfare of both the employer and employee can be attained only through a steady increase of the efficiency of the workers, as well as the managers. It seems to me essential that any plan for increasing efficiency shall be undertaken in conjunction with representatives of the workers through the Union. But it is obvious that the mere existence of the Union will not secure advance in efficiency. The experiment which you and your associates are making must, therefore, prove of great interest to all seeking to improve trade condition; and is good evidence that you are doing your part in bringing on the "brighter dawn of the better day."   Very cordially yours,

1. Dudley E. Sicher (1876–1939) was a New York underwear manufacturer. He later became president of the Federation of Jewish Philanthropies.

2. Sicher and three other manufacturers had established a pilot plan in cooperation with the city's Board of Education, in which a number of girls working in the factories would receive some time off each week to attend special classes in the schools. The girls were to be chosen on the basis of native intelligence, but also because they had not had the opportunity for a full education.

To Woodrow Wilson

May 19, 1913 Boston, Mass. [Wilson Mss]

MY DEAR MR. PRESIDENT: Referring to our recent conference concerning the Industrial Commission:

First: Further deliberation confirms my conviction that I ought not to accept the appointment you so kindly offered.[1]

Second: I have, as you suggested, considered carefully the selection of a Chairman, and am of opinion that, all things considered, President Van Hise of the University of Wisconsin, would be the best appointment.[2] If you select him I suppose you would wish to select as the other two representatives of the general public, a sociologist and a social worker; and that one of these two would be a woman.[3]

Third: As stated to you, it seems to me very important that one of the representatives of organized labor should be an I.W.W. man.[4] I have talked over with John Graham Brooks, Lincoln Steffens, and Walter Lippman [*sic*],[5] (men whom I deem the

most competent to advise,) the question, who should be selected
to represent the I.W.W.; I thought we had found the right man;
but learn today that the man we selected has resigned from the
I.W.W. I hope to report very soon further on this.

   If you desire to talk with me, I shall, of course, be glad to go to
Washington for the purpose.   Very truly yours,

   1. See LDB to Wilson, 29 April 1913.
   2. Charles R. Van Hise did not receive the nomination; Frank P. Walsh
did. See LDB to William Gibbs McAdoo, 22 May 1913, and to Woodrow
Wilson, 26 May 1913.
   3. The three "public" representatives chosen were: Professor John R.
Commons of the University of Wisconsin (see LDB to Commons, 27 May
1913, n. 1); Mrs. J. Borden Harriman; and Frank P. Walsh of Kansas City.
   4. LDB had in mind Frank Bohn, a former Wobbly and editor of the
International Socialist Review; Wilson declined to name Bohn lest he offend
the American Federation of Labor or the National Civic Federation. For
details on how Wilson chose members of the Commission, see Adams, *Age
of Industrial Violence,* ch. 3.
   5. Walter Lippmann (b. 1889), the scion of a prosperous family, was one
of the young, brilliant luminaries of the progressive era. After an outstanding
career at Harvard, Lippmann became secretary to the socialist mayor of
Schenectady, but soon grew disillusioned with the idea that socialism could
quickly re-make society. In 1911, having been "discovered" by Lincoln
Steffens, Lippmann joined the staff of *Everybody's Magazine;* in 1914, he
was one of the founding editors of the *New Republic,* which quickly established itself as an authoritative voice for liberal reform in America. In 1913,
Lippmann published his first book, *A Preface to Politics* (New York) which
analyzed the political scene with the insights of Freudian psychology, and
which, along with *Drift and Mastery* (New York, 1914), made Lippmann's
reputation as a social thinker. Other books followed, commenting not only
on politics, but on morality and foreign policy as well. After serving as a
wartime advisor to Wilson and a period as editor of the *New York World,*
Lippmann turned to writing books and syndicated columns which marked
him as one of the most influential and important social analysts in twentieth-
century America. See Forcey, *The Crossroads of Liberalism,* or Charles
Wellborn, *Twentieth Century Pilgrimage: Walter Lippmann and the Public
Philosophy* (Baton Rouge, 1969). A good sampling of his writing is Clinton
Rossiter and James Lane, eds., *The Essential Lippmann* (New York, 1963).

To Felix Frankfurter

                        May 20, 1913 Boston, Mass. [Brandeis Mss, NMF 58-1]

MY DEAR FRANKFURTER: Thank you for your telegram and letter
of the 19th.

The two new men [1] you mention would not do. I will tell you why when we meet.   Yours cordially,

1. Frankfurter had suggested two men to represent the employers on the Industrial Commission: Harry A. Wheeler (1866–1960), a Chicago banker who was president of the United States Chamber of Commerce, and George Platt Brett (1858–1936), president and chairman of the board of the Mac-millan Company, the publishers. Neither man was named; Wilson's three choices for the employer positions were Frederic Adrian Delano (1863–1953), a railroad executive (for LDB's view of Delano, see LDB to Katharine Buell, 6 July 1914); Samuel Thruston Ballard (1855–1926), a Louisville mill-owner; and Harris Weinstock (1854–1922), a California businessman with a record of government service.

To Herbert Sherman Houston

May 20, 1913 Boston, Mass. [Brandeis Mss, NMF 59-7]

MY DEAR MR. HOUSTON: [1] Replying to yours of the 19th: [2]

I have rewritten the draft of article as enclosed, and hope this will meet with your approval. I have, however, left unchanged, as you requested, the editorial note and the closing statement, for which you assume the responsibility.

I am glad that you think that my remarks were of some service.[3]   Very cordially yours,

P.S. I am enclosing the copy of my remarks at last Wednesday's meeting.

1. Herbert Sherman Houston (1866–1955) was a vice-president of Double-day, Page & Co., publishers, and wrote occasional magazine articles.

2. Houston had combined parts of LDB's testimony before the House Committee on Patents in May 1912 and a speech LDB had given 14 May 1913 at the banquet of the National Association of Advertising Managers at the Astor Hotel in New York. He sent it to LDB for corrections or additions; he planned to syndicate it to about twenty magazines with a combined readership of over two million. See next note.

3. The article appeared as "On Maintaining Makers' Prices" in *Harper's Weekly* 57 (14 June 1913): 6, and is reprinted in Osmond K. Fraenkel, ed., *The Curse of Bigness: Miscellaneous Writings of Louis D. Brandeis* (New York, 1934), 125–28. In the article LDB drew a distinction between "a manufacturer fixing the retail selling-price of an article of his own creation and to which he has imparted his reputation, and the fixing of prices by a monopoly or by a combination tending to a monopoly." LDB supported the former as supportive of competition, since it involved the personal reputation of individual products or manufacturers; price cutting by re-

tailers in these instances undermined the public's faith in the integrity of the product or manufacturer. Over the next few years LDB worked, albeit in vain, to secure passage of a workable price-fixing law.

To Frederick J. MacLeod

May 20, 1913 Boston, Mass. [Brandeis Mss, NMF 1-M-3]

MY DEAR MR. MACLEOD: Absence from the city and urgent matters upon my return yesterday prevented my considering before this afternoon the draft of the provisions—Sections 15 and 16—in the so-called Washburn Bill, transmitted with yours of the 13th. Since that date I note that the bill has passed the House, and I have before me the report of the Bill as it appears in the May 17th Boston Post.

It is, perhaps, not too late now to submit for your consideration some suggestions for amendment of the Bill, which have nothing to do with the fundamental objection of incorporating these provisions in a railroad control bill.

First: The fact that under this bill, taken in connection with the general law, there is no control over the issue of short term notes seems to me to present a serious danger. The fact that short term notes cannot under the provision be funded, unless they were issued for a lawful purpose, affords no real protection. The fact that they have been issued and are outstanding would be apt to present a moral compulsion upon the Board in view of the great desirability of removing the danger of floating indebtedness; and many a purpose would be lawful which would be distinctly unwise. Furthermore, a company desiring to engage in some enterprise, which would not be lawful under the Massachusetts Statute, might use some of their free money for the unlawful purpose and then ask to have funded notes given for a purpose which would be lawful under our law.

I have been trying to think of a method of protecting debenture holders against floating indebtedness, and it seems to me that if the right to issue additional debenture bonds is granted, there ought to be embodied in the law a provision that debenture bonds should take precedence over short term notes and other floating indebtedness or contingent liabilities, excepting only such liabilities as would have priority over mortgage under the equity practice; namely, recent current indebtedness incurred in the operation of railroads. Such a provision would be in accordance with the spirit of our law. Generally throughout the United States bond holders have insisted upon having their bonds secured by mortgage. Our Massachusetts bond holders have been content to take an unsecured indebtedness relying upon the provisions of the law which limited the bonds to an amount equal to the capital stock. They should have priority over short notes not issued under specific authority from your board.

Second: The limitation of the amount of bonds to be issued to an amount which "when added to the amount of all its then outstanding bonds, notes, or other evidences of indebtedness, shall not cause the aggregate amount to exceed twice the amount of capital stock of the corporation actually paid in at the time" etc., seems to me to leave open the door to issue obligations considerably in excess of twice the amount of the stock actually outstanding in the hands of the public.

Note that the amount of stock is not measured by the amount outstanding in the hands of the public, but by the amount "actually paid in".

On June 30, 1912, the New Haven had, according to its books, outstanding stock of $179,583,100, but of this amount $21,719,800 of stock were held by the New England Navigation Company and other subsidiary companies. Under the law as proposed the New Haven, therefore, could issue $43,400,000 of bonds in excess of the amount of stock outstanding in the hands of the public, disregarding for this purpose altogether the question of premium on the stock.

It seems clear to me that if any limitation upon the amount of the bonds is to be prescribed at all, that limitation should be based upon the amount of stock outstanding in the hands of the public, and not upon the stock "actually paid in".

Third: The law as proposed includes, in determining the amount of bonds to be issued, only "then outstanding bonds, notes, or other evidences of indebtedness". This would undoubtedly be construed as meaning direct liabilities. It would not include contingent liabilities. As a matter of fact, the New Haven Railroad has to an important extent guaranteed obligations of subsidiary companies. The aggregate of these obligations, as shown by its recent report, is in the neighborhood of $80,000,000. Some of these obligations though in terms contingent are practically direct. For instance; the Providence Securities Company, a $50,000 corporation, issued debenture bonds guaranteed by the New Haven for $19,899,000. The New York, Westchester & Boston Railroad, which is not yet paying operating expenses, has issued about $20,000,000 of bonds guaranteed by the New Haven; and there are a number of other New Haven System securities issued by subsidiary companies whose present market value is largely dependent upon the guaranty of the New Haven Railroad Company. Surely the mere form of the obligation ought not to preclude its being considered in determining the amount of bonds to be issued, if there is to be any limitation at all.

Fourth: The suggestion made by you,—that it is not necessary to require by specific statutory provision returns from subsidiary companies because they can be required under the general powers of the Commission—does not seem to me to meet the requirements of the public. As to whether or not they could be required under the general powers of the Commission, I do not express an opinion, for I have not had the opportunity to examine the other provisions of the Washburn Bill; but it seems to me clear, that what the public needs for its information and protection is not merely that the Railroad Commission should have power to require such returns under certain circumstances, but that full returns of the conditions and operation of subsidiary corporations should be made to and filed with the Commission, so that he who is interested may examine them; for without them nobody can know the true condition of the railroad. This was amply established by the results of examiner Brown's investigation presented at the recent hearing before Commissioner Prouty.

It seems to me that the Bill should be amended by specifically providing for full reports of the operation of all subsidiary companies, and that the filing of reports should not be limited to those companies which are controlled by the ownership of all or a great majority of the stock. Any railroad corporation which applies for the approval of its stock or bond issues in this Commonwealth should be obliged to file such reports of any other company in which it is substantially interested; say, if it owns twenty per cent of the stock.

Fifth: I doubt whether the provision of the proposed Bill would fully protect the community against the use of its securities for unlawful purposes, because it contains no prohibition against the use of these securities by subsidiary companies. For instance,— what under the law as passed would prevent the New England Navigation Company from again exchanging the New Haven stock which it has on hand for the stock of some other railroad or steamship company, as it did when it acquired the Boston & Maine and the Merchants & Miners Transportation Company?

Sixth: Again, does the Bill as drawn give the protection against a repetition of such acts as the consolidation of the company with the Consolidated Railway Company and the incidental creation of $30,000,000 of New Haven stock?

Seventh: Is it clear that under the law as drawn whether any fixing the standard for the amount of bonds and debentures to be issued you are to take the New Haven's outstanding capital stock with or without the premiums which have been paid in?

Statute 1908, Chapter 620, appears to report only premiums paid in compliance with our Massachusetts law. The $52,000,000 of premiums paid into the New Haven since 1900 appear not to have been paid in under our law, but to have been the result of the terms voluntarily made by the Company.

I am sending you these suggestions without waiting for a more thorough study of the sections, because I am anxious to have you get them at the earliest possible moment.

I shall, of course, be glad to talk these matters over with you, as you desire.[1]   Yours very truly,

1. Although the Massachusetts House had passed the Washburn Bill on 17 May, the Senate refused to go along, and the measure died in the upper house.

To Henry Bourne Joy

May 21, 1913 Boston, Mass. [Brandeis Mss, NMF 59-7]

MY DEAR MR. JOY: [1] Replying to your two letters of the 17th.[2]

First: I am very glad to know that your attitude is not that of attacking the Sherman Law. I feared from some things that you said that you were disposed to attack the law, and also the methods of some of those in office who were proclaiming its merits or attempting to enforce it; and it seemed to me, as stated in my talk, that such a course would be detrimental to the cause of legitimate price fixing, in which we both believe.

Second: I am sending you herewith a revision of my remarks of May 14th before the Association of National Advertising Managers. It read so badly that it seemed necessary to revise it.[3]

Very cordially yours,

1. Henry Bourne Joy (1864–1936) was president of the Packard Motor Car Company and a member of the American Fair Trade League, an organization that also was working on price maintenance.

2. Joy had spoken just before LDB at the Association of National Advertising Managers, and he felt that LDB had misinterpreted some of his remarks to mean that he favored repeal of the Sherman Law. He sent to LDB a copy of his testimony before the Senate Commerce Committee the preceding December in which he explicitly stated that he supported the Sherman Law, although he believed that the phrase "restraint of trade" was much too vague.

3. See LDB to Herbert S. Houston, 20 May 1913, n.3.

To William Cox Redfield

May 21, 1913 Boston, Mass. [Brandeis Mss, NMF 53-1]

MY DEAR MR. REDFIELD: In addition to the two lines of investigation suggested to you a fortnight ago, I venture to suggest the following:

While we have acquired much information concerning the great monopolistic trusts like the Oil, Tobacco, Steel, Sugar and Beef Trusts, which have been investigated by the Bureau of Corporations or Congressional Committees, little data have been collected and made public concerning the many competitive concerns engaged in many different lines of business which have entered into some sort of agreement with one another to limit prices or output, or concerning trade rules and practices.

Some of these agreements are doubtless reasonable and beneficent restraints upon trade and should be permitted; others are doubtless vicious and should be abrogated or prevented. But in the absence of comprehensive and detailed knowledge on the subject we are not in a position to lay down general rules, or to legislate intelligently concerning them.

The Bureau of Corporations could perform a most valuable service to the Country by entering upon a full and comprehensive inquiry into this subject.[1]   Yours very cordially,

1. See LDB to Redfield, 27 May 1913.

To William Gibbs McAdoo

May 22, 1913 Boston, Mass. [Brandeis Mss, NMF 58-1]

MY DEAR MR. McADOO: Replying to yours of the 21st.[1]

I met Frank Walsh only once, and then but for a few moments, and know little of him, except that he is held in very high esteem by a number of the social workers in New York. However great his other qualifications, I should doubt whether he is sufficiently known throughout the Country to command the attention which the Chairman of the Commission should; and I should also greatly doubt whether he would be willing to substantially give up his practice, which he would be obliged to do if he gave to the Commission's work the time and intense thought which it deserves.

I wrote the President on the 19th suggesting President Van Hise as Chairman of the Industrial Commission. After considerable thought, it seemed to me that Mr. Van Hise combined, on the whole, more fully than any other probably available person, the qualifications which the President deemed necessary for the position. I wrote the President that I should be glad to go to Washington to discuss the matter if he desired.[2]

Very cordially yours,

1. McAdoo had requested LDB's opinion of Frank Walsh as possible chairman of the Industrial Commission. During Wilson's deliberations on the appointment, McAdoo was one of Walsh's strongest supporters.
2. See LDB to Wilson, 19 May and 26 May 1913.

To Frederick Chamberlin

May 23, 1913 Boston, Mass. [Brandeis Mss, NMF 58-1]

MY DEAR MR. CHAMBERLIN: [1] A reply to your letter of April 18th was delayed by the long hearings on the New Haven and our railroad situation before the Interstate Commerce Commission, of which you may possibly know if the Boston papers reach you. It was not until yesterday that I had an opportunity of reading in your most interesting "Philippine Problem",[2] and I have taken great pleasure in sending it to the President.

I suggested in the letter that you would be glad to go to the Philippines in the Government's service, and if the opportunity arises, I shall be glad to talk with the President.[3]

The present Japanese problem [4] gives a special interest to what you say in your concluding chapter.

I trust that your occupation in London is a pleasant and profitable one. Every part of the world is full of interest now, but I sometimes think that London, in the midst of the English revolution, must be the most interesting place of all.

With every good wish,   Most cordially yours,

1. Frederick Chamberlin (1870–1943), an American who enjoyed a mixed career of law and journalism, settled down to a life of letters in Europe, where he wrote numerous popular histories.

2. *The Philippine Problem, 1898–1913* (Boston, 1913).

3. Chamberlin did not receive an appointment to a Pacific post, but in 1920 he was named vice-consul in Palma de Mallorca.

4. On 16 April, the California legislature had passed a measure forbidding land-ownership to those aliens ineligible to become citizens, an indirect violation of the Japanese-American Treaty of 1911. This act, of which Wilson quietly approved, undid much of the diplomatic work of Theodore Roosevelt in smoothing out relations between the two countries. See *Papers Relating to the Foreign Relations of the United States, 1913, 1914, 1915* (Washington, 1920–24), *passim*.

To William Harrison Ingersoll

May 24, 1913 Boston Mass. [Brandeis Mss, NMF 59-7]

MY DEAR MR. INGERSOLL: I have yours of the 22nd enclosing the papers in the Kellogg Corn Flakes Co. case. I will look into the matter and see what can be done.[1]

I may say now that it is all right for you to get in touch with the Retail Dealers' Association, but there is no occasion to trouble them about raising funds to pay any fees to me.[2] If I should act in capacity as counsel, it would be as unpaid counsel, as I should regard this matter merely as a public service, and a part of my general effort to aid in establishing a proper understanding of the trust problem, and undue restraint of trade.

Very truly yours,

1. The Justice Department had begun an investigation of the Kellogg Corn Flake Company to see whether its marketing policy violated the Sherman Act. The Company enforced, as part of its wholesale agreement, a provision that a box of its cereal could not be sold for less than ten cents. The case was ultimately decided against the company, and it ceased this policy. See *United States v. Kellogg Toasted Corn Flake Company et al.*, 222 Fed. (E.D. Mich.) 725 (1915).

2. Ingersoll had written that the Retail Dealers' Association supported the company, and he hoped that LDB would serve as their counsel in the matter. Although the Association as a whole had little money, Ingersoll believed there would be no problem in securing enough to pay LDB through an assessment on the individual members. LDB, however, did not get directly involved in the case.

To Maurice Barnett

May 26, 1913 Boston, Mass. [Brandeis Mss, NMF 47-2]

MY DEAR MR. BARNETT: Thank you for sending me your noble appeal for Profit Sharing.

Profit sharing is undoubtedly an important step forward; but it seems to me that profit sharing, unless it be combined with a real labor co-partnership, which you suggest, will bring many disappointments. To attain real efficiency we must overcome the sense of injustice; and I doubt whether a sharing of profit, without a sharing of responsibilities,—in other words, without real co-operation,—will accomplish what we long for. In the end, industrial democracy must attend political democracy.

Yours very truly,

To Woodrow Wilson

May 26, 1913 Boston, Mass. [Wilson Mss]

MY DEAR MR. PRESIDENT: Replying to yours of the 22nd: [1]

First: As to Frank P. Walsh: I met Mr. Walsh for a moment in New York last Fall, and heard favorable reports of him and his work from Boyd Fisher, and one or two others, but I have no information concerning him which entitles me to an opinion as to whether or not he would be desirable for Chairman. The only reason I have for any doubt is the fact that he lacks a national reputation, for I found that others, of whom I have recently inquired about him, knew as little of him as I do.

Second: As to an I.W.W. man: John Graham Brooks, Lincoln Steffens and Walter Lippman [*sic*] agreed that Frank Bohn would be the best man to represent the I.W.W. I do not personally know Bohn, or indeed anything about him, save what I have heard from them. I enclose a memorandum concerning him prepared by John Graham Brooks, and in his handwriting. I understand that Bohn is from the West; that he was for some time an instructor at Columbia; that he resigned to become an I.W.W. organizer. His brother, William E. Bohn,[2] was instructor at the University of Michigan. They are both on the editorial staff of the International Socialist Review.

My only doubt about Bohn is a technical one. I am told that about a year ago he resigned as an active member of the I.W.W. I presume that means that he ceased to be an organizer. He certainly appears, from his contributions to the International Socialist Review to be actively working for the cause.

Section I of the Industrial Relations Act speaks of "representatives of organized labor", and the question might be raised whether Bohn, under these circumstances, is a representative.

After this possible technical obstacle to selecting him was brought up in conference, Steffens recommended Vincent St. John, the Secretary of the I.W.W. and the founder of the organization. Steffens says St. John is able, intelligent and representative; that he has a big reputation in labor circles; and that he is confident that St. John would contribute greatly to the work of the Commission. But Brooks says that St. John has a record of past violence, which would make his selection impossible.[3]

I have found in making inquiries about the various I.W.W. men, that the personal records of several of those who might naturally be selected as representative, are such as to preclude their selection.   Very cordially yours,

1. See LDB to Wilson, 19 May 1913.
2. William E. Bohn (1877–1967) wrote for numerous liberal and radical

journals, especially the *New Leader* later in his life; he was active in Socialist Party politics.

3. Vincent St. John (1873–1929) had originally worked for the Western Federation of Miners, but in 1905 joined the International Workers of the World, becoming general secretary in 1908. He had been heavily involved in the bitter internecine fighting of the I.W.W., and had been shot by a Wobbly belonging to another faction in 1907. Although he had left the I.W.W. in 1914 to go prospecting, the Wilson administration put St. John and dozens of other radicals on trial in 1918 for attempting to obstruct the war effort. He was convicted, but later impartial reviews declared that the evidence against him was negligible, and President Harding released him from prison. See Patrick Renshaw, *The Wobblies* (Garden City, 1967).

To John Rogers Commons

May 27, 1913 Boston, Mass. [Brandeis Mss, NMF 58-1]

MY DEAR MR. COMMONS: [1] *First:* Your letter of the 18th, transmitting a copy of the market commission bill, did not come to my attention until today owing largely to my absorption in our fight against the New Haven Railroad monopoly.

I have not yet had an apportunity to more than glance at the bill; but I find on page 22, Article 13, the provision—

"Making any factors agreement or other agreement under which persons dealing in a certain article are pledged not to sell such article at a certain figure."

Apparently this clause purposes enacting into law the rule declared by the Supreme Court of the United States, and extended yesterday even to the case of patented articles,—that the maker may not fix the retail selling price.[2] It seems to me that this rule is economically unsound when applied to the proprietary or patented articles, or articles sold in original packages or under a trade mark, in competitive business; and that the adoption of this rule will, in practice, promote monopoly and capitalistic combinations.

Please read on this subject my talk before the House Committee on Patents, May 15, 1912.[3] Chairman Oldfield will be glad to send you a copy if you have none on file.

Second: Kindly let me know what the status is of your market commission bill.   Cordially yours,

1. John Rogers Commons (1862–1944) was professor of economics at the University of Wisconsin and was one of the outstanding authorities on labor law and economics. Commons worked closely with progressive forces in the state in drafting a number of bills, and he directed numerous studies that provided factual information for social reformers. Perhaps his most famous work was the *History of Labor in the United States* (New York, 1935, 4 vols.), of which LDB's daughter Elizabeth wrote part.

2. In *Bauer* v. *O'Donnell*, 229 U.S. 1 (1913), the Court dealt a sharp setback to those who favored retail price maintenance by declaring that copyrights and patents did not carry with them any inherent right to set price and that attempts to fix retail rates were therefore illegal.

3. U.S. Congress, House Committee on Patents, *Hearings . . .* , 62d Cong., 2d Sess. (Washington, 1912), 1–25; the testimony is excerpted in Alfred Lief, ed., *The Social and Economic Views of Mr. Justice Brandeis* (New York, 1930), 400–403.

To Robert Marion LaFollette

May 27, 1913 Boston, Mass. [LaFollette Mss]

MY DEAR BOB: I have your letter of the 21st enclosing a copy of your anti-trust bill S.4931, saying that you wish to re-introduce it, and asking whether I have any suggestions for changes and additions.

First: I am enclosing you a re-draft of that bill. It differs from S.4931 practically only in the following respects:

1. By the introduction of definitions it is made possible to greatly simplify the language of the bill, and make it more easily understood.

2. The amendments are made to apply exclusively to civil suits. Most of the provisions in the amendment necessarily apply only to civil suits. Practically the only ones that would apply to criminal cases are those relating to the presumptions and burden of proof. It seemed to me on the whole wiser not to imperil the passage of the bill by making its provisions apply to criminal proceedings. Several objections were raised as to the constitutionality of the provisions of the burden of proof when applied to criminal proceedings,—objections which seemed to me wholly groundless, but which apparently made such impression upon certain members of the Judiciary Committee that it seems wiser to avoid that reaction.

With the exception of Section 20, the bill now sent you is substantially in the form of the revision which I sent for the consideration of the House Judiciary Committee in May 1912, and which was printed as "Confidential Committee Print", but never acted upon.[1]

Second: I have another suggestion to make which bears upon the general question of restraint of trade, and which is appropriate to your Federal Trade Commission bill. (Possibly there are provisions in that bill now which cover the point—I have never seen a copy of this bill as printed). The suggestion is embodied in paragraph 4 of Article Third in the enclosed statement, which I have prepared, entitled "Needed Anti-Trust Legislation", which possibly you or LaFollette's may find some use for when you introduce your Anti-Trust bills.

My purpose is to set in motion the acquisition of that knowledge necessary to deal intelligently with those agreements between competitors that do not kill competition.[2]

Third: Yesterday's decision denying the patentees the right to fix selling prices is, in my opinion, radically wrong economically. What should be done is to extend that right to all makers or individuals of trademark products. For my reasons for this view please read my statement before the Patent Committee, May 15, 1912.[3]

I have attempted a more popular statement of the argument in the enclosed article "Price Fixing and Monopoly", which is to appear in some of the July magazines, and which I have, therefore, marked not to be released before June 20th.[4] I think that we should frame a bill covering this point, and I shall want to discuss this with you when I am next in Washington, which I hope will be within a fortnight.

Fourth: It seems to me very important that we, who are endeavoring to maintain the competitive system in business, should do our best to erect barriers against the excesses of competition, and draw very clearly the distinction between those restrictions upon competition which are harmful, and those which serve to preserve competition. It is with this in view that I urge the points set forth in Articles Second and Third.

We are much in the situation of those who love peace so much that they are ready to fight for it. There must be reasonable re-

strictions upon competition else we shall see competition destroyed.　　Yours very cordially,

1. LaFollette re-introduced his bill as S.2552 on 17 June 1913.
2. Many of the suggestions which LDB made to LaFollette were incorporated into the Clayton Anti-trust Act of 1914, which LDB helped to
write. See his article, "The Solution of the Trust Problem: A Program,"
Harper's Weekly 58 (8 November 1913): 18–19, reprinted in *The Curse of
Bigness,* 129–136.
3. See preceding letter, notes 2 and 3.
4. See LDB to Herbert S. Houston, 20 May 1913, n. 3.

To William Cox Redfield

May 27, 1913 Boston, Mass. [Brandeis Mss, NMF 58-1]

MY DEAR MR. REDFIELD: Replying to yours of the 23rd: [1]

First: You ask what was in my mind when I wrote: "the many
competitive concerns engaged in many different lines of business
which have entered into some sort of agreement with one another
to limit prices or output, or concerning trade rules and practices."

It was this:

We know concerns which are actively competing in many
lines of trade have agreements of one kind and another regulating
the conduct of business and trade practices, which tend rather to
preserve than to suppress competition; for instance, some agreements concerning discounts, payment of freight, dating, cancellation of orders, opening and closing of shops, temporary shutdown
of factories, and agreements for reports as to production, stock on
hand, or prices actually prevailing or charged.

Some of these agreements may not be restraints of trade at all;
some are restraints, but are clearly not unreasonable. There are
also other agreements made which are clearly unreasonable.

It seems to me very important that, before we undertake to
legislate specifically,—and before the Department of Justice takes
action in regard to such agreements or arrangements between
competitors, we should have a comprehensive knowledge of the
facts,—what agreements actually exist, and how they came to
exist, what their justification, if any. With that knowledge we
shall be able better to determine what so-called restraints of trade
aid, and what suppress competition.

Second: Yesterday's Supreme Court Decision,—denying to patentees the right to fix retail selling prices,—suggests a kindred investigation.[2]

My own opinion is that the decision is economically wrong. That the right to fix the retail selling price is not an injury, but an aid to business, so far as the particular branch of business is competitive; and that the cry against retail price-fixing is based upon a misconception. Instead of denying this right to patentees, the right should be conferred, not only upon patentees, but upon all who make an article stamped with individuality, as by a trademark or sold as a named article in the original package.

The decision of the Supreme Court will not settle this question. It will, on the contrary, lead to renewed effort to establish a rule consistent with sound business and the maintenance of the small concern. The decision plays into the hands of the capitalistic undertaking the chain of stores of the great concern which, like the Standard Oil, can retail an article as well as manufacture.

In my opinion, your Department would perform a service of the greatest value by undertaking at once an investigation into the question:—

To what extent the fixing of retail prices by manufacturers is beneficial or harmful.

It seems to me very important that we, who are endeavoring to maintain the competitive system in business, should do our best to erect barriers, or enable business men to erect barriers against the excesses of competition. We must draw very clearly the distinction between restrictions which are harmful and those which serve to preserve competition.

Third: The two investigations suggested above would aid very much through the ascertainment of trade facts in enlightening public opinion upon this subject. It would enable us to carry out the policy which President Wilson has proclaimed,—of preserving competition by regulating it. Unless we preserve the right of reasonable restrictions upon competition, we shall lose competition altogether.

Please read in this connection, my talk before the House Committee on Patents, May 15, 1912.   Yours very cordially,

1. In response to LDB's letter of 21 May (see above), Redfield had expressed interest in the idea, and asked LDB for more information.
2. See LDB to John R. Commons, 27 May 1913, n. 2.

To Woodrow Wilson

May 27, 1913 Boston, Mass. [Wilson Mss]

MY DEAR MR. PRESIDENT: Since writing you yesterday I have another communication from Steffens in which he says that he disagrees with Mr. Brooks' judgment as to St. John, — "not his facts perhaps, but his point of view"; that "St. John is loyal and representative". Mr. St. John's address is: 164 Washington Street, Chicago.

My opinion remains that Mr. Bohn would be much the better appointment.

If you have any doubt as to the advisability of appointing any I.W.W. man, I hope you will look at Brooks' book on "American Snydicalism".[1]   Yours cordially,

1. John Graham Brooks, *American Syndicalism: The I.W.W.* (New York, 1913).

To Norman Hapgood

May 28, 1913 Boston, Mass. [Brandeis Mss, NMF 52-1]

MY DEAR NORMAN: Pursuant to the request in yours of the 22nd, I am sending you a list of some persons to whom I think it would be worth while to send Harper's Weekly circular.

I shall hope to send you an additional list later.[1]

Cordially yours,

1. In order to help Hapgood launch his editorship of *Harper's Weekly*, LDB sought a number of ways to increase the magazine's circulation. He personally bought subscriptions for a number of New England public libraries; he refused to accept fees from the journal for his articles; he used *Harper's* as a vehicle for his series of articles on the money trust; and he constantly sent Hapgood lists of possible subscribers. On 31 May LDB suggested that Hapgood try to secure the subscription lists from the *Boston Common, LaFollette's Weekly* and *The Public.*

To Henry Moskowitz

May 28, 1913 Boston, Mass. [Brandeis Mss, NMF 35-2]

MY DEAR MOSKOWITZ: I duly received yours of May 22nd about a postponement of the proposed conference,[1] and saying that you expected to write again within a few days.

I have not heard from you, but have today a letter from Hour-wich, of which I enclose copy.[2] I shall not answer it, at least until I hear from you. The attitude of ominous threats disclosed by Hourwich is rather disconcerting. I think you and some of our other friends ought to get in touch with him at once.

Cordially yours,

1. The unions had submitted proposals for a new contract to the employers' association and had requested a conference by the end of May. The employers, however, declared that it would be impossible to have any meeting until the end of June since many members were away and would not be back until then.

2. Hourwich attacked the employers' justification for delaying the conference as "dilatory. . . . This delay will bring the Association face to face with the Unions at about the same time as in the memorable summer of 1910. If the Association persists in its unyielding attitude, I do not want to foretell the consequences." Hourwich to LDB, 27 May 1913.

To William Harrison Ingersoll

May 29, 1913 Boston, Mass. [Brandeis Mss, NMF 59-7]

MY DEAR MR. INGERSOLL: I have yours of the 20th.[1]

I should be glad to have a talk with you as soon as you send me the opinions in Bauer vs. O'Donnell.

It seems to me the interests of the manufactuers, the retailers, and the consumers are identical; and my statement of a desire to act if at all without receiving any compensation, applies equally to any advice that I may be able to give the manufacturers.

Yours very truly,

1. Ingersoll wrote that since the Bauer decision (see LDB to John R. Commons, 27 May 1913, n. 2), he had been flooded with inquiries from manufacturers for interpretations of what the law meant in terms of everyday affairs. Ingersoll, who belonged to a number of manufacturers' associations, asked if LDB would be willing to counsel the manufacturers as well as the retailers on future policy.

To Thomas Watt Gregory

June 2, 1913 Boston, Mass. [Brandeis Mss, NMF 1-N-1]

MY DEAR MR. GREGORY: [1] Pursuant to yours of the 31st I am sending you under another cover three copies of my pamphlet entitled, "Financial Condition of the New York, New Haven & Hartford Railroad Company and of the Boston & Maine Railroad".[2]

Colonel House[3] spoke to me of you when we last met a fortnight ago, and I have this morning a letter from Secretary McAdoo, with a very cordial note of introduction to you. I trust I may have the pleasure of seeing you soon.

Yours very truly,

1. Thomas Watt Gregory (1861–1933), a Texas attorney and protégé of Colonel Edward House (see note 3), had been brought into the Justice Department as a special assistant attorney-general in charge of prosecuting the New Haven for anti-trust violations. In 1914 he succeeded James McReynolds as Attorney-General. He is credited by a number of historians with suggesting LDB's name to Wilson in 1916 for nomination to the Supreme Court.

2. See LDB to Alfred Brandeis, 2 January 1908, n. 1.

3. Edward Mandel House (1859–1938) was for several years President Wilson's closest political confidant. A self-effacing man, he delighted in his shadowy role as a power behind the scenes. Wilson consulted him on all major appointments and deferred to House's judgment when the Texan argued that appointing LDB to the Cabinet in 1913 would cause irreparable dissension within Democratic ranks. Prior to 1917, House traveled in Europe attempting to convince the warring European powers to allow Wilson to mediate their differences. He and the President broke in 1919 over the conduct of the Paris peace talks. He played a minor role in 1932 in securing the Democratic presidential nomination for Franklin D. Roosevelt. House's philosophy of society can be seen in his *Philip Dru: Administrator* (New York, 1912), which he published anonymously; his involvement with New Freedom policies and politics is clear in Charles Seymour, ed., *The Intimate Papers of Colonel House*, (4 vols., Boston, 1926–28); his relationship with Wilson is examined in the controversial *Woodrow Wilson and Colonel House: A Personality Study* by Alexander and Juliette George (New York, 1956).

To Charles Caldwell McChord

June 2, 1913 Boston, Mass. [Brandeis Mss, NMF 1-N-1]

MY DEAR SIR: [1] In connection with the investigation of yesterday's wreck [2] on the New York, New Haven & Hartford R.R., I venture to suggest that the Commission make inquiry into the number of employees laid off during the month of May.

Ten days ago I was told by a man of seeming knowledge that after the final hearing before the Commission on May 7th, a large number of men were laid off, and my informant then stated that some of them were laid off in departments which affected safety, and expressed apprehension as to the result.

Yours very truly,

1. Charles Caldwell McChord (1859–1937), after service on the Kentucky Railroad Commission, was a member of the Interstate Commerce Commission from 1911 to 1926.

2. See LDB to Hiram Belnap, 6 June 1913.

To James S. Harlan

June 3, 1913 Boston, Mass. [Brandeis Mss, NMF 1-N-1]

MY DEAR SIR: [1] You will recall that when I discussed with you in March the accounting methods and practices of the New York, New Haven & Hartford Railroad Company, I suggested the importance of having one or two of the Commission's accounting force at work on the books of the New Haven and its subsidiaries at the time of the closing of the books for the fiscal year. I venture to repeat that suggestion, and to add that it seems to me desirable that the Commission's accountants enter upon such work as early in June as possible.[2]   Yours very truly,

1. James S. Harlan (1861–1927), son of the former Supreme Court justice and a Chicago attorney, had served as attorney-general of Puerto Rico before Theodore Roosevelt named him to the Interstate Commerce Commission in 1906.

2. Harlan referred LDB's letter to Fred W. Sweney, Chief Examiner of Accounts, who replied on 5 June. Sweney said that he did not believe it was necessary to have I.C.C. accountants in the New Haven office in June, since the fiscal year did not end until 30 June. However, he promised to have a man on the spot immediately after the closing of the books, "to secure any benefits that may be gained through the influence of his presence."

To Charles Edward Knoeppel

June 3, 1913 Boston, Mass. [Brandeis Mss, NMF 8-3]

MY DEAR MR. KNOEPPEL: [1] Pardon my long delay in acknowledging your courtesy in sending my report of your most interesting lecture on "The Psychology and Ethics of Wage Payment." [2]

I hope to have some day the opportunity of discussing this with you. Meanwhile I want to suggest this:

Is it not essential to satisfactory conditions of employment that the conditions, however admirable in all other respects, be arrived at by some method of collective bargaining?

Yours very truly,

1. Charles Edward Knoeppel (1881–1936) wrote on industrial management and efficiency techniques.

2. *The Psychology and Ethics of Wage Payment: A Lecture on Piece Work and the Bonus System* (New York, 1912).

To Charles Azro Prouty

June 3, 1913 Boston, Mass. [Brandeis Mss, NMF 1-N-1]

MY DEAR SIR: Advocates of the New Haven Monopoly have insisted that the attitude of the New England legislators and of the press on this subject shows that the advocacy of a dismemberment of the New Haven System is confined to but a few men.

Before accepting that conclusion I venture to suggest that the Commission have made a thorough investigation in regard to the expenditures by the New Haven and its subsidiary companies to control legislation and to "accelerate" public opinion. You will recall that Mr. Brown's examination into the blind vouchers, which pointed to lobbying in Massachusetts was confined to a single month and to a single company.[1]

As the distinguished Massachusetts Senator said some years ago—

"In the great American electorate money has few votes; but it can command many voices and cause many birds to sing".

Yours very truly,

1. For an indication of how correct LDB's "hunch" about New Haven publicity was, see LDB to Massachusetts Public Service Commission, 26 September 1913, to Norman Hapgood, 22 December 1913, and to Alex G. Barrett, 31 January 1914.

To Roy E. Ressler

June 3, 1913 Boston, Mass. [Brandeis Mss, NMF 56-3]

MY DEAR SIR: [1] Replying to yours of May 27th, in which you ask for my ideas as to what I consider "the best in and what is the best for" our Judicial Procedure.

A comprehensive answer to this will, I hope, be made in due course by a committee of the National Economic Association of which I am a member, together with Professor Roscoe Pound and others.[2] At present I take the liberty merely of calling your attention to the simple procedure in practice adopted in Massachusetts, and which in many respects appears to be a nearly ideal system.   Yours very truly,

1. Roy E. Ressler was a Gary, Indiana, attorney who was trying to write a paper on judicial procedure reform.
2. See LDB to J. W. Beatson, 6 July 1914.

To George Weston Anderson

June 6, 1913 Boston, Mass. [Brandeis Mss, NMF 1-N-1]

MY DEAR ANDERSON: I have yours of yesterday.[1]

To my mind it makes little difference what the laws are concerning our Railroad Commission or the issuing of railroad securities, so long as we establish one huge transportation financial power which controls legislatures, public officials, and cows the individual. The greatest of all objections to the New Haven–Boston & Maine merger was just that; and unless we can break this monopoly's power in some way, we shall be frittering away our time in dealing with details.   Very cordially yours,

1. Anderson had raised some technical points about proposed bond limits and liabilities under the proposed Washburn Bill (see LDB to Fred J. Macleod, 20 May 1913) as opposed to the general railroad law of 1912.

To Hiram W. Belnap

June 6, 1913 Boston, Mass. [Brandeis Mss, NMF 1-N-1]

DEAR SIR: [1] Replying to yours of the 4th:

The wreck referred to on the New York, New Haven & Hartford Railroad on June 1st was the one which occurred in Boston, described in the enclosed clipping from the Boston Journal of June 2nd.[2] This wreck, fortunately, did not result in any death.

There was another wreck on the Berkshire Division of the New York, New Haven & Hartford Railroad, which resulted in one death. A clipping relating to this is herewith enclosed, dated June 3rd.[3]

There have also been a series of accidents, or narrow escapes from accidents, on the Boston & Maine, described in clipping[s] from the Boston Globe of June 3rd, and the Boston transcript of June 4th.[4]

The assertion made to me,—that large numbers of men have been laid off—applies to the Boston & Maine as well as to the New Haven.[5]   Yours very truly,

1. Hiram W. Belnap (1867-1918) was chief safety inspector for the Interstate Commerce Commission. In reply to LDB's letter to Commissioner McChord of 2 June, Belnap replied that he had received no information of any wreck on the New Haven on 1 June.

2. A crowded train from Providence, Rhode Island, ran through a stop signal as it entered Boston's South Station and plowed into the 3:00 P.M. New Haven Shore Line train which was about to leave for New York. Of 450 passengers on both trains, only eight were injured, and miraculously no one was killed, despite the extensive damage done to the Pullman cars.

3. A special passenger train ignored signals to pull onto a siding and ran head-on into a milk train at North Kent, Massachusetts, on the Berkshire line of the New Haven on the evening of 2 June. The fireman on the special train was killed and the engineer seriously hurt.

4. The New Haven had been plagued by numerous accidents during early June. In addition to the two described above, a shuttle train and a regular passenger train collided in Lawrence, with a dozen people seriously hurt; another Boston & Maine train ran past a stop gate and stopped only feet away from an open drawbridge over the Mystic River.

5. See LDB to Belnap, 27 June 1913.

To Alfred Brandeis

June 8, 1913 New York, N.Y. [Brandeis Mss, Unmarked Folder]

DEAR AL: Nothing from you for an age. Frank [Taussig] says you were not looking well. Let me know how you are.

Arrived here this AM. Shall spend the day on Zionism and the evening with Norman H[apgood] & [Charles R.] Crane. Leave

for Washington at midnight and expect to stay there until
Wednesday noon, then to speak in Baltimore and be back in
Boston Thursday or Friday.¹ Was here last Wednesday at Con-
ference on Price Maintenance. Your friend [Henry B.] Joy of
Detroit has become my most ardent admirer. The Supreme Court
is all wrong in declaring price maintenance agreements on trade-
marked goods illegal,² & I want to set machinery in motion to get
this straightened out. Also want to see I.C.C. people; & Dept. of
Justice on New Haven matters & LaFollette on some legislation.
So I have occupation enough in W[ashington].

Elizabeth & I are riding again, she on a hired horse, I on Robert
Son of Battle, who is worthy of the name. Susan is in Geneva,
N.Y. with Ruth Ingersoll.

Walter Child has ret[urne]d from Europe.

1. At a meeting of the Associated Advertising Clubs in Baltimore on 11
June, LDB departed from his attacks on big business to praise the growth
of business morality among average businessmen. He noted that there seemed
to be greater truth in advertising, a greater commitment to service among
businessmen, and that it was this type of commercial enterprise which he
supported as opposed to that practiced by the trusts. See *Baltimore News
American*, 12 June 1913.

2. See LDB to John R. Commons, 27 May 1913, n. 2.

To Henry Bourne Joy

June 12, 1913 Boston, Mass. [Brandeis Mss, NMF 59-7]

MY DEAR MR. JOY: Upon my return to the city I find your letter
of the 6th, with interesting enclosures, for which I thank you.¹

Occurrences since we met in New York last week have confirmed my conviction that, with the proper campaign of education, our cause will win. It is, however, very important that
nothing should appear in public or private literature or communications which could be construed as criticism either of the Department of Justice or of Mr. [William A.] Oldfield. All of the
gentlemen concerned have the highest motives, and are seeking
the public good. Like the majority of the Supreme Court, they
lack, in this instance, the necessary knowledge of business practice
and conditions. It is very important that nothing which is said by
any of us, which could be twisted into a criticism of individuals,

should appear; and as the danger of such misconstruction is very great, I am inclined to think it would be best to fight our cause affirmatively, without making any reference directly either to Mr. Oldfield or to the Department of Justice.[2]

Yours very truly,

1. Joy had enclosed part of a letter from the Justice Department to its special agents, in which the Department affirmed its intention to press the Kellogg Corn Flakes case to a final determination.

2. See next letter.

To William Cox Redfield

June 12, 1913 Boston, Mass. [McReynolds Mss]

MY DEAR MR. REDFIELD: Upon my return to Boston today I find a letter under date of June 6th concerning price maintenance, which encloses copy of a letter from some one in the Department of Justice to one of its special agents relating to the Kellogg Toasted Cornflake case and similar proceedings, which I enclose herewith.

The enclosure was, of course, written some time before our conference with the Attorney General on the tenth. I shall call this to his attention, but I hope that you will say something to him also, lest, without his knowledge, some further proceedings of action be taken inconsistent with the policy discussed between us.[1]

Yours very truly,

1. At the meeting, McReynolds, Redfield, and LDB had agreed to allow the Kellogg case to remain dormant until the administration had worked out an overall anti-trust policy which would include direction on price maintenance.

To Edgar Augustus Van Valkenberg

June 13, 1913 Boston, Mass. [Brandeis Mss, NMF 59-7]

MY DEAR MR. VAN VALKENBERG: Mr. Henry B. Joy of the Packard Motor Car Company has sent me a copy of the letter of your Mr. Graham to Mr. Joy, of the 26th, in relation to price maintenance.

It seems to me very clear that the majority of the Supreme Court in holding void contracts for the maintenance of the price of trade-marked articles in competitive business, proceeds upon an entire misapprehension of the business facts—an instance of reasoning from false promises [sic] and analogies.[1]

It is very important that we, who believe in competition, should undertake to remove the restriction which the Court's decision has imposed upon legitimate business practice. For we must, in order to curb or prevent monopoly, allow reasonable regulation of competition. And in such regulation of competition the action taken voluntarily by business men is quite as important as compulsory action by the State through legislation. We must afford protection to those agreements between competitors which preserve and make continued competition possible; and we must protect also those agreements which the individual makes with his customers, and such sales systems as the individual engaged in competitive business develops for the prevention of "cut-throat" competition,—so long as there is nothing in them against the public welfare. The denial of this right would inevitably further capitalistic combinations.

I was very glad to find that Mr. Joy had called this matter to Mr. Graham's attention; and I hope that the North American will take an active part in the campaign of enlightenment on this subject. Ultimately we must get an express legislative recognition of the right of the individual manufacturer engaged in competitive business to market his goods through retail channels at a uniform price. It is good morals and is essential to the existence of the smaller business concerns.   Yours very truly,

1. See LDB to John R. Commons, 27 May 1913, n. 2.

To Woodrow Wilson

June 14, 1913 Boston, Mass. [Wilson Mss]

My dear Mr. President: As requested at our conference on the 11th I am writing you the substance of the opinion expressed by me on the proposed currency legislation: [1]

First: It is, of course, desirable to enact at an early date a currency bill, if an adequate, confidence-inspiring bill can be passed.

But full and free discussion of any proposed measure is essential both to safety and to public confidence in its wisdom. Up to this time there has been little discussion of the currency question except that organized by the bankers.

Second: The power to issue currency should be vested exclusively in Government officials, even when the currency is issued against commercial paper. The American people will not be content to have the discretion necessarily involved vested in a Board composed wholly or in part of bankers; for their judgment may be biased by private interest or affiliation. The function of the bankers should be limited strictly to that of an advisory council. Merely placing in the Government that ultimate supervision and control over the currency issues would not afford the public adequate protection.

Third: It was suggested that a bill, providing for local boards of nine members, of whom six would be bankers, could be passed now, because of the public opinion which the bankers have been making within the past two years; that it would be desirable to so pass such a bill in order to prevent panic conditions, and that later, when the public should have become educated not to heed the cry against the Government entering the banking business, the law might be modified so as to transfer the power over the currency issue to Government officials. But a bill vesting the immediate currency-issuing power in the bankers is almost certain to meet with serious opposition, and there is little probability of securing the passage of such a bill in time to prevent any early financial disturbance, or to quickly allay it.

Fourth: The effect which the enactment of an improved currency law would have in preventing or allaying financial disturbances has, I believe, been greatly exaggerated. The beneficent effect of the best conceivable currency bill will be relatively slight, unless we are able to curb the money trust, and to remove the uneasiness among business men due to its power. Nothing would go so far in establishing confidence among business men as the assurance that the Government will control the currency issues and the conviction that whatever money is available, will be available for business generally, and not be subject to the control of a favored few. Any currency bill which is enacted, should embody provisions framed so that the people may have some assurance that the change will enure to their benefit.

Fifth: It is a serious question whether, in case we should pass a currency bill satisfactory to the banking interests, and which contains no provisions limiting the power of the money trust, the probability of enacting later legislation to curb the money trusts would not be greatly lessened.

Sixth: The conflict between the policies of the Administration and the desires of the financiers and of big business, is an irreconcilable one. Concessions to the big business interests must in the end prove futile. The administration can at best have only their seeming or temporary cooperation. In essentials they must be hostile. While we must give the most careful consideration to their recommendations and avail ourselves of their expert knowledge, it is extremely dangerous to follow their advice even in a field technically their own.   Very cordially yours,

1. This letter marks a turning point in the debate that had been going on within the Wilson administration over the nature of the currency reform bill. The United States had been without a central banking mechanism ever since Andrew Jackson had destroyed the Bank of the United States in the 1830's. Periodic business recessions had been magnified by the absence of a flexible monetary system that could adjust to varying needs and conditions. The Panic of 1907 had been due in large part to a shortage of currency.

Wilson had realized since 1896, when he was a gold Democrat, that little of the unrest in the country would subside until this vexatious problem was solved. Shortly after his election, he began a series of meetings with Representative Carter Glass (1858–1946), chairman of the House Banking and Currency Committee, and Henry Parker Willis (1874–1937), an economist working with Glass's committee. Glass and Willis proposed a private system of twenty regional banks, each with the power of currency issue, and a central board in Washington to coordinate their efforts. Essentially a conservative plan, it followed basic lines laid out by banking interests over the preceding seven years.

As the Glass-Willis plan circulated within the administration, strong opposition was voiced by Secretary of State William Jennings Byran, who pointed out that the Democratic Party had pledged itself to make issuing currency a governmental function. Senator Robert L. Owen, Samuel Untermyer, and William Gibbs McAdoo joined Bryan in his criticism of the Glass-Willis scheme, and noted that it would not reduce the vast power then held by private banking interests. They favored a government-controlled banking system but realized that the most they could hope for was a federal central bank. In early June, Wilson had to decide between the two factions; the Glass proposal would certainly have the bankers' support, while the Bryan plan for a federally managed central bank would appeal to the more radical progressives and agrarian interests.

On 11 June Wilson met with LDB to get his opinion of the two plans. Wilson had relied heavily on LDB for advice on a business plan during the

1912 campaign, and LDB was one of the few men in the country whom the
President trusted on financial questions. LDB convinced the President not
only of the justice of Bryan's arguments in light of past Democratic pledges,
but also of their rightness in terms of economic reform. Banking had to be
brought under federal control in order to curb the money trust; and currency issue, even if backed by commercial notes, had to be solely a governmental function. One week later, on 18 June, Wilson called in his major
advisers and informed them that he would agree to Bryan's plan. The Federal Reserve system would consist of a series of regional banks, a central
board in Washington, and all currency issue would be under the Board's
control; moreover, a majority of members would be federal appointees, with
advisers drawn from the banking community.

With the Bryanites and the conservative Glass now reconciled, Wilson
was able to maneuver the bill through Congress before the end of the year.
The Federal Reserve Act was probably the single most constructive act of
Wilson's entire administration, and despite some imperfection, solved the
basic problems that had resulted from the lack of a central banking appa-
ratus. It struck a fine balance between private control and public supervision, and exemplified LDB's ideal of using government to establish and
then regulate competition. While the literature on the Federal Reserve
system is large, see Link, *Wilson: The New Freedom*, ch. 7; William Gibbs
McAdoo, *Crowded Years* (Boston, 1931); H. Parker Willis, *The Federal
Reserve System* (New York, 1923); and Carter Glass, *An Adventure in
Constructive Finance* (Garden City, 1927).

To Joseph Edward Davies

June 16, 1913 Boston, Mass. [Brandeis Mss, NMF 59-7]

MY DEAR MR. DAVIES: [1] At our conference on the 9th you asked
me for any suggestions as to businesses to be investigated, with a
view to showing the relative efficiency of large and small units:

I think the comparison of the Department Store with the smaller
or specialty business would afford a particularly interesting and
fruitful subject of investigation. The impression prevails generally
that the Department Store operates at a lower average cost than
the smaller stores. I am informed that this is a mistaken view; that,
on the whole, the operating expenses,—including interest upon
capital—is larger in the department stores than in the smaller
stores. [2]

A very careful investigation of this subject has been made by
Charles Coolidge Parlin, Manager of the Division of Commercial
Research of the Curtis Publishing Co. His address is Barristers

Hall, Boston. Mr. Parlin is a Wisconsin University graduate of 1893, and spent about a year making the particular investigation. During this inquiry Mr. Parlin has also collected much information which will be of value in connection with your proposed inquiry relating to the one-priced article.

Yours very truly,

1. Joseph Edward Davies (1876-1958) had practised law in Wisconsin before becoming Commissioner of Corporations in Wilson's administration; in 1915 he went on to the Federal Trade Commission. Davies later held a number of special posts, including that of economic adviser to Wilson at the Paris conference. President Franklin Roosevelt named him ambassador to the Soviet Union, and during World War II he was a personal envoy to Joseph Stalin.

2. See LDB's dissent in *Liggett* v. *Lee*, 288 U.S. 517, 541 (1933).

To Norman Hapgood

June 16, 1913 Boston, Mass. [Brandeis Mss, NMF 52-1]

MY DEAR NORMAN: I am to be in New York on the 19th for an arbitration and shall breakfast at the Harvard Club. If you have nothing better to do, of course I shall be glad to have you breakfast with me.

It occurs to me that Aaron Aaronsohn, "the wild wheat discoverer", head of the Palestine Agricultural Experiment Station, might write an interesting and subscriber-making article on "Zionism". As a talker, he is one of the most interesting men I have met. I suppose that he would write very poorly, particularly because he had only recently learned English; but if his material were good it could, of course, be rewritten. He planned to sail for the Mediterranean early in June, but a recent letter from him leads me to think that he may still be here. If you would like to see him I will wire him to call on you; or perhaps you would prefer to have me suggest to him that he write an article and send it to me with a view to my having it published somewhere, if possible, and that would leave you entirely untrammeled.[1]

Cordially,

1. Two days later, LDB wrote to Aaronsohn suggesting that he contact Hapgood about an article; however, no article on Zionism by Aaronsohn appeared in *Harper's* or any other magazine at this time.

To William Harrison Ingersoll

June 16, 1913 Boston, Mass. [Brandeis Mss, NMF 59-7]

MY DEAR MR. INGERSOLL: I have yours of the 14th.

First: I return the article and have noted in pencil thereon certain verbal changes which it seemed necessary to make; otherwise I have left it in its present condition, assuming that you deem that the most effective.

Second: Please send me a copy of the book entitled, "Modern Business" referred to on page 22 of your testimony before the Patent Committee.[1]

Third: I assume that Mr. Nims [2] is making further investigation as to foreign laws relating to price maintenance, and that you will send me the result of that investigation as soon as possible.

Fourth: Your schedule of prices,—pages 19–21 of your testimony,—is extremely interesting. There are in it some obvious typographical errors. I should like to have you go over that list and make any necessary corrections and any additions and any changes involved in bringing it up to date.

The schedule presented seems to me extremely important, and of particular persuasive force, in so far as it appears to show that trade-marked articles which are not price restricted are sold at a higher profit than those that are price restricted.

I should like to make liberal use of this schedule in so far as you feel absolutely certain of the data on which it is based. In going over this schedule (and in adding to it) I wish you would let me know specifically the evidence on which you based your statements as to the price paid by the retailer and the consumer's price, both of the restricted and the unrestricted trade-marked articles; and on what evidence you based your statements as to price paid by retailers and consumers on non-trademarked articles. I should like also to have you indicate to what extent the non-restricted trademarked articles have indicated on the original package a selling price, even if that price is not observed or enforced.

This seems to me a most promising line of data, but it is of the utmost importance that no erroneous statement should be made.

"One bad oyster spoils the stew."

On pages 30–31 of your testimony you refer to the percentage of dealers who declared themselves in favor of price maintenance. I shall be glad of some detail to this canvass.

Fifth: As I stated to you at Baltimore, I propose to write an article or a series of articles on this subject, and shall be glad to have data from time to time as soon as you can furnish it.

Sixth: What have you done in the way of starting the education with the newspapers? Mr. Joy sent me the copy of his correspondence with Mr. Graham of the Philadelphia North American; and I judge from a remark in a letter received today that the North American had a favorable report of my Baltimore talk.[3]

If you will send me a few copies of the enclosed statement when revised, I will write the Scripps-McRea people on the subject. Also Mr. [Treadwell] Cleveland of the Newark Evening News, who is particularly enlightened on industrial questions.[4]

Yours very truly,

1. J. F. Johnson, general editor, *Modern Business* (13 vols., New York, 1910–1913). This series dealt with a variety of business topics, such as economics, organization and management, accounting, etc.

2. Harry Dwight Nims (1876–1968) was recognized as a leading authority on trademark law. He was also interested in court reform, and in 1931 Governor Franklin D. Roosevelt named him to the New York Commission on the Administration of Justice.

3. See LDB to Alfred Brandeis, 8 June 1913, n. 1.

4. See LDB to Treadwell Cleveland, Jr., 18 June 1913.

To Robert Marion LaFollette (Telegram)

June 16, 1913 Boston, Mass. [LaFollette Mss]

Recommended VanHise for Chairman, and made one recommendation for labor representative; these being the only positions as to which my advice was asked. Not having been asked about woman member have not recommended Elizabeth. Hope that you will see the President and recommend her, and that you will mention my knowledge of her qualifications so that he may ask for my opinion.[1]

1. Elizabeth Glendower Evans was not named to the Industrial Commission; Wilson did, however, name a woman, Mrs. J. Borden Harriman.

To Treadwell Cleveland, Jr.

June 18, 1913 Boston, Mass. [Brandeis Mss, NMF 59-7]

MY DEAR MR. CLEVELAND: I do not know whether you have considered the question of price maintenance of trademarked articles, —the subject matter of the Dr. Miles Medical Remedy case, 220 U.S.,[1] which came up more recently in connection with patented articles in the Sanatogen case.[2]

The Sanatogen case and the Bobbs Merrill (the copyright case)[3] seem to me right as decisions of questions of patent and copyright law. The possession of a patent or copyright, as such, ought not to give the owner a right to fix the resale price; but every individual manufacturer of trademarked goods ought to have a right to determine the price at which the goods are to be sold in original packages. His position in the market ought to be the same whether he is both manufacturer and retailer,—as the Standard Oil Company is—or must, like the less powerful concerns, use the jobber and the retailer as a means of distribution; in fact, the jobber and retailer are to him as much a means of distribution as the railroad, the mail, and the express.

It seems to me that the decision of the Supreme Court in the Dr. Miles Remedy Company case was due to a failure to understand trade facts,—to differentiate between the case of rival manufacturers combining and forming a monopoly in a staple article, and independent manufacturers engaged in competitive business, each determining for himself the method of marketing goods most favorable to him.

If we are to prevent monopoly, we must regulate competition; regulate it, not only by law, but by the voluntary acts of those engaged in business; and the system of marketing goods devised by such concerns, as the Ingersoll Watch people, are entirely in accord with the principles of regulating competition.

It seems to me that public opinion should be educated in this matter preparatory to the introduction of Federal legislation expressly authorizing price maintenance of articles sold under a trademark or trade name in competitive business. Of course this principle of price maintenance has no application to the sale of goods in bulk not under a trade name. There the goods lose themselves in the mass as soon as the first sale is made.

The suppression of this system of price maintenance of individual trademarked articles must result to a large extent in the substitution of capitalistic chains or stores, mail order houses, or actual monopolistic concerns for the numerous independent manufacturers and dealers.[4]   Yours very truly,

1. The Dr. Miles Medical Company required its distributors to sign a price-maintenance agreement, so that the company's products would not be sold at less than the prices set by the firm. The Court refused to distinguish between price maintenance and monopolistic price fixing, and held the agreements to be in violation of the anti-trust laws. The sole dissenter, Mr. Justice Holmes, opposed his colleagues on the grounds that they were interfering in the natural laws of economics when there was no reason to do so. *Dr. Miles Medical Company* v. *Park & Sons Company*, 220 U.S. 373 (1911); Holmes's dissent is at 409.

2. "Sanatogen" was the trade name of the article involved in *Bauer* v. *O'Donnell* (see LDB to John R. Commons, 27 May 1913, n. 2.).

3. In this case the Court held that the granting of a copyright does not carry with it the right to qualify future sales by a vendee, or to limit or restrict future sales as to price. *Bobbs Merrill Co.* v. *Straus*, 210 U.S. 339 (1908).

4. The same letter was sent to Livy S. Richard of the Newspaper Enterprise Association.

To William Harrison Ingersoll

June 18, 1913 Boston, Mass. [Brandeis Mss, NMF 59-7]

DEAR MR. INGERSOLL: I have your letter of the 17th about Henry Siegel Company selling your watches at less than $1.00.

By good fortune Mr. Henry Siegel[1] was in Boston and came into my office this morning. I have talked the matter over with him and he has stated to me that in view of what I have told him he will not advertise or sell the watches in the Boston Store for less than $1.00 unless some other person is cutting here; and that he will do nothing in this matter until you have had an opportunity of taking the matter up with him in New York.

Mr. Siegel will be in New York again on Friday.

Yours very truly,

1. Henry Siegel (1852–19[?]), an immigrant from Germany, started as a peddler and worked his way up to ownership of five large department stores in New York and Boston.

To Selden Osgood Martin

June 18, 1913 Boston, Mass. [Brandeis Mss, NMF 59-7]

MY DEAR MR. MARTIN: [1] Dean Gay,[2] in compliance with my request, has sent me a copy of the interesting bulletin [3] on shoe retailing with an invitation to ask for any further information, and I am therefore troubling you:

First: I should like to know whether your investigation has resulted in the collection of any data tending to show to what extent, if any, the establishment of a fixed price for shoes,—as the Douglas $3.50 shoe, etc.,—has upon the selling cost. A priori it ought to reduce materially the selling cost. I should be glad to have any data you have collected, and a memorandum of any conclusions reached by you on this subject.

Second: Will you kindly send me a copy of circular 10a and the rest of the Harvard Systems of Accounts for Shoe Retailers?

Yours very truly,

1. Selden Osgood Martin (1881–1942) was an assistant professor of marketing and director of the Bureau of Business Research at the Harvard Business School; he was later involved in a number of business ventures.

2. Edwin Francis Gay (1867–1946), a professor of economics, was dean of the Harvard Business School; during World War I Gay served in several important positions with the War Industries Board and War Trade Board.

3. Harvard University, Graduate School of Business Administration, Bureau of Business Research, *Management Problems in Retail Shoe Stores* (Cambridge, n.d.).

To Hiram W. Belnap

June 27, 1913 Boston, Mass. [Brandeis Mss, NMF 1-N-1]

DEAR SIR: Referring again to my letter to Commissioner McChord of June 2nd, to you of June 6th, and later correspondence, and my conference with you on June 24th concerning the wreck at Canaan, Conn. on the preceding day: [1]

I now call to your attention: —

1: The accident on the Connecticut River Express on June 24th, reported caused by the blowing out of a cylinder head while crossing the Norwalk River Bridge. (See report in New York World of June 25th.) [2]

2: The accident at Ore Hill on June 25th (reported in the New York Times of June 26th), said to be due to "a broken plate on the first of the cars." [3]

3: The collision at Laconia, N.H., on June 26th, (reported in the Boston Transcript of that date.) [4]

Yours very truly,

1. Two mill cars being shunted inside the Canaan, Connecticut, yard collided with a New Haven passenger coach, causing the coach to crash into a local freight train of the Central New England Road. Eight passengers were hurt, one mortally; witnesses ascribed the wreck to the absence of a flagman in the yard.

2. Engine #1328, drawing the crack Connecticut River Express, blew out a cylinder head while crossing the Norwalk River Bridge near South Norwalk, Connecticut. The train was stuck on the bridge, forty feet over the water, and many passengers were near hysteria. In 1853, more than fifty people had been killed when a train plunged through an open section of that bridge.

3. A westbound passenger train of the Central New England Road barely missed serious damage and injuries to passengers when two of its cars derailed near Ore Hill, Connecticut. The cause of the derailment was a broken plate on the baggage car; inspection of the plate disclosed that it was badly worn, and should have been replaced.

4. A northbound freight train, which fortunately was traveling slowly, bumped into a southbound passenger express while the latter was standing in the station; one man suffered slight injuries.

To Raymond Bartlett Stevens

June 27, 1913 Boston, Mass. [Brandeis Mss, NMF 1-N-4]

MY DEAR MR. STEVENS: Upon my return to the city I find your letter of the 25th.

It was an odd coincidence that I should have called upon you yesterday; and I was sorry not to have seen you.

Replying to your question: [1] I think it would be advisable for you and Senator Hollis [2] to call at once on Commissioner Prouty. He has heard so much which misrepresents, I think, the attitude of the public towards the New Haven, that it would be effective for him to hear from you two (and promptly) some real facts. I hope you will make clear to him also, what we all feel so strongly, that the issue is not Mellen, but the policy which Mellen has been carrying out at the instances of those who have employed him.

We shall never have good transportation conditions in New England unless the policy of monopoly is abandoned, and unless we also reduce the size of our units so that they can be properly managed; and this proper management means not merely management of operation, but financial management, and the ability to raise money. I am confident that the large unit which has been created has curtailed very seriously the possibility of raising money. New Englanders in the past could distribute their investments among a half dozen or a dozen New England transportation companies. Today, all of their transportation investments practically must be made in the New Haven System, unless possibly an investment in the Grand Trunk or the Bangor & Aroostook. No prudent New Englander, even if he thought well of the New Haven management, would think of putting all his eggs in one basket. Through monopoly the New England railroads have cut off their means of raising money, as well as their chance of efficiency in operation.

I understood that Commissioner Prouty was due to return to Washington yesterday afternoon; and I think it would be well for you and Senator Hollis to see him at once.

Each day seems to bring a new accident,[3] and we greatly need the help which the Interstate Commerce Commission can give us.

Yours very truly,

1. Stevens reported that he had heard of pressure being brought upon the Interstate Commerce Commission to withhold its report on the New Haven until the fall. Stevens wanted the report disclosed on time, and he sought LDB's advice on what to do.

2. Henry French Hollis (1869–1949) was serving, in 1913, his only term as United States Senator from New Hampshire.

3. See preceding letter.

To Hiram W. Belnap

June 28, 1913 Boston, Mass. [Brandeis Mss, LtB]

DEAR MR. BELNAP: Referring again to my letter of June 2nd to Commissioner McChord, and to you of June 6th, and subsequent correspondence:

I am enclosing you herewith two clippings from the Boston Post of today covering two wrecks on the New Haven yesterday,

—the first covering the wreck at Wellfleet;[1] the second the wreck near Quincy Adams.[2]   Yours very truly,

1. The afternoon train from Boston to the Cape ran through an open switch near Wellfleet and crashed into a freight train standing on a siding. Although the passenger engine was overturned and several cars of the freight demolished, no one was seriously hurt.

2. Two cars of a New Haven freight train derailed because of a wrong switch, and piled up near the Quincy-Adams station just south of Boston.

To Norman Hapgood

July 7, 1913 Boston, Mass. [Brandeis Mss, NMF 52-1]

MY DEAR NORMAN: Upon my return to the city I find your two letters of the 30th.

First: As to the articles on the one price system: I have done considerable work on these without, however, satisfactory results. There probably ought to be three, not very long, articles; the first, "Competition that Kills"; the second, "Efficiency and the One-price Article"; the third, in substance "How Europe deals with the one-price goods".[1]

The material for the second and third articles is in process of collection,—much of it very difficult to get; however, I hope to have it soon, and I think some of the facts which will develop will be very interesting.

My article "Competition that Kills" is nearly finished and I can send it to you soon. I do not like it very much, and I shall want you to tell me how to make it better.

Second: As to the article on Bird for Governor: I think it best that I should not try that; among other reasons, because there are several other subjects in the economic and financial field that I want to write on during the year. How would Richard Washburn Child do for the Bird article? When I met him recently he said that he would be West most of the time until the middle of August, but you could, of course, reach him through Stone & Webster, Boston.[2]

Third: I may be called to New York before the week is over in connection with labor matters, and will wire you if I am.

                    Cordially yours,

1. Of these three proposed articles, only the first was ever published, and not until later in the year. In "Cutthroat Prices: The Competition That Kills," *Harper's Weekly* 58 (15 November 1913): 10–12, LDB traced the evolution of trade from primitive barter through the use of currency to the point where the consumer could rely upon trademarked, nationally advertised merchandise, and know that the value received would remain constant. But to insure this benefit to the consumer, it was necessary to allow the manufacturers of such articles to establish the retail price, and this was the purpose of price-maintenance contracts between manufacturer and retailer. If the Ingersoll brothers advertised their standard watch at one dollar, and certain retailers undercut that price, then all consumers would be led to question the veracity of Ingersoll's advertising and the value of the watch. This price-cutting undermined fair competition, since those retailers who worked to support Ingersoll's policies were put at an unfair disadvantage. LDB went on to draw his customary distinction between price maintenance to uphold competition of manufacturers between their products and price-fixing by firms seeking monopoly. The article is reprinted in *Business—A Profession*, 236–54.

2. Charles S. Bird had been the unsuccessful candidate for Massachusetts governor on the Progressive ticket the previous fall; Child did not write such an article for the magazine.

To William Allan Oldfield

July 7, 1913 Boston, Mass. [Brandeis Mss, NMF 58-1]

MY DEAR MR. OLDFIELD: Replying to yours of the 30th, which I find upon my return to the city: [1]

First: I think it would be a mistake to abolish the Commerce Court. Many of its decisions have been notably bad, but the Supreme Court had doubtless taught its judges many valuable lessons, and we may expect less erroneous decisions in the future.

Some time ago I talked with Assistant Attorney General Denison about the Commerce Court. He has represented the Government in many cases which would naturally come before it. He was strongly in favor of retaining the Commerce Court. He is a man of high public spirit and of ability, and I suggest your talking with him about it.

Second: I entirely agree with you,—that it is desirable to have a patent court of appeals. I am not sufficiently familiar with the work of the Commerce Court to know whether that Court could take on the work of the patent court of appeals; but if the situation is such that it could, your suggestion might lead to a very simple solution of the problem. I suggest your talking this matter over also with Assistant Attorney General Denison; and if it seems feasible ask him to prepare an amendment to the Commerce Court Act which would accomplish the desirable result. I should, of course, be glad to look over the bill drafted by him, if you desire.

Third: I have really no knowledge of Mr. Ewing; [2] but the fact that he has been selected by the President and Secretary Lane gives me confidence to believe that he is all right.

Fourth: I do not know yet when I shall next be in Washington, but I shall arrange to see you when I am. I want to talk over with you then the matter of price maintenance. The decision of the Supreme Court in the Sanatogen case has greatly simplified the situation.[3] Now that all question of special privilege through patent monopoly has been removed, and the special objection of jurisdiction of the Federal Court is eliminated, I think it important that we should develop the right of producers of trademarked articles, growers as well as manufacturers, to establish by contract the price at which their products shall be sold.

Very cordially yours,

1. Oldfield was trying to prevent the abolition of the federal commerce court at the hands of congressmen who thought it had no use. He asked LDB if the utility of the court would be improved if the power to hear patent appeals were added to it. Oldfield also asked LDB what he thought of the new Patent Commissioner (see next note). See LDB to James C. McReynolds, 25 September 1913.

2. Thomas Ewing (1862–1942), a New York patent attorney, had been named by Wilson as Commissioner of Patents, a post he held until 1917.

3. See LDB to Treadwell Cleveland Jr., 18 June 1913 and to John R. Commons, 27 May 1913.

To Alfred Brandeis

July 9, 1913 Boston, Mass. [Brandeis Mss, unmarked folder]

DEAR AL: Was just on the point of writing you about Uncle William's marvellous improvement when yours of Monday came.[1] Hope your Saint Louis trip won't tire you too much.

Mellen's resignation from the B. & M. is interesting.[2] I enclose Journal clipping & Herald editorial.[3] The latter is particularly interesting, as accepting my principle of merit of efficiency, as it has been & is my bitterest foe here, being controlled by Shoe Machinery & New Haven interests.

Yr $225 draft received.

1. Next day, William Taussig, Alfred's father-in-law, died in St. Louis.

2. In a surprise move, Charles S. Mellen handed in his resignation as president of the Boston & Maine to that line's directors on 8 July. The official announcement explained that the duties of being president of both the B. & M. and the New Haven had proven too heavy, and that he had chosen to devote his full energies to the New Haven's problems. Foes of the merger claimed, however, that Mellen was trying to stave off further anti-trust prosecution by the government. In a statement to the press, LDB said: "The action today is a step in the right direction, but it does not go far enough. The traveling public will not be entirely satisfied until there is complete severance of the control of the Boston & Maine and Maine Central by the New Haven Road."

3. The *Herald*, in its editorial of 9 July, ignored most of the antimerger-ites' arguments regarding fiscal control, violation of state and federal stat-utes, and even poor service. Rather, the paper suggested that the problems of the two lines were different, and each would require the full energies of a capable man to lead it through troubled times. Without mentioning LDB, the paper echoed his argument that one man could not properly perform too many tasks without a loss in quality of work done.

To Norman Hapgood

July 9, 1913 Boston, Mass. [Brandeis Mss, NMF 52-1]

MY DEAR NORMAN: Yours of the 8th received.

First: I am enclosing herewith the article, "Cutthroat Prices—Competition that Kills." I am not at all satisfied with it; and I wish you would consider it carefully and let me know how to make it better.[1] [Frederick L.] Collins, or your advertising man, might have some valuable suggestions.

Second: I had a letter from Aaronsohn, (who I understand sailed yesterday) saying that he had called on you while you were out of town. I hope he called again and saw you.

Third: Mellen's resignation from the Boston & Maine Presi-dency is interesting. I enclose a clipping from the Journal, and an editorial from the Boston Herald, which is even more interesting considering the hostility of that paper to me and my economic views.

Fourth: This may interest you, as further evidence that the Massachusetts opposition to my going into the Cabinet [2] was not in its essence political: George W. Anderson, the Democratic nominee for Attorney General for the past two years, recently appointed Public Service Commissioner, a very good Public Franchise League man, and Skeffington, a Democratic labor man,— both good friends of mine,—came to me separately yesterday to urge me, on behalf of the Democratic machine leaders, to run for the Massachusetts Attorney Generalship. Of course, I declined, as I did in 1910, I think it was.   Cordially yours,

1. See LDB to Hapgood, 7 July 1913.
2. See LDB to Alfred Brandeis, 2 March 1913.

To Robert Marion LaFollette

July 9, 1913 Boston, Mass. [LaFollette Mss]

MY DEAR BOB: *First:* I have just wired you as follows: "Mondays telegram received. Will make no decision before seeing you." [1]

Second: You must have been interested to read this morning of Mellen's retirement from the Presidency of the Boston & Maine System. I enclose you a clipping from the Boston Journal; and what is more interesting, an editorial from the Boston Herald, accepting our propositions in regard to the limit of efficient unit, and the inefficiency of too great concentration.[2] The Herald was and is my bitterest foe here, the paper being controlled by the financial interests,—notably the New Haven and Shoe Machinery.

Third: I expect to send you before the week is out a memorandum of "Diamond Jim" Brady's [3] contracts with the New Haven.[4]

Fourth: I have not seen the full report on the Commission's decision on the New England railroad conditions, but it is about what I expected when I talked with you a fortnight ago.[5] I am sorry for even its limited and conditional approval of monopoly; and I think that it would be a mighty good thing if you would come out with an editorial in LaFollette's declaring that no possible regulation or control can make the railroad monopoly tolerable. Please read, in this connection, my article on "The New Haven—An Unregulated Monopoly", which was reprinted in the Senate Trust Hearings as Part no. 35.[6]

Fifth: Another evidence of the inconsistency of the worldly wise: I had yesterday urgent entreaty, through those representing the Massachusetts Democratic machine, to go on their ticket this fall for the Attorney Generalship. Of course I declined. It is rather amusing in view of the fact that I was not a good enough Democrat for them a few months ago.

Cordially yours,

1. LDB had been invited to participate in another investigation regarding railway valuation, and he was reluctant to get involved. LaFollette had wired that he hoped LDB would not make a final decision until the two men had a chance to confer.

2. See LDB to Alfred Brandeis, 9 July 1913, n. 3.

3. James Buchanan Brady (1856–1917) began his career as a bellhop and worked his way up to the presidency of several corporations involved with the railroad industry. He got his nickname by his ostentatious display of diamonds, and his gem collection was worth more than two million dollars. Brady was one of the few New York financiers who participated in theatre and cafe society.

4. See LDB to LaFollette, 11 July 1913.

5. The Interstate Commerce Commission report on the New Haven was released on this day; it castigated the railroad for its financial practices. Moreover, the Commission took care to point out that many of the charges raised by the roads' opponents had been true; the fault lay not in the criticism, but in the practices. "Had the stockholders of the New Haven, instead of vilifying the Road's critics, given some attention to the charges made, their property would today be of greater value and the problem an easier one."

6. See LDB to Alfred Brandeis, 8 December 1912, n. 1.

To Henry French Hollis (Telegram)

July 10, 1913 Boston, Mass. [Brandeis Mss, NMF 1-N-1]

A telegram from one of my friends leads me to think you may have some question as to confirmation of Newman [1] as District Commissioner. I dare say inference is wholly unfounded. Newman seems to me uncommonly good man for office.

1. Oliver Peck Newman (1877–1956), a newspaperman, had been nominated by Wilson as one of the commissioners of the District of Columbia. Some senators questioned whether he met the technical requirement of continuous residence in the District, but Newman was confirmed after the facts were straightened out.

To Henry Bourne Joy

July 10, 1913 Boston, Mass. [Brandeis Mss, NMF 59-7]

MY DEAR MR. JOY: Replying to yours of the 7th.

The argument made in your letter of the 3rd seems to me sound and very forcefully put.[1] I would make, however, these suggestions:

First: It seems unwise to give currency to the statement made by Mr. Calkins.[2] We ought not to assume that the attitude of the Department of Justice is, or will be, hostile; on the contrary we should assume that the Department of Justice will act in accordance with what we deem to be the best interests of the community. Furthermore, it is highly important that for the present, and while we are seeking to develop constructive legislation, the manufacturers and dealers should co-operate in maintaining prices so far as possible. Some sacrifices will be necessarily involved, but everyone directly interested ought to take the decided stand that he will do his utmost to maintain prices, even though it be temporarily without full support of the legal machinery.

Second: It seems to me wise to make it very clear that we are not quarreling with the decisions of the Court so far as they declare that the grant of a patent or copyright does not of itself confer the right to fix prices; in other words, we are not quarreling with the fact that owners of patents and copyrights are not given especial privilege. What we insist upon is that all men, who produce and market their goods under their own name, shall have the right to determine the price at which those goods shall be sold to the ultimate consumer; and you are, of course, entirely right in saying that no goods are usually sold until they reach the ultimate consumer.

Third: It seems to me wise to substitute for the word "manufacturer", *producer.* The latter is really in precisely the same position as the manufacturer; and in respect to trademarked goods, to a greater and greater extent, the latter is building up a reputation, and his goods are being sold on that reputation. Prominent in this respect are dairy products, and, to a certain extent, vegetable and fruit, and to a marked extent, the growers of grain to be used as seed.

Our case is so clearly right that I feel sure of success, if our education proceeds vigorously on the right lines. We ought to secure adequate legislation at the first regular session of the present congress.[3]   Yours very cordially,

P.S. I am glad to learn of your safe return from San Francisco.

1. Joy had written to the Winchester Arms Company setting forth ideas that he and LDB shared regarding the right of a manufacturer to set a fair retail price. He did, however, warn that under current court interpretations there was danger of prosecution for insistence of price-maintenance agreements between manufacturer and retailer.

2. Grosvenor Calkins, a Boston attorney, had written Joy: "Confronted by this series of [Court] decisions, by the aggressive attitude of the Department of Justice, and by statutes in almost every State too numerous to even keep track of, there is no course open to an attorney today but to advise his manufacturing client to get the best price he can and to abandon his loyal jobbers to the mercy of the unscrupulous and cut-throat competition." Joy had cited this passage in his letter to the Winchester Company.

3. See LDB to George Rublee, 18 November 1913.

To Charles Henry Jones

July 11, 1913 Boston, Mass. [Brandeis Mss, LtB]

MY DEAR MR. JONES: Thank you for your letter of the 10th.

The struggle [against the New Haven], in which you took a large part, was well worth while. The improvement in conditions, —social and political, as well as transportation—will come; and perhaps the greatest benefit will be a renewed respect for truth and the law.   Most cordially yours,

To Daniel Kiefer

July 11, 1913 Boston, Mass. [Brandeis Mss, NMF 36-1]

MY DEAR MR. KIEFER: [1] Replying to yours of the 9th: [2]

It seems to me clear that charters should confer upon cities the right of municipal ownership of public utilities. When and to what extent that right should be exercised is a matter for consideration in the particular place, at the particular time, and with respect to a particular utility.

With best wishes,   Most cordially yours,

1. Daniel Kiefer (1856–1923), after becoming financially independent in the clothing business, devoted himself to municipal reform in Cincinnati.

An advocate of Henry George, he became chairman of the National Single Tax League in 1917.

2. The People's Municipal-Ownership League, of which Kiefer was treasurer, was fighting for a new city charter, and Kiefer had asked LDB for a brief statement of his views on municipal ownership.

To Robert Marion LaFollette

July 11, 1913 Boston, Mass. [LaFollette Mss]

MY DEAR BOB: *First:* I hope you will find time to read Prouty's report on the New Haven, and McChord's on the recent New Haven accident. They contain abundant material for your second speech on the New England Railroad situation.

Second: The next step that ought to be taken now is for the Department of Justice to move with reasonable promptness, and not allow its action to be delayed by any suggestions financial in nature.

Third: You asked me to send you some data on "Diamond Jim" Brady: I am enclosing a memorandum (six pages),[1] prepared by Joseph B. Eastman, Secretary of our Public Franchise League, who was associated with me in the recent hearings; and I am also sending you under another cover a copy of Mr. Eastman's brief, which you may care to examine.   Cordially yours,

1. The document noted that Brady and New Haven president Mellen were good friends; that Brady was involved in a number of firms manufacturing railroad equipment; and that his firms received a very large percentage of New Haven contracts for these articles. Brady had also assisted Mellen in the New Haven's fictitious disposition of Massachusetts trolleys after the road had been ordered to do so by the Massachusetts Supreme Court.

To Arch Wilkinson Shaw

July 11, 1913 Boston, Mass. [Brandeis Mss, NMF 59-7]

MY DEAR MR. SHAW: [1] *First:* I hope from your long studies concerning efficiency in distribution, you will be able to give me this information:

1: What, in staple articles of production,—like flour, sugar, shoes, cottons, woolens, hardware, ready-made clothing, eggs, poultry, vegetables,—is the markup or difference between the producers' selling price and the price paid by the consumer?

2: To what extent has there been progress in reducing the percentage of cost of distribution?

3: Can you give me any figures which show what part of the total cost of distribution is absorbed by the retail selling?

And if you have written on this subject, or have anyone else's article upon it available, will you be good enough to send me a copy?

Second: It seems to me very important to secure such change in the law as will establish the right of a producer (independently of any patent or trademark) to protection for such price as he may establish for his trademarked articles. It is only necessary that the system of price maintenance should be clearly understood by our people. If it is, I am confident that laws will be enacted to give it protection.

I hope you will agree with me and that System will do its part in the work of education.   Very cordially yours,

1. Arch Wilkinson Shaw (1876–1962) was the editor of *System*. He was also the head of a company that published a number of magazines devoted to business; he served as chairman of the President's Committee on Recent Economic Changes from 1927 to 1940.

To Winfred Thaxter Denison

July 12, 1913 Boston, Mass. [Brandeis Mss, NMF 1-N-1]

MY DEAR MR. DENISON: Thank you for your letter.[1]

The Interstate Commerce report is, of course, a great satisfaction, and I hope it will result in a renewal of Massachusetts respect for the truth and for law; and will aid in its emancipation from a thraldom of which the transportation monopoly is but a part.

As to Frankfurter: In suggesting to Pound that he call on Stimson I had no thought of what Stimson personally would give, but rather what Stimson could do in bringing the matter to the attention of men in New York, who would recognize the great opportunity for public service that was offered.[2] My own recent clashes with the capitalistic world seem to disqualify me for that task.

I was very sorry not to see you when I dined at your house recently.   Yours very cordially,

1. Denison had written to congratulate LDB on his victory over the New Haven and to tell him that all reformers felt he had been completely vindicated by the I.C.C. report. See LDB to Robert M. LaFollette, 9 July 1913, n. 5.
2. Negotiations were already underway to offer Felix Frankfurter a position at Harvard Law School. There had been some questions raised about his fitness, and the school required some aid in financing the position. See LDB to Pound, 5 November 1913.

To Arthur Dehon Little

July 12, 1913 Boston, Mass. [Brandeis Mss, NMF 59-7]

MY DEAR ARTHUR: [1] I want a few dramatic examples showing how the costs of products were reduced:
   (1) By chemical discoveries;
   (2) By utilization of waste products—which of course may include chemical discoveries.
I shall be glad if you can give me in addition to these also the figures showing not merely the reduction in costs of production, but also the reduction in manufacturers' selling prices before and after.

For my purposes it is not necessary that these should be "modern instances".[2]   Very cordially yours,

1. Arthur Dehon Little (1863–1935) was one of America's first consulting chemical engineers; he headed his own company based in Boston.
2. Little replied on the 16th, with a brief list for LDB's use.

To Roscoe Pound

July 12, 1913 Boston, Mass. [Pound Mss]

MY DEAR POUND: I wrote Frankfurter about Stimson after receiving your letter, and have had a reply which leads me to think that you will have no difficulty in securing Stimson's co-operation. Probably Stimson has been convinced by a later letter from Frankfurter; but in any event, as his objection was solely on the ground of what was best for Frankfurter, he will not hesitate to

give all possible assistance, since he now definitely knows that it is
Frankfurter's desire to come to the School.[1]

Most cordially yours,

1. See LDB to Winfred T. Denison, 12 July 1913, and to Pound, 5
November 1913.

To Charles Azro Prouty

July 12, 1913 Boston, Mass. [Brandeis Mss, NMF 1-N-1]

DEAR JUDGE PROUTY: You have performed a great public service,
not only for New England, but for the whole country.[1] The
report is so clear and forceful that it has won assent to its conclusions practically from everyone, except the convicted management of the New Haven. You must have been particularly
gratified at its reception by the New York Press.

Your service is by no means confined to the improvement in
transportation conditions, which is bound to result. It will help
much in securing greater safety for investors; and its greatest
service will be in reawakening in Massachusetts respect for law
and for truth.   Most cordially yours,

1. See LDB to Robert M. LaFollette, 9 July 1913, n. 5.

To Bureau of Labor Statistics

July 14, 1913 Boston, Mass. [Brandeis Mss, NMF 59-7]

DEAR SIRS: *First:* I am desirous of ascertaining whether or not the
relative cost of distributing merchandise at retail is higher than it
was on the average for the period from 1890 to 1899.

With this in view I desire to make a comparison between relative increases in wholesale prices and in retail prices of the same
articles, comparing the average price of 1890 to 1899 with the
price for the year 1911. I turned, therefore, to the reports of
your Bureau on wholesale prices, and also those on retail prices
for those years.

From my examination of the reports (which has not been
thorough) I have been unable to find data for retail prices which

appear comparable to the data on wholesale prices. For instance,—
I find in Bulletin No. 99 that the wholesale prices for the year
1911 were 29.3 per cent higher than the average prices for the
ten years 1890–1899; and I find likewise in Bulletin No. 114 that
the wholesale prices for 1912 were 33.6 per cent higher than the
average prices for the ten years 1890–1899.

Have any retail prices been collected by the Bureau which are
comparable with these wholesale prices, and if so, what.

I find in the Bulletin on Retail Prices of August 23, 1912, page
8, retail prices of fifteen food articles for 1911 compared with the
ten year period, 1890–1899. Has the Bureau collected wholesale
prices for the same fifteen articles properly comparable, and if so,
where would they be found?

Second: I desire also to determine to what extent, if any, the
increased cost of manufactured articles (comparing, for instance,
1911 with the ten year period from 1890 to 1899) is due to the
increased cost of raw material, and to what extent, if any, it is due
to the increase in the cost of converting the raw material into the
manufactured product. Can your Bureau furnish me with any
data showing this, and if so, what?

Third: I should be glad to have generally any data bearing
specifically upon the increase or decrease during the last twenty-
three years of the costs of distribution.

Fourth: Among other things, I should like to have as of today,
or any recent period, comparable figures showing the difference
between the wholesale and retail prices of beef, of vegetables, of
fruit, of flour, of sugar.

Will you have the kindness to let me hear from you at the
earliest possible moment? [1]   Yours very truly,

1. Similar letters were sent to the Department of Agriculture, the Filene
Company, and the McElwain Company.

To Norman Hapgood

July 15, 1913 Boston, Mass. [Brandeis Mss, NMF 52-1]

MY DEAR NORMAN: I received today from McClure's the enclosed check for $100, for the article on "Cutthroat Prices".

I don't want to be paid for anything I do for Harper's until after it has reached the stage of earning dividends on common stock, so I am returning you the check. I am delighted to see that [Frederick L.] Collins is starting out with the policy of making such prompt payment for contributions.

Most cordially,

To William Gibbs McAdoo

July 15, 1913 Boston, Mass. [Brandeis Mss, NMF 51-1]

MY DEAR MR. McADOO: There is a persistent rumor here that Mr. [John Torrey] Burnett is to be appointed collector.

From my talk with you sometime ago I suppose this rumor is wholly without foundation; but the appointment of Mr. Burnett would be so particularly unfortunate that I venture to trouble you with this letter.[1]   Very cordially yours,

1. Burnett was not appointed collector of customs; see LDB to McAdoo, 17 July 1913.

To William Harrison Ingersoll

July 16, 1913 Boston, Mass. [Brandeis Mss, NMF 59-7]

MY DEAR MR. INGERSOLL: Replying to yours of the 14th:

First: My inquiry as to the origin in America of the price maintenance system was merely with a view to getting the history of its development in America. I should be glad to have such further data as you can give me, showing its development; and should also be glad to have data as to the history of any price-fixing through the license system. In other words, I want to understand fully the efforts which have been made to maintain prices, and the measure of success obtained by them. In this connection, I should be glad to know the several lines which have been pursued to attain the one end of price maintenance.

Second: I should be glad to have any data of which you have knowledge, bearing upon the question whether or not the cost of distribution has been increasing or decreasing. We have, undoubtedly, had in industry a constant decrease in the cost of converting raw material into finished product. What has been the tendency as to the cost of distribution?

Third: In Mr. [Charles C.] Parlin's chart 28, entitled, "Cost of Retail Business including Corporation Salaries, Buying Expenses and Freight" he shows an average cost in cities of 600,000 and upward in the East, 26.5%, and gradually reducing in smaller communities, until it reaches 17% in the rural stores. Are his figures comparable; that is, do the rural store figures include rent, salary for the owner, and interest on capital?

I assume that in the data you are expecting to send me this week this general subject will be covered.

Fourth: I assume also that in the material you are gathering will be the result of the investigation which Mr. Noyes planned to make into the various questions raised, including relative expense of selling, price maintained, and other goods.

                                        Yours very truly,

To Albert Sonnichsen

July 16, 1913 Boston, Mass. [Brandeis Mss, NMF 59-7]

MY DEAR SIR: [1] I was much interested, in your article [2] in the April number of the Review of Reviews, in the reference to the effect of the wholesale co-operative associations on the trusts. You speak there of the effect in Sweden on the Sugar and Oleomargine Trusts; in Switzerland on the Shoe Manufacturers' Association; and of the possible effect in England on coal operators.

I should be glad if you could send me some detail[ed] data on this particular subject, or refer me to publications where the subject is discussed.   Yours very truly,

1. Albert Sonnichsen (1878–1931) was a free-lance journalist who was also involved in the consumer cooperative movement. At one time he was secretary of the Cooperative League of America.

2. "Consumers' Cooperation, the New Mass Movement," *Review of Reviews* 47 (April 1913): 455–64. In the article, Sonnichsen argued that the cooperative movement forced monopolies to provide more favorable terms when they competed against cooperative producers.

To William Gibbs McAdoo

July 17, 1913 Boston, Mass. [Brandeis Mss, NMF 58-1]

DEAR MR. McADOO: Replying to yours of the 15th: [1]

I assume that you would consider it to the interests of the Administration to select someone on the list you enclose, and that Mr. [Charles S.] Hamlin will be selected by you for the Assistant Secretaryship.[2] Of the other men on the list I should think William Taylor [3] might be the best, but I should not advise selecting Mr. Taylor without first discussing the situation with Mr. E. A. Grozier, proprietor of the Boston Post. I should expect Mr. Grozier to tell you frankly what he thought of Mr. Taylor for the office.

I shall hope to see you here Sunday.

Very cordially yours,

1. McAdoo had sent a list of Boston-area Democrats to LDB for his advice regarding patronage.
2. See LDB to McAdoo, 23 July 1913.
3. William Taylor was on the editorial staff of the *Boston Post*.

To Judson C. Clements

July 18, 1913 Boston, Mass. [Brandeis Mss, NMF 1-N-1]

DEAR MR. CLEMENTS: [1] I was extremely glad that you and Mr. Harlan made the addition which you did to the general opinion of the Commission in the report of the New England Railroad investigation.

The position taken by you on the excessive bigness seems to have been accepted quite generally as sound; and Mr. Mellen himself recognized it in the statement issued by his Publicity Bureau last week when he resigned from the presidency of the Boston & Maine and Maine Central.   Yours very truly,

1. Judson C. Clements (1846–1917), after five terms in the Congress representing Georgia, had been appointed to the Interstate Commerce Commission in 1892.

To Louis Lipsky

July 18, 1913 Boston, Mass. [Brandeis Mss, Z 1-4]

DEAR MR. LIPSKY: I accept the election as a member of the Associate Executive Committee of the Federation of American Zionists, transmitted in your letter of the 13th.[1]

I read with much interest the report of the Convention, and am glad to know that substantial progress has been made during the year.   Yours very truly,

1. The associate committee was primarily an advisory body, with little power. Despite LDB's willingness to join (in light of the many such offers he refused), he attended very few meetings of this body during the following fourteen months.

To Charles Caldwell McChord

July 18, 1913 Boston, Mass. [Brandeis Mss, NMF 1-N-1]

MY DEAR MR. McCHORD: Your and Mr. Belnap's work in connection with recent New Haven accidents have undoubtedly contributed largely to the resignation of Mr. Mellen, which we hope is the beginning of the reorganization of the system.[1] Another man might avoid Mr. Mellen's faults; but, in my opinion, actual relief will be impossible unless the recommendations of the Committee are followed,—the separation of the trolleys, and the competing steamship lines disposed of; and the Boston & Maine is completely divorced from the New Haven.

                    Yours very truly,

1. On 17 July, Mellen also resigned from the New Haven presidency, as he had previously done from the B. & M., marking the end of the battle he had waged for control of New England's transportation system. LDB wasted little time on gloating, and immediately called for the resignation of the directors who had supported Mellen's policies. "The directors," he charged, "are obviously not to be trusted to introduce those radical changes which the Interstate Commerce Commission recommended and which are essential to a restoration of the railroads to their former prosperity." See LDB to Alfred Brandeis, 19 July 1913.

To John Hobart Marble

July 18, 1913 Boston, Mass. [Brandeis Mss, NMF 57-1]

DEAR MR. MARBLE: Pursuant to our conference with Morris Llewellyn Cooke on June 25th I am enclosing herewith a memorandum of certain inquiries which it seems advisable to make now of all railroads in connection with the advance rate case.[1]

If full answers are given to these inquiries, some light will be thrown upon efficiency in operation, and the comparative data collected should at least serve to show the insufficiency of present accounting, and the necessity of scientific cost keeping, and the ultimate establishment of a Federal Bureau of Railroad Costs.

The data enclosed have reference:

1. As to Freight Cars
2. As to Rails etc.
3. As to Coal User
4. As to so-called legal and public expenses
5. Concerning Interlocking Directorates.

The Commission might find it worth while to employ in some capacity F. Lincoln Hutchins,[2] who has done some work for Harrington Emerson. Mr. Hutchins has considerable railroad experience. He has some quite obvious limitations; but in view of the paucity of men who are connected with railroads, who have a proper appreciation of the importance of ascertaining costs, Mr. Hutchins might prove of considerable value to the Commission. He is no longer a young man, and is not a man who would be extravagant in his demands.

I think you would find it of value to look at two articles of his published in the Engineering Magazine, especially the later:

January 1912   "The Railroad Problem: Rates, Unit Costs and Efficiency."

February 1912   "The Railroad Problem: Capitalization and Regulation, The Deduction from Unit Costs of 20 American Railways."

Mr. Hutchins address is: Box 322 Port Chester, New York.

As to efficiency in purchasing, Mr. Cooke wrote me under date of July 10th as follows:

"In the matter of the purchasing, I expect to be able to do

something. I have secured from France some information in regard to the French system, the essentials of which I will have translated. I will also draft out what I consider to be the fundamentals of a proper purchasing system for the railroads, and I have secured the services of a thoroughly competent man who will pick out ten or twelve sufficiently standardized articles, upon which prices can be asked. In other words, I hope to have say by the end of the present week, the essentials of the things we discussed in connection with the purchasing."

I presume that he will send either direct to you or to me his suggestions on this subject.   Yours very truly,

P.S. I was exceedingly glad that you and Mr. [Judson C.] Clements added a memorandum of your individual views to the opinion on the New England transportation situation.

1. After having lost their bid in 1910–11 for a rate increase, the railroads filed a new request on 14 May 1913, asking for an average five per cent advance. At first LDB was not sure whether he would get involved, and this letter represents a tentative probing rather than a full-scale commitment. On 15 August, however, the Interstate Commerce Commission formally requested LDB's aid. His role would be unique, representing neither railroads nor carriers, but the public, with the specific task of "seeing that all sides and angles of the case are presented of record." See LDB to James S. Harlan, 21 August 1913.

2. F. Lincoln Hutchins was the statistician for the Iowa Board of Railroad Commissioners.

To Alfred Brandeis

July 19, 1913 Dedham, Mass. [Brandeis Mss, unmarked folder]

DEAR AL: Mellen's resignation looks as if the seven year war were drawing to a close. Of course there is much to be done besides getting a new man, if one man must be Overlord again, & I think our community is settling down pretty well to that idea.[1]

The real disgrace to our community is the past attitude of our Pillars of Society—Higginson et al.[2]

1. To replace Mellen, the directors chose Howard Elliott (1860–1928), the president of the Northern Pacific line. Although Elliott eschewed Mellen's monopolistic tendencies, he proved to be almost as irresponsible on fiscal matters. Under his leadership (although he had inherited the situation), the New Haven quit paying dividends altogether.

2. According to Richard Abrams, Henry Lee Higginson and other members of the State Street financial group probably were aware of Mellen's irregularities, since they floated his bond and stock issues. However, instead of insisting that the line reform, they attacked the New Haven's critics. *Conservatism in a Progressive Era* (Cambridge, 1964), 205n.

To Felix Frankfurter

July 19, 1913 Boston, Mass. [Frankfurter Mss-HLS]

MY DEAR FRANKFURTER: I have yours about the Philippines.[1]

I do not think that it would be wise for me to make any suggestion to the President, unless I should see him, or he should chance to write to me on the subject.   Yours very cordially,

1. Secretary of War Garrison (see LDB to Norman Hapgood, 23 July 1913, n. 1) was leaving on an inspection tour of the Philippines, and Frankfurter thought that there were some social and economic facts of which he should be aware; he wanted LDB's advice on how to get these matters before the President.

To Norman Hapgood

July 19, 1913 Boston, Mass. [Brandeis Mss, NMF 52-1]

MY DEAR NORMAN: *First*: Pursuant to yours of the 16th I am sending you under another cover a copy of what is supposed to be the best of my more recent photographs.

Second: There is considerable delay in getting together the material for my other articles on price-fixing. I had expected a large batch of data today from William H. Ingersoll, who is in general charge of the collection of data, but a letter just received leads me to fear that it may not come promptly.

Third: In connection with Mellen's resignation, you may be interested in having recalled my letter to you of September 25, 1911, of which I enclose a copy.[1]   Very truly yours,

1. In that letter, printed in its entirety in Volume 2, LDB wrote: "Anticipating the future a little, I suggest the following as an epitaph or obituary notice:--Mellen was a masterful man, resourceful, courageous, broad of view. He fired the imagination of New England; but, being oblique of vision, merely distorted its judgment and silenced its conscience. For a while he trampled with impunity on laws human and divine; but as he was obsessed

with the delusion that two and two make five, he fell at last the victim to the relentless rules of humble arithmetic. Remember, O Stranger: 'Arithmetic is the first of the sciences and the mother of safety.'" Hapgood used the letter in his editorial, "Arithmetic," which was published in the first issue of *Harper's* under his editorship, 16 August 1913.

To Robert Marion LaFollette

July 19, 1913 Boston, Mass. [LaFollette Mss]

MY DEAR BOB: I have yours of the 18th about Roe.[1] I expect to be called to New York in a few days and think it would be better for me to talk to a few of my friends on the Committee, rather than to write them.[2]   Very cordially yours,

P.S.   Does not Mellen's complete resignation offer a good opportunity for a ringing editorial on the need of a complete breaking up of the monopoly? And there is a great opportunity for effective work by the Department of Justice.[3]

1. LaFollette had written asking LDB's support in a movement to run Gilbert Ernstein Roe (1865–1929) for Supreme Court justice in New York City on a fusion ticket. Roe, a New York attorney, had once been LaFollette's law partner and had continued to work closely with him on political and reform matters. See LDB to Charles C. Burlingham, 24 July 1913.

2. As it turned out, the Fusion Committee passed by Roe and chose instead a man who was fast developing into one of the foremost jurists and legal philosophers in the country, Benjamin Nathan Cardozo.

3. See LDB to LaFollette, 28 July 1913.

To Joseph Russell Marble

July 21, 1913 Boston, Mass. [Brandeis Mss, NMF 1-N-1]

MY DEAR MR. MARBLE: Thank you for your letter of the 18th and for the interview.[1]

I suppose it is unnecessary to tell you that I not only was not paid for my services, but that I necessarily expended, in cash disbursements during this six-year struggle, a very considerable sum of money in endeavoring, both to curb the monopoly, and to free the individual from the thraldom to which this great power has subjected so many of our fellow citizens.[2] I hope too that the result may serve to renew the traditional respect in New England for law and for the truth.   Very cordially,

1. Marble congratulated LDB upon the overthrow of Mellen and said the entire Commonwealth owed him its thanks. "Whether you were retained or not I do not care," he said, and enclosed an interview he had given to a local paper castigating the New Haven management and praising LDB.

2. LDB had in fact paid $25,000 to his law firm in compensation for the time he had devoted to the case, as well as for services performed by members of his staff. This figure does not, of course, include the very large sums that LDB could have been earning had he devoted his entire energy to private practice. See LDB to E. Louise Malloch, 4 November 1907.

To Philip Patterson Wells

July 21, 1913 Boston, Mass. [Brandeis Mss, NMF 51-7]

My dear Mr. Wells: Thank you for yours of the 18th: [1]

If the War Department seems to be going wrong on water power questions, I hope you will discuss them fully with Frankfurter. He is thoroughly with us on conservation, and is so intelligent that I consider him a power for the right.

Yours very truly.

1. Wells had expressed worry that some of the water policies proposed for land under control of the War Department violated sound conservation ideas.

To Norman Hapgood

July 23, 1913 Boston, Mass. [Brandeis Mss, NMF 52-1]

My dear Norman: Replying to yours of the 19th:

First: It looks as if there would be considerable delay before the material is collected for my other articles on Price Maintenance; and I agree with you that it would be better to use in the issue of the 16th, the Secretary of War's article.[1] Probably it would be better for the price-maintenance cause also to have the articles come at a later date, when the movement for new legislation takes more definite form.

Second: I am enclosing an article entitled "The Failure of Banker-Management—A lesson from the New Haven," which I want you to read. This article sets forth what I believe to be a new and important truth which should aid in combatting the bankers' control of business. The article was not prepared with a view to its publication in Harper's, as I thought for several reasons you would not want it; but, of course, you are welcome to it. If you do not want it, please send it back by return mail.[2]

Third: I am enclosing you an additional list of possible subscribers to whom it might be well to send the Harper circular letter.   Yours very truly,

P.S. If you don't want the article, let me know where you would prefer to have it published.

1. Lindley Miller Garrison (1864–1932), after a law career in New Jersey, had worked himself up to the state's Chancery Court, from which Wilson had named him as Secretary of War. Garrison was competent but unable to make necessary political adjustments, and he resigned in 1916 when the President refused to accept the preparedness plan he and the army staff had devised. Garrison's article was "Vital Needs of the Army," *Harper's Weekly* 58 (16 August 1913): 6–8.

2. Hapgood ran the piece as "Banker-Management; Why It Has Failed: A Lesson from the New Haven," *Harper's Weekly* 58 (16 August 1913): 14–15; it was reprinted as ch. 9 of *Other People's Money, and How the Bankers Use It* (New York, 1914). In the article LDB attacked banker control as essentially opposed to good management, since it created divided loyalties and confused sound practices. LDB used the New Haven example to show the evils of bigness, monopoly, banker management, and interlocking directorates.

To Louis Lipsky

July 23, 1913 Boston, Mass. [Brandeis Mss, LtB]

DEAR MR. LIPSKY: I am in receipt of yours of the 23rd, notifying me of my election as a delegate to represent the American shekel-payers [1] organized as the Federation of American Zionists by the Cincinnati Zionist Convention held on Tuesday, the 24th.

I regret that other engagements will prevent my attending the congress.[2]

With high appreciation.   Very truly yours,

1. See LDB to Chaim Weizmann, 11 October 1914, n. 10.
2. The fact that LDB had been chosen by the American Zionists to be one of their delegates to the World Zionist Congress in Vienna does not

indicate the extent of LDB's involvement at this time so much as it shows the small number of available leaders upon whom the Zionists could draw. See LDB to Nahum Sokolow, 1 August 1913.

To William Gibbs McAdoo

July 23, 1913 Boston, Mass. [McAdoo Mss]

MY DEAR MR. MCADOO: If you do not select Charles S. Hamlin for the Assistant Secretaryship, I think he would be much preferable for the Collectorship to any of the others whom we considered; and if you do want him for the Assistant Secretaryship I think it would be advisable to talk with him before you commit yourself on the Collectorship.[1] It might make a difference as to whether or not he would accept.

I met him at the Club today, and he spoke of not getting, until after you had left the city, your message sent through the Mayor's office.   Yours very cordially,

1. Hamlin received an appointment as Assistant Secretary of the Treasury; see also LDB to McAdoo, 30 July 1913.

To Massachusetts Board of Railroad Commissioners

July 23, 1913 Boston, Mass. [Brandeis Mss, NMF 1-N-1]

DEAR SIRS: It was reported in last evening's paper that the New York, New Haven & Hartford Railroad Company has called a meeting of stockholders for August 22nd, with a view to securing the approval of an issue of $67,552,400. of 6% convertible debenture bonds, to be offered to stockholders and holders of previous issues of convertible debenture bonds at par.

The New Haven Railroad will presumably make application to your Board for leave to issue these securities; and I desire to present for your consideration the following, among the many other questions, which your board must consider before authorizing such issue:

The need of money to be raised from these debentures is said to be the $40,000,000. of short-time notes maturing December 1st, 1913, $5,000,000. of 4% debenture bonds maturing February 1st, 1914, and certain necessary improvements.

The report of the Interstate Commerce Commission recommends that the New Haven dispose of its trolleys, calls attention to the provisions of the Panama Canal Act,—under which its interest in steamships must be disposed of—and strongly recommends generally that the New Haven withdraw from its outside operations.

From the report of the New Haven to its stockholders, dated June 30, 1912, it appears that the company then held the following securities:

Securities of Proprietary, Affiliated and Controlled Companies—	$151,741,668.35
Miscellaneous Investments—	69,746,299.28
Securities issued or assumed held in treasury—	202,650.00
Marketable Securities—	27,643,782.64
	$249,334,400.27

I respectfully submit that in view of the facts disclosed by the report of the Interstate Commerce Commission, the New Haven should be required to meet its accruing indebtedness, and provide for its other financial needs, by a sale of a part of these securities held by it.[1]

If this proposed issue is authorized and placed, and thereafter the New Haven,—following the recommendations of the Commission, or acting under compulsory process of the Courts,—parts with its other properties acquired in pursuit of the monopoly in transportation, the Company would have available a large amount of cash or other assets for which, apparently, it would have no need in its legitimate business of railroading, and would, in its capacity as holding company, be tempted to make further investments prejudicial to the interests of stockholders and the public.[2]　Very truly yours,

1. The stockholders did approve the issue, and the New Haven immediately requested the Massachusetts Public Service Commission (which replaced the Board) for approval. LDB objected at that time in a tone similar to the one he used in this letter, and he also requested the Commission to show all the disbursements made by the New Haven during Mellen's tenure. The Commission did find widespread misuse of funds, with very large amounts of money used for lobbying and publicity, although the funds were supposedly allocated for "educational" activities. Nevertheless, the Commis-

sion approved the issue and drew forth a bitter minority opinion from George W. Anderson. See LDB to Norman Hapgood, 15 October 1913.

2. This same day a similar letter was sent to Thomas W. Gregory, urging the Justice Department to keep close watch on the proceedings and possibly to investigate the matter.

To Charles Culp Burlingham

July 24, 1913 Boston, Mass. [Brandeis Mss, NMF 58-1]

MY DEAR CHARLIE: I hear that Gilbert E. Roe has been suggested by a nonpartisan judiciary committee for the Supreme Court.[1] I am wondering whether he will not be also the fusion committee's candidate.

My meetings with Roe have been few, but I have heard much of him through Senator LaFollette; and think he made a distinct contribution to the supremacy of law by his "Our Judicial Oligarchy".[2] Although one may not agree with all he says, or approve entirely the way he puts it, he has performed an important service. If we are to preserve proper respect for the law, I think we need some men on the bench of his views.

I wonder whether you saw, in a recent number of the New Statesman, how even the English are having trouble with the class judiciary.[3]   Very cordially,

1. See LDB to Robert M. LaFollette, 19 July 1913.
2. (New York, 1912). Burlingham replied that he had read the book at a sitting: "It is certainly interesting and so far true as to be rather depressing. It would be a satisfaction to have some men on the Bench who had a little sense of what really is important."
3. A minor fury had arisen in Parliament over the *obiter dicta* of a judge in a labor case, which the members felt had cast a slur on their integrity. The article noted a widespread feeling that all was not well nor fair in the dispensation of judges. "Politics and the Bench," *The New Statesman* 1 (5 July 1913): 391-92.

To Bernard Abraham Rosenblatt

July 24, 1913 Boston, Mass. [Brandeis Mss, NMF 11-2]

MY DEAR MR. ROSENBLATT: I am returning you herewith Chapters 8, 9, and 10 of your book, which I have read with unusual interest.[1] The program which you set forth is well worthy of the most careful study by the student of our social problems. Your argument is forceful; and the manner of treatment, logical and convincing. There is throughout a combination of vision and practical sense which is full of promise.

Your general purpose of maintaining competition and developing agencies which shall stimulate and be stimulated by private agencies of production and distribution, seems to me sound.

I doubt whether there is anything of value which I can suggest, but possibly you would care to consider this.

First: You have assumed an efficiency of the trusts and large organizations. My own belief is that there is a limit of size of the efficient unit, which has already been over-stepped by a large part of our institutions. There is, of course, danger that you may be confronted with this same difficulty in the public industrial units; for instance, the State Grange. There is some evidence to the contrary, however, namely, that afforded by the Co-operative British Wholesale Society, which is a relatively large unit and apparently very well managed.

Second: As to the single tax: I think your argument differentiating the farm lands from other lands has in it much of political value. I am disposed to think, however, that one of the strongest arguments in favor of the single tax is the development of the landlord class in America. I suggest your looking up the statistics on Tenant Farmers. My recollection is that in Illinois or Iowa the percentage of absentee owners of farms is about 43 per cent. You will, I think, also find that the increase of the value of farm land during the last twelve years has been much greater on the average than the increase in value of urban property. This, of course, has a very strong bearing upon the cost of living. As I said the strength of your argument, from the political standpoint, is considerable.

In connection with the tendency toward a single tax, you might make mention of the recent action in Pittsburg [*sic*], under which the tax on improvements is being gradually eliminated.

I congratulate you on your work.   Very cordially yours,

1. *The Social Commonwealth: A Plan for Achieving Industrial Democracy* (New York, 1914).

To Henry Robinson Towne

July 25, 1913 Boston, Mass. [Brandeis Mss, NMF 59-7]

My dear Mr. Towne: [1] Thank you for yours of the 24th.

The process of education on this subject [price maintenance], energetically pursued, must result in securing legislation sanctioning individual price maintenance in competitive business.

I have borne well in mind your remarks to me in the lobby of the New Willard two years ago, about collective price maintenance. The inroads of monopoly demand that we should protect competition; and to this end certain agreements among competitors must have legal sanction. It is more difficult, however, to define exactly what should be legalized and what not.

Legislation should be preceded by careful investigation into the facts. I hope such an investigation will be undertaken by the Government; and I suggested some time ago, to those who had the investigation under consideration, that the best starting point would be to tap your great reservoir of knowledge on this subject.

Very cordially yours,

1. Henry Robinson Towne (1844–1924) was the cofounder of the Yale & Towne Lock Company, and he also served as president of the Merchants Association of New York.

To Henry Bruere

July 28, 1913 Boston, Mass. [Brandeis Mss, NMF 64-1]

Dear Mr. Bruere: [1] *First*: I am investigating the question of unnecessary costs incident to municipal loans; and, among other things, the interest burden incident to the issue of loans in large amounts and then depositing the proceeds of the loan in the banks at a low rate of interest until the funds shall be used.

Has your Bureau any data bearing upon this subject, and specifically upon the following: The amount of New York's balance from time to time in the banks; the rate of interest thereon; and, in connection therewith, the dates of issue of loans and receipt of proceeds thereof.[2]

If you have any such data will you kindly send same to me?

Second: In connection with the above, I am also considering the possibility of municipalities selling their bonds direct to the investor; and, among other things, selling them "over-the-counter" as distinguished from public bidding. If you have, or can refer me to any data on this subject, I shall be greatly obliged.[3]

Yours very truly,

1. Henry Bruere (1882–1958), a well-known progressive, was in 1913 a director of the New York Bureau of Municipal Research; later he was involved in a number of civic improvement and efficiency movements.

2. Bruere replied on 31 July that New York had devised a method to avoid this problem, through the issuance of corporate stock certificates against the sale of bonds.

3. A similar letter was sent this day to Clinton Rogers Woodruff.

To Robert Marion LaFollette

July 28, 1913 Boston, Mass. [LaFollette Mss]

MY DEAR BOB: The editorial in last week's issue of the magazine was fine.[1] The appointment of Howard Elliott is not reassuring. He is said to be personally thoroughly honest, and a good operating man; but there is reason to think that he has not the same regard for public rights, and that he is a monopolist by nature. At all events the Board of Directors is unchanged.

The New Haven's proposal to issue $67,500,000 of 6% twenty-year debentures indicates, also, an intent to disregard the recommendation of the I.C.C.,—to dispose of the outside properties. The New Haven had, according to its own accounts, on July 30, 1912, $249,334,400.27, book value of securities. A large part of these represent the subsidiaries which were acquired for the purpose of suppressing competition. Many of the securities are clearly marketable. If the New Haven intends to dispose of the properties acquired for the purpose of suppressing competition, it could easily raise $67,500,000, which it desires to pay the $40,000,000 of notes maturing December 1st, and for other purposes. Or, if it merely doubted its ability to close the transaction, in disposing of those properties in time to be in funds to pay the December 1st notes, why does it not issue short term notes as it has been in the habit of doing of late?

It seems to me clear, at least, the present management of the New Haven (the Old Board of Directors remain) can learn nothing; and that we cannot get compliance with the law without action by the Department of Justice.

Yours very cordially,

P.S.   I made an effort to have Roe endorsed;—do not know yet whether it will have any results.[2]

1. "The Eight Hour Day will Come," *LaFollette's Weekly Magazine*, 5 (19 July 1913): 1. In the front page editorial, LaFollette wrote a miniature Brandeis brief, citing numerous facts and figures on the relation of the workday to efficiency and health; much of the data came from Josephine Goldmark, *Fatigue and Efficiency*.

2. See LDB to LaFollette, 19 July 1913.

To William Gibbs McAdoo

July 30, 1913 Boston, Mass. [Brandeis Mss, NMF 58-1]

MY DEAR MR. MCADOO: Replying to yours of the 25th, and referring further to our conference at Col. House's:

I am convinced now that it would be unwise to appoint [William] Taylor; and I am strongly of the opinion that the best man on the list of eligibles is Hayes, of Springfield.[1] He is a lawyer,—and we need a lawyer; he has been Mayor of Springfield, and State Senator; and would properly represent the administration.

It would seem to me unwise to select for the Collectorship [of the Port of Boston] any of the other men on the list.

As to the Collector of Internal Revenues: Have you considered John T. Wheelwright? [2] He too, is a lawyer and of the highest character; he has always been a Democrat; has held public office; and could be relied upon to guard the interests of the administration.[3]   Very cordially,

1. William P. Hayes (1866–1916), a Springfield attorney, served in the Massachusetts senate in 1907; he was mayor of the city in 1900 and 1901.

2. John Tyler Wheelwright (1856–1925) had held a number of public positions in Massachusetts, including chairman of the Board of Gas and Electric Light Commissioners, assistant corporation counsel of Boston, and Boston park commissioner.

3. See LDB to McAdoo, 13 September 1913.

To Mary Boyle O'Reilly

July 30, 1913 Boston, Mass. [Brandeis Mss, Z 1-2]

MY DEAR MISS O'REILLY: [1] Thank you for your letter of the 29th and the copy of the interview. My statement is greatly improved under your skillful handling.[2]

I am delighted to know that you are to go to Russia on so important a mission. You are undertaking a work worthy of your father's daughter.[3]

I hope that you can arrange to supplement your Russian visit with one to Palestine. No treatment of the Russian Jewish question is adequate without a study of Zionism, and the hope which that presents. If you go to Palestine see Mr. Aaron Aaronsohn, the chief of the Jewish Agricultural Experiment Station at Haifa,—a very remarkable man, the discover of the wild wheat; and also see, if she is still there, Miss Eva Leon, who is introducing district nursing in Jerusalem. Mr. Aaronsohn has spent much time in America,—possibly you have met him. Miss Leon is the sister-in-law of Professor Gottheil of Columbia.[4]

If you should chance to be in Boston before you go, see Mr. Jacob DeHaas, the Editor of the Jewish Advocate, who was an associate of Dr. Herzl,[5] and had an important part in the inauguration of the Zionist movement.

With best wishes. Yours very cordially,

1. Mary Boyle O'Reilly (1873–1939) wrote extensively on a number of humanitarian reforms; among other public offices, she was a Massachusetts prison commissioner from 1907 to 1911.

2. Miss O'Reilly had interviewed LDB on the New England rail situation for the Newspaper Enterprise Association papers.

3. John Boyle O'Reilly (1844–1890), an ardent Irish patriot, had been sentenced to death for conspiracy against Queen Victoria. When he was shipped with other prisoners to Australia, he escaped and came to America where he edited the influential *Boston Pilot*, an organ of liberal Catholicism. For his career as a reformer, see Arthur Mann, *Yankee Reformers in the Urban Age* (New York, 1966), 27–44.

4. Richard James Horatio Gottheil (1862–1936) was professor of Semitic studies at Columbia University. He was one of the pillars of the early Zionist movement in the United States. A reluctant leader, he gladly welcomed LDB's direction after 1914. His history, *Zionism* (New York, 1914), was widely read.

5. Theodore Herzl (1860–1904) was the founder of modern political Zionism. Growing up as an assimilated Jew in Austria-Hungary, Herzl received a law degree in Vienna and practiced for a while before he found his true vocation as a journalist. He was the Paris correspondent for the Viennese *Neue Freie Presse* during the Dreyfus affair, and the shock of the scandal brought him back to Judaism. In 1895 he penned his classic statement of Zionism, *The Jewish State*, which set forth in detail how the Jews should reestablish themselves in their homeland. Although Leo Pinsker and others had written along similar lines in the 1880s, Herzl reached his conclusions ignorant not only of their work but also of the Chibbath Zion (Love of Zion) movement then flourishing in Russia.

For the rest of his brief life, Herzl was possessed by his dream of recreating the Jewish homeland. Distrusted by many of the Russian Zionists because of his "non-Jewish" habits, he nonetheless sparked the imagination of the Jewish masses. He saw himself as a prophet, and contemporary descriptions employ that imagery. In 1897 he convened the first World Zionist Congress at Basle, and he later confided in his diary that at Basle he founded the Jewish State. Always confident of success, he said that "if you will it, it is no dream," a phrase that LDB used over and over again in his Zionist talks.

Herzl's Zionism was based on the premise that Jews were discriminated against because they had no homeland; the restoration of a homeland would thus give the Jews dignity and relieve the gentiles of the burden of anti-Semitism. He believed that the fastest way to secure such a homeland was through political negotiation with the Sultan of the Turkish Empire, and he tried several times to interest the Sultan in allowing the Jews to reestablish Palestine as a Jewish state in return for large loans. He died in 1904, having won the love of the masses and the admiration of many western Jews but having failed totally in his efforts to influence Turkey.

The literature on Herzl is immense, but one place to start is with his *Diaries;* a good abridgement in English has been prepared by Marvin Lowenthal (New York, 1956). The best biography is Alex Bein, *Theodore Herzl,* tr., Maurice Samuel (Philadelphia, 1942). *The Jewish State* exists in many editions and many languages; also useful is Joseph Adler, *The Herzl Paradox* (New York, 1962).

To James Waldron Remick

July 31, 1913 Boston, Mass. [Brandeis Mss, NMF 1-N-1]

MY DEAR REMICK: I have yours of the 30th about the Railroad Conference Commission.[1] I have not supposed that the Commission would contribute anything material to the solution of our railroad problem; but I think it may, and as at present constituted, is quite likely to make the solution of the problem more difficult, because of the men on it who favor monopoly, or are otherwise distinctly representative of the railroad interests.

If you went on the Board the public would be properly represented, and you could, I think, be of distinct service to the community in counteracting the influence which the Board might otherwise have in preventing an early and proper settlement of our transportation problem.

I should not think that the demands upon your time, involved by serving on the Conference, would be very great; and I hope you will accept the appointment if it is again offered.[2]

Very cordially yours,

1. Remick had been offered a seat on the New England Railroad Conference, and he had so far declined. However, he wanted to know if his accepting the New Hampshire position might aid the public interest in solving the rail problem.

2. Remick did not become a member of the Conference.

To Aaron Aaronsohn

August 1, 1913 Boston, Mass. [Brandeis Mss, Z 1-2]

MY DEAR MR. AARONSOHN: Miss Mary Boyle O'Reilly, the daughter of the Irish patriot John Boyle O'Reilly, wrote me recently that she was planning to go to Russia, on behalf of the Newspaper Enterprise Association, to study conditions in the Pale of Settlement.[1] (The Newspaper Enterprise Association, as you doubtless know, is closely associated with the Scripps McRae newspapers,—a leading progressive force in America.)

I said to Miss O'Reilly [2] that a study of the Pale of Settlement ought to be supplemented by a study of Palestine, and the Zionist movement; and suggested that she extend her journey to Palestine; and, of course, mentioned you as an important source of information concerning conditions there. She writes me that she was planning, in any event, to go to Palestine for some Christmas and Easter stories; and I take great pleasure in giving to her this note of introduction to you.   Very cordially yours,

1. Established by the Empress Catherine II in 1791, the Pale of Settlement was that area of czarist Russia to which Jews were restricted. The Pale varied in its boundaries from time to time and was finally abolished after the Russian Revolution.

2. See LDB to Mary B. O'Reilly, 30 July 1913.

To Nahum Sokolow

August 1, 1913 Boston, Mass. [Berlin Office]

MY DEAR MR. SOKOLOW: When you were in Boston I promised to consider your request that I attend the coming Zionist Congress.[1] It has proved impossible for me to leave the United States this summer; and I, therefore, ask you to be good enough to convey my greetings and good wishes to all my fellow Zionists, from whose deliberations we hope so much.

The Congress should know that your visit to this country has greatly stimulated and developed the interest in the Zionist movement; and I believe that the Jews of the United States will support well matured and carefully devised plans tending to bring about the ends we are seeking to attain.

I venture to suggest the following for the consideration of the Congress:

First: That we concentrate our efforts upon a few undertakings.

Second: That as the pressure upon the Jews is increasing so rapidly, our efforts should now be directed mainly toward opening up Palestine to the masses.

Third: That we need for this purpose the possession of large tracts of land, coupled with such concessions from the Turkish government as will give to our people freedom of movement, control of our operations, and security for the investments necessary to the development of the land we may own.

Fourth: That at this juncture the offer of our movement to introduce into Turkish possessions an intelligent and industrious population cannot fail to have great weight with her statesmen; and the public offer to sell the Crown Lands presents to us a much sought opportunity to achieve a position of permanent value to our people.

Fifth: That while we need the land, we need at the same time a large immigration of our people into Palestine. Numbers are necessary to rendering our position secure.

Sixth: That we must have such conditions of settlement as will leave our people free from such entanglements as have arisen in the past, and which must necessarily arise in the future if the Jews are not afforded an opportunity to act in their own behalf with the mutual consent of the Turkish government.

Any plan which shall combine these necessary factors will, I feel sure, meet with the hearty approval and financial support of the Jews in the United States.

The Committee formed to organize the American Palestine Company has so far done only some preliminary work.[2] Its plans are not yet formulated. The Committee will, I am sure, cooperate heartily in carrying out a policy which shall be broad enough to demand the support of our people in this Country.

With Zion's greetings,[3]   Very cordially yours,

1. See LDB to Louis Lipsky, 23 July 1913.
2. The American Palestine Company was an organization designed to persuade American Jews to invest in the economic development of Palestine.
3. This letter was read before the Congress.

To John M. Walton

August 1, 1913 Boston, Mass. [Brandeis Mss, NMF 64-1]

DEAR SIR: [1] In connection with the study of financial efficiency in municipal affairs, I am investigating the experience and possibilities of cities dispensing with the banker as middleman in the placing of its [*sic*] loans, and the circumstances under which it is possible to sell bonds direct to the investor.

I have in mind, not only the possible saving to the city from not paying commissions, or profit to the banker, but also the advantages of the creation of a continuous market for such bonds, which would obviate the necessity of issuing loans in large amounts and then depositing the proceeds of the loans in banks at a low rate of interest until the funds can be used.

I understand that Philadelphia has succeeded on several occasions in selling bonds "over-the-counter"; and I should be greatly obliged if you would let me know fully the experience of Philadelphia in this respect; and the advantages which have flown [*sic*] from it, or any disadvantages which may have presented themselves.[2]   Yours very truly,

1. John M. Walton was comptroller for the city of Philadelphia. This letter was typical of many which LDB sent to officials in a number of cities, gathering material for his forthcoming series in *Harper's*.

2. See LDB to Morris L. Cooke, 25 September 1913.

To William Gibbs McAdoo

August 9, 1913 Boston, Mass. [McAdoo Mss]

MY DEAR MR. McADOO: I duly received your letter of the 6th, and have now come from the Court.[1]

First: I am very glad to report that upon a full hearing Judge Dodge [2] decided to retain Mr. Fisher as receiver; and he showed some little impatience at the attack which had been made upon Mr. Fisher.[3]

Second: Mr. Morris,[4] representing a Committee of Creditors of which Mr. Curtis is chairman,[5] requested that the Court should not determine whether or not to appoint a co-receiver until after a meeting of creditors which he would call for Thursday or Friday of next week. The Court assented to this request, stating that he would be glad to have them vote as expressed at the meeting whether a co-receiver should be appointed; but he indicated pretty strongly an intention to appoint a co-receiver, not so much because he thought it necessary, as because an appreciable number of the creditors and some stockholders believed that it was necessary, and he wanted them, as well as himself, to feel satisfied. However, he left the matter open.

Third: My impression is that the Judge will decide to appoint a co-receiver and it seems likely that he will prefer to have as such receiver some Massachusetts lawyer. I discussed this matter with Mr. Morris, and he said that he would take the matter up with the creditors who have already signified their assent to the formation of a Creditors' Protection Committee, and he will then communicate with my office.

Fourth: There was the fullest cooperation today between counsel representing Mr. Curtis and Mr. Fisher,—that is, Mr. Morris, Mr. Friedman,[6] and myself; but I rather felt that Mr. Friedman was not entirely happy at the thought of my "taking charge of the entire situation so far as the interests of the Department are concerned."

Probably you may want to say something to Mr. Curtis and Mr. Fisher on this subject.

I tried to reach you on the telephone at Beverly, and also at the Touraine, but found that you had not yet arrived. I shall hope to get in touch with you at South Yarmouth, where I can be reached through Pay Station Hyannis 9056–11.[7]

Yours very cordially,

1. McAdoo explained to LDB that the Treasury Department had been drawn into a complex business matter. The Atlantic National Bank of Providence, R.I., had failed and was in the hands of a government-appointed receiver; subsequently, the Walpole Tire and Rubber Co., a heavy debtor to the bank, had also failed and was in the hands of a receiver. In litigation some disgruntled stockholders wanted a coreceiver appointed to act jointly with the government-recommended receiver. McAdoo asked LDB if he would "take charge of the entire situation so far as the interests of the Department are concerned."

2. Frederic Dodge (1847–1927) was the United States circuit judge for the First Circuit.

3. Robert C. Fisher was a New York businessman, an acquaintance of McAdoo; at McAdoo's urging, he was chosen receiver of the Walpole Tire and Rubber Co.

4. Morris was the counsel for the Creditor's Protective Committee.

5. Rennselaer Curtis was the government-appointed receiver of the Providence bank.

6. Friedman was the lawyer for Fisher.

7. LDB and McAdoo discussed this matter again on 18 August at which time LDB reported to McAdoo that Judge Dodge had instead appointed ex-Congressman Robert Orr Harris (1854–1926) of Massachusetts to be the coreceiver. LDB wrote: "So far as I can see the Department's interests are fully protected."

To James Clark McReynolds

August 13, 1913 Boston, Mass. [Brandeis Mss, NMF 58-1]

MY DEAR MR. MCREYNOLDS: Since our meeting in New York last week I have given much thought to your inquiry as to a proper man for United States Attorney for Massachusetts and also one for Assistant Attorney General from New England.

As to the latter I have no suggestion to make as yet. Most of the men whom I had in mind proved either not to be Democrats or they are distinctly obnoxious to the Democratic leaders in

Massachusetts, and their appointment would be deemed an unfriendly act.

As United States Attorney for Massachusetts I think it worth while for you to consider Michael J. Sughrue of Boston.

Mr. Sughrue was for many years the leading Assistant District Attorney for Suffolk County (Boston), and for a short time was District Attorney, by appointment, to fill a vacancy. He was defeated in the subsequent election for District Attorney under very peculiar circumstances although he had the very general recommendation of the Bar.[1] He has since that time been Counsel for the Boston Finance Commission and has performed important service. He has always been a Democrat; is an Irishman, and his appointment would, I think, be accepted as a compliment to the Irishmen. He has been a very good public servant, and bears an excellent reputation. He has, however, incurred the enmity of such men as Mayor Fitzgerald and his associates, and this fact may make it unwise to appoint him.

Assistant Secretary Dudley Field Malone, who has thoroughly canvassed our local situation in connection with proposed appointments under the Treasury Department, could probably tell you whether the hostilities of certain factions toward Mr. Sughrue, would make it unwise to appoint him.

The fact is that no man who has been active in public or private life and does his duty, would be acceptable to most of the Democratic leaders in Massachusetts.[2]

I hope to report further to you later.

Very cordially yours,

1. See LDB to Lawrence Veiller, 15 November 1905.

2. See LDB to Charles Warren, 8 October 1913 and to McReynolds, 18 October 1913. Ultimately, the position went to LDB's close friend George W. Anderson. See LDB to Thomas W. Gregory, 18 September 1914.

To Joseph Bartlett Eastman

August 21, 1913 South Yarmouth, Mass.
[Brandeis Mss, NMF 57-1]

DEAR EASTMAN: I have been asked by the Interstate Com. Commission to act as its special counsel in the advance rate case and expect to do so.[1]

I shall want to retain you as assistant and hope you have no engagement which will prevent your entering upon the work after you complete Elevated Arbitration matter.[2]

Cordially,

I suppose I shall have to begin on advance rate work middle of September.

1. See next letter.

2. After a strike during the summer of 1913, the newly organized union of Boston Elevated Railroad workers agreed to arbitration. Eastman, upon LDB's recommendation, assumed the responsibility of presenting labor's case; and in January 1914 he had the satisfaction of seeing his contentions upheld by the arbitrators. There is no record of Eastman's interrupting his work in this arbitration to accept LDB's proposal regarding the freight case.

To James S. Harlan

August 21, 1913 South Yarmouth, Mass.
[Brandeis Mss, NMF 57-1]

MY DEAR MR. HARLAN: Reply to yours of 15th has been delayed by my absence from Boston.

I appreciate most highly the invitation to act as special counsel of the [Interstate Commerce] Commission in the Advance Rate case and shall be glad to lend my aid as you suggest.[1]

You do not say when the hearings are to begin. I trust that no date will be fixed earlier than October, as my vacation was delayed this year and I should be unable to do any work in the case before the middle of September. After that date I should be glad to go to Washington for a conference if you are to be there.[2]

Very cordially yours,

1. The railroads did not take lightly their defeat of 1910-11, at the hands of Brandeis and the I.C.C. They remained convinced of the need for higher rates, and by 1913 they felt prepared once again to request rate increases, this time to average five per cent. Faced again with a complex case, the Commission asked for LDB's help (see LDB to John H. Marble, 18 July 1913). Unfortunately, in the letter of 15 August, Harlan's definition of LDB's role was ambiguous, and the resulting confusion ended in bad feeling and charges of hypocrisy and cowardice. Harlan had written that LDB's task would be "seeing that all sides of the case are presented of record, without advocating any particular theory for its disposition." In addition, another passage in Harlan's letter added to the confusion: "We are of course aware of the fact that the carriers will not fail fully to present their side of the

case and the Commission has felt that every effort should be made in the public interest adequately to present the other side. Would you care to undertake that burden?" The question of LDB's precise role was to become important. While it was widely believed, because of his previous record in this area, that he had been retained to attack the railroads, he took Harlan literally and attempted to aid the Commission in impartially weighing the arguments of all sides. Consequently, when he concluded that in the East freight rates were inadequate to provide sufficient revenue for the railroads, some shipping spokesmen accused him of bad faith. For the details of this controversy, see Mason, *Brandeis*, ch. 21, and the testimony of Clifford Thorne at LDB's confirmation hearing in 1916, *Nomination Hearings*, I, 5–62, and also the testimony of others in *Ibid.*, 62–103.

2. Preliminary hearings began on 24 November 1913; the Commission handed down its final verdict on 29 July 1914.

To Charles Azro Prouty

August 21, 1913 South Yarmouth, Mass.
[Brandeis Mss, NMF 1-N-1]

MY DEAR JUDGE PROUTY: I thank you for yours of the 15th, reply to which has been delayed by absence from Boston.

By the same mail came Mr. Harlan's letter inviting me to act as special Counsel of the Commission in the Advance Rate Case and I have accepted. This will prevent my giving much time specifically to Boston and Maine matters now; but our New England problem raises so many of the considerations involved in the general enquiry as to the propriety of rate advances that I trust you will deem it advisable to defer final action in respect to Boston & Maine rates until the broader investigation shall have been completed.   Most cordially yours,

To Alfred Brandeis (Fragment)

August 29, 1913 South Yarmouth, Mass.
[Brandeis Mss, Unmarked folder]

DEAR AL: I suppose you noticed New Haven dropped to 91⅜ the other day. It will doubtless go on to a 4 percent dividend basis by January 1.[1]

1. On 18 December, the directors of the New Haven decided to pass the dividend completely for the first time in forty years.

To Alfred Brandeis

September 2, 1913 Dedham, Mass.
[Brandeis Mss, Unmarked folder]

Dear Al: Nothing from you for a long time, and I didn't get a chance to ask Madie about you on Wednesday.

Have had a rather quiet time since South Yarmouth, trying to write some articles on the money trust for Harper's.[1] There will be some crys [*sic*] of "Holy Murder" if the legislation I propose ever gets past [*sic*]; but less than that will do little good.

New Haven matters are active as ever. The government lawyers are steadily at work and we should get some action before the middle of October.

1. These important articles, printed in *Harper's Weekly* in the last months of 1913 and through January 1914 as "Breaking the Money Trust," were compiled and published as *Other People's Money and How the Bankers Use It* by Frederick Stokes Co. in 1914. The book summarized and popularized the findings of the Pujo committee (see LDB to Samuel Untermyer, 18 March 1913, n. 2), and revealed the extent to which American business was dominated by what LDB called, in his first chapter, "our financial oligarchy." The work hit hard at many of LDB's most common themes: the evils of monopoly, the inefficiency of gigantic corporatism, the autocratic power of bankers, and the threat that is everywhere present to traditional American free enterprise. For an intelligent and provocative discussion of the origins, the social and intellectual context, and the long-range value and effect of the book, see Richard M. Abrams's introduction to the 1967 Harper Torchbook edition.

To James S. Harlan

September 6, 1913 South Yarmouth, Mass.
[Brandeis Mss, NMF 1-N-1]

Yours of 4th received. You are right in your assumption that I am entirely content to leave the matter of compensation to the discretion of the Commission.[1] I leave here Monday early after which time my Boston office will be my address.

1. The Commission paid LDB $12,500 for his services at the original hearings and $1,250 for the supplemental hearings.

To R. E. Steed

September 8, 1913 Boston, Mass. [Brandeis Mss, NMF 16-4]

My dear Sir: [1] Upon my return to the city I find yours of the 20th.

The sliding scale as applied to the Gas Company in Boston, has been eminently successful. You will find an article on this subject in the Review of Reviews for November 1907. The experience since the date of that article has been equally satisfactory. I am not aware of any Public Service Corporation of any kind in the country which has succeeded equally well in satisfying investors and the public. Since the sliding scale plan was put into operation there has been absolute satisfaction on the part of the public, and the Company's securities have been great favorites in our market.

Of course the great success has been due to a combination of the method and the man. [2] The management of the Company has been enlightened, and, among other things, has extended the sliding scale to the compensation of the employees,—most of whom now receive a dividend upon their wages at the same rate which stockholders receive on their stock.

Yours very truly,

1. R. E. Steed was the clerk of the Public Utilities Committee of Norfolk, Virginia.

2. A reference to James L. Richards, Chairman of the Board of the Boston Consolidated Gas Company.

To Herbert L. Harley

September 9, 1913 Boston, Mass. [Brandeis Mss, NMF 56-3]

My dear Mr. Harley: [1] I find upon my return to the city yours of August 11th, inviting me to become a member of the Council.

Your Society is undertaking a very important work. Although I feel that I should probably be able to contribute little to the work which is being undertaken, I shall be glad to do that little, and therefore accept the invitation which you so courteously transmit.

I find also a letter from Mr. Higgins [2] of August 14th following yours. Will you kindly express to him my appreciation, and say that I shall be glad to submit any suggestions which may come to me from time to time.

With best wishes,   Very cordially yours,

1. Herbert L. Harley (1872–1951) was the founder of the American Judicature Society, a newly established organization designed to promote the efficient administration of legal procedure. He had written to ask LDB to allow his name to be used as a member of the organization's council.

2. William Edward Higgins (1865–1920) was a lawyer and professor of law at the University of Kansas. He had accepted the position of director of drafting for the American Judicature Society, and had written to ask LDB if he might occasionally request advice on various drafts before submitting them to the larger public.

To William Gibbs McAdoo

September 9, 1913 Boston, Mass. [Brandeis Mss, NMF 1-N-1]

MY DEAR MR. McADOO: During my absence from Boston I noticed a reference to an investigation which the Comptroller made concerning the alleged excessive loan of the National City Bank of New York to the Chicago Traction interests.

I wonder whether there has been brought to your attention the evidence disclosed in the New Haven hearings before Commissioner Prouty in relation to the $11,000,000 loan by the National City Bank to J. L. Billard. According to the testimony of David E. Brown, the Examiner of the Interstate Commerce Commission, the bank loaned Billard $11,000,000 on his note, with the Boston & Maine stock as collateral. The facts appear on pages 3990 to 4000 of the typewritten record of the testimony, of which a copy is in the possession of Mr. T. W. Gregory.

Very cordially yours,

To Stuart D. B. Morrison

September 9, 1913 Boston, Mass. [Brandeis Mss, NMF 48-2]

DEAR MR. MORRISON: [1] I find your letter of August 31st upon my return to the city, and shall bear it in mind.

I feel that there is a great future for legal work along industrial lines, and think it would be desirable for you to get in touch now with those who are doing some of the best practical work on these lines,—Dr. Henry Moskowitz, 216 Madison Street, New York City, and Miss Josephine Goldmark, National Consumers' League, 116 East 19th Street, New York City. It might lead at almost any time to an opportunity for legal work of this character.

Yours very truly,

1. Stuart D. B. Morrison had graduated from the Columbia Law School in June. He was anxious to practice law in the area of industrial relations, and asked if LDB's firm had any openings. If not, he wanted any advice LDB could offer: "I'm very much in earnest about the practice of the law and its application to our changing economic and industrial needs."

To Samuel Untermyer

September 9, 1913 Boston, Mass. [Brandeis Mss, NMF 1-N-1]

MY DEAR MR. UNTERMYER: It was good to have your letter about the New Haven.

You are entirely right about the responsibility of the Morgans. I have insisted upon this much; among other ways, in an article on Banker Management in Harper's Weekly of August 16th, which possibly you have seen.[1]

I hope to bring out such responsibilities more fully in some articles on the Money Trust dealing with your most valuable investigation.[2] There is one line of inquiry which was developed in the testimony far less fully than other lines;—namely, the huge amounts taken for underwriting and other commissions, and the extent to which these are distributed. I suppose that this was a matter on which full data was asked and not furnished, and it occurs to me that you may have collected from other sources a mass of information on this precise subject. It seems to me very important to bring out these facts. They are easily understood. The bankers' extortions for relatively slight services are of a character to shock the conscience. If you have such information, and there is no objection to my using it, I should be very glad to have the data. Of course some flagrant illustrations would be most instructive.[3]   Very cordially yours,

1. "Banker-Management; Why It Has Failed: A Lesson from the New Haven" began with LDB's discussion of the connections between the Mor-

gan banking interests and the New Haven Railroad. See *Other People's Money*, 189–90.

2. The Pujo investigation. See LDB to Untermyer, 18 March 1913, n. 2.

3. LDB discussed the problem of bank commissions and fees in "Our Financial Oligarchy," the article for *Harper's*, on 22 November 1913. See *Other People's Money*, 22–26.

To Robert Marion LaFollette

September 11, 1913 Boston, Mass. [LaFollette Mss]

MY DEAR BOB: We are delighted with your vote on the tariff bill. It is just like you.[1]

I long very much to see you and Belle. There are many things to talk over. Perhaps I shall be able to get down to Washington by the time you get through your duties on the Conference Committee.   Very cordially yours,

P.S. I had a nice letter from Phil on the New Haven matters the other day.[2]

1. The Underwood-Simmons tariff bill had come to a vote in the Senate on 9 September. There had been much speculation about whether LaFollette would follow the Republicans in this intensely partisan debate or desert the party and vote for the Democratic-sponsored bill. The *Springfield Daily Republican*, for example, ran a story under the headline, "What Will LaFollette Do?" Although every other progressive Republican voted against the bill, LaFollette decided to vote for it, and his response to the roll call caused two minutes of applause in the chamber. The bill passed the Senate forty-four to thirty-seven with fourteen Senators not voting. See LaFollette and LaFollette, *Robert M. LaFollette*, 1: 458–83. The Democratic press, including Hapgood's *Harper's Weekly*, gave LaFollette extravagant praise for this vote.

2. Probably LaFollette's son, Philip Fox LaFollette (1897–1965), later an important political figure in his own right and governor of Wisconsin for a number of terms in the 1930s.

To William T. Chantland

September 13, 1913 Boston, Mass. [Brandeis Mss, NMF 59-7]

MY DEAR MR. CHANTLAND: [1] I thank you for your letter of July 30th on price maintenance which I find upon my return to the city, and I wish you would send me the legal argument to which you refer prepared in connection with the Bauer v. O'Donnell case,[2] and any other data you have bearing on the subject. I shall hope to talk this matter over fully with you when I am next in Washington, and to get the benefit of all of the facts which have come to your knowledge against the position which I have taken. That which you speak of as my argument is only a part of the argument. Indeed most that I have to say has not yet been published, and I shall be very glad to have the full benefit of your views before anything is published hereafter.[3]

Perhaps you may care to read my so-called testimony on this subject before the House Committee on Patents on May 15, 1912 (Part No. 18).   Very cordially yours,

1. William T. Chantland was a special assistant attorney connected with the Department of Justice.

2. See LDB to John R. Commons, 27 May 1913, n. 2.

3. LDB's fullest statement was "Competition That Kills," *Harper's Weekly* 58 (15 November 1913): 10–12. It is reprinted in *Business–A Profession*, 243–61.

To William Gibbs McAdoo

September 13, 1913 Boston, Mass. [McAdoo Mss]

MY DEAR MR. McADOO: Congressman [William F.] Murray called on me today in regard to the proposed appointment of Mr. Billings as Collector. He said that I had been quoted in Washington and here in many ways as to my views in regard to the appointment; and that he, Murray, proposed to see the President on Tuesday, and to urge on him:

First: That politically it was unwise to make any appointment of Collector at the present time, and

Second: That it would be particularly unwise politically to appoint Mr. Billings.

I told him that I had no candidate for Collector; but that when inquiry was made of me in regard to Mr. Billings, I had expressed the high opinion which I have of him; that I had not expressed any opinion on the political question, and did not consider myself particularly competent to express an opinion on that phase of the matter; and that I was quite prepared to believe that from a political standpoint it would be wiser to defer making an appointment until after election.[1]

I stated to Mr. Murray also what I said to you: that I thought the situation here was a practically insoluble one; that the local politicians would vigorously oppose any man fit for the office, who had either in official life or otherwise attempted to improve our local conditions; that the men on whom the politicians would unite are either not fit for the office, or like Joseph B. Russell, would not accept it.[2]   Very cordially yours,

1. Wilson appointed Edmund Billings, LDB's old friend from the Good Government Association, to the collectorship of Boston on 8 October 1913. He served until 1 July 1921.

2. Joseph Ballister Russell (1852–1929) was a leading Boston businessman, a director of many of the companies LDB had opposed, including the Boston Consolidated Gas Co., the New Haven, and the Boston Elevated.

To George Carroll Todd

September 13, 1913 Boston, Mass. [Brandeis Mss, NMF 64-1]

MY DEAR MR. TODD: [1] I happened to see in the Milwaukee Journal of October 24, 1912 the report of the testimony in the Harvester Trust case to the effect that J.P. Morgan & Company had received as underwriting commissions for the promotion of the trust, 165,000 shares of the Harvester stock, which netted $13,500,000.

Will you kindly let me know whether in that statement the testimony is accurately reported, and if possible send me a copy of the part of the testimony bearing specifically upon that statement? [2]   Yours very truly,

1. George Carroll Todd (1879–1947) was serving in 1913 as an assistant to Attorney General McReynolds, in charge of anti-trust cases.

2. On 20 September Todd replied that the story was not accurate. J. P. Morgan & Co. had received 165,000 shares, but they had paid $13,500,000 for them; their profit, assuming the shares to be valued at par, was $3,000,000. LDB covered the matter in *Other People's Money*, 139.

To William Mackintosh Macnair

September 16, 1913 Boston, Mass. [Brandeis Mss, LtB]

MY DEAR MR. MACNAIR: [1] I thank you for yours of the 15th.

Just at the moment I do not know that there is anything that a

Congregational minister can do in connection with the railroad bond issue, but a little later I may have something to suggest, and in that event will take the liberty of letting you know.

Very cordially yours,

1. William Mackintosh Macnair (1870–19[?]) had been pastor at the Prospect Street Congregational Church in Cambridge since 1908; he was also president of the Cambridge Law Enforcement Society, and active in other civic affairs.

To Grenville Stanley MacFarland

September 18, 1913 Boston, Mass. [Brandeis Mss, NMF 1-N-1]

MY DEAR MACFARLAND: Charles W. Proctor [1] has brought in your telegram to him, in which you ask me to let you know my opinion, or suggestions in regard to the Railroad situation.

I don't think it is very satisfactory.

First: The appointment of Stone, a former employee of the Boston & Albany and closely associated with the Boston & Albany, raises a considerable doubt.[2] I know nothing about the man; but he is not the kind of a man that Anderson wanted. (Anderson wanted a lawyer, and was particularly urgent to have Hammond). I was surprised at Governor Foss appointing Stone in view of the fact that two days before, in a long talk with him, he had expressed a great desire not to appoint anyone that was not entirely agreeable to Anderson, and would give Anderson the support that he desired.

Second: The old financial pressure, against which we have fought for six years, is still manifest and in a somewhat more dangerous form than heretofore. The notion of giving Elliott a fair chance, and of not driving matters too hard when the New Haven is down, is getting support for a great deal of unwisdom in regard to the New Haven financial affairs.

The first obligation of the Commission is to secure public safety; the second is to make the New Haven bond-safe; and third is to improve the condition of the stockholders.

To do the first two, it is, in my opinion, essential that the New Haven should suspend its dividends for a time sufficient to enable it to recover from its financial debauch. There is, I think, a deficiency in assets (not taking into consideration unearned increment or the increased value of the right-of-way) of very near $100,000,000, due partly to bad investments, and partly to the payment of unearned dividends. The New Haven admits by its books of about $10,000,000 unearned dividends in the last six years; and I fancy the amount not admitted (represented by a failure to make proper equipment depreciation charges) would add at least another $10,000,000 and probably $15,000,000 more to the admitted deficit. Under these conditions, if the New Haven continues to pay dividends, either rates must be largely advanced, or there will be a constant tendency to skimp repairs or to let them appear as improvements. And there is ultimate danger to bond-holders and stockholders.

There is some reason to think that the pressure upon the Commission is so great that they will be disposed to allow so-called improvements to be made from bonds, or note issues, when they ought to be made out of earnings; and that the views of conservative finance, for which we have been contending, will not prevail.[3]

I trust you are having a very enjoyable vacation, but hope that it is nearly over and that you will be returning soon to take up the fight.

I have not lost any of my confidence in "arithmetic" or the Wilson Administration; but it will be too bad if the difficulties shall be increased by further unwise action on the part of Massachusetts authorities.   Very cordially yours,

1. Charles W. Proctor (1871–1953) was a hotel owner and a minor Democratic politician.

2. Edward E. Stone had been appointed to the Public Service Commission (the successor to the defunct Board of Railroad Commissioners) along with LDB's friend, George W. Anderson. These two new appointees, plus the three former Railroad Commissioners constituted the new body. The Commission was hearing testimony regarding the issuing of $67,000,000 in New Haven bonds. See LDB to Norman Hapgood, 9 October 1913.

3. LDB's fears were justified. See LDB to Norman Hapgood, 15 October 1913.

To William Harrison Ingersoll

September 20, 1913 Boston, Mass. [Brandeis Mss, NMF 59-7]

DEAR MR. INGERSOLL: I write to acknowledge receipt of yours of the 16th, which pressing work prevents my examining at present.

I have been somewhat disturbed at your report of the lack of progress and effectiveness in the collection of data; [1] and I hope that you will be able soon to reorganize the work, if you have not already done so, in order to get results which you would deem adequate.

We can win only on the facts, and our investigation of them should be thorough and comprehensive.

Have you had your talk with the Commissioner of Corporations? [2]   Yours very truly,

1. Regarding the legalization of price maintenance of trademarked items.
2. Joseph E. Davies.

To V. H. Kriegshaber

September 20, 1913 Boston, Mass. [Brandeis Mss, Z 1-2]

DEAR MR. KRIEGSHABER: [1] Thank you for yours of the 17th with the clipping from the Constitution.

I am so busy now that I cannot take time to answer it at present, but before long I hope to be able to make a comprehensive statement of my reasons for supporting the Zionist movement, which should remove such misconceptions, and I hope will allay any doubts which you may feel. [2]

Of course the purpose of the Zionist movement is not to compel a return to Palestine of the twelve million Jews scattered over the earth, but to make it possible for those, who wish to return, to find there freedom and opportunity of development for which they long, and to preserve and advance the noble traditions and high ideals of the race.   Very cordially yours,

1. V. H. Kriegshaber was an Atlanta, Georgia, businessman. He had sent LDB an editorial from the 17 September *Atlanta Constitution*, entitled "Brandeis' Inconsistency," which berated LDB for his Zionism: "Louis D. Brandeis, of Boston, is a smart lawyer and a useful public character, but, like many other big men, he is guilty of the sin of inconsistency. Here he is . . . advising the Jews to return to Palestine. . . . The principal inconsistency about the counsel of Brandeis is that he has not himself seen fit to follow it. Snugly and profitably ensconced in America, he is forcefully pleading with his compatriots to return to the home of the race." America, the editor continued, has "plenty of room for the right sort of Jews." The editorial closed: "It is up to the Boston lawyer, if he is sincere, to put himself right by catching the first boat for the Mediterranean."

2. For LDB's early statements on Zionism and American citizenship, see the compilation by Solomon Goldman, *Brandeis On Zionism: A Collection of Addresses and Statements by Louis D. Brandeis* (Washington, 1942), or Jacob deHaas, *Louis D. Brandeis, A Biographical Sketch* (New York, 1929), which contains the full text of LDB's statements on Zionism between 1912 and 1924.

To Thomas Watt Gregory

September 22, 1913 Boston, Mass. [Brandeis Mss, NMF 1-N-1]

MY DEAR MR. GREGORY: Replying to yours of the 19th: [1]

First: Mr. H. LaRue Brown, counsel for the Public Service Commission, tells me that Mr. Robbins did not state [that] the New Haven controlled the Billard Company.[2]

Second: The best statement as to what companies were stated as controlled by the New Haven Company will appear in a schedule of the companies included in the combined balance sheet of the New Haven System. A copy of this is being prepared and will be sent you promptly.[3]

Third: I will also endeavor to have sent you promptly a full copy of the testimony taken before the Commission. But you will find that most of this so-called testimony is of little value. The really valuable data are contained in the exhibits and statements submitted by the New Haven in response to requests of the Commission, and I think it would be desirable for you to have a full set of those statements, which can be prepared if you so desire.

Please wire me if you would like to have copies of the exhibits.

Very cordially yours,

1. Gregory had written regarding the newspaper report that a New Haven attorney (see next note) had admitted that the New Haven controlled the Billard Company (see LDB to Alfred Brandeis, 13 July 1908). The reported admission was in connection with the Public Service Commission's hearings regarding the proposed New Haven bond issue of $67,000,000.

2. Edward Denmore Robbins (1853–1932), a former member of the Connecticut legislature and a former professor of jurisprudence at Yale, was in 1913 serving as general counsel for the New Haven.

3. LDB sent this material the next day.

To Mark Sullivan

September 22, 1913 Boston, Mass. [Brandeis Mss, NMF 46-3]

MY DEAR SULLIVAN: Replying to yours of the 16th:

I have had no time to check up the statements contained in the editorial.

But "The Real Question" treated as an argument strikes me as very clever and interesting. Undoubtedly the decisions before the last twenty years contained in them much of which we must now complain.

I should think, however, that the editorial, if published, ought to contain some statement making a little clearer the Court's change of heart. In this connection Mr. Justice Holmes is entitled to high appreciation for his persistent refusal to usurp legislative powers.[1]

I am returning the editorial and Warren article.[2]

Yours very truly,

1. On this point of Holmes's judicial philosophy, see particularly Samuel Konefsky, *The Legacy of Holmes and Brandeis*, ch. 2.
2. Neither the editorial nor the article were published in *Collier's*.

To Norman Hapgood

September 23, 1913 Boston, Mass. [Brandeis Mss, NMF 52-1]

DEAR NORMAN: You and Collins may care to know what I learned at one of the news stands in the South Station about the sale of the Weekly: The man in charge told me that he is now selling 200 copies a week, whereas the sales of the old Harper's had dropped to about 15; and that he sells now about the same number of Harper's and Collier's.

This is only one of three or four stands in the South Station.

I called up Charles Crane Sunday at Woods Hole, and found that he and Mrs. Crane were still in New York. That was contrary to their plans, and I hope Charles is getting on well.

Hope you and Ruth had a good outing in New Hampshire.

Very cordially,

To Charles Azro Prouty

September 23, 1913 Boston, Mass. [Brandeis Mss, LtB]

MY DEAR MR. PROUTY: I was sorry that pressing matters prevented my taking part in the Boston & Maine hearing this week.

So much has been disclosed in regard to the financial transactions as to make it, in my opinion, clear that no general increase in rates should be allowed until the financial management of the Boston & Maine during at least the last six years, since the New Haven acquired its large holdings, shall have been fully investigated.

You will remember how insistent (I fear you deemed it unduly insistent) I was last spring in urging a continuation of the New Haven investigation to include not only the smaller subsidiaries but also the Boston & Maine and Maine Central. The few facts disclosed by Mr. Hobbs at the recent hearing may be merely illustrations of what exists.[1]   Very cordially yours,

1. William J. Hobbs (1854-[?]) was the financial vice-president of the Boston & Maine. He testified before the I.C.C. in an attempt to explain the railroad's disastrous financial report for the year ending 30 June 1913. The line had lost over $1.3 million.

To George Weston Anderson

September 25, 1913 Boston, Mass. [Brandeis Mss, NMF 1-N-1]

MY DEAR ANDERSON: *First:* You were so busy with your bond hearing yesterday that you may not have noticed the testimony which was given in regard to the Boston and Maine purchase of 30,000 additional shares in the Maine Central at 110.[1] The answers elicited were not full, and I think that your Commission ought to get accurate information as to the time of the purchase and the circumstances.

The fact stated that this stock was purchased through Estabrook of course means nothing, and it would not be surprising to find that Estabrook was selling it to the Boston & Maine for Ricker or some other director, as there are of course very few large stockholders.[2]

It seems also quite possible that this purchase was a part of a deal to secure consent to the increase of the extraordinary method pursued by the Maine Central in financing its supposed needs. The plan adopted of issuing this $20,000,000 of new stock is, from a financial standpoint, so incomprehensible that the probability of official impropriety seems strong. The Boston & Maine Annual report taken in connection with Mr. Hobbs' testimony that the stock was purchased just before the new stock was issued, suggests the possibility that the parties with whom the deal was made either made the delivery largely out of new stock which they got through subscriptions at par, incident to their then holdings, or that they purchased rights in the market.[3]

I have not seen the Boston & Maine report, but I understand that statements in that report, taken in connection with Hobbs' testimony will show that the money with which the Maine Central stock has been purchased is costing the Boston & Maine 7½ percent.

Second: I think also that your Commission ought to get the data in regard to the payment by the Boston & Maine and the Maine Central, as well as the New Haven, to Mellen and the voting of the future salary. I was told the other day, on what seemed to me very good authority, that the whole story has not been told; and that Mellen got, in addition to the money paid and promised, an agreement indemnifying him against any possible claim which might be made in connection with his management of any of these properties. It is my opinion that the directors of the New Haven are liable in millions to the stockholders, not only for illegal investments, but for the payment of dividends in excess of earnings. Sometime a suit ought to be brought to enforce that liability, and it seems not at all improbable that Mr. Mellen anticipated such a suit, and insisted upon an indemnity agreement as the price of his retirement and silence.[4]

Third: I don't know what attitude your Commission has taken on the question of raising rates, but it seems to me that, until the financial transactions of the Boston & Maine are examined thoroughly, and the public can know authoritatively how much money has been wrongfully expended, your Commission ought to resist strenuously any increase in present rates. When all the facts are known, the matter can be considered on its merits.

Fourth: As to Maine Central stock: I suppose you noticed the very small surplus of last year. Does it seem at all possible that the Maine Central can continue its 6% dividend on the present large issue of stock without repeating some of the Boston & Maine and New Haven performances?

Very cordially yours,

1. The testimony was given by officials of the Boston & Maine before the Interstate Commerce Commission in hearings relating to the rate increase question.
2. Arthur F. Estabrook (1847–1919) was a Boston banker. E. P. Ricker was a director in the Maine Central.
3. See preceding letter.
4. See LDB to Henry L. Stimson, 18 July 1914.

To Morris Llewellyn Cooke

September 25, 1913 Boston, Mass. [Brandeis Mss, NMF 64-1]

MY DEAR MR. COOKE: I enclose herewith a copy of a letter which I wrote on August 1, 1913 to Mr. John M. Walton, your City Comptroller, to which I have not had any reply, and which I have not followed up before because I was off on my vacation.

I presume Mr. Walton overlooked the letter among his many duties, and I am writing you so as to assure a full and early reply.

One of the important questions, not only of financial efficiency, but of industrial liberty, is how to free ourselves from banker control. And it seems to me it ought to be possible for all our great cities to market their own bonds direct to the people.

I would like to have a clear statement of Philadelphia's experience, and, among other things, how the bankers treated them. From what I have heard, it seems as if the bankers had failed the city at a crucial moment, and were unwilling to give their aid except upon exorbitant terms.[1]   Very truly yours,

1. Cooke turned LDB's letter over to Mayor Rudolph Blankenburg (1843–1918), a German immigrant who had made a fortune in manufacturing and who served as Philadelphia's mayor from 1912 to 1916. Blankenburg replied on 1 October 1913: "I have, for years, considered it the poorest kind of business for municipalities to float loans through the aid of bankers, paying them either a commission or selling them the bonds at a lower rate than they can be purchased by the general public." He went on to detail Philadelphia's recent "over-the-counter" loans.

To James Clark McReynolds

September 25, 1913 Boston, Mass. [Brandeis Mss, NMF 58-1]

MY DEAR MR. McREYNOLDS: I was glad to note that you are urging the continuance of the Commerce Court. From what I have been able to gather, I should judge that the House has provided for the abolition not only of the Court, but the judgeships.[1]

If such is the fact, I hope that there is some vacancy to which Judge [Julian W.] Mack can be appointed. It would be a calamity to lose him from the public service. He is a good Democrat in every sense of the word.   Most cordially yours,

1. See LDB to William A. Oldfield, 7 July 1913.

To Massachusetts Public Service Commission

September 26, 1913 Boston, Mass. [Brandeis Mss, NMF 1-N-1]

DEAR SIRS: *First:* The disclosures made of the New Haven System's "publicity, legislative and other expenses" appear, from the newspaper reports, to be confined to the seven months ending June 30, 1913.[1]

I respectfully suggest the importance of your Commission obtaining similar data for the seven years ending June 30, 1913; and in addition, for the three months ending September 30, 1913.

In view of the occurrences of 1913, the data for July, August and September may be more enlightening than any others.

Second: I have not had an opportunity to examine the report on "other expenses" etc. received by the Commission, but if as I understand, it does not include the expenditures made by the Boston & Maine and all of its subsidiaries, including the Maine Central, the Commission ought, in my opinion, to call for such a statement covering the period beginning with April 1907, when the New Haven acquired its control of the Boston & Maine.

Third: The Public Service Commission ought also to obtain from the New Haven and all of its subsidiaries, including among others the Boston & Maine and Maine Central, a full statement, not only of the payments made and agreed to be made to Mr. Mellen, but copies of the actual agreement entered into with Mr. Mellen. Information has come to me from a source which seems to be authentic that the New Haven management has undertaken to indemnify Mr. Mellen against all possible claims arising out of the mismanagement of the properties.

Fourth: The facts developed in the recent hearings before Commissioner Prouty concerning the purchase of upwards of 30,000 shares of the Maine Central stock at about 110, at a time when the Boston & Maine was in financial distress, and Maine Central stock was gravitating to par, demand thorough investigation by your Commission, particularly in view of the fact that at an earlier hearing it had been disclosed that the Maine Central had purchased from one of its directors hotel property believed to be unremunerative.

Fifth: I respectfully submit that your Commission ought resolutely to oppose any increase in rates on the Boston & Maine, and refuse to authorize any agreement with the Hampden Railroad, or otherwise to pass any order concerning the finances of the Boston & Maine, until a thorough investigation has been made of the transactions of the Boston & Maine management.

                              Very respectfully yours,

1. The explosive revelation of the New Haven's "Other Expenses" report showed that the railroad had spent $337,469.71 on publicity, newspapers, magazines, and lobbyists in the period between 1 December 1912 and 30 June 1913. Included were handsome payments to editors, reporters, and lecturers; the anti-Brandeis *Boston News Bureau* alone had received $133,000. The papers, particularly the *Boston Journal* and the *Boston American*, seized on the disclosures and demanded further investigations. See Staples and Mason, *Fall of a Railroad Empire*, 156-62.

To Manuel Levine and Fielder Sanders

September 27, 1913 Boston, Mass. [Brandeis Mss, NMF 58-1]

DEAR SIRS: [1] Replying to your very interesting letter of the 22nd: [2]

In my opinion all fees should be abolished, and the Court maintained by general taxation, as other Governmental agencies.

I do not happen to know of any Court in which this policy is applied today, and I trust that your Court will not lose the opportunity of being the pioneer.   Very truly yours,

1. Manuel Levine (1881-1939) and Fielder Sanders (1876-19[?]) were Associate Judges of Cleveland's Municipal Court.

2. The Municipal Court of Cleveland, established in 1911 to hear small claims cases, was trying to decide how fees should be set. The choices were to make the court self-sustaining through fees charged to the litigants, to abolish all fees and support the court through general taxation, or to compromise and use both sorts of funds.

To Thomas Watt Gregory

September 30, 1913 Boston, Mass. [Brandeis Mss, NMF 1-N-1]

MY DEAR GREGORY: Will you kindly send me a copy of the bill or petition in the recent suit commenced by the Government against the Reading? And also if available a copy of the bill in the old Reading case and in the Union—Southern Pacific case? [1]

I wonder whether you are getting the Boston papers, particularly the Boston Journal. For the last ten days we have been uncovering the scandal of the New Haven's "other expenses"; that is, the amount expended in lobbying and accelerating public opinion.[2] The data as to seven months' expenditures were obtained as a result of a request made by our Public Service Commission in connection with the new bond issue; and the disclosures were such as to lead to Governor Foss making a specific request upon the Commission for a thorough investigation, and every day discloses some facts in this connection. They have no direct bearing upon your inquiry, but you may find them of value later.

The indications now are that our Public Service Commission will refuse to approve the new bond issue on the ground of lack of power.[3]   Very truly yours,

1. The two Reading cases involved prosecution of the company as a coal trust; the first had miscarried earlier in the year, and the second was to be based on the prior investigation. The Union-Southern Pacific case was an outgrowth of the Supreme Court's decision in January that the two roads should submit a plan for dissolution. The case dragged into the Wilson administration although it was begun by Taft's attorney-general, George W. Wickersham.

2. See LDB to Massachusetts Public Service Commission, 26 September 1913, n. 1.

3. Contrary to LDB's prediction, the Commission granted the New Haven's request for the $67,000,000 bond issue on 14 October. See LDB to Norman Hapgood, 15 October 1913.

To Norman Hapgood

September 30, 1913 Boston, Mass. [Brandeis Mss, NMF 64-1]

MY DEAR NORMAN: The articles are so far advanced that I think you may safely arrange to begin the publication in the first or second week of November.

As the title of the series I suggest "Breaking the Money Trust". Possibly you would prefer "Breaking up the Money Trust"; or you may have a better suggestion. The individual articles are— [1]

1: "Our Financial Oligarchy".
2: "How the Combiners Combine".
3: "Interlocking Directorates".
4: "Serve One Master Only".
5: "What Publicity Will Do".
6: "Where the Banker is Superfluous".
7: "The Curse of Bigness".
8: Probably, "Banks that are not Such."
9: "The Inefficiency of the Oligarchs".

No. 1 is all ready; and I hope to send it to you tomorrow. Nos. 2, 3, and 4 are practically ready. Nos. 5 and 6 are written and being revised; and 7 is in process. Nos. 8 and 9 are thought on, but not completely thought out.

The first two articles are largely diagnosis of the situation. The next six deal mainly with remedies; and the 9th is to show the general gain in economic and social efficiency which may be expected as a result of the decentralization of power. I want to bring out in this connection the rather remarkable results which have been attained in England in connection with the Wholesale Cooperative Society; where 36 men, none of whose salary exceeds $1800.00, are conducting a $150,000,000 business in very successful competition with the best capitalistic, manufacturing, producing and merchandising businesses in England.

George Rublee came over last Friday to tell me that he had severed his connection with Spooner and Cotton, and wanted to take hold in some of my public work. I was delighted to have him take up the Money Trust; and he has started to work with me today. This will be of very great value, not only in checking up and perfecting the articles, but in preparing the necessary legislation and the making of converts.

I approve, in the main, of the remedies suggested by the Pujo Committee; but consider them entirely inadequate.[2] I am inclined to think that Untermyer was not satisfied with the recommendations of his Committee, and went merely as far as he could; because the facts in the report call for much more drastic legislation than the Committee recommends.

I expect to be in New York the latter part of this week and want to have a full talk with Untermyer.

Walter Rogers called me up last evening to ask me to go to New York Thursday on Crane Company matters, which I expect to do. If you are free I hope we can breakfast together Thursday at the Harvard Club; but I am to be there Friday, and probably Saturday, on Labor Arbitration matters; so that we can breakfast together on Friday if Thursday is not convenient for you.

                                        Very cordially,

1. With some slight variations of title this outline was fairly close to the actual appearance of the articles. Number Seven became "Big Men and Little Business," and Number Eight was "A Curse of Bigness." The series began with the 22 November issue and ended with the issue of 17 January 1914. When published as *Other People's Money*, a new ninth chapter, "The Failure of Banker Management" (from LDB's article in the 16 August 1913 issue of *Harper's*) was inserted, giving the book version ten chapters.

2. See LDB to Samuel Untermyer, 2 October 1913.

To William T. Donaldson

                    October 1, 1913 Boston, Mass. [Brandeis Mss, NMF 55-1]

DEAR SIR: [1] I regret delay in replying to yours of September 9th in regard to industrial conciliation and arbitration.

Answering your several questions:

First: Whether there is any way of avoiding strikes in cases where the labor unions have been recently forming and seeking recognition.

I do not think it can be said definitely that strikes cannot be avoided in these cases. Considerable educational work must of course be done both with the Union and with the employers, but it seems to me not impossible to avoid strikes in many cases.

Second: Do you consider a permanent board of conciliation better than one appointed for each case in disputes.

I very much doubt the efficiency of a permanent Board of Conciliation, unless you happen to have upon it a man who possesses the necessary qualifications to a very high degree.

Third: Can I suggest any means of enlisting employers and unions in an industry which would have for its object the establishment of some sort of working scheme with fixed machinery for the settlement of grievances?

This seems to me to be largely a matter of educating employers, and the probability of effectively educating them is rarely very great, unless employers have suffered through a strike.

My own belief is that most conciliations and arbitrations are proceeding upon a wrong basis, namely: —that of mutual concession. In a large percentage of the cases mutual concession results in not properly solving the difficulties which has [sic] given rise to the grievance. Instead of mutual concession, the parties ought to be brought together for the purpose of devising some new means of overcoming the difficulty which was presented. In other words,— the need is not mutual concession, but invention,—constructive improvement, just as much as the difficulty in manufacturing are [sic] to be overcome by devising some new way of avoiding each difficulty which has been met.

Such success as has been obtained in the garment trade,—particularly the Cloak and Suit Manufacturers, is, in my opinion, due to the adoption of this as the underlying policy.

When we began the work something over three years ago, the material with which we were working seemed to be particularly unpromising. The results attained have been due largely to open-mindedness on the part of the representatives of employers and of employees, and a recognition that a wide field is open for progressive action.   Very truly yours,

1. William T. Donaldson was a minor Ohio public official, currently with the Legislative Reference Bureau in Columbus. In 1915 he would move to the state budget department and become assistant commissioner and then commissioner of the budget, 1916–1919.

To Charles Caldwell McChord

October 1, 1913 Boston, Mass. [Brandeis Mss, NMF 1-N-1]

MY DEAR MR. McCHORD: Your report on the recent New Haven accident seems to have pierced at last the thick hide of the Directors. It will do much good here and elsewhere.

Will you kindly have sent to me two or three copies of your report? [1]   Yours very truly,

1. The most serious of the recent string of New Haven accidents occurred on 2 September near North Haven, Connecticut. The White Mountain express ploughed into the rear of the Bar Harbor express leaving twenty-one passengers dead and another thirty-three injured. The incident received wide coverage, and the Interstate Commerce Commission conducted a month-long investigation. On 25 September McChord, who conducted the investigation and who wrote the report, released the document to the press. It condemned not the switchman nor the engineer but the New Haven board of directors. The *New York Times* for 26 September made it a front-page story under the headline, "New Haven Ills Put on Directors: Commerce Commission Assails Board for Neglect to Safeguard Railroad's Passengers: 'Main Failure' High Up."

To Bernard Abraham Rosenblatt

October 2, 1913 Boston, Mass. [Brandeis Mss, Z 1-2]

MY DEAR MR. ROSENBLATT: Immediately after our meeting in New York I considered with Mr. DeHaas the work of our committee.[1] It seemed clear that no effective discussion could proceed until he had gathered data concerning the present industrial conditions in Palestine. This Mr. DeHaas undertook to do, and has, I understand, been steadily at work upon it since June. It has required much foreign correspondence, and when I saw him last, a fortnight ago, he was not yet ready to submit a report for consideration.

I hope to take the matter up with him as soon as he is ready.

Very cordially yours,

1. Probably the committee to guide the American Palestine Company. See LDB to Nahum Sokolow, 1 August 1913.

To Samuel Untermyer

October 2, 1913 Boston, Mass. [Brandeis Mss, NMF 58-3]

MY DEAR MR. UNTERMYER: Since our conference on [the] Money Trust last spring, I have given much thought to the subject;— particularly during the last two months in connection with the articles about which I wrote you.

Further study of the testimony and of the report deepened my admiration for the work which you have done.[1] It is a great public service.

I am, however, confirmed in the belief, already expressed to you, that the legislation recommended by the Committee should be broadened. The specific recommendations made seem to me sound, as far as they go; and I should reserve a doubt only as to one or two. But the provision in regard to interlocking directorates, and the prohibition of trade contracts in which the management is interested, must be applied far more widely, if the money trust is to be broken up; and some additional remedies seem to me advisable.[2]

I am leaving tonight for New York on a labor arbitration matter, which will occupy me tomorrow and possibly Saturday; and I should like very much to arrange in some way for our having an uninterrupted hour or two together to talk matters over. Will you have the kindness to send word to the Harvard Club in New York whether you would be free to see me Saturday afternoon or evening, and if that is impossible, when will you be free?

I am treating the subject in a series of articles,—devoting the first two to a diagnosis, and the later ones to a discussion of the remedies. Possibly you may have time before we meet to look over the first,—"Our Financial Oligarchy", of which I enclose a copy, which will give you some idea how I am treating the subject. I shall, of course, welcome any criticism.

Very cordially yours,

1. As counsel to the Pujo Committee. See LDB to Untermyer, 18 March 1913, n. 2.
2. Untermyer had wanted prohibitions against interlocking directorates written into the banking reform bill. Wilson and his advisors, while recognizing the need for such an act, chose not to imperil the banking program

by additional measures, and they incorporated the proscription into the Clayton Anti-Trust Act.

To Thomas Watt Gregory

October 7, 1913 Boston, Mass. [Brandeis Mss, NMF 1-N-1]

MY DEAR MR. GREGORY: Thank you for the papers.

I presume you noticed that our Democratic Convention [1] inserted in the platform a plank demanding the complete divorce of the Boston and Maine from the New Haven. Some of the most worthy and prominent of our democrats have expressed to me, in the last two days, great concern over the newspaper rumor that the Attorney General is willing to consider before filing the Dissolution bill, any proposals of the Directors looking towards dismemberment; and they fear that the Attorney General may be misled by the siren song. I have told them that in my opinion their fears were groundless, as I feel sure that you know the local situation, and have had ample experience before in dealing with similar situations.

I think it would be quite unfortunate for the administration if there should be much delay now before filing the bill, or anything which looks like secret negotiations. [2]

Very cordially yours,

1. Massachusetts Democrats met in convention on 5 October.
2. Despite LDB's urging, it took a passed New Haven dividend, another fury in the nation, and a fresh Interstate Commerce Commission investigation before the Justice Department moved to dissolve the merger. The effort was finally made in June 1914, and on 11 August of that year the two roads were separated.

To Henry Bourne Joy

October 7, 1913 Boston, Mass. [Brandeis Mss, NMF 59-7]

MY DEAR MR. JOY: In connection with an investigation which I am now making, the results of which are to be published, I should like to know definitely the extent to which the great successes in the automobile business, including automobile supplies, can be said to be due to aid given by great banking houses.

My own impression has been that in the automobile business, as in most other new industries, the great banking houses did not begin to finance the concerns until success had been attained, or was practically certain. Of course it was necessary to finance the business, but I have assumed that they were financed either from within, or through individuals, — often local interests, which were brought into contact with the able and enterprising men who have conducted these businesses, or by largely local banks.

Will you have the kindness to write me fully on this subject as soon as you can? [1]   Very cordially yours,

1. LDB published Joy's response in "Big Men and Little Business," *Harper's Weekly* 59 (3 January 1914): 11–15; see *Other People's Money*, 148–49: "When a few gentlemen followed me in my vision of the possibilities of the [automobile] business, the banks and older business men (who in the main were the banks) said, 'fools and their money soon to be parted'—etc., etc. Private capital at first establishes an industry, backs it through its troubles, and if possible, wins financial success when banks would not lend a dollar of aid. The business once having proved to be practicable and financially successful, then do the banks lend aid to its needs."

To William Gibbs McAdoo

October 7, 1913 Boston, Mass. [Brandeis Mss, NMF 64-1]

MY DEAR McADOO: Replying to yours of the 3rd enclosing Commissioner Osborn's letter of the 2nd, which I return: [1]

My immediate desire for the information was for use in one of the articles on The Money Trust, which I am writing for Harper's Weekly. The need for that article alone would not justify the work which Commissioner says is involved; but my real reason for wanting the information is for use in connection with the drafting of certain bills relating both to money trusts and to industrial trusts; and for that purpose I am very anxious to have the data, and I should like to have it before I trouble you to consider some definite suggestions for legislation, which I have in mind.

Would it be possible for Commissioner Osborn to send me now a statement of the total number of corporations which have made returns, and let me have, say, by November 15th the additional information?

I trust that the President's victory on the Currency bill will not be long postponed, and that he will then take up as vigorously the needed money trust legislation.[2]

Very cordially yours,

1. On 29 September, LDB had written ten complex questions for McAdoo, for "use in an article I am writing." The questions involved the number of business corporations in the United States and a breakdown of the total by capital strength. The letter was forwarded by McAdoo to William Henry Osborn (1856–1921), a North Carolina businessman and politician who was serving as Commissioner of Internal Revenue. Osborn pointed out that, with his other duties, it would be most difficult to comply with LDB's request. McAdoo had written, "I will go the limit for you, however, so let me know the least that you can get along with." Osborn forwarded the information on 10 November 1913.

2. Wilson's victory on the currency act would not come until 23 December, after six months of debate.

To Charles Warren

October 8, 1913 Boston, Mass. [Brandeis Mss, NMF 58-1]

MY DEAR WARREN: I have your letter about Sullivan.[1]

My relations with the administration are such that I have carefully refrained from recommending anybody to any office except where my advice has been asked.[2]   Yours cordially,

1. See LDB to James C. McReynolds, 18 October 1913.
2. For evidence that LDB did not always adhere to this rule, see LDB to Woodrow Wilson, 10 October 1913.

To Thomas Watt Gregory

October 9, 1913 Boston, Mass. [Brandeis Mss, NMF 1-N-1]

DEAR MR. GREGORY: Referring to our conversation about the Fitchburg Railroad: You may be interested in the statement made by Mr. Mellen yesterday at the hearing before our Public Service Commission on the Hampden Railroad (a report in today's Journal) to the effect that the Boston & Maine is now losing $750,000 a year on the Fitchburg lease.   Yours very truly,

To Norman Hapgood

October 9, 1913 Boston, Mass. [Brandeis Mss, NMF 1-N-1]

MY DEAR NORMAN: Possibly you may care to give the Boston Journal a boost for the fight that it is making for free journalism; and incidentally, also to George W. Anderson, our new Public Service Commissioner.

For three years I had been trying in various proceedings to get an itemized account of the expenditures of the New Haven for lobbying and publicity, without success until recently. In connection with the proposed $67,000,000 bond issue, I suggested to the Counsel of our Public Service Commission, that the Commission call for such a statement. Our Public Service Commission is a revamping, under the Act of 1913, of our moribund Railroad Commission.[1] Under the Act, the three old Railroad Commissioners were continued; but the Governor was authorized to make two new appointments, and was induced to appoint Geo. W. Anderson as one of the new men. Anderson is a good lawyer; for many years a member of the Public Franchise League; and ran twice for Attorney General on the Democratic ticket, but was defeated. In response to the call for this information by the Public Service Commission the Railroad filed a statement which has created great consternation, because it disclosed, not only payments to many lobbyists and some legislators, but disclosed the wide extent to which newspaper writers had been in the pay of the New Haven. And the Journal has been particularly fearless in uncovering the amounts paid, not only to such sheets as the Boston News Bureau, but the amounts paid to many State House and other reporters of our Massachusetts papers.[2]

I am enclosing you the clipping containing the summary of disclosures,—Boston Journal, Sept. 24th,—and the clippings from the Journal of the 6th, 8th, and 9th.

Anderson is making a splendid fight on the Commission; but it is questionable whether he will be able to overcome the reactionary forces, as Foss, quite like himself, balanced the good appointment of Anderson with another appointment of a former railroad engineer, who seems to have lined himself, quite naturally, with the reactionaries of the Board.[3] The Chairman of the Board,

Macleod, who was on the old Board, also generally sides with Anderson, and is a pretty good man.[4]   Cordially,

1. For a contemporary view of the Commission by one of LDB's close allies, see Joseph B. Eastman, "The Public Service Commission of Massachusetts," *Quarterly Journal of Economics* 27 (1913): 699–707.

2. See LDB to Massachusetts Public Service Commission, 26 September 1913, n. 1.

3. Edward E. Stone. Other members of the Public Service Commission were Chairman Fred J. Macleod, George W. Bishop, and Clinton White.

4. Hapgood used the material in this letter in an editorial, "Freedom in Massachusetts," *Harper's Weekly*, 58 (8 November 1913): 4.

To James S. Harlan

October 10, 1913 Boston, Mass. [Brandeis Mss, NMF 57-1]

MY DEAR MR. HARLAN: I want to thank you for your kindly expressions concerning me which appear this morning regarding my connection with the advance rate cases.[1]

You will recall writing me in August that you would let me know in October when I might have a conference with you concerning the conduct of the investigation, and that you would defer fixing any date for a hearing until after our conference. If agreeable to you, I should like to defer the conference until after October 26th.

I am engaged in engrossing work which it is important to finish before I give any thought to the rate cases, and which I think it will be possible to get out of the way in a fortnight, if I am not interrupted.[2]   Very cordially yours,

1. See LDB to Harlan, 21 August 1913. On 9 October Harlan had released to the press the information that LDB would participate in the hearings. For Harlan's comments, see Mason, *Brandeis*, 336.

2. The preliminary hearings began on 24 November 1913.

To Judah Leon Magnes

October 10, 1913 Boston, Mass. [Magnes Mss]

MY DEAR MR. MAGNES: [1] I thank you for yours of the 8th advising me of Dr. Franz Oppenheimer's contemplated trip to America.[2] I shall look forward to meeting him when he is here.

I hope it will be possible for him to address the various Menorah
Societies of the country, which seem to me a particularly hopeful
field for Zionism.[3]   Very truly yours,

1. Judah Leon Magnes (1877–1948), a Reform rabbi, played a key role in
both the New York Jewish community and the American Zionist movement. Born in America, trained at both the Hebrew Union College and the
University of Heidelberg, he was one of those rare Reform leaders accepted
by both the uptown German Jews and the new immigrants. Related by
marriage to Louis Marshall (see LDB to Louis Marshall 31 August 1914),
he had easy access to the established leaders of the American Jewish Committee, and for a time he served as leader of the prestigious Temple Emanu-
El in New York. One of Magnes's outstanding efforts was the formation
of the New York Kehillah, which for over a decade managed to unite all
segments of the nation's largest Jewish community. (See Arthur A. Goren,
*New York Jews and the Quest for Community: The Kehillah Experiment,
1908–1922* [New York, 1970]). From 1905 to 1908, Magnes was secretary of
the Federation of American Zionists, and he played an active role in the
movement until his interests in pacifism led him to retire. Magnes moved to
Palestine in 1921 to further the work of the Hebrew University in Jerusalem, which he led as chancellor after 1925 and as president after 1935. A
pacifist and a humanitarian, he constantly sought ways to lessen Arab-Jewish
tensions, devising at one point a plan for a jointly-controlled state. See
Norman Bentwich, *For Zion's Sake: A Biography of Judah L. Magnes*
(Philadelphia, 1954).
    2. Franz Oppenheimer (1864–1943) was a German social scientist and
liberal socialist. He was a Zionist and was influential in applying socialist
theories to Palestinian communities. He settled in the United States after
the Nazis gained power in Germany.
    3. Founded by Henry Hurwitz (see LDB to Magnes, 14 September 1914),
the Menorah movement began at Harvard in 1906 and spread to other
American and Canadian universities. In 1913 the Intercollegiate Menorah
Association was founded and in 1915 the group began publishing *The
Menorah Journal* under Hurwitz's editorship. The Association, dedicated to
fostering Jewish culture, disbanded in 1961 at Hurwitz's death.

To Frank L. Neall

October 10, 1913 Boston, Mass. [Brandeis Mss, LtB]
MY DEAR MR. NEALL: [1] Thank you very much for your kind letter of the 9th and the interesting clippings.
    It took six years to open the eyes of our New England people

to the New Haven iniquities. I think they see now, but have not enjoyed the process of awakening.

Yours very truly,

1. Frank L. Neall of Philadelphia sent LDB some clippings relating to the New Haven controversy.

To Woodrow Wilson

October 10, 1913 Boston, Mass. [Wilson Mss]

MY DEAR MR. PRESIDENT: The rumor is persistent that Judge Prouty intends to resign soon from the Interstate Commerce Commission. If he does, I wish to recommend for that office Mr. David O. Ives of Boston.

No man in New England is better qualified by character or ability; and I know of no other man anywhere who possesses the unique experience which would enable him preeminently to aid in solving our serious transportation problems.

Mr. Ives has been, since May 1909, the Transportation Manager of the Boston Chamber of Commerce. Immediately before that he was Chairman of the Official Classification Committee, with headquarters in New York, a position to which he was appointed by joint action of the trunk lines; after some twenty years of service in various capacities on important western railroads.

Mr. Ives is a native of Massachusetts, and graduated from Harvard in 1879. He then entered a manufacturing business; but was compelled to give up the work on account of his health, and spend several years ranching in the West. He then entered the employ of the Atchison; was later for many years with the Burlington, and after that became General Manager of the Wabash under President [Frederick A.] Delano. He resigned that position in order to take the chairmanship of the Classification Committee.

Mr. Ives would therefore bring to the Commission, at the time of New England's greatest need, not only a special knowledge of local business and transportation conditions, but the benefit of a wide practical experience in railroading, which would be of great service to the commission in the solution of its important problems.

Mr. Ives is and always has been a Democrat.

Mr. Ives' salary as Transportation Manager of the Chamber of Commerce is such that acceptance of a position on the Commission would involve an important financial sacrifice; but he is a man of such fine public spirit that I feel convinced he would be willing to make that sacrifice.

Secretary Lane has known Mr. Ives well for many years.[1]

Very cordially yours,

1. On 13 October Wilson replied that he would give careful attention to Ives if a vacancy on the I.C.C. should occur. This letter marks the start of an intensive campaign by LDB to get Ives appointed. On 3 February 1914 Prouty did resign; but Ives was passed over by Wilson and six weeks later, at the age of fifty-six, he unexpectedly died. To replace Prouty, Wilson nominated Henry C. Hall (see LDB to Alfred Brandeis, 30 May 1914).

To Norman Hapgood

October 15, 1913 Boston, Mass. [Brandeis Mss, NMF 62-1]

MY DEAR NORMAN: I am enclosing herewith, as promised, the article "Solution of the Trust Problem. A Program".

The article seems to me rather tame and stale as compared with the Money Trust articles, and I am not so sure as I was then of the advisability of publishing it and the "Competition that Kills" article, before the Money Trust series begins.[1]

As I said to you, you must exercise the stern judgment of the editor, and not hesitate to exclude or postpone altogether the publication of one or both of these. I was perhaps made unduly apprehensive by the Clayton incident.[2]

The proof of the Money Trust articles I and II has just come.

Cordially yours,

P.S. You may have noticed that the $67,000,000 bond issue was authorized by Public Service Commission, Anderson alone dissenting, and dissenting vehemently.[3] I think the decision of the Commission indicates the financial concentration of our community. I am told that there never was more lobbying at the State House than was practised about the Public Service Commission's office during the last six weeks; and that Governor Foss has been using all his influence to sway the Commission.[4]

1. Hapgood showed no hesitation about printing the two pieces before the "money trust" series. "The Solution of the Trust Problem: A Program" appeared in the 8 November issue of *Harper's;* it is reprinted in *The Curse of Bigness*, 129–36. Essentially the article is a nearly word-for-word copy of LDB's long campaign letter to Woodrow Wilson, 30 September 1912, printed in Volume II of this collection. Hapgood published LDB's "Cutthroat Prices: Competition that Kills," in the 15 November issue; it is reprinted in *Business –A Profession*, 243–61. The article is a defense of price maintenance of trademarked goods and a condemnation of price-cutting such products. The piece grew out of his efforts, with Ingersoll, to change the doctrine in *Bauer* v. *O'Donnell* (see LDB to John R. Commons, 27 May 1913), and LDB used the Ingersoll watch as an example in his argument.

2. In an unprecedented move, President Wilson wrote a letter to Henry DeLamar Clayton (1857–1929), the anti-trust expert in the House of Representatives and the man who gave his name to Wilson's anti-trust legislation. In his letter, the President asked Clayton to withdraw from the Alabama senatorial race in favor of his rival, Oscar Underwood. Wilson couched his request in terms of Clayton's importance in the approaching anti-trust fight in the House, but the incident was widely interpreted as paying a debt to Underwood, the sponsor of the new reform tariff Wilson had wanted so badly. On 10 October Clayton complied with Wilson's wish and left the field to Underwood.

3. For Anderson's remarks, see the *New York Times*, 15 October 1913. Anderson accused his fellow commissioners of "arrogance" and of abridging Massachusetts law by their own fiat.

4. The decision of the Public Service Commission was immediately taken to court, and on 9 January 1914, the Massachusetts Supreme Court ruled unanimously against the bond issue, charging that the Public Service Commission had exceeded its authority when it approved the proposal.

To Franklin Knight Lane

October 15, 1913 Boston, Mass. [Brandeis Mss, NMF 58-1]

MY DEAR MR. LANE: I enclose herewith copy of letter of October 10th which I sent to the President about appointing Ives on the Interstate Commerce Commission, and a copy of his reply of the 13th.

It would be a calamity if Ives were not appointed. I had some doubt whether it would be better for me to go to Washington to see the President, but concluded on the whole that it was wiser not to do so.

I feel quite sure that you share my views in respect to Ives' fitness, and I should be glad if you would telegraph me whether there is anything more which you think I could wisely do which would further his appointment.[1]

Very cordially yours,

1. For Lane's reply, see LDB to David O. Ives, 20 October 1913.

To Henry Bourne Joy

October 17, 1913 Boston, Mass. [Brandeis Mss, NMF 57-1]

MY DEAR MR. JOY: There is another question on which I want information from you.

My investigation of the railroad problem, particularly that in connection with the advance rate case three years ago, convinced me that the terminals and the short hauls presented to the railroads their most serious problems. Adequate terminals in the older communities are attainable only at an almost prohibitive price; and the many junctions and the exigencies of terminal service render short haul quick deliveries extremely expensive, and almost impossible.

Of course my mind on this question is directed largely to conditions such as we have in New England and the middle Atlantic States.

It has seemed to me probable that the relief to our transportation system lies on these lines:

First: That water ways must be developed, as in Germany wherever possible to carry the very heavy traffic, and

Second: The auto truck and good roads must be resorted to for the short haul traffic, say, within fifty miles, at least in the more congested communities; and that we may reasonably look for decreasing costs both in the construction, and in the operation of the auto truck.

I wish you would write me fully your views on this subject and supply me with any data that may be available,—data as to the relative costs of auto truck transportation and rail transportation, and the present relative cost, all things considered, by which I mean to conclude, of course, the fact that rail transportation involves at least double loading and unloading, and hauls to and from the station.[1]   Yours very truly,

1. On 27 October Joy replied in a long letter. He argued that water traffic would never supplant the railways, and that if the railroads were given a free hand, they might displace all water traffic with ease. He favored the development of waterways, "but never will they *pay*." As far as trucks were concerned, Joy thought their operation and maintenance cost "is three times what it should be, by reason of rough pavements." The first priority was better roads, particularly around docks and railroad yards. Still, Joy himself found trucks convenient for small loads (less than a railroad car) and for short distances. The outlook depended so heavily upon local conditions, he contended, that it was hard to generalize about trucking's potential service to business.

To Frederic H. Sidney

October 17, 1913 Boston, Mass. [Brandeis Mss, NMF 59-2]

MY DEAR SIR: [1] I am in receipt of your letter of the 16th in which you advise me of the vote of your Association requesting me to act as the counsel of the Association in the effort to secure cooperative pensions substantially on the lines of the Act passed in 1909 relating to the pensions on the Boston and Maine System.[2]

I see no reason for any doubt as to the constitutionality of that Act, and, if amended with respect to certain provisions which were introduced at the time as concessions to the Railroad, in order to secure the passage of the Act, I still believe that the system set forth in that statute is the one most desirable.[3]

I am glad to know that your association desired to secure the adoption of this plan on the Boston & Maine and its extention to the other railroads of New England.

So far as it is possible, I should be glad to aid your Association in this effort, acting, to this end, as its unpaid counsel; but I shall be obliged to be away from Boston much during this winter, and may not be able to give the matter full attention. Later on I should, therefore, wish to confer with you with regard to the employment of some younger man who could give the matter continuous attention.

With best wishes,   Yours very truly,

1. Frederic H. Sidney was the secretary of the New England Association of Railroad Veterans.

2. See LDB, "Boston and Maine Pensions," *The Survey* 22 (19 June 1909): 436.

3. See LDB to Frank O. Hardy, 20 April 1909.

To Norman Hapgood

October 18, 1913 Boston, Mass. [Brandeis Mss, NMF 62-1]

MY DEAR NORMAN: Replying to yours of the 16th about Altman and Russell's letter, which I return: [1]

Russell's fundamental thought is right; as is also his feeling that employment ought to be continuous. But the problem is one on which much hard thinking will have to be done, and I am inclined to think that the best thing to do in connection with the Altman incident is gently to call attention to this fact: After all, this great successful merchant has sought to express his success outside of the business instead of in it. That is,—in art collection and charity, instead of advancing the art in which he achieved his fortune; and that the true line of progress is through making a business a profession and solving the problems, as I indicated in my Brown University Commencement address, of which I enclose a copy.[2]   Yours very truly,

1. Benjamin Altman (1840–1913) was a wealthy New York businessman who had made a fortune in dry goods. He had died on 7 October and left his unusually important art collection (valued at $12,000,000) to the Metropolitan Museum of Art. Apparently Russell (whose name and letter are irrecoverable) wrote Hapgood complaining that while Altman did much valuable art collecting, his employees suffered from irregularity of employment. Hapgood did not touch upon the matter in *Harper's*.
2. See LDB to J. Franklin McElwain, 18 June 1912, n. 1.

To Carl Hovey

October 18, 1913 Boston, Mass. [Brandeis Mss, NMF 1-N-1]

MY DEAR MR. HOVEY: [1] I am so weighed down with burdens already assumed, and so little fitted to act as Judge on your prize offering, that I feel obliged to decline the very kind suggestion contained in yours of the 17th.[2]

I am going to try to make some amends. You remember my talking to you about writing up the Boston attitude and state of mind, as developed in connection with New Haven matters. C. P. Connolly, 76 North Munn Avenue, East Orange, N.J., whose articles in Everybody's and Collier's you of course know, spent a great deal of time on the New Haven situation, particularly this aspect of it, in connection with an article he was going to write for Hearst's, and which is not to be published. I should think you could get hold of him for the Metropolitan.[3]

Very cordially yours,

1. Carl Hovey (1876–1956) was the editor of the *Metropolitan Magazine* and also of *Hearst's International*. He later moved to Hollywood and became the story editor for Cecil B. DeMille, the motion picture producer.

2. The *Metropolitan* intended to publish an article by George Bernard Shaw in its December issue. The magazine then proposed a contest for the best reply to Shaw and Hovey asked LDB ("as the leading thinker on economic topics in America") to join Thomas A. Edison and *Chicago Tribune* editor James Keely as judges.

3. The magazine did not carry an article on the New Haven.

To James Clark McReynolds

October 18, 1913 Boston, Mass. [Brandeis Mss, NMF 58-1]

MY DEAR MR. MCREYNOLDS: Replying to yours of the 15th about Francis M. Carroll and John A. Sullivan: [1]

First: It does not seem to me that either of these two gentlemen would be desirable for United States District Attorney at Boston. Neither of them has the professional experience which should be demanded of a United States attorney,—at least in so important a district as this.

Second: I do not recall having met Mr. Carroll [2] but once, and then for a very short time. He made a very pleasant impression upon me, but I am told by one who knows him, and is well versed in local political matters, that he lacks stamina, and that he is pre-eminently Mayor Fitzgerald's man. I don't know that being Mayor Fitzgerald's man is worse than being the man of some other of our local Democratic leaders; but we certainly need for District Attorney a man of ability who is nobody's man.

Third: John A. Sullivan I have known somewhat for many years. He is a man of character and independence, and has given evidence of ability in his public service as a member of the Finance Commission; but his appointment would be a direct slap in the face of most of the Democratic leaders, and while one might be glad to have the slap administered, and for that reason have Mr. Sullivan appointed to some position of prominence, if consistent with the policy of the administration, Mr. Sullivan's professional standing would offer no justification for selecting him for the position of District Attorney.

You will remember my writing you sometime ago about Mr. Sughrue.[3] He is doubtless a very good friend of Mr. Sullivan, originally acting as counsel for the Finance Commission. He is a man of professional experience.

Very cordially yours,

1. McReynolds had requested LDB's opinion regarding the two men as possible choices as the United States district attorney for Boston. See also LDB to Charles Warren, 8 October 1913.

2. Francis M. Carroll (1874–1941) was a Boston lawyer who had been an early supporter of Wilson in Massachusetts. He served as Mayor Fitzgerald's fire commissioner.

3. See LDB to McReynolds, 13 August 1913, and to Thomas W. Gregory, 18 September 1914.

To David Otis Ives

October 20, 1913 Boston, Mass. [Brandeis Mss, NMF 58-1]

MY DEAR DAVE: I have your letter of Saturday. This morning comes a letter from Lane which reads as follows:

"I can think of nothing further you can do except to see the President personally when here." [1]

My own judgment is that it would not be wise for me to go to Washington specifically on this matter. The President might think that I am pressing you because I think you will aid in carrying out the New Haven policy I have advocated; but I expect to be in Washington next week to see Harlan about the advance rate case, and there are other matters about which I can properly see the President. It seems to me best to defer speaking to him until I can do that.

If, as your Washington friends think, politics is going to play so important a part, I am quite sure that I would not fit into the game; but I am not prepared to believe it.

I do not think it would do any harm to let such of your trade association friends as volunteer in different parts of the Country, urge your nomination.   Very cordially yours,

1. See LDB to Franklin K. Lane, 15 October 1913.

To Garet Garrett

October 22, 1913 Boston, Mass. [Brandeis Mss, NMF 64-1]

MY DEAR MR. GARRETT: [1] Every time that I take up the Annalist, which is once a week, I am impressed anew with the excellent work which you are doing.

The paper is informing and enlightening and thrillingly interesting.

I was particularly glad to learn from it today that Senator Owen had taken the position that a bank is a public utility.[2] That is the position which I have taken in one of the articles on the money trust which I am writing for Harper's Weekly.

Very cordially yours,

1. Garet Garret (1878-1954) served at one time or another as the financial editor for many of the leading New York newspapers, and he wrote many books and essays. In 1913 he was the editor of the *New York Times Annalist*.
2. Robert Latham Owen (1856-1947) was a liberal Democrat who served as Oklahoma's senator from the territory's achieving statehood, in 1907, to 1925, when he decided not to seek another term. LDB also wrote to Owen on this date congratulating him on his view and asking permission to quote him in one of the *Harper's* articles.

To F. Lincoln Hutchins

October 22, 1913 Boston, Mass. [Brandeis Mss, LtB]

MY DEAR MR. HUTCHINS: Thank you for yours of the 20th.

I am very glad to know that the Iowa Commission is planning to take part in the advance rate hearings, and I hope to have the pleasure of seeing much of Mr. Thorne in that connection.[1]

Yours very truly,

1. Clifford Thorne (1878-1923) became one of LDB's bitterest enemies. He was an Iowa lawyer whose whole career was devoted to defending the interests of shippers against the railroads. In 1913 he was serving as the chairman of Iowa's Board of Railroad Commissioners, and he greeted the news of LDB's role in the approaching rate hearings with glee. The two men had been associated in the 1910 hearings, and as this letter announces, Thorne came to Washington to join LDB in presenting the shippers' side. It was clear that Thorne, like so many others, was confused about LDB's position in the hearings—Thorne thought that LDB, as the public's representative,

would naturally side with the shippers. (See LDB to James S. Harlan, 21 August 1913, n. 1.) When LDB argued that the Eastern freight rates were inadequate, Thorne and others felt betrayed and angry. See Mason, *Brandeis,* 342–45 for an account sympathetic to LDB, and for Thorne's side, his testimony against LDB's confirmation to the Supreme Court, *Nomination Hearings,* 1: 5–62.

To Felix Frankfurter

October 24, 1913 Boston, Mass. [Brandeis Mss, NMF 58-1]

MY DEAR FRANKFURTER: Of course you know that Valentine is being urged as our Labor Commissioner. Mrs. Davis R. Dewey [1] is one of the members of the Board. Last evening Mrs. Brandeis met her, and Mrs. Dewey said that she personally would appoint Valentine eagerly, but that she thought some of the other members were afraid to appoint him, on account of his record in the Indian Department on Catholicism. Mrs. Dewey said that she had heard that some high Catholic potentates,—Cardinal Gibbons,[2] or some others, had said that Valentine had done the only thing he could under the circumstances, and she said that if a letter could be obtained from some distinguished Catholic, the scruples of other members of the Board might be overcome. Of course this is all confidential.

I thought that if any such thing were possible, you would not only know about it, but be able to arrange it, so I am writing you.[3]

I expect to be in Washington the latter part of next week, and look forward to seeing you.   Very cordially yours,

1. Mary Hopkins Dewey was the wife of the well-known M.I.T. economist, Davis Rich Dewey.

2. James Cardinal Gibbons (1834–1921) was one of the most influential religious leaders of his time. Often credited with smoothing the way for the huge influx of Catholic immigration at the end of the nineteenth and beginning of the twentieth centuries, Cardinal Gibbons was known for his charm, persuasive abilities, and talent for cooperating with leaders of other faiths. See his own *Retrospect of Fifty Years* (Baltimore, 1916), or the old two-volume study, Allen S. Will, *Cardinal Gibbons* (New York, 1922).

3. Robert G. Valentine was appointed in 1913 the first chairman of the Massachusetts Minimum Wage Board.

To Thomas Watt Gregory

October 25, 1913 Boston, Mass. [Brandeis Mss, NMF 1-N-1]

DEAR MR. GREGORY: In connection with the recent election of the directors of the New Haven you doubtless noticed that Galen L. Stone was elected a director.[1]

Mr. Stone is the leading,—almost the only force, in the Eastern Steamship Corporation and the Atlantic, Gulf, and West Indies. His election would indicate a purpose on the part of the present management to fasten, in some other form no less effective, the existing suppression of all steamship competition.

I trust you are making good progress with your bill.

Cordially yours,

1. In a stormy stockholders' meeting on 22 October, the New Haven management attempted to prepare the stockholders for the approaching dividend cut, hinting that it would be lowered to 4% (actually the dividend was passed completely in December). Their relations with J. P. Morgan were called into question by a minority of the stockholders, and it was announced that the retired Charles S. Mellen had declined his salary ($30,000 per year for the next five years). Two new directors were elected. One was James L. Richards, LDB's friend from the days of the gas consolidation fight. But the second was Galen Luther Stone (1862–1926), a leading investment banker and a director of at least six steamship companies and other transportation concerns.

To Elihu Thomson

October 25, 1913 Boston, Mass. [Brandeis Mss, NMF 64-4]

DEAR MR. THOMPSON [*sic*]:[1] I thank you for your very kind letter of the 24th, and shall look forward to receiving the pamphlets and statements which your Secretary may be able to find.[2]

I did not want to put you to the trouble of preparing a statement, however brief, of the facts which I am particularly anxious to know, but I venture to do so in view of the courteous suggestion with which you close your letter.

What I have in mind is this:

The success of the best inventions is of course dependent upon the supply of money and of managerial ability to develop them; and the men who supply that money and the management in the early history of the invention should share in the glory of the success. My impression had been that the Thompson-Houston [*sic*] Company, particularly in the first five years of its life, presented a conspicuous instance of the aid so given by business men accustomed to take risks with their money, or by what might be called neighborhood investors. I want to know who they were and what they did.

I had supposed that the early history of the Thompson-Houston [*sic*] Company had in this respect some slight resemblance to the early history of the telephone, which was so much aided by Thomas Saunders [*sic*].³ I shall greatly appreciate it if you will let me know the facts.⁴   Yours very truly,

1. Elihu Thomson (1853–1937) was an English-born teacher and an inventor of electrical devices. He patented over seven hundred inventions related to electricity and was a cofounder of the Thomson-Houston Electrical Company and a pioneer in General Electric.

2. On 23 October LDB had written Thomson asking for information on the early financing of the electrical industry. On 24 October Thomson replied, in a cordial letter, that his secretary would forward some pamphlets on the early history of the Thompson-Houston company and that, if LDB desired, he would be glad to undertake to write a sketch of the early days of the industry.

3. Thomas Sanders is described by LDB (in *Other People's Money*, 141) as "a simple, enthusiastic, warm-hearted, business man of Haverhill, Massachusetts," who was willing to make pioneering investments of his own money in the telephone business. From 1874 to 1878, Sanders, a shoe manufacturer, invested nine-tenths of all the money invested in the telephone. This was a case when the early investor did not get his share "in the glory of the success," as Sanders is not remembered today despite the fact that his money bought the first five thousand telephones in the country.

4. LDB was interested, of course, in showing how in the early stages of a business the bankers were cautious and unfriendly while the businessmen themselves were pioneering and venturesome. See LDB to Henry B. Joy, 7 October 1913. For his remarks on the electrical industry, with particular reference to the story of Thomson-Houston, see *Other People's Money*, 146–47.

To Norman Hapgood

October 28, 1913 Boston, Mass. [Brandeis Mss, NMF 62-1]

MY DEAR NORMAN: I am expecting to take the 1:00 o'clock train for New York tomorrow. I have a number of appointments at the

City Club during the evening, and shall leave at midnight for Washington.

If you are free about 10:15, I will come over to the Harvard Club when I get through my appointments at the City Club, and if you have nothing on hand, should like to see you at that time. If that time is inconvenient, perhaps we could get together for a little at 6:15 at the Harvard Club. There is nothing special that I want to talk over with you, but I don't like to pass through New York without seeing you.   Yours very truly,

To Louis Lipsky

October 28, 1913 Boston, Mass. [Brandeis Mss, Z 1-4]

DEAR MR. LIPSKY: *First:* You will doubtless hear from Mr. De-Haas, with whom I have conferred today, that I am to be in New York on Sunday, November 9th, in connection with one of the Garment Workers' arbitration matters. I am afraid that it may not be possible for me to attend the meeting of the council, but I will if I can.

Second: Mr. DeHaas is also reporting to you that the difficulty in collecting the data concerning conditions in Palestine, which difficulty has not yet been wholly overcome, has prevented our taking the matter up with the members of the Special Committee, and that we, therefore, cannot make even a partial report at this time.

I regret very much the delay resulting.

Very cordially yours,

To Henry French Hollis

November 3, 1913 Boston, Mass. [Brandeis Mss, NMF 58-1]

MY DEAR SENATOR HOLLIS: I thank you for yours of the 1st.

I am extremely glad that you have seen the President. I was in Washington on Thursday for the day, and tried to do so, but found the President too busy to see me.[1]

Yours very cordially,

1. Senator Hollis was working with LDB to get David O. Ives appointed to the Interstate Commerce Commission (see LDB to Woodrow Wilson, 10 October 1913) and his interview with Wilson was for that purpose: "I hope I made some impression; but you know the President is rather noncommital."

To Jacob Henry Schiff

November 3, 1913 Boston, Mass. [Brandeis Mss, NMF 64-1]

MY DEAR MR. SCHIFF: I have occasion to refer publicly to the underwriting commissions paid by the Union Pacific in connection with the dissolution of the Union Pacific-Southern Pacific merger. Desiring to avoid the possibility of any inaccurate statement, I wrote Judge Lovett under date of October 22nd, and have his telegraphic reply under date of October 29th, copies of both being enclosed.[1]

I had not supposed, when I wrote Judge Lovett, that there was anything in the transaction which the company would hesitate to disclose, and I believe that you cannot have any objection to the facts being known.

I shall be glad, therefore, if you will give me the information, unless you deem it improper to do so in view of Judge Lovett's refusal.[2]　　　Yours very truly,

1. Robert Scott Lovett (1860–1932) had risen from a railway attorney in Texas to a powerful force in American railroading. He had been president of the Harriman system's Union Pacific and Southern Pacific lines until 1913. He then became chairman of the executive committee of the Union Pacific, and later its president and finally its chairman of the board. He had telegraphed LDB that "our rule is to give no information respecting our business transactions to unofficial persons except as published for information of all alike. I know of no reason for departing from that rule in this instance."

2. Schiff replied on 5 November that, although there was nothing which Kuhn, Loeb & Co. desired to hide, in view of Lovett's refusal, it was deemed best not to accede to LDB's request. For LDB's comments on Schiff's firm, see *Other People's Money*, 45–46.

To Walter Edward Weyl

November 3, 1913 Boston, Mass. [Brandeis Mss, NMF 35-2]

MY DEAR WEYL: [1] I am returning, as you requested, with my O.K. the carbon of Mr. Winslow's letter to you of the 20th, reporting on the arrangement made by him with the Bureau of Labor.[2]

I saw Winslow in passing through New York last Wednesday, and thought that he had handled the matter exceedingly well, and I am entirely content with the arrangement with this understanding:

It seems to me that we are engaged in what is perhaps the most important investigation yet made with a view to improving the industrial conditions. In that work you are taking a very important part. You understand the processes, and will understand the results. You have the ability to express your ideas in words. I feel that for your sake, as well as for that of the cause, you should be the interpreter to the world of the results attained, and I should be careful that any arrangement made leaves the matter in such a situation that the results will first be published through your discission of the subject.[3]   Very cordially yours,

1. Walter Edward Weyl (1873–1919) was an important writer, reformer and social thinker of the progressive period. He earned his doctorate in economics under the guidance of the progressive economist Simon Patten and became a free-lance writer and muckraker, publishing articles in most of the leading reformist journals. All of his work, like that of LDB, was guided and informed by a passion for statistics and fact-gathering. In 1912 he had written the book for which he is chiefly remembered, *The New Democracy*, which espoused a Rooseveltian "new nationalist" position; he had, however, a greater faith in grass-roots democracy than did many other new nationalists. In 1913 he was serving as a member of the Board of Arbitration in the garment industry, a position which threw him into frequent contact with LDB. He was already negotiating with Herbert Croly for a position as editor of *The New Republic*, and would become one of the founding editors when the magazine began publishing in November 1914. Weyl was a gregarious and likeable man, who, despite his independence and growing radicalism, retained the respect and affection of his co-workers. He "looked like a saint," Alvin Johnson once said, "and fundamentally was one." See the excellent account of his life and thought in Forcey, *Crossroads of Liberalism*, ch. 2.

2. In early August, while trying to settle a wage dispute, the Board of Arbitration determined to conduct that kind of exhaustive statistical study

which was so congenial to both LDB and Weyl. The study would involve detailed investigations of every aspect of the garment industry and would have the full support of both the unions and the manufacturers. Weyl was placed in charge, and he quickly hired more than fifty field investigators to undertake the work. LDB also telegraphed Secretary of Labor Wilson for the loan of Charles H. Winslow (1866-19[?]), a special agent in the Bureau of Labor Statistics who had experience in the garment industry. The correspondence referred to dealt with the division of responsibilities between Weyl and Winslow, and the precise role of the Bureau in the investigation.

3. In the end it was Winslow and the Bureau of Labor Statistics who published the results; see Winslow, *Conciliation, Arbitration and Sanitation in the Dress and Waist Industry of New York* (Washington, 1914). See also LDB to William C. Redfield, 17 November 1913 and to Weyl, 1 January 1915.

To Roscoe Pound

November 5, 1913 Boston, Mass. [Pound Mss]

DEAR MR. POUND: Thank you for Seligman's letter, which I am returning herewith.

As I wrote Thayer yesterday, I am extremely glad we had the frank talk about Law School matters. With you, Thayer and Frankfurter there, the school ought to do great things.[1]

Very truly yours,

1. Frankfurter wrote of his invitation to join the faculty at the Harvard Law School: "If I had received a letter from an Indian princess asking me to marry her, I wouldn't have been more surprised." After extended consultations with Holmes, Stimson, Croly, Roosevelt, and LDB, Frankfurter accepted the position — and he remained at Harvard until his appointment to the Supreme Court in 1939. When he expressed to LDB his doubts about his qualifications, LDB replied: "I would let those who have the responsibilities for selecting you decide your qualifications and not have you decide that." See Phillips, ed., *Felix Frankfurter Reminisces*, ch. 9.

To Dix W. Smith

November 5, 1913 Boston, Mass. [Brandeis Mss, NMF 47-2]

DEAR MR. SMITH: [1] The plan suggested in yours of the 3rd is very interesting. Every instance of humane and rational treating of industrial enterprise helps on the great cause, and I have no doubt that the plan developed on the lines you have in mind, would be of service. I doubt, however, whether it would go far towards checking Socialism, which you say is now spreading so rapidly in the mining world. It seems to me that the prevailing discontent is due perhaps less to dissatisfaction with the material conditions, as to the denial of participation in management, and that the only way to avoid Socialism is to develop cooperation in its broadest sense. Mere profit sharing, while a step in advance, will not go far in solving our problem. I trust, however, that you will have the opportunity of trying out your most interesting experiment.

Yours very truly,

1. Dix W. Smith was an attorney from Elmira, New York. He had written to LDB asking his opinion of a plan for improving the lot of miners in the bituminous coal fields of Pennsylvania. His plan included a model community, baths, gymnasium, health facilities, a store which would deal fairly with the men, lectures, reading rooms, parks and the like. He would also pay the miners on the basis of their productivity and introduce profit-sharing. His hope in all of this would be "checking socialism now so rapidly spreading in the mining world. . . . "

To James Walton Carmalt [1] (Memorandum)

November 13, 1913 Boston, Mass. [Brandeis Mss, NMF 57-1]

I have your letter of Wednesday evening and will think that point over. Since our talk yesterday it occurred to me that we might get important assistance from the Department of Commerce bearing upon the question of the raising of prices of materials and supplies through the combinations. You will recall that, in connection with the investigation of the Standard Oil Company, the Bureau of Corporations developed the excessive prices paid the Galena Signal Oil Company. I have talked today with Mr. [Joseph E.] Davies and as a result of my conference with him he is directing an investigation of their records to see what material they have which will bear upon this aspect of our inquiry.

It seems to me also that the Department of Justice might have valuable matter. It, of course, has the data in connection with the steel rail pool, and I thought might have considerable other data bearing upon this subject. I spoke to Assistant Attorney General

Adkins [2] today and he is having made an investigation as to what data there may be available among their files.

There is also one other line of inquiry which I took up tentatively yesterday with Mr. Bemis, about which I will want to talk with you.

1. James Walton Carmalt (1872–1937), an attorney with the Interstate Commerce Commission, would become the Commission's chief examiner in 1914. He was working closely with LDB in preparation for the advanced rate hearings, and this memorandum is typical of many which passed between them.

2. Jesse Corcoran Adkins (1879–1955) in 1913 was serving his second term as Assistant Attorney General. He was appointed an associate justice of the supreme court of the District of Columbia in 1930.

To Max Pam

November 17, 1913 Boston, Mass. [Brandeis Mss, NMF 64-1]

MY DEAR MR. PAM: [1] I think you will be interested in my articles in Harper's Weekly on "Breaking the Money Trust", which begin November 22nd.

In the third article I had quite a long passage discussing your important contribution to the subject. The article itself seemed to Mr. Hapgood too long, and he has, therefore, taken the liberty of cutting out, among other things, the discussion of your article in the Law Review, but I have the promise that he will use editorially the matter omitted from the article, and perhaps that will show an even better appreciation of your service in this connection. [2]   Very cordially yours,

1. Max Pam (1865–1925) was a leading Chicago corporation lawyer.
2. Pam's article was "Interlocking Directorates, The Problem and Its Solution," 26 *Harvard Law Review* 467 (1913). The omitted material from Pam's article was restored in the book version; see *Other People's Money*, 60–61. There was no editorial reference to Pam in *Harper's*.

To William Cox Redfield

November 17, 1913 Boston, Mass. [Commerce Department]

MY DEAR MR. REDFIELD: Referring to our conference on the investigation into the clothing trade to be made by your Department, I am sending you, as requested, a memorandum of the investigation now being made in those branches in which I have been interested through the introduction of the preferential union shop.

First: Garment Trade Workers.

The workers in this industry are represented by two international unions,—both affiliated with the American Federation of Labor:

In the men's garment trade,—The United Garment Workers of America.

In the women's garment trade,—The International Ladies' Garment Workers Union.

Second: The International Ladies' Garment Workers Union,—New York being the chief seat of the industry,—is represented there by seven distinct locals dealing with specific trades:

1. In the cloak and suit trade, by the Joint Board of Cloak, Suit and Skirt Makers' Union, comprising five locals.

2. In the dress and waist trade, by the Ladies' Waist and Dress Makers' Union, Local 25.

3. In the children's dress trade,—by the Misses and Children's Dressmakers' Union, Local No. 50.

4. Wrapper, kimona and house dresses trade,—by the Wrapper, Kimona and House Dress Makers' Union, Local No. 41.

5. The underwear and white goods trade,—by the Underwear and White Goods Workers' Union, Local 62.

6. Raincoat trade,—by the Rain Coat Makers Union, Local No. 20.

In addition to the above there is also (7) Union of Ladies' Tailors.

Third: There is no general employers' association corresponding to the International Ladies Garment Workers Union, but there are special employers' organizations in each of these trades, namely:

1. In the cloak and suit trade,—The Cloak and Suit Manufacturers' Protective Association.

2. In the Dress and waist trade,—The Dress and Waist Manufacturers' Association.

3. In the children's dress trade,—The Children's Dress Manufacturers' Association.

4. In the wrapper, kimona and house dress trade,—The New York Association of House–dresses and Kimona Manufacturers.

5. The underwear and white goods trade,—The Cotton Garment Manufacturers' Association.

6. The raincoat trade,—The Water-proof Garment Manufacturers' Association.

In addition to the above there is also some association of employers in the ladies' tailoring industry.

Fourth: In each of these branches of the women's garments trade in New York City there has been introduced a protocol embodying the principles of the preferential union shop, but the degrees of organization, and the extent to which the preferential union shop idea has been put into practice, varies greatly. It was first introduced September 2, 1910 in the cloak and suit industry, and a full report, by Charles H. Winslow, on its organization is found in Bulletin #98 of the United States Bureau of Labor, January 1912. In this industry practically all of the workers in New York are organized, and a majority of the shops are subject to the protocol.

In the dress and suit industry the protocol was introduced in January 1913, and a much smaller part of the workers and of the shops are within its provision. In the other branches of the women's garment trade the process of development of the protocol idea is likewise far less developed than in the cloak and suit trade.

This is true also of the development of the protocol idea in Boston,—where early in 1913 an agreement was signed in the cloak and suit trade by the Boston Ladies' Garment Manufacturers Association on the one hand, and the Cloak and Skirt Makers' Union Local No. 12, Local No. 56 and Local No. 73 on the other; and likewise some agreement in the dress and waist trade.

Fifth: In the cloak and suit trade an important investigation is now in process.[1] Early in August 1913 the Board of Arbitration, of which I am Chairman, had submitted to it an application for increase in wages. Upon investigation the Board concluded that the question submitted could not be properly determined without an investigation into the state of the trade, bearing particularly upon the character and extent of employment or unemployment of the workers, and the reasons therefore and the possible remedies.

It seemed to us probable that upon ascertaining the facts in this and related industries, it would be possible to secure greater regularity of employment. With this in view a careful investigation of the cloak and suit industry was undertaken. The services of Mr. Charles H. Winslow of the Department of Labor were secured, and for some months also those of Mr. Manley as chief statistician.[2] Mr. Manley has recently become connected with the Industrial Commission as statistician. The work of investigation, which has been under way for 3½ months, will be continued until this branch of the trade in New York is fully covered.

In the dress and waist industry the board of Arbitration, of which I am also Chairman, is having a careful statistical inquiry made by Mr. Stone, and it is expected that his report will be ready in about a month.

Sixth: In order to adequately solve the problem in any department of the garment trade, it is probably necessary to consider all branches of the trade in the principal garment manufacturing centers of the United States, and the end sought to be attained would be greatly advanced by full cooperation between your Department, the Department of Labor, the Industrial Commission, and the parties to the protocols. Through Mr. Charles H. Winslow we have already arranged for co-operation with the Department of Labor, and I have had a conference with Mr. W. J. Lauck[3] concerning cooperation with the Industrial Commission.

As I have already suggested, it would seem to me advisable for your Department to direct its investigation particularly to branches of the trade other than the New York cloak and suit industry, and the New York dress and waist industry, in which our investigations are proceeding. If your investigations should cover the other branches of the women's garment trade, and of the men's garment trade, particularly in New York, and extend, in conjunction with the Department of Labor, your investigation of both men's and women's garment trades in cities other than New York, we ought to be able to obtain in a comparatively short time a comprehensive knowledge of the whole garment trade of the United States, and be enabled to suggest and develop means for advancing the efficiency of the concerns engaged in various branches of the trade and improve the conditions of the workers.

Yours very truly,

1. See LDB to Walter E. Weyl, 3 November 1913.

2. Basil Manley (1886–1950) was an economist who would be in and out of government service, serving as technical advisor to the Bureau of Labor Statistics, the Federal Trade Commission, the War Industries Board and numerous other federal and New York state agencies. He also worked occasionally in journalism and wrote a number of books on economic topics.

3. William Jett Lauck (1879–1949) was one of America's leading labor and economic experts, and he served as consultant and executive secretary for numerous government investigative agencies, including the U. S. Tariff Commission and the Commission on Industrial Relations. During the war he was secretary of the National War Labor Board.

To E. M. Tousley

November 17, 1913 Boston, Mass. [Brandeis Mss, NMF 47-2]

MY DEAR MR. TOUSLEY: [1] Upon my return to the city I find your letter of the 6th, for which I thank you.

I am not familiar with the Constitution of North Dakota, but the ruling of the Attorney General, to which you refer, seems preposterous. If the court should uphold it, it would give a great opportunity for a state wide campaign of cooperation.[2]

I have asked Mr. Norman Hapgood to send you copies of my article on "Breaking the Money Trust" which closes with Co-operation as the great remedy, and which I think you may find of interest to yourself and the readers of "Co-operation".

Yours very truly,

1. E. M. Tousley (1859–1934) was secretary-treasurer of the Right Relationship League, Inc., a Minnesota organization to promote the principles of cooperation and the establishment of cooperative societies. He had written to LDB in response to a request for information for the *Harper's* articles.

2. Tousley wrote: "Are you aware of the fact that the Attorney General of North Dakota has ruled that those portions of the cooperative statute of the State which provide for one vote per stockholder regardless of investment and distributing net earnings pro rata among the patrons, are unconstitutional? If this ruling is upheld by the courts it will completely stop all cooperative work in that State."

To Arthur Williams

November 17, 1913 Boston, Mass. [Brandeis Mss, NMF 64-1]

MY DEAR MR. WILLIAMS: [1] Upon my return to the city I find your interesting letter of the 10th. With much that you say I entirely agree, but it has seemed to me that you do not lay sufficient stress upon the importance of industrial liberty. No amount of material well-being can make up for the lack of that, and in the end it is only industrial liberty that can give the fullest material well-being.

If you are not already wearied with reading my articles, I hope you will follow the series on "Breaking the Money Trust", which begins in the November 22nd number of Harper's Weekly.

Cordially yours,

1. Probably Arthur Williams (1868–1937), a former vice-president of the Edison Company, and an engineer connected with a number of electrical concerns. Williams was a director of the Metropolitan Insurance Company. He had written a long letter commenting upon LDB's article on old-age pensions ("Massachusetts's Substitute for Old Age Pensions," *The Independent* 65 [16 July 1908]: 125–28; see LDB to Alfred Brandeis, 20 July 1908).

To George Rublee

November 18, 1913 Boston, Mass. [Brandeis Mss, NMF 59-7]

MY DEAR GEORGE: May I add to your labors by suggesting that you consider carefully appropriate legislation to carry out the price maintenance principles advocated in my Harper's article of November 15th.

It is clear that if we specifically authorize price maintenance, the act ought specifically to guard against certain evils:

First: The privilege should not be granted to any manufacturers or producers who have a monopoly of the market.

Second: It ought not to be granted to any who agree with competitors upon selling prices.

Third: It ought (probably) not to be granted to those who give quantity discounts. And I mean by "quantity discounts" those who make a difference between jobbers and retailers,—between fair quantities and very large quantities.

Fourth: Some right ought to be given to dispose of stocks on hand, either in case of bankruptcy, or of damaged goods, if the manufacturer had not himself agreed to take the goods back at cost, or some reasonable percentage of cost to the dealer.

There may be other provisions to be considered, and the above may not all be sound. I am merely sending this for your consideration so that you may be thinking over provisions of the bill.[1]

Cordially yours,

1. A bill drawn by Rublee and LDB was introduced by Representative Raymond B. Stevens, and in January 1915, LDB appeared in support of it before the House Committee on Interstate and Foreign Commerce. See 64th Congress, 1st Session, *Hearings on Regulation of Prices* (9 January 1915) 198–243; excerpts are published in Alfred Lief, ed., *The Social and Economic Views of Mr. Justice Brandeis*, 398–99. The bill was watered down and forgotten during the war, but it was reintroduced in 1924 and again in 1931. Not until 1937, twenty-four years after LDB became involved, did victory come with the passage of the Miller-Tydings Act. See Mason, *Brandeis*, 424–28.

To William Hard

December 1, 1913 Boston, Mass. [Brandeis Mss, NMF 57-5]

MY DEAR HARD: Upon my return to Boston I find yours of Nov. 18th.

You ask what I think of the land question: Possibly the enclosed memorandum, which I dictated in July, 1911, will indicate my thought on that subject, altho it relates to Alaska.[1]

I am afraid that I shall have to leave to you the development of my economic ideas into a "system".[2]

Very truly yours,

1. See LDB to Robert M. LaFollette, 29 July 1911.
2. See William Hard, "Brandeis," *The Outlook* 113 (31 May 1916): 271–77.

To William Harrison Ingersoll

December 1, 1913 Boston, Mass. [Brandeis Mss, NMF 57-9]

MY DEAR MR. INGERSOLL: My friend, Mr. George Rublee, with whom I have discussed price maintenance from time to time and certain essentials of a bill, has prepared the enclosed draft of bill on that subject.[1] I have not had a chance to read it, as I am only passing through the city today, but I am sending it to you so that you and your associates may look it over and return this draft to me with your suggestions.

The extent to which, and conditions under which price maintenance shall be permitted must be carefully thought out in the light of the experience of manufacturers and producers.

I am about to return to Washington, and shall be glad to hear from you there.   Yours very truly,

1. See LDB to George Rublee, 18 November 1913.

To George Weston Anderson

December 6, 1913 Washington, D.C. [Brandeis Mss, NMF 58-1]

DEAR ANDERSON: Yours of 5th rec'd.[1] I think you had better write the President yourself. He is not seeing anyone now.

I think he will appoint Ives, if he is given a chance. The other man you mention won't do at all.[2] There are a dozen men available who would be better even if they don't come from New England as Prouty's successor should.

Prouty said to me today that the New Haven ought to pass its dividend.[3]

1. Anderson had written to inform LDB of a meeting of forty New England businessmen and shippers "for the purpose of trying to get concerted New England action" for the appointment of Prouty's successor on the I.C.C. Anderson also informed LDB that Prouty, with whom he had talked several times recently, was convinced that Wilson would not appoint Ives.

2. The man Anderson had mentioned was Andrew James Peters (1872–1938), a Massachusetts Democrat serving in Congress. He later became Assistant Secretary of the Treasury, 1914–1917 and mayor of Boston, 1918–1922.

3. The New Haven passed its dividend for the first time in forty years, the announcement coming a week after this letter.

To Franklin Knight Lane

December 12, 1913 Boston, Mass. [McReynolds Mss]

MY DEAR MR. LANE: As requested at our discussion on Tuesday concerning trust and cognate legislation I am sending you herewith an outline of my suggestions for an administration program:

First: The President's policy of New Freedom involves necessarily the hostility of the great banking and financial interests; for they want industrial and financial absolutism, while we want industrial democracy. The conflict between us is irreconcilable. On the other hand, the business men, large and small, will be benefited by the policy of New Freedom. Their antagonism rests upon apprehension—indeed misapprehension. It will vanish if the administration makes clear now by overt acts how it proposes to aid business. Then the active support of business men can be secured. To accomplish this an affirmative constructive policy must be adopted; one which will show that the business man is as much the subject of governmental solicitude as are the farmers and the working man. To this end we should:

(1) Establish an Interstate Trade Commission with substantially the powers suggested by me in paragraph third of my article in Harper's of November 8, entitled, "A Solution of the Trust Problem." [1]

(2) We should differentiate clearly capitalistic industrial monopolies from those relations between competitors in industry which are really a regulation of competition. Capitalistic monopolies have been fully investigated and we know how to deal with them. But we have no comprehensive detailed information concerning the character and effect of these trade agreements between competitors; and in the absence of such data we cannot deal with them intelligently. To obtain such information an investigation should be undertaken, and meanwhile those who supply the necessary data should be protected against criminal prosecution, as set forth in paragraph fourth of my article of November 8.

(3) We should undertake to aid commerce and industry by means similar to those now employed in aid of agriculture. This aid should be both wide in scope and intensive in character. We should establish industrial experiment stations and other bureaus for research and for the dissemination of education in industry. By this means only can the smaller manufacturers and others secure equality of opportunity in business. We shall erect a great bulwark against the trusts when we thus offer to the small business man what now is procurable only by the great industrial concerns through their research laboratories and bureaus of information. To a very limited extent the Government is already doing this work in the Bureau of Standards.

You may recall that I suggested in 1911 the establishment of a similar bureau of costs and experiment stations in connection with railroads.[2]

(4) The rule which prohibits a manufacturer, producer or distributor of a trade-marked article engaged in competitive business from fixing the price by which his article shall be sold to the consumer tends to discourage competition and should be abrogated. The reasons are discussed in my article in Harper's of November 15 on "Price Maintenance, Competition that Kills."[3]

The policy outlined above would not only remove paralyzing apprehension among business men. It would directly stimulate new business. It would give assurance that the administration appreciates the efforts and the needs of those engaged in industry.

Second: These constructive measures will not, however, be effective unless the policy of New Freedom is carried out by removing the obstacles to business now existing. This involves:

(1) Supplementing the Sherman Law by provisions which will:

(a) Make it easy of application and,

(b) Make its judicial enforcement effective.

The most important of the necessary legislation is suggested in paragraphs first and second of my article in Harper's of November 8, "A Solution of the Trust Problem."

(2) Abolishing interlocking directorates and other conflicting relations by which men are interested on both sides of the transaction, as set forth in my article in Harper's of December 4, "Endless Chain," and December 13, "Serve One Master Only."

(3) Supplementing the interstate commerce law and other statutes by provisions which will:

(a) Confine railroads to their own transportation business.

(b) Abolish the terminal allowance and service abuses.

(c) Make the commodity clause effective, and not only prevent railroads from being interested in industries, but also industries from controlling railroads.

In other words, embody in legislation largely the recommendations made by you in the report on the Harriman merger and, more recently, in the Commission's opinion on the New Haven investigation.[4]

There are certain other desirable provisions designed to prevent discrimination in favor of the powerful industrial concerns which it seems unnecessary to discuss now.

Third: In my opinion the enactment of laws of this character is not only essential to carrying out the policy of New Freedom, but is politically necessary to satisfy the demands of the very large number of progressive Democrats and the near Democrats, who are already beginning to express some doubt whether the administration will have the courage (in view of indicated business depression), to carry out the policy which it has hitherto declared. The depression can not be ended or lessened by any course which the administration may take. Neither the tariff act nor the currency bill have materially contributed to it.[5] Nor will it be appreciably augmented by the administration pursuing undeterred its policy of New Freedom. — The fearless course to the wise one.[6]   Most cordially yours,

1. This article, referred to repeatedly in this letter, was essentially a repetition of LDB's campaign memorandum to Wilson. See LDB to Woodrow Wilson, 30 September 1912.

2. See LDB to Rudolph G. Leeds, 9 November 1910, and to Lane, 18 November 1912.

3. See LDB to Norman Hapgood, 7 July 1913, n. 1.

4. See LDB to Robert M. LaFollette, 9 July 1913, n. 5.

5. Wilson's message to Congress included many of the measures suggested by LDB in this letter. See LDB to Alfred Brandeis, 23 January 1914.

6. Probably LDB meant to write "The fearless course is the wise one."

To Alice Goldmark Brandeis

December 15, 1913 Washington, D.C. [EBR]

DEAREST: Have been all day in my sunny room (& a delightful day it is) working over some interesting papers. I have much to tell you about yesterday's interviews first with J.R[andolph]. Coolidge, then with [Thomas R.] Lamont, & then with Gregory after his & the Atty General's seance with Howard Elliott. Indeed there is too much to tell for a letter & some of it had better not be written.

Just as I supposed the day's work was done, Frank Scott blew in with an hour's tale on C.R.C. affairs. (I told him of Prince Forzell).

Mrs. J. Borden Harriman wanted me to dine with her & the Willard Straights[1] (on whom she seems to have developed a mash)—but I missed both that & other joys; but did get about 10 miles in the open.   Lovingly,

1. Willard Dickerman Straight (1880–1918) married Dorothy Whitney, and then had been the Morgan firm's representative in the Far East. A friend of Theodore Roosevelt's, he too was influenced by Herbert Croly's *The Promise of American Life* (New York, 1909), and in 1914 the Straights founded *The New Republic* with Croly as the editor. Straight died in the influenza epidemic in France in 1919. See Herbert Croly, *Willard Straight* (New York, 1924).

To Alice Goldmark Brandeis

December 16, 1913 Washington, D.C. [EBR]

DEAREST: It is fine you had such day[s] in Dedham. Only the poor retailers must suffer from this unseasonable weather.

Dined last evening with [Samuel] Untermyer, who came with message from W[illiam]. R[andolph]. Hearst to get me to take up suit to make directors of the New Haven pay for their mismanagement. I declined again with thanks but gave them my blessing and recommended Untermyer to employ LaRue [Brown] and Eastman.[1]

U. is not pleased with the effect of his Springfield speech and says he was misreported.

As I was leaving here at the Willard, ran into Billy Kent, U'Ren[2] & Mark Sullivan, who were distressed over [Francis] Heney allowing himself to be edged out of the Senatorial race by Hiram Johnson. Heney thinks he will run for Governor now. My interlocutors thought he could make it. Kent thinks he might have had Senatorship himself but stood back for Heney.

Watson came in yesterday. Apparently nothing was accomplished in N.Y. I gave him in 5 minutes some bill & law work re railroads which ought to last 5 weeks.   Lovingly,

1. See LDB to Henry L. Stimson, 18 July 1914.

2. William Simon U'Ren (1859–19[?]) was an Oregon attorney and reformer, who had founded and led the Oregon Direct Legislation League, and played active roles in reform struggles over direct primaries, proportional representation, and anti-trust legislation.

To Alice Goldmark Brandeis

December 17, 1913 Washington, D.C. [EBR]

DEAREST: Poor Norman has so many problems that I[t] seems best to breakfas[t] in N.Y. Saturday and take the 10 AM train—so you can get your rest before we drive to Dedham.

Please order good weather.

Met Justice Holmes on street yesterday which resulted in my dining there pleasantly alone. He is at last growing older but Mrs. is a bit younger.

The Torreys asked me for Sunday dinner & hoped to see you after Xmas. I shall dine with Mr. Palfrey this evening & then go at 8³⁰ to talk New Haven with the Atty G[eneral] & [Thomas W.] Gregory.

H[erman] LaRue [Brown] is to lunch with me today; & Miss Grady advises that Elmer Bliss is to descend upon me later.

It was good D[avid] O[tis] I[ves] go[t] a unanimous endorsement. Hope it will do some good.[1]

Did you see what a fix Prouty got into—talking too much.[2] Howard Elliott had better beware also.[3]

1. The transportation committee of the Boston Chamber of Commerce voted unanimously to recommend Ives to President Wilson to fill the vacancy on the I.C.C. left by Prouty's resignation. The committee announced that it wanted a man who had railroad experience, knew railroad conditions, and came from New England, and that Ives satisfied all of these conditions. For details see Boston *Herald*, 17 December 1913.

2. Prouty, in an address before the Lotus Club of New York City on 13 December, advocated tighter government control of the railroads. His remarks were interpreted as a clue about his attitude toward the requested freight rate advance. Despite a long clarifying statement in which he denied having touched the issue, the *New York Times* editorially condemned his lack of judicial discretion in discussing such matters at all.

3. Elliott, of the New Haven, had also spoken to the Lotus Club. In addition, the night before he had addressed the Railway Business Association. In both speeches he was sharply critical of government interference in railroad affairs. A *New York Times* editorial accused him of sounding like his predecessor, Charles S. Mellen.

To Alice Goldmark Brandeis

December 18, 1913 Washington, D.C. [EBR]

DEAREST: Had 1 ½ hours with McR[eynolds] & [Thomas W.] Gregory last evening. The former is very tired and I think must look back longingly to the days of obscurity. Before that I dined (1 ¼ hours) at the Rublees with our old friend Raymond Stevens of Landoff—the New Hampshire legislator who came down with Bob Bass nearly three years ago. He confirmed what is evident on all sides—the political apprehension resulting from the business depression. Moses Clapp used to be eloquent in prophesying it. The one pervading thought is re-election, even now at the beginning of the first regular session of the Congress.

Bliss wanted to talk Shoe Machinery and Merger. He is a Chamber of Commerce man & I told him my views of the State assisting stockholders.

"Of all the wonders that I yet have heard, the greatest is [sic] that men should fear." [1]   Lovingly,

1. "Of all the wonders that I yet have heard, it seems to me most strange that men should fear. . . ." *Julius Caesar*, II, 2:32.

To Norman Hapgood

December 22, 1913 Boston, Mass. [Brandeis Mss, NMF 64-1]

MY DEAR NORMAN: *First*: I am enclosing you herewith my check to the order of Harper's Weekly for $822, being payment for the 274 yearly subscriptions to Massachusetts libraries.

Will you kindly let me know when I see you tomorrow or the next day the number of libraries in Maine, New Hampshire and Vermont not now subscribers to the Weekly? [1]

Second: I am enclosing you herewith a clipping from today's Boston Journal, containing the sensational resignation of Bruce Wyman of Harvard, on account of his secret connection with the New Haven; also an editorial on that subject, and a clipping from the editorial page summarizing the results of the investigation into these "other expense payments".[2] This subject, it seems to me will be most effective for an editorial bringing out the improper use of railroad money, the influence exercised by large units, and tainted news. I am endeavoring to get the specific portions of the testimony bearing upon the Associated Press, and on that tainted news. I am inclined to think, however, that whatever guilt there is on the part of the Associated Press is the guilt of a subordinate, plus the New Haven Road, and not specifically attributable to the wrong intent of his superiors.[3]   Very cordially yours,

1. See LDB to Norman Hapgood, 28 May 1913, n. 1.

2. Bruce Wyman (1876–1926) was a Harvard-trained lawyer who had taught at the Law School since 1901. After the "other expense" of the New Haven became public (see LDB to the Massachusetts Public Service Commission, 26 September 1913, n. 1), it was learned that Wyman was receiving $10,000 yearly from the railroad to give "scholarly" lectures on current transportation problems. See LDB to Alex G. Barrett, 31 January 1914.

3. In the 10 January 1914 issue, Hapgood noted that the Associated Press on several occasions had served as an agent for reactionary railroad interests, and that propaganda was not distinguished from news.

To William Harrison Ingersoll

December 22, 1913 Boston, Mass. [Brandeis Mss, NMF 59-7]

DEAR MR. INGERSOLL: Your letter of the 17th concerning the question of restraint of trade and restraint of competition presents a subject which could be much discussed, and on which much could be said, if it were a new and open one. As a matter of fact the law of England and America have recognized for centuries the difference between reasonable and unreasonable restraint of trade, and it would not be profitable to attempt at this time to undermine the existing structure.

I expect to return to Washington in a few days.

With best Xmas wishes,   Yours very truly,

To Horace Meyer Kallen

December 22, 1913 Boston, Mass. [Brandeis Mss, Z 3-1]

MY DEAR MR. KALLEN: [1] I have yours of the 20th.

The statement that the organization of the American Palestine Company [2] is complete and its program formulated, is entirely unfounded. Upon taking up the matter with my associates last summer I found that the necessary data to formulate any plan were not at hand. A preliminary report was made by Mr. Jacob DeHaas at the Executive Committee meeting in November, and further investigation of the subject was agreed upon. There is no chance of the final plan being formulated for some time.

I regret that I am leaving Boston again tomorrow, and so shall not be able to see you, but I hope that you will talk this matter over fully with Mr. DeHaas, and submit also a memorandum of your views in writing, so that they may be considered by all of the members of the committee.

The urgent engrossing matters which have taken me to Washington have prevented my giving as much time to the Zionist question as I had wished, and hope later to do. I may say that I have great sympathy with your point of view.

Very cordially yours,

1. Horace Meyer Kallen (b. 1882) has been called by one authority "the outstanding intellectual in the American Zionist movement." A philosopher (who was a pupil and a friend of William James) and a gifted social analyst (most famous for his work on "cultural pluralism"), Kallen was a devoted Zionist. In the controversies within American Zionism, he remained in the LDB faction of the movement. He has written widely on many topics, but for his early views on Zionism, see his *Zionism and World Politics: A Study in History and Social Psychology* (New York, 1921). During these years he taught philosophy at the University of Wisconsin, but in 1919 he would begin his long and distinguished service with the New School in New York.

2. See LDB to Nahum Sokolow, 1 August 1913.

To George Rublee

December 23, 1913 Boston, Mass. [Brandeis Mss, NMF 57-1]

DEAR GEORGE: *First*: You may care to look at the December number of the Harvard Law Review, at "Predatory Price-Cutting as Unfair Trade." [1]

Second: I notice some new Railroad bills have been introduced bearing on our problems. I think it would be well for you to get through Stevens a full set of all the bills before the House Committee.[2]   Yours very truly,

1. Edward S. Rogers, "Predatory Price Cutting as Unfair Trade," 27 *Harvard Law Review* 139 (1913). The article took the view that the law ought to move toward protecting manufacturers of trademarked goods from price cutting by retailers.
2. The index to the *Congressional Record* lists four dozen railroad bills that were introduced during the session.

To Alice Goldmark Brandeis

December 28, 1913 Washington, D.C. [EBR]

DEAREST: Nothing from you today, but Friday's letter tells of your plan of returning Monday to Boston. Bon Voyage.

Have had a quiet day & after a good walk some hours on my papers—then 1 ¼ hours with McReynolds, lunch with [Jesse C.] Adkins, a nap (yesterday it was 1 ½ hours at that—quite equalling you & Do) & now some more papers.

Belle [LaFollette] has just telephoned me to be sure to come to supper this evening as John R. Commons is there. I shall be glad to hear what he will say on the Moyer episode. It looks as if we might have a new trouble there. Cong. McDonald [*sic*] has started for Mich. to look into the situation further. He wants a Congressional enquiry that would offer an opportunity for the Industrial Commission as an alternative; but the Court declared some time ago against further investigations.[1]

Spent last evening in my room alone, after a dinner at the Tea Cup Inn which looks forlorn.

Resisted an invite to lunch at the Hamlins.

Lovingly,

Please ask Josephine to send Senator LaFollette (3320 Ave. of Presidents) copy of the opinion of the Oregon judge on minimum wages.

1. The Moyer "incident" grew out of the long, bitter strike in the copper mines of Calumet, Michigan. After a Christmas Eve tragedy that involved a panic in a workers' meeting—leaving many dead—the Western Federation of Miners's president, Charles H. Moyer, was accosted and "deported" from

the area by a group of "citizens." Congressman William Josiah MacDonald (1873–1946), a one-term Progressive from Michigan, went home to look into the situation himself.

To Alice Goldmark Brandeis

December 30, 1913 Washington, D.C. [EBR]

DEAREST: My yesterday was quiet enough to suit even your taste —three meals and a walk alone, & most of the hours day & evening in my room except for a brief visit at the ICC & on Gregory in the morning & drop in on the Social Insurance Meeting in the afternoon, leaving shortly after the business session began.

Miss [Florence] Kelley was there—after a morning with the the [sic] Industrial Relations Com^tee. which she was hopeless about—and Ann Morgan [1] strode in with her air of dashing royalty; and sonerous [sic] Gompers appeared after 2 days in New York wrestling with Hourwich and then all the small fry— Lee K. Frankel and Fredk. Hoffman of Old Savings Bank Insurance days—with finally James Lowell, Henry Dennison and Prof Doten of Boston to give real respectability.[2] Business began some ¾ hours after called time—& I after encountering [Ralph M.] Easley and Arthur Williams, flew to Potomac Park.

Lovingly,

1. Anne Morgan (1874–1952), the daughter of J. P. Morgan, was active in a large number of social reform and philanthropic movements.

2. Probably James Arnold Lowell (1869–1933), a Boston lawyer and member of the legislature, interested in workmen's compensation and other labor questions. He was later appointed U. S. District Judge for Massachusetts. Henry Sturgis Dennison (1877–1952) was a Massachusetts manufacturer and author of books on industrial problems. He served on a number of federal commissions and committees under several Presidents. Carroll Warren Doten (1871–1942) was a professor of economics at the Massachusetts Institute of Technology, also involved in workers' compensation questions.

To Alice Goldmark Brandeis

January 3, 1914 Washington, D.C. [EBR]

DEAREST: That was a lovely New Years letter.

And I am glad you called on Mrs. Angell. There are not many of the old generation left. Brand Whitlock quoted Mr. [William Dean] Howells yesterday as saying: "All the people I know ar[e] dear [dead]." I met Whitlock, (or rather he met me), as I was leaving the Commission yesterday afternoon and we had a nice walk together in Potomac Park. He is a charming fellow, a real democratic [sic] in feeling, and in manner and bearing the distinguished gentlemen. We must see him in new post as Minister to Belgium. He says he has had to listen daily to my praises from his townsman Ashley,[1] who you will recall has furnished funds for subscriptions of Harpers to the Ohio libraries.

Is J.P.M. Co. directorate withdrawal interesting?[2] Kuhn, Loeb & Co. should follow and will be kicking themselves they didn't lead.

I dined with Watson & after dinner discussed RR with Congressman Sims[3] of the Com^{tee} on Interstate & Foreign Commerce. Mat Hale has written for an appointment to discuss "an important matter" for which he will come to W[ashington] next week. If it's money for the Journal he will have his trouble for his pains.

The Govt. Printing Office is still unable to cope with the demands of our questions. I think University Press could have done as well.

1. H. W. Ashley of Toledo.

2. On 3 January, the first business day of the new year, J. P. Morgan announced that he and his vice-presidents were voluntarily resigning thirty directorships in banking, transportation, and industrial firms. The move was attributed to both the change in public sentiment and a desire to appease the Congress, which was considering harsh controlling legislation.

3. Thetus Willrette Sims (1852–1939) was a Democrat from Tennessee.

To Alfred Brandeis

January 3, 1914 Washington, D.C. [Brandeis Mss, M 4-1]

DEAR AL: G. G. Hull's letter duly rec'd. Please tell him so. Dr. L. exaggerates. I met him twice, but, of course, love him as a brother.

I don't know his project, but whatever it is, I want to divert your funds to another cause for the moment.

I conceived the idea that the best way to help Harper's influence & give it some financial support is to make sure that for a year it is in all the public libraries & to this end to arrange that it be sent to all that were not already subscribers. I provided for all New England & got others to provide for the middle Atlantic states, Ohio, Illinois & the North Western states. I have hopes of covering N.C., Ga. and Fla. I thought you might care to take Ky. I will let you have soon the list of libraries not already subscribers. The cost is $3 per subscription.[1]

When we meet I will tell you of my recent talks with [Thomas W.] Lamont (of J. P. Morgan & Co.) about withdrawal from directors.

1. See LDB to Alfred Brandeis, 11 January 1914.

To Editor, *New York Times Annalist*

January 5, 1914 Boston, Mass. [*Annalist*]

In connection with unemployment, don't fail to discuss the even more important question of regularization of employment. The amount of waste and suffering in times of good business, due to seasonable industries and the jaggedness of employment in even all-year businesses is the most serious blemish on our industrial system. The recognition of this by Ford is the greatest single reason for commending his action.[1] In this connection, credit should be given to William H. McElwain for his pioneering in regularizing his great shoe business.[2]

1. Henry Ford (1863-1947), the eccentric and brilliant car inventor and manufacturer, had recently announced that he would distribute some $10 million of the company's profits among its employees. He also announced the establishment of a minimum wage of a dollar a day, and that he would try to so arrange production schedules that any lay-offs would occur during the harvest season, when it would be easier for the men to secure temporary employment.

2. Immediately below LDB's letter (which appeared in the 26 January issue) there was a brief quote from LDB's article, "Business–A Profession," dealing with the McElwain business.

To Alfred Brandeis

January 11, 1914 Washington, D.C. [Brandeis Mss, M 4-1]

DEAR AL: As I get the Ky list of unsupplied libraries I am reminded of James Speed's bathing experience. The shortness leads me to think you may want to clothe Ky and supply some other Southern states. I am therefore enclosing "unsupplied" list so you make your choice.

Please return the enclosed list after eliminating those you choose and so far as you choose, write Hapgood and send him check to order Harper's Weekly at the rate of $3 per subscription.[1]

Alice is here since Tuesday and expects to remain until Friday. Elizabeth is partly at 6 Otis Place and partly with Mrs. [Elizabeth G.] Evans.

The RR. questions were supplement[ed] by some informal enquiries—one on transit matters.

The New Haven news must interest you.[2] There was marching up the hill with 100,000 men, & coming down with a great many less.[3] Howard Elliott has a hard enough job on his hands for any man. He told me it would take years to get New Haven tracks and road bed into proper condition.[4]

1. See LDB to Alfred Brandeis, 3 January 1914. Alfred had written on the top of this letter: "Ky 12 Libraries. Tenn. 11 Libraries."

2. The New Haven was much in the news in early January. In the first place, on 10 January the Supreme Court declared that the Massachusetts Public Service Commission had acted without proper authority in permitting the new bond issue. In addition, President Elliott had been in Washington for about a week conferring with McReynolds and other government officials in the hopes of avoiding a federal anti-trust suit. For the next phase of the battle, see LDB to Charles M. Cox 5 June 1914, and to Grenville S. MacFarland, 25 June 1914.

3. From the nursery rhyme: "The King of France went up the hill/With 100,000 men/The King of France came down the hill/And ne'er went up again."

4. While he was in Washington, Elliott and LDB met for a discussion on the evening of 6 January. There followed an exchange of letters, Elliott sending LDB information on New Haven bond sales, and LDB thanking Elliott and hoping the two would soon meet again. The relatively sympathetic view of Elliott expressed afterwards comes from the good impression made during the meeting.

To Edgar Addison Bancroft

January 20, 1914 Washington, D.C. [Brandeis Mss NMF 69-1]

MY DEAR MR. BANCROFT: [1] Yours of the 9th has reached me.

I am greatly surprised at the suggestion which you make of the possible interpretation of the passage in my article on Big Men and Little Business.[2] My thought was to say something pleasant; not the opposite. As you suggest, I did not think of the possibility of such an interpretation being put upon it; and, frankly, even now, it seems to me extremely unlikely that other readers should view the matter as you do. But I have never had any doubt about the facts to which you call my attention, and I shall be only too glad, in the reprint of the article, to make some change which will remove the possibility of misunderstanding to which you call attention.[3]   Yours very truly,

1. Edgar Addison Bancroft (1857–1925) was a Chicago lawyer; in addition to representing various railroads, he was the general counsel for International Harvester.

2. The controversial passage read: "The concerns then consolidated as the International Harvester Company with a capital stock of $120,000,000 had been previously capitalized, in the aggregate, at about $10,500,000—strong evidence that in all the preceding years no investment banker had financed them." LDB contended that in the basic industries, investment bankers played a minor role until the industry became immensely profitable. He wrote the passage to show the business ability of Cyrus McCormick and others who pioneered in harvesting machinery. But Bancroft was afraid that "this statement might easily leave the inference that actual values of $10,500,000 were juggled into $120,000,000 of capitalization when the International was formed."

3. The passage was clarified when the article became part of LDB's book; see *Other People's Money*, 139.

To Alice Harriet Grady

January 20, 1914 Washington, D.C. [Brandeis Mss, NMF 63-5]

DEAR MISS GRADY: Mr. Hapgood determined that it was best to give the publication of my money trust articles, in book form, to Stokes.[1] I was sorry for this decision, because I should have preferred to let Norman White have it.

Mr. Hale,[2] of Small, Maynard & Company, called on me on

January 10th. I told him that the money trust matter was wholly in Mr. Hapgood's hands; but I talked with him then also about the publication, in book form, of other articles [of] mine, and in respect to this I feel free to give the book to Small, Maynard & Company, if they want it and are prepared to publish it *at once*. My suggestion to him was substantially as follows:

That the title of the book be "Business—A Profession," and that the book should include the following: (1) Business—A Profession; (2) Competition that Kills; (3) Trusts and Efficiency (In Collier's, September 14, 1912); (4) Trusts and the Export Trade (In Collier's, September 21, 1912); (5) The Solution of the Trust Problem, a Programme (Harper's, November, 1913); (6) The Relation of Employers to Employees (the Typothetae address); (7) Organized Labor and Efficiency; (8) How Boston won 80-cent gas; (9) The Road to Social Efficiency; (Outlook, June 1911); (10) The New Peonage; (11) The New England Transportation Monopoly; (12) The New Haven, an Unregulated Monopoly.

I am inclined to think there might also be inserted the New York Economic Club address on efficiency, which, if I remember right, was reprinted by the La Salle University; an address that I made before the Civic Federation in New York on hours of labor or leisure, and possibly there ought to be included the articles on Life insurance, the abuses and remedy, and the original savings bank article, and some others you may think of.

I wish you would take this matter up at once with Mr. Norman White and Mr. Hale, and let me know what they say.[3]

Cordially,

1. The Frederick A. Stokes company published LDB's articles as *Other People's Money* in 1914.

2. Ralph Tracy Hale (1880–1951) was a member of the editorial staff of the Small, Maynard publishing company of Boston. In 1927, he became president of Hale, Cushman & Flint publishing company.

3. *Business—A Profession* was published by Small, Maynard & Co. in 1914 It consisted of eighteen articles previously published by LDB, and it began with Ernest Poole's article, "Brandeis," from the February 1911 number of the *American Magazine*. The final version includes most of the articles LDB lists in this letter, but not all of them. Moreover, the order which LDB suggests here was radically changed in the finished work. The book was reissued and revised, newer articles being included, by Hale, Cushman & Flint in 1933.

To Horace W. Paine

January 20, 1914 Washington, D.C. [Brandeis Mss, NMF 62-1]

DEAR MR. PAINE: [1] Thank you for yours of yesterday.

Will you kindly let me know, first, how you account for the relatively large sales of the November 1st issue, as compared with the issues of the three preceding weeks? Second, will you please give me the best information as to the sales of each of the issues since November 1st?

I assume that you must have some data from which you could form a fairly definite idea as to what the sales have been for each number since, even if the full returns have not come in, and that you are also able to determine what markets and conditions are relatively favorable or unfavorable.

It is, of course, of the utmost importance to make an intensive study of this subject, by the consideration of localities and with special reference to the contents of the different issues.

I shall be glad if you will write me fully on this subject, with such detail as you are able to give, as I am sure it would aid the owners in considering their problem.[2]   Very truly yours,

1. Horace W. Paine was the treasurer of McClure Publications, publishers of *Harper's Weekly*.
2. Paine replied on 22 January that the reported figures for the 1 November issue were erroneous; instead of sky-rocketing increases in circulation, the total number of copies sold were much closer in line to the other weeks of October and November. *Harper's Weekly* had been selling between fifteen and twenty thousand copies each issue. In order to economize, Paine reported, the magazine was printing up only twenty-four thousand copies each week, as opposed to the optimistic fifty-five thousand of 1 November.

To Alice Goldmark Brandeis

January 21, 1914 Washington, D.C. [EBR]

DEAREST: It was good to have your postal & yr Monday evening letter. You should have had by that time the N.Y. letter mailed at Penn[sylvania]. Station in Watson's presence at 11[50] Sunday night.

The President[']s Trust Message is all right. He says considerable & the rest can be read into it.[1] He really overdoes a bit his *suaviter in modo;* [2] but that balance has its uses & makes it possible for the big interests to swallow his pills somewhat more easily.

It is so warm here that I took my long Potomac Park walk unovercoated—which will please Elizabeth.

Dr. Nathan's [3] Zionist row, explains Mary Boyle.[4]

Dined with Do at the Teacup yesterday & we shall dine somewhere together today possibly at Watsons & then go to the Senator's [5] whom she wants to see.   Lovingly,
I finished up Fels [6] & Stein Bloch for the present today.

1. On 20 January 1914, President Wilson appeared before a joint session of Congress to announce his trust program. Among the concrete suggestions he made, there were some that could be traced directly to LDB's advice and many more that LDB must certainly have greeted with approval. Wilson suggested a prohibition of interlocking directorates in the same terms as LDB had used in his *Harper's* articles. He made a direct assault on the manipulators of "other people's money" by complaining that "the men who have been the directing spirits of the great investment banks have usurped the place which belongs to independent industrial management. . . ." In addition, Wilson demanded tighter Interstate Commerce Commission regulation of railroad security issuse and a separation of production and transportation, a better definition of the anti-trust laws (something LDB had advocated for many years), a federal commission to help trusts comply with the law (one of LDB's original suggestions to Wilson during the campaign of 1912), relief for private litigants against monopolistic business (another old LDB proposition), and the prohibition of holding companies. The text of Wilson's message can be found in the *New York Times*, 21 January 1914; Ray Stannard Baker and William E. Dodd, eds., *The Public Papers of Woodrow Wilson* (New York, 1925–27), I: 81–88; or in the *Congressional Record*, 63rd Cong., 2nd Sess. 51:2:1962–64, 1978–79. See next letter.

2. "Sweetness of manner." Professor Link also described Wilson's address as using "honeyed words." His tone was one of peaceful reconciliation with businessmen, many of whom, the President insisted, recognized the wisdom and the justice of the measures he was urging. He talked about "The atmosphere of accommodation and mutual understanding which we now breathe with so much refreshment. . . . The antagonism between business and government is over." See next letter.

3. Dr. Paul Nathan (1857–1927) was a German-Jewish philanthropist. He had recently issued a pamphlet critical of Zionist activities in Palestine. Their chauvinism and intense nationalist spirit, he charged, imperilled the success of the movement. He accused the Zionists of organizing mob actions similar to the Russian pogroms. American Jews tended to discount his charges, ascribing the tension to a dispute between those who advocated Hebrew and those

who preferred German as the official language of the new technical institute in Haifa.

4. A reference, no doublt, to a private report to the Brandeises of Mary Boyle O'Reilly's recent trip to Palestine. See LDB to Aaron Aaronshon, 1 August 1913.

5. Robert M. LaFollette.

6. Joseph Fels (1854–1914), a soap manufacturer, was a longtime client and friend of LDB's. One of America's leading disciples of Henry George, Fels was a lifelong advocate of applying single-tax methods both in America and in Palestine.

To Alice Goldmark Brandeis

January 21, 1914 Washington, D.C. [EBR]

DEAREST: Do & I dined at the Rublees. George came in at six to talk trust message & walk. Of course the omnipresent Felix [Frankfurter] "occurred" to us on 16ᵗʰ St., and almost the same moment, the almost omnipresent Mrs. J. Borden Harriman who wanted to know about Sunday's performance.

We made a brief stay after R[ublee] dispatched trust talk. Done fixing bills & [Victor] Morawetz letters & proceeded to the Senator's whom Do wanted to see. Found him in better trim, tho with neuritis; but Belle had a bad accident, burning her legs by overturned Alcohol lamp while taking a steam bath or the like.

The Senator was quite delighted with the substance of the President's bill, but questions the RR part. He is agin the I.C.C. passing on securities in any way.[1]

Bob's cousin Marion LaFollette who is in with the financiers quite confirms my view of their present game, i.e. that [with] that fine talk they are trying to lure the lambs and W.W. is trying a bit of Christian Science.

1. See preceding letter.

To Alfred Brandeis

January 23, 1914 Washington, D.C. [Brandeis Mss, M 4-1]

DEAR AL: You are right about the Pres[iden]t's message.[1] He has paved the way for about all I have asked for & some of the provisions specifically are what I got into his mind at my first interview.

Confidentially I think he rather overdid the Era of good feeling. I am convinced that the Wall St. gents are playing a game — want to unload their securities on the men with hoarded money & they have to appear pleased. Doubtless the Pres[iden]t is playing his game a little as well as they & he is a fine player.

I have yours about Transit; hope we can do something with that some day.

Saw Thruston Ballard last week at the Industrial Relations Com[tee].

1. See LDB to Alice Brandeis, 20 January 1914.

To Alice Goldmark Brandeis

January 23, 1914 Washington, D.C. [EBR]

DEAREST: Do [1] got the usual scare (about the Ohio case brief) yesterday. Case may be reached next Thursday instead of April.[2] So brief had to be gotten ready. I invoked Watson's aid and this he did up nicely within the day & it has gone to Boston for the printing.

Do intended to leave at 3 yesterday; but Col. [John J.] Hannan found her at the train and brought her back as Sen. LaFollette wanted her here today to round up folks to get the bill into working [*].

Lunched at Mrs. Harriman's yesterday as I wanted to see Col. House about D[avid] O[tis] I[ves]. (Confidentially I. has a very good chance—don't mention this.) [Edwin A.] Van Valkenburg and Victor Murdock [3] were there also.

Am laboring with my suggestions to Com[missione]r Harlan.

1. "Do" was the family name for Josephine Goldmark.

2. On 24 February 1914, the Supreme Court upheld the Ohio 10–hour law for women, confirming the principle of *Muller* v. *Oregon* (See LDB to Louis B. Wehle, 10 February 1908). The Ohio case, for which LDB was listed as lawyer, was *Hawley* v. *Walker*, 232 U.S. 718 (1914).

3. Victor Murdock (1871–1945) was the progressive congressman from Kansas between 1905 and 1915. He was appointed to the Federal Trade Commission in 1917 and served until resigning in 1925.

To Alice Goldmark Brandeis

January 26, 1914 Washington, D.C.[?] [EBR]

DEAREST: Just arrived. Have yours about this.[1] Think you should ask A[lice]. H. G[rady]. to come in with the articles & her suggestions & consider them together; but I want to be consulted before the matter is closed & the papers and their order agreed upon.

If you will reread [Frederick] Stokes' letter I think you will see that Everybody's Money is to come out at once.[2] It is going thru the press now.

I enclose you letter to the Pres[iden]t.[3]

1. LDB's letter was written by hand on the bottom of a letter from his secretary, Alice Grady. Miss Grady had reported on the progress of plans for compiling the book, *Business—A Profession* (see LDB to Alice H. Grady, 20 January 1914).

2. A reference to LDB's other book eventually entitled *Other People's Money*, about to be published by Frederick Stokes.

3. Unfortunately, there is no trace of this letter either in the Brandeis collection or in the Wilson Mss.

To Alice Goldmark Brandeis

January 29, 1914 Washington, D.C. [EBR]

DEAREST: Charles & Mrs. Crane called me up last evening. The[y] had arrived in the morning and leave tonight for N.Y. & from there West Tuesday.

Charles says the lawyers are still at work getting the papers ready to put the agreement into shape & he seems to expect that it will be done next week.[1]

Shall probably see him for a moment today.

Had a call from George Hewitt Meyers [sic].[2] Madame is trying the rest cure after wrestling with getting into the new house. The mechanics are still torturing them at the rate of 5 to 10 a day. He is very sore on Glavis and the apple farm[3]—so much so that he didn't see Glavis while here.

I was thinking he might do something for Harper's; but don't see any likelihood.

Talked at Common Counsel Club yesterday some more on business legislation. Seated between Sec[retar]y [William Jennings] Bryan & Sec[retar]y Wilson.⁴ You see I am quite a Democratic[*] Besides advising Mrs. J. Borden H[arriman]. & the Industrial Commission.

Hope to see you Sat. A.M.

1. Probably in relation to *Harper's Magazine*, in which Crane was financially interested.

2. George Hewitt Myers (1875–1957) was a financier who was also an authority on textiles and forestry, having served in the Forest Service under Theodore Roosevelt.

3. After the 1911 investigation, Louis Glavis had retired for a brief period to his apple farm in Oregon.

4. William Bauchop Wilson (1862–1934) was a Scotch immigrant and former miner who rose through Congress to become Wilson's Secretary of Labor.

To H. W. Ashley

January 31, 1914 Boston, Mass. [Brandeis Mss, NMF 69-1]

MY DEAR MR. ASHLEY: Returning today to Boston I find your letter of December 29th in regard to Harper's. You ask whether the ten cent price does not prevent its being read by many who should read it. Doubtless more would read it if it was sold at five cents; but no such paper sold at five cents can, under any conceivable circumstances, pay but for the returns from advertising. And the paper which is dependent for its life on advertising cannot be really free; and it is a free organ which Harper's hopes to be. The cost of manufacturing such a paper as Harper's, exclusive of all the editorial services and over-head expense, is between three and four cents. To my mind our cheap papers and periodicals have in them the vice of dependence, either upon definite controlling interests, or the less definite advertising contingent.

Of course, I do not mean that a paper should not accept advertisements, but a paper ought to be built upon a foundation that it can, if it sells enough copies, stand financially independent of its advertisers. A five cent weekly of the Harper type could not exist without dependence either upon advertisers or the "interests" or an "angel". What it needs now is circulation.[1]

Very cordially yours,

1. Ashley had agreed to pay for subscriptions to *Harper's* for Ohio libraries.

To Alexander Galt Barret

January 31, 1914 Boston, Mass. [Brandeis Mss, NMF 1-N-3]

DEAR MR. BARRET: [1] I find your letter of the 2nd upon my return to the city today.

For an accurate account of the Bruce Wyman matter, I think you had better write to Dean Thayer.

The substance is this: Wyman, while Professor, was employed by the New Haven and Boston & Maine at an aggregate salary of $833.00 a month; and his main service appeared to be writing and speaking in favor of the New England transportation monopoly. The fact of his employment was kept secret. The question of whether the New Haven should be allowed to maintain its monopoly was a controverted public question. People naturally supposed they were receiving from Professor Wyman a disinterested judicial opinion from one who purported to be an expert on public service corporations.

Immediately after the circumstances of his retainer were disclosed, his resignation was tendered and immediately accepted.

Cordially yours,

1. Alexander Galt Barret (1870–1931) was a Louisville lawyer and a member of the Harvard Club of Kentucky. He had graduated from Harvard Law School in 1893.

To Horace Bookwalter Drury

January 31, 1914 Boston, Mass. [Brandeis Mss, LtB]

MY DEAR SIR: [1] Replying to yours of the 30th:

Mr. Going's [2] views seem to me substantially correct.

The term "scientific management" was not adopted as synonymous with the Taylor system, but as expressing the fundamental conception of the new movement, to which Mr. Taylor's contribution was of course greater than any other.

The term was adopted as the general consensus at a meeting at Mr. Gantt's apartments, at which Mr. Gilbreth, Mr. J. M. Dodge [3] and others were present. Neither Mr. Taylor nor Mr. Emerson were there. It was in October 1910 when I was about to bring this movement forward in connection with the rate advance case. It seemed to me important that all differences between the various advocates of efficiency should be eliminated, and some term be adopted to express the new idea which was common to them all; and I asked all who were to be witnesses to agree on this subject. Several names, like "Taylor System", "Functional Management", "Shop Management" and "Efficiency" were proposed. It seemed to me that the only term which would properly describe the movement and also appeal to the imagination, was "Scientific Management", and as I recall it all present were ultimately unanimous in the adoption of that term.

It was agreed that in presenting the matter to the Interstate Commerce Commission, the fundamental conception, rather than a particular system, should be presented. Mr. Emerson and Mr. Gantt were both important witnesses, but of course everyone recognized the conspicuous contributions which Mr. Taylor had made to the movement.   Yours very truly,

1. Horace Bookwalter Drury (1888–19[?]) was a graduate student at Columbia University working on his doctoral dissertation. The dissertation, a history of scientific management, was published as *Scientific Management: A History and Criticism* (New York, 1915). Drury used this letter from LDB as a source (see p. 18 of his book).

2. Charles Buxton Going (1863–19[?]) was the author of *Principles of Industrial Engineering* (New York, 1911).

3. James Mapes Dodge (1852–1915) was a Pennsylvania mechanical engineer and a manufacturer of conveying machinery. His scientific management ideas were mentioned in LDB's brief in the first advanced rate hearing.

To Charles Sumner Hamlin

January 31, 1914 Boston, Mass. [Brandeis Mss, NMF 67-2]

MY DEAR HAMLIN: On my desk I find yours of the 5th asking about Moskowitz.

He is a splendid fellow; now president of the Civil Service
Commission of New York; for many years head of the Down
Town Ethical Society, an offshoot of Professor Felix Adler's
Ethical Culture Society.

Remind me to tell you more about him when we next meet.

Yours very truly,

To Roger Benton Hull

January 31, 1914 Boston, Mass. [Brandeis Mss, NMF 48-2]

MY DEAR MR. HULL: [1] Upon my return to the city I find your
letter of January 7th.

I am glad to hear from you and will certainly bear you in mind
as you suggest. I presume you have written Felix Frankfurter,
who has a faculty, rarely equalled, of hearing about "possible
opportunities" for men capable of doing good work.

With best wishes,   Very cordially yours,

1. Roger Benton Hull (1885–1942) had graduated from the Harvard Law
School in 1911, and after a short term in a Boston law office, went to Puerto
Rico as an assistant to the Attorney General. He was later appointed to the
Committee on Franchises and Public Service Corporations in San Juan. He
was anxious to return to America, and requested LDB to keep him in mind
for any possible professional opportunities. After serving as a major during
the war, Hull entered a firm in New York and specialized in railroad and
insurance law.

To Howard White

January 31, 1914 Boston, Mass. [Brandeis Mss, NMF 68-2]

MY DEAR MR. WHITE: Upon my return to the city I find your
letter of January 3rd in regard to the judiciary:

First: I am a strong believer in appointed judiciary such as we
have in Massachusetts.

Second: I am against the recall of judges by vote of the people.
In my opinion they should be merely subject to impeachment, as
in Massachusetts. That is, all judges, high and low, are appointed
by the Governor to serve during good behavior.

Very truly yours,

To Henry Bourne Joy

February 2, 1914 Boston, Mass. [Brandeis Mss, NMF 66-3]

MY DEAR MR. JOY: I have yours of the 28th:

I had thought long and hard on the subject of interlocking directorates. The result of my thought is embodied in the articles in Harper's Weekly beginning November 22nd, which I hope you have had time and patience to read.

I am convinced that, subject to the possible limitations therein stated, the system of interlocking directorates is an inevitable breeder of evil. The fundamental law that no man can serve two masters cannot be safely ignored as a general working rule, however great the merits or virtues of particular individuals or enterprises.

I have also your letter of January 17th with the courteous invitation to address your local Board of Commerce, for which I thank you.

My work at Washington is so engrossing at present that I cannot accept invitations for public speaking elsewhere.

Very cordially yours,

To Joseph Russell Smith

February 2, 1914 Boston, Mass. [Brandeis Mss NMF 62-1]

MY DEAR MR. SMITH: [1] In passing through the city today I find your letter of January 6th.

Many have suggested to me, as you did, that perhaps it might have been better had my articles been published in the Saturday Evening Post or possibly Collier's, in view of their large circulation, than in Harper's Weekly. But I regard Mr. Hapgood as so important a factor in the American advance movement that if I have been of any service in helping Harper's Weekly, as his instrument, I shall feel well content with the decision made.

Since Mr. Hapgood left Collier's I have read it but rarely. I have, however, a high opinion of Mr. Mark Sullivan.

Very truly yours,

1. Joseph Russell Smith (1874–1966) was a professor of economic geography at the University of Pennsylvania. In 1919 he moved to Columbia Uni-

versity and he taught there until 1944. He wrote more than thirty books by the time of his death and was considered a pioneer in the study of the relationship between human societies and their geographic settings.

To Alice Goldmark Brandeis

February 5, 1914 Washington, D.C. [EBR]

DEAREST: Elizabeth's free days and your theatre dissipations make me quite envious. I should be delighted to be off for a few days & collect my thoughts. This business of general guide, counsellor and friend grows a bit wearisome—particularly when friends stop at the Gordon [Hotel]. [George W.] Anderson was here & has left. Mrs. B. H. Meyer[1] longs to call on you, as does Mrs. Adolph Miller[2] who bad [*sic*] me to dine (in vain) for this evening as did Mrs. Thruston Ballard last.

I[nterstate] C[ommerce] C[ommission] affairs are proving intensely interesting.

I must be off to the General Croziers.[3]　　Lovingly,

1. Probably the wife of Balthasar Henry Meyer (1866–1954), a former professor at the University of Wisconsin, who had moved from LaFollette progressivism in that state to service as an economist with the Interstate Commerce Commission, 1910–1939. He was an authority on railroad economics.
2. Probably the wife of Adolph Caspar Miller (1866–1953) another former economics professor (at the University of California) who entered government service. Miller was assistant to the Secretary of the Interior, but he soon began his twenty-two year service on the Federal Reserve Board.
3. General William Crozier (1855–1942) rose through the Indian campaigns to an instructorship first at West Point and then to the Army War College where he served as president. In 1914 he was Chief of Ordnance at the War College and a leading authority on that subject.

To Alfred Brandeis

February 7, 1914 Washington, D.C. [Brandeis Mss, M 4-1]

DEAR AL: Don't believe all you hear about that B & M Chairmanship.[1] There was a suggestion somewhat of that character. I refused to admit or deny or to be communicated with simply to "*tease*" those Boston folks.

I[Interstate] C[ommerce] C[ommission] matters seem to be progressing well, except that we lost out on Ives.[2] I think the rebate indictment did it.

1. Rumors had begun to fly that LDB would be appointed a member of the board of Boston & Maine trustees, perhaps even chairman of that board. See, for example, *New York Times*, 7 February 1914. See next letter.
2. See LDB to Woodrow Wilson, 10 October 1913.

To George Weston Anderson (Telegram)

February 9, 1914 Washington, D.C. [Brandeis Mss, NMF 1-N-3]

Your telegram received.[1] I deem it clear that in view of my employment as counsel for the Interstate Commerce Commission in the Eastern Advance Rate Case it would be improper for me to accept Boston and Maine trusteeship. Have so advised [Thomas W.] Gregory.[2]

1. Anderson, who had been handling negotiation of the Boston & Maine trustee appointments, had telegraphed: "Apparent agreement on you. Wire suggestions of names and number of desired associates."
2. See next letter.

To George Weston Anderson (Telegram)

February 11, 1914 Washington, D.C. [Brandeis Mss, NMF 1-N-3]

Today's telegram received.[1] I have discussed situation with Gregory, [Jesse C.] Adkins and Prouty. Think they agree with me that it would be improper for me to serve as trustee. Have heard nothing from Governor. Your presence here desirable very soon.[2]

1. Anderson had persisted in urging the Boston & Maine trusteeship upon LDB: "Wire suggestion of your associates at once. Delay embarrassing."
2. See next letter.

To George Weston Anderson (Telegram)

February 13, 1914 Washington, D.C. [Brandeis Mss, NMF 1-N-3]

Letter Received.[1] [Charles P.] Hall excellent. [James L.] Richards or [Joseph B.] Russell would be good if he sold all his New

Haven securities. The others seem to me undesirable. Charles H. Jones would be good as trustee or director. Allen Hollis or Bass should be selected from New Hampshire if Stevens will not serve.[2]

1. Anderson had written lamenting LDB's decision not to accept: "When all the parties recognize that you are acting adversely on the rate question, and yet agree that you are the best available man to go on to this Board of Trustees, I think you would have done better to accept." In addition, Anderson suggested a long list of names which were being considered for directors for the B. & M.

2. Of this list, only Charles P. Hall was chosen as a new director for the railroad.

To Alfred Brandeis

February 22, 1914 Washington, D.C. [Brandeis Mss, M 4-1]

DEAR AL: I have your several letters:

First: I can see Abrams Monday M[ar]ch 2, at the Gordon [Hotel] at 6³⁰ PM.

Second: Transit matters will come up in due time, taking its turn with other free services.

Third: Did I really see your Toledo man in Boston? If so, when? I can't recall—probably a dreadful confession.

The ICC matters are so interesting that I greatly begrudge the time which trust & kindred legislation are taking.

"Zu fragmentarisch ist Welt und Leben."[1]

I long for the days of Ballinger isolation.

Alice is still with me, & will doubtless stay a few days longer. Elizabeth is in Wallingford Conn. with Chris at a St. George school celebration.

You may want to be reminded that Susan's 21st birthday comes Friday.

I guess I am raising up several new crops of disgruntled critics in the I.C.C. field among the big shippers.

1. "The world and life are too much fragmented."

To James Clark McReynolds (Fragment)

February 22, 1914 Washington, D.C. [Brandeis Mss, NMF 66-3]

DEAR MR. MCREYNOLDS: Have been working as you requested on the so-called "Trust Bills" and am handing you herewith my suggestions, although I shall want to work over the details further before I have a talk with you.[1]

First. As to the interlocking directorate bill: The main purpose of this bill is to stop the concentration of money power. The prevention of combination between competitors, the prevention of injury to minority stockholders and the incidental injury to the public in the case of railroad and public service corporations, are of secondary importance. For a general discussion of this subject you may care to look at my article "Serve One Master Only," in Harper's Weekly for December 13th. This concentration is attained (1) through a common directorship between competing concerns (2) through a common directorship between concerns engaged in different lines of business but which do business with one another. The term director is used above as including officer or employee and in certain cases as extending to conflicting financial interests.

In applying the prohibition it is desirable to apply somewhat different rules to banks than to other corporations. For this reason I propose that as to all banks within the Federal reserve system, the prohibitions be confined to banks in cities of more than one hundred thousand inhabitants.

As to other corporations, I suggest that the prohibition extend to all corporations having capital or resources of Five Million Dollars and that there be included among these corporations state banks and trust companies not in the Federal reserve system and life insurance companies so far as they may be held to be engaging in interstate commerce.

As you will see from the bill following, I have endeavored to kill what is ordinarily referred to as "dummy director:"

"A Bill to prohibit certain persons from being or becoming directors, officers or employees of certain banks or corporations and making contracts in which they have conflicting interest.

Section 1. In this act, except as hereinafter otherwise provided or unless the context otherwise requires:

(a) the word "bank" means any national banking association or any bank or trust company organized under state law which has a place of business in a city with a population, according to the latest national census, of more than one hundred thousand inhabitants and which is a member of a reserve bank under the provisions of the act approved December 23, 1913, entitled "An Act Providing for the establishment of reserve banks, etc."

(b) The word "financial concern" means (1) any bank, trust company or banker which has a usual place of business within the United States and which receives deposits subject to check or draft payable on demand, whether such concern is incorporated under the laws of the United States, of a State or of a foreign country or is an unincorporated corporation, firm or individual or (2) any life insurance company which has a usual place of business within the United States which has resources of Five Million Dollars.

(c) The word "corporation," except as used in Section 4, line 1, means any bank or association, whether incorporated or unincorporated, and any firm which has a usual place of business within the United States. The word "corporation" as used in Section 4, line 1, includes among other things, (1) any bank or trust company, whether incorporated under the laws of the United States, of a State or of a foreign country, which is not a member of a reserve bank under the provisions of the act approved December 23, 1913, entitled "An Act Providing for the establishment of reserve banks, etc," and which receives deposits subject to check or draft payable on demand, and (2) any life insurance company which has a usual place of business within the United States.

(d) The word "director", except as used in (   ), means director, officer or employee or a partner or representative of such director, officer or employee.

Section 2. No bank shall have among its directors any person who is at the same time a director or who holds a financial interest, through stock ownership or otherwise, in another financial concern having a usual place of business in the same city or any partner or representative of such person.

Section 3. After December 31, 1915, no bank shall lend any money, or credit to, or, except as hereinafter expressly provided, make any other contract with any of its directors or with any corporation in which any of its directors is also a director or holds a financial interest, through stock ownership or otherwise. The above prohibition shall not apply to contracts for usual banking services which the bank actually performs in the ordinary course of business indiscriminately for all its customers.

Section 4. After December 31, 1915, no corporation or association having a general place of business within the United States which has a capital or resources of Five Million Dollars or more, shall transact any commerce among the states or with foreign nations except upon compliance with the following requirements:

A. It shall not have among its directors any person who is a director or who holds a financial interest, through stock ownership or otherwise, in another corporation which is naturally a competitor doing business in whole or in part in the same line in the same territory.

B. It shall not make any contract, except as hereinafter expressly provided, with any director or with any corporation in which any of its directors is also a director or holds a financial interest, through stock ownership or otherwise. The above prohibition shall not apply to contracts for services as corporate officers or employees or to such contracts as the corporation is bound by law to perform for the public generally or which in the ordinary course of business it actually performs for its customers, without discrimination.

Section 5. Any loan or other contract made by any bank which is prohibited by Section 3 and any contract made by any corporation engaged in interstate commerce contrary to the provisions of Section 4, paragraph B, shall be absolutely void and not voidable merely.

Section 6. Every bank subject to the provisions of Sections 2 and 3 shall, on or before the first day of March, 1917, and on each first day of March thereafter, file with the Comptroller of the Currency a report signed by its president or other chief executive officer and by its treasurer and verified by their oaths and affirmation, covering the year ending the next preceding thirty-first day of December and showing in such form as said Comptroller shall from time to time prescribe:

A. Whether or not any director of said bank was a director of or had any financial interest, by stock ownership or otherwise, in any other financial concern having a usual place of business in said city; and, if so, the facts relating thereto.

B. Whether or not said bank made any loan to or other contract (except as permitted in Section 3) with any director or with any corporation in which any director was financially interested, by stock ownership or otherwise; and, if so, the facts relating thereto.

Section 7. Every corporation or association subject to the provisions of Section 4 shall file with the Interstate Trade Commission on or before the first day of March, 1917, and of each first day of March thereafter, a report signed by its president or other chief executive officer and by its treasurer and verified by their oaths and affirmation, covering the year ending the next preceding December 31st and showing in such form as said Commission shall from time to time prescribe:

A. Whether or not any director of said corporation or association was a director of or had any financial interest, by stock ownership or otherwise, in any other corporation contrary to the provisions of Section 4, paragraph A; and, if so, the facts relating thereto.

B. Whether or not said corporation or association has entered into any contract, except as permitted by Section 4, paragraph B, with any director or with any other corporation in which any of its directors or any of his partners or representatives was also a director or was financially interested by stock ownership or otherwise; and, if so, the facts relating thereto.

Section 8. There should be a provision authorizing the Comptroller of the Currency to enjoin from doing business a bank violating Sections 2 or 3 and empowering the Attorney

General or Trade Commission to enjoin a corporation which violates Section 4 from doing business in interstate commerce.

Section 9. Any person who becomes or acts as director contrary to the provisions of Section 2 or of Section 4, paragraph A, or who knowingly participates in causing a bank or corporation to make a loan or other contract contrary to the provisions of Section 3 or Section 4, paragraph B, shall be deemed guilty of a misdemeanor, and, upon conviction thereof, shall be punished by a fine not exceeding Ten Thousand Dollars or imprisonment not exceeding thirty days, or by both said punishments, in the discretion of the court.

Section 10. Any bank which violates Section 2 of this act and any corporation which violates Section 4, paragraph A, of this act, shall be deemed guilty of a misdemeanor, and, upon conviction thereof, shall be punished by a fine not exceeding One Thousand Dollars for every day such violation continues.

Any bank which violates Section 3 of this act and any corporation which violates Section 4, paragraph B, of this act, shall be deemed guilty of a misdemeanor, and, upon conviction thereof, shall be punishable by a fine not exceeding Ten Thousand Dollars.

Failure or neglect of any corporation to comply with the provisions of Section 6 of this act and failure or neglect of any corporation to comply with the provisions of Section 7 of this act, shall constitute a misdemeanor, and, upon conviction thereof, such bank or corporation shall be subject to a fine of not more than One Thousand Dollars for every day such failure or neglect continues.

Section 11. Any person authorized hereby to verify any report or declaration to be made and filed under this act, who shall verify any such report or declaration knowing the same to be false in any particular, shall be guilty of perjury and shall, upon conviction thereof, be punished by a fine of not more than Ten Thousand Dollars or by imprisonment for not more than one year, or by both such punishments, in the discretion of the court.

Second. As to the bill to supplement the Sherman law:

I.

It seems clear that this law should be supplemented by certain provisions improving the legal machinery or making clear the existence of certain legal powers which the court of chancery probably possesses now but might hesitate to exercise, including,

A.

The provision making the decree in the Government's suit an estoppel enuring to the benefit of all persons, as the President has recommended.

B.

Provisions granting private individuals or a State the right for certain limited purposes to intervene in a Government suit and also the right to bring proceedings in equity to protect their individual interests.

C.

A provision expressly giving the court power, where the market has been monopolized, to insure a supply from the monopoly, of the necessary article until some substitute can be obtained.

D.

A provision expressly giving the court power to make such orders as are essential to an effective disintegration and restoration of competition.

E.

The right to have forfeited a patent used in violation of the Sherman Act.

The provisions carrying out each of the above purposes should be made a part of the Sherman law by way of supplement. That is, the statute enacting them might read "That the act approved July 2, 1890, entitled 'An Act to protect trade and commerce against unlawful restraints and monopoly' is hereby supplemented by adding thereto the following Section. . . ."

A.

For the purpose of "A", above set forth, I suggest the following:

(1) (which is with some change in phraseology the same as the first half of Section 12 in the first of the Clayton Bills)

"That whenever in any suit or proceeding, civil or criminal, brought by or on behalf of the Government under the provisions of this act, a final judgment or decree shall have been rendered to the effect that a defendant in violation of the provisions of this act has entered into a contract, combination, in the form of trust or otherwise, or conspiracy in restraint of trade or commerce among the several states or with foreign nations, or has monopolized or attempted to monopolize or combine with any person or persons to monopolize any part of the trade or commerce among the several states or with foreign nations, such judgment or decree shall, to the full extent to which it would constitute in any proceeding an estoppel between the Government and such defendant, constitute as against such defendant conclusive evidence of the same facts and be conclusive as to the same issues of law, in favor of any other party in any other proceeding brought under or involving the provisions of this act."

(2) There should be a provision allowing injured parties to obtain redress by intervention about as follows:

"That in any civil suit or proceeding brought under the provisions of this act by or on behalf of the United States, in which a judgment or decree, interlocutory or final, has been entered that the defendants or any of them have been guilty of conduct prohibited by Section 1, Section 2, or Section 3 of this act, if it shall appear to the court by intervening petition of any other person that such person claims to have been injured by such conduct, such person shall be admitted as party to the suit to establish such injury, if any, and the damages resulting therefrom; and such person may have judgment and execution therefore or any other relief to the same extent as if an independent suit had been brought under Section 7 of this act. In the course of such proceedings the court may grant orders of attachment, or may appoint a receiver or may take such other proceeding conformable to the usual practice in equity as to insure the satisfaction of any claim presented and the protection of the petitioner's rights. Nothing done under this Section shall be permitted to delay the final disposition of said principle proceeding in all other respects, and nothing contained in this section shall be taken to abridge the right of any person to bring an independent suit as provided under Section 7 of said act; but, if any person proceeds both by intervening petition and by independent suit, the court may order an election."

(3) To prevent the running of the Statute of Limitations against parties awaiting the result of a pending suit, the following:

"That an intervening petition under Section ( ) of this act or an original suit for the same cause under Section 7 of this act, shall not be barred by lapse of time if begun within two years after final decree or judgment entered in a suit brought by or on behalf of the United States establishing such violation by the defendant or defendants of Section 1, Section 2, or Section 3, provided, that in case an appeal is taken such petition or suit shall not be so barred if begun within two years after entry of the order, affirming such decree or judgment, by the Supreme Court of the United States or the entry of a decree or judgment establishing such violation in accordance with the mandate of said Supreme Court."

B.

For the general right of intervention to protect against threatened injury,

(1) "That whenever a suit has been instituted under Section 4 of this act any person who shall be injured or is threatened with injury in his business or property by any other person by reason of anything forbidden or declared to be unlawful by this act and any State of the United States, may at any time intervene in said suit to protect his interests, or, if the intervener be a State, the interests of a citizen of such State, and may, after final decree in said case, petition said court for protection or redress in case of any violation of said decree; and the court shall have power to take such action as may be appropriate in the premises. Nothing done under this section shall be permitted to delay the final disposition of said principal proceeding in any other respect, and nothing contained in this Section shall be taken to abridge the right of any person to bring an independent suit as provided in the following Section; but, if any person proceeds both by intervening petition and by independent suit, the court may order an election."

(2) For the purpose of giving private individuals a right to injunctive relief, Section 13 of the first of the Clayton Bills seems adequate.

C.

To insure continued supply of an article subject to monopoly, a provision substantially in the form of Section 15 of the Lenroot Bill or Section 16 of the LaFollette Bill, namely:

"That whenever after the institution of proceedings in equity under Section 4 of this act, it shall appear to the court in any preliminary hearing that there is reason to believe, or upon final hearing the court shall find, that any contract, combination in the form of trust or otherwise, or conspiracy was entered into, existed, or exists, which was or is in any respect or to any extent in restraint of trade or commerce among the several States or with foreign nations, and that as a result thereof the defendants or any of them have the control of supplying the market with any machine, tool, or other article, whether raw material or manufactured, reasonably required in the manufacture or production of any other article or for general consumption or use, and that no adequate opportunity exists to immediately substitute another article therefor of equal utility, the court shall have power to make such order, by injunction or otherwise, as it may deem necessary, as will secure to purchasers or users of such article full opportunity to continue to acquire or use the same upon payment of a reasonable compensation, to be fixed by the court in such order, until some other adequate substitute can be provided: provided, however, that in so far as at the time of the application for such order such machine, tool, or article is being supplied to any person under any contract the amount of compensation therefor to be paid him under said order shall be that actually payable in accordance with the terms of such contract, unless or until such contract is found or declared to be void or expires."

D.

To make clear the powers of the court on final decision adjudging a combination illegal, the following provision, which is substantially the same as Section 16 of the Lenroot Bill and Section 17 of the LaFollette Bill:

"That whenever in any proceeding under Section 4 of this act any contract, combination or conspiracy has been adjudged illegal under Section 1 or Section 2 of this act, the court before which such proceedings are pending shall have jurisdiction (a) to partition any property owned under any contract or by any combination or pursuant to any conspiracy (and being the subject thereof) mentioned in Section 1 and Section 2 of this act, in severalty among the owners thereof, or groups of owners thereof, and, if the owners include one or more corporations, among the several stockholders thereof or among groups of the several stockholders thereof in proportion to their respective interests;

(b) "If sales of such property are necessary or proper, either to pay encumbrances thereon or to recreate conditions in harmony with the law, to sell such property as a whole or in parcels; and the court may forbid the said owners, and if the said owners include one or more corporations, the stockholders thereof, from purchasing at such sales, and may prescribe the conditions on which any purchase may be made by any person or corporation whatsoever;

(c) "To make such restraining orders or prohibitions as may be necessary or proper to recreate conditions in harmony with the law, including prohibitions of any acts, conduct, methods, or devices tending to create unreasonable restraint of trade;

(d) "To declare void as against the defendants or any of them any contract entered into as a part of the contract, combination or conspiracy found to be in restraint of trade.

"The relief granted in this Section shall be in addition to and not exclusive of other relief permitted by law or by this act."

E.

To provide for the power to declare void a patent used in violation of the Sherman law, the following:

"Any patent which shall be used to restrain or to monopolize or to attempt to monopolize any part of the trade or commerce among the several States or with foreign nations in violation of the provisions of this act, shall be forfeited to the United States and may be condemned by like proceedings as are provided by law for the forfeiture, seizure and condemnation of property imported into the United States contrary to law.

"Whenever in any proceeding brought under Section 4 of this act it shall appear that any patent granted by the United States has been used as a part of any contract, conspiracy or combination to restrain, or to monopolize or to attempt to monopolize any part of the trade or commerce among the several States or with foreign nations in violation of the provisions of this act, the court shall have jurisdiction to declare such patent forfeited upon petition duly filed by the Attorney General in such proceeding; and, when any petition is so filed, the court shall, so far as possible, expedite the hearing thereof if so requested by the Attorney General.

(2) The abuse of patents in this connection is so infrequent that it might be advisable to provide as follows:

"That it shall be a complete defense to any suit for the infringement of any patent that the plaintiff or the real party in interest at the time of the alleged infringement or at the time of the beginning of said suit was engaged in carrying on business in any manner or to any extent in violation of the provisions of this act."

F.

You have already suggested that the Statute of Limitations in criminal proceedings under the Sherman law should be extended to six years.

II.[2]

III.

A potent reason for the ineffectiveness of the Sherman law in the past was a lack of whole-heartedness on the part of the previous administrations in enforcing its provisions. This manifested itself, among other ways, in the fact that, while the Department of Justice was proceeding against certain persons for violating the law, other Departments of the Government were aiding the defendants by purchasing supplies from them. This course was in my opinion most unseemly. It was the function of the Department of Justice to determine whether the defendants were presumably guilty of violating the law. Having so determined, the administration ought not to lend aid and comfort to the supposed lawbreakers unnecessarily.

It is, I understand, the practice in at least some of the European Governments not to accept bids for supplies from persons against whom the Government is proceeding, and this would seem to be a proper course to be pursued here. It is, of course, largely a question of administrative policy; but it might be well to embody it as a provision of law, somewhat as follows:

"That whenever in any suit under Section 4 of this act it shall be alleged that the defendants or any of them have entered into a combination which was or is in restraint of trade, no Department or official of the United States shall unless and until such allegation shall be found on final decree to be unfounded, enter into any contract with any such defendant for the purchase or supply of any article, or purchase from such defendant or any other person any article manufactured by such defendant or any subsidiary or controlled company, association or firm, except so far as required so to do by some existing contract, unless.

"First, the article so manufactured is reasonably necessary for the purposes of the Government and no adequate opportunity exists to substitute another article of equal utility at a reasonable price; and

"Second, the officer authorized to make contracts or purchases of that nature shall, after full investigation and before such contract or purchase is made, have certified in writing to the facts set forth in the preceding paragraph and have filed with or mailed to the Department of Justice and the Interstate Trade Commission copies of such certificate."

Third. As to the trade commission bill.[3]

1. Once Wilson had achieved tariff revision and currency reform, he turned squarely to face the problem of anti-trust legislation. In addition to this "input" from LDB, the administration had to consider a wide variety of bills put in by a number of legislators (see the able discussion in Link, *Wilson: The New Freedom*, ch. 13). After a spring and summer of debate and compromise, including a strenuous and successful campaign by organized labor to exempt labor unions from anti-trust definitions, two key pieces of legislation were passed in early autumn of 1914. On 26 September the Federal

Trade Commission Act became law. It attempted to define and prevent unfair competition in interstate commerce and it replaced the old Bureau of Corporations with a watchdog Federal Trade Commission of five members. On 15 October, a measure even closer to LDB's heart, the Clayton Anti-trust Act, became law. Exempting labor, the act tried to extend the Sherman Act by prohibiting monopolizing price discriminations and interlocking directorates. The Clayton act also provided relief for injured individuals and the possibility of punishing corporation officers for violations. Although LDB's suggestions played an important part in the final form of those enactments, the finished work was the product of the views of a large number of legislators, economists, and presidential advisers. See Nelson B. Gaskill, *The Regulation of Competition* (New York, 1936); and George Rublee, "The Original Plan and Early History of the Federal Trade Commission," *Proceedings of the Academy of Political Science* 11 (January 1926), 114–120.

    2. There is a break in LDB's letter at this point.

    3. The letter ends abruptly at this point.

To Alice Goldmark Brandeis

February 27, 1914 Washington, D.C. [EBR]

DEAREST: *Susan's Birthday*.

Trust you will have a good trip home with Bessie [Evans] & a joyous reunion with Elizabeth.

The Conference with Atty Genl. was not exciting. He is weary & I think almost wishes he were out of the job. New Haven, B & M matters are going none too smoothly & it is by no means clear that both roads won't land in receiverships before the end is reached. I think Winsor is beginning to realize how heavy the load is he was assuming.[1]

The weather is promising again. I am convinced Arctic exploration would be a mistake for me.   Lovingly,

Other People's Money seems pretty stupid now.

    1. Robert Winsor (see LDB to Patrick A. Collins, 28 May 1902) was deeply involved in New Haven financing.

To Alice Harriet Grady

March 7, 1914 Washington, D.C. [Brandeis Mss, NMF 63-5]

AHG: Have written S[mall], M[aynard] & Co "How Boston Solved the Gas Problem" should precede "Life Insurance: Abuses & Remedies." Have returned them that & Savings Bank Ins.[1]

I hope to [be] at the office next Friday & Saturday. *Don't* tell Mr. Beatson.

1. These were the final editorial arrangements of articles for the forthcoming *Business—A Profession.*

To George Rublee (Telegram)

March 14, 1914 Boston, Mass. [Brandeis Mss, NMF 66-3]

Telegram received.[1] Matter must await my return Tuesday.

1. Rublee had telegraphed: "[Henry D.] Clayton wants your interlocking director bill on Monday. If you are willing to let him have it how can I get it."

To Norman Hapgood

March 16, 1914 Boston, Mass. [Brandeis Mss, NMF 62-1]

MY DEAR NORMAN: *First:* This is the quotation from Lord Morley's "Notes on Politics and History", which I could not lay my hand on when I saw you Friday:

"Our fashionable idolatry of great states cannot blind us to the cardinal fact that self government, threatened with death when Protestantism appeared upon the stage, was saved by three small communities, so little in imperialistic scope and ideals as Holland, Switzerland and Scotland." [1]

Second: As carrying forward the "Bankers' Superfluous" thought, you may care to comment on the success of the $4,000,000 Third Avenue Railroad 4s which Whitridge [2] put out successfully last week. I am enclosing you two clippings from the Boston Transcript of the 14th bearing upon this issue, and one of them also mentioning the completion of the Massachusetts sale over the counter.

You will recall that in my article I specifically pointed out that public service corporations might wisely apply directly to their stockholders for financing; and also pointed out the importance of not calling for too much money at a time.[3]

Third: I am returning herewith Hart, Schaffner & Marx's letter and the clippings. After their great strike three years ago, they took up the idea of collective bargaining with their help. In the course of time they adopted our preferential union shop, and a large part of the ideas which were worked out in New York; and in this they were aided partly by Charles H. Winslow, who was making a specific study for the government (U.S. Bureau of Labor, Bulletin #98, 1912) of the New York Protocol.

Hart, Schaffner & Marx's experience has been very successful, and is particularly important in view of the fact that the attitude of both the trade unionists and of the employers towards one another has been far less reasonable in Chicago than in the East.[4]

Fourth: You may care to see A. Mitchell Inness's letter to me of January 21st, which please return, for its reference to the Weekly.[5]   Cordially yours,

1. John Morley, *Notes on Politics and History* (New York, 1914), pp. 47–48. Hapgood used the quote in an editorial, "Imperialism," in the 4 April 1914 issue of *Harper's*.

2. Frederick Wallingford Whitridge (1852–1916) was the president of the Third Avenue Railway Co. and a president or director of a number of other urban transportation corporations.

3. In the 4 April edition, Hapgood noticed both stories in editorials, praising LDB's contribution in the article, "Where the Banker is Superfluous."

4. Also in the 4 April issue, Hapgood editorialized on this matter as well, borrowing LDB's wording for the editorial "Success and Friendliness."

5. See next letter.

To Alfred Mitchell–Inness

March 16, 1914 Boston, Mass. [Brandeis Mss, NMF 69-1]

MY DEAR INNESS: [1] I was very glad to have your letter of January 21st, which I shared with our good friends at the House of Truth.[2]

I do not think there is any objection to your project of compulsory loan,[3] but it seems to me that we are not today in a situation where compulsion need be applied. The loans of states and municipalities, at least in America, will, I think, be readily accepted without the intervention of bankers, if the proper means of education and publicity are applied. We have just had one such example in Massachusetts where the recent loan of $6,325,000 was taken in small amounts in the course of a month, being sold by the State Treasurer direct.

I have been in Washington most of the last four months, pursued by problems of deepest interest. I wish you were there that we might talk them over,—particularly the problems involved in our international relations. My own time is being given mainly to the railroad rate advance case, which has many ramifications.

With most cordial greetings,   Sincerely yours,

1. Alfred Mitchell–Inness (1864–1950) had entered the British diplomatic service in 1890. After assignments in Egypt and Siam, he became Councillor of the British embassy in Washington, where he associated with Frankfurter, Denison, Valentine, Eustace Percy and others (see next note). In 1913 he was sent to Uruguay and served as minister there until his retirement from the diplomatic service in 1919.

2. The House of Truth was the name whimsically given to the bachelors' quarters at 1727 Nineteenth Street, N.W. in Washington. Centering around Felix Frankfurter, Robert G. Valentine and Winfred Denison, the house was frequented by bright young diplomats and intellectuals, and became well-known for its stimulating atmosphere, the men often talking into the morning. Holmes and LDB were frequent guests. Frankfurter wrote "How or why I can't recapture, but almost everybody who was interesting in Washington sooner or later passed through that house. The magnet of the house was exciting talk, and it was exciting because talk was free and provocative, intellectually provocative." See *Felix Frankfurter Reminisces*, ch. 12.

3. Mitchell–Inness had made a suggestion based on his reading LDB's articles in *Harper's*. He believed that one way to avoid exorbitant bankers' commissions on municipal and state bonds would be to "compel" each citizen to purchase a quantity of bonds for which he would receive interest. As long as the quantity assigned each individual was in proportion to his income, it seemed to Mitchell–Inness that no injustice would be done. "I see no more reason why a citizen should not be compelled to assist in the building of a railway, than in lighting the streets or in educating the people, or in any other work of public utility."

To Alfred Brandeis

April 29, 1914 Washington, D.C. [Brandeis Mss, M 4-1]

DEAR AL: It seems to me that you are as taciturn as an Indian. Why haven't you been heard from[?] Suppose you have noticed Advanced Rate arguments are on—mine will come probably tomorrow PM and Friday.[1] But I expect to be busy here now considerably longer—how much longer can't tell yet. Alice & I have thought you ought to be ou[t] here loafing a while.

Charles N[agel] was here last week.

Our united family had some good Easter days together & Alice will probably stay here until May 10th.

1. On 30 April, LDB told the commission that although a general freight rate increase should be resisted, nevertheless it was true that operating revenues in the East were not adequate to the expenditures of the railroads. Steps ought to be taken at once, he said, to alleviate that situation. For LDB's remarks, see *Five Per Cent Case* (1913–14), Sen. Doc. No. 466, 63rd Cong., 2nd Sess., 6: 5233–66. See also, LDB to F. L. Hutchins, 22 October 1913, n. 2.

To Alice Harriet Grady

May 2, 1914 Washington, D.C. [Brandeis Mss, NMF 63-5]

DEAR MISS GRADY: I enclose draft of Small Maynard contract you left with me.[1]

My purpose is to assign to the Mass[achusetts] S[avings] B[ank] I[nsurance] League the proceeds of this contract, so that your League is primarily interested.[2] Therefore I am sending it [to] you to get it into such shape on conferring with Mr. [Norman] White as you & he think proper. Provision for due advertising seems to me the most important consideration.

1. The contract for *Business—A Profession*.
2. Miss Grady had assumed the duties of financial secretary of the league. She later became deputy commissioner in charge of the system.

To E. Louise Malloch

May 13, 1914 Washington, D.C. [Brandeis Mss, NMF 1-N-3]

ELM: Thanks for the RR securities schedule. Continue collection of current data. I will let you know when I want supplemental list sent.

I enclose my income tax notice ($1763.22).[1]

Let me know of any promising bond offering, including Public Service.

1. The Underwood Tariff of 1913 had instituted an income tax, the first since the Civil War. According to Professor Mason, LDB's annual income from his law practice during this time averaged $73,000, and his investments amounted to nearly $2,000,000.

To Alfred Brandeis

May 30, 1914 Washington, D.C. [Brandeis Mss, M 4-1]

My dear Al: We seem to have returned to very primitive conditions when all communications are per messenger by word of mouth. Louis Wehle brought some word of you, and yesterday Com[missione]r Hall [1] introduced me to his Louisville brother who had some vague data. If you don't speed up and let me know something about yourself I may be forced to run down to Kentuck myself and begin an investigation.

I am afraid Dan Willard didn't like my enquiry of yesterday into the CH & D.[2] The financial end puts a terrible strain on their operating men.

Gruesse aus die Familie.[3]

1. Henry Clay Hall (1860–1936) was a Colorado lawyer who served as a commissioner on the Interstate Commerce Commission, 1914–1928.
2. Cincinnati, Hamilton & Dayton Railroad; see LDB to Norman Hapgood, 1 June 1914.
3. "Greetings to the Family."

To George Weston Anderson

June 1, 1914 Boston, Mass. [Brandeis Mss, NMF 1-N-3]

My dear Anderson: I have yours of the 29th enclosing the copy of my letter to Wolcott of May 20, 1909, which I return herewith.[1]

I do not see any reason to doubt the legal correctness of the conclusions set forth in the letter. Of course the embarrassment suggested in the second paragraph beginning on page 5 will regularly present itself, and in case New Hampshire, Maine and Vermont should take a hostile attitude there would undoubtedly be a situation presented which would cloud the title.[2] I have not given this subject any consideration since that time, and I do not know what, if any decision, there may have been rendered by the United States Supreme Court bearing upon the subject since that time.

I do not consider the right of the commonwealth to take over the Boston & Maine stock of any substantial value. I cannot conceive of any conditions arising under which I should be willing to advocate the commonwealth exercising its option to take over the Boston & Maine stock. It could not take that course without practically becoming a guarantor on the existing leases and the outstanding indebtedness of the Boston & Maine. To do that would be acting as fairy godmother to many investors in many states, but it would be doing an act of great injustice to the tax payers of Massachusetts.

No one ought to take over the Boston & Maine without a thorough financial reorganization. The leased line stocks ought to be converted into a preferred stock of the new company. A large part of the existing Boston & Maine debentures ought also to be converted into preferred stock. Unless a reorganization is worked out on such conservative lines, there will be hereafter in the first place a failure to raise enough money to thoroughly rehabilitate the Boston & Maine physically, and in the second place the money which is raised will be purchased at such a high interest rate as to be an undue burden upon the company. We shall simply enter upon a new chapter of railroad errors in New England if an attempt is made to carry forward the Boston & Maine staggering under its present leases and its outstanding debentures.

I had a call yesterday from Howard Elliott and I expressed to him in substance the views stated above, so far as they concern the method of reorganizing the company. He spoke of having just received Expert Miller's report on the condition of the Boston & Maine.[3] I think you ought to see that. I trust that Governor Walsh will overcome his hesitation and send in a message,[4] and that any arguments based upon the desirability of the commonwealth's retaining the control over the stock will not be given much attention. Some of our best-intentioned people who have not given this subject much thought will be playing into the hands of the enemy if they continue to present obstacles. Forcing the withdrawal of Richards was, in my opinion, a grave error.[5]

It is a great satisfaction to feel that you are so closely in touch with the situation.   Very sincerely yours,

1. That letter, printed in Volume II of this collection, gave LDB's views on the rights of the commonwealth of Massachusetts with respect to Boston & Maine stock.

2. LDB had written: "It is undoubtedly true that if each of the states into

which a consolidated corporation extends undertook to exercise all the powers that it possesses, some embarrassing questions of conflict would arise...."

3. Perhaps L. C. Miller, who was serving as president of the New York, Westchester, and Boston Railroad and who, on 7 June, testified on various aspects of New Haven finance.

4. On this very date, Governor Walsh sent a message to the legislature recommending a referendum on the possibility of the state's buying the Ballard shares of the Boston & Maine. The proposal was not acted upon. For the text of the governor's message, see *New York Times*, 2 June 1914.

5. In early May, Governor Walsh put pressure on James L. Richards to resign from the Boston Railroad Holding Company, the corporation which was holding the Ballard stock. Walsh was reported to have felt that Richards was too closely tied to Morgan interests, and suggested, as an alternative to resignation, giving up all of Richards's Boston Elevated stock.

To Norman Hapgood

June 1, 1914 Boston, Mass. [Brandeis Mss, NMF 65-1]

MY DEAR NORMAN: It is quite possible that you may not care to go at all into the following matter, but I am calling it to your attention as you may possibly care to take it up, as it presents a striking example of the power and bad habits of the money trusts. They preach conservatism, and are reckless in financial management. They complain of the public's having a lack of confidence, and almost every important matter which one investigates should convince us that the people have far more confidence than the facts justify.

Read the article in Saturday's and Sunday's Times on the Interstate Commerce hearing concerning the relations of the Baltimore & Ohio and Cincinnati, Hamilton & Dayton. The subject there discussed is part of one of the most dramatic stories in high finance.[1] Frederic Drew Bond wrote on the earlier phases in the October Moody's Magazine an article entitled The Destruction of the Great Central Merger. Look at that, I should think he might write a good story for Harper.

A matter of broad interest brought out on Saturday and on which you may comment is that: The Baltimore & Ohio has been led into an enterprise in which it appears that it has a good chance of losing from thirty to forty-five million dollars, becoming more and more heavily involved from year to year.[2] The precariousness of this enterprise was fully known at least a year ago and doubtless was known a year or two before that; but the annual report of the Baltimore & Ohio to the stockholders does not disclose in any way the existence of this skeleton in the closet; and I myself, who had made a very careful study of the Baltimore & Ohio annual stockholders' reports, was not aware of the situation until recently when it was called to my attention by one who knew the inside. It seems to me that this extraordinary suppression of information amounting to ingenuity and misrepresentation, is a great disgrace to those who have been charged with management; and among them as bankers is Kuhn Loeb & Company, who are represented on the Baltimore & Ohio Board of Directors by Paul Warburg;[3] Speyer & Company, represented on the Board by James Speyer;[4] and the New York City Bank, who are represented on the Board by James Stillman.[5] The Board of Directors contains the names of such other estimable citizens as Norman B. Ream, Robert S. Lovett, and Robert Garrett.[6]

In the second place, in spite of this impending loss, the directors of the Baltimore & Ohio have been going on quietly giving their regular six per cent dividend as if there were no trouble brewing.

In certain ways the evil practices exhibited remind of the New Haven—a suppression of truth, of course, in the interests of the stockholders less they be unduly frightened, and the maintenance of confidence in order to maintain credit. The Baltimore & Ohio recently had occasion to borrow about $35,000,000 which they obtained through Kuhn Loeb & Company.

Your financial editor Atwood[7] is probably familiar with this situation, and if Paul Warburg is available it would be well to see him to ascertain what he can say in justification.

Very sincerely yours,

1. The Interstate Commerce Commission had just turned to an examination of the purchase of the Cincinnati, Hamilton & Dayton by the Baltimore & Ohio in 1909. The suspicion of the Commission had been raised by an Illinois congressman who wrote a letter charging fraudulent practices. It emerged that the Baltimore & Ohio had purchased this small railroad, but that it had also taken close to $100,000,000 in that railroad's indebtedness. The full story, involving J. P. Morgan, Edward H. Harriman and others, involved postponed payment and the shuffling of the road back and forth between giant organizations. As a result of this indebtedness, the plea for a 5 percent

rate increase on the part of the Baltimore & Ohio was more urgent, and, in the view of some, less justifiable.

2. This is a reference to the same purchase of the Cincinnati, Hamilton, & Dayton.

3. Paul Moritz Warburg (1868–1932) was a member of an illustrious family of bankers and philanthropists, deeply involved in high finance and in Zionism. He left Kuhn, Loeb & Co. soon after this letter was sent in order to accept President Wilson's appointment to the Federal Reserve Board.

4. James Speyer (1861–1941) was a powerful New York banker also involved in a wide variety of philanthropic work.

5. James Stillman (1850–1918) had been president of the National City Bank from 1891 to 1909, when he became its chairman of the board. He also had connections in many other corporations.

6. Norman Bruce Ream (1844–1915) was a leading Chicago and New York capitalist; Robert Garrett (1875–1961) was a director of a family banking firm in Baltimore.

7. Albert William Atwood (1879–[?]) wrote a weekly column, "Finance," for *Harper's*. He went on to write dozens of books and articles on financial topics.

To Charles Marshall Cox

June 5, 1914 Boston, Mass. [Brandeis Mss, NMF 1-N-3]

MY DEAR COX: Some time ago you asked me for my suggestions on the New England railroad situation. I am writing you now, because I have heard that several of the Progressive party leaders have expressed hostility toward the agreement reached between the Department of Justice and the New Haven.[1] I hope you are not among these objectors, as the settlement agreed upon seemed to me an eminently wise one and the proposed disposition of the matter the best possible under the circumstances.

First: In securing through decree of court the complete separation of the New Haven Railroad from the Boston & Maine, from the Massachusetts, Rhode Island, Connecticut, and New York trolleys and from some at least of the steamship lines, the New England transportation monopoly will be effectively broken and what is, perhaps, more important the financial concentration involved in that monopoly will be greatly curtailed. Without such financial concentration, the debauch of lawlessness and unwisdom in which Massachusetts indulged for nearly seven years would have been impossible. When once the monopoly is broken and the financial concentration curtailed, the people of Massachusetts will have no serious difficulty in protecting their transportation interests. We had laws enough on the statute books seven years ago to enable this to be done. What we lacked was wisdom and courage to battle against the forces of concentration.

Second: It has, I am told, been urged that the proposed agreement between the Department of Justice and the New Haven fails to protect the interests of Massachusetts in that it "surrenders" the right over the Boston & Maine stock which was secured through the holding company act. The proposed agreement does not involve the relinquishment of any substantial right. Massachusetts will, nevertheless, retain the right of eminent domain, and that right of eminent domain may be exercised not only upon the physical property of the Boston & Maine, but also upon the stock holdings in that company, as the Boston & Maine is a Massachusetts corporation. But the right to take the Boston & Maine stock is itself of no substantial value. Under present conditions Massachusetts could not acquire the Boston & Maine stock without in effect guaranteeing the existing Boston & Maine leases and the outstanding Boston & Maine debentures and, incidentally, giving greatly enhanced value to the outstanding minority Boston & Maine stock. The acquisition by the Commonwealth of the Boston & Maine stock from the holding company would, of course, bring great joy to investors in leased line and Boston & Maine stocks resident in New Hampshire, Maine and Vermont and would give added value to the holdings of the New Haven in leased line stocks. It would likewise prove a great boon to J. P. Morgan & Company, Kidder, Peabody & Company, and many other bankers scattered throughout the Union, who now hold in large part the $27,000,000 of outstanding Boston & Maine notes. But in conferring these great advantages upon investors, Massachusetts would impose a very heavy burden upon its own citizens and taxpayers, and it is hardly thinkable that Massachusetts should be guilty of so great an act of injustice to them.

Third: The Boston & Maine cannot be put into proper condition to serve New England without a complete financial reorganization. Such a reorganization must involve:

1. The cancellation of all leases and the conversion of the stock of such leased lines as become a part of the system into new preferred stock of the Boston & Maine.

2. The conversion into new preferred stock of the Boston & Maine of a part of the outstanding debentures and notes of the Boston & Maine.

3. Probably an assessment on Boston & Maine common stock.

Such a reorganization would, by reducing the fixed charges of the Boston & Maine, effect such a necessary reduction in the fixed charges as would enable it to secure the additions to capital required for its complete physical rehabilitation at a cost consistent with adequate development of the system, and the maintenance of reasonable rates. Without such a scaling of interest charges, the company will inevitably be either hampered in its development through lack of funds or have to pay so heavy for its new money that its financial stability will be imperiled and a temptation developed to charge unreasonably high rates. The conversion of fixed charges into preferred dividend charges will, on the other hand, enable the management to do full justice to leased line stockholders and debenture and note holders. They will, without suffering an arbitrary reduction of their income, be able to receive their fair proportion of what the railroad earns.

Obviously, such a reorganization of the Boston & Maine could be effected by private parties only. The Commonwealth should have no part in it beyond the performance of its general obligation to see that all are treated fairly.

Fourth: While opposing any participation of the Commonwealth at present in the ownership and reorganization of the Boston & Maine, I am not unmindful of possible advantages of public ownership. But if the Boston & Maine is to be owned by the public it seems obvious that ownership by Massachusetts alone would be undesirable, even if otherwise feasible. It would have been better for Massachusetts to undertake to own the Boston & Maine system rather than endure the complete transportation monopoly, which was undermining not only the business but the morale and manhood of New England. But since we are able to break the concentration and monopoly, we ought not to think of incurring heavy financial and political obligations which would be involved in any scheme by which Massachusetts attempted to control alone a railroad system extending into Maine, New Hampshire, Vermont and New York. If the time comes when public ownership of this system seems imperative, it should clearly be ownership by the Federal Government and not by Massachusetts. But, even if ownership by Massachusetts were desirable, that ownership should be acquired not through the purchase of Boston & Maine stock but through purchase of the physical property of the company in Massachusetts. In that way only could the payment of an excessive price be averted.[2]   Very cordially yours,

1. See LDB to Alfred Brandeis, 11 January 1914, n. 2.
2. See LDB to Grenville S. MacFarland, 25 June 1914.

To Albert William Atwood

June 6, 1914 Boston, Mass. [Brandeis Mss, NMF 62-1]

DEAR MR. ATWOOD: I thank you for yours of the 5th. I trust in the article that you write the obligation of directors and bankers to make full disclosure will be brought out. It seems to me that this failure to deal fairly and frankly with stockholders is one of the most serious aspects of present financial management, and one of the causes of growing lack of confidence.[1]

Yours very truly,

1. See LDB to Norman Hapgood, 1 June 1914.

To Alfred Brandeis

June 7, 1914 Washington, D.C. [Brandeis Mss, M 4-1]

DEAR AL: Returned yesterday from Boston after 5 days at home —4 horseback rides, 1 paddle, 3 drives with Alice, 2 motorings to Dedham with Herbert [White], Harvard class day with Elizabeth & Ruth Adler [1] were my chief accomplishments there other than getting oral reports about you

First: from Lee Callahan

Second: from Oscar Findley & Anderson.

On train to N.Y. met Joe Morningstar who gave a glowing account of his affairs—domestic and professional.[2] One son has just graduated at Harvard Law School.[3] One is assistant to the sculptor Borglund [*sic*].[4] One is in some construction engineering business. One at Wesleyan College. The elder daughter married one [*], a Mass. Institute of Technology graduate & has a son, the remaining daughter is about 13 years old.

Joe is doing a sort of combination starch & other specialties business & expert work. Ed Werdenbach retired & is abroad. Joe says they keep up their weekly musicales. Joe says business in general is worse than he has known it. Even in 84, 93, or 1907.

Saw Frank Taussig, 3 daughters, Lucy & Frank Jr. at class day.

1. Ruth Adler was the youngest daughter of Felix Adler and LDB's sister-in-law, Helen Goldmark Adler. She later married Horace L. Friess.

2. Joseph Morningstar (1859–1916) was head of a family gun and drug business, Charles Morningstar & Co. Besides business, he was interested and active in musical circles in New York City. Probably the Brandeis brothers knew Morningstar from their schooldays in Dresden, where Morningstar, too, was educated.

3. Joseph Morningstar Jr. (b. 1890) graduated from the Harvard Law School in 1914 and set up practice in New York City.

4. Gutzon Borglum (1871–1941) was already a celebrated sculptor. He would not begin his most famous work, the carving of Mt. Rushmore, until 1927. See Robert J. Casey and Mary Borglum, *Give the Man Room: The Story of Gutzon Borglum* (Indianapolis, 1952), or Gilbert C. Fite, *Mount Rushmore* (Norman, 1952). Neither book mentions any Morningstar as an assistant to Borglum.

To David Lubin

June 13, 1914 Boston, Mass. [Brandeis Mss, NMF 47-2]

MY DEAR MR. LUBIN: [1] Upon my return to Boston I find your letter of April 14th.

Your work in connection with cooperative rural credits has been much appreciated by me, and I had an opportunity to refer to it in an article published in Harper's Weekly last winter, and which has since been reprinted in a volume entiled "Other People's Money".[2]

During the past winter I have been obliged to confine my work substantially to our urgent railroad problems, and so could not give much time to the consideration of legislation concerning rural credits. I am confident, however, that on both the House and Senate Committee are men of ability and public spirit, and that their minds are open in spite of recommendations already made as embodied in bills which have been reported.

I shall hope to find time to give some attention to the subject after the summer, but I suggest that if you have not already done so, you put yourself directly into communication with Senator Henry F. Hollis and Representative Robert J. Bulkeley.

Very cordially yours,

1. David Lubin (1849-1919) was a merchant who pioneered in the concept of rural credits; he represented America at the International Institute of Agriculture in Rome, from 1905 until his death.

2. See *Other People's Money*, 214.

To M. R. Trauerman

June 13, 1914 Boston, Mass. [Brandeis Mss, NMF 68-1]

MY DEAR SIR: [1] I have your letter of the 9th.

In my opinion your contention is erroneous, and the error arises from the fact that in considering the application of public regulation, you are directing your attention to the consumer instead of to the provider of a service which is in its nature public.

A manufacturing concern,—whether incorporated or unincorporated,—is as much a part of the public as the individual. A manufacturing concern is entitled to protection against unreasonable railroad rates as much as the individual traveler. Why should not the manufacturer be also protected against unreasonable charges for gas and electricity?   Very truly yours,

1. M. R. Trauerman was a Pittsburgh attorney. He had written LDB in order to argue that public service commissions had no right to regulate the prices of energy to manufacturing enterprises—what a factory owner paid for his gas or electric power was merely another of his "raw material" expenses. Commissions could no more determine that price, Trauerman argued, than they could determine the price of any raw material entering into the finished product.

To Robert Marion LaFollette

June 20, 1914 Washington, D.C. [LaFollette Mss]

My dear Bob: [Irvine] Lenroot tells me of the paper-marker's demand for $1500, and I am sending you herewith check for that amount—so that we may have more time to see whether it is possible to get the $12,000 a year fund guaranteed.[1]

Most cordially,

1. In addition to his support of Hapgood's *Harper's*, LDB had also interested himself in the financially ailing *LaFollette's Weekly*. The senator's sudden and unexpected illness in June 1914 had forced the cancellation of $8,000 worth of speaking engagements and his income, never very large, was so precariously low as to endanger the life of the magazine. The $12,000 fund which LDB and others tried to raise never materialized, and in November LaFollette was forced to convert the weekly into a monthly. See LDB to Gilbert E. Roe, 18 September 1914.

To Grenville Stanley MacFarland

June 25, 1914 Washington, D.C. [Brandeis Mss, NMF 1-N-3]

My dear Mr. MacFarland: I am just in receipt of your telegram reading as follows:

"Please give me your opinion both as to legal and practical advantage of the so-called string in the bill reported by the railroad committee carrying out the agreement between railroad and government."

and hasten to reply: [1]

First: As to the "legal advantage". In my opinion no substantial legal advantage would be gained by the Commonwealth through the so-called string over that which it now possesses. As the Boston & Maine is a Massachusetts corporation, the Commonwealth could take not only the company's property but the stock in that company under the power of eminent domain. I expressed my views on the subject fully in a letter addressed to Mr. Wolcott, Chairman of the Committee on Railroads, in May, 1909, while the Railroad Holding Company bill was under consideration and I have seen no reason for modifying the opinion expressed by me in that letter.[2] But aside from the questions especially considered in that letter, there is in my mind no doubt that Massachusetts had at that time ample power to protect the citizens of Massachusetts in respect to control of the Boston & Maine by parties who might be hostile to New England's best interest. It has such power now independently of the control which it exercises over the Railroad Holding Company stock. All that is needed is wisdom and courage to utilize the power possessed; and in the absence of such wisdom and courage all legal provisions are futile. The fact that the most valuable property of the Boston & Maine system is situated in Massachusetts; that it will require from time to time in the future additional legislation to meet the new needs that will arise makes it certain that the Boston & Maine can never be superior to the laws of Massachusetts, whether or not its dependence on the will of the Commonwealth is expressed in general laws or on the certificate of stock.

Second: As to the "practical advantage". I see no practical advantage in attaching the "string" to the Boston & Maine stock and certain rather obvious disadvantages of doing so. What the Boston & Maine needs now primarily after its separation from the New Haven is financial reorganization. To put the road in first-class condition and to supply the additional facilities which northern New England requires considerable money must be raised annually, for a series of years. In order to do this (at least at reasonable rates) the fixed charges of the company must be greatly reduced. This cannot be done without radical changes in the relations of the company to the leased lines and to its own debenture bondholders. Fixed charges must be converted into charges contingent upon their being earned. Attaching a string to the Boston & Maine stock would in my opinion tend to discourage the accomplishment of this readjustment of securities and the providing of the funds which are required. Indeed there seems great probability that the attaching of the "string" to the stock would completely block the financial reorganization and would result in an early receivership.

The agreement made by the Department of Justice with the New Haven seems to me a wise one—and in every way in the interest of the Commonwealth; and Massachusetts ought not to prevent its being put into effect.[3]   Yours very truly,

1. The Fisher-Ellis bill providing for the separation of the Boston & Maine from the New Haven, contained a provision which LDB had long opposed;

namely, that the state reserved the right to purchase the Boston & Maine stock. Despite LDB's opposition from Washington, the bill was passed and on 8 July signed into law by the governor. The refusal of the New Haven to abide by this law would force another confrontation between the railroad and the Department of Justice in July and August.

2. See LDB to Roger Wolcott, 20 May 1909.

3. See LDB to Alfred Brandeis, 11 January 1914, and to Charles M. Cox, 5 June 1914.

To George Weston Anderson

June 27, 1914 Washington, D.C. [Brandeis Mss, NMF 1-N-3]

MY DEAR ANDERSON: I have yours of the 24th about the Sliding Scale Bill. It seems to me that it would be very unfortunate to have the Sullivan Bill become a law.[1] I am enclosing herewith a letter to Senator Wells which I have written in pursuance of Richards' suggestion, and am sending it to you with the request that you mail the same to Wells, provided you approve of it. We certainly ought to kill the Sullivan Bill. Possibly you are not in a position to do much effective work in this matter, but Eastman ought to be able to gather some of the Public Franchise League fragments sufficient to accomplish this result.

Yours very truly,

1. House Bill 1674, the so-called Sullivan Bill, would have effectively abolished the "sliding scale" mechanism which had been so laboriously constructed in 1906. The bill proposed 70¢ gas and its backers argued that the sliding scale was not a "contract" which was legally binding upon the state. To the members of the old Public Franchise League, in Anderson's words, "it is manifest that the whole system of dealing with the regulation of public utilities will break down unless substantial good faith is exercised by the state." Anderson reported that James L. Richards, president of the gas company, "is a good deal disturbed and somewhat irritated at the prospect of the Legislature's cutting loose from the arrangement." For LDB's detailed views on the Sullivan Bill, see his letter of this date to Henry G. Wells, and to Editor, *Boston American*, 17 April 1915.

To George Weston Anderson

June 27, 1914 Washington, D.C. [Brandeis Mss, NMF 1-N-3]

MY DEAR ANDERSON: I have yours of the 24th about the "String" bill.[1] After you wrote the letter Gregory talked with me after his talk with you over the telephone on that day, and he has doubt-less also seen the letter which I wrote to McFarland [*sic*] in response to his telephone message and telegram a day or two later. If it were not for the follies committed by the people of Massa-chusetts in the past in connection with its railroad legislation, I should not suppose it possible to prevent the agreement made by the Department of Justice with the New Haven going into effect.

Yours very truly,

1. See LDB to Grenville S. MacFarland, 25 June 1914.

To Charles Marshall Cox

June 27, 1914 Washington, D.C. [Brandeis Mss, NMF 1-N-3]

MY DEAR COX: I thank you for yours of the 25th advising me of the course which you and other progressives plan to take with respect to the New Haven legislation.[1] In my opinion the course is an extremely unwise one. The arrangement made between the Department of Justice and the New Haven is the best possible solution of a difficult situation.   Very cordially yours,

1. Cox had written to inform LDB that the Massachusetts progressives would make an attempt for state ownership of the Boston & Maine, but when that failed, as Cox was certain that it would, they would fall in behind the Fisher-Ellis "string" bill (see LDB to Grenville S. MacFarland, 25 June 1914).

To James Lorin Richards

June 27, 1914 Washington, D.C. [Brandeis Mss, NMF 16-4]

MY DEAR MR. RICHARDS: I was very sorry to learn from yours of the 24th of the passage to a second reading of the Sullivan Gas Bill. I agree with you that it will be very unfortunate to have this bill passed, and I have written Senator Wells as per enclosed copy, and sent the letter to Mr. Anderson with the request that he mail it to Senator Wells if he approves of it.[1]

Yours very truly,

1. See next letter.

To Henry Gordon Wells

June 27, 1914 Washington, D.C. [Brandeis Mss, NMF 16-4]

MY DEAR SIR: [1] I notice that on June 23rd the House, by vote of 107 to 102, passed to a second reading of the bill proposed by Mr. Sullivan [2] entitled "To Promote the Reduction of the Price of Gas in the City of Boston and Its Vicinity." I do not know what action may have been taken on this bill since that time, but the proposed legislation seems to me so unwise that I venture to call the matter specifically to your attention.

The Sliding Scale Gas Act of 1906 is probably the most successful piece of progressive legislation which has been enacted in Massachusetts within a decade. It gave to Boston much cheaper gas than it has ever had before. What is perhaps more important, it assured for us an exceptionally honest and efficient management of the Gas Company. The success of this measure has attracted widespread attention through the country, as presenting a plan of private ownership which was just alike to the public and the investor. As long as the public is supplied with gas by private companies is it important that those who own and manage these companies should be permitted to conduct the enterprise under conditions which in ordinary business have proved a sufficient incentive to attract men of large ability and to insure for them their utmost effort for its advancement. These essential conditions are:

(a) The right to enjoy a fair share of the fruits of successful effort.

(b) The opportunity of devoting one's whole efforts to developing the business.

(c) The probability of pursuing for a reasonable time without interruption such business policies as may be adopted.

The Public Franchise League believed that the Sliding Scale system supplied in large measure these conditions essential to the successful conduct of this public service—conditions which are in no respect inconsistent with the restrictions demanded for a proper protection of the public interests. The expectations of those who were particularly active in securing this legislation have been fully realized. Gas properties which throughout the greater part of the preceding twenty years had been the subject of financial and political scandal, developing ultimately bitter hostility on the part of the people, have been conducted since the enactment of that law in a manner so honorable as to deserve and to secure the highest public commendation.

Mr. Sullivan's bill proposes to imperil this highly satisfactory condition. It undertakes arbitrarily to reduce to 70 cents per 100 cubic feet the cost of gas in Boston after June 30, 1916. What justification can there be for such arbitrary action by the Legislature, in view of the provision carefully inserted in the Sliding Scale Act by which it is provided that after the expiration of ten years (that is after June 30, 1916), the Gas and Electric Light Companies may, upon petition, "lower or raise the standard price per thousand cubic feet to such extent as may be justly required by reason of greater or less burdens which may be imposed upon the company by reason of improved methods in the art of manufacture, by reason of changes in the price of materials and labor, or by reason of changes in other conditions affecting the general cost of manufacture or distribution of gas."

This bill undertakes to determine what the price shall be after two years from the present time. Besides many other considerations it is obviously impossible to determine now what will be a just price two years hence. It may be that the cost of manufacturing and distributing gas may rise within the next two years, or it may be that it will fall. Is there any reason why the Legislature should determine now, in view of such uncertainty, what the price shall be at that remote period? If the Legislature sees fit to take from our Board of Gas and Electric Light Commission the power to determine upon due investigation what the price should justly be, there can certainly be no reason why it should do so now rather than in the year 1916.

But it would be extremely unwise for the Legislature to undertake to fix definitely the price of gas. That is a matter which should be left to the operation of the Sliding Scale Act. The provision quoted above affords the community the full opportunity of protecting itself upon due investigation by a competent Commission in the only manner consistent with justice.

It should be borne in mind that when the standard price of gas was fixed at 90 cents in the Act of 1906, it was done not only with the consent of the gas company, but after a most exhaustive investigation as to the then cost of manufacturing and distributing gas.

It may be worth noting that in the recent period in which the cost of the necessities of life have been so largely increased, the cost of gas to the people of Boston has been substantially decreased; and though a further reduction in the price of gas is desirable, it seems clear that the interests of the people of Massachusetts can only suffer through such action as is proposed by the Sullivan Bill.[3]   Yours very truly,

1. Henry Gordon Wells (1879–1954), after receiving his degree from the Harvard Law School in 1905, entered practice in Boston. He served in the Massachusetts House of Representatives from 1910 to 1912, and in the Senate from 1913 to 1918, the last two years of which he was the powerful and respected president of that body. He later moved to New Hampshire, served in the legislature there also, and was ultimately named to the New Hampshire Public Utilities Commission.

2. Lewis R. Sullivan (1874–1928), a grocer in Dorchester, was that town's state representative from 1913 to 1917, and later a member of the Governor's Council.

3. The bill was defeated on the third reading on 30 June, by a vote of 93–106. Sullivan, however, re-introduced the bill again the following year; see LDB to Editor, *Boston American*, 17 April 1915.

To Alfred Brandeis

July 5, 1914 Washington, D.C. [Brandeis Mss, M 4-1]

DEAR AL: The Mrs. Avery whose letter appears in the July 4th Harpers is Mrs. B.F. Avery. Is she one of the Louisville family? [1]

I saw Colston of the L[ouisville] & N[ashville] at the I[nterstate] C[ommerce] C[ommission] the other day.[2] Said he hadn't seen you for 6 weeks, but that then you were looking thin.

Don't you think you had better arrange to spend August in South Yarmouth? I guarantee you as much loafing as you want & will furnish you a conveyance to W. Yarmouth to see your good friend Capt. Baker.

Am hoping to get away from here in about a fortnight.

1. Mrs. Susan Lake Avery, an elderly resident of Wyoming, New York (and probably not related to the Louisville plow manufacturing family), had written to *Harper's* praising LDB's articles and book, *Other People's Money*, which she was circulating among her friends and neighbors. She noted that no other civilized nation would put up with such horrid conditions, and hoped that if LDB were ever in upstate New York he would drop in so they

could discuss banking problems. "An Old Lady's Views," *Harper's Weekly*, 58 (4 July 1915): 3.

2. William Ainslie Colston (1873–1934) was a Louisville lawyer who worked his way up to general solicitor for the Louisville & Nashville Railroad. In the 1920s he joined the New York Central system in Cleveland.

To J. W. Beatson

July 6, 1914 Washington, D.C. [Brandeis Mss, NMF 56-3]

MY DEAR MR. BEATSON: I am so nearly innocent of participation in the preparation of the preliminary report on "Efficiency in the Administration of Justice", which you sent me, that the demands of modesty will not be violated by declaring it excellent.[1]

There is nothing which, it seems to me, should be changed in this preliminary report. There are two points on which I think we may hear criticism:

First: Our discussion of the evils incident to the elective judiciary omits reference to the evils incident to the Federal appointive judiciary, which in some of the western and southern states has been, I think, the main cause of the demand for recall of judges in the judicial decisions.

Second: The suggestion as to the advisability of eliminating jury trials in commercial cases, seems to me of doubtful wisdom.

There are a few other matters as to which I may have suggestions to make, but in respect to all I feel that the matter can well await the preparation of the final report, in connection with which I hope to be a little more active.   Yours very truly,

1. The report, a product of the National Economic League, was the work of a committee of two hundred, with LDB as a marginal member. Much of the writing was done by Roscoe Pound. It was being distributed for final revision prior to submission to the National Council of the League for final approval.

To Katharine Buell

July 6, 1914 Washington, D.C. [Brandeis Mss, NMF 62-1]

DEAR MISS BUELL: [1] I am enclosing a leaflet entitled "Some Suggestions for the Owners of Railway Securities and Railway

Officials", containing communications from Mr. F.A. Delano. Mr. Delano was for many years president of the Wabash Railroad and is now president of the Chicago, Indianapolis & Louisville. He is a thoroughly trained railroad man, high minded and right minded. At present he is also a member of the United States Industrial Relations Committee.

The suggestions made by Mr. Delano, that the railroad men should undertake to supplement the work of the commissions by an association of their own number, which makes them in a sense their brothers' keepers, seems to me eminently wise and a course which should have long ago been pursued. To my mind the fact that no railroad man throughout the country and no banker throughout the country undertook, publicly, to denounce the New Haven's reckless and lawless methods when so many of them must have been thoroughly cognizant of the fact, is the strongest indictment against bankers and railroad men. It will be a long time before bankers or railroad men can recover from the evil repute into which the New Haven action and their supine silence has placed them, but Mr. Delano's intelligent and high-minded suggestions ought to have hearty support and I hope you will write an editorial on the subject.[2]   Yours very truly,

1. Miss Katharine Buell was an editorial assistant and occasional writer for *Harper's*.

2. An editorial, "Their Brother's Keeper," following LDB's wording closely, appeared in the 1 August edition of *Harper's*.

To James Lorin Richards

July 9, 1914 Washington, D.C. [Brandeis Mss, NMF 1-N-3]

DEAR MR. RICHARDS: I opposed the legislature's attaching the "string" to the railroad bill both because it was unjust to the New Haven, in view of the agreement reached by it with the Department of Justice, and because it was unwise from the point of view of the people. But the legislature having passed the act with the string attached, we must deal with the situation as it exists.

In my opinion, it would be very unwise for the New Haven to refuse to accept the act on that account.[1] New Haven stockholders might conceivably lose some millions in the market value of Boston & Maine shares through the attachment of the string, although the effect of that provision upon market value is by no means clear, but the loss to New Haven stockholders through the system's being plunged into dissolution litigation would be much greater and such litigation or the acceptance of the act appear to be the only alternatives.

Litigation resulting in receivership might ultimately be the best thing for New England, however great the suffering of individuals, but for New Haven stockholders there would appear to be only loss in litigation, no matter what the outcome of that litigation might be in respect to the precise issue involved. Litigation would necessarily occupy years, it would prevent the management from deciding definitely upon the course to be pursued in developing the property and would add greatly to the difficulties of financing.

There does not appear to be any question of principle involved so far as the New Haven is concerned, and I have still hope that your board will carefully reconsider the question and reach the conclusion that it is consistent with the interests of that company to accept the act.[2]   Very cordially yours,

1. Upon passage of the Fisher-Ellis "string" bill (see LDB to Grenville S. MacFarland, 25 June 1914), the New Haven announced that it would refuse to comply with its provisions; the railroad contended that enabling the state to purchase the B. & M. stock would prevent the rise of that stock in open trading. The alternative to compliance, of course, was the entrance of the Department of Justice to compel dissolution of the New Haven and Boston & Maine, and Attorney General McReynolds was reported as ready to move in that direction if the railroad maintained its adamant position.

2. See LDB to James L. Richards, 17 July 1914.

To Katharine Buell

July 15, 1914 Washington, D.C. [Brandeis Mss, NMF 62-1]

MY DEAR MISS BUELL: Replying to yours of the 14th. I regret that I am so much driven at this time it will be impossible for me to write the editorial which you suggest.

If you will look at my two articles in "Business—A Profession" entitled "The New England Transportation Monopoly" and "The New Haven—An Unregulated Monopoly", you will find that the

Commission have confirmed all of my statements and prophesies.[1]
Then if you will take my articles in "Other People's Money" entitled "The Failure of Banker Management" and "The Inefficiency
of the Oligarchy" you will find that the Commission adopts practically my diagnosis of the causes of the trouble.

Remedies against similar occurrences are in part to be found in
the proposals for legislation as recommended in what is known as
"The Brandeis Substitute", which are now being considered by
the Senate Committee as an amendment of the Railroad Securities
Bill which passed the House a month or so ago, and is now being
considered by the Senate Committee on interstate commerce.[2]
You will find this substitute referred to in the clipping from the
Christian Science Monitor of July 14 entitled "Senate Action on
New Haven Report Due", which I enclose herewith.[3]

Very truly yours,

1. On 14 July, the Interstate Commerce Commission issued its final report
on the New Haven investigation. It was an unqualified denunciation of the
New Haven management under Charles S. Mellen and a full vindication of
LDB's long battle against the railroad. Calling the whole sordid story "one of
the most glaring instances of maladministration in all the history of American
railroading," the report labelled the Ballard purchase a "fraud" and contended that not only did the railroad's management break the law frequently,
but they were fully aware of the illegality of their acts. The Commission
called for vigorous prosecution of the officials of the railroad. For a full summary of the report see the front page article in *The New York Times*,
14 July 1914. For the articles which LDB refers to in this letter, see LDB to
J. C. B. Smith, 16 January 1908 and LDB to Alfred Brandeis, 8 December
1912.

2. The Rayburn bill would have extended the power of the Interstate
Commerce Commission to the supervision of new issues of railroad securities.
On 19 June LDB appeared before the Senate Committee on Interstate Commerce to argue against the proposal. In the first place, the Commission was
simply too busy already to undertake so burdensome a supervisory role.
Moreover, the Commission lacked sufficient information to be able to judge
such matters wisely. And finally, Commission approval might be taken to be
a kind of government "guarantee" of the soundness of the stock issues. In-
instead, LDB proposed a substitute: the Commission should be empowered to
pass upon the acquisition by the railroads of new lines. LDB's amendment
also made it unlawful for a railroad to issue securities for the purpose of
acquiring interests in enterprises not directly related to its own railroad
system; specifically prohibited were purchases of trolley and steamship lines.
As was the case with so many other reform measures, this one was forgotten
after the outbreak of the war.

3. The 1 August issue of *Harper's* contained three editorials on the New Haven question. The first, entitled "He Told Us So" was a hymn of praise to LDB for having warned about New Haven conditions so long ago: "It is seldom that it can be said of any man, even in his official capacity, that he is always right. Yet we have never known Mr. Brandeis . . . to make a prophecy on economic problems that has not been proved true by subsequent events." The final editorial advocated the "Brandeis substitute."

To James Lorin Richards

July 17, 1914 Washington, D.C. [Brandeis Mss, NMF 1-N-3]

MY DEAR MR. RICHARDS: The morning papers report that the New Haven directors voted unanimously yesterday to adhere to their decision of refusing to accept the Massachusetts Act.[1] The reports leave it uncertain whether some course has been decided upon which might obviate the necessity of a Government suit. I trust that if a suit should become necessary you will have retired from the Board before the suit commences.

I do not think you can afford, in justice to yourself, to remain in a position which would necessitate your being joined as a defendant in a Government suit, and I am sure that the community cannot afford to have you there. You are one of the few men connected with big business in New England in a position to be of great public service, and your usefulness would be much impaired by the mere fact of your being joined as defendant in such a suit. Such a suit is necessarily based, among other things, upon the assertion of participation by the defendants in a present violation of the law. The inference would be drawn generally by the community that you approved of the present course and you would be held, among other things, responsible, in such opinion, for the attendant losses to stockholders and the community. In view of the opinion which you actually hold as to the course which the company should pursue, it seems clear that no obligation of loyalty to the company, on your part, would require putting yourself in such a position.

I trust, therefore, that you will not hesitate to retire from the Board and make known to Mr. Gregory the fact that you have done so in ample time before the Government suit shall have been commenced.[2] Very cordially yours,

1. See LDB to James L. Richards, 9 July 1914.

2. Richards chose not to follow LDB's advice in this instance, and on 23 July, when the Department of Justice filed suit, at the direction of President Wilson himself, Richards was named as one of the defendants. See *New York Times,* 24 July 1914 for the full list of corporations and individuals charged under the federal suit.

To Henry Lewis Stimson

July 18, 1914 Washington, D.C. [Brandeis Mss, NMF 1-N-3]

MY DEAR MR. STIMSON: Your letter of the 14th reaches me here. It is quite uncertain when I shall again have a day in New York, but whenever it is I hope to give myself the pleasure of calling on you.

Answering your specific inquiry: [1]

First: I have long been of the opinion that the directors of the New Haven are personally liable civilly for a large part of the losses which have been incurred by the stockholders, and which are somewhat accurately reflected in the present market value of the stock. The ground of this liability seems to me rest upon

1. The authorizing or approving of transactions which were illegal.

2. The authorizing or approving the payment of dividends that were not earned.

3. Neglect of duties of director which resulted in great waste of corporate funds, aside from 1 and 2.

It would seem that the liability of the directors was far more clear than in most, at least, of the adjudicated cases where directors have been held liable, among other reasons because in a formal pamphlet which I prepared and published on the condition of the New Haven in 1907, the wrong doing and weaknesses of the company were fully pointed out and no action was taken by the directors to protect the stockholders. On the contrary the directors persisted in their fatal policy of illegal expansion and the paying of dividends in spite of their losses.

Second: I do not know whether there is any likelihood of the company undertaking itself to enforce this liability of directors. It seems probable that no such action will be taken on the part of the company so long as the Board of Directors is composed, as it still is, largely of those who participated in the wrongful acts, or their friends. I do not know of any existing attempts on behalf of stockholders to enforce this liability to which I should at present recommend your clients to ally themselves.

Third: I hope your clients will conclude that it is wise for them to retain you to represent their interests in this respect. It needs a man who combines your capacity and your character to do full justice to the case, in the interest both of the stockholders and the public. If you should take up the case, it would probably be desirable for you to secure as an assistant in it either H. Larue [*sic*] Brown, of Boston, or Jos. B. Eastman, of Boston, both young men thoroughly familiar with the New Haven situation. Brown was Special Counsel of the Public Service Commission last year in the New Haven's proceeding for authorization of the $67,000,000 bond issue. Eastman is not a member of the bar, although he has studied law for some time and for a number of years was secretary of our Public Franchise League. He spent about a year on the financial aspects of the New Haven case, acting as Mr. Ives' and my assistant, in connection with the investigation of the New England Railroad by the Interstate Commerce Commission, which resulted in the opinion delivered by Commissioner Prouty in June, 1913. It is possible that Mr. Eastman may not be able to assist you in view of the fact that, as I understand, he has been consulted by some other counsel acting for stockholders.[2]

Very cordially yours,

1. Stimson wrote to say that his law firm was managing the affairs of many individuals who had large quantities of New Haven stock. He wondered if there was any likelihood of stockholders recovering damages due to mismanagement of the company and, if so, who would be the best men to contact about the situation. See LDB to Alice G. Brandeis, 16 December 1913.

2. Eventually a suit was brought against the New Haven to recover $150 million. The contending parties ultimately settled on a compromise figure of $2.5 million, about half of which went to lawyers. An attempt to convict eleven directors of criminal conspiracy failed in 1916 when six were found not guilty and the jury could not agree on the other five. See Mason and Staples, *Fall of a Railroad Empire*, 192.

To Roscoe Pound

July 20, 1914 Washington, D.C. [Pound Mss]

MY DEAR MR. POUND: I have your letter of the 17th, and am glad to know that you have succeeded in inducing President Lowell [1]

to invite Professor Ehrlich to lecture before the Lowell Institute.[2]
I should suppose that many of our law schools would be glad to
secure a course of lectures from him, and doubtless you will take
this matter up with [George W.] Kirchway and Bates.[3] You will
hardly find difficulty in securing engagements which would
furnish the additional five hundred dollars; but if you desire, I
am quite ready to underwrite that amount; or, if you prefer it, I
am willing to defray the expenses of a course at the Harvard Law
School to an amount not exceeding five hundred dollars, in case
you and Frankfurter think that this would be a desirable part of
the work which you have undertaken.

Very cordially yours,

I can see no possible impropriety in your writing the President
your opinion of Mack.[4]

1. A. Lawrence Lowell had been appointed president of Harvard in 1909.
2. Eugen Ehrlich (1862–1922) was a well-known German legal philosopher.
For an examination of his approach to the philosophy of law, see Pound's
"Introduction" to Ehrlich's *Fundamental Principles of the Sociology of Law*
(Cambridge, Mass., 1936). Because of the war, Ehrlich never delivered the
Lowell Institute lectures; see LDB to Pound, 10 December 1914.
3. Henry Moore Bates (1869–1949) was dean of the University of Michi-
gan Law School and past president of the Association of American Law
Schools.
4. Pound wanted to write to President Wilson, urging that he appoint
Julian W. Mack to the vacancy on the Supreme Court, but he was uncertain
if this would be a breach of legal ethics. The nomination ultimately went to
James C. McReynolds.

To Charles McCarthy

August 1, 1914 Washington, D.C. [McCarthy Mss]

MY DEAR MCCARTHY: Thanks for the clippings & yours of 30th. I
am sorry the outlook is not more cheerful.[1]

The rate decision came out today & I leave for Massachusetts
for a rest.[2]

With best wishes.   Cordially,

1. McCarthy had enclosed a gloomy assessment of the Wisconsin gubernatorial race shaping up for November. He saw the "reactionaries" as having
the preponderant strength in both parties, and the only hope he saw was the
direct intervention of Wilson behind a progressive.

2. The decision, made 29 July 1914, with two commissioners dissenting, denied a rate increase except in the Central Freight Association territory. The commission followed LDB's argument so closely that many private citizens and public sources assumed that LDB had written the opinion himself. The railroads were not any more willing to accept this second unfavorable decision than they had been willing to accept the first in 1911. They were soon busy raising the issue again, and this time they had a source of unexpected help: the war that broke out in Europe on the very day this letter was written.

To John E. Warren

August 3, 1914 Boston, Mass. [Brandeis Mss, NMF 69-1]

MY DEAR MR. WARREN: As I pass through the city today I find your very kind letter of the 13th, and am glad to know that the views which I have expressed meet with your general approval.

I have deemed my work with and for S.D. Warren & Company a most important part of my education in business, and you among my tutors.

I trust all goes well with you,   Most cordially yours,

To C. A. Whittier

August 7, 1914 South Yarmouth, Mass.
[Brandeis Mss, NMF 68-2]

DEAR MR. WHITTIER: [1] The country and the Democratic party have great need in Congress of such men as Robert J. Bulkeley. Progressive minded and serious, he has the ability to understand the important social and industrial problems which confront us and the courage to grapple with them.

His work on the patent committee and on rural credits has been of high order; and those who are making the fight against the forces of monopoly hope for his continued aid in Congress. [2]
Very truly yours,

1. This letter was solicited by C. A. Whittier of Cleveland, who introduced himself as Congressman Bulkeley's campaign manager. He thought that an endorsement by LDB would be useful in the primary campaign. But the letter was returned a few days later the addressee being unknown, and by then it was too late for the primary.

2. Bulkeley was reelected for one more term in November 1914.

To Thomas Watt Gregory

August 13, 1914 South Yarmouth, Mass.
[Brandeis Mss, NMF 1-N-3]

MY DEAR MR. GREGORY: I write to confirm the conclusions reached at our recent conference.

The provision in the Clayton bill under which findings of violation of the Sherman law in a suit brought by the government creates an estoppel (or prima facie evidence) against defendants in favor of other parties, should be amended so as to permit the Department of Justice to continue its practice of securing future compliance with the law by agreement for consent decrees.

This can be done effectively and safely by providing that the entry of decree etc shall not operate as an estoppel (or as prima facie evidence) if entered into by consent before any evidence is taken in the case.[1]

I hope you will be able to secure such amendment of the pending bill.[2]   Yours very cordially,

1. This change related to the possibility of private citizens' recovering damages on the basis of a government suit under the act. The Justice Department was fearful that the act, without the proposed amendment, would stiffen the resistance of corporations and would prevent the practice of proceeding under decrees to which the company consented.

2. This change was incorporated into the final law as an amendment to Section 5. See 38 *United States Statutes* 731 (1914).

To Thomas Watt Gregory

August 20, 1914 South Yarmouth, Mass.
[Brandeis Mss, NMF 1-N-3]

MY DEAR GREGORY: My heartiest good wishes.[1] I know how reluctant you were to assume office; but it will be a great satisfaction to you that you are at least aiding our noble President in carrying his heavy burdens.   Most cordially,

I trust my duplicate letter of August 13 reached you duly.

1. Upon the appointment of James C. McReynolds to the Supreme Court, Wilson sent Gregory's name to the Senate for Attorney General. The nomination was confirmed by the Senate on 30 August, and Gregory was sworn in 4 September.

To Zionists of America [1]

The war in Europe has brought a crisis upon the Zionist organization. The members of our Actions Comité are scattered.[2] Our Central Bureau at Berlin is crippled. The Federations of England, Germany and Austria are partially or wholly disabled. The Zionists of these countries and of Russia are forced to take thought for themselves alone, and Palestine, which they have hitherto aided in amplest measure, is bereft of their support.

The achievements of a generation are imperilled. The young Jewish Renaissance in the Holy Land, the child of pain and sacrifice, faces death from starvation.

In this unprecedented emergency, the Zionists of America are called upon to take energetic measures, lest Zionist work in Europe and Palestine suffer interruption and irreparable harm. At an Extraordinary Conference of American Zionists held at New York on August 30, 1914, a Provisional Executive Committee for General Zionist Affairs was formed, to act until such time when the Actions Comité shall reassemble.

The Provisional Executive Committee is fortunate to have the co-operation and advice of one member of the Actions Comité, Doctor Schmarya Levin.[3] It has put itself into touch with other members of the Actions Comité and with the Federations here and in all neutral countries. It has inaugurated the work of administration. It has made plans for the maintenance of the institutions of Zionism in Palestine—its schools, its colonizing enterprises, all the manifold social and cultural interests that have been originated and fostered by our movement. It is in communication with our pioneers in the land of the fathers, and they have received the assurance that we shall not fail them in this catastrophe. It has entered into relations with other bodies of Jews, in the hope that a united American Jewish community may be ready to act at the opportune moment.

Fellow Zionists, the work of safeguarding the continuity of our movement is begun. Upon you depends the successful issue. Grave as the Provisional Executive Committee knows its undertaking to be, so grave is your part in its accomplishment. It requires men, it requires money. You must furnish both. You must give of your devotion without reserve, of your means without stint.

For the Jew in America, at peace in a strong, neutral country, these are momentous days pregnant with serious tasks. He will be called upon to raise in large part the relief funds that will be needed to alleviate the distress and repair the losses of the millions of our people who are now groaning under the pitiless exactions of war. He will be called upon to rescue the Jews in Palestine, who have always looked to the Diaspora for sustenance, and who are now overwhelmed by want and anxieties. In these respects we urge you to do your fullest duty as Jews when the proper time is at hand.

But you, Zionists of America, have another, a paramount duty to perform. You have a particular charge devolving upon you, a peculiar treasure to cherish. Your organization, your institutions are looking to you for succor. To safeguard the one and maintain the others will require immediately the sum of One Hundred Thousand Dollars. Without this sum the Provisional Committee cannot discharge the obligations it has assumed. With this sum we may hope to tide our sacred movement over these critical times.

Zionists, the duty of the hour is supreme. Strain every nerve to obtain at once the One Hundred Thousand Dollar fund that is essential to the welfare of our movement. Put the machinery of all your organizations into motion without delay. Let every individual Zionist heed the solemn appeal to render service and bring sacrifices. And who knows but that opportunity may yet be wrested from disaster! Who knows but that our tried people everywhere, hearing the message of Zionism ring above the din and clash of battle, will strive, united with us, for permanent justice, peace, and liberty for the Jewish people in the Jewish land.

1. LDB had become increasingly interested in Zionism since his meeting with Jacob deHaas in August, 1912 (see LDB to Eugene N. Foss, 13 August 1912). The press of other business had prevented him, however, from playing a very active role in Jewish affairs. He made a number of speeches for Zionism and was involved in some minor committee work but was in no way a "leader" of the American movement. In August 1914, while vacationing at South Yarmouth, LDB embarked upon a concerted study of Jewish history and of contemporary Jewish problems. The outbreak of World War I caused immense dislocations in the European Jewish community, disrupting and

scattering the established Zionist leadership, and the war also threatened the fledgling Jewish institutions in Palestine with destruction. On 30 August about 150 American Zionists met in New York City and founded the Provisional Executive Committee for General Zionist Affairs. (For the details of the meeting, see LDB to Chaim Weizmann, 11 October 1914.) At Jacob deHaas's urging, LDB was unanimously elected president. This letter, which was printed in Yiddish and English and sent on various dates to hundreds of individuals, marks the announcement of the Provisional Executive Committee (P.E.C.) and the start of LDB's leadership within the movement; until the end of his life scarcely a day would go by without LDB's giving some attention to Zionist affairs. LDB began the task with a frank admission of his weaknesses: "I have been to a great extent separated from Jews. I am very ignorant of things Jewish." His willingness to learn, however, and his unparalleled administrative skill and relentless energy made him a genuinely vitalizing force in the American Zionist movement. There were approximately 12,000 members in the Zionist movement in 1914; in 1919 there were 176,000. The budget of the American Zionists in 1914 was about $15,000; under LDB's leadership it grew, by 1919, to $3,000,000. The literature is vast, but see Jacob deHaas, *Louis Dembitz Brandeis: A Biographical Sketch with Special Reference to his Contribution to Jewish and Zionist History* (New York, 1929); Yonathan Shapiro, *Leadership of the American Zionist Organization, 1897–1930* (Urbana, Illinois, 1971); Melvin I. Urofsky, "The Progressive as Zionist," in *A Mind of One Piece: Brandeis and American Reform* (New York, 1971); Mason, *Brandeis,* chapter 29, or the article on Brandeis by S. Z. Abramov in *The Encyclopedia of Zionism and Israel* (New York, 1971).

2. The Actions Comité was the supreme advisory and supervisory arm of the congress of the World Zionist Organization.

3. Schmarya Levin (1867–1935) was a Russian-born Jew, active in Zionism even before Herzl. He was forced out of Russia in 1908 because of anti-Czarist pronouncements and settled in Germany. Levin was stranded in the United States by the outbreak of the war and was responsible for calling the meeting which led to the formation of the Provisional Executive Committee. He was in close touch with LDB and American Zionist leadership throughout the war years. A powerful orator, he is credited with converting many people to support for Zionism. His three-volume autobiography has been translated and condensed as *Forward From Exile* (New York, 1967).

To Louis Marshall

August 31, 1914 New York, N.Y. [Marshall Mss]

DEAR SIR: [1] The Provisional Committee for International Zionist Affairs was constituted at a conference of representative Zionists in New York City, on Sunday, August 30, 1914. This committee

is to act on behalf of the International Zionist Organization pending the reconstruction of that organization, which has been dis-
rupted by the present war. The Committee is endeavoring to
maintain and strengthen the Zionist organization and to support
such Palestinian Institutions as have heretofore been supported by
that organization.

The Committee regards it also as its function to emphasize the
importance of Palestine for the Jews of the world in any negotiations that may be entered upon by the Powers before or upon
the conclusion of the war.

That any diplomatic negotiations on behalf of the Jews shall
have due effect, the Committee believes that action should be
taken by a united American Jewry.

To this end, the Committee invites you to cooperate with it in
calling a conference of representatives of all the important Jewish
organizations and groups in the country.[2]

For the Committee,

1. Louis Marshall (1856–1929) was the president of the American Jewish
Committee, which he had helped to found in 1906. By any standard, he was
one of the most important and influential leaders in the American Jewish
community. At first an open anti-Zionist, Marshall moderated his stand but
could never join the movement despite his acquaintance with many of its
leaders. The relations between Marshall and LDB were always formal and
courteous but also strained and somewhat uneasy although both men were
interested in many of the same projects and programs. Marshall played an
important role at the Versailles peace conference and helped to establish
Jewish rights in the newly formed countries of Central and Eastern Europe.
He also took the lead against the counterfeit and anti-Semitic *Protocols of
the Elders of Zion* and eventually secured an apology from Henry Ford for
his part in publishing the hoax in 1927. Besides his Jewish activities, Marshall
worked in the NAACP and was a lawyer in many civil liberties and civil
rights cases. See Morton Rosenstock, *Louis Marshall: Defender of Jewish
Rights* (Detroit, 1965), and Charles Reznikoff, ed., *Louis Marshall: Champion
of Liberty*, 2 vols. (Philadelphia, 1957).

2. The American Jewish Committee had been meeting in New York, and
was therefore able to take up the request immediately. On the same day,
Marshall replied that his committee had already begun to take appropriate
wartime measures not unlike those the Zionists were proposing. Nevertheless,
"This Committee welcomes your co-operation," Marshall wrote, and he suggested a meeting of three officials from each group to work out the details of
cooperation. See LDB to Louis Lipsky, 18 January 1915. Despite this note of
encouragement, the two committees were soon locked in bitter struggle over

the nature of an agency representing all of America's Jews. The Zionists, led by LDB, favored a democratically elected congress, while Marshall and his allies preferred a select committee of the established Jewish leaders. Ultimately, the Zionists won out, and the American Jewish Congress was established in 1918.

To George F. Graham

September 8, 1914 Boston, Mass. [Brandeis Mss, NMF 65-1]

MY DEAR SIR: [1] I am returning herewith as per your instructions, voucher dated September 2, 1914 for $11,500, for legal services rendered in connection with the Five per cent Rate Increase Case signed by me.

Kindly acknowledge receipt.   Yours truly,

1. George F. Graham was the disbursing clerk of the Interstate Commerce Commission.

To Benjamin Perlstein

September 8, 1914 Boston, Mass. [Brandeis Mss, Z 3-2]

MY DEAR MR. PERLSTEIN: [1] Yours of the 6th and 7th received.

First: I note that the meeting is called for Friday the 11th at 10:30. I expect to reach the office on that day about 9:00 o'clock, and it is possible that I may be in New York already on Thursday, in which event I will come to the office at about 9:00 o'clock on Thursday also.

Second: I enclose my check for $1,000 in payment of my subscription to the general fund.[2]

Third: I enclose check for $10.00 to my order from Joseph Levenson, 177 Blackstone Street, Boston, as a contribution to the fund, which I have endorsed.   Yours very truly,

1. Benjamin Perlstein was the administrative secretary of the Provisional Executive Committee for General Zionist Affairs. Never a Zionist of first-rank importance, Perlstein was nevertheless an efficient and hardworking member of the movement. LDB would be in virtually daily contact with Perlstein (sometimes several letters a day passed between them) and in LDB's attempt to introduce efficiency, discipline, and order into the movement, Perlstein was his chief lieutenant.

2. At the meeting establishing the P.E.C., an emergency fund of $100,000 was projected. LDB started the fund with his announcement of a contribution of $1,000 — a total of $12,000 was raised that very day. Prof. Mason reports that LDB's gifts to Jewish charities and Zionism totaled over $600,000 before his death. In addition, his will granted one-half of his estate (after his family had been provided for) to Zionist causes.

To Judah Leon Magnes

September 14, 1914 New York, N.Y. [Magnes Mss]

MY DEAR DR. MAGNES: The Committee to consider the political problems of Zionism, so far as appointed, are yourself as Chairman, Dr. Stephen S. Wise,[1] Prof. Gottheil, Prof. Kallen and Mr. Hurwitz.[2]

I should be glad to have your suggestions as to any other persons whom you may think it desirable to add to the Committee.[3]

Yours very truly,

1. Stephen Samuel Wise (1874-1949) was one of the most influential American Jews of the twentieth century. Ordained as a rabbi in 1893, Wise served briefly in New York City and in Portland, Oregon, before establishing the Free Synagogue (now known as the Stephen S. Wise Free Synagogue) in New York in 1907. He served there until his death over forty years later, and the Free Synagogue was the chief forum for his views: liberal politics, social reform, and Zionism. He was active in progressive politics supporting labor and helping to found the NAACP and the ACLU. Wise had been a Zionist since the 1890s, and it was at Herzl's request that he served as the American secretary of the movement. He worked closely with LDB, Mack, and Frankfurter, helping to found the P.E.C. and playing an important part in the American reception of the Balfour Declaration in 1917. He attended the Versailles conference on behalf of Zionist programs in Palestine and followed the Brandeis faction out of the movement after the schism of 1921. Wise was one of the first American Jews to warn of the impending troubles in Germany. He later advised Franklin D. Roosevelt regularly on Jewish and Zionist affairs and was a generally accepted spokesman for a large portion of the American Jewish community.

Wise devoted the November 1941 issue of his magazine, *Opinion*, to a series of tributes to LDB. In his editorial introduction, Wise wrote: "One felt as one sat with him in his modest little study, unadorned save by the radiance of his personality, that one had drawn a little nearer to the sources of truth and justice. . . . I, who, in common with a number of the older American Zionists, am — alas, was — privileged to be in close touch with him, thank God for that privilege — which I cherish as few things in life — of having worked year after year, and day after day with a man whose spirit has given me a fresh insight into the possibility of the Jew at his highest." Wise's sermons and letters have been published in various volumes and he wrote an autobiography, *Challenging Years* (New York, 1949).

2. Henry Hurwitz (1886–1961) was the founder of the Menorah movement (see LDB to Magnes, 10 October 1913), and the editor of *The Menorah Journal* from 1915 until his death.

3. See LDB to Benjamin Perlstein, 18 September 1914.

To Thomas Watt Gregory

September 18, 1914 Boston, Mass. [Brandeis Mss, NMF 68-2]

MY DEAR MR. GREGORY: I learn that there is a possibility of Mr. George W. Anderson being nominated for United States Attorney for the District of Massachusetts.[1] Such an appointment would in every way be admirable.

Mr. Anderson is a lawyer of ability and of high public spirit; who has already served effectively in the people's cause. You yourself know the excellent work that he has done as Public Service Commissioner, and particularly in connection with New Haven matters.

Mr. Anderson is a good Democrat; highly respected by the community, and twice the nominee of his party for Attorney General of the State.

The appointment of Mr. Anderson to this position would reflect great credit on the administration.[2]

Yours cordially,

1. LDB learned this from Gregory himself, who on 14 September wrote to tell LDB of his intention to nominate Anderson and to ask LDB for a letter praising Anderson to place in his file.

2. Anderson became the United States Attorney for Massachusetts on 1 November.

To May Childs Nerney

September 18, 1914 Boston, Mass. [Brandeis Mss, NMF 69-3]

DEAR MISS NERNEY: [1] Absence from the city from which I returned today has caused delay in replying to your letter of the 10th.

So far as I know, I shall be in the city on next Wednesday, and could see you at 11:00 o'clock on that day. I have great doubt, however, whether it would be worth your while to come to Boston for that purpose alone, as it does not seem to me possible that I should be able to give you any advice of value in regard to the Jim Crow car situation, and the work which I have on hand would prevent my entering upon an investigation of the matter.

I shall probably be in New York in the near future, and if you should prefer, will make an appointment there.

Yours very truly,

1. May Childs Nerney (1876–1959) was a researcher and a librarian who was serving as secretary for the National Association for the Advancement of Colored People; she joined the Thomas A. Edison laboratory as a librarian in 1928. She had written LDB to request his aid in filing a complaint to the Interstate Commerce Commission regarding Jim Crow railroad cars. See LDB to Chapin Brinsmade, 29 September 1914.

To Benjamin Perlstein

September 18, 1914 Boston, Mass. [Brandeis Mss, Z 3-2]

DEAR MR. PERLSTEIN: *First:* I have yours of the 17th enclosing copy of letter from Dr. Wise, and am sending you copy of my reply. Please show Mr. Nathan Strauss [*sic*] [1] my original letter to Dr. Wise, his reply of the 16th, and copy enclosed. I trust that Mr. Strauss [*sic*] will be able to induce Dr. Wise to accept the Chairmanship.[2]

Second: I duly received your telegram of the 15th as follows: "Magnes thinks political aspects require careful deliberation. Suggests no further action nor appointments for present." [3]

In view of the above I should of course make no further appointments until I see Dr. Magnes, and I had no thought of the Committee taking any external action whatsoever at present. What I desired was that Dr. Magnes and each of the other members of the Committee should begin a careful study of this subject, so that we might eventually think out the problems, and have a basis for some clear thinking on the subject. This was the idea underlying Miss Zold's [*sic*] [4] motion for the appointment of the Committee.

Third: I conferred with Dr. [Schmarya] Levin about your telegram concerning the Anglo-Palestine Bank. Dr. Levin is strongly of the opinion that we ought, at least until the $100,000 fund is raised in accordance with the original vote,[5] refrain from extending our activities, or as he put it "that we ought to be modest in our undertakings". I entirely agree with him, and for that reason, among others, made no mention of the needs of the Anglo-Palestine Bank at Rochester. Of course if Dr. Magnes has been able to arrange in New York, by application to some of our richer friends, who could understand fully the situation, that would be fine.

Dr. Levin and I are also strongly of the opinion that it is very important that we should avail of the present need, not only to raise the $100,000 fund, but to secure attention to the general subject of Zionism, so that it may be better understood. To this end we ought to arrange, as I indicated in my letter to Prof. Gottheil, for many small meetings. The propaganda work of Zionism can be best carried on in that way, and it ought to be possible during the course of the year for us to arrange, at least in the eastern part of the Country, for some discussion of the subject before practically each one of the Jewish societies, whether Zionist or non-Zionist. I presume this is a subject which has already been considered with considerable care by the Propaganda Committee of the Federation, but I hope that you will arrange to have Professor Gottheil and Mr. Hurwitz take up the subject with Mr. Lipsky for comprehensive planning.

Fourth: I enclose for your files letter of the 4th from Dr. Magnes to me with enclosure.

Fifth: Referring to your [*sic*] of the 17th: For the present I do not think it will be necessary to have any special stationery struck off for me with my Boston address. Even when I write letters from Boston I should ordinarily prefer to have the answers go to the central office, and in the event I do not, I can easily indicate it in my letter.   Yours very truly,

1. Nathan Straus (1848–1931) was a leading New York merchant, the head of the R. H. Macy department store since 1896. He was a devoted Zionist who made many trips to Palestine in connection with his philanthropic work there. By the time of his death he had given around $2,000,000 to Zionist causes, particularly in the fields of education and public health.

2. See next letter.

3. See LDB to Magnes, 14 September 1914.

4. Few Zionists, men or women, enjoyed such universal love and respect as Henrietta Szold (1860–1945). The daughter of a prominent Baltimore rabbi, she early became interested in Zionism and in the plight of Russian immigrants to America. She established the first evening school in the country where the English language and useful crafts were taught to the immigrants, an educational experiment that soon spread across America. On her first visit to Palestine, in 1909, she decided that the health program there was in need of help. Adopting the motto of "Healing the daughter of thy people," she founded the immensely influential Hadassah, the Women's Zionist Organization of America, which has developed a comprehensive program in health services in the Holy Land over the last sixty years. At an age when most women retire, she moved "temporarily" to Palestine to take over the social service program under the Jewish Agency, and in 1927 she became the first woman member of the Agency and a politician in spite of herself. Her greatest work was undertaken when the Nazis came to power in the 1930s; she organized the Youth Aliyah, which brought thousands of German children to Palestine, thereby saving their lives. Her story is best told in Marvin Lowenthal, ed., *Henrietta Szold: Life and Letters* (New York, 1942); what she meant to American Jewish women is beautifully expressed in Midge Decter, "The Legacy of Henrietta Szold," *Commentary* 30 (December, 1960): 480.

5. See LDB to Perlstein, 8 September 1914, n. 2.

To Stephen Samuel Wise

September 18, 1914 Boston, Mass. [Brandeis Mss, Z 6-2]

MY DEAR MR. WISE: A copy of your letter of the 16th reaches me here. I trust you will not definitely decline the appointment as Chairman of the Committee on Finance.[1] As I have implicit confidence in Mr. Nathan Strauss' [sic] judgment, I cannot entertain the doubt which you expressed as to your ability to be of help in this connection. Please talk this over with Mr. Strauss [sic]. I think that he will be able to convince you to accept the Chairmanship, and if by any possibility he should not, I hope to reinforce his plea when we next meet.[2]

Yours very truly,

1. See preceding letter.

2. Wise accepted the position. See LDB to Wise, 16 November 1914.

To Gilbert Ernstein Roe

September 18, 1914 Boston, Mass [Brandeis Mss, NMF 67-1]

MY DEAR MR. ROE: Upon my return to the city today I find yours of the 16th.

Of course I am very sorry to learn that Mr. Pierce [1] has declined to take over the Weekly.[2] The Senator's opponents will doubtless seek to have their followers draw unfavorable inferences from the discontinuance of the paper. But it seems to me clear that a monthly would prove a serious burden to the Senator, not only financially, but otherwise; and that it would be a great mistake to make a new start now with a monthly. We must try to free the Senator from this magazine burden; and I cannot believe that it will be done if the Weekly is merely transformed into a monthly.[3]   Very cordially yours,

1. Dante Melville Pierce (1880–1955), of Des Moines, was the largest publisher of agricultural journals in the country. Among his magazines was the influential *Wallace's Farmer*.

2. Roe had journeyed to Des Moines in order to persuade Pierce to take over the ailing *LaFollette's Weekly*, both because of its financial losses and because of the burden upon Senator LaFollette's fragile health. After studying the matter, Pierce felt he could not undertake the task despite his loyalty to and friendship for Senator LaFollette. He recommended instead that the journal become a monthly. See LDB to LaFollette, 20 June 1914.

3. Despite LDB's misgivings, LaFollette decided to bring the magazine out on a monthly basis, starting in November.

To Nathan Pinanski

September 23, 1914 Boston, Mass. [Brandeis Mss, Z 1-2]

DEAR MR. PINANSKI: [1] I understand that an appeal has been made in your Congregation, on the New Year, for aid for the Jewish people abroad as a consequence of the war. I also learn that the appeal, as might be expected from your Congregation, was generously responded to.

At this time there are no Jews who need aid more than the Jews of Palestine. Their need is urgent, and I trust your Board of Directors will recognize the propriety of having this contribution made a part of the fund which our Committee is endeavoring to raise.

If this meets with the approval of your Board, it would, I am sure, be very helpful to have you and your Directors attend the meeting on Sunday, and present the list of donors in open meeting.

Cordially yours,

1. Nathan Pinanski (1862–1936) was an immigrant from Russia who had become a successful Boston real estate dealer. A member of the American Jewish Committee and involved in numerous Jewish charities, he was also president of Congregation Adath Jeshurun, the largest synagogue in Massachusetts.

To Harry Friedenwald

September 24, 1914 Boston, Mass. [Brandeis Mss, Z 1-2]

MY DEAR DR. FRIEDENWALD: [1] Yours of the 26th reaches me here.

There will be a meeting of our Provisional Committee on a date which will doubtless be fixed tomorrow, and we shall have an opportunity of discussing fully the several matters stated in your letter. It may be well, however, to say this now:

First: I had not heard before receiving your letter that Dr. Max Nordau [2] was coming to America. If he is coming, it is not upon the invitation of our Committee. The question of inviting him to come was fully discussed at one of our Committee meetings, and it was understood that Dr. Gottheil would communicate with Dr. Nordau as to the possibilities of his coming sometime, and the conditions, but making it clear that he was not now invited to come, and that we made inquiries merely with the view to ascertaining the possibilities for the future. I entirely agree with you that we have not the spare money nor the energy in our Committee which it will be necessary to devote to any tour which Dr. Nordau might undertake, although he could at some other time be of the greatest service in spreading Zionistic education.

Second: In regard to the disposition of our share in the $50,000 fund. I shall be glad to hear further from you when we meet. My disposition was to yield in this respect to any recommendation which Ambassador Morganthau [*sic*] might make, which had the approval of the American Jewish Committee; since it was through the Ambassador that the fund was raised, and he appeared to be in close cooperation with Dr. Rupin [*sic*].³ I was the more inclined to yield in respect to the course proposed by reason of the fact that it probably had the hearty approval of Mr. Nathan Straus, to whom we are indebted for the $12,500 contribution.

Very truly yours,

1. Harry Friedenwald (1864–1950) was a leading Baltimore Zionist and a member of the P.E.C. He, like his father before him and his son after, was an ophthalmologist and a teacher of medicine in Baltimore. He was an authority on Jews in the history of medicine. Friedenwald had been a Zionist since the 1890s, and from 1904 to 1910 he was president of the Federation of American Zionists. See Alexandra Lee Levin, *Vision : A Biography of Harry Friedenwald* (Philadelphia, 1964).

2. Max Nordau (1849–1923) was one of the elder statesmen of the world Zionist movement. A philosopher and social analyst of considerable repute, Nordau had met Herzl in Paris where both were working as reporters. Nordau drafted the crucial Basle Program at the first Zionist Congress in 1897 and was Herzl's personal choice as his successor. Nordau, however, refused the presidency of the Zionist organization and maintained a fierce independence; he opposed both that faction led by Ahad Ha-Am (which advocated a "cultural" center rather than a political one) and that faction led by Weizmann (the so-called "practical" Zionists). Nordau favored immediate, massive migration of Jews to Palestine, the establishment of a Jewish majority there, and the speedy creation of an independent Jewish state. His wife and daughter collaborated on a biography: Anna and Maxa Nordau, *Max Nordau* (New York, 1943).

3. Dr. Arthur Ruppin (1876–1943) was a sociologist who pioneered in the collection of concrete data regarding the Jews, and thereby helped to elevate the study of the Jewish people above the level of stereotype, myth, or mere cultural patriotism. He went to Palestine for a sociological investigation in 1907 and became an active Zionist. Head of the Zionist Organization's Palestine Office in Jaffa from 1908 until his death, Ruppin was responsible for the day-by-day development of Jewish settlement in the region. Called the "father" of Zionist settlement, Ruppin placed his highest priority on the purchase of new lands, and under his direction, and at his urging much territory was purchased with Zionist funds. See Alex Bein, ed., *Arthur Ruppin: Memoirs, Diaries, Letters* (New York, 1972).

To Norman Hapgood

September 24, 1914 Boston, Mass. [Brandeis Mss, NMF 62-1]

MY DEAR NORMAN: ¹ I enclose clipping from today's Boston Post concerning the proposed new treaty with Russia.²

In this connection I think you may care to look at President Harrison's message to Congress on December 9, 1891 concerning the immigration of Russian Jews, due to the Russian disabilities; and Secretary Hay's note of August 11, 1902 concerning Roumania's violation of the provisions in the Treaty of Berlin designed to protect its Jews.[3] These two documents are in the Appendix to Samuel Joseph's essay on the Jewish Immigration to the United States,[4] which was published by the faculty of political science of Columbia University this year, and is presumably in the University Club Library.

Read in Joseph's essay the description of the disabilities imposed by Russia (as well as Roumania), which shows that H.G. Wells' statement in his article published in Harper's last week, to the effect that Russia has treated its Jews no worse than its other subjects, has little foundation in fact.[5]

Very cordially yours,

1. It is a measure of LDB's Zionist fervor, and of his ability to persuade others, that Hapgood became a committed Zionist under his tutelage. Hapgood writes: "One of the firm interests of my life, started in me by Mr. Brandeis, is connected with a race to which he belongs and I do not. . . . [F]rom his mind it passed into mine." Hapgood, *Changing Years*, 196–97. Hapgood was attracted by the potential for building democratic institutions which LDB saw in the creation of a Jewish homeland in Palestine.

2. The newspapers carried rumors that Secretary Bryan was about to complete one of his arbitration treaties, this time with Russia. The new treaty would replace one that had been allowed to lapse under President Taft because of the Congressional interpretation of it: namely that under its provisions American Jews might be denied the right of free travel in Russia. It was now rumored that the new treaty would simply fail to make any reference to the matter.

3. President Harrison's message complained that the harsh treatment of Jews in Russia and the passage of anti-Semitic laws was cruel and inhumane and that this persecution was forcing many Jews to escape to other countries, especially the United States. Secretary Hay's note charged that Rumania, in violation of the treaty of 1878, persecuted her 400,000 Jews and enforced economic and political disabilities upon them.

4. Samuel Joseph, *Jewish Immigration to the United States from 1881 to 1910* (New York, 1914). The Harrison message and the Hay note may be found at pages 199–205.

5. H. G. Wells, "The Liberal Fear of Russia," *Harper's Weekly*, 49 (19 September 1914):268. Herbert George Wells (1866–1946) was the immensely prolific British novelist, social reformer, socialist, and historian. For Hapgood's view, see his editorials, "Zionism's Crisis," in the 26 September issue of *Harper's* or "Jews and the War" in the issue of 3 October.

To Chapin Brinsmade

September 29, 1914 Boston, Mass. [Brandeis Mss, NMF 69-3]

MY DEAR MR. BRINSMADE: [1] Replying to yours of the 28th:

I should greatly doubt whether the Interstate Commerce Commission would, upon the filing of a formal petition, enter upon a general investigation of conditions of service to colored people on interstate trains.

My advice to Miss Nerney was that petitions be filed with the Commission, seeking redress for failure to provide reasonable accommodations on such railroads as appeared to be particularly serious offenders, and be prepared to make full proof in those cases.[2]

After the presentation of a number of such petitions, the Commission might be induced to undertake a general investigation, but I should greatly doubt whether it would do so in the first instance. I am inclined to think that before instituting any proceeding, it would be advisable for you to talk this matter over with Mr. James W. Carmalt, one of the attorneys of the Commission, who is associated with Chairman Harlan's office. He could probably give you much better advice than I. If you will show him this letter, it will make clear to him the point I have particularly in mind.

Very truly yours,

1. Chapin Brinsmade (1885–1928) was a lawyer and a teacher who was serving his only year as attorney for the National Association for the Advancement of Colored People. Brinsmade had written requesting clarification of LDB's advice to Miss Nerney, 18 September 1914.

2. The Interstate Commerce Commission did not become involved in problems of racial discrimination until the late 1930s; Jim Crow laws on the railroads continued to exist until the Supreme Court acted in 1941. See *Mitchell* vs. *United States*, 313 U.S. 80 (1941).

To Norman Hapgood

September 29, 1914 Boston, Mass. [Brandeis Mss, NMF 62-1]

MY DEAR NORMAN: In connection with the editorial in this week's Harper's [1] the following which I just found in Sir Harry H. Johnston's [2] article on "The German War and Its Consequences" in the September Nineteenth Century, page 522, is interesting:

"But I can see as in a Sidney Carton[3] vision many good things for humanity emanating from this holocaust of men and horses, this destruction of famous buildings and ruin of the arts. I can see a Poland once more taking shape; at first a vassal power under the wing of Russia, but by degrees a splendid West Slavic Nation, developing in central Europe a brilliant literature and an original genius in painting and music. I see far better conditions of life granted to the Jews in Russia, and a Jewish State in Palestine, guaranteed by Britain, France, and Russia" etc.

Cordially yours,

1. "Jews and the War," in the 3 October 1914 issue.
2. Sir Harry Hamilton Johnston (1858–1927) was a British novelist and African explorer.
3. Sidney Carton was the young idealist who went to the guillotine in place of Charles Darnay in Charles Dickens's *A Tale of Two Cities*.

To Benjamin Perlstein (Telegram)

September 29, 1914 Boston, Mass. [Brandeis Mss, Z 3-2]

Request Lipsky to caution organizers of my meetings to select rather small halls. Overcrowded small hall meeting better than large hall nearly full. Every man turned away for lack of room is worth two who get in. This request previously made of Lipsky was ignored in Philadelphia, Pittsburgh, and Rochester.

To Norman Hapgood

October 1, 1914 Boston, Mass. [Brandeis Mss, NMF 62-1]

MY DEAR NORMAN: *First*: I return herewith the copy of the Scripps correspondence, which seems to me very satisfactory.[1] Charles and Mrs. Crane dined with us last evening, and Charles seemed particularly happy over this correspondence, and with the recent numbers of Harper's.

Second: Replying to yours of yesterday: I will think over your suggestions as to a New Haven article, but on first thought it seems to me that it would not be desirable.[2] With respect to the

New Haven: The important thing now is the future, not the past; and the story of the future should be largely the uninteresting one of patience, virtue, and attention to details.

Third: Referring to our discussion with Moskowitz: To secure a proper peace treaty now, as well as to protect ourselves against future wars, we must secure acceptance of a fundamental idea, namely:—the equal rights of all nations and races to live, and to develop their own individuality. In other words,—an extension to Nations and races of the now recognized rights of the individual man, including specifically the equality of opportunity. The democratic doctrine of equality of opportunity involves the assumption that the common weal will be most advanced by allowing all classes and individuals the opportunity of full development. Lasting peace must rest not upon the basis of toleration of unlike nations, but upon the belief that civilization will be most advanced through permitting each nation and race to develop. In other words,—what we want is not a dominant race or races,—not uniformity, but what Felix Adler expresses as "the utmost differentiation of the type of culture,—the utmost variety and richness in the expression of fundamental human faculties". That was the thought which underlay the organization of the First Universal Races congress of 1911,[3] at which Adler, in subordinating the practical devices of disarmament, treaties and the so-called parliament, declared: "If humanity is ever to become a corpus organicum spirituale—and that is the aim—then a conception based on reciprocity of cultural influence, favourable to the greatest possible variety of types, and assuring to the different groups of mankind their integrity as distinct members, in order that they may make manifest the distinctive gifts with which Nature has endowed them, seems unavoidable." [4]

Dubnow, in his Essay on the Philosophy of History,[5] called "national intolerance the modern substitute for the religious bigotry of the middle ages.", and thought that a study of Jewish history might have a not inconsiderable share in the spiritual change that was to annihilate that intolerance.

Cordially yours,

1. Hapgood had enclosed copies of letters he exchanged with Edward W. Scripps about the quality of *Harper's Weekly*, and about the serialization of parts of John Galsworthy's *Forsyte* books. Both Scripps and Congress-

man William Kent argued that Harper's was not hitting hard enough, that there was "too much pink tea" in the articles, and neither one of them cared for Galsworthy. Hapgood took exception to the comments and defended his editorial policy.

2. LDB did not write any further articles for *Harper's* on the New Haven.

3. A conference to discuss relations between Eastern and Western nations, as well as between blacks and whites in the United States, "in the light of modern knowledge and the modern conscience" was held three years before this letter. The sponsors of the conference hoped it would lead to friendlier relations and good will. See W.E.B. DuBois, "The First Universal Race Congress," *The Independent* 71 (24 August 1911): 401–03.

4. *Papers on inter-racial problems, communicated to the first Universal races congress* . . . (London and Boston, 1911), 261–68, at 266.

5. Simon Markovitch Dubnow, *Jewish History: An Essay in the Philosophy of History* (Philadelphia, 1903).

To Stephen Samuel Wise

October 1, 1914 Boston, Mass. [Brandeis Mss, Z 6-2]

MY DEAR DR. WISE: Replying to yours of the 29th: [1]

First: Possible imperative demands in connection with my Washington work have made it necessary for me to refrain for the present from making any speaking engagements after the 16th. It was for that reason that I was unable to accept the arrangement made for Chicago for the 17th, 18th, and 19th, and have found it not yet possible to fix a later date; but I shall not forget that I am to answer you later in reference to your very kind call.[2]

Second: It is possible that DeHaas could get away to go to Stockholm [*sic*],[3] but I feel that he is very much needed here. Intensive organization work, in the first place with a view to raising the $100,000, and then to marshall the American forces, is essential; and I feel that if we are to send any emissary abroad, it would be better to postpone doing so until after we have made more progress in our mobilization here. There will doubtless be occasion for another meeting at Stockholm or elsewhere within a few months.   Cordially,

1. Wise had invited LDB to speak at the Free Synagogue on 18 October 1914.

2. LDB did speak to the Free Synagogue on 25 October 1914 on the topic "Why I Am a Zionist." Voicing what would become a familiar theme, LDB

explained that his approach to Zionism was through Americanism, and that prior to his involvement in the garment strike he had had very little contact with Jews. Once he met them, however, he was impressed by the similarity of the ideals of American society and of the Jewish ethos. He also explained that Zionism was not a movement to compel all Jews to go to Palestine, but rather to provide a homeland for those who did wish to emigrate there.

3. The Central Zionist Bureau had called a special meeting in Copenhagen in December to discuss international Zionist problems and requested all national organizations to send representatives. See LDB to Chaim Weizmann, 11 October 1914.

To Richard James Horatio Gottheil

October 2, 1914 Boston, Mass. [Gottheil Mss]

MY DEAR PROFESSOR GOTTHEIL: *First*: I thank you for yours of the 1st [1] enclosing the memorandum which seems to state clearly and forceably the position taken by our committee in connection with the conference of the American Jewish Committee. I am, however, a little troubled by two sentences,—the one referring to the English Alien Law; the other,—that referring to the United States. I think it would be well to lay this memorandum before the Political Study Committee at its next meeting.

Second: I trust that you are making good progress in organizing a band of speakers among the intellectuals. It seems to me very important that this work should be pressed forward as rapidly as possible, and that intensive work of educating through small groups and meetings should be undertaken.

Third: I feel also clear that we ought to have further favorable comment on the movement similar to that in Harper's [2] and I hope that you and Dr. Wise will press this work forward.

Very cordially yours,

1. In the memorandum Gottheil noted that there would undoubtedly be some conference after the war to settle outstanding questions, and that at that meeting the Jews must be prepared to press their demands for the right to a homeland in Palestine. The memorandum further argued that existing alien and immigration laws would not help the Jews in any of the European countries, and it predicted that the hitherto unrestricted flow of people into America would be drastically curtailed.

2. See "Zionism's Crisis," *Harper's Weekly*, 59 (26 September 1914): 289.

To Norman Hapgood

October 2, 1914 Boston, Mass. [Brandeis Mss, NMF 62-1]

MY DEAR NORMAN: I enclose clipping from this morning's New York Times announcing that Gary has retired from all of the directorates except the Steel Board.[1]

It is just a year since we were bombarding the inter-locking directorate evil.[2] Now the Clayton Bill is embodying the prohibition into law.   Cordially yours,

1. Earlier in the year, in an effort to forestall federal anti-trust legislation, members of the House of Morgan had resigned from numerous directorships (see LDB to Alice Goldmark Brandeis, 3 January 1914, n. 1.). Gary, who headed the Morgan-sponsored U. S. Steel Corporation, had announced the preceding day that he was also resigning from all boards except those of the affiliated steel companies. On 9 October LDB dropped a note to Hapgood informing him that Charles M. Schwab, president of Bethlehem Steel, had also resigned from all other directorships.

2. LDB, "The Endless Chain: Interlocking Directorates," *Harper's Weekly*, 58 (6 December 1913): 13–17, reprinted as ch. 3 of *Other People's Money*. LDB reiterated his arguments against the divided loyalties of such arrangements in "Interlocking Directorates," *Annals of the American Academy of Political and Social Sciences*, 57 (January 1915): 45–49. Hapgood developed LDB's observation into an editorial, "A Year's Progress," in the 17 October issue of *Harper's*.

To Alfred Brandeis

October 3, 1914 Boston, Mass. [Brandeis Mss, M 4-1]

MY DEAR AL: I am determined to put an end to your absence and silence, & for this reason have agreed to speak on Zionism in Cincinnati October 14. Shall expect you to be on hand on my arrival. Indeed I am considering the possibility of spending an extra day there—the 13th—so as to see something more of you. Will let you know later.[1]

1. LDB did go to Cincinnati, and Alfred joined him there, but LDB's plans to speak on Zionism were frustrated by the hostility of Reform Rabbi David Philipson. See LDB to Louis Lipsky, 5 October 1914.

To Louis Lipsky (Telegram)

October 3, 1914 Boston, Mass. [Brandeis Mss, Z 1-4]

Yes, will arrive Cleveland in time for afternoon luncheon, but should favor luncheon only if Committee convinced it will be financially profitable. Cleveland ought to produce at least five thousand dollars.[1] Write me fully concerning character Cleveland audience, and also about Masliansky.[2]

1. LDB's speech repeated the now-standard Zionist message that no one would be forced to go to Palestine. He also used what would become a famous phrase: "To be better Americans we must be better Jews; to be better Jews we must become Zionists."
2. Zvi Hirsch Masliansky (1856–1943) had been a member of the early Chibbath Zion in Russia before emigrating to the United States in 1895. Although a strong Zionist, from 1902 to 1904 he had been the editor of the New York Yiddish newspaper sponsored by Louis Marshall, *The Jewish World*.

To Augustus Owsley Stanley

October 3, 1914 Boston, Mass. [House Mss]

MY DEAR STANLEY: Replying to yours of the 1st: [1]

If the President should consult me concerning appointments on the Trade Commission, I shall be very glad to tell him about Mr. Woolley.[2]

I am distressed to have you say that your "relations with the public service are to be severed".[3] I hope it will mean merely that your activity is to have another field. You have done the Country, the State, and yourself a great credit. Your investigation of the Steel Trust has been a large factor in educating public opinion generally in regard to big business. You have had a large part in producing the revulsion of feeling against interlocking directorates. In a world where there is so much fighting to be done, even in a "neutral country", we can ill afford to lose you.

Most cordially yours,

1. Stanley had written to urge that LDB recommend to President Wilson the appointment of Robert Woolley (see next note) to the newly created Federal Trade Commission.

2. Robert Wickliffe Woolley (1871–1958), after working on several newspapers, had become chief investigator for the Stanley Committee investigation of U. S. Steel in 1911. Active in Democratic politics in the 1912 election, he had been rewarded with appointments in the Treasury Department, and Wilson named him to the Interstate Commerce Commission in 1917.

3. Although Stanley had written that he would soon retire from politics, he ran successfully for the governorship of Kentucky the following year, and he was elected to the Senate for one term in 1918; from 1925 until 1954 he served as chairman of the International Joint Commission between Canada and the United States.

To Richard James Horatio Gottheil

October 5, 1914 Boston, Mass. [Gottheil Mss]

MY DEAR MR. GOTTHEIL: I have yours of the 3rd, and am glad to know that you have commenced to organize the college men. It is very important that I have as soon as possible accurate information in regard to the following:

First: What the Turkish Law, regulations and practices are in regard to the admission to and the treatment of Jews in Palestine, and specifically to what extent, if any, they are subjected to discriminations in comparison with the Mussulmans or Christians.

Second: Like information in regard to the treatment of Jews in Palestine from time to time during the last thirty or forty years.

Third: Like information in regard to the treatment of the Jews in other parts of the Turkish Empire.

In connection with this information I should like the data to cover both the attitude of the Government, and the attitude of portions of the Turkish subjects,—like the Arabs.

Will you undertake to secure for me, so far as possible, this information? I suppose that Mr. Oscar Straus [1] has considerable data of value on this subject. I shall hope to see him when I am next in New York, but I do not wish to delay even so long the getting together of the data on this subject, which may be called for at any moment.

I am enclosing copy of a letter from Dr. Ruppin's office of September 8th, which seems to me very encouraging, after the sombre reports which we have received from there. [2]

Cordially yours,

1. Oscar Solomon Straus (1850–1926), a New York lawyer and merchant, was the first Jew appointed to serve in an American cabinet; he was Secretary of Commerce and Labor from 1906 to 1909. In addition, he was three times ambassador to Turkey. Straus was active in numerous Jewish organizations, but his Zionist sympathies were not as strong as those of his brother Nathan. See his *Under Four Administrations* (New York 1922), and Naomi Wiener Cohen, *A Dual Heritage: the Public Career of Oscar S. Straus* (Philadelphia, 1969).

2. Ruppin, having learned of the formation of the PEC, had sent LDB some statistics on conditions in Palestine. While cautioning that the war could yet inflict great hardship and damage, he argued that with sufficient outside help the Jewish settlement (the Yishub) would be able to ride out the storm with minimal hardship. Because of the confusion created by the war, there was now ample opportunity to buy land and make preparations for an anticipated immigration from Europe. The Jewish Colonial Trust was solvent, relief agencies were functioning, and so far none of the major institutions or schools had been closed. On this same day, LDB wrote to Ruppin (see below) urging him to be sure that all needs for preservation of existing colonies be met before any new land be purchased; the $100,000 relief fund could not be utilized to expand Yishub holdings.

To Nathan D. Kaplan

October 5, 1914 Boston, Mass. [Brandeis Mss, Z 3-1]

MY DEAR MR. KAPLAN: [1] Answering your letter of the 3rd:

First: About Das Volk: [2] The advisability of making an appropriation of $2500 to Das Volk was very carefully considered, at an unusually full meeting of the Provisional Committee, at which Dr. Levin, Mr. Lipsky and Mr. Barondess [3] were present. It appeared to be clear that Das Volk must receive this subsidy or be discontinued, and in view of its part in helping us to raise the $100,000 fund, it was believed by all to be unwise to allow the paper to be discontinued. The subsidy is not made by the Provisional Committee to Das Volk. It is made by the Provisional Committee to the Federation, but with a view to its necessity of relieving Das Volk. This seemed necessary because we have diverted, for our purposes, the efforts of the Federation officials. The Federation had appealed specifically for the maintenance of Das Volk; and it was believed that these appeals would interfere with the appeals we were making for the general fund; and that all of the energies of the Federation officials ought to be given, for the present, to the raising of our $100,000 fund. For this reason the Provisional Committee concluded to make this advance to the Federation.

Second: As to the membership of Dr. Gottheil and Dr. Max Heller: [4] A question was raised as to the power of the Committee to increase its membership; and upon consideration there appeared to be a serious doubt on that point. It seemed best to make Professor Gottheil and Dr. Heller, as well as Mr. DeHaas, Professor Kallen and Mr. Hurwitz, and the members of the Administrative Committee of the Federation, Associate members.

Third: I am enclosing a copy of a letter of September 8th from Dr. Ruppin's office, which, after the dark reports we have had from Palestine, seems to be very encouraging. It shows in the first place that Dr. Ruppin is still there, and that he is at work upon our great national problems of permanent value, as well as the immediate and pressing demands for relief.

Cordially yours,

1. Nathan D. Kaplan (1877–1952), a Chicago attorney, was one of the leading Zionists in the midwest. In addition to being president of the Knights of Zion, he was active in numerous Jewish charities and agencies. In 1927 he moved to Palestine, and was a member of the Tel Aviv municipal council from 1936 to 1941. Kaplan was chosen to be mayor, but refused the post, saying that it should go to a native-born citizen.

2. *Das Volk* (The People) was the Yiddish-language newspaper sponsored by the Federation of American Zionists.

3. Joseph Barondess (1863–1928) had been among the chief ogranizers of Jewish immigrants into the New York trades unions as well as a prominent Zionist. A founder of the American Jewish Congress, he was a member of its delegation to the Paris Peace Conference.

4. Maximilian Heller (1860–1929) was the long-time rabbi of the Sinai Temple in New Orleans and professor of Hebrew at Tulane University. From 1909 to 1911 he was president of the Central Conference of American Rabbis, despite the fact that he was an ardent Zionist and the Reform movement at that time was strongly opposed to Zionism. For many years Heller and Stephen Wise were practically the only Zionists in the C.C.A.R.

To Nathan D. Kaplan

October 5, 1914 Boston, Mass. [Brandeis Mss, Z 3-1]

MY DEAR MR. KAPLAN: I have your telegram and letter of the 3rd selecting November 7th, 8th and 9th for the days in Chicago.

I expect that Dr. Levin will be with me and he will no doubt be prepared to stay in Chicago a longer time, if you believe in that way he can advance the cause, and particularly the present urgent work of raising our $100,000 fund. I had supposed that you planned in addition to the banquet, the address at Dr. Hirsch's [1] Synagogue, and the mass meeting, a large number of small meetings which Dr. Levin could attend, and at each of which a collection could be taken up.

I venture to suggest that the collections from Chicago ought to reach in the aggregate $20,000. In Boston we raised about $7,000 at our meeting on the 27th, and the work is being continued with the expectation of increasing this amount for Boston and vicinity to at least $15,000. Considering the large Jewish population in Chicago, $20,000 would seem a fairly modest demand.

We are very conscious of the difficulty to which you call attention of the several relief funds. It does not seem to me possible, however, to arrange satisfactorily with the American Jewish Committee for a joint collection, and a proportionate distribution. We must make our demands specifically for the needs of Palestine looked out for through the Zionist organization. This includes of course relief work. There is no better way of effecting relief, even quite directly, than through the maintenance of our institutions. If we maintain our schools, our district nursing, and our various other institutions, those to whom we pay money will be effective directly and indirectly in relieving Palestinian distress.[2]

I am quite sure that you will agree with me that the only way to make our November meetings a success is for all of our Chicago friends to undertake very persistent missionary work in advance, and secure contributions in advance, of which reports can be made at the meeting. It was such intensive work, carefully planned, and persistently carried out, which made the Boston meeting so great a success; and we are through this building up an organization from which we are expecting very great support in the future. I have no doubt that the month intervening before the meeting will be put by you to the best possible use.

Very cordially yours,

1. Emil Gustav Hirsch (1851–1923) had been rabbi of the Sinai Congregation in Chicago since 1880, as well as professor of rabbinical philosophy and

literature at the University of Chicago. He stood among the more liberal Reform rabbis, and was sympathetic to Zionism.

2. Eventually it was necessary to combine the various relief groups into the Joint Distribution Committee, although the Zionists retained discretion over funds earmarked for Palestine.

To Louis Lipsky

October 5, 1914 Boston, Mass. [Brandeis Mss, Z 1-4]

MY DEAR MR. LIPSKY: I have yours of the 4th.[1]

As you have already accepted the conditions proposed by Dr. Philipson,[2] there is nothing for me to do but to acquiesce, but I thoroughly disapprove of them. I am at a loss to know what justification there is in my appearing at a meeting which is not only "not held under Zionist auspices", but in which "no Zionist propaganda be made", and in which speakers may not appeal for aid for the Zionist movement. I should like to have you write me a speech that would be appropriate for such a meeting.

Please make no such conditions for any future meeting at which I am to speak. I am perfectly ready to recognize that before certain audiences Zionism is not to be unduly obtruded, and should expect to observe proper discretion in this respect. I should expect that would be the case in connection with certain meetings which are to be held in Chicago, as I found it in regard to the meeting held at Pittsburgh. I do not believe our cause will be advanced by subscribing to any such terms as Dr. Philipson proposed and you yielded to. Other speakers may feel different about this, and I of course am perfectly content that they should speak at such meetings. I am not particular either about a declaration that a meeting is held under Zionist auspices, but a meeting which undertakes to restrict my liberty of speech is not a meeting which I want to address.[3]

How much money do you expect to get from Cincinnati for the educational and agricultural institutions in Palestine?

Very cordially yours,

1. Lipsky had agreed to send speakers, including LDB, to Cincinnati upon the urging of Zionists there who had secured the consent of Rabbi Philipson (see next note) for a fund-raising meeting, provided that it not be held under Zionist auspices.

2. David Philipson (1862–1949) had been one of the first graduates of the Hebrew Union College, the Reform seminary established by Isaac Mayer Wise. From 1888 to 1938 he served the B'ne Israel Congregation in Cincinnati, teaching also at Hebrew Union. A past president of the Central Conference of American Rabbis, he used his vast influence within the Reform movement to oppose Zionism, and even after the Balfour Declaration continued in his opposition to a Jewish homeland in Palestine. He once declared: "The United States is our Palestine, and Washington our Jerusalem." See his autobiography, *My Life as an American Jew* (Cincinnati, 1941); for information on Reform Judaism's opposition to Zionism, see Naomi Wiener, "Reform Judaism in America and Zionism, 1897–1922" (master's essay, Columbia University, 1949), and Robert E. Flexner, "In Quest of Security: the Controversy over Zionism in the American Jewish Community, 1897–1920" (master's essay, University of Oklahoma, 1968).

3. The proposed speech was never delivered, and the entire meeting was called off after LDB arrived in Cincinnati. Philipson and several other influential Reform leaders met privately with LDB the afternoon of 13 October and convinced him that if he insisted on talking about Zionism it would mean an open war among Cincinnati's Jews. Although LDB refused to comment on the meeting, merely echoing Philipson's assertion that there had been a "misunderstanding," he did respond to reporters' questions, asserting that the center of the Zionist movement had shifted from Berlin to the United States. He also praised the Wilson administration, and endorsed the women's suffrage movement. See *Cincinnati Enquirer*, 14 October 1914.

To Arthur Ruppin

October 5, 1914 Boston, Mass. [Brandeis Mss, Z 10-3]

MY DEAR DR. RUPPIN: I have received from your office a letter of September 8th, which I have read with great satisfaction.

The assurance that your office is undertaking not merely to relieve the immediate distress, but to continue and extend our great National work, is most encouraging. I agree with you entirely as to the importance of acquiring, when possible, additional tracts of fertile land. It seems to me that money available could not be put to better use. Dr. Epstein is in this country at present in the interest of the National Fund,[1] and I hope that he will have success in adding to the resources of that fund.

Our Committee must at present confine itself to the task of raising the $100,000 fund to support the Zionist organization, and the Zionist Palestinian institutions, about which Dr. Levin has no doubt written you fully. Until that task is completed, it would be unwise for us to attempt to raise money specifically for land purchases. Indeed the task of raising the $100,000 fund is a serious one, owing partly to the fact that the demand upon the Jews of America to meet the distress among their bretheren in Europe is very great,—which diverts them from the specific demands of Palestine and Palestinian work, and partly because business in America also has not been good for sometime, and even here is seriously affected by the great war. The present distress may, however, enable us to secure to a much greater degree than otherwise would have been possible, the attention of the Jews in America to the Zionist movement, and to lay now the foundation for greater support in the future.

I am greatly relieved to know that it has been possible for you to remain in Palestine, and to continue without interruption your able administration of Zionist affairs. Please send me, say, monthly, a report on Palestinian conditions, covering, among other things, not only specifically our Zionist institutions, but also the condition of the several colonies. I do not wish to burden you unduly, but must impress upon you that it is essential for the effective prosecution of our work here that we should have comprehensive and up to date information in regard to the Palestinian work.

I agree with you entirely as to the importance of the Hebraic schools.   Very cordially yours,

P.S. Let me express to you also my thanks for sending me your admirable volume "The Jews of Today", which has deepened my insight into our problems.[2]

---

1. The Jewish National Fund (Keren Kayemet le-Yisroel) had been founded at the Fifth Zionist Congress (1901) for the purpose of acquisition, development, and afforestation of land in Palestine. It began to acquire land in 1905, primarily under the direction of Ruppin, and by the time of the founding of the State of Israel in 1948, had purchased 235,523 acres, including large tracts in the Galilee, Samaria, Huleh, the Negev, and the Valley of Jezreel. Benjamin Epstein was a JNF organizer who had previously worked primarily in Russia. Fluent in Yiddish and German, he was then traveling around the United States raising money for the Fund.

2. Ruppin, *The Jews of Today* (London, 1913) was originally published in German in 1904. It was the first scientific effort to collect data about the Jewish communities of Europe, and has remained a classic work for the study of pre-Nazi Jewry.

To Alice Stone Blackwell

October 6, 1914 Boston, Mass. [Brandeis Mss, NMF 47-3]

DEAR MRS. BLACKWELL: [1] I think it best not to attempt an answer to the questions contained in yours of the 5th. Of course I am strongly in favor of women voting, but I am not so sure that votes for women would make an important difference in the frequency of wars. The causes of war lie I think far deeper than the absence of the franchise for women, and the categorical answer to your question one would be apt to exaggerate unduly the importance of that fact.   Cordially yours,

1. Alice Stone Blackwell (1857–1950) was a newspaperwoman who edited a series of feminist magazines. She was actively involved in both the peace and the women's suffrage movements. Mrs. Blackwell had asked if LDB believed that wars would be less frequent if women voted, and if so, why.

To Jacob deHaas

October 9, 1914 Boston, Mass. [deHaas Mss]

DEAR MR. DEHAAS: *First*: I received your letter of the 5th with memorandum; also yours of the 7th, both of which have been very helpful.[1] You will find that the course recommended by you has been in most respects adopted.

Second: Mr. Lipsky stated that after your return to Massachusetts, he was purposing to have you go South. I am inclined to think that it would be wise for you to devote yourself during November to the thorough mobilization of the forces in Massachusetts, on the lines which we discussed. Intensive work in Massachusetts will probably be more productive of financial results than work in the South, in view of their great feeling of poverty over cotton conditions;[2] and aside from that, it seems to me particularly important to have thorough work done in Massachusetts, among other things, as an example to other cities and States. With the admirable start that you have made, it seems to me that we ought, within a month or two, have progressed far in our work of mobilizing the forces here.

Third: The meeting in Cleveland was excellent in quality, and I think we have made a distinct impression on the non-Zionists,—

particularly at a small luncheon in which professed Zionists did not participate.   Very cordially yours,

1. In his letter of the 5th, deHaas had recommended that the lines of authority and responsibility in the Provisional Committee's office staff be made clearer, since many of the resolutions were policy statements rather than specific directives, thus leading to much confusion. The memorandum noted that the Central Zionist Bureau in Berlin should be considered defunct for the duration of the war. Moreover, since the colonization associations had always followed the leads of those who supplied the cash, now was the time for the American Zionists to make clear their proper role of leadership in the world movement. The letter of the 7th consisted primarily of gossip about minor matters and individuals.

2. The wartime disruption of transoceanic trade had caused a severe drop in cotton prices, from 12½ cents a pound in July to less than 7 cents a pound in mid-October. For the administration's efforts to save the South from bankruptcy, see Link, *Wilson: The Struggle for Neutrality, 1914-1915* (Princeton, 1960), 91-102.

To George Rublee

October 9, 1914 Boston, Mass. [Brandeis Mss, NMF 68-2]

MY DEAR GEORGE: I have yours and Farrand's [1] letters, and have just written him as per copy enclosed.

If it is possible to go to Manchester, I want to do it, and to tell New Hampshire people how valuable a man Stevens would be. [2]

I am delighted to know that the Trade Commission Bill is in a form satisfactory to you. [3] Your season in Washington has been well worth while.

Best greetings to Mrs. Rublee. It is fine to have her come back so well.   Most cordially yours,

1. George E. Farrand was chairman of the New Hampshire Democratic State Committee; he had written inviting LDB to speak in the state on behalf of Stevens's candidacy for the Senate.

2. Stevens was challenging incumbent Jacob H. Gallinger (1837-1918); he lost by 3,000 votes. See LDB to Alfred Brandeis, 28 October 1914.

3. Because of LDB's work with the I.C.C., Rublee had taken over the task of drafting the bill creating the Federal Trade Commission. He recalled his role in "The Original Plan and Early History of the Federal Trade Commission," *Proceedings of the Academy of Political Science*, 11 (1926): 114-20. For details on LDB's part in winning over Wilson to the idea of a strong trade commission, see Melvin I. Urofsky, "Wilson, Brandeis and the

Trust Issue, 1912–1914," *Mid-America*, 49 (1967): 3–28, especially 24–27. See also, LDB to Edward M. House 31 December 1914, and to Gilson Gardner, 7 September 1915.

To Thomas Watt Gregory

October 10, 1914 Boston, Mass. [Brandeis Mss, NMF 68-2]

MY DEAR GREGORY: Replying to yours of the 8th: [1]

The only one of the six men whom you name for marshall whom I know or know about, is the third man.[2] It seemed to me clear that he was not a man whom the Administration could afford to put into an office where, as you say, the qualities required are that the man be "honest, fearless, and not easily influenced". I thought it wise, however, to call up our friend MacFarland to find out what he knew about the six men. Without any intimation of any kind from me as to what I thought of your third man, he expressed himself far more emphatically as to the dangers of appointing him then I should have from my meagre knowledge. MacFarland knew little about the other five, but stated that he felt it clear that No. 4 was unfit.[3] He added that he would make some further inquiry and suggested that you defer for a week making any selection. I think it would certainly be wise not to make a selection without getting a definite report from MacFarland.[4]

I am going West next week for a few days, and expect to reach Washington a day or two before Monday the 19th, when the hearings before the Interstate Commerce Commission begin again, and I shall get into touch with you as soon as I reach Washington.[5]

Very cordially yours,

1. Gregory had solicited LDB's advice regarding the patronage appointment of a United States Marshal in Boston. He wrote: "It is my earnest desire to appoint an Irish Catholic to this place if a suitable man can be found. I am disposed to announce this before the general election."

2. The third name on the list was that of Thomas P. Riley (1875–1928), the assistant attorney-general of Massachusetts, and former chairman of the Democratic State Committee.

3. The fourth man was Joseph T. Lyons.

4. The appointment finally went to Guy Murchie.

5. See LDB to Alfred Brandeis, 21 October 1914.

To Chaim Weizmann

October 11, 1914 Boston, Mass. [Weizmann Mss]

DEAR SIR: [1] Letters addressed to Dr. Schmarya Levin by Mr. Hantke,[2] from Berlin, and Mr. Berger,[3] from Copenhagen, acquaint us with the fact that a conference of the Greater Actions Comite is to be convened at Stockholm on October 27. Circumstances make it next to impossible for anyone here to be present. We would therefore request you to act as the representative of the Provisional Executive Committee for General Zionist Affairs. We assume that it has been your intention to go to Stockholm in any case, and now we hope that you will let nothing stand in the way of your acting as our delegate and putting the contents of this letter before our European comrades.[4] It is of the utmost importance that the conference should have a clear understanding of what has been done here, chiefly at the urgence of Dr. Levin, and of what may yet be done to help our organization weather the difficult times that have overtaken it.

We desire to give you, first a comprehensive statement of what led up to the formation of the Provisional Executive Committee, as well as of subsequent action and happenings.

Dr. Levin was prompt in utilizing his enforced return to the United States on the Kronprizessin Cecilie for the benefit of the Zionist organization. Believing it inevitable that the war should interrupt the activities of the Inner Actions Comite for a shorter or longer period, and desiring that no interregnum hurtful to Zionist interests should intervene, he, together with the Chairman of the Executive Committee of the Federation of American Zionists, Mr. Louis Lipsky, called an extraordinary conference of American (that is, United States and Canadian) Zionists, to meet in New York City on August 30. A copy of the call is enclosed (Appendix A). About one hundred and fifty Zionists came to New York in response to their invitation. Canada was not represented *officially*. Dr. Levin opened the conference with a statement in which he pointed out the imperative need of providing for the administrative work and for the institutions hitherto supported by the Inner Actions Comite.

In accordance with his exposition of Zionist needs, the following resolution was adopted by the conference:

"WHEREAS, conditions prevailing in Europe have completely disorganized the Zionist organization and its committees and institutions, it, therefore, behooves us to assume the duties of the international administration, therefore,

BE IT RESOLVED, that we accept these duties through a Committee hereafter to be selected; that this committee shall act in co-operation with or in substitution for the members of the Actions Committee, until such time as it shall be able to resume its functions, or until a general congress can be summoned, and be it further,

RESOLVED, that the Provisional Committee for International Zionist Affairs shall be composed of eleven numbers, who are citizens of the United States."

The next action of the conference was the appointment of a committee of eleven: nine members at large, one representing the Mizrachi Federation, and one, the Poale Zion. The Committee, which took the title "Provisional Executive Committee for General Zionist Affairs", is composed of the following.

Chairman of the Provisional Committee, Louis D. Brandeis of Boston,

Vice-Chairman, Dr. J. L. Magnes, of New York,

Treasurer, Mr. E. W. Lewin-Epstein of New York, as representing Palestinian interests,[5]

Dr. Stephen S. Wise, of New York,

Dr. Harry Friedenwald of Baltimore, as Honorary President of Federation of American Zionists,

Mr. Louis Lipsky of New York, as Chairman of Executive Committee of Federation of American Zionists,

Mr. Joseph Barondess, as President of Nasi, Sons of Zion,

Miss Henrietta Szold, of New York, as President of Daughters of Zion,

Nathan D. Kaplan of Chicago, as President Knights of Zion,

Rabbi A. M. Ashinsky of Pittsburgh, Nominated by the Mizrachi,[6] and

Dr. Nochum [sic] Syrkin, nominated by the Poale-Zion.[7]

The Committee began its deliberations without delay. It appeared that its immediate task was twofold:

First, to put itself into communication with the members of the Inner Actions Comite, with the federations in all the neutral countries, and with Palestine; and,

Second, to proceed to raise a fund sufficiently large to ensure the continuity of the administrative work of the Zionist organization and maintain the institutions in Palestine, such as schools, etc. *Besides*, it was agreed that it was a proper function of the Provisonal Executive Committee, in view of possible developments, to establish relations with the American Jewish Committee, the agency which would naturally concern itself with the situation of the Jews in all countries affected by the war.

Appendix D [8] will indicate what means have been taken to execute the threefold task assumed by the committee. Correspondence (Appendix E) has been begun with the Inner Actions Comite, with the Federations of other neutral countries and with Palestine. Telegrams and letters have been received from Messrs. Warburg,[9] Hantke, and Sokolow, Mr. Berger, Dr. Ruppin, The Hague and Canada.

Appendix F is an appeal for a fund of $100,000. This sum was fixed by Dr. Levin as the minimum required for all the purposes enumerated above, for about two years. Collections are now in progress in all cities and towns in the United States in which there are societies affiliated with the Federation of American Zionists. In the large centers mass meetings have been held, at which the speakers have been Mr. Brandeis and Dr. Levin. A number of other prominent public speakers have offered their services, and the Federation of American Zionists is making arrangements for a series of similar meetings to be addressed by them.

Appendix G is a copy of a memorandum which has been presented to the American Jewish Committee. This requires a word of explanation. The Provisional Executive Committee approached the American Jewish Committee with the suggestion (Appendix D, Page 3) that a conference of all the large Jewish bodies in the United States (about seventy-five in number) be summoned for the purpose of discussing the whole Jewish situation created by the war and devising ways and means of meeting its exigencies. The subject was given consideration by a subcommittee of the Provisional Executive Committee in consultation with a subcommittee of the American Jewish Committee. As a consequence, the latter body will call such a conference on October 25. The Federation of American Zionists, as the American branch of the organization, will participate in the conference. The memorandum purports to represent the *minimum* programme on the basis of which the Zionist organization can take part in the conference. On the other hand, it is understood that its acceptance by the American Jewish Committee or by the conference of National (American) Jewish bodies does not preclude further steps on our part for safeguarding the Zionist organization in any way or ways that may present themselves in the course of time or through the development of events.

At the cabled request received from Ambassador Morgenthau, the American Jewish Committee raised a fund of $50,000 to be used partly as a loan fund and partly as a relief fund, and to be disbursed (at the suggestion of Ambassador Morgenthau) in Palestine by a committee headed by Dr. Ruppin. The American Jewish Committee appropriated the sum of $25,000 from its Emergency Fund; Mr. Jacob H. Schiff subscribed $12,500, and the Provisional Executive Committee also $12,500 (from funds other than the $100,000 fund projected).

Less than two weeks after the formation of the Provisional Executive Committee (though after the above threefold plan had been inaugurated and wide publicity had been given to the programme of the committee) it appeared, greatly to our satisfaction, that the central office of the Zionist organization was in a position to conduct its affairs. The Provisional Executive Committee at once took steps to bring about co-operation between itself and the members of the Inner Actions Comite. Through telegraphic communications, the Provisional Executive Committee has been authorized to proceed independently in all matters affecting the maintenance of the Palestinian institutions. With regard to the Shekel,[10] the correspondence is not complete. The Federation of American Zionists, as such, has received authority to issue a Shekel receipt. What has not yet been made clear is whether this authority was for America alone, or whether the Shekel was to be issued by the Provisional Executive Committee, for the world at large. The Committee awaits a reply touching this point.

A few isolated facts ought to be recorded.

The National Fund Bureau for America is not making deposits

in London nor in The Hague, because of the uncertainty of the situation in Europe. It has remitted $4,000 direct to Dr. Ruppin in Jaffa, on account of the Jewish National Fund, taking advantage of an opportunity to send gold to Palestine. Dr. B. Epstein has arrived here as the emissary of the National Fund, and is about to begin a propaganda for it. He will receive the moral and practical endorsement of all three American offices, the National Fund Bureau for America, the Federation of American Zionists, and the Provisional Executive Committee for General Zionist Affairs. A few days ago, the information reached us that Mr. K. [*sic*] Kaplansky [11] is on his way to this country, also for the purpose of furthering National Fund collections.

Mr. Kann,[12] of The Hague, and Mr. Cowen,[13] of London, have both written and cabled us as to the necessity of raising a fund of $500,000 for the bank, either through the sale of shares or through a loan for two years at a low rate of interest. (Appendix H)

This completes the resume of the work in this country since Dr. Levin's representation, made in the first instance to the Administrative Committee of the F.A.Z., spurred us on to the action we took. He succeeded in making the Zionists of America feel deeply the gravity of the situation. In all parts of the country, there have been manifestations which encourage the belief that the Zionist contingent in the United States will strain every nerve to maintain the organization and its institutions. The feeling that has been displayed indicates that there prevails intensive loyalty towards the Inner Actions Comite.

Now that it appears, contrary to our first thoughts, that the Actions Comite may be able to function in one way or another, we hold ourselves ready to carry out its mandate, and to support its work in the future as we have in the past.

In view of the above, the Provisional Executive Committee for General Zionist Affairs recommends to the Stockholm conference the following:

1) That it be authorized to represent not only one or another federation, but the Zionist organization as a whole, in all matters requiring action in connection with the Palestinian institutions and with the National Fund.

2) That it be authorized, in case of necessity, to represent the Zionist organization as a whole in any conference or pourparlers

that may eventually take place, having for its object the adjustment of the claims of the European nations.

(In both instances the authorization naturally is to be regarded as temporary, until such time when the Inner Actions Comite is again able to resume its normal duties, though the withdrawal of the authorization ought to be as explicit as the authorization we now recommend.)[14]

With Zion's greetings, we beg to remain,

Sincerely yours,

1. Chaim Weizmann (1874–1952) devoted his entire life to two causes, Zionism and chemistry. Born in the Russian city of Pinsk, he was educated at German and Swiss universities because anti-Jewish quotas kept him out of Russian schools. Even before Herzl founded the Zionist movement, Weizmann belonged to the Chibbath Zion society, and at the age of eleven he wrote a letter to his teacher advocating the creation of a Jewish homeland in Palestine. At the early Zionist congresses, he opposed Herzl's political Zionism as ignoring the cultural and religious values of Judaism, which he claimed formed the only possible bases for a true Jewish state.

In 1904 he moved to England as a lecturer in biological chemistry at the University of Manchester, and he gradually rose to the unofficial leadership of the Zionist movement. At the same time he was doing important work in chemistry, and becoming director in 1916 of the Admiralty Chemical Laboratory. With the fragmentation of the Zionist movement caused by the war, and with the important contacts he had made in the British government, Weizmann came to assume the leadership of the world movement, a position that was confirmed by his election to the presidency of the World Zionist Organization in 1919.

Undoubtedly Weizmann's most important contribution to Zionism during this period was the Balfour Declaration, which he guided from conception to fruition. In 1918, the British named him head of the Zionist Commission to go to Palestine to lay the groundwork for the eventual mandatory government there. While there, he laid the cornerstone for the Hebrew University in Jerusalem, which he hoped would be a central agency in the regeneration of Jewish life in the Holy Land.

Although LDB and Weizmann cooperated closely during the war, they clashed in 1920 and 1921 over the future management of the Zionist movement. LDB insisted on more practical work, while Weizmann was unsure of the political basis of the settlements in Palestine and wanted to continue developing the legal foundation for the homeland. Moreover, the two disagreed over the creation of the Keren Hayesod, a fund for the economic development of Palestine (see Zionist related letters in 1921). Weizmann challenged LDB's leadership of the American movement, and in 1921 he managed to force him out.

Weizmann's over-cautious leadership, as well as his great faith in Britain, gradually led to a weakening of his own position in the world movement, and he was ousted from the presidency in 1931. Although he was reelected in 1935, he never again enjoyed the prestige of his earlier regime. A new group of Zionists who mistrusted England, led by David Ben Gurion, gradually came to power, and Weizmann was again ousted in 1946. During 1947 and 1948, however, he played an important role in international negotiations over the partition of Palestine and the establishment of the state of Israel. He was the unanimous choice for the first presidency of the state, and was nominated by his foe Ben Gurion, who said: "I doubt whether the Presidency is necessary to Dr. Weizmann, but the Presidency of Dr. Weizmann is a moral necessity for the State of Israel." In ill health, he occupied the ceremonial position for only four years. At his death, he was buried at Rehovoth at the famed Science Institute which he founded.

The best source for his life is his autobiography, *Trial and Error* (New York, 1949), but it is highly defensive, and must be read with care; a useful corrective is Oskar K. Rabinowicz, *Fifty Years of Zionism: A Historical Analysis of Dr. Weizmann's 'Trial and Error'* (London, 1952). The publication of his papers has recently begun: Leonard Stein, in collaboration with Gedalia Yager, eds., *The Letters and Papers of Chaim Weizmann*, series A ⌐Letters (London, 1968 –).

2. Arthur Menahem Hantke (1874–1955), a German lawyer, had also belonged to a pre-Zionist group, the Judische Humanitatsgesellschaft, and later held a number of positions as a Zionist executive; his most important work, however, was as a director of the Jewish National Fund from 1905 to 1928. In 1926 he moved to Palestine and was an executive on the Keren Hayesod until his death.

3. Julius Berger (1884–1928) had begun his career as a Zionist executive in the central office in Cologne under David Wolffsohn (1856–1914), Herzl's successor as president of the movement. Berger edited the official Zionist paper, *Die Welt*, for many years, and when the war broke out, moved Zionist affairs to Copenhagen. In 1923 he settled in Palestine, and he was active in the Jewish National Fund until his death.

4. Weizmann did not go to Copenhagen and in fact scrupulously avoided contact with the Copenhagen office. Since the bureau was staffed primarily by Germans, he feared that the British government would consider the Zionists pro-German. Weizmann claimed later that his circumspection won the approval and support of key British leaders.

5. Elias Wolf Lewin-Epstein (1863–1932), another member of the Chibbath Zion movement, had been involved with several Jewish groups including one that established a Palestinian colony. He came to the United States in 1900 as a representative of the Carmel Wine Company and immediately became active in the Federation of American Zionists. During the war he went to Europe on a diplomatic mission representing the American Zionists, and in 1918 he headed the American Zionist Medical Mission to Palestine. His memoirs have been published in Hebrew, *Zikhronatai* (Tel Aviv, 1932).

6. Aaron Mordecai Ashinsky (1867–19[?]), born in Poland, had come to

the United States in 1886 and served as rabbi of Congregations Beth Hami-drash Hagadol and Beth Jacob in Pittsburgh. He had helped to found the first Zionist group in Canada and was a founder of the Mizrachi, the ortho-dox Zionist group. He later served as vice-president of the Keren Hayesod in the United States.

7. Nachman Syrkin (1867–1924) was one of the leaders of the Socialist Zionist (Poale Zion) movement. He had been at the first Zionist Congress in Basle in 1897 but had left the movement for a brief involvement with territorialism after the Uganda offer in 1905. (See *Encyclopedia of Zionism and Israel*, 1:263–64, 636–37.) He moved to the United States in 1907 and rejoined the movement in 1909, supporting himself as a Yiddish journalist. During the war he helped found the American Jewish Congress and served on the delegation to the Paris Peace Conference. See Marie Syrkin, *Nachman Syrkin: Socialist Zionist* (New York, 1961).

8. Appendix D consisted of LDB to Louis Marshall, 31 August 1914, and the reply.

9. Otto Warburg (1859–1938), a German botanist, had been instrumental in moving the Zionists toward more practical work by founding colonies in Palestine. Warburg was president of the World Zionist Organization from 1911 to 1920; in that year he moved to Palestine and founded the agri-cultural experimental station at Rehovoth.

10. The *shekel* was an ancient silver coin of Palestine, and also the tax paid for maintenance of the Sanctuary (Exod. 30:13); in the period of the second temple, it was an annual levy upon all Jews, and the Mishnah tractate *Shekalim* deals with its collection. The Zionists revived the idea of a shekel tax to support their activities, and all Zionists had to purchase at least one shekel stamp each year. The sum was small, less than a dollar, but it repre-sented a commitment to Zionism.

11. Shelomoh Kaplansky (1884–1950), a Polish-born Labor Zionist, was in charge of settlement affairs for the Jewish National Fund at its main office in The Hague. In 1919 he assumed direction of the movement's economic affairs and was a founder of the Keren Hayesod. In 1924 he settled in Pales-tine and was a director of the Haifa Technion.

12. Jacobus Henricus Kann (1872–1945), a Dutch banker, had been an early associate of Herzl and a member of the Zionist executive. He died in the concentration camp at Theresienstadt.

13. Joseph Cowen (1868–1932), an English businessman, had also been a colleague of Herzl, whom he accompanied on his mission to the sultan. Cowen was a founder of the Jewish Colonial Trust, the official bank of the Zionist movement.

14. On 18 October, Weizmann replied: "I consider the activities of the old Actions Committee impossible and even dangerous for the future of our cause. I cannot help thinking that the conference at Copenhagen would prove absolutely useless for our movement, and actually harmful for the future. The American Provisional Executive Committee should be given full power to deal with all Zionist matters, until better times come." See Weizmann, *Trial and Error*, 165.

To William Jennings Bryan

October 12, 1914 Boston, Mass. [Brandeis Mss, Z 1-2]

MY DEAR MR. BRYAN: I am enclosing herewith a letter from Mr. N. Syrkin, representative of our Zionist committee of the Poale Zion; and also a letter to me from Dr. J. L. Magnes, another member of that Committee, and a highly esteemed citizen of New York.[1]

The detention of Mr. Chazenovitch, as a prisoner of war is, we believe, due to a serious misapprehension on the part of the Austrian Government, and his detention there is depriving us of a zealous and efficient worker.

I trust it may appear to you proper to lay this correspondence before the Ambassador of Austria-Hungary with a view to his causing an investigation to be made into the facts by his Government.[2]   Very cordially and respectfully yours,

1. Both Syrkin and Magnes had requested LDB to use his good offices to secure the release of Leon Chazenovitch, a Canadian citizen being detained in Austria as an Allied agent. Chazenovitch (1882–1925) was a Labor Zionist leader and Yiddish journalist who actively promoted the Poale Zion. He was very effective in securing support for Zionism at various socialist congresses.

2. On 15 October, Acting Secretary of State Robert Lansing (see LDB to Stephen S. Wise, 15 October 1915) informed LDB that the American Ambassador at Vienna had been instructed to bring the matter to the attention of the Austrian Foreign Office; on 22 October, Lansing wrote that the department had been able to secure the release of Chazenovitch and his wife from prison, but that Austria would not allow him to leave the country.

To Alfred Brandeis

October 16, 1914 Detroit, Mich. [Brandeis Mss, M 4-1]

DEAR AL: Ran into Carmalt and some other I.C.C. men here of which I was glad, as it enabled me to talk over the Washington situation in advance of my going there. Es ist nicht sehr enfreulich.[1] "Man delights me not," [2]—and my appreciation of Bob son of Battle grows.[3]

At this hotel I was introduced to the modernist stunt of having not only an orchestra at dinner & singers, but also dancers.

Pompeii & Alexandria are being emulated. I guess a heavy batch of adversity wouldn't hurt American morals.

By the way, Anti-Semitism seems to have reached its American pinnacle here. New Athletic Club with *5000* members & no Jew need apply. Ich könnte es Ihnen kaum übel nehmen [4]—if the other 4600 were excluded also. But as Percy Lowell said of our Athletic Club: "It is the most inclusive club in Boston."

Off for Washt. 11⁵⁵ pm.

1. "It isn't very satisfactory." See LDB to Alfred Brandeis, 21 October 1914, n. 2.
2. *Hamlet*, II, 2: 321.
3. Alfred Ollivant, *Bob, Son of Battle* (New York, 1898), was a children's story about horses, and also the name of LDB's horse.
4. "I couldn't take offense."

To Alfred Brandeis

October 18, 1914 Washington, D.C. [Brandeis Mss, M 4-1]

DEAR AL: Prof. Ross (The Old World in the New [1] p. 143) gives the number of Jews in the U.S. in 1848 as 50,000, in 1861 about 150,000, in 1888 400,000. Now the number is about 3 million.

Situation here is further complication [*sic*] by fact that Harlan is a sick man (confidential) and it is uncertain whether he will be able to sit tomorrow. He certainly will not be able to work on the case during the next six weeks—the crucial period.

McGinty [2] told me (when I reported to him on Mrs. Marble) that neither Lane nor he had heard a word from her since she left Washington & that she left W. without saying goodbye or indeed giving any of them any intimation of her intention to do so.[3] McGinty's were very intimate with the Marbles, as of course the Lanes were. I guess you are the only person who has heard from Mrs. M.

1. (New York, 1914); see LDB to Prescott F. Hall, 8 April 1915, n. 3. More recent scholarship has only slightly adjusted these figures.
2. George Banks McGinty (1878–1937) was secretary of the Interstate Commerce Commission.
3. John Hobart Marble had died the preceding November.

To Henry Hurwitz

October 19, 1914 Washington, D.C. [Brandeis Mss, Z 6-2]

MY DEAR MR. HURWITZ: Your letter of the 14th reaches me here, as does also a letter of Mr. Philip Barnet [1] of the 12th and another from him of the 17th, with copy of his correspondence with Dr. Eliot. I think on the whole that it is fortunate that Dr. Eliot has declined. [2] In my mind our case can be best furthered at this time if the talk which I am to make should be somewhat more intimate in character than would be possible at a meeting open generally to the University public. I think it will be much better to limit the meeting to present and past members of the Zionist and Menorah Society and others you and Mr. Barnet may think it desirable to invite. I should suppose in that event you would select as the place of meeting the hall customarily used for your Menorah Society meetings.

I expect to be in Boston on election day, November 3, as well as on the 2nd. If Mr. Hermann should determine to hold his meeting on the 2nd I could speak on the evening of the 3rd at Harvard.

I am very glad to know that you are taking up actively with the committee of the Harvard Zionists Club the task of mobilizing the students and of collecting data. The more I have thought of these plans the more important and pressing this work seems to be, and I trust you will be ready upon my return to Boston to submit in some detail your suggestions on this subject.

I note your suggestion that I speak at the Chicago Menorah Society. I shall hope to do that, and also to speak at Ann Arbor, possibly in connection with my next visit to Chicago.

I have a telegram from Mr. [Walter] Kaplan, indicating that it will be desirable to postpone the Chicago meeting. I shall probably arrange to go there for November 21st.

Very truly yours,

1. Philip Barnet (b. 1892) a senior, was secretary of the Harvard Zionist Society. After Harvard Law School he joined the Federal Trade Commission and then established a practice in Bedford, Massachusetts. He represented Bedford in the state legislature from 1928 to 1942.

2. The Harvard Zionists had invited Charles W. Eliot, president emeritus of the University, to serve as chairman of the meeting at which LDB was to speak. He had declined, saying: "I am not clear in my mind that [Zion-

ism] is the best direction to give to the money of charitable American-Jews during this terrible war time."

To The Zionists of Philadelphia

October 19, 1914 New York, N.Y. [Brandeis Mss, Z 1-4]

You are all doubtless aware of the creation of The Provisional Executive Committee for General Zionist Affairs, of which I have the honor of being Chairman. This Committee was formed to maintain the institutions founded by the Zionist organization in Palestine through the present crisis, and to continue all Zionist activities pending the resumption of its functions by the Inner Actions Comite.

In line with this work, we have initiated a campaign of propaganda for an Emergency Fund of at least $100,000. We have received satisfactory co-operation from many of the larger Jewish centres, but regret to say that Philadelphia has not responded adequately. You do not seem to appreciate the seriousness of the present situation, else you would have organized your forces and presented our cause to our brethren in your city in a more energetic manner. We appreciate the fact that you have local problems which make this task a difficult one, but, in the name of our cause, we appeal to you again to organize your forces and begin now the work which must be done as soon as possible, if it is to be efficacious.

Together with the chairman of your Zionist Council,[1] I therefore call you to a special meeting of the organized Zionists of Philadelphia, to be held on Sunday evening, October 25th, at eight o'clock, at the Zion Institute, 1514 South Sixth Street. The Provisional Committee will be represented by several of its members, and you will receive from them information regarding the present status of our organization and our institutions in Palestine, which will aid you in forming plans for the Propaganda, to be inaugurated by you in Philadelphia.

Every Zionist who is earnest and loyal will respond to this invitation. This is the time when we expect of every sincere Zionist loyal and self-sacrificing service.

                              With Zion's greeting,

1. The letter was cosigned by Max Leopold Margolis (1866–1932), professor of Biblical philology at Dropsie College and chairman of the Zionist Council of Philadelphia.

To Alfred Brandeis

October 21, 1914 Washington, D.C. [Brandeis Mss, M 4-1]

DEAR AL: Otto [Wehle] may care to see enclosed from Karl.

Meeting many of your friends here. Huies of Louisville introduced himself yesterday (who is he?) also one Beech (?).[1] Hopkins of Chicago assures me of his undying admiration of you.

Met Col. Watterson, blooming like a rose, who greeted [me] as "Louis."

No doubt about Phillipson's [sic] power nor that he is a son of a gun.

Have had some fun in cross-examination these days & don't think the railroad folk are very happy. Their present application seems to me an impertinence.[2]

Descried Charles N[agel] at Bar Assn Reception yesterday; but we didn't "see" one another.

1. The Veech family was a prominent Louisville family with several branches. It is impossible to know which particular member LDB was introduced to. See LDB to Alfred Brandeis, 28 October 1914.

2. Claiming that they were confronted by unprecedented financial conditions aggravated by the war, the railroads had petitioned the Interstate Commerce Commission for a rehearing on their application for at least a 5 percent rate advance. The opening witness on 19 October was B. & O. president Daniel Willard, who presented a mass of evidence supporting the railroad's contention that they had been adversely affected by the wartime disruptions. Questions by the commission members indicated that they had anticipated this line of argument, and they demanded to know why the railroads should be treated any differently than other industries hard-hit by the war.

In cross-examination, LDB tore into the financial picture presented by Willard and wanted to know how the B. & O. had managed to maintain a 6 percent dividend in the face of an operating loss of $3,000,000 in net revenue. LDB also noted that an increase in rates would shift the burden of industrial accommodation from the stockholders, where it belonged, to the consumers. As the hearings moved into their second day, LDB and the commissioners hammered on the theme that the railroads were asking the public to assume costs inherent in the risk-taking nature of investment, and that businesses had to absorb these costs first via reduced dividends before they could justify a rate increase.

To Jacob deHaas

October 21, 1914 Washington, D.C. [Brandeis Mss, Z 6-1]

MY DEAR MR. DEHAAS: I have yours of the 16th.[1]

First: I am glad to know that you are satisfied with the success of your western trip. I trust that your trip to Cincinnati also has met with good results.

Second: From such data as I have been able to obtain I agree fully with the opinion which you express, that there has been a great lack of organization in the western and southern country and that there is opportunity for extensive development there. My conviction, however, was and is that the most fruitful of all territory is Massachusetts, and that both for immediate results and for ultimate benefit to the cause we should obtain most by thoroughly developing the Massachusetts field, for its own sake and as an example to others; and not only as an example but as affording a basis of experience which could be applied elsewhere.

I note, however, that there are a "number of reasons," which you do not set forth, why you deem it advisable to undertake the proposed southern and western trip which you and Mr. Lipsky plan before undertaking an extensive campaign in Massachusetts; and if you and Mr. Lipsky are, upon further consideration, both of the opinion that it will be more desirable for you to make the southern and western trip first I am entirely content to defer to your judgment.

I expect to return to Boston in order to vote, and to reach there not later than Monday, November 2, so that presumably I shall have an opportunity of talking matters over generally with you in any event. Of course you will have to make your plans for the tour, if you do leave, as I suppose you plan, immediately after election, and I do not wish to have you and Mr. Lipsky await my return to Boston before reaching a decision on the above.

Third: I have today a telegram from Mr. Julius Meyer reading as follows:

"Jewish Chronicle London reports received letter from Doctor Nordau stating now located Madrid Spain.[2] Know the men received letter London. You think advisable to communicate with London to Get Nordau's address so we may get in touch with him at Madrid."

I am not certain of the purpose that Mr. Meyer may have had in mind. I presume it is clear that we do not wish to invite Mr. Nordau to come to America at present.

                                        Very cordially yours,

1. deHaas reported that his swing through the Midwest had been fairly successful, raising money and also starting several new Zionist societies. He believed that the best place for him to go next would be through the West and South, since that was territory that had never been developed by Zionist organizers before.

2. Max Nordau, although pro-Allied, had been expelled from France as an Austrian citizen, and he spent the rest of the war in Spain.

To Henry Morgenthau

                October 22, 1914 New York, N.Y. [Morgenthau Mss]

DEAR SIR: We are enclosing for your information, copy of a letter sent by this Committee to Dr. Arthur Ruppin.[1]

We desire to bring to your particular notice, the paragraph referring to the centralizing of the Palestine charitable work. It is our hope that you will appreciate the importance of this and assist by your influence and advice in this very important step.

We feel that the opportunity is now in our hands to bring about a more orderly and more systematic arrangement for the distribution of charitable funds in Palestine and especially in Jerusalem.

We thank you for the courtesies that you have in the past shown to us and we trust that we may have your valuable cooperation in the future.[2]

With Zion's greetings, we are,   Very truly yours,

1. See LDB to Arthur Ruppin, 5 October 1914.

2. As ambassador to Turkey, Morgenthau played a crucial role in the early months of the war. He assured the Turkish officials that America was in fact neutral, and that aid to the Jewish population of Palestine was no

more and no less than an act of mercy. He intervened several times to prevent local officials from harassing the Palestinian Jews, although he was unable to prevent the mass expulsion of those who retained Russian citizenship, since Turkey was at war with Russia. Morgenthau, however, was never overly friendly to Zionism, and after the war ended, he became an aggressive anti-Zionist. See his article, "Zionism a Surrender, Not a Solution," *World's Work*, 42 (July 1921): 1–8 [supp.].

To Ben Campbell

October 23, 1914 Washington, D.C. [Brandeis Mss, NMF 65-1]

MY DEAR MAYOR CAMPBELL: [1] Your letter of the 13th reaches me here. You say that you learned from press reports that I am attorney for "an organization formed in New York City, of Eastern commercial organizations and twenty-three commercial bodies scattered from Bellows Falls, Vt., and Rochester, N.Y., to Richmond, Va., united in a compact to resist any further encroachments upon the business welfare of the Atlantic Seaboard." I did not see the press report to which you refer and did not hear before the receipt of your letter that any such organization had been formed. Possibly it has, but I doubt it. I know, however, that I am not attorney for such an organization and have not been approached by anyone in respect to acting for or with any organization or individual proposing activity in that direction.

My only connection with traffic matters at present is as special counsel for the Interstate Commerce Commission in connection with the proposed advance in rates in Official Classification Territory.

I desire to express my appreciation of your courteous invitation. I have not such a knowledge of relative rates to the seaboard and the Gulf ports to entitle me to an opinion as to whether the rates to the Gulf ports are discriminatory or whether they are just, but if my other engagements did not prevent I should be only too glad to attend your convention and to learn from others what the situation is. It would be a great satisfaction also to me to attend for an entirely different purpose, that is to express to the people of Texas our gratitude for the men they are at present furnishing for high places with the administration.[2]

Very cordially yours,

1. Ben Campbell (1854–1942) was mayor of Houston from 1913 to 1917, and was responsible for a number of civic and industrial improvements in the city during his administration. He had invited LDB to address a civic convention in Houston on the problems of differential rates between the various I.C.C. rate zones.

2. Among Texans appointed by the Wilson administration were Albert S. Burleson and Thomas W. Gregory; E. M. House, the President's confidant, was also a Texan.

To Jacob deHaas

October 23, 1914 Washington, D.C. [Brandeis Mss, Z 6-1]

MY DEAR MR. DEHAAS: I have a telegram this morning from Mr. Prussian [1] stating that the local charities were to send a delegation to Sunday's conference with a view to organizing a war relief fund in Massachusetts, which will interfere with our meeting, asking whether necessary arrangements for our representation in conference will be made and whether we are to fight or cooperate with local charities.

First: You doubtless know that arrangements have been made for quite a full Zionist representation,—three specific delegates of the Federation and Dr. Magnes and Mr. Lewin-Epstein as representatives of other organizations.

Second: As to the attitude to be taken with respect to our meetings, that is whether they should be separate or in connection with general charity meetings, you will know best. My own opinion, however, is that we shall do better to have our meetings separate and apart from the others. The only instance of definite combination which was carried out—that of Pittsburgh—has been by no means satisfactory, and the futile attempt in Cincinnati proved quite embarrassing. I am inclined to think that our own cause would to a considerable extent be dwarfed by the combination. We can not afford to make our cause subordinate to any other, although, of course, we must take the occasion of the war to advance in every way the Zionist cause.[2]

Very cordially yours,

1. Aaron Prussian was a member of the Boston Zionist group; he referred in his telegram to the 25 October meeting that would discuss overall strategy for raising relief funds in the United States.

2. In the end, it proved impossible for the Zionists to operate their own fund-raising program. Many of the wealthy Jews in the country were either non-Zionists or openly anti-Zionist, while smaller donors were primarily concerned with relief to their relatives in Europe. The Zionists finally settled for a dominant role in the disposition of funds earmarked for Palestinian work.

To Alfred Brandeis

October 24, 1914 Philadelphia, Pa. [Brandeis Mss, M 4-1]

DEAR AL: I came over on the midnight [train], on my way to Atlantic City to have a little talk with Harlan & then to N.Y., where Alice & Susan are.

Tomorrow, unfortunately, must be devoted to Zionism. Then I return (with Alice I hope) to Washington for about a week. The arguments begin Thursday; & we shall go back to Boston to vote. The later moves are not yet settled, but shall probably return to Washington after Election for a[t] least a short time.

The RRs & Bankers did not do themselves much credit. If they have their way they will utterly break down the Commission & even if they are beaten they will have succeeded in greatly impairing its standing and their own defense against lawlessness and public ownership.

To Richard James Horatio Gottheil

October 27, 1914 Washington, D.C. [Gottheil Mss]

MY DEAR PROFESSOR GOTTHEIL: Your letter of the 26th reached me this morning.[1]

First: I telegraphed you at once, suggesting that you see Dr. Magnes in regard to the treasurership of the committee if the matter is serious, as you suggest. I have no doubt that it is not too late to arrange now for the withdrawal of Mr. Warburg as Treasurer.[2]

Second: As to the collection for Palestinian charities: Your Committee should, of course, not take any action which the Executive Committee of the National Conference deems a violation of our obligations to it, and if Mr. Sulzberger's[3] and Judge

Mack's view is entertained by others I suppose that you are clearly limited in your work so far as Palestinian charities are concerned; but it must be clear on the other hand that our Zionist work is in no way restricted.

Third: I called up the French embassy today asking for an appointment tomorrow afternoon, and the clerk who answered the telephone said that it would be necessary for him to confer with the Ambassador and that he would send me word.[4]

Cordially yours,

1. At the meeting of the National Conference of Jewish Charities on 25 October, a special committee had been created to coordinate all Jewish charities; Gottheil believed this would hamper the work of the Federation of American Zionists on its own Palestinian relief efforts, but the F.A.Z. was a member of the conference. He also worried about the effects on Allied opinion of the election of Felix M. Warburg (see next note) as treasurer of the special fund, since Warburg was reputedly pro-German in sentiment.

2. Felix Moritz Warburg (1871–1937), a partner in Kuhn, Loeb and Company, and a son-in-law of Jacob Schiff, was heavily involved in a number of Jewish charitable organizations.

3. Cyrus Leo Sulzberger (1858–1932), a New York merchant, had participated in several anti-Tammany campaigns, including an unsuccessful election bid for the Manhattan borough presidency in 1903. He was on the boards of numerous Jewish charitable agencies and was secretary of the American Jewish Relief Committee. Sulzberger was the father of Arthur Hays Sulzberger, the future editor of the *New York Times*.

4. See LDB to Jean A. A. J. Jusserand, 16 November 1914.

To Alfred Brandeis

October 28, 1914 Washington, D.C. [Brandeis Mss, M 4-1]

DEAR AL: You will be interested in enclosed which please return. Alice came down with me Monday & we plan to leave for Boston Saturday pm. As a true patriot I must go home to vote & even go to Manchester, N.H. to speak in aid of Stevens' candidacy for the U.S. Senate (Democratic).[1] Tuesday I am to talk to the Harvard Menorah. Expect to go to N.Y. again on Thursday pm on Labor matters for 2 days & am uncertain whether then to Washington or Boston. Don't you think Commercial Travellers Assn would take me?

Sorry I didn't appreciate who Veech [2] was.

1. See LDB to George Rublee, 9 October 1914, n. 1.
2. See LDB to Alfred Brandeis, 21 October 1914, n. 1.

To Oscar Solomon Straus

October 29, 1914 Washington, D.C. [Brandeis Mss, Z 1-2]

MY DEAR MR. STRAUS: First: I hope that Dr. Magnes conveyed to you my telegraphic message of Monday, that in my opinion you ought to be the Chairman of our Organization Committee.[1] I should have resisted your very kind nomination of me at the time but for the fact that when you made it I was thinking of our own conference at the City Club.

Second: Professor Gottheil has written to me his views in regard to the selection of Mr. Warburg for the treasurership of the National Committee, and although he may possibly have exaggerated the danger, I think his objection is well taken; and I hope that Mr. Marshall has been convinced that it is advisable to make a change as we must be very careful to avoid the possibility of a misunderstanding in dealings involving foreign relations.[2]

Third: I am returning to you herewith the letters of Dr. Nordau, Dr. Yahuda and Mr. Marshall, which did not reach me until yesterday.[3]

Fourth: I had a talk yesterday with the French Ambassador,[4] about which I shall wish to confer with you when we next meet.

Cordially yours,

1. Of the American Jewish Relief Committee. Straus did accept.
2. See LDB to Richard Gottheil, 27 October 1914.
3. There are no copies of this correspondence in the Brandeis collection. The Dr. Yahuda referred to is undoubtedly Abraham Shalom Ezekiel Yahuda (1877–1951). A Biblical scholar and Orientalist, he was presently teaching at Madrid (where Nordau himself was located during the war). Yahuda worked to bring the problems of Palestinian Jewry to the attention of Straus and other American Jewish leaders. After the war he and Nordau went to England, and then Yahuda settled in the United States where he died.
4. Jean Adrien Antoine Jules Jusserand (1855–1932) was the extremely cultivated long-time ambassador of France to the United States. The author of several books on French, English, and American history, he served as president of the American Historical Association in 1921. See LDB to Jusserand, 16 November 1914.

To Howard S. Graham

October 30, 1914 Washington, D.C. [Brandeis Mss, NMF 69-1]

MY DEAR MR. GRAHAM: [1] I am very glad to have your letter of the 28th, the copy of your statement and the other enclosures. I read Charles Francis Adams' "A Chapter of Erie" many years ago, and it seemed to me then extremely illuminating. I have had frequent occasions since to think of it and to appreciate Mr. Adams' remarkable foresight.

I am glad to know that you are prepared to help in the work which the Commission has undertaken and in which I have endeavored to aid it. To succeed two things must be established: First, a proper respect for truth; and, secondly, a recognition by bankers and corporation men that we are our brothers' keepers. It has long seemed to me that false accounting was in our age a far more serious offense than counterfeiting. The ordinary individual does have some reasonable chance of detecting a counterfeit bill or counterfeit coin. The counterfeit money soon reaches a final resting place, and is apt to result in the prompt punishment of those who engage in circulating it. But even the most intelligent investor in securities has no protection against the pitfalls incident to false accounting. And yet neither the corporation men who require credit nor the bankers who are instrumental in giving credit have been willing to take a determined stand in favor of sound accounting, or to show in any effective way their disapproval of false accounting.

The false accounting of the New Haven was exposed seven years ago. Every honest railroad man and every honest banker had really a professional interest in protecting his craft from the evil effects of permitting false accounting to continue in a company of such prominence as the New Haven; but no one of those occupations thought truth in accounting to be of enough importance to insist upon its observance in the case of so conspicuous a corporation. I realize, of course, the limitations of the individual man, but certainly if such an association as that of the American Investment Bankers is to have any justification, ought it not make it its first task to insist upon truth, and even if that involves some immediate sacrifice on the part of the members of the association?

I hope that we may meet soon and talk these matters over.

Yours very truly,

1. Howard S. Graham was an investment banker in Philadelphia. He had met LDB in Washington at the rate hearing and had been bothered by LDB's comments that the bankers should have known about the financial irregularities of some of the railroads. Graham admitted that the bankers did indeed know, but he thought most of them accepted the problem as an unavoidable social evil and took it into account whenever dealing with railroad securities. Those bankers who were bothered found some comfort in the fact that the Interstate Commerce Commission, as well as some of the state agencies, had finally begun to regulate railroad securities to a minor degree. The statement enclosed dealt with this fact, and Graham sent it on to the I.C.C. Graham also enclosed a copy of Charles Francis Adams's exposé of the Erie Railroad published forty years earlier.

To Maurice Robert Hely-Hutchinson

October 30, 1914 Washington, D.C. [Brandeis Mss, NMF 66-3]

MY DEAR SIR: [1] I have read with great interest your very courteous letter of the 28th, your published letter to the Evening Post and that of the 23rd to the Evening Post which I trust has been published since. There is hardly a word in what you say in which I do not fully agree.[2]

Your plan of forming an Institute of Directors is in substance similar to that suggested by Mr. Frederick A. Delano last summer, in which he proposed to bring home to the bankers and railroad men the obligation of enforcing business honor in their respective professions.

It has seemed to me that we could never secure the proper conduct of big business until bankers and corporation men generally recognized that they were their brothers' keepers. Unfortunately, there has in the past been no recognition of this obligation. The tendency has been rather the contrary, that is to protect their brother whether right or wrong.

The most serious sin of which those connected with big business have been guilty has been the failure to recognize the importance of truth, and specifically the importance of correct accounting, to which you call attention. I am not aware that anyone connected with the banking world has commented favorably on any exposure by the Interstate Commerce Commission of false accounting, such as it made in connection with the St. Paul, the Frisco and the New Haven. When false accounting by the New Haven was exposed seven years ago the effort of the financial interests was to cover up and minimize the false accounting (And, as you say, the certificate of the Chartered Accountant, instead of proving a protection, added to the pitfall).

Justice is but truth in action, and we cannot hope to attain justice until we have the proper respect for truth.

If by chance you see a little volume of mine entitled "Other People's Money", I wish you would read the chapters on "Bankers,—management" and "Inefficiency of the Oligarchs."

I am much interested to hear that you are a friend of Lord Eustace Percy,[3] for whom I have a very warm regard. I trust that I may have the pleasure of meeting you some day.

Yours very truly,

1. Maurice Robert Hely-Hutchinson (1887–1961) was a member of the family of the Earl of Donoughmore. He was the American representative of several British industries.

2. In two letters signed "Signa Severa," Hely-Hutchinson had attacked the morality of American corporate enterprise and had proposed that the corporate directors themselves be held criminally responsible for corporate wrong-doing.

3. Eustace Sutherland Campbell Percy (1887–1958), later Baron Percy of Newcastle, was in 1914 at the beginning of a lengthy career first in government service and later in education. In addition to diplomatic work, he was a member of Parliament and an official in several cabinets. From 1937 to 1952, he was rector of the Newcastle division of the University of Durham. Among his many books were *The Responsibilities of the League* (London, 1920), *Democracy on Trial* (London, 1931), and the autobiographical *Some Memories* (London, 1958).

To Richard James Horatio Gottheil

October 31, 1914 Washington, D.C. [Gottheil Mss]

MY DEAR MR. GOTTHEIL: Replying to yours of the 30th:

I regret that Mrs. Brandeis, who is with me, is not very well, so that it will not be possible for me to stop over at New York as you suggest. We shall take the through train for Boston which does not go via New York. I expect to be in New York again on Friday next.

I doubt whether there is anything that I can suggest in regard to your interview [1] that will not occur to you and Miss Szold. This only I think is imperative—Nothing must be said which could by any possibility be understood by the Turkish or German authorities in indicating a lack of sympathy with Turkish government or as indicating particular sympathy with the allies. I know how difficult it would be to write anything which might not be subject to misconstruction at this time; and perhaps you may find it wiser to defer the interview.   Very cordially yours,

1. A reporter from the *London Times* wanted to interview Gottheil on the future of Palestine, especially since Turkey had entered the war against Great Britain. Gottheil realized that this was a sensitive issue, and he wanted LDB to stop in New York and advise him.

To Alfred Brandeis

November 1, 1914 Washington, D.C. [Brandeis Mss, M 4-1]

DEAR AL: 42 years ago today we were on the Huzzarrenberg. (I am not quite sure which to double, the z's or the r's.)[1] Those were better days for poor Europe—and for Austria in particular.

I omitted to tell you that [Schmarya] Levin described his Cincinnati meeting as a "Reinfall,"[2] & was quite as disgusted with the local material as we were.

Alice & I plan to leave on the Federal today,—should have left yesterday, but for her annoying headache, which Alice thought would be humored into decency by a day's waiting. May be back here again before many days. The railroads made a pretty poor showing in many respects,—in wisdom as well as in earnings.

1. See LDB to Alfred Brandeis, 1 November 1889.
2. "Disappointment, let-down."

To Alfred Brandeis

November 4, 1914 Boston, Mass. [Brandeis Mss, NMF 65-1]

MY DEAR AL: I have yours of the 31st about the advance in grain rates.[1] I have no doubt that the grain rates ought to be advanced. They, and particularly the rates on grain products, are too low, and this is particularly true of export rates. Of course I do not know to what extent discrimination exists, or may be aggravated by the proposed increases, and I also know nothing as to what the

Commission will do. I should not be surprised, however, if they declined to exercise their discretion of suspending the rate, and reserve for later hearings the question of its propriety and discrimination.[2]

My progressive friends suffered severely yesterday.[3]

    1. Alfred had sent on a letter he received regarding a one-cent increase in the rate for grain shipment from Chicago to New York, and noting that a lower price on transshipment of grain originating beyond Chicago had not been affected. While he did not deny the possible need for the increase (which amounted to 5 percent), he noted the opportunity of all grain shippers to claim an Illinois origin and thus receive the lower rate for transshipment.

    2. On 6 November Alfred replied that he was objecting, not to an increase in rates, but to the failure to apply such an increase uniformly and in those areas where an increase would not affect business. He cited as an example grain shipped across country for export to Europe. With the European nations eager to buy grain, an increase of even 1.5 cents per 100 pounds would merely be passed on to the buyer without any affect on the market.

    3. Progressives experienced genuine setbacks in the 1914 elections. The Democratic majority in the House of Representatives was reduced from 73 to 25, and Republicans returned to power in the key states of New York, Pennsylvania, Ohio, Illinois, Wisconsin, and Kansas. Actually, the vote reflected the return of many Progressive Party members to the G.O.P. as much as dissatisfaction with Democratic policy and depressed business conditions.

To Howard Elliott

November 4, 1914 Boston, Mass. [Brandeis Mss, NMF 1-N-3]

MY DEAR MR. ELLIOTT: Upon my return to the city I find your letter of October 12th with enclosures, and the annual report which you were good enough to send me.[1]

Despite results which must appear to you in some respects unsatisfactory, I think you are to be congratulated on the great progress which has been made. It seems to me that the hope which you expressed is fully justified.

With best wishes,   Very truly yours,

    1. Elliott had sent LDB reports indicating that the New Haven had effected economies in all departments except maintenance. He also noted that the "path ahead does not look very bright," but hoped that the efforts at economy and a possible business upswing would bring better times.

To Henry French Hollis

November 4, 1914 Boston, Mass. [Brandeis Mss, NMF 68-2]

MY DEAR HOLLIS: It is too bad that Stevens has been defeated, but I think we may still pluck victory out of defeat by securing his appointment as the New England member of the Federal Trade Commission.

Will you take this up with the President? [1]

Most cordially yours,

1. Stevens was ineligible under the provisions of a law which prohibited any member of Congress from holding an office created by a Congress of which he was a member. Stevens was later named counsel to the F.T.C.

To Gifford Pinchot

November 4, 1914 Boston, Mass. [Brandeis Mss, NMF 68-2]

MY DEAR GIFFORD: The morning news is disappointing to the progressive minded.[1] We are saddened by many defeats; but you made a grand fight, and I am sure have laid the foundation for later victories. Your campaign, what you said, and particularly what you are, must have made a deep impression on Pennsylvania. The State and the Country will be much the better for it.

You must take a short rest after the strenuous campaign, but I hope it will be but a few weeks before you, with Amos, will be again planning other attacks upon the omnipresent enemy.

My most cordial greetings to Mrs. Pinchot, who, I am told quite equals her husband as a campaigner.

Most cordially yours,

1. Pinchot had been badly defeated in his race for the Senate by Pennsylvania boss Boies Penrose. The tally in the three-way fight was: Penrose (Rep.) 489,346; Pinchot (Prog.) 252,853; and A. Mitchell Palmer (Dem.) 251,433.

To Raymond Bartlett Stevens

November 4, 1914 Boston, Mass. [Brandeis Mss, NMF 68-2]

MY DEAR RAY: I am deeply disappointed at the morning's returns. It would have been a great thing for New England and the Country to have had you in the Senate, but I feel sure that in office or out we shall have you in the public service.

Most cordially yours,

To Meyer London

November 5, 1914 Boston, Mass. [Brandeis Mss, NMF 68-2]

MY DEAR LONDON: I am delighted to read in the morning papers of your election to Congress.[1] It shows the appreciation of your work by our people, and through it will come a wider appreciation of what you have done and are doing.

With every good wish,   Cordially yours,

1. In the heavily Jewish Twelfth Congressional District of New York, Meyer London was elected to Congress on the Socialist ticket by a plurality of 924 over incumbent Democrat Henry M. Goldfogle (1856–1929).

To Samuel Randall

November 5, 1914 Boston, Mass. [Brandeis Mss, Z 1-2]

MY DEAR SIR: Upon my return to the city I find your very courteous letter asking permission to use my name as the name of your Club.[1]

I appreciate the compliment, but venture to suggest that there are so many other names worthier of adoption that it would be preferable to make some other selection.

Yours very truly,

1. Randall belonged to a newly formed Zionist club in Boston, and he and his friends wanted to name the club after LDB.

To Max Harris Wilensky

November 5, 1914 Boston, Mass. [Brandeis Mss, NMF 78-1]

MY DEAR MR. WILENSKY: [1] I have yours of the 3rd.

If I attend the National Conference of Mayors next week, I shall be glad to arrange the interview which you suggest. As it is doubtful whether it will be possible for me to be there, I venture to suggest the following:

Anti-Semitism is no doubt an obstacle which it is necessary to overcome in many situations, and under many conditions, but I am convinced, nevertheless, that in this Country good work in many departments of activity will soon be recognized, even if not necessarily at 100 per cent of its value. I am convinced also from my own observation that there is little difference in this respect between the different cities. The wise thing for you to do is to endeavor to meet such feeling as you may find to exist in the place in which you are working, and not endeavor to escape by removal to another city.

I see no reason whatever to believe that you would find conditions better in Boston than in Philadelphia, and in leaving Philadelphia you would abandon the start which you have already made,—a matter serious in itself.

Bear in mind also that the real success in life is to be measured by one's own accomplishments in advancing the welfare of the community, and that most men will be doomed to disappointment if they measure accomplishment by the degree of appreciation which they receive.

I am glad to note that you are assisting Mr. Morris L. Cooke, for whom I have great admiration. I am returning herewith the elaborate brief which you enclosed.[2]

With best wishes,   Very cordially yours,

1. Max Harris Wilensky (1887–1946), after graduating from law school, had joined Morris L. Cooke in the Philadelphia Department of Public Works to assist in the Utilities Bureau's legal work. He wrote that while his work had been praised by Cooke, he believed he had been the victim of blatant anti-Semitism in the course of his career.

2. Despite LDB's advice, Wilensky left Philadelphia to settle in Atlanta, Georgia, where he enjoyed a prosperous career both in business and in law; for many years, however, he maintained a law office in Philadelphia as well.

To Israel J. Biskind

November 6, 1914 Boston, Mass. [Brandeis Mss, Z 1-2]

MY DEAR MR. BISKIND: [1] I find upon my return here that up to date, $2,000 has been received from Cleveland. We have hoped that Cleveland would contribute at least $5,000 and I trust that the amount sent represents a part only of what has been already subscribed.

My talk with Mr. Baker [2] at luncheon, led me to believe that if your Committee presented this matter to the Committee of the Federation of Charities, of which Mr. Baker is Secretary, that a substantial amount would be made available for our purpose.

Will you kindly confer with your associates and let me know when we may expect further remittances from Cleveland and what the result has been of your application to the Federation. I felt very confident after my talk with some of those present at the luncheon, that they would give their substantial support. Awaiting your reply, I am,[3]   Very truly yours,

1. Israel J. Biskind, a Cleveland physician, was an officer of the Zionist organization of that city. He was the chief surgeon for the first American Zionist Medical Unit for Palestine and the consulting physician for the government of Palestine, 1924–25.

2. Newton Diehl Baker (1871–1937), the mayor of Cleveland, had given the welcoming speech to LDB when the latter visited Cleveland. A leading Ohio progressive, Baker served as mayor of Cleveland from 1912 until he was appointed by President Wilson to be Secretary of War in 1916. Although reputedly a pacifist, Baker proved a competent war official; in 1928, Calvin Coolidge named him to the Permanent Court of Arbitration in The Hague. For an analysis of his service in the War Department, see Daniel R. Beaver, *Newton D. Baker and the American War Effort, 1917–1919* (Lincoln, Neb., 1966). See also, Frederick Palmer, *Newton D. Baker: America at War* (2 vols., New York, 1931), which is practically idolatrous.

3. There is no reply from Biskind in the Brandeis MSS.

To Benjamin Perlstein

November 9, 1914 Boston, Mass. [Brandeis Mss, Z 3-2]

DEAR MR. PERLSTEIN: Please attend to the following:

First: Reimburse Mr. Sachs [1] promptly for the expense paid by him of the taxi which took me from Columbia to the Bronx, and then to 43rd Street,—an appreciable amount.

Second: You will recall a letter I dictated to Mr. Wilfred A. Oppenheim saying I sent by another mail copies of two pamphlets on Zionism. I omitted to specifically request you to send those pamphlets, but presume you have done so. If you have not, please send them at once.

Third: Send me a copy of the report prepared by you and Mr. Lipsky for the November 8th meeting, showing in detail the receipts to date, and sources thereof, distributed among the cities etc., and also the schedule of estimated amounts already subscribed.

Send similar reports to me on Monday of each week bringing up the data to the preceding Saturday.

Fourth: Send to members of each of the Committee having matters in hand not yet disposed of, a request to send a report to the office in writing not later than next Monday and let me have carbons of letters that you send.

Fifth: I desire to have on file here a complete report of all meetings, beginning with the report of the conference on August 30th and of meetings of the Provisional Committee since.

I have on my files now copy of the following:

Minutes of meeting on August 30, 1914.

Minutes of meeting on August 31, 1914.

I am enclosing a copy of letter of today to Mr. Lipsky.[2]

Yours very truly,

1. Possibly Alexander Sachs (b. 1893), who had recently joined the New York office of Lee, Higginson & Co. as an economist; he later became a director of research for Lehman Brothers and for the National Recovery Administration. He served on the political economy committee of the Zionist organization.

2. See LDB to Perlstein, 18 January 1915.

To Judah Leon Magnes

November 11, 1914 Boston, Mass. [Magnes Mss]

DEAR DR. MAGNES: Further consideration has confirmed the opinion expressed by me at our meeting of the National Relief Committee on the 6th that my name ought not to go in as a member of the Executive Committee.[1] I cannot emphasize too much the importance of care in the selection of the list of nominations for that Committee, and as soon as the full list of names for the general committee is ready, each member of our Committee on Organization should be furnished this list, as was agreed, so that we may before our next meeting of the Committee on Organization, give it careful study.

I learned that Dr. Wise did not receive any invitation to join the General Committee. This I presume must have been an oversight, in view of the large number of invitations sent out, and I wish you would ask Mr. Fromenson [2] to send him an invitation at once.

I have heard much criticism of the large number of invitations to join the General Committee which were issued. It was contended that this great increase in the number above 100 deprives the Committee of the democratic character which was to have been secured by the election of representatives of the 50 organizations. Of course those 50 representatives who would have constituted a large part of the Committee of 100 become a negligible minority in a committee of 1000 or possibly 2000, and the large number of the general committee dilutes also very much the honor of the appointment. How did it happen that so great a modification in the plans was made?

Very cordially yours,

1. At the meeting of 25 October which had decided to form a unified relief agency, it had also been decided to form both national and local committees to head the fund-raising drives. LDB did not want to sit on the executive committee of what ultimately became the American Jewish Relief Committee, primarily because he felt it might restrict his activity as head of the Provisional Committee.

2. Abraham H. Fromenson (1874–1935), a former writer for the *New York Evening World,* did publicity work for a number of Jewish organizations, writing articles in both the English and Yiddish presses. He later worked with LDB in the Palestine Economic Corporation.

To Max Shulman [1] (Telegram)

November 11, 1914 Boston, Mass. [Brandeis Mss, Z 1-2]

Your yesterday's telegram received. Impossible to speak in Milwaukee Tuesday, twenty-fourth, but will re-arrange other plans so as to speak there Monday, twenty-third, if a net contribution of at least two thousand dollars is effectively guaranteed. Let me have answer not later than next Saturday morning. [2]

1. Max Shulman (1885–1937), a lawyer, was also president of the Community State Bank of Chicago. In 1914 he was vice-president of the Chicago Zionist Association, and he later served as vice-president of the Zionist Association of America.

2. Shulman wired back that the change of date was satisfactory, and that "prominent people interested desired success assured." But see LDB to Nathan D. Kaplan, 18 January 1915.

To Chaim Weizmann (Telegram)

November 11, 1914 New York, N.Y. [Weizmann Mss]

Levin and Provisional Committee insist absolutely necessary central bureau be temporarily in United States as neutral land and second largest Jewish center.[1] Therefore imperative Tschlenow[2] and either Sokolow or Jacobson[3] come immediately.

1. With the disruption of communications caused by the war, and the necessity for the Zionists to maintain a strictly neutral position, a number of leading Zionists urged the transfer of organizational headquarters from Berlin to New York. Weizmann himself believed this to be necessary and had urged that the Provisional Committee be given greater power. (See LDB to Weizmann, 11 October 1914, n. 14.) Although the P.E.C. assumed large powers and responsibilities, the Berlin office refused to abdicate its powers. In 1917, after the entry of the United States in the war, *de facto* control was exercised in London with close communication and consultation with the P.E.C.

2. Jehial Tschlenow (1864–1918), a Russian physician, had played an important role in the Zionist movement since the days of the Hoveve Zion. In 1915 he moved to Copenhagen, and worked with the Zionist bureau there until his death.

3. Victor Jacobson (1869–1934) was the political representative of the Zionist Executive in Constantinople. Later in the war he managed the Copenhagen office, and after 1925 was permanent representative of the Organization to the League of Nations.

To Alfred Brandeis

November 14, 1914 Boston, Mass. [Brandeis Mss, Z 1-2]

My dear Al: I am to be in Chicago and Milwaukee from the 21st to the 23rd, and our friend Mr. M.W. Ades, who you remember came to Cincinnati, is urging me to come to Louisville for a Zionist meeting.[1] I have written him that I cannot do that at present. I notice on the letterhead of the Louisville Zion Society, besides Ades:

Charles Strull, Vice-President
Samuel J. Levy, Treasurer
Nat W. Weissberg, Financial Secretary
Dora Goldstein, Recording Secretary

Let me know about the standing of these people, and what may be expected of them. What can they do in raising funds?[2]

I find your letter of the 10th with enclosures upon my return from Philadelphia, where I had, among other things, a good time with Susan, and met at the Mayor's Conference a Louisville man, whose name I did not get, a friend of Louis Wehle's.

Upon my return I find a birthday present from Mr. Bernheim,— some twenty-one year old whiskey decked in roses.[3]

My greetings to the ??? ???

The razor shall be given a fair trial. It is good to have Jennie's letter.

1. Moses W. Ades was the chairman of the Louisville Zionist Society.

2. Alfred replied on 16 November that money in Louisville was controlled by a group of people who, he believed, had little sympathy with Zionism (see next note for example). The men LDB named were "full of enthusiasm . . . but the trouble is they cannot command much money." Alfred also reported that some of the local Zionists believed LDB's coming to Louisville would help to raise large sums of money, but Alfred himself doubted it. LDB finally did make a Zionist appearance in Louisville in January 1916.

3. Isaac Wolfe Bernheim (1848–1945) was a whiskey distiller from Louisville and a man of strong and decided Jewish philanthropic interests. A violent anti-Zionist, he served as treasurer of the American Jewish Committee from 1906 to 1921. He proposed, in 1918, a "Reform Church of American Israelites" which would be composed of "100 percent Americans." He favored a Sunday Sabbath and the abandonment of such "foreign" terms as "synagogue," "temple," "Jew" and "Judaism." He was a leading contributor to and long-time member of the executive board of the Union of American Hebrew Congergations. Doubtless the whiskey was a birthday present to LDB, whose fifty-eighth birthday was on 13 November.

To William Jennings Bryan

November 14, 1914 Boston, Mass. [Brandeis Mss, Z 1-2]

MY DEAR MR. SECRETARY: I am enclosing a letter from Mr. Lewin-Epstein of our Provisional Committee which sets forth clearly the great need which the Jewish resident of Palestine, including American citizens, have of relief, and the present difficulties in forwarding funds to them. Enclosed is also a copy of letter from the Vice-President of the National City Bank of New York referred to by Mr. Lewin-Epstein.

Will it not be possible for you to arrange so that we may send funds through our Embassy in Turkey and our Consuls in Palestine? The situation is an urgent one.

Awaiting your reply.[1]   Very truly yours,

1. While there are no copies of the letters mentioned, nor an answer from Bryan, in the Brandeis MSS, the State Department did extend full cooperation to the Provisional Committee in the transfer of funds to Palestine, some of which went through the embassy in Turkey.

To Jacob deHaas

November 14, 1914 Boston, Mass. [Brandeis Mss, Z 6-1]

DEAR MR. DEHAAS: *First:* Mr. Lipsky wants to reprint my Symphony Hall speech as a pamphlet.[1] I have not thought that it was really good enough to print, but he is urgent to have it, and I am ready to let it be so used upon revision, after it has been carefully considered by you and Dr. Levin.

Will you kindly let me have such suggestions or corrections as you think advisable.

Second: I am enclosing for your consideration a memorandum of November 13th from our good friend, Mr. Halvosa [2] of the Boston American, concerning the boarding out of Jewish Children. This is not a matter which it seems desirable for me to take up, but I call it to your attention for such action, if any, may be deemed desirable.

Third: On your return to the city I should like to have you consider the suggestions contained in Mr. Lipsky's letter of the 11th concerning an Assistant Secretary for New England.

Very cordially,

1. In this talk, LDB openly acknowledged how far he had been from Judaism, and explicitly noted that his approach to Zionism came about because of its approximation to progressive ideals. In a widely quoted section he said: "During most of my life my contact with Jews and Judaism was slight. I gave little thought to their problems, save in asking myself from time to time, whether we were showing by our lives due appreciation of the opportunities which this hospitable country affords. My approach to Zionism was through Americanism. In time practical experience and observation convinced me that Jews were by reason of their traditions and their character peculiarly fitted for the attainment of American ideals. Gradually it became clear to me that to be good Americans, we must be better Jews, and to be better Jews, we must become Zionists." He went on to note the economic growth of Palestine and the revival of Hebrew through the efforts of Eliezar Ben Yehuda, and urged American Jews to take up the burden of supporting the homeland. The speech is reprinted as "The Rebirth of the Jewish Nation" in Jacob deHaas, *Louis D. Brandeis: A Biographical Sketch*,

163-70. The Federation issued an expanded version of the talk as "Zionism and Patriotism," reprinted in *Curse of Bigness*, 209-17.

2. Philip J. Halvosa (1869-1915) was the City Hall reporter for the *Boston American*; he also wrote much of the labor news and was an organizer for the state A. F. of L.

To Harry Friedenwald

November 14, 1914 Boston, Mass. [Brandeis Mss, Z 1-2]

DEAR MR. FRIEDENWALD: Replying to yours of the 12th enclosing letter and papers from Mr. J. H. Kann of Octber 27th, which I return herewith:

Dr. Kaplan Kaplansky,[1] representing the Jewish National Fund, and a special emissary from Mr. Kann, brought me papers from Mr. Kann, and had a long conference with Dr. Levin, Mr. DeHaas and myself on November 3rd.

In my opinion Mr. Kann does not overrate the importance of protecting the Anglo-Palestine Company,[2] and I am greatly impressed with the excellent management of the Company. It seemed to us, however, clear that our Provisional Committee is not in a position to aid in securing the large funds required to put the bank on a safe basis. We advised Dr. Kaplan Kaplansky that the only course which offered any hope was to have either Mr. Katzenelsohn [*sic*] [3] or Mr. Kann himself come to America to lay this matter before Mr. Schiff and other important Jewish bankers, and presumably Dr. Kaplan Kaplansky cabled Mr. Kann to that effect immediately after our interview on the 3rd.

Cordially yours,

1. LDB undoubtedly refers to Shelomoh Kaplansky, representing the Jewish National Fund. See LDB to Chaim Weizmann, 11 October 1914, n. 11.

2. In 1903 the Jewish Colonial Trust, the official fiscal agent of the Zionist movement, established the Anglo-Palestine Company with capital of £40,000 as the main bank of Palestine. During the war the Turks closed the bank, but it was later revived during the mandate. In 1951 its name was changed to the Bank Leumi Le-Israel, and is now one of the largest banks in Israel.

3. Nissan Katzenselsohn (1863-1923) was a prominent Russian banker and physicist, and a pioneer in the Russian Zionist movement. A former member of the Actions Comité, in 1904 he had been involved in financial negotiations with Jacob Schiff.

To Alex Kanter

November 14, 1914 Boston, Mass. [Brandeis Mss, Z 1-2]

MY DEAR MR. KANTER: [1] I am glad to have your letter of the 9th.

I am to be in Chicago from the morning of the 21st to the morning of the 23rd, but shall be so much occupied with various engagements that have been made for me, that I fear I shall not have enough time to give you and your friends to justify your making the long trip to Chicago. I think it may be better, therefore, for you to get into direct communication with Mr. David Rubin,[2] 52 Irving Street, Cambridge, Mass., a Harvard Law School man, who is with much energy and intelligence taking steps to develop the Zionist movement among college men in the East. He has discussed with me recently the formation of an Intercollegiate Zionist Organization, and is developing a plan for taking up Zionist research work. I am writing him that you will communicate direct with him, as I think you two men ought to get into direct touch.

You ask specifically the definite purpose which our Zionist work should have. The efforts are being directed towards establishing a publicly recognized, legally secured home for Jews in Palestine. Such a home will serve both as a haven for persecuted Jews from European countries, and also a center for Jewish ideals and Jewish culture. We must in America support the movement in two ways, —financially and culturally, and as a means to both of these ends, we must develop a body of young Jewish men who thoroughly understand the aims and purposes of Zionism, and are familiar with what has been accomplished both culturally and practically in Palestine, and who can themselves become leaders of thought, and can, through writing, speaking, and organizing, extend the Zionist movement in America.

It was with this broad purpose in view that I have taken up the work at Harvard. We had recently also a joint meeting of the several Menorah Societies in New York City.

I hope you will write at once to Mr. Rubin.

My address in Chicago will be La Salle Hotel.

Cordially yours,

1. Alex Kanter was a young insurance adjuster in Minneapolis who was very interested in the Intercollegiate Zionist Society and in progressive politics. He had written a lengthy letter to LDB about his hopes and questions regarding Zionism, and about LDB's role in the recent election. He emphasized that he believed Jews must act and be treated just as all citizens are, with no special privileges granted to them nor restrictions placed on them. For LDB's view of Kanter, see LDB to Nathan D. Kaplan, 20 October 1915.

2. David Rubin (b. 1891) was then in the Harvard Law School; he later moved to Los Angeles where he became active in civic affairs and in the Sierra Club, a conservationist organization.

To Louis Lipsky

November 14, 1914 Boston, Mass. [Brandeis Mss, Z 1-4]

MY DEAR MR. LIPSKY: Replying to yours of the 13th: [1]

First: I approve most heartily of your project of publishing new literature for distribution in connection with the propaganda for the emergency fund. I shall be entirely ready to have you use my address a little later, but I should prefer first to make some amendments to it, and to have it considered somewhat carefully by Mr. DeHaas and Dr. Levin. I will do this as soon as possible and let you know.

Second: For general instruction in Zionism it would seem to me that Israel Cohen's [2] pamphlet entitled "The Zionist Movement", of which I have the edition of 1912, is the most informing.[3] I wonder whether it will not be possible to get Mr. Cohen to bring his data down to practically the opening of the war. The progress made in the last two years preceding the war seems to me so great as to make it very desirable that we should have a picture of conditions at that time. Will you take this up with Mr. Cohen? [4]

Very truly yours,

1. Lipsky wanted to increase the number and variety of propaganda pamphlets that the federation was distributing, and he proposed using LDB's speech at Symphony Hall (see LDB to Jacob deHaas, 14 November 1914).

2. Israel Cohen (1879–1961) was a long-time member of the world Zionist secretariat; he wrote widely on Jewish topics.

3. *The Zionist Movement: Its Aims and Achievements* (London, 1912).

4. Cohen did not revise the pamphlet, but thirty years later he expanded it into a book-length history of Zionism, with a chapter on American Zionism written by Bernard Richards: *The Zionist Movement* (London, 1946).

To Judah Leon Magnes

November 14, 1914 Boston, Mass. [Magnes Mss]

DEAR DR. MAGNES: *First:* I hope in preparing the list for the General Committee there have not been created elsewhere the troubles due to inclusion and omission of names, which I find has resulted in the selection of names for Boston, in addition to those selected at the first meeting of our Committee on Organization. Here in Boston a serious complication has arisen, [*sic*] due, among other things, to the fact that a Mr. Heller has apparently interpreted the letter of November 4th as a power for him "to designate persons of local importance in Massachusetts, whose co-operation should be invited by the New York Committee", instead of interpreting it merely as an invitation to send our Committee names which he deems desirable. Mr. Heller, under the title of Central Jewish Relief Committee for War Sufferers, has sent out such notices to some of our prominent Jews who did not receive invitations from our Committee, and who are considerably an-noyed by the situation. I shall give notice that the local committee has not yet been formed, and that when the necessary preliminary steps have been taken by organization of the Executive Committee I will call a meeting in Boston.

Second: Will you kindly send me by return mail a list of all in Massachusetts to whom invitations to become members of the General Committee have been sent. Am I right in assuming that these were all sent in the form of the circular letter of November 4, 1914? [1]   Yours very truly,

1. This letter is indicative of the trouble LDB encountered in trying to organize Zionist relief activities. The Jewish community in the United States was relatively unorganized, many different groups claimed leadership, and each had established its own fund-raising drive for relief. Eventually, the larger groups united in the American Jewish Relief Committee.

To Joseph Isaac Brody

November 16, 1914 Boston, Mass. [Brandeis Mss, Z 6-2]

DEAR MR. BRODY: [1] I have your telegram advising that the time allotted for my talk on Monday morning, November 23rd, is twenty minutes, and asking me to let you know the topic.

Had I known that the time allotted was not more than twenty minutes, I should have declined to speak, as what I wish to say cannot be said in twenty minutes; and I will, therefore, ask you to cancel the appointment unless public notice of the talk has already been given. If it has been given so that it would be embarrassing to cancel the engagement, you may give notice that my talk will be on Zionism.[2]   Yours very truly,

1. Joseph Isaac Brody (1889–1963) was in 1914 in law school at the University of Chicago, and a local Zionist worker. He later practiced law in Des Moines and was active in Jewish affairs, serving a term as national commander of the National Conference of Christians and Jews.
2. Brody quickly agreed to extend LDB's speaking time to "forty-five or fifty minutes."

To Jean Adrien Antoine Jules Jusserand

November 16, 1914 Boston, Mass. [Brandeis Mss, Z 1-2]

SIR: I have the honor of enclosing herewith the memorandum of our recent conversation concerning the desirability of securing from Russia a modification of the laws relating specifically to her Jewish subjects. I trust you may deem it proper to call this memorandum, and a report of our conversation, to the attention of your Government.

The sending of the memorandum was delayed owing to my inability to confer with Professor Gottheil.

Please believe me to be, with expressions of high esteem,
                              Yours very respectfully,

To Stephen Samuel Wise

November 16, 1914 Boston, Mass. [Brandeis Mss, Z 6-2]

DEAR DR. WISE: Your letter of the 13th concerning Adolph Lewisohn [1] reaches me via Washington.[2]

It seems to me unlikely that a conference between Mr. Lewisohn and me would be productive of good results for the following specific reason:

I was counsel in important litigation of the Old Dominion Copper Mining & Smelting Company [3] against the Leonard Lewisohn [4]

"Citizen Brandeis"

James Clark McReynolds

William Gibbs McAdoo

Thomas Watt Gregory

Norman Hapgood

David Philipson

Cyrus Adler

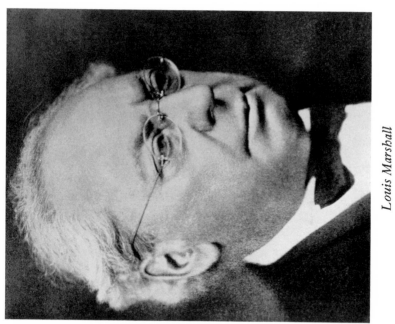

Jacob Henry Schiff

Louis Marshall

Louis Lipsky

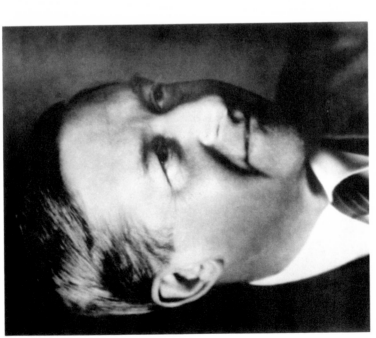

Judah Leon Magnes

Jacob DeHaas

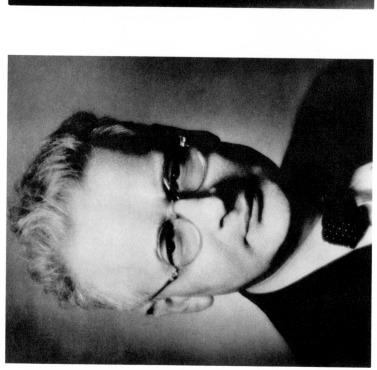

Horace Meyer Kallen

Provisional Executive Committee for General Zionist Affairs. Seated (left to right): Henrietta Szold, Stephen S. Wise, Jacob DeHaas, Robert D. Kesselman, Louis Lipsky, Charles Cowan, Shmarya Levin, Meyer Berlin;

Estate (and in which Adolph Lewisohn was also involved). The litigation involved the recovery of secret profits, and we actually obtained a decree for about $2,500,000 in that part of the litigation which was conducted in Massachusetts. No recovery was made against the Lewisohns, not because of any difference in the facts, but because of the different application of a rule of law by the New York courts. The litigation covered a period of ten years. It involved secret promoters' profits, and I presume there was some feeling on the part of the Lewisohns. For this reason alone I should expect that Mr. Lewisohn would be little inclined to aid a cause in which I showed much interest. But with the rich Jews of New York, particularly those with financial connections, I should expect to find a general feeling of disinclination to aid at my insistence, on account of the persistent attitude that I have taken in regard to the financial practices of Wall Street and allied interests. On the other hand I have believed that it was quite possible that among the rich New Yorkers were many who would be glad to contribute to our cause, if approached by the proper person. My own opinion that you would be the proper person was confirmed by Mr. Nathan Straus. It was for this reason that I appointed you Chairman of the Finance Committee nearly two months ago, and I deferred naming the other members of that Committee, desiring that you should recommend whom you would like to have as your associates. I feel sure that you can raise in New York a considerable amount of money, and I hope you will undertake this now. Mr. Perlstein reports that only comparatively few small sums have come as a result of the meeting on the 25th, and I presume that individuals of your Congregation are merely awaiting your own magic touch.   Very cordially yours,

P.S. Thank you for the memorandum for the French Ambassador.[5]

1. Adolph Lewisohn (1849–1938) headed several mining firms; he gave money to a number of causes, including Columbia University and various agencies; and he built Lewisohn Stadium in New York.

2. Wise had urged LDB to meet with Lewisohn in an effort to secure a large contribution from him for Palestinian causes.

3. See LDB to William Francis Fitzgerald, 2 January 1904, n. 2.

4. Leonard Lewisohn (1848–1902), Adolph's brother and associate, had built up a fortune as president of the United Metals Selling Company.

5. See preceding letter.

To Max Mitchell

November 17, 1914 Boston, Mass. [Brandeis Mss, Z 1-2]

DEAR MR. MITCHELL: [1] I hope you have already undertaken to get the large subscriptions about which you spoke to me. Try to make them at least $500 a piece; and one or two $1000 subscriptions would go a long way towards giving the proper impetus to the work throughout the Country and in putting Massachusetts where it belongs in this movement.

I hope that you will have these checks in hand before Friday when I start for Chicago.   Very cordially yours,

P.S. Miss Grady tells me you made an excellent speech after I left on Sunday.

1. Mitchell served as head of the local Massachusetts committee of the American Jewish Relief Committee.

To Stephen Samuel Wise

November 17, 1914 Boston, Mass. [Brandeis Mss, Z 6-2]

MY DEAR DR. WISE: I shall not be able to attend the meeting of the Relief Committee of One Hundred which is called for Sunday, as I am to be in Chicago on Zionist propaganda that day. I hope that you will attend.

First: At the first meeting of our Organization Committee we agreed upon National Jewish Relief Committee as the name, the precise name being suggested by Mr. Oscar Straus. Last week I found that without taking the matter up with the members of the Organization Committee, the name had been changed to American Jewish Relief Committee. I called the attention of the fellow members of the Committee, and of Dr. Magnes, to this at the second meeting of our Committee last Thursday, and expressed my strong conviction that it was very undesirable to adopt the name American Jewish Relief Committee, in view of the similarity of that name to the name of the American Jewish Committee. Dr. Magnes writes me that he will bring this matter up at the meeting next Sunday, and I hope that you will be able to prevail upon those present to change the name to that originally adopted by us at the first meeting of the Organization Committee.[1]

I have spoken of this matter also to Mr. Louis E. Kirstein [2] of Boston, who will attend the meeting.

I should suppose that Mr. Meyer London, Mr. Fischel,[3] and Judge Mack would all approve of a return to the name originally adopted, as they certainly acquiesed in my request to Mr. Magnes to restore the original name. Mr. Oscar Straus was not present at our second meeting.

Second: You will note in the list of suggestions for the Executive Committee submitted by our Committee that there are 24 and not 25 names. Some of my associates felt that I ought to be a member of that Committee. I have very great doubt whether that is desirable. In any event I am perfectly clear that the Committee, of which I am Chairman, should not nominate me, and with a view to overcoming that obstacle, Dr. Magnes induced your Committee to confine its recommendation to 24 names.

Yours very truly,

P.S. I am enclosing herewith my proxy for the meeting on Sunday.

1. The name "American Jewish Relief Committee" was kept.

2. Louis Edward Kirstein (1867–1942) had worked his way up to the vice-presidency of Filene's by 1911, and he was also a director of the nationwide Federated Department Stores. He was active in both civic and Jewish agencies in Boston and was later chairman of the American Jewish Committee.

3. Harry Fischel (1865–1948), a New York philanthropist, was treasurer of the Hebrew Sheltering and Immigrant Aid Society for over fifty years.

To Charles McCarthy

November 18, 1914 Boston, Mass. [Brandeis Mss, NMF 11-2]

MY DEAR MR. McCARTHY: Yours of the 16th reaches me here.[1] I have not been in Washington since the election, and shall probably not be able to go there again until the early part of December, when I go on to argue the Oregon Minimum Wage [2] and the California Eight Hour law cases,[3] so it will not be possible for me to see the President before his message is completed.

There are few subjects that are so urgent as properly to have preference over the regulation of labor; but I suppose that it would take some time to bring the President to a full realization of the problem if he has not yet given it attention. If he became convinced of the urgency, he might be willing to send in a special message.[4]

I presume you or Mr. Leiserson [5] will be in Washington in December, and I shall be glad to consider the bill then.

Very truly yours,

1. McCarthy believed that Wilson should issue a special message on a proposal for the regularization of employment, and he wanted LDB to talk to the President urging this course upon him.

2. In 1913 Oregon had established an Industrial Welfare Commission to regulate conditions of employment in that state. The Commission promptly issued an order setting minimum wages for women employed in factories and stores, and just as promptly it was challenged in the courts. LDB submitted a brief to the Oregon Supreme Court, which unanimously upheld the law on grounds similar to those argued in the *Muller* case (see LDB to Louis B. Wehle, 10 February 1908). On 17 December 1914 LDB argued the case before the United States Supreme Court. He reviewed the background and arguments which had led the state to enact the law, and then proceeded to justify the law primarily on economic and social grounds; his brief contained 369 extracts from various documents supporting the necessity for minimum wage legislation. While all of this was familiar in the light of *Muller*, LDB anticipated his own general attitude on the bench when he urged the justices to exercise judicial restraint, to ignore their own prejudices and allow the states the right to experiment within a broadly conceived constitutional framework. "This court is not burdened with the duty of passing upon the disputed question whether the legislature of Oregon was wise or unwise, or probably wise or unwise, in enacting this law. The question is merely whether . . . you can see that the legislators had no ground on which they could, as reasonable men, deem this legislation appropriate to abolish or mitigate the evils believed to exist or apprehended. If you cannot find that, the law must stand." (The brief was published by the National Consumers' League, and portions appear as "The Constitution and the Minimum Wage" in *The Curse of Bigness*.) The Court split four-to-four on the case, thus upholding the law. *Stettler* v. *O'Hara*, 243 U. S. 629 (1917).

3. California had passed a law establishing a maximum eight-hour workday for women, with certain exemptions, notably registered nurses. The statute was attacked on the ground that the exemption constituted an arbitrary and unlawful exercise of the state's police power. LDB argued that the Court had already upheld the validity of eight-hour laws for men and also the right of state legislatures to define the public good. In doing so, they thus permitted legislatures to make reasonable exceptions to general rules in order to promote the public welfare. The Court accepted LDB's arguments and held that reasonable exemptions fell within the allowable exercise of the state's powers. *Bosley* v. *McLaughlin*, 236 U. S. 385 (1915).

4. Wilson did not send in a special message on the subject.

5. William Morris Leiserson (1883–1957) was an economist working under McCarthy for the United States Industrial Commission. He later held numerous government positions involving labor economics.

To Benjamin Perlstein

November 20, 1914 Boston, Mass. [Brandeis Mss, Z 3-2]

DEAR MR. PERLSTEIN: *First:* As to the Dannenbaum letter: My own impression is that the arrangement Mr. Dannenbaum made is entirely proper.[1] I see no inconsistency between it and the work of the National Relief Committee. I do not see that there is any occasion for us to say anything further to him, or to do anything about the matter at present.

If the B'nai Brith should conclude to join the National Relief Committee, I suppose their part would be transferred into the National Fund. Somewhat similar questions are apt to arise here and elsewhere in connection with the National League. Of course in each instance there will have to be some arrangement made by the local committee. My idea is that the local National Committee ought to give distinct notice where they contemplate doing anything for Zionist work, that they will receive contributions earmarked "wholly for general relief purposes" or "wholly for Zionist purposes", and that any funds of which the purpose is not designated, will be distributed on a basis of certain proportions to one and certain proportions to the other. This of course would apply only where in the opinion of the Committee it is deemed desirable to consolidate the appeals to the community.

Second: As to the publication by the Committee. In my opinion the only discretion left to the Lewin-Epstein, Szold, Magnes Committee is the form of the notice to be published, and I should hope that two members of that Committee could be able to agree on the form.[2]

Third: Referring to yours of the 19th: I called the attention of Dr. Magnes and the Committee to the adoption of the word "American" instead of "National", and the objection to so doing, and he writes me that he will bring the matter up before the Committee of One Hundred next Sunday. I have also called it to the attention of Dr. Wise and Mr. Kirstein, who will attend that meeting, and also to Mr. Max Mitchell's attention.[3]

Fourth: I was glad to receive copies of the various letters and reports transmitted, and hope you will be able to send me, upon my return, additional papers referred to in mine of Nov. 9th.

Fifth: As to Mr. Cohen's letter: I do not see that there is anything for me to say to him now; but I may have occasion to write him later and can then refer to his letter.

Sixth: Referring to the contribution of the children of the Religious School of the Free Synagogue: I have written Dr. Wise as per enclosed two letters.[4]

Seventh: I enclose also copy of a letter of the 19th from Mr. Lewin-Epstein referring to the proposed letter to Mr. Marshall, and the letter which he enclosed.

I think a letter ought to go to Mr. Marshall. My impression, however, is that something somewhat more diplomatic than this letter ought to be written. I wish you would call together Mr. Lewin-Epstein, Miss Szold and Dr. Magnes at the earliest possible moment, and have them go over this draft of letter, and prepare a draft of letter which may reach me here by the 25th, when I expect to return to Boston. I think the letter ought to go forward at the earliest possible moment. I was impressed by what Dr. Yellin [5] said, and what could be read between the lines of Mr. Wertheim's report.[6]   Very truly yours,

P.S. Since dictating the above, Mr. Max Mitchell has called upon me. Mr. Mitchell and Mr. Ratshesky,[7] the two strongly opposing Boston forces, are both to be on the Committee of One Hundred, as well as Mr. Louis E. Kirstein. Some of the German Jews of Boston have contemplated getting up a collection for Zionist purposes, but have postponed doing so in view of the program of the National Relief Committee, and suggested to me that the thing to do was to have the local committee reach some agreement among themselves that the undesignated funds would be devoted in a fixed percentage between the general relief and the Zionist Palestine institutions, and relief through Zionist sources. I mentioned this to Mr. Mitchell who called on me this morning, and he thought that would be very undesirable, but that it would be very desirable, and he thought it ought to be possible to arrange, to assign a definite proportion of all funds, say, one-tenth for Zionist institutions and relief through Zionist sources, and that he proposed to take the matter up at the meeting in New York on

Sunday. We agreed that it would be well to have a discussion of this matter with some of our Zionist delegates before the meeting on Sunday, and I suggested that he ask you to have Dr. Wise and Dr. Levin-Epstein, Mr. Lipsky and others attend for a discussion of that situation at our Committee's office at 9:00 o'clock on Sunday morning. Mr. Mitchell said he would ask Mr. Kirstein to be present.

I have not thought this matter out myself, and do not know what it may be possible to do, but it may be that this matter will have to be left to the Executive Committee of the National Committee, but it seems pretty clear that the people who, like the Boston German Jews, want to raise some funds for Zionist purposes through the general appeal, ought to be able, directly or indirectly, to insure the Zionist institutions getting a fair share. Of course none of the money that is raised through this National Relief Committee ought to go for Zionist propaganda, or the expenses of the Zionist organizations in countries other than Palestine.

1. Harry Dannenbaum, an official in the Texas B'nai Brith, had suggested that the fraternal organization assume fund raising chores in the South because of the lack of a large Zionist group that could handle the work; the receipts, of course, would be turned over to the National Relief Committee.

2. There had been disagreement among members of the Provisional Committe over the wording of an announcement that the Committee would handle transfer of money to Palestine.

3. Despite LDB's protest, the name of the committee continued to be the American Jewish Relief Committee.

4. The children of the Free Synagogue's Religious School had sent in fifty dollars as a contribution, and Perlstein had suggested that LDB thank them personally. In forwarding the money, Wise had proposed that letters be sent to religious schools all over the country to encourage similar donations.

5. David Yellin (1864–1941) was one of the first teachers of secular Hebrew in Jerusalem, where he later headed the Hebrew Teachers College. A noted philologist, Yellin was also active in the political life of the Jewish settlement, serving as deputy mayor of Jerusalem and head of the Vaad Leumi, the elected Jewish committee which advised the mandatory government.

6. Maurice Wertheim (1886–1950), an investment banker, was the son-in-law of Henry Morgenthau and during this period served as an aid to him in distributing relief in Palestine. See LDB to David Rubin, 31 December 1914.

7. Abraham Captain Ratshesky (1864–1943) was president of the U.S. Trust Company in Boston and heavily involved in Boston Jewish charities. As an executive of the Union of American Hebrew Congregations, it is doubtful if he was overly sympathetic to Zionism. President Hoover named Ratshesky to be ambassador to Czechoslovakia in 1930, and he served until 1932.

To Alfred Brandeis

November 27, 1914 Boston, Mass. [Brandeis Mss, M 4-1]

MY DEAR AL: Your letter of the 25th is so searching in some of its inquiries that I am resorting to a stenographer.

First: The Chicago experience was as successful as the Cincinnati was unsuccessful. In fact Chicago was successful far beyond expectation.

Dr. [Emil G.] Hirsch, who is ordinarily a pretty difficult factor to deal with, and has declared himself repeatedly, non-Zionist, was helpful in every way, and the meeting at his Temple was really a perfect meeting. There were 2200 present, and my talk which I limited to thirty-five minutes, was unquestionably effective. [Julius] Rosenwald, who had been quite anti-Zionist in his inclinations recently, was not content with a mere call for immediate relief, but insisted that the donors should bind themselves to continue contributions, and he rose and stated that he would give $1000 a month during the war and for twelve months thereafter.[1] A number of others gave contributions of similar character in small amounts, and Dr. Hirsch himself said he would make small monthly contributions for life. The other meetings,—the mass meeting Sunday evening, and the luncheon with the reformed rabbis on Monday, were also successful. In addition there was a banquet on Saturday evening, and a Menorah talk at the University on Monday afternoon. The general feeling was that we had captured the town, and I don't think the editorial in the Chicago Tribune, which you doubtless saw, will do any harm.[2] There must be people who won't agree with us, and it is well enough to have the subject definitely discussed.

The Milwaukee meeting also was successful. We had a dinner before the meeting with the Germans, who really had no sympathy with the Zionist movement, and who came in to it merely out of personal regard for me,—one of them being interested in the Independent Shoe Machinery fight,—another in the Fair Trade. The leader of the German community there stated to me at the dinner that he was opposed to Zionism, and no argument could move him; but when I got through my talk, he said that I had converted him, and I think that was true of some of the others.

The B'nai Brith men are very friendly. [Schmarya] Levin is to talk at the Annual Convention in Chicago, December 26th, and I had a very urgent letter from Samuel Sale [3] of St. Louis asking me to speak there in his Temple at a joint meeting of the Temple and the St. Louis B'nai Brith,—their annual meeting. In the South-western States Dannenbaum of Texas is working in cooperation with the B'nai Brith in joint meetings, on the basis of their taking one-quarter of the proceeds, and a similar arrangement has been made with the B'nai Brith in Norfolk. It occurs to me that something of that sort might be worked up in Louisville. What do you think?

Second: I believe that when the war is over there will be a great increase in immigration, and particularly of the Jews.[4] The indications are that if the Polish monarchy is re-established, the condition there will be worse than it now is. Of course the possession of means will probably be the only serious limit upon the volume of immigration. Hirsch, in his talk which followed mine, bore heavily upon the subject of immigration, and the importance of keeping Palestine open for this purpose. Of course immigration to Palestine would involve far less initial cost than to America.

Third: Mrs. R. C. Nicholson, 5471 Kimbark Avenue, who you remember was Oscar's landlady, sent me a letter while I was in Chicago, telling me that he was in the hospital, and suggesting that I see her and her husband, which I did on Monday morning. I was very favorably impressed with them. He seemed a very nice fellow, and she a fine woman, and they speak in the highest possible terms of Oscar. I told her that I had not communicated with her before because I did not care to say how the family had felt about him. I did tell her substantially the family feeling, and why they had not given relief. On the whole I was firm that I would not take over his support, but I told her I would send her $100 to be used in her discretion for Oscar; but I did not want Oscar to know that I had sent it. I have sent her that sum. She says that Oscar was operated on, and the doctors thinking that there was one chance in four that he would recover; but that the operation was successful, and he seems now on the road to recovery. She said that she was convinced that it was nothing but ill health that stood in Oscar's way; that whenever he was well, he had good positions, and was most highly thought of. She wanted to know whether she should keep me advised in regard to Oscar, and I told her that I might write her again on the subject. I have relieved my feeling a little by sending the $100 but I don't feel very comfortable in not doing more,—particularly as I am inclined to think that Oscar is now being helped by the Nicholsons and other friends who are probably less able to help him. The immediate situation is doubtless taken care of.

Let me know what you think.

Met the young Fisher brother on the Twentieth Century of which he is conductor. He told me he recognized me by my resemblance to you & treated me quite royally.

Had intended each day while west to write you but was excessively occupied. The Cincinnatians are pretty unhappy over Phillipson's [sic] performance & have been trying to get me down there for the Intercollegiate Menorah meeting, but they won't.

1. See LDB to Nathan D. Kaplan, 30 November 1914.

2. The editorial of 25 November, entitled "Patriotism Begins at Home," attacked LDB's contention that the lack of a homeland was responsible for the rise of crime among Jews. The paper said that the Jews had maintained high ethical principles for two thousand years without a homeland, and that immigrants must adopt the United States as homeland.

3. Samuel Sale (1854–1937) had been rabbi of Congregation Shaare Emeth in St. Louis since 1887.

4. The expected immigration failed to materialize because of the enactment of several restrictive quota laws.

To Treadwell Cleveland, Jr.

November 27, 1914 Boston, Mass. [Brandeis Mss, NMF 66-3]

MY DEAR MR. CLEVELAND: Upon my return to the city I find your letter of the 20th in regard to the Federal Trade Commission.[1]

I certainly should not censure you for desiring a position offering so great an opportunity for usefulness.

The administration has seen fit from time to time to ask my advice in regard to appointments, and particularly some as to which they thought I might have opinions of value. I have, therefore, made it a rule not to proffer my advice, and I am particularly anxious to avoid doing so in the case of the Federal Trade Commission, because I had some part in framing the legislation,[2] and also because several of those likely to be considered for the position are among my friends. If, however, your name should be suggested by someone else, and the President should ask my opinion, I should be only too glad to tell him what I know of your qualifications.[3]   Very truly yours,

1. Cleveland had asked LDB to recommend him to the President for appointment to the Federal Trade Commission.
2. See LDB to James C. McReynolds, 22 February 1914.
3. Cleveland did not receive an appointment to the commission.

To Nathan D. Kaplan

November 27, 1914 Boston, Mass. [Brandeis Mss, Z 3-1]

MY DEAR MR. KAPLAN: Replying to yours of the 25th:

First: As to the Tribune editorial: [1] My present impression is that it is not advisable to answer the editorial. We do not wish to enter upon a realm of controversy, and a controversy with a newspaper, which always has the last word, is particularly unsatisfactory. My Boston address on this subject entitled "Patriotism and Zionism" will have to be published in pamphlet form soon, and I think that that will be a better way of meeting this position. Of course we cannot expect wholly to eradicate the belief in the policy of assimilation.

Second: I am sending to Miss Szold today a copy of that portion of your letter which deals with the Palestine Welfare Society, telling her that I approve of your suggestion.

Third: I saw a stenographer taking notes of my address last Sunday morning. If there is any stenographic report, I wish you would send it to me. It may be that the Chicago address might be better, in pamphlet form, for relief work than the Boston address.

Cordially yours,

1. See LDB to Alfred Brandeis, 27 November 1914, n. 2.

To *The New York Times*

November 27, 1914 Boston, Mass. [Brandeis Mss, NMF 65-1]

DEAR SIRS: Upon my return to the city I find your day message of the 25th.

I do not know definitely what you refer to in saying that I "have been quoted in dispatches as saying the railways would use receipts from increased rates to buy materials, etc." I have made no formal statement bearing upon that subject, but I recall that in the course of a discussion with some newspaper men on many subjects, including the war and business prospects, I said that I thought there would certainly be an increased demand for railroad materials and supplies, because many of the companies had had large stocks of these which were being exhausted, and they would have to replace these supplies soon, and that mere operation and maintenance of property would compel purchasing from current earnings, which were now being augmented on many roads by increased passenger and certain freight rates.[1]

Yours very truly,

1. The paper did not use LDB's reply.

To Benjamin Perlstein

November 27, 1914 Boston, Mass. [Brandeis Mss, Z 3-2]

DEAR MR. PERLSTEIN: As you know, it will be impossible for me to attend the meeting of the Provisional Committee on Monday because of the long-standing speaking engagement in Worcester on Sunday.

I wish you would call to the attention of the Committee the importance of agreeing upon and publishing at once a notice that the Committee will receive money for transfer to Palestine.[1] When I was in Chicago, as elsewhere, I had specific inquiries on this point, and since we have now re-established financial communication with Palestine, I am sure it will be of great service to the people of Palestine, as well as to the Zionist cause, to give wide publicity to the fact that we are ready to so receive money.

Very cordially yours,

1. Through several American embassies and the foreign offices of American companies such as Standard Oil, the Provisional Committee became the main conduit for transmission of money from Americans to their relatives in Europe and the Middle East until this country entered the war in 1917. Millions of dollars were handled with virtually no loss; in fact, the Committee functioned so well in this area that it also acted in money matters for non-Jews.

To Roscoe Pound (Special Delivery)

November 27, 1914 Boston, Mass. [Pound Mss]

MY DEAR POUND: In talking with Frankfurter this morning about the Frank case [1] and Justice Holmes' memorandum, he told me that you were convinced that Frank had not had a fair trial, and that he was not guilty, and that this was another Dreyfus case.[2]

It seems to me of great importance that you should, in a public letter, give expression to your opinion on this subject. Your standing among the lawyers of America is such that what you say men will heed, and it is important that this protest should be made by a non-Jew.[3]   Very truly yours,

1. Leo Max Frank (1884–1915) was a factory superintendent in his uncle's pencil plant in Atlanta, Georgia. On 26 April 1913, the body of Mary Phagan had been found in the plant, and it was later determined that Frank had been the last person to see her alive. He was accused and tried under bizarre circumstances, and a mounting crescendo of anti-Semitic propaganda marked the whole episode. During the trial, his defense was almost incompetent, and the judge did nothing to prevent mobs of people outside the courthouse from chanting "Hang the Jew." After Frank had been convicted and sentenced to death, Northern civil rights lawyers became interested in the case and began planning for appeals. Governor John Marshall Slaton (1886–1955) of Georgia, recognizing the gross irregularities in the trial, commuted Frank's sentence to life imprisonment, an act for which he was hounded out of office. While in prison, Frank was almost killed by another inmate; then, on 16 August 1915 a mob plucked Frank out of the hospital where he was recuperating and lynched him. Although many of the mob members were known, a Georgia grand jury brought in a verdict of "death at the hands of persons unknown." The Frank case was the first serious outburst of anti-Semitism in the United States, and it worried many people; some scholars have seen it as the most extreme manifestation of a latent anti-Semitism among the Populists, who identified corporate capitalism with Jewish financiers. The case led directly to the founding of the Anti-Defamation League of the B'nai Brith, which for over half a century has worked

against any form of prejudice. For the case, see Leonard Dinnerstein's *The Leo Frank Case* (New York, 1968).

2. Alfred Dreyfus (1859–1935), a brilliant captain in the French general staff, was accused of selling secrets to the Germans, and in 1894 he was condemned to life imprisonment on Devil's Island. The trial was marked by a number of irregularities, and it was tinged with anti-Semitism. Dreyfus protested his innocence, but the French generals had found a scapegoat, and when evidence was produced identifying the real culprit, they quickly acquitted him. Emile Zola (1840–1902) a non-Jew, recognized that anti-Semitism had convicted Dreyfus, and in a famous article published in 1898, *J'accuse*, attacked the verdicts in both cases. In 1899 a retrial took place amid great tension; Dreyfus was again found guilty, but this time the verdict was not unanimous and "extenuating" circumstances were admitted. Dreyfus was pardoned by President Loubet, and in 1906 the Court of Cassation announced him completely innocent. The case had wide repercussions both for France and for the Jews. It shocked many Jews out of their belief that they had been fully accepted into gentile society and led them to a reevaluation of their status; one of these "assimilated" Jews was Theodore Herzl, who covered the trial as a reporter.

3. On 30 November Pound answered that he believed it would be a "grave reproach to American justice if the sentence were to be carried into execution . . . . There can be no excuse for permitting passion and clamor to affect or even determine the course of justice." He urged that there be a review of the case, and added that LDB was "at liberty to make any use of this letter which you think expedient."

To Richard James Horatio Gottheil

November 28, 1914 Boston, Mass. [Brandeis Mss, Z 6-1]

MY DEAR MR. GOTTHEIL: I have yours of the 27th.[1]

I am extremely sorry that you sent to the Russian Ambassador the memorandum which you did, and that you did it in my name. I should not have done it. If any memorandum was to be sent to the Russian Ambassador, I think it should have been couched in a different form; and I do not think that the matter was of such urgency that I should not have been communicated with. As a matter of fact I was in constant communication during this period with our Secretary, Mr. Perlstein, and happened to be also in communication with Dr. Wise.[2]

We had a most satisfactory experience in the West, and made a very great advance in Chicago. And our progress in Milwaukee was on the whole gratifying.

I shall not be able to attend the Committee meeting tomorrow, as there is a long standing engagement at Worcester.

Very truly yours,

1. Gottheil wrote about the memorandum that LDB had written to the French ambassador regarding the plight of the Jews in Russia (see LDB to Jean A. A. J. Jusserand, 16 November 1914). Charles R. Crane, misunderstanding Gottheil, had mentioned the memorandum to the Russian ambassador, George Bahkmeteff. The Russian had not seen the document, and he requested a copy of it through Crane. Gottheil sent it to him.
2. See LDB to Gottheil, 1 December 1914.

To Joseph Saffro [1] (Telegram)

November 28, 1914 Boston, Mass. [Brandeis Mss, Z 1-2]

Much disappointed by smallness of collection made in Milwaukee. Feel confident that if you will call on all the members of the Committee that entertained us at dinner, and their friends with whom we spoke after the meeting, you will be able to secure the expected contribution of five thousand dollars from Milwaukee.

1. Joseph Saffro, an insurance salesman and investment counsellor in Milwaukee, was involved in Zionist affairs there; LDB sent a similar telegram to Israel J. Biskind in Cleveland.

To Herbert Seely Bigelow

November 30, 1914 Boston, Mass. [Brandeis Mss, NMF 16-4]

MY DEAR MR. BIGELOW: [1] Replying to yours of the 28th.

Our Sliding Scale Gas Law is: Statutes 1906, Mass., Chapter 422. The origin of the Act and its results were discussed by me in the Review of Reviews for November 1907. This law has never been applied to the electric light and power business. The propriety of so applying it was recognized, and the subject was much considered, but it was believed that the electric light and power cost possibilities had not been sufficiently developed to justify then an adoption of the principle for fear of fixing a standard which would prove too high, in view of improvements which were likely to be made in the art. Perhaps the time has now come for applying the principle to the electric light business, but the facts should be worked out very carefully before it is so applied. And in this connection it would be desirable to use the Utilities Bureau, which has been developed under the inspiration of Mr. Morris L. Cooke, Director of Public Works, Philadelphia.

Very truly yours,

1. Herbert Seely Bigelow (1870–1951) was an Ohio legislator from Cincinnati; in the 1930s he served in the United States House of Representatives for one term.

To James Davis

November 30, 1914 Boston, Mass. [Brandeis Mss, Z 1-2]

MY DEAR MR. DAVIS: [1] Replying to yours of the 28th.

Please send to the office of the Provisional Committee at the above New York address, the $2,000 which you have on deposit, and any additional sums from time to time as often as you have available, say, $1,000, for transmittal.

It is important to have these funds reach the Committee as soon as possible, and I trust that you will do all that you can to expedite collection.   Very truly yours,

1. James Davis was a paint and wallpaper dealer. He served as treasurer of the Chicago fund-raising committee.

To Nathan D. Kaplan

November 30, 1914 Boston, Mass. [Brandeis Mss, Z 3-1]

MY DEAR MR. KAPLAN: *First:* I have yours of the 27th and will defer answering it until I have talked again with Dr. Levin, whom I expect to see tomorrow. In a brief talk which I had with Dr. Levin yesterday in Worcester, I infer that he was convinced that Mr. Rosenwald's intentions were entirely in harmony with our wishes, and that he had arranged with Mr. Rosenwald definitely that all the funds should go through our Committee; that $500 of each monthly allowance should be for our general Zionist purposes; the remaining $500 divided in amounts of $200, $200, and $100 among the specific institutions for the benefit of pupils of institutions which he had agreed upon with Mr. Rosenwald, namely: the Gymnasium at Jaffa, the Girls' School, and one other that I do not definitely recall.

Second: In replying to a letter from Mr. Davis under date of the 28th, inquiring what disposition he should make of the funds, I have written him as per enclosed.

I am somewhat disappointed to learn that more has not been collected as yet, and I trust that every effort will be made to make collections promptly. The small amount that he has named leads me to think that it does not include the sum which you had previously collected, as I understand that you had $2000 in hand before our first meeting on the 21st.

Third: What have you and Mr. [Max] Shulman arranged in regard to the $12,000 collected for general relief purposes? I trust you have got that into shape now so that the fund can be turned over for transmittal through our Committee. I heard from Dr. Levin yesterday that we had forwarded $35,000 on Friday last.

Fourth: What have you accomplished in Milwaukee? You will remember that the Milwaukee people agreed that we should have a minimum of $2,000 net in case I went to Milwaukee. Of course that is a minimum only, and we ought to get $5,000 from there.

Very truly yours,

To Bernard Abraham Rosenblatt

November 30, 1914 Boston, Mass. [Brandeis Mss, Z 1-2]

MY DEAR MR. ROSENBLATT: Replying to yours of the 25th:

First: I am glad to know that your Social Commonwealth is about to appear, and look forward to the copy which you are good enough to say you will send me.[1]

Second: I think now that I can arrange for a December 30th dinner of the Zion Association of Greater New York; but before considering that as a definite arrangement, I wish you would make thorough inquiry and let me know whether we can rely upon a thoroughly successful meeting. I must say to you frankly that in no part of the Country, with the exception of Cincinnati, have the results of the Zionist propaganda seemed to me as unsatisfactory as they are in New York; and I am inclined to think that unless a thorough change can be made with respect to New York, it will be better for us to devote what time and energy we possess to other parts of the Country.

I have not made a sufficient study of New York conditions to know what the reason is why we are so lacking in success there, but I should not want to agree to participate in any other meeting in New York unless after a careful survey you concluded that a thoroughly successful meeting could be had, and were able to make also arrangements to insure success.

I will therefore hold the date open for the present, but please do not consider it an engagement until you have made such a survey, and have communicated to me the result.

Very truly yours,

1. Rosenblatt's *The Social Commonwealth: A Plan for Achieving Industrial Democracy* (New York, 1914), was dedicated to LDB.

To Richard James Horatio Gottheil

December 1, 1914 Boston, Mass. [Brandeis Mss, Z 6-1]

MY DEAR PROFESSOR GOTTHEIL: I have yours of the 30th enclosing copy of Mr. Crane's telegram, which I return herewith.

I understand fully how you came to act, and I trust we shall have no occasion to regret it; but I think it was a dangerous thing to do, and we ought not to run such risks. I still feel that there was no emergency calling for such action without communicating with me.[1]

I was glad to hear that Miss Leon is coming to Boston, and regret much that both Mrs. Brandeis and I are leaving the city.

Most cordially,

1. See LDB to Gottheil, 28 November 1914.

To Abraham Kolinsky

December 1, 1914 Boston, Mass. [Brandeis Mss, Z 1-2]

MY DEAR MR. KOLINSKY: [1] Replying to yours of the 24th:

I strongly believe in an appointed judiciary, but if judges are to be elected, election expenses are inevitable for a proper representative conduct of the campaign. The expenses of such a campaign ought to be borne by the community which decrees the election of judges. But since the State does not provide for paying election expenses, they must be paid by some portion of the people, either by the candidate himself, if he is able and willing, or by others. The candidate is usually not able to bear the expenses, and it is very doubtful whether it would be desirable for him to do so, if he were; and since the expenses must be borne by some part of the community, I can conceive of no part which could more appropriately be intrusted with making the contribution than the lawyers themselves. They are usually best able to judge of the fitness of the candidate, and are certainly most disposed to observe the proprieties of the offices of judge and lawyer. It seems to me, therefore, that generally speaking, the contributions by the Bar to the expenses of the campaign for judicial office are entirely proper. There may, I think, be some question as to the amount of the contribution of any person, and particularly of the proportion which any individual should bear. This limitation I think has no special reference to contributions to a campaign for judge, but it seems to me undesirable that any office holder should feel indebted for contributions to only one person, particularly if that person is one likely to have a particular interest in the administration of the office.   Very cordially yours,

1. Abraham Kolinsky was a Cleveland attorney, and a member of the Zionist group there. He wrote that in the recent election a number of attorneys had contributed heavily to the campaign funds of the various judicial candidates, and questions had arisen regarding the propriety of such actions. Kolinsky wanted LDB's views on the matter.

To Lydia Littman

December 2, 1914 Boston, Mass. [Brandeis Mss, Z 1-2]

DEAR MISS LITTMAN: [1] I desire to urge upon the members of the Texas Zionist Association gathered at their ninth annual convention, the importance not only of raising funds to meet the urgent needs of our institutions in Palestine, but also of intense propaganda work.

The war has in large measure suspended the activities of those able and devoted Zionists who have hitherto led the movement, and we Americans are called upon not only to fill the gap thus created, but to give that greater aid in wise counsel and in financial support which the exigencies of war render necessary. But while the war has greatly increased the responsibilities resting upon the Zionists of America, it has immeasurably increased the opportunities for usefulness.

The manifest seriousness of present and prospective Jewish problems enables us to secure from many Jews, who heretofore have been hostile or indifferent to our cause, careful consideration of the Zionist program. What we need is careful consideration of our arguments, and a greater opportunity is afforded for securing such consideration than has ever existed heretofore. The time has come when practically every Jew should be made to see that loyalty to America, as well as loyalty to the race demands adhesion to the Zionist cause; and I desire to urge upon your members the development of a campaign with a view to securing as members of the Zionist organizations practically all the Jews in Texas.   Very truly yours,

1. Lydia Littman was secretary of the Texas Zionist Association.

To Charles McCarthy

December 2, 1914 Boston, Mass. [Brandeis Mss, NMF 66-3]

DEAR MR. MCCARTHY: Your letter of the 23rd has just reached me from Washington.[1]

With your fundamental proposition, namely that it would be desirable to have upon the Trade Commission a labor man of ability, experience and reputation, I fully agree; and I also agree with that statement contained in Mr. Walsh's letter that "it is a mistaken idea perhaps to uniformly appoint labor men as such to the heads of labor departments, and other municipal, state and National bodies which have to do directly with industrial questions."

I think, however, that it would be a mistake in selecting a labor man, to select a person who may be deemed to be a representative of labor, be it organized or unorganized. The men who go upon the Trade Commission should be selected, not because they are representatives of any particular body, but because they have the experience and associations which give them specific knowledge, and breadth of view. I have no doubt that with that general principle you and Mr. Walsh would entirely agree.[2]

Very cordially yours,

1. McCarthy wanted LDB to urge Wilson to name John Brown Lennon (1850–1923) to the Federal Trade Commission; Lennon was treasurer of the American Federation of Labor.
2. Lennon did not receive the appointment.

To Alfred Brandeis

December 8, 1914 Washington, D.C. [Brandeis Mss, M 4-1]

DEAR AL: Sorry I had to wire declining. Your several letters have come. You would find Ross' book reviewed in leaflet sent you very interesting.

Am here on I.C.C., Oregon Minimum wage & California 8 hour law cases. Expect to stay until 18th & then return to Boston via N.Y.

Alice has just come, plans to stay with me until I leave for N.Y. & then stop with Susan until they go to Boston together on the 22nd.

Haven't run across any of your friends here, but saw Colston in Supreme Court yesterday.

Harlan said he would like to talk with you some day on billing in transit. My greetings to Jennie et al.

You cannot possibly conceive of the horrible sufferings of the Jews in Poland & adjacent countries. These changes of control from German to Russian & Polish anti-semites are bringing miseries as great as the Jews ever suffered in all their exiles.

To David Rubin

December 9, 1914 Washington, D.C. [Brandeis Mss, Z 1-2]

DEAR MR. RUBIN: I enclose Berman's letter of 4th. I deem it important that the Harvard [Zionist] Society should have speakers from time to time & I am willing personally to bear the expense of their coming from New York, when necessary, during the present academic year, if and so far as you may deem this advisable from time to time. It is, of course, important that the men should feel that they too are making some sacrifices for Zionism.

DeHaas returns to Boston about December 17.

Cordially,

To Roscoe Pound

December 10, 1914 Washington, D.C. [Pound Mss]

MY DEAR POUND: I saw Ass. Secy Phillips [1] about Ehrlich, and he will take the matter and see what can be done about safe-conduct, but doubted whether the British would consent.[2]

Cordially,

1. William Phillips (1878–1968) was one of the first career officers in the foreign service. He began as secretary to Ambassador Joseph H. Choate in London in 1903, and then held many State Department jobs including one term as Assistant Secretary and two terms as Under Secretary, as well as several ministerial appointments. During World War I, he was Chief of the Far Eastern Affairs Division and, as such, was able to help the Zionists frequently. A friend of Franklin Roosevelt's since their Harvard days, he came out of retirement in 1941 at the President's request to establish a special services office in England. In 1946 he served on the Anglo-American Commission of Inquiry on Palestine.

2. Professor Eugen Ehrlich had been invited by Harvard University to give a series of lectures (some of which LDB had agreed to subsidize; see LDB to Pound, 20 July 1914). At the outbreak of the war, however, the Germans had refused Ehrlich a passport because of his pacifist views, and some conservatives in the American embassy at Vienna had reported that he had radical social ideas. Pound hoped that the State Department could arrange a safe-conduct with the British to bring Ehrlich to the United States from Vienna, where he was interned. It proved impossible to arrange for Ehrlich's passage.

To Edward Albert Filene

December 11, 1914 Boston, Mass. [Filene Mss]

MY DEAR MR. FILENE: The American Jewish Relief Committee, formed to aid the sufferers from the war, is now perfecting its organization with the establishment of local committees in the leading cities.

I take pleasure in inviting you to attend a meeting at the Elysium Club, 218 Huntington Ave., on Wednesday, December 23rd at 8:00 o'clock P.M., for the purpose of forming a Greater Boston Committee to cooperate in this important work.

The enclosed appeal of the Committee indicates how urgent the need is. Awaiting your reply.[1]   Very truly yours,

1. This letter was sent to over one hundred people in the Boston area.

To Alfred Brandeis

December 12, 1914 Washington, D.C. [Brandeis Mss, M 4-1]

DEAR AL: I have yours of 8th with copy of letter from Cornelius. I don't think grain rates are high enough, but they may be absolutely unfair otherwise & I have no faith in the RRs or Chicago & see no reason why you shouldn't fight if you have a mind to. I told Harlan of your letter. Anytime you are here he will no doubt be glad to talk with you on grain matters. Am confirmed in views expressed to you in October about I.C.C.

The Cranes, Rublees & we (including Josephine) dined at the LaFollettes last evening. Wisconsin situation is pretty bad,[1] and reactionaries are pretty well buttressed the country over.

Terrible stories of suffering in Palestine & generally. The Jews are having a sad time — [Leo] Frank included.[2]

1. LaFollette-backed candidates had done poorly in the November elections in Wisconsin. The candidate for lieutenant-governor, John J. Blaine, had finished a weak third, while Paul Hastings defeated Governor McGovern, an ally of LaFollette, in the race for United States Senator.
2. See LDB to Roscoe Pound, 27 November 1914.

To Alfred Brandeis

December 17, 1914 New York, N.Y. [Brandeis Mss, M 4-1]

DEAR AL: Yours about L & N decision reached me too late to look at it while in Washington. Send me your copy to Boston.[1] Saw Helm Bruce,[2] Senator Beckham & one or two other

Kentuckians whose names I didn't get in the Supreme Court today & told Bruce of our attempt to visit him at West Harwich [Mass.]

Have just learned of Ed Meier's death. Whom should I write to, if anyone?

1. See LDB to Alfred Brandeis, 1 January 1915.
2. Helm Bruce (1860–1927) was a prominent Louisville attorney.

To Norman Hapgood

December 22, 1914 Boston, Mass. [Brandeis Mss, NMF 62-1]

DEAR NORMAN: The enclosed two letters, which please return, one from Delos F. Wilcox[1] of December 18th, and one from Milo R. Maltbie of the 17th, will bear on our discussion of commissions.

First: As to Wilcox's letter:[2] I have a high opinion of Maltbie, and hope that if you agree with me, you will be able to do something to keep Maltbie on the Commission. As Wilcox says, Maltbie is pretty nearly the saving remnant of your Commission. I should not think it would be wise for me personally to act on Wilcox's suggestion by addressing a letter to Whitman.[3]

Second: The Artaud matter referred to by Mr. Maltbie is sent merely for your information.[4] I do not suppose that there is anything that you could do at present, but you ought to know the dangers. I have the gravest apprehension as to the effect on the public interest, of the valuation of railroads now in process; mainly because of the character of the men who in one way or another are being insinuated into the service.

Third: I expect to reach New York Sunday morning, and shall breakfast at the Harvard Club.   Very truly,

1. Delos Franklin Wilcox (1873–1928) had recently resigned as chief of the Bureau of Franchises, New York Public Service Commission, to become deputy commissioner of public utilities for New York City. He wrote widely on problems of public utility regulation.

2. Wilcox was worried that the Tammany politicians were trying to prevent the reappointment of Milo Maltbie to the Public Service Commission, and he was urging LDB and other prominent men to write Governor Whitman (see next note) in support of reappointment. See LDB to Maltbie, 1 May 1915.

3. Charles Seymour Whitman (1868–1947) had been district attorney of New York City before successfully running for the governorship the previous month; after two terms he resumed private law practice in 1919.

4. Maltbie had noted that there would probably be a shakeup among some lower staff on the Interstate Commerce Commission, and he thought it important that the right type of people be appointed. Artaud worked in the evaluation section, which played a key role in determining future rates.

To James S. Harlan

December 22, 1914 Boston, Mass. [Brandeis Mss, NMF 65-1]

MY DEAR MR. HARLAN: Upon my return to the city I find the copy of the December 16th opinion, together with your memorandum.

First: You will recall that the only evidence we had of the removal of the limitation in price was the news item in the Washington Post, which we examined together early last week. When the Stock Exchange was opened, the order allowed some of the stocks to be dealt in without limitation, and on others, a limit was fixed.[1] That article stated that the Committee in charge had concluded to remove the limitation. When I reached New York I found a notice in the papers stating that certain minima would be reduced, which showed that the plan of removing all limitations had not been adopted, and I therefore wired you Friday morning to that effect before 9:00 o'clock. I hope the telegram reached you.

Second: You may be interested in looking at the articles in yesterday's New York Times Annalist on the rate decision,[2]—particularly the remarks of Onlooker.[3]

You probably noticed that President Elliott of the New Haven and President Huestis [*sic*][4] of the Boston & Maine both gave out the statements to the effect that their roads would not gain respectively more than $250,000 under the decision. That was in accord with Mr. Elliott's previous statement in his letter to me, but the gain on the Boston & Maine is even less than I had supposed. There are some indications from the editorials that there are many doubts as to the railroads being really the gainers by the decision. I noticed in the Springfield Homestead an article on "Increased Rates and Increased Wages" indicating that the benefit of the rate increase would likely be absorbed now by increased wage allowances.[5]   Very truly yours,

1. Shortly after the outbreak of war in August, all trading had been suspended on the New York Stock Exchange. Trading resumed on 11 December, with minimum prices established for most of the stocks to avoid panic selling. This restriction proved unnecessary, and most prices advanced in the first few days of selling. Once the governors of the exchange saw this, they quickly removed the minimums on most issues.

2. Under the pressure of an intense propaganda campaign, as well as the claims of unusual expenses induced by the war, the Interstate Commerce Commission had reversed itself on 16 December and agreed to a general five percent rate increase in all classifications. For details of the railroad campaign, see Mason, *Brandeis*, ch. 21; see also LDB to Alfred Brandeis, 23 December 1914.

3. The *Annalist* had editorialized that the rate decision made good sense, in its recognition that railroad rates could not be arbitrarily set, but should be tied to general prices. If the Commission had decided this sooner, the editorial concluded, there would have been fewer railroad wreckages. (*New York Times Annalist*, 4 [21 December 1914]: 479.) "Onlooker" argued that much of the prosperity of the country should be credited to the railroads, and that the government should interfere with their operations as little as possible. In direct opposition to LDB, the columnist argued that all technological and efficiency improvements had been made, and that it would be impossible to reduce the per-unit costs any further. While admitting that some of the roads were over-capitalized, he said that nothing could be done about it at this point ("Relevant Annotations," *Ibid.*, 480.).

4. James Humphrey Hustis (1864–1942), a veteran railroad administrator, had been named president of the Boston & Maine in August. He served in the Railroad Administration during the war, but returned to the presidency of the B & M until his retirement in 1926.

5. The article grew out of an interview originally concerned with Zionism; LDB, however, led the reporter into the realm of railroad politics, and was pleased when that subject received a separate notice.

To Bloch Publishing Co.

December 23, 1914 Boston, Mass. [Brandeis Mss, Z 1-2]

DEAR SIRS: Please send me by return mail the following of your publications:

1. "Aspects of the Jewish Question."   .50
2. "Judaism and Its History" by Dr. Abraham Geiger   2.50
3. "The Sufferings of the Jews in the Middle Ages"   .50
4. "Jewish Questions" by Dr. Ignatz Zollschan   .25

I enclose check for $3.75 to cover same.

Yours very truly,

To Alfred Brandeis

December 23, 1914 Boston, Mass. [Brandeis Mss, M 4-1]

DEAR AL: My Xmas greetings.

I have yours about A.J.R.C. Collection. It is pretty hard raising money now for any purpose.[1] We have our first try here at a Com[tee] meeting this evening. The cry of home needs is loud, but men must realize that even taxes do not yield to customary standards. The situation abroad among the Jews is worse than man can tell.

Alice & Susan arrived today. Haven't seen either yet.

Confidential: The I.C.C. decision will prove a misfortune to both the RR's & the Comm[n] & will do much to hasten government ownership.[2]

Shall be in St. Louis January 3 & 4.

1. The American Jewish Relief Committee did a rather remarkable job of fund-raising, but the bulk of the money was brought in through the connections of the wealthy German-American Jews affiliated with the American Jewish Committee. The Zionists, despite great efforts, did not raise a large portion of the total. For an analysis of the fund-raising effort, see Yonathan Shapiro, *Leadership of the American Zionist Organization, 1897–1930.*

2. See LDB to James S. Harlan, 22 December 1914.

To Louis Lipsky

December 23, 1914 Boston, Mass. [Brandeis Mss, Z 1-4]

DEAR MR. LIPSKY: You will recall our correspondence with Dr. Krauskopf [1] in regard to my speaking in Philadelphia, and the conclusion we reached that it was not desirable to speak there unless we were assured of financial success. Since then I have had the following urgent invitations:

First: From Miss Emily Soles [*sic*] Cohen [2] of the Mikve Israel Association, who wanted me to talk at one of their Association meetings which were held at Dropsie College, and has been urging that I fix a date for January or February.

Second: From the Y.M.H.A., which, through Miss Soles Cohen offers to cooperate with the Mikve Israel Association for a joint meeting.

Third: From the Menorah Society of the University of Pennsylvania, of which Jacob Rubinoff [3] is President.

Fourth: From the Alumni Keneseth Israel, of which Jerome J. Rothschild [4] is President, and Sidney L. Olsho,[5] Chairman of the Committee on Lecture Courses, who are the alumni of Dr. Krauskopf's Association.

I had suggested to Miss Soles [*sic*] Cohen in November the possibility of these four organizations joining and holding a meeting. I enclose a copy of my letter of November 30th and of her letter of December 7th. In talking this matter over with Mr. DeHaas this morning, he suggested that he thought it would be undesirable for me to go to Philadelphia, at all events to speak for the Keneseth Israel, without satisfactory arrangement being made which would insure a good financial return, and he deemed the City of Philadelphia of enough importance to justify your going there and taking up the whole situation of Philadelphia,—conferring with these various parties, and see whether a satisfactory meeting could be arranged. I had not felt entirely certain whether or not it would be better to leave Philadelphia alone for the present.[6]

I shall be obliged to go to Washington immediately upon, or shortly after my return from St. Louis: and could with least inconvenience attend a meeting or meetings in Philadelphia on Sunday, January 10th (and indeed a meeting on the evening of Saturday the 9th would be possible). If those dates are not feasible, I would possibly be able to fix some date the latter part of January, but am unable to set it yet.

Please let me know by tomorrow's mail what you think of Mr. DeHaas' suggestion, and let me have generally your advice on the matter.   Very truly yours,

1. Joseph Krauskopf (1859–1923) was rabbi of the Reform Congregation Keneseth Israel in Philadelphia and founder of the Jewish Publication Society of America. He was also involved in several efforts to place Jewish immigrants on farms.

2. Emily Solis-Cohen (b. 1890) wrote widely on various subjects for Jewish journals.

3. Jacob Rubinoff (1884–1948) became a manufacturer of poultry feed in New Jersey after his graduation from college.

4. Jerome J. Rothschild (1884–1964), a Philadelphia lawyer, was later prominent in both the American Jewish Committee and the National Conference of Christians and Jews, of which he once served as president.

5. Sidney L. Olsho (1879–1964) was a Philadelphia ophthalmologist and consultant to the United States Public Health Service.

6. See LDB to Lipsky, 31 December 1914.

To Leon Sanders

December 23, 1914 Boston, Mass. [Brandeis Mss, NMF 56-2]

DEAR MR. SANDERS: [1] Yours of the 21st, requesting me to serve as a member of the Committee in connection with a contemplated citizens' meeting to manifest an objection against the Smith Immigration Bill [2] now pending before the Senate of the United States, just received.

I have not been able to follow this matter, but if, as I assume, the holding of this meeting meets with the approval of Dr. Wise and Judge Mack, I shall be glad to have my name appear as a member of the Committee. My engagements for the immediate future are, however, such that it will not be possible for me to be active.   Yours very truly,

1. Leon Sanders (1867–1937), former judge in the New York Municipal Court, was president of the Hebrew Sheltering and Immigrant Aid Society and was also grand master of the Independent Order of Brith Abraham.

2. Ever since the wave of so-called "new immigrants," primarily Jews and Catholics, began to arrive in large numbers there had been attempts to restrict immigration. A literacy test passed Congress in 1913, but it was vetoed by President Taft upon the recommendation of Charles Nagel, to whom illiteracy merely meant lack of opportunity, not of ability. Although the House failed to override Taft's veto, proponents of restriction began their campaign again almost as soon as Wilson took office. Shortly after the 1914 election, Congress acted and sent the Smith Bill to Wilson in January 1915. Wilson had already given indications that he opposed a literacy test, despite his basic sympathy with some of the restrictionists' aims; he vetoed the bill, and used the patronage powers to prevent the Congress from overriding the veto. See John Higham, *Strangers in the Land: Patterns of American Nativism, 1860–1925* (New Brunswick, N. J., 1955).

To Henry Green Hodges

December 24, 1914 Boston, Mass. [Brandeis Mss, NMF 11-2]

MY DEAR MR. HODGES: [1] Replying to yours of December 19th: [2]

The subject of unemployment is so vast and difficult a one, and I have in my own thinking made such slight advances towards even a partial solution, that I do not feel competent to pass any judgment of value upon your comprehensive plan for a State Bureau of Employment, which you enclosed. I venture, however, to suggest the following:

First: In all thinking on this subject a clear distinction must be made between unemployment because of special periods of depression, like the present, and that unemployment which is incident to irregularity of employment at times even of normal conditions. So far as concerns the unemployment due to depression, it ought to be possible to mitigate the evil by arranging that public work necessary to be done is done at such times that it will tend to equalize employment. That is, it should not be done at periods when work is abundant, and it should be done at periods when work is slack.

Second: That unemployment which is due to irregularity of employment should be met by a gradual development of the demands of labor, so that they include not only proper wages, hours and factory conditions, but also continuous employment. And where trades are seasonal, so that employment cannot be continuous, provision should be made by which the worker in a seasonal trade secures work in a supplementary trade.

Third: So far as concerns irregularity of employment in private concerns, I am convinced that a large part is avoidable, and that ways will be found of making employment continuous, provided adequate incentives to regularity are provided. Among other things, there should be a penalty worked out for under-employment, similar to the double pay for over time.

In the volume of my addresses entitled "Business—A Profession", I discuss this general subject in the article of that name,[3] and made some reference to the subject of unemployment in another article in the volume entitled "The Road to Social Efficiency."

I think the fundamental proposition that we must establish is that irregularity of employment is an industrial disease that may be cured.[4]   Very truly yours,

1. Henry Green Hodges (1888-[?]) taught at the Wharton School of the University of Pennsylvania.
2. Hodges had written that he and a number of other people were trying to tackle the unemployment problem through the establishment of a free state employment bureau.
3. See LDB to J. Franklin McElwain, 18 June 1912, n. 1.
4. See LDB to Abraham L. Filene, June 1911.

To Thomas William Churchill

December 31, 1914 Boston, Mass. [Brandeis Mss, NMF 69-3]

MY DEAR MR. CHURCHILL: [1] Absence from the city has delayed a reply to your letter of the 22nd.[2]

I do not feel competent to express an opinion on any matter of detail in respect to the division of the work involved in administering the school system of the City of New Work. But I have no doubt that so large a Board as yours now is cannot be the most efficient instrument to accomplish this purpose. It seems to me clear that the Board of Education should consist of only a few members; that the Board when it meets should be able to consult instead of making speeches, and that the work of the Board itself should be similar in character to that performed by the ideal board of directors of a corporation. In other words, the Board should determine the broad questions of policy, administration and supervision, and should leave to paid employees the carrying out of the policies and directions determined upon by the Board.[3]

Yours very truly,

1. Thomas William Churchill (1862-1934), a New York attorney, was president of that city's board of education.
2. Churchill was seeking a reorganization of the board, which then consisted of forty-six members. He wanted a smaller board, with much of the committee work relegated to a paid professional staff, and the members limiting their duties to policy making.
3. A reorganization of the board of education did ultimately take place, and it followed LDB's general suggestion of a small policy-making group relying on a professional staff. For the ultimate consequences of this decision, see David Rogers, *110 Livingston Street* (New York, 1968) and Marilyn Gittell, *Participants and Participation* (New York, 1967).

To Frederick Morris Feiker

December 31, 1914 Boston, Mass. [Brandeis Mss, NMF 11-2]

MY DEAR MR. FEIKER: [1] I am much interested by the introduction in System of the department entitled "The Human Factor". The importance of that factor in industry is becoming more and more widely recognized, and contributions which your department will make to a proper consideration of it cannot fail to be useful.

I was particularly interested in your reference to the Minimum Wage laws, as I had just come from arguing their constitutionality before the Supreme Court of the United States, where the validity of the Oregon law was being challenged. The subject was discussed with great fullness. No decision has yet been rendered.[2]

1. Frederick Morris Feiker (1881–1967) was chairman of the editorial board of *System*. Although trained as an engineer, Feiker's professional life was spent in writing for numerous trade and industrial journals until he became dean of the George Washington University engineering school.

2. See LDB to Charles McCarthy, 18 November 1914.

To Norman Hapgood

December 31, 1914 Boston, Mass. [Brandeis Mss, NMF 62-1]

MY DEAR NORMAN: *First*: Governor Walsh has appointed Eastman to the Public Service Commission to fill the vacancy left by George W. Anderson's retirement (Anderson has become United States Attorney for Massachusetts.) Governor Walsh ought to have commendation for this appointment, and something should be said to introduce Eastman to the country. I enclose clipping from the Boston Herald of a brief statement of his "career".

Eastman is a man of ability, a hard worker, of high character, and fine public spirit. It is particularly satisfying that a man who has in all the time I have known him never shown the slightest thought of his own interest when that of the public was concerned, should have had the success of attaining at the age of 33 a position of distinction, with a very good salary. It ought to prove to be great encouragement to others.

The appointment of Eastman was much opposed by some of the public service magnates, but I feel confident that he will prove absolutely just to them, and that the vested interests as well as the public, will be safe in his hands.[1]

Second: Have you seen Morris [*sic*] Wertheim about writing an article on Zionism and the Palestinian Colonies? He talked the other evening on the subject in a very interesting way. Of course I do not know what kind of an article he could write. He has also some interesting photographs.[2]

Third: You will recall my talking to you about Morris L. Cooke, the Director of Public Works in Philadelphia.

He has been most active in starting the project of a Utilities Bureau. When in Philadelphia yesterday I suggested his writing you as soon as he is ready for some publicity on this subject.[3]

Yours,

1. LDB sent similar letters praising the Eastman appointment to Hamilton Holt of the *Independent* and Lawrence F. Abbott of *The Outlook;* Holt did run a brief notice of the appointment in the 25 January 1915 edition. Hapgood's editorial on Eastman, "Good for Walsh," appeared in the 23 January 1915 issue of *Harper's*.

2. Wertheim did write an article on this subject, but it appeared in another magazine; "Palestine and the War," *Survey*, 33 (2 January 1915): 353. See also LDB to David Rubin, 31 December 1914.

3. *Harper's* did not publish any articles by or about Cooke in 1915.

To Edward Mandel House

December 31, 1914 Boston, Mass. [House Mss]

MY DEAR COLONEL HOUSE: Norman Hapgood has sent me a copy of his letter to you of the 28th concerning the suggested appointment of J.P. Cotton, Jr., to the Federal Trade Commission. I agree entirely with what Norman says.

Cotton would be an ideal Commissioner,—a man of unusual ability, wide experience, public spirited,—combining legal and business training.

The success or failure of the Commission will depend largely upon the quality of men selected, and I can think of no one who would be more likely to insure success of this new experiment than Cotton.[1]

Very cordially yours,

1. Cotton, who had worked with LDB on the Ballinger investigation, was not appointed to the trade commission. The appointees were Joseph E. Davies, the Commissioner of Corporations; Edward Nash Hurley (1864–1933), a tool manufacturer and later chairman of the United States Shipping Board during the war; and George Rublee (but see LDB to Norman Hapgood, 23 February 1915, n. 1). Of the three, only Rublee shared the original Wilson-Brandeis concept of regulation. In an interview with Ray Stannard Baker in the late 1920s, LDB commented that Wilson had ruined the entire idea of the F.T.C. because of the men he had named to it (Ray Stannard Baker MSS, Library of Congress, File I–B–21). See LDB to Gilson Gardner, 7 September 1915.

To Louis Lipsky

December 31, 1914 Boston, Mass. [Brandeis Mss, Z 1-4]

DEAR MR. LIPSKY: I am in receipt of yours of the 30th enclosing memorandum entitled "Suggestions for Publicity".[1] I am in accord with you as to the need of proper publicity. I have, however, very grave doubt whether the proper course for us to pursue at the present time is to enter upon a new publication. What we need particularly is some means of getting our views properly before the public generally in newspapers and periodicals, and one of the first requisites for this is to secure writers of sufficient ability, knowledge and distinction.

With every day I am becoming more convinced that what we need is able, zealous, efficient workers. Of these there is at present a terrible lack, and until we get a larger supply, we must be very careful not to take on additional burdens.

Yours very truly,

1. The memorandum reflected the sentiment of a number of American Zionists that the leadership of the world movement had passed to the United States as a result of the European war. Lipsky proposed that the P.E.C., in connection with the Inner Actions Committee, publish a fortnightly magazine which would embody "the official" views of the Zionist movement regarding the pressing questions arising out of any peace settlement. Arguing that "the desired impression cannot be made by individual utterances or by inspired articles in the general press," Lipsky thought that only a special periodical could both press Jewish demands effectively and at the same time assert the hegemony of the American branch of the movement.

To Louis Lipsky

December 31, 1914 Boston, Mass. [Brandeis Mss, Z 1-4]

MY DEAR MR. LIPSKY: Miss Emily Soles [*sic*] Cohen got in touch with me while I was in Philadelphia yesterday, and told me of the letter which she had received from you, and also that she had now arranged so that they could have a meeting there in which the four organizations,—the Mikve Israel Association, the Y.M.H.A., the Menorah Society, and the Alumni Keneseth Israel,—would cooperate; but that it would not be possible to make this meeting an occasion for the collection of money.[1]

It seemed to me that the fact of cooperation was, in Philadelphia, an important one, and that it was worth while for me to speak there as soon as I reasonably could, at a joint meeting conducted by the four organizations, which would be held at the rooms of the Alumni Keneseth Israel. I therefore told her that as soon as I could arrange for such an evening I would let her know, giving her approximately two weeks' notice.

Yours very truly,

1. See LDB to Lipsky, 23 December 1914.

To David Rubin

December 31, 1914 Boston, Mass. [Brandeis Mss, Z 2-3]

MY DEAR MR. RUBIN: At the meeting of the Zeta Beta Tau Fraternity in New York Tuesday evening, Morris [*sic*] Wertheim gave a talk on Palestine with stereoptican [*sic*] views. I think he will become one of the most effective speakers on Zionism, because he apparently had no interest whatever before he went to Palestine, but it took great hold of him, and he talked of it in a way which should have great influence on young men.

I think the members of the Zionist Society would be greatly interested in having him come over. It might be better to have him talk before the Menorah Society, and thus get a larger audience.   Very truly yours,

To Earnest R. Stevens

December 31, 1914 Boston, Mass. [Brandeis Mss, NMF 68-1]

MY DEAR MR. STEVENS: [1] Replying to your letter of the 30th enclosing a petition concerning the regulation of the price of electricity:

It seems to me that the bill in the lines proposed in the petition would be highly unwise. I have no doubt that the charges for electricity are inequitable, and are in the main too high, but I think the method proposed by the petition should not be pursued. To my mind the first step proper to be taken is, however, the determination of the actual cost of production, and the actual cost of distribution,—such work as was proposed at the Conference of Mayors held in Philadelphia in November in connection with the formation of the Utilities Bureau, of which Mr. Morris L. Cooke, Director of Public Works in Philadelphia, is deeply interested. I would suggest your communicating with him on this subject.
                                                      Very truly yours.

1. Earnest R. Stevens was Massachusetts state deputy for the National Association of Stationary Engineers. He wanted LDB to support a petition to regulate the price of electricity between fixed limits based on the costs of production.

To Robert Grosvenor Valentine

December 31, 1914 Boston, Mass. [Brandeis Mss, NMF 11-2]

MY DEAR VALENTINE: Your letter of the 10th asking me to become a member of the Massachusetts Committee on Unemployment should have been answered before.

I dislike very much being a member of any committee when there is a great probability of my being inactive; but the subject of unemployment is so important a one that I cannot altogether refuse to give assistance if you think that I can be of any help in talking matters over with you and the others from time to time.
                                                      Cordially yours,

To David Ignatius Walsh

December 31, 1914 Boston, Mass. [Brandeis Mss, NMF 65-3]

MY DEAR GOVERNOR: My hearty congratulations to you and to the Commonwealth on your appointment of Eastman. I am sure that he will reflect great credit on your administration, and that the public, including many who now oppose him, will recognize his sterling qualities.

I came to town this morning, and leave again tomorrow for the West, and then for Washington, so that I shall not have the pleasure of hearing your Inaugural address.[1]

With every good wish for 1915.   Most cordially yours,

1. Walsh had just been reelected governor.

To Felix Moritz Warburg

December 31, 1914 Boston, Mass. [Brandeis Mss, NMF 66-1]

MY DEAR MR. WARBURG: I was very sorry that I did not have an opportunity while in New York to discuss with you the following matters, and I am writing you as I am about to leave for the West, and may not be able to attend the next meeting of the Executive Committee or of the Committee on Distribution.

The American Jewish Relief Committee has assumed these serious obligations:

First: To collect for the war sufferers the greatest possible sum.

Second: To secure a wise and equitable distribution of the funds collected.

It is obvious that the amount of our collections will be dependent, to a large extent, upon the confidence which the Jews of America have in the wisdom and fairness of the distribution to be made; and that we should not select as a representative, charged with the duty of distribution, any person whom a large number of Jews regard with suspicion.

I have received from many persons strong protests against the selection of Dr. Ephriam Cohen [*sic*],[1] as our representative in Jerusalem. I realize of course that it might be very embarrassing to remove Dr. Cohen [*sic*], and I was, therefore, very glad to learn that at the last meeting of our Committee on Distribution (which I was unable to attend) two additional residents of Jerusalem were added to the Committee, and that the character of the men elected was such as to minimize, if not wholly remove the objections to the selection of Dr. Cohen [*sic*].[2] It seems to me particularly unfortunate, therefore, that the action taken by your Committee was later nullified.

At the meeting of the Executive Committee on the 27th a reference was made to the fact that Dr. Paul Nathan had offered his services in making distribution in the three Polands. I find that the feeling regarding Dr. Nathan is similar to that expressed in regard to Dr. Ephriam Cohen [*sic*]. I have no personal knowledge of the qualifications of character of either of these two men; but it seems to me clear that with the large field of choice open to us, we ought not to select men whom any appreciable number of Jews regard with suspicion. I am confident that employment by us of the services of Dr. Nathan would greatly embarrass the confidence in and success of our Committee.[3]

Very cordially yours,

1. Ephraim Cohn–Reiss (1863–1943) was director of the German-sponsored Hilfsverein schools in Palestine, and the objections were due to the pro-German attitude expressed by Cohn–Reiss and other officials of the schools.

2. In addition to Cohn–Reiss, Arthur Ruppin and Aaron Aaronsohn were named.

3. The Committee did not accept Nathan's offer.

To Editor, *Menorah Journal*

[January, 1915] Boston, Mass. [*Menorah Journal*]

The formation at Harvard University on October 25, 1906, of the first Menorah Society is a landmark in the Jewish Renaissance. That Renaissance, in which the Society is certain to be a significant factor, is of no less importance to America than to its Jews.

America offers to man his greatest opportunity—liberty admidst peace and natural resources. But the noble purpose to which America is dedicated cannot be attained unless this high opportunity is fully utilized; and to this end each of the many peoples which she has welcomed to her hospitable shores must contribute the best of which it is capable. To America the contribution of the Jews can be peculiarly large. America's fundamental law seeks to make real the brotherhood of man. That brotherhood became the Jews' fundamental law more than twenty-five hundred years ago. America's twentieth century demand is for social justice. That has been the Jews' striving ages-long. Their religion and their afflictions have prepared them for effective democracy. Persecution made the Jews' law of brotherhood self-enforcing. It taught them the seriousness of life; it broadened their sympathies; it deepened the passion for righteousness; it trained them in patient endurance, in persistence, in self-control, and in self-sacrifice. Furthermore, the widespread study of Jewish law developed the intellect and made them less subject to preconceptions and more open to reason.

America requires in her sons and daughters these qualities and attainments, which are our natural heritage. Patriotism to America, as well as loyalty to our past, imposes upon us the obligation of claiming this heritage of the Jewish spirit and of carrying forward noble ideals and traditions through lives and deeds worthy of our ancestors. To this end each new generation should be trained in the knowledge and appreciation of their own great past; and the opportunity should be afforded for the further development of Jewish character and culture.

The Menorah Societies and their Journal deserve most generous support in their efforts to perform this noble task.[1]

1. This letter appeared with several others of a similar nature in the inaugural issue of *The Menorah Journal*, 1 (January 1915): 4.

To Alfred Brandeis

January 1, 1915 Boston, Mass. [Brandeis Mss, NMF 71-5]

MY DEAR AL: I heard Chief Justice White deliver the opinion in United States vs. L. & N., and I read the opinion, which I return herewith.[1]

I do not know what the doubt is that you have in mind for your letter has been mislaid. It seems to me the decision established merely this rule: That the fourth Section applies to cases of rebilling, as well as to ordinary through shipments, and that, therefore, a rate is illegal if

(a) it is lower to a more distant point than to an intermediate point measured from the point of origin, or

(b) if it is lower from a more distant point than to an intermediate point measured from the rebilling point.

That in this instance the rate in question was lower measured either from the Ohio River or from Nashville to the point of ultimate destination than to an intermediate point, and was therefore illegal.

I am leaving at noon today for St. Louis, and I leave there Monday night for Washington, and to be there until the arguments of the California eight hour cases are finished.[2] The cases are on the list for next week, but may not be reached until the week after. I shall probably go from Washington to Boston.

Yours,

1. The Louisville & Nashville Railroad had been ordered by the Interstate Commerce Commission in 1911 to cancel special reshipping rates for grains at Nashville, since the rate gave that city an unfair shipping advantage. The railroad appealed to the Commerce Court, which vacated the commission ruling, and the I.C.C. in turn appealed to the Supreme Court. The high court held that findings of fact by the I.C.C. were not disputable in courts of law, and reversed the Commerce Court, upholding the original I.C.C. order. *United States* v. *Louisville and Nashville Railroad Co.*, 235 U.S. 314 (1914). Interestingly, LDB's cousin Albert Brandeis represented the railroad.

2. See LDB to Charles McCarthy, 18 November 1914, n. 3.

To Richard James Horatio Gottheil

January 1, 1915 Boston, Mass. [Brandeis Mss, Z 6-1]

MY DEAR MR. GOTTHEIL: *First*: Replying to yours of the 31st: [1]

I know nothing of Mr. Bernstein,[2] but so far as Dr. Magnes is concerned, I think you are mistaken in assuming that there is any deliberate attack on you. The discussion was a general one, applicable of course to everybody, and I do not recall that any specific reference was made in the discussion to your talk in Philadelphia. There was a reference made to the article in the Sun. The discussion was conducted with great fairness, and wholly as a matter of the policy which is best for the Zionist cause.

Second: You say: "I find it strange also that I have not been informed of what took place at the meeting and have only in a general way had a word from Dr. Wise concerning it." Dr. Wise was especially deputed to explain this matter fully to you as the best means of communication, and with a view to avoiding any false interpretation by you.[3] If Dr. Wise has not made this clear to you, it must have been because the opportunity did not serve for a full statement from him.[4]   Most cordially yours,

P.S. I am glad that you feel that an impression was made on the boys the other evening.[5]

1. Gottheil was extremely upset at what he took to be a personal attack upon him at the previous meeting of the Provisional Committee, which he had missed. Moreover, he accused Herman Bernstein (see next note) and Judah Magnes of deliberately misrepresenting comments he had made at a Menorah Society meeting in Philadelphia in late December. The gist of the dispute lay in conflicting attitudes towards the war. Gottheil and some other members on the Provisional Committee privately favored the Allies, but had agreed that it would be best for Jewish interests to maintain an official neutrality. Many of the Eastern European immigrants, the natural constituency of the Yiddish press, supported the Central Powers primarily in opposition to Russia, which they hated for its persecution of the Jews. Gottheil charged Bernstein with distorting his comments in an article in the *New York Sun* to make it seem that he favored the Russians.

2. Herman Bernstein (1876–1935) was the founder and editor of the Yiddish daily, *Der Tag* (*The Day*), and also wrote numerous articles for the English language press. He was named by President Hoover as minister to Albania in 1930.

3. See LDB to Stephen S. Wise, 13 January 1915.

4. On 12 January Gottheil repeated his irritation, and sent LDB copies of the offending article; he again complained that he felt left out of some of the Provisional Committee deliberations.

5. LDB had spoken to the Columbia University Menorah Society the preceding week.

To Walter Edward Weyl

January 1, 1915 Boston, Mass. [Brandeis Mss, NMF 67-2]

MY DEAR WEYL: I have yours of the 31st, which by the way I am extremely glad to get.[1] My understanding had exactly accorded with yours in regard to what the Board of Arbitration, as distinguished from Mr. Winslow, was to do in respect to this report, and furthermore that you were to prepare for the Board of Arbitration the summary of the report, with a statement of the conclusions and of the proposals which we were eventually to make. I had, therefore, felt a deep regret that your other work, had as I supposed, compelled not only your resignation from the Board, but a withdrawal from the task of preparing the summary and reports of the conclusions and proposals.[2] I am more than glad, therefore, to find that there has been a misunderstanding, and that you are now prepared to go forward on the lines originally planned by all of us, and I am writing Commissioner Meeker,[3] expressing my gratification that you will do so; and asking him to withhold the publication until this shall have been done.[4]

I am also writing Dr. Moskowitz and Holt by this mail, sending each a copy of my letter to you.   Cordially yours,

1. Weyl had written that the Bureau of Labor Statistics was ready to publish a second report on the Protocol (for the first, see LDB to Weyl, 3 November 1913), and that it was his understanding that this new report would not be released until he prepared a preliminary statement representing the policy of the board of arbitration.

2. Weyl had joined Herbert Croly and Walter Lippmann as an editor of the *New Republic*.

3. Royal Meeker (1873–1953) had come from a professorship in economics at Princeton to accept the position of Commissioner of Labor Statistics under Wilson. After 1920, Meeker went on to a distinguished career in teaching and in various state governments' statistical branches.

4. The Bureau of Labor Statistics could not delay publication because the report had already been set in type. See *Wages and Regularity of Employment in Cloak, Suit and Skirt Industry* . . . (Washington, 1915); the first part of the report, on wages, was written by Charles H. Winslow, while the second, dealing with education of apprentices, was prepared by William T. Bawden.

To Charles Bren Strecker

January 13, 1915 Boston, Mass. [Brandeis Mss, NMF 66-1]

DEAR MR. STRECKER: You doubtless received notice of your appointment as Chairman of the Committee on Speakers and Public Meetings, as per my letter to you of December 31st.

Upon my return to the city today I find that no action of any kind appears yet to have been taken by you. The need is so great

that it is imperative that prompt action be taken. Will you, therefore, kindly arrange at once for completing the membership of
your Committee, and getting it into active service.[1]

Yours very truly,

1. This letter was typical of many that LDB sent urging Zionists to greater
and greater action.

To Stephen Samuel Wise

January 13, 1915 Boston, Mass. [Brandeis Mss, Z 6-2]

MY DEAR DR. WISE: I have had two letters from Professor Gottheil
in both of which he complains that he has not "yet had a report
of that meeting, but have only heard in a vague sort of a way
about it from Dr. Wise." [1]

My own feeling was that the discussion at the meeting was
conducted in a way that it was most considerate—and that as to
communicating the result to him no better way could have been
found than that you, who are so fully in sympathy with him,
should tell him what happened; and this I understood to be also
your own view.

I trust that you will arrange to see Professor Gottheil immediately, and remove if possible the feeling of irritation which
appears to exist.   Cordially yours,

P.S. Have you done anything about articles in the Independent
or Outlook?

1. See LDB to Richard Gottheil, 1 January 1915.

To Boris Baer

January 14, 1915 Boston, Mass. [Brandeis Mss, NMF 65-5]

DEAR MR. BAER: The Executive Committee of the American
Jewish Relief Committee of New England appointed a Trade
Committee, of which Mr. Max Mitchell is Chairman, and in his
absence Mr. Al. A. Rosenbush serves as Acting Chairman. The
special duty of the Committee is to secure from members of their
respective trades or businesses subscriptions to the relief fund.

I have taken the liberty of selecting you as the representative of the wool business.

Will you kindly get in touch at once with Mr. Rosenbush with a view to pushing the work of the Committee? [1]

Yours very truly,

1. Notes similar to this were sent to numerous Jewish business men in the Boston area.

To Richard James Horatio Gottheil

January 14, 1915 Boston, Mass. [Gottheil Mss]

MY DEAR PROFESSOR GOTTHEIL: *First*: I hope you will be able to make a report to me soon embodying the results of your investigation into Herzl and other negotiations with the various powers.[1] I realize how much you have been hampered in getting material from abroad bearing on this matter, but I hope you will let me have soon whatever is available.

Second: I think it would be desirable also to have the data concerning the action taken in behalf of the Roumanian Jews at the conference resulting in the Treaty of Berlin;[2] and that the Jewish Chronicle of London, obtainable at one of the New York libraries, would prove a proper source as also reports of the Israel Alliance Universalle and the Anglo-Jewish Association.[3] Could you also have this matter looked up?

Cordially yours,

1. Theodore Herzl believed that the creation of a Jewish homeland would result from "political" actions, namely negotiations with heads of state who would then guarantee a Jewish nation. Herzl met with the sultan of Turkey and the emperor of Germany, but he received nothing except good wishes from them.

2. In 1878 Bismarck convened a conference in Berlin in an effort to settle some of the differences between Russia and Turkey; on the agenda was the treatment of the Jews in the Balkan states. At the initiative of the French, Bulgaria, Serbia, and Rumania were recognized as independent nations conditional upon their granting political and religious rights to all minorities, irrespective of religion. Rumania ratified the treaty but then found a technical loophole and continued to deprive Jews of civil rights. See LDB to Norman Hapgood, 24 September 1914, n. 3.

3. The Alliance Israelité Universalle was founded in 1860 to protect Jewish religious and civil liberties. It organized public protests against anti-Semitism and conducted relief drives to help oppressed Jews. In 1870 the

Alliance established the pioneer agricultural school in Palestine at Mikveh Israel, but the organization was decidedly anti-Zionist. Since World War II its main function has been conducting a variety of Jewish schools in France, North Africa, and the Middle East. The Anglo-Jewish Association was founded in 1871 in imitation of the Alliance, and it was also anti-Zionist until the mid-1920s. It has maintained several schools for deprived Jews, as well as the Evelina de Rothschild School in Jerusalem (see LDB to Stephen S. Wise, 27 December 1915).

To Horace Meyer Kallen

January 14, 1915 Boston, Mass. [Brandeis Mss, Z 3-1]

MY DEAR KALLEN: Your letter of the 1st reached me in St. Louis.[1]

First: I am glad to learn of the ferment in Cincinnati; and what you say has been confirmed by Dr. Levin, who went there from St. Louis, and had most satisfactory experiences. He was particularly delighted with Mr. Fechheimer's sympathetic interest.[2]

Second: Our St. Louis experience was most satisfactory, particularly with the German Jews. The meeting at Dr. Harrison's [3] Temple was of much the same character as at Dr. Hirsh's, and the interest manifested by those at the banquet in the evening even more promising than what we found in Chicago. We are making unmistakable progress, but our crying need is for educated workers trained to the task.   Very cordially yours,

1. Kallen had written that while in Cincinnati he had spoken to a number of Jews outside the influence of Rabbi Philipson, and that real possibilities existed for developing Zionist sentiment there. Moreover, there was much resentment against Philipson for not allowing LDB to speak there (see LDB to Louis Lipsky, 5 October 1914).

2. Samuel Marcus Fechheimer was a Cincinnati clothing manufacturer with strong Zionist sympathies.

3. Leon Harrison (1866-1928) had been rabbi of the Reformed Temple Israel in St. Louis since 1891, and he was also active in several civic reform groups.

To Louis Lipsky

January 14, 1915 Boston, Mass. [Brandeis Mss, Z 1-4]

MY DEAR MR. LIPSKY: Referring to our talk of yesterday concerning the financing of the Zionist Bureau for New England:

I am willing for the present to pay, in addition to the rent, clerical services and office expenses, an amount equal to one-half of Mr. DeHaas's salary from January 1, 1915, which salary I understand to be at the rate of $2,000 a year. If it is agreeable to the Federation, I will make this payment direct to Mr. DeHaas,— to wit, $83.33. monthly.

From my talk with Mr. DeHaas today, I should think that the added income which the Federation will derive from the additional members obtained through the Bureau would be more than the expense of the balance payable to Mr. DeHaas by the Federation.   Very truly yours,

To Benjamin Perlstein

January 14, 1915 Boston, Mass. [Brandeis Mss, Z 3-2]

DEAR MR. PERLSTEIN: *First*: I am enclosing herewith check for $1,000 from Mr. Samuel S. Fels,[1] being a contribution to our Emergency Fund.

Second: I have your financial report of January 10th, and am disappointed to find that the amount of cash received in the Emergency Fund is not larger. Are our representatives in each of the communities being pressed to make prompt contributions? I have spoken to Mr. DeHaas and learn that Mr. [Charles B.] Strecker is to send $2,000 today.

What is the significance of the item in the balances "On hand $10,436.38" as distinguished from the amounts in the two banks.[2]

Third: I am uncertain whether I shall be in New York before Tuesday morning, but I expect to call at the office Tuesday morning shortly after 9:00, for about an hour. At 10:30 I go into an arbitration meeting. I suggest that you call a meeting of our committee for Thursday, late afternoon and evening.

Will you kindly send me by return mail a memorandum of the matters which you think should be taken up at our meeting.

Yours very truly,

1. Samuel S. Fels (1860–1950) was a wealthy soap manufacturer and the brother of LDB's former client, Joseph Fels.

2. Jeanette Jacobson replied for Perlstein that all deposits were made at noon; the $10,436.38 had been received by the office after noon, and was therefore "on hand" until the next day's deposit.

To Lillian D. Wald

January 16, 1915 Boston, Mass. [Wald Mss]

DEAR MISS WALD: Mr. Kellogg tells me that the Peace Conference is adjourned to January 23rd at 11:00 o'clock.[1] I am to be in New York on the day, but I regret that I have promised to speak before the Industrial Relations Committee in the morning,[2] and at a Minimum Wage meeting in the afternoon.[3]

Cordially yours,

1. See LDB to Paul U. Kellogg, 16 February 1915.
2. In his testimony before the Commission on Industrial Relations, LDB pleaded for greater democracy in industry. Employers had to learn to trust their workers and to confide in them; the age of benevolent absolutism was over, and both management and labor had to adjust to this fact. As usual, LDB lashed out at large corporations as the worst tyrants over labor and blamed much of the current social unrest on the unwillingness of giant monopolies to treat their men fairly. LDB's testimony can be found in Senate Document 415, 64th Cong., 1st Sess. (Washington, 1915). 26:7657–81; excerpts can be found in *The Curse of Bigness*, 70–95.
3. At a luncheon of the City Club, LDB joined several other speakers in endorsing minimum-wage legislation, not as a philanthropic measure, but as an overall societal benefit. A brief summary of LDB's comments can be found in *The New York Times*, 24 January 1915.

To Nathan D. Kaplan

January 18, 1915 Boston, Mass. [Brandeis Mss, Z 3-1]

DEAR MR. KAPLAN: *First*: Under date of November 10th Mr. Shulman wired me:

"Milwaukee just informed us that they are arranging Gigantic Demonstration for Tuesday, twenty-fourth, to be addressed by you. They promise to raise substantial sum. Wire whether your stay in Chicago will permit you to visit Milwaukee."

To which I replied under date of November 11th:

"Your yesterday's telegram received. Impossible to speak in Milwaukee Tuesday, twenty-fourth, but will rearrange other plans so as to speak there Monday, twenty-third, if a net contribution of at least two thousand dollars is effectively guaranteed. Let me have answer not later than Saturday morning."

To which Mr. Shulman replied under date of Nov. 13th.

"Milwaukee wires 'Meeting for Brandeis arranged for Monday evening, twenty-third. Prominent people interested. Desired success is assured. Wire Brandeis to that effect. Answer if satisfactory.' "

My last reports from New York in regard to Milwaukee collections were very unsatisfactory. I had hopes after our visit there that it might be possible to raise in all $4,000 or $5,000; but we must certainly hold all interested up to their guaranty of $2,000.

Will you kindly write me to the New York office, where I expect to be this week, when we may expect further remittances.

Second: I hope to hear when I reach New York of substantial reports from our St. Louis meeting.

Yours very truly,

To Louis Lipsky

January 18, 1915 Boston, Mass. [Brandeis Mss, Z 1-4]

MY DEAR MR. LIPSKY: Replying to yours of the 17th: [1]

I think it unwise for me to make any public statement, or for any member to discuss in a way which might become public, the subject of an American Jewish Congress or Convention, until this subject has been fully considered by the Provisional Committee.[2]

I hope we shall have a full attendance of Associate as well as regular members of the Committee at the meetings assigned for next Thursday and Sunday, so that this and other matters may receive due consideration.   Very truly yours,

1. Lipsky had prepared a press release and statement for LDB calling for a Jewish Congress to meet and discuss the situation of the Jews after the war.

2. The subject of a Jewish Congress had been under discussion since the outbreak of the war. At the extraordinary meeting of 30 August which had elected LDB to head the Provisional Committee, a resolution had been introduced "to call a convention of Jewish organizations and Jewish committees." Following this, LDB had invited the American Jewish Committee to join the Provisional Committee in convening such a meeting (see LDB to Louis Marshall, 31 August 1914). It soon became clear, however, that the Provisional Committee and the American Jewish Committee had widely differ-

ing views on the exact nature of this gathering. The A.J.C., used to dealing with small committees of influential people, preferred, in effect, a mere extension of their own group, one that they could control. LDB and the so-called "downtown" Jews favored a more democratically chosen congress, in which the will of the American Jews could be expressed by freely chosen delegates. By mid-1915, the congress question was the burning issue in American Jewry, with those groups representing the more recent immigrants backing the congress, while the older German-American Jews favored the A.J.C. proposal of a "conference." In late July LDB met with Cyrus Adler in an effort to reach agreement, but these talks broke off in mid-August (see LDB to Cyrus Adler, 28 July and 10 August 1915). By late 1915 the A.J.C. had recognized that the pressure for a Congress was too great to resist any longer, and agreed to cooperate provided the meeting did not take place until after the war. The Congress Organizing Committee, however, plunged ahead and held a preliminary meeting in Philadelphia on 26–27 March 1916; further meetings were delayed due to American entrance in the war, and the first full-scale meeting did not take place until December 1918. By that time Louis Marshall had been partially won over; he played an important role in the first Congress meeting, and was chosen to head the congress dele-gation to the Paris Peace Conference. The A.J.C. had supposed that the congress would dissolve after it had made its representations to the Paris conference, and were bitterly upset when a rump session led by Bernard Richards turned a one-time meeting into an ongoing organization. The best collection of documents and materials on the congress fight is Alvin Sidney Roth, "Backgrounds and Origins of the American Jewish Congress," (rab-binic thesis, Hebrew Union College, 1953).

To Charles McCarthy

January 18, 1915 Boston, Mass. [McCarthy Mss]

MY DEAR MR. McCARTHY: The enclosure with yours of the 14th as to the Governor's activities is certainly disturbing.[1] He seems to be radically reactionary, but I have confidence that Wiscon-sin's leaders in progressive thought and action will in the end be able to protect the State and the Nation.[2]

With every good wish,   Most cordially yours,

1. Emanuel Lorenz Philipp (1861–1925), a Wisconsin industrialist, had just been elected to the first of his three terms as governor; in his inaugural mes-sage he proposed abolishing the Legislative Reference Bureau.

2. The bureau was not abolished. For the story of the fight, see Fitzpatrick, *McCarthy of Wisconsin,* ch. 7.

To Benjamin Perlstein

January 18, 1915 Boston, Mass. [Brandeis Mss, Z 3-2]

DEAR MR. PERLSTEIN: Referring to my letter to you of November 9th:

First: I asked then to have you send me a copy of a report showing in detail receipts to date and sources thereof distributed among the cities etc. Also the schedule of estimated amounts already subscribed. And I then added "Send similar reports to me on Monday of each week bringing up the data to the preceding Saturday."

I never received any such report from you, but suppose you have it at the office. I wish you would have such a report prepared to and including Saturday, January 16th, and have it ready for me by Thursday morning.

Second: I also asked you to "Send to members of each of the Committees having matters in hand not yet disposed of, a request to send a report to the office in writing not later than next Monday, and let me have carbons of letters that you send."

I have received no communications of this kind from you.

I wish you would have prepared a statement showing every matter referred to a Committee, which has not yet been acted upon, giving dates etc., so that I can go over this matter on Thursday morning.

Third: In that letter I wrote that I desired to have a complete report on all meetings, stating that the only report of the meetings on my file were August 30th and 31. Since then I have received reports of the following meetings:

September 11th, November 29th, December 6th.

I trust that the reports of all meetings are now ready, and I should like to complete the file.   Yours very truly,

To Carl Vrooman

January 18, 1915 Boston, Mass. [Brandeis Mss, NMF 1-N-3]

DEAR MR. VROOMAN: Replying to yours of the 16th: [1]

From my own observation I was inclined to think that Commissioner Prouty's finding in respect to the transportation conditions of the New England roads at the time that he examined them, was perhaps a little too generous to the companies,—due perhaps in part to this: That as a result of the investigation conditions were improved, and his findings were rather with respect to conditions at the end of the investigation than what they had been at the time the investigation, which lasted a year, was commenced. What he said about long distance rates was absolutely true. Some of the short distance rates also were unduly low, but others were very high. Since that time, as a result of the investigation, freight rates have been thoroughly revised in New England. The general trend has been upward; and this is also more true of passenger rates, which were lower than operating costs warranted.

Important improvements have been made under the new management of the New Haven and the Boston & Maine.

Cordially yours,

1. Vrooman had followed up a statement of LDB's that train service in New England was inferior to that in the rest of the nation. He found that while certain roads were in bad shape, the Department of Agriculture's Bureau of Markets considered the major part of the service equal to service in other sections. He wanted LDB's comment on these findings.

To John Hollis Bankhead

January 25, 1915 Boston, Mass. [Brandeis Mss, NMF 69-3]

MY DEAR SENATOR BANKHEAD: [1] I hope that your committee will find time to consider, and having considered, will report favorably at an early date, Senate Bill 6770 for increasing the deposits in savings banks.

The development of these banks is a distinct step in the direction of financial democracy, and the recent failures of smaller private banks, to which savings of our wage earners have been entrusted, make the proposed legislation particularly urgent.[2]

Yours very truly,

1. John Hollis Bankhead (1842-1920) represented the Sixth Alabama District in Congress from 1887 to 1907, when he was elected to the Senate, where he served until his death. Bankhead was chairman of the Senate Committee on Post Offices and Post Roads.

2. Bankhead responded on 29 January that if the legislative program permitted consideration of anything other than emergency legislation, he hoped to secure passage of the bill. The measure was never reported out of committee.

To Jacob Billikopf

January 25, 1915 Boston, Mass. [Brandeis Mss, Z 7-1]

MY DEAR MR. BILLIKOPF: [1] Replying to yours of the 21st:

In my address on Zionism and Patriotism,[2] which I enclose, and another in the January Menorah Journal which I am having sent to you,[3] I stated in part my reasons for advocating Zionism, even if it were impossible to answer altogether satisfactorily the two questions put in your letter. For in my opinion the only thing of real value in life is the ideal, and in this I am certain that Professor James, from a "pragmatic view point", would have wholly concurred.[4]

As to the practical questions which you suggest, pray bear in mind "wer Nichts wagt gewinnt Nichts" [5] and that it never has been possible for the Jew "to play safe" or for anyone else indeed "to play safe," who has sought advances in conditions. But to my mind the thing involving the greatest risk in the world is not to attempt to advance, and if not Zionism, what is the alternative?

Answering your specific questions:

First: As to the assurances that we have had or may get: I suppose we have had nothing that may justly be called assurances. Certainly we have no charter rights, and if we had them, they would be of little value. Belgium's recent experience should teach us that there is no assurance for the Jew except that which his own intelligence and courage, wisely applied, can give him. And it seems to me clear that a large successful settlement in Palestine would give much greater assurance than that which could come from any or all of the powers. Indeed no assurance could be of any value without possession through successful, intensive and extensive occupation. If we had 500,000 settlers in Palestine today, the problem there would settle itself.

Second: You ask whether we can hope to solve the Jewish question since Palestine would be capable of accommodating only 2,000,000 or 3,000,000. We certainly would have a very much better chance of solving it. We should then have a standing among the peoples of the world. Montenegro, with 250,000 inhabitants, and no past, has a standing; has all rights now in a Congress of Nations. Think of our condition in comparison.

You say that "unless our people enjoy complete autonomy, the work of the Zionists would be in vain".

To my mind if all the Palestinian colonies were wiped out tomorrow the work of the Zionists there, and elsewhere, in the last forty years would stand as the best achievement for the Jews, not only during that period, but for a century. What is best in Jewish life has been its idealism; its ability to conceive great things; and it is the conception, rather than the carrying out, in which greatness ordinarily manifests itself. But in this particular instance we have an accomplishment as well as conception.

I presume you have read Wertheim's story in the Survey.[6]

I want you to read, indeed to study carefully, the story told in the ten-year work of the Anglo-Palestine Company,—the Zionist Bank, which I am sending you under separate cover. To one working as you are for social justice, this achievement should appeal particularly.[7]   Most cordially yours,

1. Jacob Billikopf (1883-1950), a leading social worker in Kansas City, Missouri, held a variety of high offices in both Jewish and national social work organizations. He later moved to Philadelphia, and was active in unemployment relief work during the depression and aiding the refugees during World War II.

2. See LDB to Jacob deHaas, 14 November 1914, n. 1.

3. In this article, LDB praised the Jewish love of learning and suggested that it lay at the root of Jewish character. But learning, in the Jewish culture, was valued not in the abstract but for how it could ennoble one's life. Moreover, education was closely connected to the Jewish ideal of democracy, and both traits were part of the American tradition as well. Education imposed duties, and in time of crisis those best fit to deal with the emergency were obliged by their heritage and by their training to meet the need. Now was the time for the educated Jew to help his less fortunate brethren, both by raising funds for relief and by joining the Zionist movement. "A Call to the Educated Jew," *The Menorah Journal*, 1 (January 1915): 13-19, reprinted in *Brandeis on Zionism*, 56-69.

4. William James (1842-1910) had been one of the leading spirits of his age —a prominent and pioneering psychologist and the most important American philosopher since Emerson. The leader, if not the founder, of the "pragmatic" school, James taught at Harvard from 1872 until his death. See Ralph Barton Perry, *The Thought and Character of William James* . . . (2 vols., Boston,

1935), or Gay Wilson Allen, *William James: A Biography* (New York, 1967).

5. "He who wages nothing, wins nothing."

6. Maurice Wertheim, "Palestine and the War," *The Survey*, 33 (2 January 1915): 353.

7. See LDB to Billikopf, 16 June 1916.

To David Maurice Bressler

January 25, 1915 Boston, Mass. [Brandeis Mss, NMF 73-5]

MY DEAR MR. BRESSLER: [1] It would give me great satisfaction to accept the Chairmanship of the Conference of the National Association of Jewish Social Workers to be held in Baltimore in May, as you so kindly suggest in yours of the 22nd; but the work which I have on hand is such that I dare not undertake it.

I am particularly glad that the Conference is to discuss the protocol. Each year adds to my conviction of the soundness of the underlying principle, and my appreciation of the high qualities of the employers and employees who are engaged in advancing this experiment in industrial democracy.   Yours very truly,

1. David Maurice Bressler (1879–1942) was chairman of the National Association of Jewish Social Workers; in 1915 he was assistant secretary of the American Jewish Relief Committee and the following year became the first secretary of the American Joint Distribution Committee. In the 1930s he served as a non-Zionist member of the Jewish Agency.

To Jacob deHaas

January 25, 1915 Boston, Mass. [Brandeis Mss, Z 6-1]

MY DEAR MR. DEHAAS: Please arrange that I receive not later than the 5th of each month a report covering the activities of the Zionist Bureau during the preceding month.

I should be glad if you would give some care to the form of the report, so that it may be possible, by a comparison of the reports from month to month, to note readily the progress that has been made in each line of activity, and serve as a current reference to the achievements of the Bureau.   Very truly yours,

To Horace Meyer Kallen

January 25, 1915 Boston, Mass. [Brandeis Mss, Z 3-1]

MY DEAR KALLEN: Yours of the 21st enclosing Fechheimer's letter of the 20th has just reached us.[1] Your own report of conditions in Cincinnati was confirmed by Levin and Wise, who have both been there, and it looks as if we should gain much through the errors of our opponents. My own impression is this:

What the Jews need most is unity, and [one] of the many good things which Zionism promises is the opportunity for unity. I feel that for us to go to Cincinnati to speak on Zionism, unless it follows an invitation from Dr. Philipson to speak at his Temple, would tend to an intensification of the existing feeling. My hope, therefore, was that there would come to me from Mr. Fechheimer and his associates an invitation to speak, to which I would answer expressing the views stated above. If we go to Cincinnati to speak it ought to signify a closing of the breach, and I know of no way in which that could be manifested except through an invitation from Dr. Philipson himself. To go there in any other way would appear to be "beating him", which we don't want to do because of the inevitable effect of developing opposition into animosity.

I should like to include in the condition, if it is feasible, that Dr. Kohler [2] should join in the invitation, because we certainly don't want to have opposition from him.[3]   Very truly yours,

1. Kallen was urging LDB to preside at a proposed Zionist meeting in Cincinnati, and had enclosed a letter from S. Marcus Fechheimer predicting success if Brandeis and Julian Mack would preside at the gathering.

2. Kaufmann Kohler (1843–1926), born and educated in Germany, was rabbi at the prestigious Temple Beth El in New York from 1879 to 1903. During that time he became a powerful figure in the American Reform Judaism movement and played a major role in drafting the Pittsburgh platform of 1885, which defined Reform principles and explicitly denied any expectation for returning to Palestine. From 1903 to 1922 Kohler headed Hebrew Union College and was honorary president of the Central Conference of American Rabbis.

3. See LDB to Kallen, 10 February 1915.

To Emily Solis-Cohen

January 25, 1915 Boston, Mass. [Brandeis Mss, Z 2-2]

MY DEAR MISS COHEN: Thank you for your very kind letter.

It is my practice to pay my own expense on such occasions,[1] but I am taking the liberty of sending the check which you enclosed to the Provisional Committee as your Association's contribution to the Emergency fund.   Cordially yours,

P.S. I think your members would be interested if you could get Morris Werthiem to lecture on Palestine.

1. LDB's trip to Philadelphia to speak to a combined meeting of Jewish organizations.

To Samuel Untermyer

January 25, 1915 Boston, Mass. [Brandeis Mss, Z 7-1]

MY DEAR MR. UNTERMYER: I am venturing to send you herewith my address on Zionism and Patriotism, and am having sent you a copy of the Menorah Journal for January containing an article of mine, and also a report of the Anglo-Palestine Company,—the Zionist Bank. I want you to take time to read my two addresses, and more particularly to study the report of the Zionist Bank. You and I have had so much occasion to criticize what has been done through banks and bankers, that I feel sure that you will rejoice with me in the accomplishments of this institution in aid of the rebirth of Palestine and the development of social justice.
                          Very cordially yours,

To Louis Lipsky

January 27, 1915 Boston, Mass. [Brandeis Mss, Z 1-4]

DEAR MR. LIPSKY: *First*: The format of the Maccabaean seems to me a great improvement, but the smallness of the print seems to me most objectionable. Zionists are great readers, and we ought to preserve their eyes. I realize that larger print with the same number of pages would mean less reading matter, but I am convinced that we should be a great deal better off with less reading matter if it were presented in a form in which it could be conveniently and not injuriously read.[1]

Second: I hope that the proposed meeting discussed on Sunday, for the development of the work in New York, will have been held before this reaches you, and that important results will follow.

It seems to me of great importance that this work should go forward energetically, and that, among other things, we should utilize to the full every day the very valuable services which Dr. Levin can afford in developing Zionist understanding and interest.

Very truly yours,

1. Lipsky replied the following day that to avoid curtailing the material, the journal would be expanded four pages and a larger print size used. The *Maccabaean* was the official publication of the Federation of American Zionists.

To Benjamin Perlstein

January 27, 1915 Boston, Mass. [Brandeis Mss, Z 3-2]

DEAR MR. PERLSTEIN: Mr. DeHaas was with me when you telephoned the Alexandrian cable which you received from Washington, and we have since carefully considered the situation, and I am now dictating this letter in his presence.[1]

It seems to us very improbable that there is anything that America do under the circumstances. It would seem as if any protection that could be afforded would have to come either through Germany or England.[2] I presume that our English friends have the same information that we have; for the Consul in Alexandria must have been importuned to communicate with the home Government. But in case you and Mr. Lipsky have any doubt as to our English friends being informed of the situation, it might be well to send a cable indicating briefly the situation, and asking for information as to prospects. It would not seem necessary or advisable for us to make any recommendation or to cable the details.

The closing paragraph of the cable seems hardly consistent with the earlier statement and the whole rather rhetorical.

As I told you, I shall not be able to go via New York, but

expect to reach Washington Saturday morning, and could have a conference there, if it were deemed advisable. You may think it preferable to have a conference in Boston on Friday. I expect it would be sufficient if one or two of our members were here for conference with Mr. DeHaas and me. If the conference is to be held, it might be most advisable to have Mr. Lewin-Epstein as one of the conferees. I understand that he is expected in New York on Friday, and if you are purposing to have a conference in Boston on Friday, you could by telegram divert him so that he would come to Boston direct.

I assume that you have refrained from giving any publicity to the cable. It certainly seems quite inconsistent with the message we had a few days ago.

I expect to be in New York on my return from Washington,— possibly Wednesday or Thursday and Friday of next week.

Cordially yours,

P.S.   Since dictating the above I have talked this matter over with Dr. Wise quite fully on the telephone.

1. It was agreed that he would telegraph Mr. Bryan personally to try to get confirmation from Ambassador Morganthau [*sic*].

2. That he would advise a brief cable to Mr. Cowan [*sic*] in London.

3. That the New York members would hold an informal meeting this evening, and let me hear tomorrow morning the results of inquiries and deliberations.

1. Although there is no copy of this cable in the Brandeis MSS, it is possible to reconstruct, tentatively, the situation that prompted it. In early 1915, the Turkish government took several steps against the Jewish population in Palestine. First it insisted that all Jews had to become naturalized Turkish citizens and expelled over 4,000 who refused. Jemal Pasha, the Turkish governor, ordered several of the Zionist leaders into exile, banned the use of Zionist stamps or emblems, and closed the Anglo-Palestine Company, which most Palestinian Jews used as their bank. See LDB to David Rubin, 10 February 1915 and to Stephen S. Wise, 13 February 1915.

2. That is, to protect their nationals threatened by Turkish laws.

To L. Hollingsworth Wood

January 27, 1915 Boston, Mass. [Brandeis Mss, NMF 73-4]

MY DEAR MR. WOOD: [1] I thank you for yours of the 26th calling my attention to the American League to Limit Armaments.

There is of course much work to be done in educating public opinion on this subject, but I have not been able to give time to the consideration of the problems involved, and feel, therefore, at present that I ought not to join any of the various Leagues working for peace on different lines.[2]   Very truly yours,

1. L. Hollinsgworth Wood (1874–1956), a New York attorney, devoted much of his life to the causes of peace and racial harmony. He was secretary of the American League to Limit Armaments.
2. The previous day LDB had sent a similar letter to Henry S. Haskins, secretary of the Massachusetts Peace Society, declining membership.

To Bernie F. Green

January 28, 1915 Boston, Mass. [Brandeis Mss, NMF 66-1]

MY DEAR MR. GREEN: [1] I deeply regret than an imperative call to Washington will prevent my being present at your meeting on Sunday.

I desire to urge upon the citizens of Lynn the urgent need of liberal contributions. At no time since the expulsion of the Jews from Spain has their plight been so serious as now, and even then the number affected was small as compared with those subjected to dire suffering today.

The more fortunate Jews in America must give quickly and liberally, not from their incomes merely but from their capital also. I trust that you will make this clear to your fellow citizens.
                    Very cordially yours,

1. Bernie F. Green was a member of the Lynn (Massachusetts) Jewish Relief Committee.

To Alfred Brandeis

January 29, 1915 Washington, D.C. [Brandeis Mss, M 4-1]

MY DEAR AL: Nothing from you for a short age. Alice & I arrived today coming a little earlier because of Palestinian affairs, which are disquieting.[1]

Susan is at the LaFollettes. Elizabeth's holidays commence Monday & she will either go to New Hampshire on a winter party or meet us in New York next week.

We plan to stay here until Wednesday taking in the Attorney General's dinner to the Justices of the Supreme Court on Tuesday.

Tumulty says the House will sustain the President's veto [2] & seems to think the ship bill will be passed.[3]

1. See LDB to Benjamin Perlstein, 27 January 1915.
2. See LDB to Leon Sanders, 23 December 1914.
3. In his most energetic effort to meet the economic emergency created by the war, Wilson sought thirty million dollars from Congress to purchase and operate a government shipping line. Since the only vessels available for sale were the interned German boats, the measure sparked a bitter debate in Congress. Republicans, led by Henry Cabot Lodge and Elihu Root, opposed it because it would interject the government into an area previously controlled by private enterprise and also because they feared purchase of German ships would embroil the country in the Atlantic war. Despite intense lobbying by the administration, the bill was defeated in early March 1915.

To Alfred Brandeis

February 3, 1915 Washington, D.C. [Brandeis Mss, M 4-1]

DEAR AL: Nothing from you here. We start this afternoon for N.Y. Shall probably be there until Thursday. Elizabeth is to be at [*].

Democrats becoming rather doubtful of passing Ship bill, & generally as to political outlook.[1]

We dined with Justices last evening at the Atty General's invitation. Have known of as interesting dinners with less distinguished guests.

Wheat is behaving disreputably.[2]

1. See preceding letter.
2. The price of wheat had climbed steeply in January on the impetus of

European demand. On 17 January Wilson ordered an investigation following widespread protests by housewives, and the following day wheat prices dipped considerably.

To Julius Rosenwald (Telegram)

February 4, 1915 [New York, N.Y.] [Brandeis Mss, Z 12-3]

At our meeting held this day we read exchange of telegrams between you and Dr. Magnes. We beg to inform you that Zionist Provisional Committee has already appropriated out of its funds twenty five thousand dollars. We regret inability to comply with your suggestion that you anticipate your pledge to us because we are already committed to expenditures for Palestine work for which we rely in part on your pledge.[1] The one hundred twenty five thousand dollars referred to in Magnes telegram to you composed as follows: Nathan Straus fifty thousand dollars. Provisional Zionist Committee twenty five thousand. Jacob Schiff twenty five thousand. American Jewish Relief Committee twenty five thousand. Our sincere hope in view of above information you may be willing to contribute also twenty five thousand dollars for relief ship.[2]

1. See LDB to Alfred Brandeis, 27 November 1914.
2. One of the projects undertaken by the Provisional Committee was to send supplies to Palestine. While there was little difficulty gathering relief supplies, the Committee could not get clearance from either the Allies or the Central Powers to guarantee safe passage from New York to Jaffa. However, a Navy collier, the *U.S.S. Vulcan,* was scheduled to sail for Alexandria, and the Committee secured Secretary of the Navy Josephus Daniels's permission to ship the relief supplies aboard the American vessel. While the relief ship was undoubtedly one of the major successes of the Committee, it also led to a great deal of friction between the Zionists and the American Jewish Relief Committee over crediting the supplies. See LDB to Judah L. Magnes, 13 March 1915.

To Otto Warburg and Arthur Menahem Hantke

February 4, 1915 New York, N.Y. [Berlin Office]

Wir sind im Besitze Ihres Geehrten vom 12. Januar 1915, so wie auch Ihre Geehrten an Herrn Dr. S. Lewin von 30/12/14, u.

7/1/15. wie auch der beiden Briefen des Herrn Berger vom 13. u. 14. Januar 1915.

Wir beehren uns Ihnen hiermit anzuzeigen, dass wir Ihnen heute telegrafisch weitere $2000 zu Ihrer Verfuegung gesandt haben. Wir haben beschlossen Ihrem Verlangen in Bezug auf weitere Sendungen, so weit unsere Mittel es uns gestatten werden, im vollen Umfange nach-zukommen.

Wir theilen Ihnen ferner mit, dass wir ausfuehrliche Berichte von Victor (letzter Bericht datirt vom 5. Januar) erhalten haben und auch seine Bitte *voll* bewilligt haben . . . Wir sandten ihm am l. d. M. $1000.00 and werden ihm heute weitere $2000.00 schieken.

Wenn auch manchmal in unserem Briefwechsel Verzoegerungen stattgefunden haben, so werden Sie es uns doch hoffentlich nicht veruebeln, dass wir in erster Reihe unsere ganze Spannkraft und Aufmerksamkeit unseren Institutionen und der Bevoelkerung in Palaestina gewidmet haben. Es war gar keine leichte Aufgabe in Anbetracht dessen, dass die juedische Catastrophe *ueberall* solche umgeheure Dimensionen angenommen hatte.

Es ist uns bis jetzt gelungen *unseren* Institutionen in Palaestina $21,700.00 zu ueberweisen. Ferner haben wir Zionisten $17,008.78 nach Palaestina fuer Relief gesandt, ausser dass wir noch andere nicht Zionistische Gruppen organisirt haben, welche durch uns circa $40,000.00 fuer Reliefzwecke nach Palaestina gesandt haben. Schliesslich haben wir auch die Ueberweisung von Geldern an Privatpersonen und wohlthaetige Anstalten in Palaestina uebernommen und ist es uns gelungen auf diesem Wege fernere $155,-000 Palaestina zukommen zu lassen.

Ferner muss noch in Betracht gezogen werden, dass wir auch in der Arbeit fuer den Relieffund fuer die anderen Laender uns mindestens ebenso intensiv betheiligen wie die nicht Zionisten, so z. B. leistet Herr Dr. Lewin immer folge, wenn und wo er nur zu einem Vortrag im Interesse des allgemeinen Relief aufgefordert wird.

Jetzt sind wir dabei ein Schiff mit Nahrungsmitteln nach Palaestina zu versenden wobei die amerikanische Regierung uns in der vornehmsten Weise jeglichen Schutz gewaehrt.[1] Dieses Schiff wird vom American Jewish Relief Committee, mit der Cooperirung unseres Prov. Comitees, verschickt. Wir betheiligen uns vorlaeufig mit $25,000.00, aber ausserdem hat unser Gesinnungsgenosse Nathan Straus, der wirklich mehr Opferwilligkeit als *jeder Andere* in America offenbart, $50,000 fuer diesen speziellen Zweck gespendet, und wir koennen ohne jede Uebertreibung sagen, dass wir in erster Reihe ihm, Nathan Straus, dank wissen fuer die Verwirklichung dieses Planes.

Sie sind auch wahrscheinlich unterrichtet dass wir auch mit dem Orangen-und Mandeln-Verkauf viel zu schaffen hatten und waren wir auch theilweise erfolgreich, leider aber hat die locale tuerkische Behoerde die weitere Ausfuhr dieser Producte verboten, zu einer Zeit wo wir auf dem besten Wege waren einen neuen Markt fuer die palaestinaensische Producte zu schaffen.

Zum Schluss muessen wir noch eins betonen. Bei all den aufgezaehlten Aufgaben, die dem Moment entsprungen sind, erblicken wir doch unsere Hauptaufgabe in dem innern Aufbau und Staerkung der Zionistischen Organization hier in Amerika. Die Stimmung in den Massen, wie auch in manchen intelectuellen Kreisen ist sehr guenstig, vielleicht mehr als je zuvor. Es muss aber emsig gearbeitet werden um die Stimmung in organisirte Kraft umzusetzen.

Wir bitten Sie sehr uns oeftere Berichte zukommen zu lassen und unsere gegenseitige Correspondenz mehr regelmaessig zu gestalten.

Mit Zions Gruss und Hochachtung [2]

1. See preceding letter.

2. "We are in possession of your letter of 12 January 1915, as well as your letters to Dr. S. Levin of 30 December 1914, and 7 January 1915, and also Mr. Berger's two letters of 13 and 14 of January 1915.

We have the honor to inform you that we have sent you today by telegraph a further $2000 for your disposal. We have decided to comply fully with your wishes in reference to further sendings, as far as our means will permit it.

We further inform you that we have received complete reports from Victor [Jacobson] (last report dated 5 January) and have also completely agreed to his request. We sent him $1000 on the first of the month and will send him a further $2000 today.

If sometimes in our correspondence delays have occurred, we hope that you will not blame us for having dedicated our whole energy and attention primarily to our institutions and to the population of Palestine. That was no easy task considering that the Jewish catastrophe had taken on such tremendous dimensions.

We have succeeded up till now in transferring $21,700 to our institutions in Palestine. Furthermore, we sent $17,008.78 to Zionists in Palestine for relief. Besides that we have organized non-Zionist groups which have sent through us about $40,000 to Palestine for relief purposes. Finally we have also taken over the transference of monies to private persons and charitable oragnizations in Palestine, and succeeded in this way to have a further $155,000 sent to Palestine.

Furthermore it must be taken into consideration that also in the work for relief funds for other countries, we participate at least as intensively as the non-Zionists, so for instance Dr. Levin always accepts whenever and wherever he is asked to give a speech in the interest of general relief.

Now we are in the process of sending a ship to Palestine with food, whereby the American government assures us every protection in the noblest way. This ship is sent by the American Jewish Relief Committee with the cooperation of our Prov. Committee. For the moment we are participating with $25,000. Besides that our fellow supporter Nathan Straus, who really has shown more willingness to make sacrifices than any other man in America, has sent $50,000 for this special purpose and we can say without exaggeration that we first of all have to thank him, Nathan Straus, for the realization of this plan.

You probably also know that we also had much to do with the sale of oranges and almonds and we are partially successful in it, but unfortunately the local Turkish authorities have forbidden the further export of these products, at a time when we were well on the way to creating a new market for the Palestinian products.

Finally we have to stress one thing. In all of the enumerated tasks which have arisen at the moment, we see our main task in the inner composition and strengthening of the Zionist organization here in America. The attitude among the masses, as in some intellectual circles, is very favorable to us, perhaps more than ever before. But we must work eagerly in order to transform the attitude into organized power.

We ask you very strongly to report to us more often and to establish our mutual correspondence on a more regular basis.

With Zion's greeting and respectfully yours,"

This letter was signed by LDB, E. W. Lewin-Epstein, and Schmarya Levin.

To Manuel Koomer

February 6, 1915 Boston, Mass. [Brandeis Mss, NMF 66-1]

DEAR MR. KOOMER: [1] Upon my return to the city I find your letter of the 1st. The matter may have been disposed of in the meantime, but I write to say that in my opinion no effort should be made to secure permission to give a vaudeville and moving picture performance on Sunday. Any Jewish war relief meeting held on Sunday should be confined to addresses and appropriate music. Very truly yours,

1. Manuel Koomer was secretary of the Brockton (Massachusetts) Young Men's Hebrew Association. He had written that up until the November election in 1914, the French society in Brockton had raised money for Belgian relief by Sunday entertainments. A new mayor had just taken office, and he insisted on enforcing the Sunday laws prohibiting entertainment, thus preventing the Jewish relief groups from holding similar events. Koomer wanted to know if the Brockton relief group should fight the mayor's ruling.

To Henry Morgenthau (Telegram)

Februray 8, 1915 New York, N.Y. [Brandeis Mss, Z 12-3]

Ruppin reports capital invested in twelve thousand dunam [1] orange groves threatened with total loss unless one hundred twenty thousand dollars can be raised. Proposed borrowing money here, repayment three years secured by groves. Would you be willing to lend your supervisory aid to securing lenders greatest protection possible? [2] Consult [Victor] Jacobsohn [sic].

1. A dunam is about one-fourth of an acre; it was the standard land measure in the Ottoman Empire.
2. A week later Morgenthau cabled back that he was "willing to render every assistance."

To D. D. Davis

February 9, 1915 Boston, Mass. [Brandeis Mss, NMF 66-1]

MY DEAR SIR: I write to acknowledge with thanks receipt of your check for $1.00 for relief of the war sufferers.

Yours very truly,

To Louis Lipsky

February 9, 1915 Boston, Mass. [Brandeis Mss, Z 1-4]

MY DEAR MR. LIPSKY: Upon my return to the city I find yours of the 28th.

First: I think it is clear, as you state that "New York cannot be captured in a month. It will require months and months of hard, persistent, and continuous application." [1]

I feel sure, however, that Dr. Levin can be of particular assistance, not only in respect to the problems in New York, but generally as to the problems of organization and development of Zionism in America. I had a talk with him on the 6th, and am sure that he will be ready to devote himself persistently, at least six or eight weeks, to aiding in such work. I have suggested to Mr. Perlstein, and also to Mr. Cowan,[2] with whom I had an opportunity of talking on this matter, the desirability of appointing some fixed time, perhaps an hour a day, for a conference with you and Mr. Perlstein, and one evening a week for a conference with all of those active in the work of the Federation. We ought to get through him the results of the Actions Committee's experience in these matters.

Second: Replying to yours of the 7th concerning the proposed mass meetings through March in aid of the emergency fund in Los Angeles: Will you please inform Mr. Fram [3] that it is impossible for me to consider going to California at that time.

Very truly yours,

1. Lipsky's comment was in reply to LDB's letter of 27 January 1915.
2. Charles Cowan, a New York Zionist, worked at the P.E.C. office.
3. Harry Fram was organizing a Zionist rally in Los Angeles with Nathan Straus presiding. He had wired that LDB's agreeing to come to California would practically guarantee that large sums would be raised.

To Horace Meyer Kallen

February 10, 1915 Boston, Mass. [Brandeis Mss, Z 3-1]

MY DEAR KALLEN: I have considered most carefully yours of the 1st,[1] and have discussed it with Wise. No invitation has come from Cincinnati, so there has been no occasion to make a formal decision. But I feel very strongly that our policy should be to avoid controversy and to win those who at present are indifferent. We can cover but a small part, with our present forces, of the field that is open to us. If we develop Zionism in those communities where prospects are bright, we shall reap a much larger crop; and if our work is well done, Philipson and the like will be isolated and will shrivel up. I think Wise agrees with this conclusion, and possibly has written you. I know that Levin does.

I am more and more impressed with the amount of work that is to be done, and the small number of workers. On all hands there are those ready to be converted. We need missionaries to go to them, and I hope soon after you come east to have an opportunity to talk the situation over with you.   Cordially yours,

1. Kallen, while agreeing with the need for unity (see LDB to Kallen, 25 January 1915), argued that patience with Philipson would only alienate those who were ready to support Zionist activities in Cincinnati. He advised LDB to force the issue, by going to speak in Cincinnati. See LDB to S. Marcus Fechheimer, 23 February 1915.

To David Rubin

February 10, 1915 Boston, Mass. [Brandeis Mss, Z 2-3]

DEAR MR. RUBIN: Upon my return to the city I find your letters of the 29th and February 5th, the latter enclosing Mr. Kallen's draft and letter to you which I return herewith.[1]

First: Dr. Kallen improved the form of notice, but it seems to me we shall in part defeat our purpose if we adopt his limitations upon the number of subjects. What we desire is to encourage a comprehensive study of the Palestinian problems and life. The mere enumeration of the subjects tends to stimulate such study, and I think that we ought not to reduce the number of subjects.

Second: Replying to your inquiry and to Mr. Berman's [2] letter of January 26th concerning the Palestinian situation: No doubt the situation is unfortunate; for our colonies are being subjected to great hardships through the imposition of special governmental burdens, the prohibitions of exports, and special persecutions,— and acts which we should naturally characterize as lawless.[3] We have reason to think, however, that the central government is still favorable to Zionism, and it seems to me clear that some of our colonies, particularly those in Galilee, have been treated with relative tenderness. We must do all we can to lessen distress, as we are proposing through the relief ship.[4] But the main work which we expect from Harvard Zionists and other college men is the intensification and spread of the Zionist ideas. That is work for which the college men are eminently fitted, and which they should take up with increased zeal.   Yours very truly,

1. The correspondence dealt with the essay contest the federation was sponsoring. The prize, $100 and a bronze medal donated by LDB, would go to the college student writing the best original essay on some phase of Jewish life and culture in Palestine. Over twenty topics were listed as acceptable, and the entries would be judged by Julian Mack, Felix Frankfurter, and Richard Gottheil.

2. William Berman (b. 1893) was a leading member of the Harvard Zionist Club, and would later be active in a number of Jewish organizations, and the national commander of the Jewish War Veterans. Although trained as a lawyer, Berman became a career army officer after his enlistment in World War I. In 1946 he served as counsel to the War Crimes Trial group handling the prosecution of Nazi war criminals at Nuremberg. After his retirement from the army, he was elected Municipal Court Judge in Portland, Maine.

3. See LDB to Benjamin Perlstein, 27 January 1915 and to Stephen S. Wise, 13 February 1915.

4. See LDB to Julius Rosenwald, 4 February 1915.

To John A. Dyche

February 11, 1915 Boston, Mass. [Brandeis Mss, NMF 67-2]

DEAR MR. DYCHE: I have yours of the 9th, about which I have talked somewhat with Mr. A. L. Filene.[1]

No doubt there is a lack of discipline in the Jewish Union. Discipline is not common in democracies, and it is particularly difficult to introduce it where the privates are largely composed of thinkers. Of course discipline is essential to continuing democratic success, but I am confident that the Jewish workers, with their many good qualities, intellectual and moral, will in time learn discipline also. Meanwhile the protocol and Jewish unionism are subjected to an extraordinarily severe test, not so much by the lack of discipline as by the serious industrial situation, to which the garment trade is subjected. The bad business puts a strain upon every business relation, and upon the temper of the individual; and the friends of the protocol and of unionism should lend all possible aid. I am convinced that this is not a time when criticism is useful. What we need particularly is encouragement and tact. Criticism, however well founded, if allowed at this time, will do harm, and may prove fatal. The protocol needs nursing, and those who like yourself and Dr. Abelson have had wide experience, should lend so far as possible a gently, sympathetic helping hand.   Very cordially yours,

1. In an extremely long letter, Dyche complained to LDB that the protocol would soon be destroyed by the lack of discipline among the Jewish unions. The protocol rested on the assumption that the leaders of each side could force their followers to abide by the decisions of the arbitration board, and it had become quite obvious that the labor leaders could not control their men. Dyche's analysis was one-sided (the manufacturers were also tired of the protocol), but essentially correct. The Protocol of Peace was in deep trouble by late April 1915, and for all practical purposes it would be dead by the end of May, despite attempts made throughout 1916 to revive and save it. See Mason, *Brandeis*, 310–14.

To Leo Mannheimer

February 11, 1915 Boston, Mass. [Brandeis Mss, NMF 67-2]

DEAR MR. MANNHEIMER: [1] Referring to yours of the 9th: [2]

First: I am inclined to think that the report of the discussion at our Cloak, Suit, and Shirt arbitration meeting on the 5th and 6th will give the best indication as to what the power and duties of the Committee on Immediate Action under the Protocol should be.

Second: I thank you for sending me the article from Sunday's edition of "Der Tag". I am convinced that the publication of such articles at the present time is distinctly harmful to the cause of labor. The protocol is being subjected to a most severe test at present,—a test due not to inherent weaknesses, but to the extraordinary strain which bad business places on employer and employee alike. The protocol is as little to be blamed for most of the troubles, as is President Wilson for the unemployment common in the country at the present time. Doubtless the protocol has defects. We have made efforts from time to time to improve the machinery; but what is needed now is not the pointing out of the defects, but the use of great tact and encouragement to make the instrument work, and to make the parties to it realize that although their condition is not a happy one, it might be and indeed but for the protocol, would be much worse. I feel sure that you and Dr. Abelson can do much by way of aid in supporting the protocol at this time.   Very cordially yours,

1. Leo Mannheimer was serving on the Industrial Relations Committee of the New York Kehillah (Jewish communal organization); he later became rabbi of a Newark, New Jersey, congregation.

2. Mannheimer had sent LDB two articles from the Yiddish press extremely critical of the protocol and had also asked him what would be the duties of the "Committee on Immediate Action" of the protocol, to which he had just been appointed. See preceding letter.

To Abraham Benjamin Cohen [1] (Telegram)

February 13, 1915 Boston, Mass. [Brandeis Mss, Z 7-1]

Since the exile of the Jews from Spain no such calamity has befallen them as that incident to the present war. Never was there greater need for Jewish Rachmonoth [2] than at this moment. Everyone of us should give for the cause of our suffering bretheren [sic] to the limit of the power of his giving.

1. Abraham Benjamin Cohen (1892–1960) began his career as an errand boy with the McElwain Company. In 1915, he was their sales representative in New York and Pennsylvania; he later founded his own highly successful shoe manufacturing corporation. Cohen also served as chairman of the Jewish Relief Committee in Scranton, Pennsylvania.

2. "Compassion."

To Stephen Samuel Wise

February 13, 1915 Boston, Mass. [Brandeis Mss, Z 6-2]

MY DEAR DR. WISE: *First:* I agree with you that in view of Dr. Heller's letter there is no alternative for you and him but to go to Cincinnati.[1] I have no doubt that you two will find it possible to shape matters so that this meeting will tend to minimize controversy. Dr. Philipson's position is so obviously assailable that he will be starved out if left to himself.

Only the support incident to active controversy can maintain him in so untenable a position.

Second: Our mission to Washington which you advised has certainly proved of value. The recent messages are more reassuring, and particularly so in that Ambassador Morganthau [sic] is brought into such direct touch with the problem.[2]

Third: Our Relief Ship work here is progressing satisfactorily. New England will give good account of herself.

I have just agreed to speak in Hartford on Sunday, the 21st.

Very truly yours,

1. Max Heller had invited Wise to speak on Zionism in Cincinnati and had written to him deprecating Philipson's attitude. He said he personally believed Philipson was seeking the leadership of the Hebrew Union College, and that he was exploiting anti-Zionist feeling to achieve his ends.

2. In response to oppressive Turkish measures against the Jews the preceding month (see LDB to Benjamin Perlstein, 27 January 1915), Ambassador Morgenthau had protested to the Turkish government. He found out that the military governor of Palestine, the fanatic Arab, Jemal Pasha, had on his own authority prohibited issuance of Zionist stamps or checks drawn on the Anglo-Palestine Bank. The Turkish officials assured Morgenthau that these measures would be rescinded, and that no Jew loyal to the Turkish government would be victimized. News of this interview was transmitted in a letter from Robert Lansing (see LDB to Wise, 15 October 1915) to Wise, 9 February 1915.

To Herman Bernstein

February 16, 1915 Boston, Mass. [Brandeis Mss, NMF 66-1]

DEAR MR. BERNSTEIN: By your article in the Sun of February 14th you have performed a distinct public service.[1] You have made vivid the tragedy of Israel in Poland. You have helped Americans to appreciate the terrible suffering to which the Jews are subjected there. Their condition is indeed worse than that of the Belgians.

The Belgians, a free and united people enjoyed before the war long years of prosperity. The Jews of Poland on the other hand, hampered by restricted laws and subjected to a cruel boycott, were economically unprepared for any strain when the war came upon them. The homes of the Belgians were occupied by the enemy, but the homes of the Jews in Poland have been subjected to that devastation which necessarily attends the vicissitudes of campaigns in which the same towns pass repeatedly from the possession of one belligerent to that of another. The Belgians, united in their sorrow, have had the active sympathy and support of the

Allies and of neutrals. They may look forward to the restoration of a land which is theirs. They may look forward to indemnity so far as money can indemnify them for their long suffering. For whatever the outcome of the war, an indemnity to them seems certain,—an indemnity from Germany if the Allies win, and if they do not, an indemnity from the Allies who are in honor bound to compensate Belgium for her losses. How different is the fate of the Jews in Poland.

When the Jews of America come to realize the extent of the suffering of their bretheren [sic], they cannot fail to give liberally for such relief as may be possible.[2]

Very truly yours,

1. According to the article, the most tragic victims of the war were the Polish Jews, persecuted both by the Germans and by the Russians. More than three million of them were starving, and tens of thousands had fled their homes. Polish leaders were stirring up new anti-Semitic campaigns, using the slogan of "Blame the Jews" to account for all the troubles caused by the war. Yet, despite a history of persecution and pogroms, Jews were fighting bravely in the armies of both sides. Herman Bernstein, "The Tragedy of Israel in Poland – Worse than the Fate of Belgium," *The Sun* (New York), 14 February 1915.

2. The last two paragraphs of this letter were published in the English section of *Der Tag* on 25 February 1915.

To Paul Underwood Kellogg

February 16, 1915 Boston, Mass. [Brandeis Mss, NMF 71-3]

DEAR MR. KELLOGG: I have read with much interest your eloquent and moving appeal "To The Fatherlands"; but there are reasons why I think it wiser that my name should be omitted from the list of those who were present at the conferences.[1]

Very cordially yours,

1. At a meeting in New York on 23 January 1915, a number of well-known pacifists, including Kellogg, Lillian D. Wald, and Jane Addams, had drafted a statement deploring the death and waste and cruelty of war, calling upon all the belligerents to lay down their arms and negotiate a peace. The statement, "To the Fatherlands," was published as a pamphlet and distributed by various peace groups. Because of his role as Zionist leader, LDB took every care to do nothing which the Turks might consider not neutral.

To Paul Underwood Kellogg

February 16, 1915 Boston, Mass. [Brandeis Mss, NMF 71-3]

DEAR MR. KELLOGG: I was extremely sorry to know from your recent editorial of a public attack upon the integrity of the Survey.[1] Its fine record of service, and the character of its editors should have protected it from that.

I am enclosing check for $50 for your Industrial Department. With best wishes,   Very cordially yours,

1. George Creel (see LDB to Norman Hapgood, 29 June 1915, n.2), in the March issue of *Pearson's Magazine*, accused Paul Kellogg of being influenced —if not actually controlled—by Rockefeller money. Creel's argument rested on the fact that *The Survey* had not immediately condemned the Rockefeller Foundation's plan to investigate industrial conditions. The editorial traced the source of the accusation to Frank Walsh, chairman of the United States Industrial Commission, who resented the idea of anybody else investigating "his" area. The editors categorically denied receiving or ever having received money from the Rockefellers. See "Letting George Do It," *The Survey*, 33 (13 February 1915): 541–42.

To I. A. Abrahams

February 17, 1915 Boston, Mass. [Brandeis Mss, Z 7-1]

DEAR SIR: [1] Replying to yours of the 15th in which you inquire whether the funds collected by the "Provisional Executive Committee are used for the purpose of assisting all the Jews in Palestine or only a certain part of them, and thru what channels is the aid distributed".

First: The Provisional Executive Committee in undertaking to raise funds for Palestine, has made this clear distinction:

1. It raises money for its so-called Emergency Fund to take care of the Palestinian institutions, as schools, district nursing etc.

2. It raises funds for general relief in Palestine, such as are now being raised for the relief ship. These are for all Jews.

3. It receives and transmits funds which Americans desire to send either to particular individuals or particular institutions in Palestine. It has acted in this way as a transfer agent for large numbers of persons.

The distribution of the funds for the Zionist institutions is made mainly to Dr. Ruppin, the head of the Palestine office. The relief funds are transmitted in part to a Committee created nearly six months ago through the American Jewish Committee, and Mr. Wertheim representing Ambassador Morganthau [*sic*]; on which Committee are Dr. Ephraim Cohen, Dr. Ruppin and Dr. Aaronsohn. Other strictly Zionist relief funds are distributed through Dr. Ruppin. The individual funds transferred are sent largely through our Zionist agencies and the American Consulate.

Very truly yours,

1. I. A. Abrahams was a fur and produce merchant in Green Bay, Wisconsin.

To William Harrison Ingersoll

February 17, 1915 Boston, Mass. [Brandeis Mss, NMF 68-1]

MY DEAR MR. INGERSOLL: Mr. Rublee and Mr. [Edmund A.] Whittier have both told me of the efforts of Mr. Clarke [1] to substitute his bill for the Stevens bill.[2] Mr. Rublee has already expressed, I think in your presence, our view that the Clarke bill would meet with very serious constitutional objections. The propriety of framing a bill on those lines had been discussed by Mr. Rublee and me more than a year ago, and we concluded it would be very unwise to attempt it.

I met Mr. Lucking [3] when in Washington recently, and told him that the Clarke bill would meet with constitutional objection, and certainly it would be very impolitic to deviate from the course which we had worked out of putting through the Stevens bill. The discussion of any other measure now would simply reduce our chances of ultimate success.[4]

Very truly yours,

1. James P. Clarke (1854–1916) had represented Arkansas in the United States Senate since 1903. He was among several legislators who introduced price maintenance proposals different from the Stevens bill.

2. See LDB to George Rublee, 18 November 1913, n. 1.

3. Alfred Lucking (1856–1929), after one term as a Congressman from Michigan, returned to private practice and was for many years general counsel of the Ford Motor Company; he was interested in the fair-trade movement.

4. See LDB to Ingersoll, 1 March 1915.

To Louis Marshall

February 17, 1915 Boston, Mass. [Brandeis Mss, NMF 66-1]

MY DEAR MR. MARSHALL: The New England Committee finds itself greatly hampered in its efforts to collect funds by reason of
certain directions alleged to have been issued by the Grand Masters of the I.O.B.A. and the O.B.A.,[1] to the effect that New England members of these Orders should not make any contribution
to our Committee, but should send their contributions to their
New York office, so that the Orders may make contributions to
the relief fund in lump for the whole Country.

This course will undoubtedly result in greatly diminishing the
possible contributions from New England. There are said to be
about 20,000 members in these two Orders. Their contributions
to their own Orders are said to be very much smaller than could
be obtained if they were subject to appeals from our Committee
here. And the fact that the orders have been issued by the Grand
Masters affords these members an easy and comparatively complete answer to our appeal.

It is estimated that the members of these Orders represent about
one-third of the Jewish population of Massachusetts, and the
possibilities of our collections here are consequently greatly curtailed. At the last meeting of our Committee it was voted that I
urge you to take up this matter promptly with the Grand Masters of the two Orders to see whether it will not be possible to
have the orders rescinded. We should be very glad of course to
have all the members of the Orders who contribute give notice
of the fact to us in connection with their payments, and we will
make a separate report of the amounts collected from New
England members of the respective Orders, or in any other way
in which the Grand Masters may suggest would make the liber-
ality of their contributions obvious.

I trust you will be able to take up this matter with them immediately.[2]   Very truly yours,

1. The Order of Brith Abraham was one of the oldest Jewish fraternal
organizations in the United States, having been established in 1859. At the
1887 convention, an internal dispute led a large faction to break off and
set up a new mutual aid and insurance society, the Independent Order of
Brith Abraham. The O.B.A. reached a peak membership of 73,000 in 1913,

then dwindled and dissolved finally in 1927 after using up its insurance reserves. The I.O.B.A. continued in existence.

2. See LDB to Marshall, 20 February 1915.

To Norman Hapgood

February 19, 1915 Boston, Mass. [Brandeis Mss, NMF 62-1]

DEAR NORMAN: I am enclosing the substance of a short speech
which I made before the Economic Club at the recent Peace
meeting, and which has not been published. Possibly you may
care to have it for Harper's; but don't take it unless you really
want it.[1]   Cordially yours,

1. In his talk, LDB noted that all of the usual machinery suggested to prevent war such as an international police force or a congress of nations,
would fail unless truly democratic principles governed relations among nations. "No peace which is lasting can ever come until the nations, great and
small, accept the democratic principle that there is and shall be no super-
nation to rise through subjection of others, and the truth that each people
has in it something of peculiar value which it can contribute to that civilization for which we are all striving." Hapgood published the speech as "An
Essential of Lasting Peace," *Harper's Weekly*, 60 (13 March 1915): 259; it
also appeared in *The National Economic League Quarterly*, 1 (May 1915):
24–26, and it is reprinted in *The Curse of Bigness*, 267–69.

To Henry H. Levenson

February 20, 1915 Boston, Mass. [Brandeis Mss, NMF 66-1]

MY DEAR MR. LEVENSON: [1] I hope that your Committee will at
the earliest possible moment make known to the members of the
several Orders and other Jewish fraternal organizations the dire
and urgent need of their brethren in the war zone.

It is difficult for us in America to realize the extent and in-
tensity of this need. Every day additional information comes to
me of the extent of the suffering, which in many cases extends to
actual starvation. Included among those who suffer are many who
have heretofore been accustomed not only to comfort, but to
luxuries. Many a man formerly rich is now reported on the bread
lines among the refugees from Poland and Galicia. The suffering
of the refugees from Palestine, and of others who have remained
at their post, is known to you.

We Americans seem to be the only Jews in the world who are able to help, and no one of us should be found wanting as this call comes.   Very truly yours,

1. Henry H. Levenson was chairman of the committee on lodges and benevolent associations of the American Jewish Relief Committee.

To Louis Marshall

February 20, 1915 Boston, Mass. [Brandeis Mss, NMF 66-1]

MY DEAR MR. MARSHALL: Your letter of the 19th in which you refer "to the precedents established by the Zionist organization and the Central Committee", shows that I have utterly failed to make clear the situation in regard to the I.O.B.A. and O.B.A., since the situation in their case is exactly the reverse of that which exists in the case of the Zionists.[1]

First: In the case of the I.O.B.A. and O.B.A., those of the 20,000 members to whom I referred are declining to make any contributions to the American Jewish Relief Fund because they say that they are ordered not to do so, but to make all of their contributions to their own Orders for transmission through the New York office of their Order. The New England Branch of the American Jewish Relief Committee would have no objection whatsoever to that course, except for the fact that the result is that these 20,000 persons are contributing a very small fraction of what they would contribute if they were open to the solicitation of the active members of our Relief Committee. Our Committee therefore voted to solicit your aid in securing a revocation of the orders of the Grand Masters; thereby increasing largely the contributions of the New England Jews to the funds of the American Jewish Relief Committee.

Second: New England Zionists on the other hand have not only received no orders to withhold directly contributions to the New England Branch of the American Jewish Relief Committee, but on the contrary have been urged in every way to contribute, and to be active in securing others to contribute funds to the American Jewish Relief Committee. To demonstrate the unity in matters of relief for which we were striving, I myself became Chairman of the American Jewish Relief Committee for New England; and at the first conference of our Committee subscribed $1,000. The Boston Zionists are among the most active workers,—several of them being Chairmen, and very active Chairmen, of important committees. The zeal of the Zionists to secure large contributions from New England accounts in large measure for the generous response of the New England Jews.

I feel sure that the explanation which I have given will enable you to meet the argument which you apprehended: that Mr. Dorf [2] and Judge Sanders might refer to "precedents established by the Zionists". If they will give the American Jewish Relief Committee the same cooperation which Zionists have given, we can promise your Treasurer largely increased contributions.

Very truly yours,

1. In response to LDB's letter of 17 February, Marshall said he would do what he could to secure greater cooperation between the lodges and the relief committee, but that officers of the fraternal organizations pointed to the independent action of the Federation of American Zionists as justification of their own course.

2. Samuel Dorf (18[?]-1923) was a grand master of the Independent Order of Brith Abraham and a member of the American Jewish Committee. He was active in numerous Jewish communal and philanthropic agencies.

To Samuel Marcus Fechheimer

February 23, 1915 Boston, Mass. [Brandeis Mss, Z 2-4]

MY DEAR MR. FECHHEIMER: I am very glad to have your letter of the 19th telling of the group of men in Cincinnati, including Dr. Max Senior [1] and yourself, who are desirous that a meeting be held there for the discussion of Zionism.[2]

I would give me great satisfaction to address such a meeting; but I am convinced that it is unwise to do so unless Dr. Philipson will join in the invitation.

In these trying times unity is the greatest of Jewish needs. Discord is perilous. Public controversy may bring disaster. The power of Zionism to unify the Jewish people of all lands is among its greatest claims to support. I hope that Dr. Philipson will yet appreciate this. But as long as he, who must be regarded as the spokesman for the reform Jews of Cincinnati, maintains the attitude manifested on the occasion of my visit in October, the cause of the Jews would in my opinion suffer more from the public controversy than it would gain through the new adherents whom I should hope to win to Zionism.

I trust that you and Mr. Senior may be able to convince Dr. Philipson that such a discussion should be accepted with the same breadth of view as that adopted by Dr. Hirsch of Chicago, Dr. Leonard Levy of Pittsburgh, and Dr. Harrison of St. Louis.

Very cordially yours,

1. Max Senior (1862–1939) was a Cincinnati businessman and philanthropist. He helped establish and was president of the city's United Jewish Charities, and was also president of the National Conference of Jewish Charities. During the war he supervised Joint Distribution Committee activities in Holland.

2. LDB had received other information that the Zionist sentiment was growing in Cincinnati. Stephen Wise had written on 19 February that he, Max Heller, and a few others had convinced Emil Hirsch that the Zionists should be given a hearing. Hirsch had originally come to the meeting to sustain Rabbi Kohler's ban on Horace Kallen's speaking at Hebrew Union College, and Wise termed his change of mind "a real moral victory." See also LDB to Horace Kallen, 10 February 1915.

To Thomas Watt Gregory

February 23, 1915 Boston, Mass. [Brandeis Mss, NMF 68-2]

Personal & Confidential

MY DEAR GREGORY: I was much delayed in getting any information concerning the candidates for the United States District Attorneys of Maine and Vermont, about which you wrote me under date of the 6th.

This morning I am in receipt of the enclosed letter from my good friend William M. Bradley [1] of Portland, dated February 19th, concerning Mr. Merrill. [2]

Mr. Bradley is a man of high standing and good judgment, and was for many years partner of Mr. Bird, [3] now Justice of the Supreme Court of the State, and under the Cleveland administration, United States Attorney for Maine.

I am also enclosing Judge Prouty's letter about Wallace Batchelder, [4] which you may care to have, although I have not been able to get in touch with any Vermont man who could give me definite information in regard to Batchelder.

Very cordially yours,

1. William Mason Bradley (1853–1933) had been a classmate of LDB's in the Harvard Law School.

2. John Fuller Appleton Merrill (1866–1944) had held a number of political and minor judicial posts in Maine; he was named to the post of United States attorney for the district of Maine and held it until the end of the Wilson administration.

3. George Emerson Bird (1847–1926) had served on the Maine Supreme Court since 1908.

4. Wallace Batchelder (1875–1919), a Vermont lawyer, was counsel to the Roosevelt forces at the 1912 Republican convention; he had served with Roosevelt in the Rough Riders.

To F. A. Griffin

February 23, 1915 Boston, Mass. [Brandeis Mss, NMF 69-1]

DEAR SIR: [1] Replying to yours of the 19th:

My book on "Other People's Money", which you may possibly have read, would show you what I think of the concentration in financial power; but I have never been convinced that our panics and depressions were the intentional act of the financiers. Some others have held a different view.

Your statement is, however, very interesting, and there is much in it in which I should fully agree.

I wonder whether you have sent a copy to Senator LaFollette.

Very truly yours,

1. F. A. Griffin was a New York statistician; he sent LDB a long statement on industrial problems and offered to work with him in bringing facts to public attention.

To Norman Hapgood

February 23, 1915 Boston, Mass. [Brandeis Mss, NMF 62-1]

MY DEAR NORMAN: I expect to be in New York Thursday. Breakfast with me at the Harvard Club if convenient.

It was good to have George appointed to the Trade Commission.[1]   Cordially,

1. Although progressives applauded Wilson's appointment of Rublee, it was blocked in the Senate by Jacob Gallinger on a point of personal privilege. Gallinger may have harbored a grudge against Rublee for the active

role he had played in Raymond Stevens's unsuccessful campaign for the New Hampshire senatorial seat the preceding November. Rublee only served a relatively brief time on an interim appointment. See LDB to Edward M. House, 31 December 1914, and also to Robert M. LaFollette, 5 March 1915.

To Horace Meyer Kallen

February 23, 1915 Boston, Mass. [Brandeis Mss, Z 3-1]

MY DEAR KALLEN: Replying to yours of the 21st:

First: I am extremely sorry that I cannot agree with you, or that you do not agree with me in regard to the course to be taken in Cincinnati. The situation there is simply this:

Philipson is at present in control of his congregation, and through it of the community. He showed this in the interview which I had with him, his President, Cohen, and Rabbi Louis Grossman.[1] The two latter wished to have me speak in Cincinnati at that time, but were overridden by Philipson and yielded without a real struggle. Some of Philipson's congregants are obviously extremely uncomfortable under the situation. The contest is one which should be waged within the Congregation and the community without external aid. The moment we enter into that controversy, local patriotism will come to the support of Philipson. We are losing nothing by waiting until the community shall rise against him. We have far more field to cover than it is possible for us even to scratch with our present forces, Chicago, St. Louis, Kansas City, Indianapolis, Cleveland, and the other cities large and small where no bitterness prevails, and in some of which there is a strong longing for us, need cultivation. Your strong conviction necessarily makes me review carefully the ground upon which I reached the conclusion announced; but I am clearly of the opinion that it would be a mistake in strategy to go to Cincinnati at present. As I said to you before, if we leave Cincinnati alone in its isolation, its opposition will shrivel up. It may continue to live, but it will not grow. Only controversy can make it develop effectiveness. The situation is the reverse of what it was twenty years ago. Then Zionism needed controversy. Today controversy alone can serve the opposition.

Second: You express a view that I have been so overwhelmed with the problems of organization and propaganda that I may not have given sufficient attention to other questions which are important. The other questions have not been out of my mind; but our problem to my mind can not be satisfactorily settled unless we have forces behind us. In my opinion Zionism can accomplish nothing except through relatively large forces of men who are thoroughly disciplined, and who are willing to make sacrifices.

I am extremely glad to know of the work you have been doing in organizing and vivifying the Zionist movement in the West.

Enclosed is a copy of my letter to Fechheimer today.

Cordially yours,

1. Louis Grossman (1863–1926) had been rabbi of Congregation B'nai Yeshurun in Cincinnati since 1898; he also taught at the Hebrew Union College and wrote numerous books and articles on aspects of Jewish life and Reform religion.

To John C. Barrett

February 24, 1915 Boston, Mass. [Brandeis Mss, NMF 69-2]

MY DEAR MR. BARRETT: [1] Replying to your letter of the 16th enclosing copy of House Roll No. 27 and House Roll No. 134.[2]

You ask my opinion as to which of these two bills providing for a minimum wage is preferable. I have no hesitation in saying that your bill,—House Roll No. 134, is much to be preferred to that introduced by Representative Howard,[3] No. 27.

In my opinion

First: No minimum wage legislation should be passed which undertakes to fix as a general law an exact minimum wage.

Second: The minimum of a living wage actually varies from time to time according to the cost of living, which varies also according to the locality to which it is to be applied, and in certain respects in accordance to the occupation to which it is to be applied. No minimum wage should be introduced without a thorough preliminary investigation by a commission, and preferably upon the report of a Wage Board reporting to the Commission.

Third: It seems to me unwise at the present time to provide for any minimum wage law which extends to adult male workers.

Fourth: The exact character of the minimum wage legislation to be enacted will depend largely upon the decision in *Stettler vs.*

O'Hara,[4] which was argued before the United States Supreme Court in December, and the decision is to be expected soon. You doubtless have seen a report of my argument in the Survey of February 6th.[5] If you should care to have a copy of the brief, you can doubtless procure one through the National Consumers' League, 6 East 39th St., New York City, who have had the brief reprinted.   Very truly yours,

1. John C. Barrett was a member of the Nebraska House of Representatives.

2. House Roll No. 27, introduced by Representative Howard (see next note), provided for a minimum wage of 20¢ an hour for all adult male workers, and 30¢ per hour for overtime, regardless of the nature of the work. Roll No. 134, introduced by Barrett, proposed a commission to investigate the problems of minimum wages, to gather and maintain data, and to propose various wage levels according to industry and locale.

3. Jeremiah Howard (1855–1930) had come to the United States from Ireland in 1885. In 1915 he was serving the second of his five terms in the Nebraska House of Representatives.

4. See LDB to Charles McCarthy, 18 November 1914.

5. "The Constitution and the Minimum Wage," *The Survey*, 33 (6 February 1915): 490–94, 521–24.

To Alfred Brandeis

February 24, 1915 Boston, Mass. [Brandeis Mss, M 4-1]

MY DEAR AL: I had not suspected when I was prodding you so persistently for a letter that you had not been well. It is too bad that you should have had such pain again. Obviously you and I ought to adopt Father's policy of frequent resort to the Medicine-Man. I am sure he was very wise in this. Man ought at least to treat himself as well as a Machine.

It was good to have Fannie's assurance that you are taking the needed rest, and to know that for you exile from business, which means confinement to the farm, is not irksome.

I am off for N.Y. tonight, after more than a fortnight here. My longest stay since—well it must be more than a year. Expect to spend Thursday in N.Y., Friday in Washington, Saturday again in N.Y. Sunday I speak in Providence & Monday am due here again. Activities now are quite largely Jewish relief. We are getting our Community well organized & they are contributing quite liberally. Had an invitation from Fechheimer and Max Senior to talk Zionism in Cincinnati, but wrote them I deemed *public* controversy so unwise for the Jews that I could not go unless Phillipson [*sic*] joins in invitation—which I suppose will prove an effective obstacle.

Thank Jennie for her letter.

Tell Otto [Wehle] Harry was in Monday. He seems in excellent condition physically & mentally. You may tell Louis (Wehle) I met Rem Ogilby's brother [1] on train from W[ashington].

1. In 1915 Charles Fitz Randolph Ogilby (1879–1962) had recently opened his own law practice in Washington.

To Alfred Brandeis

February 27, 1915 New York, N.Y. [Brandeis Mss, M 4-1]

MY DEAR AL: Arriving here this morning I find your letter to Alice & am delighted to have you say you are really on the mend. But don't go too fast this time & prove yourself true to the farm. Experts tell me that appreciation of the low mutterings of Nature which precede the Spring are [*sic*] the true test of the Country-lover.

I am glad you have suppressed your discovery re chickens, for the present. The Supreme Court has decided the California 8 hour case favorably. This was argued after the Minimum Wage Case, & indicates that the Court is having some trouble with the Minimum Wage Case.[1]

The I.C.C. is greatly troubled by the L & N decision denying them access to correspondence & think it will greatly hamper efficiency of their investigations.[2] [Henry C.] Hall wanted to talk situation over with me. They look troubled & apparently feel that they are losing in public regard. "Mann kann es ihnen in der Schule ansehen." [3]

If Phil. North American is available to you look at my interview on RR costs in yesterday's issue.[4]

Shall Zionize here morning & evening & hope to see my family between times.

1. See LDB to Charles McCarthy, 18 November 1914.
2. For the major decisions in the case, see LDB to Alfred Brandeis, 1 January 1915.

3. "One can tell by seeing them in school."

4. In an interview with Einar Barfod, LDB praised the eastern railroads for their newly-adopted policy of candor in dealing with the public, a policy begun in the fight to repeal full-crew laws. LDB said he did not doubt the integrity of the roads, but expressed surprise that they had not adopted such a policy years before. Good business practices demanded honesty with the public, and strict pursuit of the truth would in the end benefit everyone.

To Israel Friedlaender

March 1, 1915 Boston, Mass. [Brandeis Mss, Z 11-2]

MY DEAR DR. FRIEDLANDER [sic]: [1] You have doubtless already received notice of your election as an associate member of the Provisional Committee, and we are exceedingly glad that we are to have your active cooperation.

I come promptly to ask you to take over certain portions of the work which has [sic] been necessarily much neglected up to the present. Our committee has been at work now for six months. There was the work of organizing the committee, of raising money, and of dealing with the many urgent problems presented by conditions abroad.

In the multitude of pressing work, our Administrative Secretary, Mr. Perlstein, was unable to find time to prepare all the reports of our committee meetings. We need a Recording Secretary and a Historian. We want from that Secretary far more than a proper record of the meetings, namely:

First: We should have prepared a report of the work accomplished.

Second: A monthly report hereafter of the work of the Committee.

Third: A consideration in connection with the Administrative Secretary in advance of each meeting of the business to be taken up at the meeting; and, to a certain extent, formulated suggestions of matters to be presented.

We hope that you will be willing to accept the position of Recording Secretary as thus defined. I am, of course, aware of the heavy burdens which you are already carrying, but I know also your deep interest in the Zionist movement; and that you realize, as we do, that the times have pressed responsibilities upon us which cannot be performed without serious sacrifices on the part of all of us. I therefore feel justified in asking you to accept the position of Recording Secretary.[2]

Very cordially yours,

1. Israel Friedlaender (1876–1920), Russian-born and German-educated, came to the United States in 1903 to be professor of Biblical literature and exegesis at the Jewish Theological Seminary. A noted Arabist as well as a Judaic scholar, he translated Ahad Ha-Am's work (see LDB to Friedlaender, 25 June 1915) into English. Friedlaender was a member of the American Jewish Committee and a strong Zionist at the same time. He expounded the thesis that Jewish life in the Diaspora would be strengthened by the existence of a Jewish homeland in Palestine. In 1917 the Joint Distribution Committee named him to a Red Cross commission being sent to the middle East to relieve suffering, but charges of pro-German activity by Richard Gottheil and Stephen Wise led to Friedlaender's resignation. After the war, while on a mission to investigate the conditions of Russian Jews, he was murdered by outlaws near Mogilev, 150 miles from Minsk.

2. Friedlaender accepted the position.

To William Harrison Ingersoll

March 1, 1915 Boston, Mass. [Brandeis Mss, NMF 68-1]

MY DEAR MR. INGERSOLL: Replying to yours of the 26th: [1]

First: You say "I appreciate that this question is in one respect at least a pretty technical question in specialized law—namely, the Trade Mark Law".

I believe you are entirely in error in this respect. The principles involved are in no sense trademark principles. The questions involved in our particular difference with Mr. Clarke are questions of constitutional law; questions on which a knowledge of technical trademark law are not apt to be helpful. I speak with some confidence on this subject, as in earlier years I spent considerable time on trademark law, having acted in many cases with the then leading authority on trademark law,—Roland Cox,[2] for some of the concerns most interested in the preservation of trademarks, and the prevention of unfair competition.

Second: I sympathize fully with your desire to reach an independent conclusion, but I think that a distinction should be drawn as to those matters in which a layman's independent conclusion would or would not be of great value. For instance, I should not consider my conclusion of great value in advising whether a particular operation which a surgeon had under consideration was valuable or not. It comes after all very much to the question of experienced judgment as to how courts would, in view of a series of decisions, be inclined to view a particular question. We have here, however, not merely a question of what a court would ultimately hold, but what the attitude would be of courts and Congressmen towards such a question. There must exist in the mind of anyone familiar with the Court's decision at least a serious doubt as to the constitutionality of Mr. Clarke's bill, and no one who has followed the course of the Trade Commission Bill would ignore the great aid which such a doubt gives opponents to a bill. It is simply courting trouble to unnecessarily assume the burden of meeting a constitutional objection.

Third: I am inclined to think you do not fully appreciate Mr. Whittier's work. It is no doubt true that there are many opportunities outside of Washington which have not been availed of. It may be that this was partly due to the fact the continuous sessions of Congress have seemed to require Mr. Whittier's constant attendance in Washington. Undoubtedly much work should be done through the country. But what I have seen of Mr. Whittier's work there has led me to believe that he has been efficient. The prejudice, due largely to ignorance or unfamiliarity with the question which the proponents of the Stevens Bill must overcome, bulks very large. I find men of ability and intelligence who are inclined to take the same view of things that I do, approach this subject with prejudice against the principles of the Stevens Bill, and it requires even from them considerable study to overcome a natural disinclination at permitting the establishment of standard prices. If Commissioner Davies should make a favorable report, which his recent statement to me led me now to hope for, our way will be much clearer. I am convinced that Mr. P. B. Noyes'[3] apostasy had much to do with the delay in the issue of that report, and that the doubts and inclinations against us long harbored by Mr. Davies, originated largely from him who had been a strong supporter of our movement at its inception. I am inclined to think that if you who have been so much identified with the general movement, make a small deviation by withdrawing favor from the Stevens Bill to another competing measure, it will tend to produce further delay and difficulties. Of course I do not mean there must be necessarily unity in respect to all the details of the bill. Amendments which are really perfecting amendments might bring strength, but the support by our friends of the Clarke bill would be a distinct division, and would prove a source of weakness.

Fourth: Among the specific work which might profitably be undertaken by the League, is to secure some specific legislation in individual states on the lines of the Clarke or Stevens bill, establishing our contention as the laws of an individual state. The enactment of such legislation in a number of states would make the burden of convincing Congress materially lighter. But let us have something far more specific and effective than the New Jersey Law.[4]   Very cordially yours,

1. Ingersoll was attempting to clarify in his own mind some of LDB's arguments against the constitutionality of the Clarke bill (see LDB to Ingersoll, 17 February 1915). He was confused over the problem of conveying rights and said that he thought the whole subject extremely complex – probably it could only be understood by patent lawyers.

2. Roland Cox (1842–1900), a New York attorney, specialized in patent law in the later nineteenth century.

3. Pierrepont Burt Noyes (1870–1959), son of the controversial utopian socialist and sex-reformer, John Humphrey Noyes, was longtime general manager and president of the Oneida Community Silver Company, where he helped develop a model labor relations program. During the world war he served as assistant fuel administrator.

4. On this same date, LDB wrote to Edmund A. Whittier that he considered Ingersoll's doubts about the Stevens bill dangerous to the ultimate success of the cause. "It seems to me that we shall seriously imperil the chances of legislation by the Stevens bill if men like Mr. Ingersoll undertake to change horses while crossing the stream, – particularly when you change for a horse that is very apt to break down before you reach the journey's end."

To Schmarya Levin

March 1, 1915 Boston, Mass. [Brandeis Mss, Z 10-3]

MY DEAR DR. LEVIN: I write to confirm the request made at the meeting of the Provisional Committee on Thursday last, namely:

First: That you should prepare at the earliest possible moment a draft of a letter to be signed by me, in which I shall make to the

Actions Comite a comprehensive report of the work of our Committee during the six months ending February 28th; and a statement of the present conditions of the organization in America.[1]

Second: That you prepare weekly thereafter a draft of a letter to be signed by me reporting to the Actions Comite such part of the work of the Committee, or of occurrences during the preceding week which it may seem proper to communicate.

Third: That you submit a list of the persons or organizations to whom a copy of the letter to the Actions Comite should be sent.

Fourth: If in your, Mr. Lipsky's and Mr. Perlstein's as in my opinion it may not be desirable to send a copy to the organizations of England, Canada, South Africa, etc. that you prepare:

1. A separate draft of letter to those organizations embodying such report of our work during the past six months, and of the present condition of the organization in America, as it may appear wise to communicate to them, and

2. That you prepare monthly thereafter a draft of such letter to those organizations, covering the work of the preceding month as may appear to be desirable to communicate to them.

3. That you prepare a list of the persons and organizations to which these letters or copies thereof should be sent.

The drafts of these letters prepared by you would thereafter be translated into English,[2] as it is our purpose to conduct our official correspondence in English.

                              Very cordially yours,

1. See LDB to Arthur Ruppin, 18 March 1915.

2. Levin's native languages were Yiddish and Russian; during his stay in the United States he developed a fine command of English as well.

To Benjamin Perlstein

                    March 1, 1915 Boston, Mass. [Brandeis Mss, Z 3-2]

DEAR MR. PERLSTEIN: With a view to improving the efficiency of the office I suggest the adoption of the following rules:

First: That no correspondence, papers, or documents shall, without the written approval of the Chairman of the Provisional Committee, be removed by any one, whether connected with the Committee or not, from the administrative offices, except for use in the Executive offices in the Aeolian Building for the purposes of meetings.

Second: That any member of the Committee who sends letters, telegrams, or other written communications on behalf of the Committee from any place other than the Administrative offices shall, on the day of sending such communication, transmit a copy of the same to the Administrative office.

Third: That no member of the Committee shall send any communication on behalf of the Committee to the Actions Comite, or any of its members, or to any of the affiliated or cooperating organizations, in other countries, except through the Administrative office, and that, with the exception of formal communications, no such communications shall be sent under any conditions without the approval of the Chairman.

Will you kindly in due time transmit to the members and Associated Members of the Comite, a copy of the above?

Yours very truly,

To David de Sola Pool

March 2, 1915 Boston, Mass. [Brandeis Mss, Z 7-1]

DEAR DR. POOL: [1] I was very glad to learn from the minutes of the Executive Committee meeting of the Federation of American Zionists on February 18th, which has just reached me, that "the plan of propaganda by means of private gatherings and home parties for the purpose of securing converts to the cause and eventual members of the organization, be accepted".

This plan of your Committee seems to me eminently wise and promising; but I hope that it will not be left merely to the Zion Association to carry out this work. Your Committee and each of its members ought to make every endeavor to arrange for such private gatherings, and the time is ripe for such a course.

During the last six months the subject of Zionism has attracted considerable attention. It is looked upon now favorably in many quarters where it was formerly regarded with disfavor. But the ignorance concerning the cause is still very great. Such private gatherings as were suggested in the vote are the really effective means of removing that ignorance; and I feel that you are among the relatively few who are most competent to conduct such meetings.

I hope therefore that you will be able to give much time to arranging and conducting such gatherings between now and summer vacation. Very cordially yours,

1. David de Sola Pool (1885–1970), after his education in England and Germany, became rabbi of the prestigious Spanish and Portuguese Synagogue (Shearith Israel) in New York, the leading Sephardic congregation in the country. He was heavily involved in Zionist activities, being president of the Zion Association of New York and also of Young Judea. In 1919 he served on the Zionist commission to Palestine.

To Norman Hapgood

March 2, 1915 Boston, Mass. [Brandeis Mss, NMF 62-1]

DEAR NORMAN: *First*: In what issue will my Peace article appear? [1]

Second: This may interest you:

See "Other People's Money" page 212 referring to cooperative concerns "A Remedy for Trusts".

The January 1915 number of the International Cooperative Bulletin, which is published in London, says, page 1 under "A resume of the Progress of Co-operation in Denmark":

"The Danish co-operative societies have to record a slow, but steady development during the past year. The Co-operative Cement Factory is an exception to this rule; this society has made remarkable progress and is at the present time engaged in a severe struggle with the trusts. One advantage of the conflict is that the newspapers throughout the country have been awakened to the importance of the co-operative societies. Another feature of the campaign is that the Fellesforeningen for Danmarks Brugsforeninger, which legally has nothing to do with the Cement Factory, has become involved in a lawsuit. A short time ago, the new Cement Factory was enlarged, as it was quite unable to meet the demands made upon it." [2]

In connection with my argument on the efficiency of the small units ("Trusts and Efficiency" in Business A Profession, page 198) note the following also from the International Co-operative Bulletin, page 2:

"The co-operative farms show an ever-increasing tendency to divide the larger into small enterprises. Naturally, the management expenses of a smaller farm are relatively greater, but on the other hand there is the advantage of the quicker transport of the milk to the farm, and this partly compensates for the disadvantage."   Cordially yours,

1. See LDB to Hapgood, 19 February 1915.
2. Hapgood covered the matter in an editorial, "Hoch der Denmark," in the 20 March 1915 issue of *Harper's Weekly*.

To Arthur Ruppin

March 2, 1915 Boston, Mass. [Palestine Office]

MY DEAR DR. RUPPIN: Dr. Kaplansky, as representing the Jewish National Fund, has submitted a request that our Committee relieve the Jewish National Fund of its present obligation to provide the funds necessary to defray the expenses of the Palestina Amt.[1] He estimates that the amount required for this purpose, including all legal expenses, will be 64,000 francs a year.[2] It is proposed that if our Committee assumes the obligation to provide the funds required, the Palestina Amt shall come into direct relations with our Committee without any intervention of the J.N.F. making its reports directly to us so far as concerns the general operations of the Palestine Office.

Members of our Committee have informally expressed themselves favorably concerning this proposal; but I have not deemed it wise to submit the matter to the Committee for definite action until we should have heard directly and explicitly from you in regard to the matter.

First: Whether it would be entirely in accord with your desires that we should assume this obligation, which would involve your coming into direct relations with us as indicated above.

Second: A comprehensive description of the work of the

Palestina Amt. Dr. Kaplansky was not able to supply us with any definite data on this subject; and indeed expressed the opinion that a description of the work should properly come from you.

Third: A financial report showing in some detail the receipts and disbursements of the Palestina Amt from year to year up to, say, August 1, 1914; and a separate statement of the receipts and disbursements since August 1, 1914.

We of course do not desire a disclosure of any facts which cover the private relations of the office with those for whom it has done business; but merely the financial results to the office, and a detailed reference to the sources of income and elements of expense.

Fourth: Detailed estimate of the expenses and receipts for the year commencing January 1, 1915.

If our Committee assumes the obligation of providing funds necessary for the conduct of the Palestina Amt, it would expect formal monthly reports of the operations of the office, both in general of the work performed, and of receipts and disbursements.

As the J.N.F. deems it important that an early decision shall be rendered by our Committee, I beg that you will give this the earliest possible attention, although I realize the pressure upon your time owing to present emergencies.[3]

May I add that the fact that you are representing so largely our interests in connection with Palestine matters is a source of great satisfaction to us, and is giving to us the assurance that whatever funds America can provide for Palestine will be wisely and efficiently administered.   Very cordially yours,

1. The Palestina Amt was the Palestine Office of the Zionist Organization.

2. The franc in 1915 was worth approximately nineteen cents.

3. The conditions attached to the P.E.C. offer to assume the costs of the Palestine Office were not an attempt by the Americans to take over part of the world organization's power and responsibilities. Rather, this was seen as a temporary measure, but LDB insisted that in all the P.E.C.'s activities strict accounting and business methods be followed. Felix Frankfurter later commented that LDB beileved that the Zionists should run their monetary operations as conservatively as a bank, and such a procedure called for direct accountability of Ruppin's office to New York. The P.E.C. did assume the expenses of the office until after the war.

To Stephen Samuel Wise

March 2, 1915 Boston, Mass. [Brandeis Mss, Z 6-2]

MY DEAR DR. WISE: Replying to yours of March 1st:

First: In view of my confidence in your judgment, I see nothing to do but to accept the invitation you transmit to address the Eastern Council of Reform Rabbis at their semi-annual conference on the subject of "The Organization of American Israel." So far as I can see the last Sunday of April, or the one before the last will be equally convenient (or inconvenient) for me.[1]

Second: The formal invitation from Cincinnati came and I answered it last week as per copy enclosed. Upon my return to the city yesterday I found another letter from Mr. Fechheimer under date of February 26th, which I presume must have crossed my letter of the 23rd, as he makes no reference to it. Copy is enclosed.[2]

I am convinced that I ought to adhere to the decision stated in my letter of the 23rd; but it occurs to me that as you are to be in Cincinnati on the 21st for the City Club luncheon, it might be well to arrange for a little meeting between you and those gentlemen named in Mr. Fechheimer's letter of the 26th, where you could talk Zionism to them and the general situation in private, and perhaps win them over definitely to our cause.

The time has come when we must undertake to win through such private conferences men of education with influence in the various cities. I had such a meeting in New York (a dinner at the Harvard Club with sixteen brought together through Mack and Frankfurter), which I hope will lead to much. I think we should arrange for similar group discussions wherever possible.

Third: You doubtless heard from Dr. Magnes that we cannot send a second representative on the Vulcan (although it is still possible that [Isaac W.] Bernheim may go independently). I have been intending for some time to suggest to you that we ought to take steps to have Edelman[3] promoted, and one of our friends appointed Vice-Consul at Jerusalem. It seems to me that if this were possible, it would be well to suggest Rosenblatt for the position. The fact that his wife is an ardent Zionist, and that they are people of means, and that Rosenblatt himself has such special interest in Palestinian development, and is young, might make him particularly available; and that the education given him might yield rich fruit.

I saw Rosenblatt yesterday, and without in any way committing ourselves, suggested to him the possibility, and asked him to talk over the matter with his wife and father, but otherwise to treat it as strictly confidential. This he said he would do. If he is willing to go, I hope that you can take up the matter with Secretary Bryan at an early date. If Rosenblatt is not willing to go, I think we ought to discuss when we meet some other possible candidate, as it is important that we should be properly represented in Palestine.[4]

Fourth: I note your talk with Wilde of the London Times, and have confidence that it was discreet. You cannot escape from the Committee by any such means.   Very cordially yours,

1. There are only a handful of books or statements in the history of the Zionist movement which capture the prevailing mood and ideology of a particular time; one of them is the speech LDB gave at the Eastern Council of Reform Rabbis in 1915, ultimately titled "The Jewish Problem: How to Solve It." This was the closest LDB ever came to a purely ideological statement of his personal belief in Zionism, and it clearly demonstrated how Zionism reflected his progressivism, for the document not only expounded his faith in Zionism but also his faith in democracy. The "Jewish Problem," as LDB defined it, consisted of a question: "How can we secure for Jews, wherever they may live, the same rights and opportunities enjoyed by non-Jews? How can we secure for the world the full contribution which Jews can make, if unhampered by artificial limitations?" All that the Jews asked was to be treated equally.

The new liberalism had undoubtedly accomplished significant steps in the nineteenth century by removing many of the legal limitations on Jews, but their new freedoms almost immediately led to the rise of modern anti-Semitism. Liberalism, in concentrating on individual rights, failed to take into account group rights, and LDB maintained that in the modern world nationality must be supported. He drew a distinction between a nation and a nationality; the former is a man-made political institution, the latter a cultural aggregate. In answer to critics, many of them within the Reform movement, LDB denied that there was necessarily a contradiction between the two. One could be loyal to the United States (a nation) and to Jewish nationalism (Zionism). "Let no American imagine that Zionism is inconsistent with Patriotism. Multiple loyalties are objectionable only if they are inconsistent." (Cf. LDB's speech, "What Loyalty Demands," delivered on 250th anniversary of the Jews in America; see LDB to Adolph Brandeis, 29 November 1905.)

Brandeis then denied that Zionism was a movement to force all Jews to move to Palestine. Rather, "Zionism seeks to establish in Palestine, for such Jews as choose to go and remain there, and for their descendents, a legally secured home, where they may live together and lead a Jewish life." In Palestine alone, he declared, could the Jewish spirit reach its full and natural development, and from there, Jewish contributions could add to the world's civilization. To those who argued that Palestine was not a good location, and that Jews did not know how to farm, he proudly pointed to the accomplishments of more than fifty Jewish settlements, which clearly proved "that Palestine is fit for the modern Jew . . . and that the modern Jew is fit for Palestine." He then ran down the litany of Jewish achievement in Palestine, and the rebirth of the Hebrew language.

Finally, LDB turned to how Jews in America could help Zionism. The burden of supporting the Palestinian settlements had fallen on America due to the war; the American Jewish community was the most prosperous in the world, unfettered by legal or political restrictions. Our generosity alone should make us want to help, he said, but there were other reasons as well. By finding our own Jewish identity in Zionism, the quality of American Jewish life, so unhinged by the recent mass immigrations, would be uplifted. In his peroration, in words reminiscent of the savings-bank fight, Brandeis declared: "Organize, Organize, Organize,—until every Jew in America must stand up and be counted—counted with us—or prove himself, wittingly or unwittingly, of the few who are against their own people."

The speech was an immediate success, and the Federation published thousands of copies for propaganda distribution. By 1919 it had gone through five large printings, and was kept in print until after World War II. It is reprinted in *Brandeis on Zionism*, 12–35; *The Curse of Bigness*, 218–32; and in deHaas, *Brandeis*, 170–90.

2. See LDB to Fechheimer, 23 February 1915; see also LDB to Max Senior, 5 March 1915.

3. Samuel Edelman was vice consul and translator at the Jerusalem consulate.

4. Although Bernard Rosenblatt moved to Israel to work for the Zionist cause, he was not appointed vice-consul at Jerusalem.

To Richard James Horatio Gottheil

March 3, 1915 Boston, Mass. [Gottheil Mss]

MR DEAR MR. GOTTHEIL: I am returning herewith President Schuman's [*sic*][1] letter of the 27th enclosed with yours of the 1st. I am not surprised at its contents.

Boris Kazmann, whom you doubtless know of as an old Kadima man,[2] saw me on the 25th and made this suggestion in connection with the Polish Jews, which it may be well enough to think over even in advance of his more definite plan of formulation:

Instead of continuing the antagonism between the Jews and Poles, and endeavoring to establish some modus vivendi between them, in case a Polish State is established, recognize conflict as irrepressible and evolve some plan by which the new Polish State shall agree to purchase all the property of the Jews, and thus provide the means for wholesale immigration, which might in large part be diverted to Palestine and surrounding countries.

The difficulties and objections are obvious, but the suggestion deserves careful consideration.   Very truly yours,

1. Jacob Gould Schurman (1854–1942) was president of Cornell University from 1892 to 1920. The author of numerous books, Schurman also served on many state and federal commissions. There is no copy of the letter in the Brandeis Mss.

2. Boris Kazman (1874–1933) was a socialist and Zionist agitator who worked with the Zionist organization between 1909 and 1919. Trained as a chemist, he settled in Palestine in 1923 near Rehovot, where he operated a small laboratory. "Kadimah," which means "forward" in Hebrew, was an early student Zionist society.

To Norman Hapgood

March 3, 1915 Boston, Mass. [Brandeis Mss, NMF 62-1]

DEAR NORMAN: I enclose an extract from the Governor's message dealing with savings bank insurance. One of his recommendations, —that of increasing the size of the policy from $500. to $1,000, became a law yesterday. Under this law it will be possible for the savings banks in the aggregate to supply $4,000 of insurance, as there are four banks now which have established insurance departments.

The other recommendation of the Governor, namely: to undertake the educational work of making known the merits of savings bank insurance, was reported adversely by the Insurance Committee (composed largely of agents of insurance companies). There were five dissenters, and the bill making the initial appropriation asking for $2,500. was passed in the House by an overwhelming majority. The bill will now go before the Ways and Means Committee of the House, where we have reason to think it will be favorably acted upon; and then go to the Senate, where the main fight will be on. The Democrats will undoubtedly support the Governor. There is a large Republican majority, however. But we hope to secure enough votes to pass the bill there. The matter will probably not come up in the Senate for ten days or a fortnight.[1]　　Cordially,

1. A large lobbying effort by the commercial insurance companies almost defeated the governor's proposal. Judd Dewey, unpaid counsel for SBLI, managed to see the president of the senate just prior to the vote on the second reading, and he convinced him that the small appropriation should be continued. When the voice vote was taken, it seemed that the bill had lost, but Calvin Coolidge, without a blink of the eye, announced that it had passed and ordered it to a third reading. According to Professor Mason, Coolidge came to the aid of SBLI several times while he was in the Massachusetts legislature. Hapgood, relying on LDB's wording in this letter, noted the Massachusetts fight in his 20 March 1915 *Harper's* editorial, "Going Ahead."

Samuel H. Hourvitch

March 3, 1915 Boston, Mass. [Brandeis Mss, Z 7-1]

MY DEAR SIR: [1] I am in receipt of yours of the 28th referring to your letter of November 30th and December 16th you say:

"Those plans are based upon years of personal research in connection with large expenditures. Now I am informed that the Zionist leaders are negotiating with bankers to capitalize my ideas behind my back. Is this a new part of Zionist activity?"

I do not know to what you may refer as "capitalize my ideas"; but I feel sure that as a good Zionist nothing could give you greater happiness than to have your ideas accepted, if it were the fact, as a basis for Zionist action.

If, on the other hand, you mean by "capitalize on my ideas", or anyone's ideas, that bankers or others are endeavoring or expecting to make any money out of Palestinian affairs, you are grievously mistaken.

The demands upon all Zionists to contribute as much money as they can to aid Palestine is very great, and if you have not already sent your contribution to the officers in Chicago, I trust we may have a check from you either to support the work of the Zionist institutions or for the Palestinian Relief Fund.

Very truly yours,

1. Samuel H. Hourvitch of Chicago had evidently submitted some proposals to LDB the previous November and December, about improving conditions for the Palestinian settlers. He had not received any reply from LDB
(who probably sent them to the P.E.C. office), and he now accused the
Zionists of turning these plans over to bankers who would make a profit on
them.

To Alexander Sachs

March 3, 1915 Boston, Mass. [Brandeis Mss, Z 7-1]

MY DEAR MR. SACHS: How far have you progressed with the
survey of Palestinian activities originally discussed by us about
September 1st.

Now that we are getting organized the urgent work of securing funds to support the institution and for relief in Palestine,
we must try to take up more fundamental problems: and it is
important that the members of our Committee and those who
work with them should have a clear understanding of the situation
in Palestine.

I have seen it stated a number of times that the aggregate
amounts contributed to Palestine for all purposes reaches nearly
$2,000,000 a year. Accurate figures are not obtainable, but the
more I have endeavored to understand [the] Palestinian situation,
the more important seems to be the preparation of the statement
which we originally discussed.

I realize the great difficulties in compiling such a statement as
well as the inevitable demands of your course at the University,
but I hope you are making appreciable progress on the work.
Won't you let me know how far you have progressed?[1]

Very cordially yours,

1. Sachs replied on 7 March that because of the press of other activities
and business, he would be unable to complete the survey for several more
months.

To Horace Meyer Kallen

March 4, 1915 Boston, Mass. [Kallen Mss]

MY DEAR KALLEN: David Rubin writes me that they are having
"a large measure of success" in securing new members, and that
"the antis or even the non-Zionists are now practically the out-

standing exceptions". This, and the suggestion of Harry Wolfson [1] in his article in the January Menorah Journal to the effect that in Germany the "distinction between the undergraduate and graduate does not exist",[2] leads me to suggest the consideration of the following:

We need preeminently in America the intellectuals and men of leadership in the community. The men whom we wish to reach do not naturally associate with most of those who are now members of existing local Zionist organizations affiliated with the Federation, and in large part cannot be led to join such local societies. The Harvard Zionist Society appears not to be affiliated with the Federation.

Could we not develop college Zionist societies, like the Harvard Zionist Society, so that it should include either:

(a) All the Harvard graduates wherever situated, or

(b) Harvard graduates located in the neighborhood of the College itself.

The adoption of such a course might facilitate greatly our task of securing the adhesion of the intellectuals to our cause, and insure their activity when once they had taken hold. It ought, for instance, to be possible to secure for a Harvard Zionist Society a large number of the former Menorah men, and other graduates in Boston and vicinity.

I have not formulated any plan, and am submitting the idea for your consideration. I will send copies of this letter to Judge Mack, Frankfurter, Hurwitz, Professor Gottheil and Rubin, with some of whom you may care to get into communication.[3]

Very cordially yours,

1. Harry Austryn Wolfson (b. 1887) taught Jewish literature and philosophy at Harvard until his retirement in 1958. He has written numerous books and articles on philosophical and Jewish subjects.

2. In his article, Wolfson noted that Jewish students in European universities had a long history of cooperating and of organizing into societies for the promotion of Jewish objectives. He suggested that Jewish aims in the United States could be furthered if the college students could be organized. "Jewish Students in European Universities," The Menorah Journal, 1 (January 1915): 26–32.

3. This idea, after much discussion and alteration, eventually led to the establishment of the Intercollegiate Zionist Association.

To Nathan D. Kaplan

March 4, 1915 Boston, Mass. [Brandeis Mss, Z 3-1]

MY DEAR MR. KAPLAN: Replying to yours of March 1st:

First: I am glad to know that the result of your "Bread for Palestine" movement has been such as to satisfy you, and I am looking forward to the full report to which you refer.

Second: As to Zionist propaganda work: I entirely agree with you that it is of the utmost importance to take up this work vigorously, and I hope that after the middle of this month all of the Zionist organizations may be able to suspend, at least temporarily, the raising of relief funds, and devote themselves for some months to energetic Zionist propaganda. Our forces in New England have been quite largely absorbed by participation in the work of the American Jewish Relief Committee, and latterly in the specific problem of the relief ship for Palestine. The financial results in both fields are fortunately very good, but we are planning after the 15th to direct our attention to the Zionist propaganda, including of course the Emergency Fund, which is in great need of replenishment. The six months' report which you have doubtless received from Mr. Perlstein will show, even when adjusted by additional amounts, only about $10,000 on hand in the Emergency School, Institution and Shekolim funds. We must send in the very near future $10,000 to Dr. Ruppin to cover the institutional etc. expenditures for the next three months. Our committee has assumed definite obligations in the way of contributions to the Actions Comite, and has now under consideration taking over direct from the Jewish National Fund its obligations to defray the expenses of the Palestina Amt, which are estimated to amount to $12,000 a year.[1]

The expenses of our office have also necessarily grown greatly. We have now seven persons on the pay roll. The rent and incidental charges are large. Of the $8,391.32, total expenses appearing in the report of February 28th,—the report presented by our accountants and Mr. Perlstein,—$4,673.68 should be charged to the Emergency Fund, and $3,717.64 to the Relief Fund.

Certain of the expenses of the six months have not yet got into this account, and it is fairly to be expected that the total operating expenses, including travelling expenses, will reach $12,000 for the year, exclusive of amounts chargeable against Relief Funds.

It is thus very clear that vigorous effort must soon be made to increase the Emergency Funds, and I hope that you and Mr. Shulman will be able to make definite efforts to secure a reasonable financial crop from the seed which we sowed in Milwaukee and St. Louis.

Third: As to your request for a subsidy from the Provisional Committee:

I am entirely in accord with you as to the importance of pushing your propaganda work, and think that the Provisional Committee should, so far as it is possible, aid you in that respect.

The financial situation of our Committee, stated above, will show you our limitations. I should suggest, however, that before the matter is presented to our Committee, you and Mr. Shulman should submit the plan of adjustment of the relations between the Knights of Zion [2] and the Federation, which it was agreed, when you, Mr. Shulman, Mr. DeHaas and I discussed the subject in November, should be submitted.

We are to have a meeting of the Provisional Committee on March 11th, and the next meeting of the Committee after that on March 20th, and presumably weekly thereafter. I suggest that you and Mr. Shulman prepare now a careful statement setting forth the grounds on which you ask a subsidy, and the amount thereof, and at the same time to send a statement carrying out the plan of adjustment of cooperation with the Federation referred to above.

With a view to greater efficiency of the Committee, we are adopting a rule of sending out, so far as possible in advance of meetings, copies of the matters to be acted upon. We should naturally submit in this way in advance of any meeting the application of the Knights of Zion. It would therefore be a convenience to us if you could present a sufficient number of multigraphed copies of the application for circulation among all of the members of the Committee.   Very cordially yours,

P.S. Miss [Eva] Leon gave me an account of her recent work in Chicago and spoke with great enthusiasm of the assistance which she had received there.

1. See LDB to Arthur Ruppin, 2 March 1915.
2. The Knights of Zion, established in 1897, was the Midwestern center for

Zionist support; it had just agreed to merge into the Federation of American Zionists.

To Henrietta Szold

March 4, 1915 Boston, Mass. [Brandeis Mss, Z 12-2]

MY DEAR MISS SZOLD: You, Miss Seligsberg,[1] Miss Sampter[2] and Mrs. Rosenblatt[3] are to be congratulated on the February number of the Hadassah Bulletin.

(Please send me for my files Nos. 1,2,3, and 4 of the Hadassah Bulletin.) It is very instructive and should prove very useful. I am particularly impressed with the effort to secure parlor conferences—Mrs. Rosenblatt was here, and is doubtless able to report on our local situation. My impression is that it is ripe for intensive work, and that if you could arrange to have Miss Leon, who made an excellent impression here, or some of your other members, here for a series of conferences, a very considerably increased Hadassah membership might be expected. Mr. DeHaas could doubtless be of assistance to you in this matter.

May I venture to urge upon you the adoption of large type? Your Bulletin very specifically urges upon Zionists and would-be Zionists the necessity of study, but your small type is ruinous to the eyes, and also deprives your Bulletin of that careful attention which it should receive. It would add much not only to the usefulness, but to the dignity of your Bulletin if it were printed in larger type. Of course, there would be a small addition to the expense in the cost of the paper, but paper is infinitely cheaper than eyes, and I know of no more effective expenditure of money [than] in securing adequate attention to your valuable Bulletin.[4]

Very cordially yours,

1. Alice Lillie Seligsberg (1883–1940), a welfare worker in New York, led the Hadassah Medical Unit to Palestine at the end of the war; she was later president of the organization.

2. Jessie Sampter (1883–1938), after an assimilationist childhood, had become attracted to Jewish life. A prolific author, she wrote widely on Jewish and Zionist subjects, and in 1919 she took up permanent residence in Palestine. During the early days of Hadassah she worked closely with Henrietta Szold.

3. Gertrude Goldsmith Rosenblatt (1891–1955) was one of the founders of

Hadassah; she also worked as an organizer for Young Judea and other Zionist youth groups.

4. See LDB to Henrietta Szold, 24 March 1915.

To Robert Marion LaFollette

March 5, 1915 Boston, Mass. [Brandeis Mss, NMF 68-2]

MY DEAR BOB: We are delighted to read this morning that the President has signed the Seamen's Bill.[1] It is a great victory for you and for Furuseth and a great advance for the Committee.

This victory brings some compensation for the failure of the Senate to confirm Rublee.[2] It may help you to appreciate the New England feeling when you learn that the Boston Transcript found in the discovery of Rublee's connection with the Ballinger case an added reason for objecting to his confirmation.

Very cordially yours,

1. After over twenty years of effort, Andrew Furuseth's campaign to free American merchant sailors from the bonds of outdated laws finally came to fruition. He had been working with Senator LaFollette on the bill since 1912, and the measure had passed Congress in March 1913, only to receive a pocket veto from President Taft. While Wilson had announced himself as favorable, the outbreak of the war led the State Department to raise the question of how the bill would affect American commerce and treaty obligations. Wilson, deeply troubled, felt he would have to veto the bill, but LaFollette and Furuseth came to the White House on 2 March, and won the President over. In turn, LaFollette promised that the Senate would give the administration all the time it needed to straighten out any problems regarding the newly signed International Convention of Safety at Sea. "The Seaman's Act," according to Samuel Gompers, "has a rightful place among those really important legislative acts that dedicated our soil to freedom."

2. See LDB to Norman Hapgood, 23 February 1915.

To Max Senior

March 5, 1915 Boston, Mass. [Brandeis Mss, Z 7-1]

MY DEAR MR. SENIOR: I am very glad to know from yours of the 1st that the attitude manifested on the occasion of my visit in October did not meet with the general approval of the Reformed Jews of Cincinnati; and that Dr. Philipson cannot be regarded as their spokesman. The fact that he was accompanied by Dr. Grossman and Mr. Cohen on that occasion, and that they apparently deferred to the views expressed by him, had led me to suppose that he fairly represented the general community feeling.[1]

I still think however, that in view of Dr. Philipson's attitude it would be very prejudicial to the cause of the Jews for me to precipitate a public controversy over Zionism in Cincinnati at this time. On the other hand, I think it is desirable that there should be a conference on this subject with you and Mr. Fechheimer, and, say, one or two others. Furthermore it is not possible for me to be in Cincinnati in the near future. But Dr. Stephen S. Wise is to be there as you know, on Saturday, March 20th and he advises me that he will be glad to attend such a conference on either the afternoon or the evening of the 20th. He must leave that night for Chicago.

Will you or Mr. Fechheimer please wire Dr. Wise (at 23 West 90th Street, New York City) whether you approve of this suggestion, and if so, what hour will be most agreeable to you?

Very cordially yours,

1. See LDB to Horace M. Kallen, 23 February 1915.

To Woodrow Wilson

March 5, 1915 Boston, Mass. [Wilson Mss]

MY DEAR MR. PRESIDENT: I desire to express the high appreciation by the Jews of America of the important services rendered by the Department of State and the Navy Department in protecting and relieving the distress of their bretheren [*sic*] in Palestine.[1]

Very cordially yours,

1. LDB wrote similar notes to Secretary of State William Jennings Bryan and Secretary of the Navy Josephus Daniels.

To Alfred Brandeis

March 6, 1915 Boston, Mass. [Brandeis Mss, M 4-1]

MY DEAR AL: Enclosed must have been intended for you. The only farming I am engaged in is in Palestine & these books throw no light on that problem. After you have mastered farming in Kentucky should like to secure your services as expert to study Palestinian conditions.

Things Jewish have been occupying my time largely. Boston is doing well on relief funds & we are getting the Jewish Community stirred [*] to attempts at Zionistic organization. Have raised between $60–70,000 here for one fund or another & expect to bring it up pretty near $100,000 before we stop.

Cincinnatians (Max Senior, Fecheimer [*sic*] et al) have been very pressing with invitation, but I have resisted saying I don't want a public controversy with Philipson.

My greetings to the family.

To Benjamin Perlstein

March 6, 1915 Boston, Mass. [Brandeis Mss, Z 3-2]

DEAR MR. PERLSTEIN: I received your telegram about going to Palestine, and was sorry to have to wire you as follows:

"No. Your presence is indispensable at the New York office. Have written."

Much as I should wish on the Committee's account as well as your own that you should have the education and experience attendant upon a visit to Palestine, it seems to me clear that at the present time you particularly are needed here, and that we could not allow either you or Mr. Lipsky, or others of our leading workers to go to Palestine when the work in America is in such early stages of organization.

With Mr. Louis Levine [*sic*][1] going to Palestine, and Dr. Ruppin there, I do not consider it imperative that we should have a second representative. It is to be regarded rather as a privilege than as a necessity. Julius Meyer would very much like to go, and although I feel that he is much needed in Boston, the need is not so great that I should wish to stand in his way if Dr. Magnes and other members of the Committee are willing to have him go. If they are not willing to select Julius Meyer, I think some other one of the younger Zionists, whom Mr. Lipsky referred to, might be selected.　　Very truly yours,

1. Louis Hiram Levin (1866–1923) was a Baltimore lawyer and editor of the *Jewish Comment*. He had helped to organize the various Jewish charitable agencies in Baltimore and later was president of the National Conference of Jewish Charities. The brother-in-law of Henrietta Szold, he represented the F.A.Z. on the relief ship *Vulcan*. See LDB to Levin, 8 March 1915.

To George Rublee

March 6, 1915 Boston, Mass. [Brandeis Mss, NMF 68-2]

MY DEAR GEORGE: I was just about to write you when your letter of the 4th came.

First: Felix was in last evening, and we rejoiced at your recess appointment, particularly as [Learned] Hand had reported that the President is confident he can have you confirmed at the next session. By all means accept. You will always be needed on the Commission, but most in getting it started; and I think that with you there, it ought to be possible to have Stevens made counsel.[1]

Second: I have met Monk from time to time and think well of him as a newspaper correspondent. I am not so sure that he would suit you as secretary.[2] At all events you ought to let him spend considerable time with you before you decide to take him. That will give you an opportunity to size him up. I suggest also that you make inquiries concerning him of Gilson Gardner, Welliver, McSween and Elisha Hanson.[3]

Third: I have had considerable correspondence with William H. Ingersoll about the Clarke bill, and think that he will give us no further trouble.   Cordially yours,

P.S. Have just received your telegram requesting me to write the President about Stevens, and have done so.

I am enclosing a letter from Treadwell Cleveland, Jr. of March 5th. Cleveland is a good progressive, and one of the most intelligent of the newspaper men. He was in the Forestry Department under Gifford. I should think it doubtful whether you wish to give out an interview on any subject, but if you should decide to do so, Cleveland would be as good a medium as could be found.

1. See next letter and LDB to Rublee, 25 March 1915.
2. Monk was not named to the post.

3. Elisha Hansen (1888–1962) was in 1915 one of the Washington correspondents of the *Chicago Tribune,* and he later served as secretary to Senator Medill McCormick. In 1924 he established his own law practice in the District of Columbia.

To Woodrow Wilson

March 6, 1915 Boston, Mass. [Brandeis Mss, NMF 68-2]

MY DEAR MR. PRESIDENT: I venture to recommend the appointment of Raymond B. Stevens of New Hampshire as counsel for the Federal Trade Commission.

Mr. Stevens has had but little experience as a practicing lawyer; but he combines the qualities which should make him particularly valuable as counsel for the Commission. He is a man of absolute integrity; is courageous, progressive minded, and able. He has a legal and a judicial mind; has capacity for hard, persistent work, and good judgment. He understands both industrial problems and the common people.

The Commission would be greatly strengthened by the selection of such a man as its counsel.[1]   Very cordially yours,

1. On 8 March Wilson acknowledged the letter, noting that "I shall be glad to bring your suggestion to the attention of the Federal Trade Commission as soon as it is organized." See LDB to George Rublee, 25 March 1915.

To Louis Hiram Levin

March 8, 1915 Boston, Mass. [Brandeis Mss, Z 7-1]

MY DEAR MR. LEVIN: I am sending to Dr. Ruppin through you, three letters:

1. A general report on the activities of our Committee since its organization.

2. A letter of introduction, stating your authority as representing this Committee in connection with the shipments on the Vulcan.

3. A letter of authority from this Committee in respect to investigations concerning Palestinian institutions.

It is our desire that you should acquaint yourself fully with Palestinian conditions, including:

(a) Conditions as they existed at the time of the breaking out of the war; and

(b) The effect of the war and resultant present conditions.

We desire that your inquiry shall be comprehensive. There is indeed no department of life in Palestine as to which we are not desirous of having information. We feel that you, as an American of wide experience, will be able to portray to us the general conditions, and also the conditions specifically of the various institutions, more accurately than it would be possible for anyone not an American to do. In other words, that you will be able not only to ascertain facts, but to interpret these facts to us. And we desire you, therefore, to gather all data available, which will lead to a thorough understanding on your part of the life and conditions in Palestine.

Among other things we wish you would make special inquiry into:

(1) The organization, work and operations of the Palestina Amt. We have a special reason for making this inquiry. We are considering taking over the financial operations of the Amt, as appears by the letter to Dr. Ruppin of March 2nd, of which I enclose a copy.

(2) The present status and prospects of the Anglo-Palestine Company. Among other things, to what extent it is still able to serve the public.

(3) The local opinion as to the extent to which the Agricultural Experiment Station is actually aiding Palestinian agricultural work; and what foundation, if any, there is for the criticism of its work of which report reaches us.

(4) The conditions and prospects of the several colonies.

(5) The condition and prospects of the Achoosa investments.[1]

(6) The conditions, attendance, and prospects of the Zionist schools, and in this connection the condition also of the schools heretofore supported by the Deutscher Hils Verein.

(7) You will, of course, get all possible data as to the political situation in Palestine; and the relations and attitude of the Government towards Zionist institutions and the colonies; and the relation of the colonies to one another, and of the Zionists to the non-Zionists.

(8) We should also like to have as comprehensive a survey as

it is possible for you to present of the general Jewish relief in Palestine. On this subject your own wide experience will enable you to know not only just what we would naturally want, but also the necessary scope of the investigation.

(9) The above request for information is in addition to that which may have been asked for also by Miss Szold, as representing the Hadassah; Mr. Perlstein, as Secretary of this Committee, and by Mr. Lipsky as Chairman of the Federation of American Zionists.   Very cordially yours,

1. The Achoosa societies had been organized in the United States to "purchase land in Palestine and improve same by plantation of fruit trees." Launched in St. Louis in 1908, its members were to buy land and then move to Palestine. By 1913, there were seven groups in the United States with an aggregate membership of 250, and capital stock of $500,000. The following year the various societies merged and continued to buy land under the advice of Arthur Ruppin. Although the society folded during the war, it did establish three colonies – Priya, Ra'anana, and Gan Yavne.

To Arthur Ruppin

March 8, 1915 Boston, Mass. [Palestine Office]

DEAR DR. RUPPIN: [1] The Provisional Executive Committee for General Zionist Affairs was formed August 30, 1914, and its activities therefore cover a period of more than six months. We desire now to give you a general outline of the activities and accomplishments of this Committee during that period. It is our purpose from now on to keep in closer and more frequent communication not only with the Inner Actions Comite, but also with the general organizations in the several countries which the I.A.C. has difficulty in communicating with regularly.

First: At the time of the formation of the Provisional Committee it was of course impossible to forecast the dimensions which the present war has assumed; and we then hoped that Turkey would not be involved in the war. We set for ourselves, therefore, in general this task: – The maintenance of the Zionist International Organization, and of the institutions which the Zionists had organized in Palestine. It seemed to us clear that Zionist activities would be necessarily limited, or possibly suspended in the belligerent countries. As Russia, Germany and

Austria had heretofore been the main support financially of the Palestine institutions, we regarded it as our duty to create as far as we could a substitute for that support. To this end we endeavored to develop further the American Zionist organization, and to collect funds in America with which to maintain the Zionist institutions already created in Palestine. We therefore undertook to collect an Emergency Fund of $100,000 on the assumption that this fund would be sufficient to meet the indispensable expenses of our organization, particularly in Palestine.

With this in view, the Committee planned for public meetings and propaganda work extending over a large part of this country. Most active in this work were Louis D. Brandeis and Dr. S. Levin, a member of the I.A.C. But they were supported throughout by the Federation of American Zionists, which undertook in large part the task of arranging the meetings with the local Zionist organizations; and we are especially indebted for assistance to its zealous Chairman, Mr. Lipsky, and to the efficient Secretary of our own Committee, Mr. Perlstein. Among the active speakers were other members of the Executive Committee, including Dr. Stephen S. Wise, Dr. J. L. Magnes, Professor Gottheil and Miss Henrietta Szold.

We found throughout the country among different classes of Jews a distinct friendliness towards our Palestine project, and a welcome reception to our Zionist propaganda. The results were satisfactory. For we were able in the first three months to raise more than one-half of the sum which we had set out to secure. But the financial return was not the sole, or indeed the main success of our efforts.

Our chief satisfaction lies in the fact that we have been able to attract to our cause men not hitherto associated with Zionism, and who promise to become active workers. We are convinced that America offers great possibilities, and that further efforts will meet with ever more encouraging results.

Second: After our Committee had been at work for a few months the accumulated information which came to us from various sources convinced us that, in spite of the war the Inner Actions Comite, and the general organizations in the several countries had been able to continue, or to resume, to a far greater extent than we had deemed possible, their activities in Zionist affairs, and that it would be feasible for us to communicate far more frequently than we had expected with the I.A.C. and its members. Since October 1914 it has, therefore, been possible for us to communicate quite frequently with the members of the I.A.C. remaining in Europe. The fortunate presence of Dr. S. Levin has greatly facilitated our communication. It was our special effort throughout this period to get into regular communication with Dr. Arthur Ruppin, as head of the Palestinian Amt at Jaffa, and this we have succeeded in doing frequently, although not without difficulties. We are particularly indebted to Mr. Lewin-Epstein, the Treasurer of the Provisional Committee, for our success in maintaining communications with Palestine, he having devoted himself to this task with great zeal. Our efforts have resulted in our obtaining gradually an ever better understanding of conditions of the organization in Palestine, as well as of the Zionist organizations of Europe; and we feel now in a position to plan more intelligently and systematically the work before us.

Third: Before the month of October had closed, we found that the catastrophe to Jews resulting from the war, had assumed even greater dimensions than we had originally expected. Our Provisional Committee was therefore obliged to extend its activities far beyond the cause of Zionism itself. The fearful distress of the Jews which developed in eastern Europe and in Palestine compelled the Jews of America to take up the work of general relief, and the broader Jewish problems incident to the war.

Members of the Provisional Committee therefore assumed a prominent part in the financial work of the American Jewish Relief Committee which has assumed the task of affording relief to the Jews of all countries suffering from the War. Mr. Brandeis was Chairman of the Committee on organization of the American Jewish Relief Committee, and later became the Chairman of its Executive Committee for New England. Dr. Harry Friedenwald is the Chairman of the Committee in Baltimore, and Mr. E. W. Lewin-Epstein and Dr. J. L. Magnes have been among the most active members of the Executive Committee,—Dr. Magnes becoming the Chairman of the Palestinian Relief Ship Committee, which was organized under the direction of the American Jewish Relief Committee. And at Boston, Jacob DeHaas and other

Zionists have been among the most active and efficient members of the American Jewish Relief Committee.

Fourth: In respect to relief work in Palestine, the Provisional Committee has been particularly active. Early in September, even before the organization of the American Jewish Relief Committee, the Provisional Committee joined with others in providing the fund of $50,000 which was sent to Dr. Ruppin, in response to a request from the American Ambassador, Mr. Morganthau [*sic*], to meet immediate needs in Palestine. Of this sum the contribution of the Provisional Committee was $12,500, the contribution being rendered possible through the generosity of Mr. Nathan Straus. Committees for the distribution of this sum were formed in Jaffa, Jerusalem and Haifa,—Dr. Ruppin and Dr. Aaron Aaronsohn being Zionist representatives of that Committee. The money was taken to Palestine on an American war ship under an arrangement made by Ambassador Morganthau [*sic*]. His son-in-law, Mr. Maurice Wertheim, was placed in charge, and proceeded to Palestine to make arrangements for proper distribution.

Fifth: The economic needs of Palestine which we hoped would in some part be met by the transmission of the $50,000 became far more severe upon Turkey's participation in the war. Almost insuperable obstacles were placed upon imports into and exports from Palestine; and Judaea, where our colonies are in the main situated, became the seat of military activities. The political dangers in which the Jews were subjected in Palestine, as a result of the war, were also considerable and caused us great concern. Thanks particularly to the friendly attitude of the American government, and the great zeal of Ambassador Morganthau [*sic*] at Constantinople, we were enabled to maintain our communications with Palestine; and also to transmit money and food to Palestine. Too much in praise cannot be said of the assistance rendered to us by the Federal Government in this connection. Through the facilities thus obtained we were able to transmit to Palestine the funds from various sources, and for various purposes:

a) The Provisional Committee has transmitted funds to maintain Zionist institutions.

For this purpose we have transmitted to date $24,700.

b) For relief purposes in Palestine and for Palestinian Jews, refugees at Alexandria, the Provisional Committee has transmitted from its funds, gathered directly for that purpose to date $24,500.

It has also transmitted from funds collected by the American Jewish Relief Committee and the Central Relief Committee to date $40,000 approximately.

c) The Provisional Committee also transmitted to Palestine to date $90,000 for individuals or institutions there. These funds have been sent to it for that purpose by at least [3500] different individuals.

Of this amount $75,000 was received directly by the Provisional Committee, and $15,000 received through the American Jewish Relief Committee.[2]

Sixth: Information received by us late in January convinced us that there was such difficulty in procuring provisions in parts of Palestine, that provisions should be sent direct from America, in order to avoid the possibility of actual starvation. The Zionist leaders therefore undertook to arrange that a relief ship be sent from America to Palestine, and steps were taken to raise money and obtain other contributions for a suitable cargo of food, and to charter a ship for that purpose. The movement was inaugurated by securing an offer of $50,000 for this purpose by Mr. Nathan Straus. The American Jewish Relief Committee, through the special efforts of Dr. Magnes, made large grants for this purpose, and the Zionist organizations in forty of the cities and towns became active in raising contributions either of money or provisions. In this movement Mr. Jacob DeHaas of Boston, and Nathan D. Kaplan and Mr. Shulman of Chicago, have been particularly helpful. The difficulties met in securing a ship were, however, very great, and appeared to be at the moment almost insuperable. At this point the American Government was induced to grant us, without compensation, the opportunity of sending 900 tons of food to Palestine on the Vulcan, which sails on March 10th for Jaffa. Mr. Louis H. Levin of Baltimore, a man of wide experience and ability, will proceed on the Vulcan, as a representative highly satisfactory to all interested in securing this shipment. He will be accompanied by Mr. Samuel Lewin-Epstein,[3] son of our faithful associate, Mr. E.W. Lewin-Epstein. The provisions consigned on the Vulcan will not be distributed exclusively to Jews. The other needy inhabitants of Palestine will also receive a fair share.

The money collected for the relief ship to Palestine is far in excess of the amount required for the shipment by the Vulcan, and it is purposed to make a further shipment to Palestine later.

Seventh: America undertook also by other means to meet the economic difficulties under which Palestine is laboring.

Oranges have constituted the chief article of export from the Jewish Colonists. The principal markets for oranges were Liverpool, Egypt, Russia and Australia. When Turkey entered the war, the colonists were precluded from shipping oranges to any of these ports. It was necessary to find some other market. For this purpose Mr. Samuel Pewsner [4] of Haifa undertook a journey to America to see whether it were possible to establish a market for Palestinian oranges here. To make a test, several thousand cases of oranges were sent to America. A special committee was formed in order to introduce them here, and through the efforts of this Committee the oranges were sold for a sum sufficient to defray all expenses in America, and leave a sum of about $9,000 for transmission to the colonists.

The result of this shipment, however, cannot be accepted as establishing in America a profitable market for oranges, as the high price obtained for these oranges rested in part upon the philanthropic desire of the purchasers to relieve Palestinian conditions. Efforts to open a market in America were, however, soon frustrated by the order issued by the Turkish Government prohibiting further exports of oranges from Palestine.

Eighth: Under direction of Dr. Ruppin, Mr. Pewsner has also occupied himself here in developing the Achoosa movement, and there is reason to believe that his effort will have reasonable success.

Ninth: Mr. Pewsner has of late been engaged in the effort to secure a loan for the orange planters of Palestine to enable them to meet the expenses of the next year. Through inability to export oranges, the colonists have lost probably 1,500,000 francs, and have thereby lost also the means of taking proper care of the plantations during the coming year. In this way they are confronted with the loss of the plantations themselves which are valued at 15,000,000 francs. Dr. Ruppin has reported that $120,000 should be raised on loans payable in five years with interest, to be secured by the joint obligations of the planters. A Committee has been formed which will endeavor to raise in America at least a substantial part of the loan required.[5]

Tenth: Two representatives of the Jewish National Fund, Dr. Kaplan Kaplansky and Dr. Epstein, have come to the United States to advance the interests of that organization. We have reason to hope that their work will produce good results, and that America's contribution to the fund will be materially increased during the coming year, in spite of the prevailing depression in business.

Purim[6] was made a Flag Day by the New York office of the National Bureau for the purpose of raising contributions for the J.N.F. The results were quite satisfactory.

Eleventh: It does not seem feasible to discuss at any length the political conditions in Palestine. Reports which came to us the latter part of December, throughout January and a part of February were very alarming in character. The more recent reports were far more reassuring. We believe that the Government at Constantinople has now become satisfied of the loyalty of the Zionists, and the Central Government there has shown entire friendliness to Zionists. The already favorable outlook is, we believe, largely due to the efforts of the Governments of both the United States and Germany, and their ambassadors in our behalf. We can speak most definitely of the action of American officials, both in Washington and in Constantinople, who have done everything that is possible to protect our interests.

Twelfth: For the present we consider it our special duty in America to meet the needs of the Palestinian institutions, and to strengthen the Federation of American Zionists. We believe that the indications are for a greater growth of our Zionist organizations here. It is probable that the number of shekel payers in the present year will be at least twice that of last year.

Thirteenth: We venture to express the hope that you also will do whatever is possible to strengthen your own organization, and the number of shekel payers; that you will make every effort to collect the needed funds for the Palestinian institutions, and also sums applicable to Palestine relief. We are fortunately in the position of being able to aid you in the transmission of any funds that may be raised for this purpose.

Fourteenth: There are needed for the maintenance of the general organization, and of the institutions in Palestine, annually at least 600,000 francs. At least one-half of this sum should be raised in countries other than the United States, and we feel convinced that with proper effort on the part of yourself and others this can be done.

Fifteenth: Even if peace should come, the ravages made by the war will call for the utmost effort from us to repair losses which have been made, and the needs of the situation cannot be met without strengthening of the organizations in all of the countries.[7]

Very cordially,

1. This letter was sent to various members of the Inner Actions Committee, to officials in Palestine, and to various branches of the Federation in the United States.

2. The figures cited vary in different copies. The letter to Ruppin has the amounts written in by Benjamin Perlstein; the form letter to the Federations has the figures typed in. In general, the amounts in the Ruppin letter are two to five thousand dollars less than in the form letter distributed domestically.

3. Samuel (Rehabiah) Lewin-Epstein (1893–1942) worked with his father for the Carmel Wine Company. In 1917 he became recruitment officer for the Palestinian Jewish Legion, and from 1932 to 1939 was director of the Palestine office of the American Economic Commission. He was considered one of the outstanding economic authorities on Palestine, and at the time of his death was in the United States as an advisor to various Zionist agencies.

4. Samuel Joseph Pewsner (1878–1930), an English pioneer in Palestine, had been the youngest delegate to the First Zionist Congress. He had settled in the Haifa area in 1905.

5. American and English Zionists managed to arrange a loan of 600,000F, one-third each to be put up by American Zionists, Jacob Schiff and Baron Rothschild, the whole to be guaranteed by the Jewish Colonial Trust and the Jewish National Fund. The British government, worried about the drain on its currency reserves, refused permission to Rothschild, and then a variety of factors led Schiff to decline.

6. Purim is the Jewish holiday celebrating the saving of the Jews in ancient Persia by Queen Esther (Hadassah) from a decree condemning them all to death.

7. The letter was signed by LDB and Schmarya Levin.

To Benjamin Perlstein

March 12, 1915 Boston, Mass. [Brandeis Mss, Z 3-2]

DEAR MR. PERLSTEIN: At yesterday's Committee meeting you called attention to the fact that from time to time deserving Zionists who had been or were faithful Zionist workers, came to the office in great need, and under such circumstances that it seemed proper to relieve them by gifts or loans in small amounts; and you asked for an appropriation of $100. or $150. to meet such needs as might arise from time to time.

Upon discussion it appeared that the adoption of that proposition was not desirable, particularly because the demands were already too heavy upon our Emergency Fund, but mainly because the knowledge of the fact that the Committee was so relieving individuals would be sure to lead to applications for greater in number than could possibly be met. You then stated that you had, out of your own pocket, personally given such relief to the amount of $40. or $50.

Confirming the statement of intention I then expressed, I am now sending a check to you personally. Out of this check I wish you would reimburse yourself for such amounts as you have paid out for the above purpose since you became Secretary. The balance I wish you would apply also as a purely personal matter in your name from time to time to relieve such worthy Zionists as you may think best. It seems to me that all amounts paid ought to be put in the form of loans, even though the chance of their repayment might be small. If any amounts are repaid, they become a part of that personal fund of yours applicable to this purpose.

Check for $150. enclosed.   Yours very cordially,

To Benjamin Perlstein

March 12, 1915 Boston, Mass. [Brandeis Mss, Z 3-2]

MY DEAR MR. PERLSTEIN: I wish that you would take up with Mr. Lipsky, and with such others as you and he think it desirable for you to consult, the following matters about which I conferred with him yesterday:

First: In order to make local Zionist organizations effective, we must give them something else to do than merely to collect money for specific purposes. And we must arrange too, in order that they effectually collect money, that they are kept constantly in touch with Zionist development, and acquire an increasing knowledge of Zionist facts. It is inherent in Zionism as an intellectual movement that our members should study and in one form or another our affiliated organizations should be the equivalent of study clubs. It is also clear that there must be worked out some scheme of organization by which the organizations will be kept alive and active, and be constantly in touch with the central organization. This could be done particularly through organizers, and through frequent communications. The system of the reports recently introduced by Mr. Lipsky is in line with that suggestion. The plans for such organization and stimulated activity must, however, be carefully worked out with careful estimates of its cost. When that is done, we shall be in a position to take up the matter of raising the funds necessary to carry on that work.

Second: I was much impressed with Mr. Lipsky's statement of the possibilities in developing the Young Judaean work, and I think you should together work out also a definite plan for development in that connection. But equally important also is the working out of a definite plan through which our Young Judaeans shall graduate into the local Zionist organizations. Just how that can be accomplished is a subject that deserves much and careful study.

As soon as these plans shall have been worked out, I shall be glad to take them up for careful consideration with you and Mr. Lipsky before they are submitted to the whole committee.

Yours very truly,

To Benjamin Perlstein

March 12, 1915 Boston, Mass. [Brandeis Mss, Z 3-2]

MY DEAR MR. PERLSTEIN: In order to render more efficient and orderly the meetings of our Committee, it seems to me necessary that we adope [*sic*] and follow quite rigidly rules for the conduct of our meetings.

I wish that you and Mr. Lipsky would prepare, with such consultations with Mr. Lewin-Epstein and Miss Szold as you may deem advisable, a draft of such rules, and have the same ready before March 20th, so that we can discuss them on the morning of the 20th, and submit them for consideration to the meeting on that evening. The rules should of course be as few and simple as will meet the situation.

Among other things I suggest the following:

First: Hour and duration of meeting. The time should be selected after the evening meal. We should certainly avoid the interruption and strain like that of last evening. The rules should also contain a suggestion as to the length of the meeting,—say, three hours,—or whatever you decide would ordinarily be required so that members may know how long they are presumably [to] be engaged.

I am inclined to think that there should also be a fine for absence or tardiness. Our financial and industrial institutions impose a penalty for absence or tardiness in the failure to secure the director's fee. Our members of course cannot be subjected to such a penalty, but instead a fine could be imposed, as is done in several quasi-political organizations. It seems to me that the irregularity in attendance is intolerable. It wastes much time for many people, and prevents the proper attention to business.

Second: There should be a rule by which no motion, calling for the expenditure of money, should be considered except upon, say, six days' previous notice, and filing with the Secretary a brief statement in writing setting forth the reasons upon which the application is made. In connection with this written statement there should then be prepared by the Secretary a memorandum of the facts bearing upon the application,—such as previous votes of the Committee, previous expenditures, funds available etc. There should also be definitely adopted the plan which we began to act upon of requiring a circulation before the meeting of written reports of all matters to be considered at the meeting which can be deemed important.

Third: Order of business.

The Secretary should make up for consideration with the Chairman prior to the hour of the meeting a memorandum of the order in which business is to be considered.

First should be taken up those matters which the Chairman and the Executive Committee deem urgent. Then matters as to which memoranda have been circulated among the members. Then reports of Committees, and perhaps last of all, communications; that is, the reading of letters and other data which members deemed desirable to bring to the attention of the fellow members; except so far as those particular communications might properly be submitted as a part of the discussion of a motion.

Fourth: Arrangement should be made so no members attending the meeting, except in case of extreme urgency, be interrupted either by telephone or call.   Yours very truly,

To Judah Leon Magnes

March 13, 1915 Boston, Mass. [Brandeis Mss, Z 5-1]

MY DEAR DR. MAGNES: *First*: I have yours of the 9th enclosing copy of the report from the Zionist leaders in regard to the distribution of relief funds in Austria. I am glad to know that you will take this matter up with the Distribution Committee.

Second: In regard to the Relief Ship work, and the two votes passed at the Zionist Committee meeting yesterday before you arrived, namely:

a) Directing the Treasurer not to make any payments to the American Jewish Relief Committee on account of any purchases, or expenses, without further order of our Committee.

b) To ask that the $5,000 sent to the American Jewish Relief Committee be returned in view of the decision of the American Jewish Relief not to pay us yet the $12,000 for transmission.

I wish to make this explanation in order that there may be no misunderstanding:

1) When the Zionists joined with the A.J.R.C. in undertaking to send the relief ship to Palestine, the subscriptions pledged were as follows:

Nathan Straus	$50,000
Zionists	25,000
A.J.R.C.	25,000
Jacob H. Schiff	25,000

and under your directions the local A.J.R. Committees were directed to raise certain funds, under which Kansas City sent, say $5,000, Boston, $10,000, and others varying amounts, which were understood to be in addition to the $25,000 originally appropriated by the A.J.R.C. Later under date of February 12th, you informed me that the American Jewish Relief Committee had appropriated a further sum of $75,000, if required. It was understood that merchandise would be accepted in lieu of cash for any of these contributions.

In addition to the above there were to be contributions from the non-Jewish sources.

2. The chartering by us of a ship for the moment not being feasible, the shipment of 900 tons or more by the Vulcan was substituted. And it was understood that the provisions sent by the Vulcan should be borne wholly by the Jews; the shipments by the non-Jews to go later. The contributions in food stuffs collected by the Zionists and shipped to the Vulcan aggregated $25,000 as appears by memo annexed prepared by Mr. Perlstein. The payments of cash obtained through Zionists and transmitted direct to the A.J.R.C., so far reported, amount to $850.00 as appears by memorandum annexed prepared by Mr. Perlstein.

3. The cost of the food stuff purchased and paid for primarily through Mr. Warburg's office was $55,000. It was arranged also by you with the A.J.R.C. to supply Mr. Levin with an additional amount of $10,000 to purchase supplies in Palestine; and that the Zionist Committee should furnish of this amount $5,000, and the A.J.R.C. $5,000.

4. The present plan is to send later a relief ship, or at all events certain food shipments, if opportunity is afforded, to Palestine; and if that does not seem feasible, to send in lieu thereof, money to Palestine.

5. Mr. Lewin-Epstein reported that at a special meeting of the A.J.R.C. held on the 11th, called on very short notice at which neither you nor I were present, it was voted to make payment for the food stuff purchased on the basis of forty percent of the original contributions; that is, take $20,000 from Nathan Straus; $10,000 from J. H. Schiff; $10,000 from the A.J.R.C. etc.; and that some vote was passed declaring that if the relief ship were not arranged for within a reasonable time, the balance of the money appropriated by the A.J.R.C. should be sent to Russian Poland. No copy of the minutes of that meeting have yet reached me.

6. It seemed to the Zionist Committee that if the action taken

by the A.J.R.C. was in accordance with Mr. Lewin-Epstein's report, it was certainly not in accordance with what was required by the understanding under which we cooperated. The cost in merchandise and money of the shipment by the Vulcan should be borne by the various contributors pro rata; and it seemed proper also that the additional fund put at the disposal of Mr. Levin should be treated likewise as a part of the cost of the Vulcan's shipment. If this were adopted, it is clear that the Zionists, whose pledge was, at most, 20 percent of the aggregate contribution,—that is, 20 percent of $125,000,—have already contributed far more than their pro rata of the total cost of the Vulcan, including the $10,000 put at the disposal of Mr. Levin; and that properly in order to adjust the accounts as between the several contributors, we ought to have paid to us in cash by the A.J.R.C. a very considerable sum.

7. Of course it is not very material to us whether we have over paid or not our pro rata, except for the fact that the A.J.R.C., according to the report of the vote made by Mr. Lewin-Epstein deems itself apparently free to withdraw the appropriations made; and therefore to deny to Palestine the full amount for relief purposes, which it and the various local organizations appropriated for that purpose. The net result of this would be to reduce materially Palestinian relief fund, unless the A.J.R.C. should be content at some future time to grant additional amounts. It seemed to the Zionist Committee that we had no right to jeopardize Palestinian relief by acquiescing in what was reported as the action of the Executive Committee of the A.J.R.C.

8. As matters relating to the relief ship have been conducted so largely through you, it seems to me that this matter ought to be taken up by you and Mr. Lewin-Epstein with the A.J.R.C. and the exact situation expressed in a letter, so that there may be no question but that we shall be entitled to have provided for purposes of Palestinian relief the full amounts which have been hitherto appropriated by the various committees for Palestinian relief.[1]   Very truly yours,

1. Relations between the Provisional Committee and the American Jewish Committee had been strained since the emergency meeting at the end of August 1914. The A.J.C., which had always considered itself the spokesman for American Jewry, resented the assumption of leadership by the P.E.C. In

addition, the Zionist propaganda alienated many members of the A.J.C., as did the emerging push for a congress. The P.E.C., on the other hand, was beset by the problem that it really did not have access to large donors. The P.E.C. felt that it was not getting sufficient credit for the money it raised, and that an insufficient amount was being utilized for relief work in Palestine.

To James S. Harlan

March 15, 1915 Boston, Mass. [Brandeis Mss, NMF 71-5]

MY DEAR MR. HARLAN: When I last saw you you asked that I should suggest the amount of my compensation for services in connection with the rehearing in the Five Percent. Advance Case.

You and the other Commissioners know just what I have done in it, and I should very much prefer that you should fix the amount of compensation. Whatever you fix will be satisfactory to me.[1]

I tried to see you when I was in Washington last month, but you were out of the city.   Very cordially yours,

1. See LDB to Harlan, 2 April 1915.

To Alfred Brandeis

March 16, 1915 Boston, Mass. [Brandeis Mss, M 4-1]

MY DEAR AL: It is great to have your telegram following Jennie's postal. Two hours seems a long time in town for you as yet. Don't overdo, & enjoy to the full the blessing of your beloved farm. A stern doctor may order you off for change of air anytime.

You may tell Otto [Wehle], Harry dined at the house Sunday evening.

I was at Portland—Zionizing.

To Philip Barnet and William Berman

March 19, 1915 Boston, Mass. [Brandeis Mss, Z 12-1]

DEAR MR. BARNET: [1] Pursuant to the vote at the conference of the Zionist Stalwarts at the City Club last evening, you are directed as follows:

First: To form a Zionist Association of the local residents of Cambridge, which shall be independent of the Harvard Zionists; and for this purpose to confer with Mr. Berman, Edward J. Cohen, 330 Western Ave., Cambridge, Jacob Promboin, 495 Windsor Street, and A. L. Webb, Old Lo Building, and upon conference with them to select your chairman. A copy of the Federation Constitution, and a model set of By-Laws are herewith enclosed.

Second: You and your associates are authorized to fix the amount of the dues at such amount as you deem wise. It is believed, however, that dues should not be fixed at less than $3.00 per annum.

Third: The membership should be increased so that on May 1st it will be not less than 25; on June 1st not less than 50; and at the date of the Convention you should be able to report not less than 60.[2]

Fourth: A weekly report should be made in writing to this Bureau not later than 4:00 p.m. on the Monday of each week beginning March 28th, reporting the progress made during the preceding week.

Fifth: This Bureau stands ready to render at all times any aid, including clerical assistance, and we shall be glad to confer with you concerning the development of the work.

Very truly yours,

1. This letter is an example of numerous directives sent out to local Zionists urging them to form Zionist clubs.

2. The 1915 convention of the Federation of American Zionists was to take place in Boston the following June, and LDB was eager for the local Zionists to make a strong showing.

To Edward Justin Bromberg

March 19, 1915 Boston, Mass. [Brandeis Mss, NMF 66-1]

MY DEAR MR. BROMBERG: [1] I regret it will be impossible for me to attend the meeting at the Vestry in the Union Park Street Temple this morning; and I therefore beg you to express my regret and my greetings to the Committee of Jewish Musicians.

Make clear to them that what we are doing is not merely raising funds to relieve the war sufferers, but that we are building for the future. We are calling upon them as upon all Jews to unite with us in work which should in large part put an end to the misery which is constantly confronting our people. What we do now is but an earnest of what we hope to accomplish later. Now we must unite the Jews, and make clear to them also that it is through the establishment of a publicly recognized, legally secured home for the Jews in Palestine that our unity must find expression. Though we are scattered throughout the world, the re-establishment of our people in Palestine will unite us all for the great common purpose of developing Jewish life, and making it in the future, as it has been in the past, one of the greatest contributors to the world's civilization.   Cordially yours,

1. Edward Justin Bromberg (1864–19[?]) was the New England manager of the General Life & Accident Insurance Company; he held several minor political offices in Boston and was active in Jewish and Zionist affairs.

To Arthur Menahem Hantke

March 19, 1915 New York, N.Y. [Berlin Office]

DEAR DR. HANTKE: We are surprised at not having received up to date of writing, acknowledgements of our last remittance of $2,000.[1]

Re the Hilfskomite[2] for suffering Jews in Poland, we have received a copy of the favor which you forwarded to the N.F. on the 25th of February. We regret that in matters of such importance we are unable to have your direct guidance. We have already mentioned in a former letter that it would be desirable for our correspondence to be more frequent, as this would assist in the furtherance of our aims.

We have received from Copenhagen the information that the Copenhagen office is making shekel appeals to the various Federations, which does not fall in with our agreement as stated in yours of February 3rd 1915. We have already written in detail on this matter to Mr. Motzkin[3] and I should be grateful for your reply. In these unsettled times it would be unadvisable for the Federations to be instructed from more than one source, as this can only result in confusion amongst the individual Federations. We still hold it expedient, that the Zionist organizations in all English speaking countries should receive their instructions from us.[4]

Unfortunately the American Steamer "Vulcan" did not leave here on the 10th of March, but a few days later. We are indeed sorry that the foodstuffs will not arrive in Palestine until after Pesach,[5] however, the matter was beyond our control.

We are glad that the American government afforded us the opportunity of fulfilling at least part of our projects, relative to the relief of Palestine with foodstuffs.

With Zions greetings [6]   Very truly yours,

1. See LDB to Victor Jacobson, 26 March 1915.
2. "Aid committee."
3. Leo Motzkin (1867–1933), a Russian-born Zionist, was the director of the Copenhagen bureau during the war. At the Paris peace conference he was secretary, then president, of the Comité des Délégations Juives. From 1925 until his death he served as chairman of the Zionist Executive. See Simcha Kling, "Leo Motzkin," *Herzl Year Book*, 2 (1959): 228–51.
4. This letter is indicative of the continuing effort of the Americans to gain a large measure of control over the world movement.
5. Pesach, or Passover, is the Jewish holiday commemorating the deliverance of the Jews out of Egyptian bondage.
6. This letter was also signed by Schmarya Levin.

To Julian William Mack

March 19, 1915 Boston, Mass. [Brandeis Mss, Z 7-1]

MY DEAR MACK: At the last meeting of our Provisional Committee there was created, at my suggestion, an Advisory Council. The purpose was to create a body of advisors which should in the first instance include Felix and yourself. I am purposing at the meeting tomorrow evening to have you and Felix formally elected members of the Council. Then I want to take up from time to time with you and Felix those who should be added. The cause demands and deserves the cooperation of our ablest Jews of high standing.

I am to be in New York all day tomorrow and probably most of the time at the Zionist headquarters, 44 East 23rd Street. If you are free tomorrow I should be glad to have some time with you. Won't you call me up there?   Very cordially,

To Joseph Barondess

March 20, 1915 New York, N.Y. [Brandeis Mss, Z 12-3]

DEAR MR. BARONDESS: The Provisional Committee considers it necessary, for the purposes of Zionist organization and propaganda, that conventions of the various national Zionist organizations be held at the same time and at the same place. Will you, therefore, see to it that your Executive Committee [1] is called together at the earliest possible date and passes a resolution favorable to the holding of your convention in the City of Boston on a date to be fixed by the Provisional Committee, some time during the last week in June.

I am writing to like effect to the Federation of American Zionists, the Hadassah and Young Judaea.[2]

We are also calling a meeting to be held on the morning of April 14th, at 10 A.M. at the Provisional Committee's offices, Aeolian Building, West 42nd Street, of the members of the Executive Committees of these various organizations to discuss the action to be taken in this connection, and various other matters of importance concerning Zionist organization and propaganda. We hope that all of the members of your Executive Committee will be present, and beg that you will at once send notices to this effect to each of them.

Will you kindly let me hear from you as soon as you have a definite decision from your Executive Committee on this point, also let me know which of your members will be present.

With Zion's greetings,   Very truly yours,

1. Of the Sons of Zion.
2. All of the groups agreed to this request.

To Alfred Brandeis

March 21, 1915 New York, N.Y. [Brandeis Mss, M 4-1]

MY DEAR AL: Delighted to have your report of condition. But Go Slow. As father used to say: Qui va piano etc.[1]

42 years ago today we arrived at Trieste. It was a happier time despite the impending crises.

Has the Jitney [2] invade[d] Louisville? It is striking our trolley lines with consternation. Stephen Edwards [3] tells me 200 swooped down on Providence like an army of locusts the other day & struck terror into the security laden trolley system which the New Haven bought the worthless equity of for 24 millions.

Yesterday saw Rudolph Spreckels (who is trying to engineer purchase by State of California of the Western Pacific). He says the San Francisco trolleys are losing $2,000 a day by the 500 jitneys which have sprung out of the Earth, mostly light Fords. If this continues the trolley companies will be squealing as hard and shrilly as the railroads.

I speak in Hartford this evening—then back to Boston.

1. "He who goes quietly, etc."

2. LDB is referring to the earliest form of automotive taxis.

3. Stephen Ostrom Edwards (1855–1916) was a prominent Providence, R.I., attorney. He was president of the Providence and Worcester Railroad Company.

To Charles Henry Ingersoll

March 22, 1915 Boston, Mass. [Brandeis Mss, NMF 68-1]

DEAR MR. INGERSOLL: [1] Thank you for sending me a copy of your letter of the 18th to Mr. Houston.[2]

Of course I thoroughly disagree with you that to reorganize businesses so as to put an end to the horrible waste which is occurring throughout the year through irregularity of employment, is not constructive. Obviously it does not cover the whole ground. No one remedy that men are proposing will remove all the ills of society, or all of any one ill of society.

Possibly you may have read my article on "The Road to Social Efficiency" in "Business A Profession", (published by Small, Maynard & Co., 15 Beacon St., Boston) which deals further with the unemployment question. Your reference to the land seems to me to point again to an exaggeration of what the single tax, or nationalization of the land can do. I am myself a strong believer in nationalization of the land; but I am a thorough disbeliever in the contention that through nationalization of land the Millennium will come, and to my mind the exaggeration of the effectiveness of a remedy throws discredit upon the arguments in its favor.

I am very glad to note that your concern is "doing everything possible to equalize employment." Would you mind giving me the data showing to what extent you have succeeded in equalizing employment in your business?   Very cordially yours,

1. Charles Henry Ingersoll (1865–1948), a cousin of William H. Ingersoll's, was affiliated with him in business and was the secretary-treasurer of the watch company. He also was active in numerous trade organizations, as well as in those advocating the single-tax idea of Henry George.

2. Ingersoll had written to Herbert S. Houston that while LDB's expose of business waste and inequity was splendid, he was disappointed with LDB's "remedy" of regularizing employment. "Moving jobs around," he noted, "might smooth off some of the rough edges of the problem and change its appearance or form, but would surely leave its substance." The only real answer lay in providing more jobs, and for this he referred back to the idea of nationalizing land.

To Richard James Horatio Gottheil

March 23, 1915 Boston, Mass. [Brandeis Mss, Z 6-1]

MY DEAR MR. GOTTHEIL: Replying to yours of the 22nd.

What I said to Professor Harper was in substance this: [1]

First: What I said was not for publication, as I deemed it important, in view of my position as Chairman of the Provisional Committee, not to make public expression of my views on this subject:

Second: That there seemed to me no logical connection in Russia between autocracy and anti-semitism or liberalism, and the absence of anti-semitism. That in view of the course of events in Russia, I did not believe that we had any reason to assume that the treatment of the Jews would be materially improved through the Liberals, unless indeed the Liberals should, as a plank in their platform, specifically declare in favor of equal rights for the Jews.

Third: That the persecution and discrimination to which the Jews were subjected in Russia, particularly through the limitations of education, and the restrictions upon their occupations, residence and movements were such that they should call forth expressions of moral indignation on the part of the non-Jews in America; and that any expressions by Americans which could be construed as an apology for existing conditions was harmful to the cause of humanity.

Fourth: That there were undoubtedly differences of opinion among Jews here and elsewhere as to whether our course in abrogating the Russian treaty was helpful or harmful to the Jews in Russia; [2] and that likewise there might be differences of opinion as to what course pursued here in respect to restrictions in Russia might be helpful or harmful, but, that I felt no confidence in our ability to gauge the probable results, but that in view of the standards prevailing in Russia, and the devious course of their statesmanship and diplomacy, I had little faith in our ability to accomplish desired results through any course that involved an apology even by way of repression of our opinions as to the quality of their actions, and that we had no reason to expect to obtain results through patient forebearance.

In my opinion Professor Harper will do our cause harm unless he couples his expressions of admiration and hope for Russia, with proper expressions of indignation at their treatment of the Jews and exhortation in our behalf.   Very cordially yours,

1. Samuel Northrup Harper (1882–1943) was professor of Russian language and institutions at the University of Chicago (which his father had founded), and wrote widely in the periodical press about Russia. He had spoken to LDB, and carried off the belief that LDB "saw no hope of a betterment in [Russian Jewish] conditions even if a liberal government were established in Russia." Gottheil noted that he too was upset over this view, since it was impossible for either the United States and/or Palestine to absorb any large-scale emigration from Russia.

2. In protest against Russia's persecution of its Jews, the Taft Administration in 1912, after intense pressure from Louis Marshall and the American Jewish Committee, had terminated the Russo-American Trade Treaty.

To Adolph Lewisohn

March 23, 1915 Boston, Mass. [Brandeis Mss, Z 7-1]

MY DEAR MR. LEWISOHN: I wish to thank you for the copy of "Liberal Judaism and Social Service", which you were good enough to send me.[1] Mr. Lewis's treatment of the subject is, as you suggest, informing and scholarly.

It is his striving for righteousness or social justice, which the prophets taught, and the true democracy which developed throughout the centuries, which fitted the Jew especially for American citizenship, and which convinced me that the espousal of Zionism was demanded by loyalty to America as well as to the Jews.

Possibly you may care to read what I have said on this subject in my address on "Zionism and Patriotism", of which I enclose a copy.   Cordially yours,

1. Harry Samuel Lewis, *Liberal Judaism and Social Service* (New York, 1915).

To William Phillips

March 23, 1915 Boston, Mass. [Brandeis Mss, Z 3-2]

MY DEAR MR. PHILLIPS: The Department of State and the Navy Department have so generously supported the efforts of the Jews of America to relieve the distress from which their bretheren [*sic*] in Palestine have been suffering that I venture to call upon your Department for a further service:

The needs of the Jews in Palestine are so great, and the demands upon the Jews of America for other relief so extensive, that we are not able to obtain for Palestine all the funds that will be required.

We are informed by friends in Russia that there are many Jews there who would gladly contribute funds for Palestine relief if the Government should grant permission to make collections for that purpose; and it has been suggested that such consent might be granted if a request were presented by our Government, and arrangements made that the money collected be transmitted to America for subsequent distribution.

It should be distinctly understood that the money collected would be used wholly for relief purposes, and it has been suggested that it would be satisfactory to our friends in Russia if the money collected there should be sent to me personally, upon the understanding that I would undertake to have it properly distributed.

If you see no objection, I should be glad to have this request submitted to the Russian Government.[1]

Very truly yours,

1. There is no answer from Phillips in the Brandeis Mss, but arrangements were never made to allow transmission of money from Russia to Palestine.

To Norman Hapgood

March 24, 1915 Boston, Mass. [Brandeis Mss, NMF 62-1]

DEAR NORMAN: In the report of our Consul General from Argentina dated January 11, 1915 appears the following:

"The year 1914 will undoubtedly be memorable for the railroads as one of heavy expenses and small earnings. In the first six months of the year the roads lost heavily because the 1913–14 harvest was poor and the excessive rains during the season prevented the grain from being transported over the roads to the railroads. In the second half of the year the traffic receipts of the Great Southern showed a decline of $2,800,000, the Buenos Aires Pacific $2,600,000, the Central Argentine $2,-680,000, and the Buenos Aires Western $660,000. The French railways (Entre Rios Railways) and the Central Cordoba system also report heavy losses. The Posario-Mendoza road went into bankruptcy and the Argentine Railway Co. passed back into the control of the Central Cordoba and Entre Rios Railways because of the inability of the Farquhar syndicate to cover its guarantees to these two companies. The Railroad of the Province of Buenos Aires (National) also lost heavily during the past year."

Has Argentina been subjected to a "Democratic administration", "tariff reduction", or other "so-called progressive legislation"? [1]   Cordially,

1. Hapgood used this ammunition to attack Elihu Root "and all the lesser tories" for blaming the business slump on reform legislation. See "To Mr. Root" in *Harper's Weekly*, for 10 April 1915.

To Benjamin Perlstein

March 24, 1915 Boston, Mass. [Brandeis Mss, Z 3-2]

MY DEAR MR. PERLSTEIN: *First:* Replying to yours of the 23rd enclosing draft of letter which you propose to send to the Presidents of the various railroad companies: [1] I am returning the draft with some corrections. I suggest that this letter be signed by Dr. Magnes. I should not wish to make any requests myself of any of the railroad companies, in view of the fact that I have criticized them considerably in the past, and more recently have made some statements which they have published as supporting their contentions.

Second: You have seen Dr. Levin's letter of the 23rd referring to the visit of Dr. Tschlenow and Dr. Sokolow, and I am enclosing the latter's original letter to Dr. Magnes of March 11th, and Dr. Magnes' letter to me of March 23rd. Dr. Magnes's suggestion is that we should cable; "Leave advisability or time your coming here to your own discretion."

In view of what has been said to me by Mr. Lipsky and others, I feel some doubt whether it is desirable to indicate any desire to have Dr. Tschlenow and Dr. Sokolow come here in the very near future. I assume from the letter that they could not sail before April 7th, and that they, therefore, would be here presumably until about May 15th. While here they would necessarily occupy a considerable part of the time of our leading workers, and in view of the fact that we have devoted the most of our time during the last three months to questions of relief, it is important that we should continue without serious interruption our propaganda and organization work. If Sokolow and Tschlenow should come to America early in June so as to remain over the Convention period, they might be of considerable service to the cause then. By the time they arrive we should have our organization work much better in hand. The subject seems to me one that requires careful consideration on which all of the members of our Committee should have an opportunity to express their views, and since Sokolow and Tschlenow would not sail in any event before the 7th, I suggest that this subject be made the first for discussion at next Saturday's meeting. And I should be very glad if in advance of the meeting the Office Committee would discuss the matter with Dr. Levin and Dr. Magnes and Miss Szold and others who may be available.[2]   Very truly yours,

P.S. Mr. Lipsky is to be congratulated on the March Maccabaean, which shows a marked advance.

But, wouldn't it be better to have the editorial page with the index of contents etc. begin the number?

1. The letter dealt with possible special arrangements and rates for delegates attending the Zionist convention in Boston.

2. The two men did not visit the United States during the course of the war.

To Henrietta Szold

March 24, 1915 Boston, Mass. [Brandeis Mss, Z 12-2]

MY DEAR MISS SZOLD: Thank you for the full report on the typographical plans connected with the Hadassah Bulletin.[1] If it would be agreeable to you to adopt the 10 point leaded for your Bulletin, I shall be glad to pay personally the extra expense for a year, which I understand to be at the rate of $4.00 a month for 1,000 copies.

I am quite sure that after it has been in use for a year your members will be more than ready to pay the added amount required to defray the cost of a more effective and presentable Bulletin.   Very truly yours,

1. See LDB to Henrietta Szold, 4 March 1915

To Wilbur John Carr

March 25, 1915 Boston, Mass. [Brandeis Mss, Z 2-1]

MY DEAR MR. CARR: [1] Public officials are more apt to hear of complaints than of praise, and I think, therefore, that you and Secretary Bryan ought to know of the very high appreciation expressed on all sides of Dr. Glazebrook's work as Consul at Jerusalem.[2]

Enclosed copies of communications which came to our office are but a few of the expressions of gratitude which have reached us.[3]   Very truly yours,

1. Wilbur John Carr (1870–1942), a career foreign service officer, was director of the State Department's Consular Service from 1909 to 1924. From 1924 to 1937 he was an assistant secretary of state, and after that he served briefly as ambassador to Czechoslovakia until his retirement in 1939.

2. Otis Allan Glazebrook (1845–1931), after a thirty year career as an Episcopal priest, had been named consul in Jerusalem; he served in that post until 1920, when he was appointed to the consulate in Nice, France.

3. LDB enclosed letters from Ephraim Cohn–Reiss and S. Raffalowich, two members of the Zionist organization in Palestine, praising American efforts to alleviate the war-caused distress.

To George Rublee

March 25, 1915 Boston, Mass. [Brandeis Mss, NMF 66-3]

MY DEAR GEORGE: I am glad to have yours of the 26th [sic],[1] and to know that the outlook seems reasonably fair to you.

I note that Joe Cotton is on an Advisory Committee of the Chamber of Commerce. It would seem to me that it might be best to leave him there for the present without any professional connection with the Commission. After the Commission has become accustomed to his advice and learned to value him properly, it might be possible to secure him as chief counsel, when the appropriations become adequate.   Very cordially yours,

1. Rublee's letter, actually dated 22 March, reported that the Federal Trade Commission had decided to employ Raymond Stevens as counsel. He also noted that it might be possible in the future to elevate Stevens to the position of head counsel, "unless some altogether exceptional man like Joe Cotton can be secured."

To Victor Jacobson

March 26, 1915 Boston, Mass. [Copenhagen Office]

DEAR DR. JACOBSOHN [sic]: First: Re Remittances to Constantinople.

Pursuant to the cable message notifying us that the last $2,000 sent for Lichtheim [1] had not been received, I caused inquiry to be made, and found that there had been an error in transmitting the money. The cable read: "For Zionist" instead of reading "for Lichtheim," and it is possible, therefore, that Henry [Morgenthau] has not paid over the money yet. We telegraphed him on the 24th to pay the money to Lichtheim. If it should be found that he had previously paid over the amount to Dr. Ruppin, we will send another $2,000 for Lichtheim. Meanwhile we are awaiting a cable reply from Henry.

Second: Re *Conference*

We regret that it will not be possible for us to send a representative to the Copenhagen Conference called for April 15th, although we should have considered it of importance that we have a representative there.[2] At present we are heavily burdened with work. The problems which we have to meet are increasing from day to day; and it is imperative that we should devote our best efforts to building up the organization in America, and increasing our membership. The number of men on whom we can rely for efficient work is relatively small, and it would be necessary to send one of our ablest representatives to the Conference if he were to be useful to you, and we need at the present here all the able workers whom we can command.

We are confirmed in the wisdom of this decision by another consideration: Our friends Jechiel [Tschlenow] and Nahum [Sokolow] have notified us recently that they were prepared to come to America for a few weeks, and are awaiting our telegraphic reply. We are, however, of the opinion that it would be much better that Jechial and Nahum should postpone their trip to America until the beginning of June. This would enable them to attend the Conference, to whose deliberations they would contribute much, and put them in possession of the views of the various members. And they would be better able to advise us of the situation and plans after having attended the Conference. Between now and the beginning of June the general situation may have cleared somewhat, and we may all be better able to determine wisely our future course. For the above and the following additional reason we desire Jechiel and Nahum to postpone their coming. The annual Convention of our Federation will take place the last week of June. It would be a great aid to our propaganda work in America to have them present. We shall therefore, cable Jechiel and Nahum that we deem it advisable for them to postpone their visit to America until June. As we cannot attend the Copenhagen Conference, we deem it desirable to express our views on the problems which seem to us at present to be most important:

1. We are of opinion that all our work in Palestine should be continued without interruption. This is of the greatest importance because our Zionist institutions there must be protected at all hazards.

2. Our attitude towards Turkey should be one of strict loyalty, and of complete friendliness. We must at all times bear in mind that our bretheren [*sic*] in Palestine are Ottoman subjects, and that reason alone must be conclusive as to the attitude of the Zionist organization.

3. Whatever may be the eventualities, it is clear that our own safety and success demands a thorough and effective organization. In that way only will it be possible for us to act as representatives of our people, and there must be complete unity within our ranks.

We do not suggest in detail how this perfected organization shall be attained. The detailed measures to be adopted will depend upon the conditions of the several countries in which we are working. But as to the fundamental principles there should not be any difference, and all members wherever resident should recognize these principles as binding.

Third: Re *Loan to Plantations*

With respect to the loan to planters, we are unfortunately still without reply to our letter to Jechiel and Nahum. We are apprehensive that in case Edmond [3] or the ICA [4] decline to participate, our American friends will decline to afford assistance and we beg, therefore, that you will use every effort to induce Edmond or the ICA to assume at least a part of the amounts requested.

Fourth: Re *Shekels*

On November 3, 1914, the E.A.C. wrote us: "Bei dieser Gelegenheit bestaetigen wir den Empfang Ihres W. Schreibens vom 16. Oktober, in dem Sie bezw das Provisorische Komitee um eine naehere Erlaeuterung unseres Telegrammes "Billigen den Druck von Schekelblocks" ersuchen. Dieser Brief des Provisorischen Komites hat uns Veranlassung gegeben, die Sachlage noch einmal zu erwaegen, und wir sind zu dem Entschluss gekommen, Ihnen und dem Provisorischen Komitee auch in organizatorischer Beziehung Vollmacht zu erteilen, soweit die aussereuropaeischen Laender in Frage kommen. Wir bitten Sie daher, sich mit einem

Schreiben an die nachstehend aufgefuehrten Adressen zu wenden und unseren dortigen Gesinnungsgenossen mitzuteilen, dass sie die neuen Schekelblocks von Ihnen bekommen werden, und dass die zionistischen Gelder im Einverataendnis mit uns an das Provisorische Komitee absuliefern sind." [5]

Communications received from our Copenhagen office indicate that the Copenhagen office also is sending the organizations of these several countries requests for shekels, Dr. Levin has already written to the Copenhagen office calling attention to this matter, but, we desire to express again our opinion that it would be wiser that the instructions to all Zionists in English speaking Countries should be transmitted through our Provisional Committee. This we believe would lead to more satisfactory results. At all events the present situation is one which leads to confusion, and the matter should be cleared up without delay. With heartiest greetings to all our friends,[6]   Very cordially yours,

1. Richard Lichtheim (1885–1963), the scion of a wealthy, assimilated Jewish family in Copenhagen, had become a Zionist in his student days. He edited the official Zionist paper, *Die Welt*, before the war, and during the conflict he served as the organization's representative in Turkey. Elected to the Zionist Executive in 1921, he resigned two years later in opposition to Chaim Weizmann's leadership. During the 1930s he tried to warn world Jewry about conditions in Germany, and in 1933 he settled in Palestine himself.

2. See LDB to Chaim Weizmann, 11 October 1914.

3. Baron Edmond de Rothschild (1845–1934), despite frequent declarations of opposition to political Zionism, was a major factor in developing the colonies of Palestine. He donated millions, bought 125,000 acres, established wineries, and sent numerous agricultural experts to the land. His officials were often accused of trying to manage too many details of the colonists life and labor, but on balance he almost single-handedly supported the Yishuv for many years. Toward the end of his life he accepted the honorary presidency of the Jewish Agency.

4. The Jewish Colonization Association (I.C.A.) had been founded by Baron Maurice de Hirsch in 1891 to assist Jews from Russia and Rumania to settle in Argentina. After the Baron's death, the I.C.A. began to assist Palestinian colonies, and in 1899 Baron de Rothschild transferred title of his colonies, plus fifteen million francs, to the I.C.A. which after being reorganized as the Palestine Jewish Colonization Association (P.I.C.A.) in 1924, played a major role in supporting the Yishuv until its disbanding in 1957.

5. "On this occasion we confirm the receipt of your letter of 16 October in which you or the provisional committee asked for a closer explanation of

our telegram 'We confirm with the printing of the Shekel blocks.' This letter of the Provisional Committee has given us cause to consider the state of affairs once again, and we have come to the decision to authorize you and the Provisional Committee also in organizational matters as far as the countries outside of Europe are concerned. We asked you, therefore, to write to the following addresses and inform our fellow believers there that they will get the new Shekel blocks from you and that in agreement with us the Zionist money is to be sent to the Provisional Committee."

6. This letter was written by Shmarya Levin in German and translated into English to be jointly signed by LDB and Levin.

To Chaim Weizmann

March 28, 1915 New York, N.Y. [Weizmann Mss]

FELLOW-ZIONIST: [1] We sent you under date of the 18th a report covering the activities of the Provisional Committee for the preceding six months. That report showed that our activities in the past were directed mainly to these ends:

First: To the raising of funds with which to sustain the institutions in Palsetine.

Second: To the raising of funds to meet the pressing relief of residents of Palestine.

The first of these obligations must in any event be a continuing one. The demand of the Palestinian institutions which must be maintained without interruption can be met only if Zionists in your country, as in others, make generous contributions both during the war, and for some time after peace is declared. For we cannot expect any large contributions for the Palestinian work from Russia, Germany and Austria-Hungary for sometime to come. We therefore urge that you redouble your efforts to raise funds for the support of our Palestinian institutions and transmit such funds to us as soon as possible.

Third: We purpose now, however, to address ourselves also to another task in which we beg that you will join throughout your Country. It will be impossible to effectively carry forward our work in and for Palestine without a large increase in the membership of our organizations, and effect a great strengthening of the organization.

Our own experience during the last eight months convinces us that at no time have conditions been so favorable for propaganda work. The great mass of the Jews are intensely interested in the problems presented. What they want is a clear understanding of these problems, and a knowledge of the detailed facts bearing upon our work and its accomplishment. The leaders of all of our organizations should realize the opportunity which now exists. The statesmen of the several countries have shown through unmistakable utterances their recognition of the fact that the Jewish problem is one requiring solution; and there are also strong indications that they recognize that its solution is indissolubly connected with Palestine. The obligation rests upon us of redoubling efforts in behalf of our cause to enable us to act effectively when the opportunity arises.

Fourth: We venture to call your attention again to our letter of September 8, 1914 to the effect that all collections for Palestinian purposes and payments of shekel monies should be sent to the Provisional Committee. Collections for the National Fund should, for the present, be sent to The Hague.

We hope to hear from you soon,

With best greetings,[2]   Very cordially yours,

1. This letter was sent to Zionist leaders in several countries.
2. This letter was cosigned by Schmarya Levin.

To Sidney S. Conrad

March 29, 1915 Boston, Mass. [Brandeis Mss, NMF 73-4]

MY DEAR MR. CONRAD: [1] I thank you for your courtesy in suggesting that I become a member of the Kernwood Country Club. Mr. Kirstein had already spoken to me about this matter before he left for the West, and I then told him that I felt I ought not to become a member of a Country Club because there is no possibility of my ever using it. Indeed I resigned only within a year from the Country Club in the neighborhood of Dedham where I live, and of which I had been a member for nearly twenty years, because throughout that period I had found that I was unable to avail myself of its privileges.   Cordially yours,

1. Sidney S. Conrad, a Boston businessman, wrote to LDB as chairman of the membership committee of the newly formed club. From his letter it

seems that the Kernwood Club was to be primarily a Jewish club, and they wanted LDB because he was "the first citizen (among our people)" in the area.

To George Rublee

March 29, 1915 Boston, Mass. [Brandeis Mss, NMF 66-3]

MY DEAR GEORGE: I agree with the substance of what Mr. Hines says.[1] The waste of time and money both to the Commission, to counsel, and the parties incident to present method of transacting business is very great. Care should, however, be taken to insure:

First: A memorandum of the contention of counsel, including under certain circumstances, offers of proof.

Second: Where there are clear issues of fact, and particularly questions of creditability of witnesses, a verbatim report of the testimony.

I think there are also many occasions where there are not formal hearings, where the Commission, in order to protect itself and the public, should have a stenographic report of what occurs at the conferences.   Sincerely yours,

1. The Federal Trade Commission had requested advice regarding the procedures it should adopt. Rublee had sent to LDB a copy of the answer received from Walker Downer Hines (1870–1934), chairman of the executive committee of the Atchison, Topeka & Santa Fe Railroad, who later headed the wartime U.S. Railroad Board. Hines noted that the practice of keeping verbatim records of all hearings resulted in voluminous records, most of which were useless. He suggested that all oral hearings be kept informal, with memoranda summarizing the consensus of the meetings drawn up at the end. He also noted that expert accountants for the Interstate Commerce Commission spent weeks examining records, and then their findings were buried in the verbatim transcript; instead, he suggested that the examiners submit a report of their findings in accounting form, and they could then be questioned on the findings.

To James S. Harlan

April 2, 1915 Boston, Mass. [Brandeis Mss, NMF 71-5]

MY DEAR MR. HARLAN: Replying to yours of the 30th:

I should have preferred that the [Interstate Commerce] Commission fix my compensation without suggestion,[1] but since you ask for one, I will say that $1250. would, under the circumstances, seem proper compensation covering both services and expenses.

Very truly yours,

1. See LDB to Harlan, 15 March 1915.

To Alfred Brandeis

April 3, 1915 New York, N.Y. [Brandeis Mss, M 4-1]

DEAR AL: Came over on the midnight [train] re Zionism which brings me here every week now. Otherwise have been very much homekeeping of late.

Susan arrived Wednesday evening. She and Alice departed for Dedham after dinner to stay until Monday. Elizabeth to join them this evening for dinner, but I fear it will be a poor Easter Day as to weather. For the first time, almost since February, there is a very grey sky and decided threat (or hope) of rain. So bright a March was unrecorded in our country & unlike you, we bore the cold without much grumbling.

It is fine to know you are progressing steadily, but go slow still. Ein Mann in der sechziger [1] must behave quite differently & if he does, ought to be good for 20 years of satisfactory living, at least in our family.

The Charles Crane[s] & others were in to dine Tuesday;—Ex Gov. Bass & another Monday to talk B & M legislation; Thursday Susan had a dinner party, and Margaret Adler [2] was in for a few days visit. Sunday evening I talked to the Harvard Law Society. So the evenings were pretty well filled, but I have been taking things easy of late.

1. A man in his sixties. Alfred had turned sixty only ten days earlier.
2. Margaret Adler was a daughter of Felix and Helen Goldmark Adler.

To Benjamin Perlstein

April 6, 1915 Boston, Mass. [Brandeis Mss, Z 3-2]

MY DEAR SIR: *First:* I am enclosing copies of my signature as you requested.

Second: I assume that the Office Committee is preparing, and will send me a draft of the proposed letter to Rabbi Berlin.[1]

Third: Confirming our talk over the telephone: I understand that Ambassador Morganthau [*sic*] has cabled that $100,000 is needed to maintain Palestinian institutions; that he himself is prepared to give $50,000, and wants the other $50,000 raised here; and that Mr. Warburg has been anxious to ascertain immediately how much our Committee will give; that Dr. Wise is cabling Mr. Morganthau [*sic*] for information, and that you will cable Alexandria.

My feeling is that the American Jewish Relief Committee should apply to this purpose the full amount originally appropriated for Palestine, and not expended; and I assume that they would have available a large part of the $50,000. They certainly would if they included in the amount appropriated the extra $75,000 which they later agreed to advance if it should be necessary. If they cannot be made to give the whole $50,000 now, possible [*sic*] Nathan Straus might contribute something on account of his $50,000 pledged. It seems to me highly probable that the need is not for Zionist institutions or colonies, but for the other local needs at Jerulsalem. Our own institutions must have been largely provided for by the money already sent; and the need of the colonies should be met by the 600,000 francs loan, which I trust is progressing satisfactorily.

I understood from you that we had $12,000 in relief funds available. My feeling is that we ought not to pay over any part of these funds unless and until it becomes clear that they are needed, because there will certainly arise unexpected needs, for which we shall not find it so easy to raise money a little later. It seems to me that we ought not to put a heavy tax upon the financial resources of our Zionist associates at present.

Fourth: As I stated, I expect to be in New York on Friday, and shall call at the office in the morning. It is barely possible that I may have to be in New York as early as Thursday.

Fifth: Mr. DeHaas is of the impression that the English Federation has found some difficulty in transmitting funds to Palestine, and that it would be desirable to notify them that we will act as transfer agent without expense to the English organization.

Very truly yours,

1. Rabbi Meyer Berlin (1880–1949), later called Meir Bar-Ilan, was the commanding figure of religious Zionism. Born in Lithuania, and a renowned Talmudic scholar, Berlin devoted his life to blending the piety of orthodox Judaism with the modernity of Zionism into the Mizrachi movement, of which he became the acknowledged world leader. He had recently emigrated to the United States, and a problem had arisen about giving him official status in the Provisional Committee, since he was not an American citizen. In 1926 he moved to Palestine, and played an important part in the birth of the state of Israel. See Meir Bar-Ilan, *Kitvai* (Jerusalem, 1950). For the letter to him, see LDB to Berlin, 25 April 1915.

To Henry Hurwitz

April 7, 1915 Boston, Mass. [Hurwitz Mss]

DEAR MR. HURWITZ: I am much gratified at receiving the pledge from the various members [of the Menorah Society] who met on April 4, 1915 at 600 Madison Avenue, and who have agreed to volunteer their services to the Zionist cause, placing themselves at my disposal for the period of six months to act as I direct.

I desire to give careful consideration to the possibilities of utilizing the services of the several men in specific work, and will write you later my conclusions in this respect.

Meanwhile, however, there is one class of work which each of the men named is requested to perform continuously during the period of six months, and which they should undertake at once, namely—By personal propaganda among those with whom they come into contact to secure adherents to the Zionist cause, and, if possible, enrollment as members of one of the Zionist societies. Special effort should be made by each to secure adherents of men in his own profession, and to develop, as far as possible, a plan for his personal work in this direction. All of the men named are University men, and the enrollment of membership would be naturally as members of the University Zionist Society about to be formed.

We should have from each of the men a report on the first day of each month covering the activities during the preceding month, which should give a list of the names and occupations of the persons whom it was sought to win for the Zionist cause, and the results of the attempts in each instance. The study of these lists will be made as presented with a view to aiding the propaganda work. An effort will also be undertaken to aid that work by

bringing the men into connection with other Zionists in their profession, with whom they can co-operate in the work of propganda.

Very truly yours,

To Robert Marion LaFollette

April 7, 1915 Boston, Mass. [Brandeis Mss, NMF 56-2]

MY DEAR BOB: The New Century Club of Boston gave a banquet
last evening in honor of the New England Representatives who
sustained the President's veto of the Immigration Bill. At that banquet I delivered the enclosed address, which I thought you might
care to have for the Magazine.[1]

We were much disturbed to hear that Robert is not well, and
hope he is much better now.[2]   Most cordially yours,

1. On 28 January 1915 Woodrow Wilson had vetoed the literacy test for
immigrants. His veto message argued that a literacy test is not a fair measure
of prospective citizenship and would prevent the government from providing asylum for those escaping from tyranny. Had such a test been in effect
in earlier years, the President noted, the country would have been deprived
of many of its finest citizens. The message is in the *New York Times,* 29
January 1915. At the banquet LDB praised the veto, but noted that they were
celebrating not a victory but an escape, since opponents of immigration
would certainly bring it up again. The literacy test, he charged, was not
really a test of literacy, but of privilege, and it was especially designed to
discriminate against immigrants from southern and eastern Europe. LaFollette
published the speech as "Twin Evils of Literacy Test," *LaFollette's Magazine,* 7 (April 1915): 8. See next letter.

2. Robert LaFollette, Jr. would be critically ill all summer after tonsillitis
developed into a streptococcic infection. He withdrew from the University
of Wisconsin and came to Washington to live with his family.

To Prescott Farnsworth Hall

April 8, 1915 Boston, Mass. [Brandeis Mss, NMF 56-2]

DEAR MR. HALL: [1] I do not recall that I reached any definite
conclusion on the question of immigration restriction "some years
ago"; [2] and I am sure that I had not given the subject sufficient
consideration to entitle me to an opinion until last year after I was
led to take up the subject by the pendency of the Burnett Bill

and Ross' book.[3] My study then convinced me that the departure from our fundamental principles involved in immigration restriction would bring to America and to civilization far more of loss than of gain.   Very truly yours,

1. Prescott Farnsworth Hall (1868–1921), a Boston attorney, was founder and secretary of the Immigration Restriction Committee. For the activities of Hall and the League, see Barbara M. Solomon, *Ancestors and Immigrants: A Changing New England Tradition* (Cambridge, Mass., 1956).

2. Hall had written that he recalled a conversation with LDB several years earlier in which he thought LDB had been won over to the literacy test; he was very disappointed, therefore, to read of LDB's speech at the New Century Club. (See preceding letter.)

3. Edward A. Ross's book, *The Old World in the New: The Significance of Past and Present Immigration to the American People* (New York, 1914), was a hysterical attack on the "new" immigrants of eastern and southern Europe. Their entrance into American life, Ross argued, served only to debase our politics, make our cities ungovernable, weaken the purity of our blood, disfigure our once handsome appearance, and lead our formerly proud and intelligent civilization to chaos, confusion and ultimate extinction.

To Judah Leon Magnes

April 9, 1915 Boston, Mass. [Magnes Mss]

DEAR COMRADE: [1] As one of the delegates of the Extraordinary Conference held August 30th last at which this committee was organized, I am enclosing for your attention a report covering the first six months' operations of our Committee. This report is necessarily brief, but it will show you how large a part America has played in saving the Palestinian Jewish settlements.

You will note that the Committee was compelled to extend the scope of the work originally planned. The critical situation which developed in Palestine through the war created imperative needs which no other organization in the world seemed capable of meeting.

Your Committee, therefore, devoted a large part of its efforts to those activities which were necessary to save the Palestinian Jewish settlement, and to relieve the distress of our brethren there. Consequently a relatively small part of our time could be spent either on strengthening organization work, or upon the raising of funds to sustain the Zionist institutions in Palestine.

The time has now come when we must devote our attention to strengthening Zionist work:

First: To the Emergency Fund.

This is necessary if the Zionist Institutions in Palestine are to continue.

Second: To perfect and extend the Zionist organization.

This is necessary if the cause we have at heart is to succeed.

We are making preparation for a new campaign for the Emergency Fund, and will lay before you soon a plan for renewed activity on your part in this connection.

Meanwhile we urge you to devote your efforts unremittingly to strengthening your local Zionist organization. Utilize to the full the intense Zionist sentiment which has been created throughout the Country. Enroll new members in your local organizations. Be not content with merely securing shekel payers, but insist upon getting also members who will stand up and be counted as workers in our organization,—men and women who are ready to make the sacrifice necessary for our success.

The Committee relies confidently upon your personal effort to secure these results, and requests that you report to us on May 1st the results of your activity.

With Zion's greetings,   Yours very Cordially,

1. This letter, together with a six-month report, was sent to everyone who had attended the 30 August 1914 meeting at the Hotel Marseilles. The "report" which is mentioned was identical to the letter sent to Arthur Ruppin and others, 8 March 1915.

To Alfred Brandeis

April 13, 1915 Washington, D.C. [Brandeis Mss, M 4-1]

DEAR AL: Riggs Bank matter called me here from N.Y. just as I was about to leave for Boston after 4 days in N.Y.[1]

This is a terrible interruption of Zionist activities, which had become chronic.

At Penn Station met Abe Flexner who was Baltimore bound.

Spoke at an anniversary celebration at Dr. Wise's Free Synagogue Sunday.[2] After the show a Mr. _____ who "had not seen me since we were at the High School together" & whose daughter is

I think married [to] one of the Taussigs [3] of Wm. Taussig & Co—
& Boston Molasses Co—came up to greet me. Apparently he lives
& has bought land in N.Y. Who is he? [4]

Beautiful green here but it is still a bit cool.

New York "ist ganz aufgelebt" [5] since the stock market rise.

1. A battle had been brewing between Secretary of the Treasury McAdoo
and the Riggs National Bank of Washington, which was affiliated with the
Morgan-First National Bank interests in New York. McAdoo had decided to
spread government deposits around among the smaller "country" banks and
had withdrawn large sums from the government accounts normally held by
the Riggs. The bankers charged that McAdoo was playing politics, and the
Riggs Bank threatened a lawsuit against the Treasury Department. There is
no good published account of this battle, in which McAdoo ultimately prevailed, although he did leave some money in the Riggs. Details can be found
in the Charles Sumner Hamlin Diaries in the Library of Congress, and in
John Broesamle, "William Gibbs McAdoo: Businessman in Politics, 1863–
1917," (Ph.D. dissertation, Columbia University, 1970). LDB was called in
several times by McAdoo for advice in the controversy.

2. LDB had spoken at the eighth anniversary of the Free Synagogue on
11 April. He praised Stephen Wise's contribution to Zionism and then discussed the idea of Palestinian colonies as laboratories for social experimenta-
tion. The success of these colonies, he said, had moved Zionism from the
realm of dreams to that of facts. Details of the speech can be found in *The
New York Times*, 12 April 1915.

3. Charles William Taussig (1896–1948) had inherited the family sugar and
molasses manufacturing business.

4. Probably Simon Adler, a New York real estate dealer.

5. "Is completely revived."

To The Editor of the *Boston American*

April 17, 1915 Boston, Mass. [Brandeis Mss, NMF 16-4]

DEAR SIR: [1] The Sullivan bill to arbitrarily reduce the price of
gas in Boston to seventy cents after June 30, 1916 should be
killed. It involves a breach of faith. It is unjust. It is oppressive.
It is reactionary. It would destroy the Sliding Scale Act of 1906.
It is the most successful piece of progressive legislation enacted in
Massachusetts during the last ten years. Under that Act the price
of gas in Boston has been reduced from $1.00 (or more) per
1,000 feet to 80 cents; and what is even more important to the
people than this great saving,—"gas was taken out of politics."

The series of lobby scandals at the State House and City Hall, which followed one another in rapid succession throughout twenty years, were, by this Act, completely eliminated; and under honorable management the Company gave to the community efficient service amidst general satisfaction.

If it be true that the Boston Company ought to sell gas for less than 80 cents after June 30, 1916, the Sliding Scale Bill provides the method for properly determining that fact,—namely:—by referring the question for decision to the Gas and Electric Light Commissioners.

To arbitrarily fix now by legislation the price of gas in Boston at 70 cents, and so limit the return on the capital stock, is both unwise and unfair. The people would in the end be the chief sufferers from such an act of injustice.[2]

Yours very truly,

1. Identical letters were sent to all the other Boston–area newspapers.

2. The bill, identical to the one which Sullivan had introduced a year earlier (see LDB to George W. Anderson and to Henry G. Wells, both 27 June 1914) was defeated in the House of Representatives on 21 April 1915, by a vote of 35-92.

To Meyer Berlin

April 25, 1915 New York, N.Y. [Brandeis Mss, Z 12-3]

MY DEAR RABBI BERLIN: *First:* I am enclosing, for the information of your Body, a report on the activity of the Provisional Executive Committee for General Zionist Affairs, for the first seven months of its existence. This report is necessarily brief and incomplete, and for this reason, we are not prepared, as yet, to publish it in the press. but it may be read before your Body, if, in your judgment, it is advisable. At any rate, you are at liberty to report on such portions of it as you see fit.[1]

Second: We were very glad to learn from you that it is the sense of the Mizrachi in America that it will bear to our Committee the same relation as your European organization bore to the Inner Actions Comite. Now that this relation is definitely established, it will be possible to proceed to a closer cooperation on the part of your Body with our Committee. The lack of this understanding, until recently, has been due to the fact that the Mizrachi has, unfortunately, not been able to have its representative present at our meetings, than rather to any lack of intent of cooperation on the part of your organization. We trust that, in the future, it will be possible for you to have your representative present at all our sessions, and assist us by his council in our deliberations.

Third: There has been, on the part of many members of your organization, a lack of full knowledge as to the significance of our various Funds. Permit me to make this clear to you: —

(a) *The Emergency Fund.*

At the time our Committee was organized, we did not fully realize the situation in Europe and Palestine, nor did we conceive the possibility of Turkey entering into the war. Based on our expectations, we estimated that the sum of $100,000 would be necessary to maintain the Zionist institutions in Palestine, and our central organization. (Under the heading of "Zionist Institutions", we class not only such institutions as were directly under the supervision and control of the Actions Comite, but such other semi-Zionist institutions as the Hashomar, Tachkemoni, Bezalel, etc.[2]) We have since found that our estimates were far too low, and that we shall need, for the next two years, at least an additional $100,000 beyond our original budget. The Emergency Fund, out of which the purely Zionist expenses are met, has also been called upon, from time to time, to meet demands of a relief nature.

(b) *Relief Fund.*

When, in the first week of our organization, reports came from Palestine, informing us of the dreadful economic situation there, we immediately found it necessary to divert a portion of our energies from the work in behalf of the Zionist institutions and organizations, to meeting the call for relief there. From our first funds, as you will find from our report, we subscribed $12,500 to a $50,000 relief fund, which was cabled on September 2nd. All through the past seven months, we have divided our energies between the purely Zionist work and the relief work, as witness our activities in behalf the relief shipment on the "Vulcan". In the Relief Fund we place all such contributions as the donors specify their desire that it be used for relief, and not for any Zionist purpose.

(c) *Transfer Fund:*

Believing that the most efficient form of relief and help was of the sort extended by families and relatives, and finding that all ordinary methods of transmission of money into Palestine had been broken down, our Committee, at great sacrifice of energy and expense, arranged for a regular safe and rapid method of transmission to Palestine. We announced this service and extended it broadcast throughout the country. The Central Relief Committee also avail themselves of our facilities. For all of the expenses in connection with this, there was no charge made to any of the transmittors or to the other committees, but all expenses were borne by our Committee. Although the public would have been glad to pay for this service, we felt it our duty to encourage this form of self-help, and to facilitate matters for those of small means, we felt it highly advisable to lend every encouragement possible to make these remittances as large as possible.

Fourth: In the collection of the relief funds we sent, through our Committee or other Committees, the reports throughout the country show that individuals, prominent in the ranks of the Mizrachi, have done very valuable work and have been instrumental in raising large sums, not only for Palestine, but for general European relief. Your adherents, however, have failed to grasp the extreme importance of the Emergency Fund, from a Zionist standpoint, and to our great regret, contributed very little to this Fund. It is, of course, impossible to trace every contribution, and it is quite likely that in certain cities, Mizrachists joined hands with the general committees and did their share towards the general collection for the Emergency Fund. However, the Mizrachi, as an organization, and the Mizrachi societies, as societies, and the Mizrachi individual members, as individual Mizrachists, have, according to our records, contributed but little to the Emergency Fund. We feel that this is due not to a lack of appreciation of the importance of the Fund, but perhaps to a misconception as to its purpose and disposition. It is quite true that it is the duty of Zionists to help all work in Palestine, but we also have an organization to maintain, and as an organization, we have assumed certain contractual obligations, formerly made by the Actions Comite, which obligations we are honor bound to fulfil, and unless the Zionists of the country support us in these Zionist obligations, we may be forced to repudiate them.

Fifth: It is our hope, therefore, now that the significance of the various Funds has been explained to you, and the importance of the Emergency Fund has been impressed upon you, that the Mizrachi of America will, as an organized Zionist group, do its share in carrying the Zionist burden which this Committee has assumed.

Sixth: The substance of this letter, as well as [3]

1. See LDB to Arthur Ruppin, 8 March 1915.
2. "Hashomar' '(literally "the watchman") was the organization of Jewish workers founded in 1909 for the defense of the Jewish settlements, and was the seed from which the Haganah (the Palestinian militia) grew. "Tachkemoni" was a Mizrachi–operated school in Palestine. "Bezalel" was the school of arts and crafts founded in 1906 by Boris Schatz to promote native craftsmanship, especially of religious articles, and was also the name of the museum Schatz founded in 1906 to collect art and objects related to Judaism.
3. The last page(s) of the copy in the Brandeis Mss are missing.

To Alfred Brandeis

April 25, 1915 New York, N.Y. [Brandeis Mss, M 4-1]

DEAR AL: Nothing from you for a fortnight. Came here on midnight [train] from Washington for a day on Zionism and Garment Workers, & met one of your Louisville Orthodox Rabbis at the Mizrachi meeting.

Alice stayed in W[ashington] and Josephine [Goldmark] is there for a day or two. I go back tonight, for at least a while longer. Perhaps may be here Sunday next again on Zionist affairs, —which are really the important things in life now.

Elizabeth has been spending her birthday with Susan.

To Leo Motzkin

April 29, 1915 New York, N.Y. [Copenhagen Office]

DEAR FELLOW-ZIONISTS: [1]
PALESTINIAN RELIEF:

A large part of our activity is still in connection with relief for Palestine. The news that we have recently received from friends, indicate that the political situation has recently improved very much, and that our bretheren [*sic*] are not in any political danger, but the economic condition is still very serious, due principally to the fact that the country is in a state of war.

The United States collier "Vulcan" bearing one thousand ton of provisions for our brethern [sic] in Palestine, arrived in Jaffa on April 24th, after having stopped at Alexandria to take on an additional thousand ton of sugar, rice and coffee, as requested by our friends in Alexandria.

THE ORANGE PLANTATIONS

The principal concern to us now is the condition of the colonists, especially the orange growers. The war has caused them great material damage, in that it has robbed them of the ability to send their oranges to the European market, and to cultivate their orange groves further. Upon the report of Dr. Ruppin that a sum of 600,000 Francs is immediately necessary, to enable them to cultivate their lands in the ensuing year, a committee was organized here, to raise this amount as a loan fund, secured by mortgages on the orange groves. Through the generosity of a number of Jewish philanthropists, we have been successful in raising a loan fund of 600,000 Francs, and we hope that this will enable us to save the Palestine orange groves from total destruction. In this connection, we must express our extreme appreciation for the efforts of Mr. Samuel Pewsner, of Haifa, who has been in this country for several months for this purpose. Mr. Jacob H. Schiff has, in this matter, rendered us great services.[2] Others who have participated are Julius Rosenwald, of Chicago, Samuel Fels, of Philadelphia, Adolf Lewisohn and Daniel Guggenheim,[3] of New York. A subcommittee has taken over this particular task. The chairman of this committee is Judge Julian W. Mack; the treasurer, Dr. Julius Goldman; [4] the secretary, Mr. Maurice Wertheim. The other members of the committee are Mr. Louis D. Brandeis, of Boston, and Mr. Lewin-Epstein, of New York. The above named gentlemen are giving a great deal of their attention to help Palestine in this respect, and for their excellent work, the new Yeshub, as well as the Zionist organization, is extremely grateful.

PETROLEUM.

The loan fund by itself, however, does not save the situation. The orange groves must be irrigated, and the work requires petroleum for motive power. Unfortunately, there is a scarcity of petroleum in Palestine, and in order to send a sufficient quantity of petroleum there for their needs, it is necessary to get special permission from the various governments. These necessary steps have been undertaken, and in spite of the many difficulties we are encountering, we still have hopes of being able to secure the necessary consent of the governments interested, to send Petroleum to Palestine.

HAIFA TECHNIKUM.

The Hilfsverein has been able, by taking advantage of the war situation, to obtain for itself the Technikum in Haifa. On the 24th of March, the auction sale took place, and, in view of the fact that others were prevented from being present, on the ground that they were enemies, the Hilfsverin was able to purchase the Technikum in a "legal manner", for the sum of Mk. 225,000. Such action on the part of a great Jewish organization, is sure to grieve those who hold dear the interest and honor of their people. We can not believe that the Hilfsverein will persist in retaining this institution in the face of united Jewish public opinion, which is bound to protest against this action, but we must wait until the close of the war, when the other directors will be in a position to take the necessary steps.[5]

ORGANIZATION.

We must, therefore, be on watch at all times, not only to guard against our external opponents, but also to watch against the internal opponents, and the difficult duties imposed upon us to strengthen our organization in these critical times, even more than in times of peace. The more organized and the more united we shall be, the more hopes we can have for eventual success.

We call upon you to strengthen your Zionist organization with all the power at your command, and to build it up, in order that Zionism may have a solid foundation. We cannot lay too much stress on the importance of our cause that the number of Shekelpayers shall increase manifold, and that large funds be gathered by you for the assistance of Palestine and its institutions.

NATIONAL FUND.

We desire to make it clear to you that the Jewish National Fund has its Head office at the Hague, Holland, Bierkade 8a. All monies collected for the Jewish National Fund should be remitted directly to the Head office in the Hague or in accordance with their instructions.[6]

1. This letter, marked as "Report #3," was sent to the various Zionist offices and federations in Europe.

2. Only two days earlier LDB had cabled to London that the Zionist executives would have to decide immediately whether or not to accept this loan. Some of the administrators wanted the sponsors, especially Schiff, to make part of the loan into a gift, but Schiff had refused.

3. Daniel Guggenheim (1856–1930), along with his brothers, had made a fortune in mining and smelting.

4. Julius Goldman (1853–1938), a New York attorney who specialized in corporate law, was a founder of the Federation of Jewish Philanthropies.

5. At the end of the war, the Zionist Organization, with the aid of a gift from Jacob Schiff, bought back the Technikum, which was then expanded into the Technion, which is now Israel's primary engineering and science college.

6. The letter was cosigned by Schmarya Levin, who probably helped draft it.

To Joseph L. Cohen

May 1, 1915 Boston, Mass. [Brandeis Mss, Z 10-2]

MY DEAR MR. COHEN: [1] Passing through the city today I find yours of the 18th. I shall hope to see you at one of the meetings arranged for tomorrow, but as there may not be time to discuss matters, I send this:

First: The Merchavia [*sic*] Situation is one which requires careful study.[2] I shall be glad to have you enter upon that study and to discuss the matter with Professor Frankfurter when you come here on May 6th, if he is able to give it the necessary time. I regret that I shall not be in the city on that day.

Second: We must make available for our members an adequate Zionist library; directing our efforts:

(a) to having the desirable works on Zionism in leading public libraries, like those of New York, and the main universities.

(b) to have some works in public libraries in all communities where there are many Jews.

(c) to provide a reasonable working library at Zionist head-quarters, and at any Zionist Bureau that may be established.

I should be glad to have you take up this subject with a view to preparing lists of books which should be in these three classes of libraries, and ascertain approximately the cost.

As bearing upon this subject I enclose a memorandum sent me by the library of the Hebrew Union College of books in that library, which may be of some aid. I am not retaining a copy and should be glad to have you return this to me for my files.

It will be desirable for you to consult in this connection Professor Gottheil and Professor Friedlander [sic]. I will instruct the office of the Provisional Committee to lend you its facilities to enable you to conduct your correspondence, and otherwise to aid you in such way as may be possible. Let me know also if there are any other of our University men whom you would like to have associated with you in carrying out this work.

Third: Your suggestion that one university man may be attached to each center seems to me a valuable one, and I shall be glad to have you furnish me a list of the centers at which such an arrangement would appear to be advisable,—together with your suggestion as to the line of work to be pursued. I suggest that you consult in regard to this, among others, with Mr. [Alexander] Sachs.

Fourth: I am glad to have Mr. Simon's Zionist pamphlet.[3] We must have available at the earliest possible moment a proper series of pamphlets on this subject appropriate for university men, and also other sections of the community. Your suggestion of ordering 1,000 of these now should receive immediate attention. I wish you would take up this specific matter, and the whole question, with Mr. Lipsky.   Very truly yours,

1. Joseph L. Cohen was a New York Zionist.
2. Merhavya was a workers' agricultural settlement in Palestine founded in 1911 on land bought by the Jewish National Fund. The settlement, drawn up on the plan of Franz Oppenheimer (see LDB to Judah L. Magnes, 10 October 1913), was subjected to harassment and persecution by Arab villagers and Turkish officials.
3. Leon Simon, "Zionism and the Jewish Problem."

To Milo Roy Maltbie

May 1, 1915 Boston, Mass. [Brandeis Mss, NMF 68-2]

MY DEAR MALTBIE: Upon my return to the city I find yours of the 12th.

You are indeed right in saying that the success of the Public Service Commissions will depend upon the character of the appointments. To my mind the qualities requisite for a good Commissioner are greater than those that are required at the head either of a private business or of a public administrative department; and for that reason I have regretted, with so many others, the failure of Governor Whitman to reappoint you.[1]

In talking with Bemis the other day in Washington he expressed hearty concurrence with the suggestion, which I understood he had talked over with Clifford Thorne, of having a man like you retained to represent the public in the valuation work. I trust that that suggestion may be made operative, and if at any time you think a word from me in that connection can be of service, do not hesitate to call upon me.[2]   Very truly yours,

1. On 30 March 1915, Governor Charles S. Whitman had appointed Col. William Hayward (1877-1944) to replace Maltbie on New York's Public Service Commission. Hayward, a New York attorney, became a war hero during World War I and was active in state Republican politics in the 1920s. By removing Maltbie, Whitman removed one of the foremost students of public franchising in the United States. See LDB to Norman Hapgood, 22 December 1914.

2. Throughout the period 1930-1949 Maltbie was to serve once again on the New York Public Service Commission, this time as its chairman.

To Johan Kremenetzky

May 5, 1915 New York, N.Y. [Copenhagen Office]

DEAR SIR: [1] The Central Bureau, in Berlin, has forwarded to us your letter of April 5th, in which you inform us that you will agree to organize a committee, as requested in our cablegram.

I am pleased to inform you that at our last meeting, the Committee has decided to institute a department to do work similar to that we have been doing in Palestine. In the past six months, we have transferred for individuals, to relatives in Palestine, more than $150,000. It is our plan now to comply with the public demand for a means of transmission to relatives in Austria and Galacia. For this reason, we have cabled you, requesting you to organize a committee.

We beg to repeat the information contained in our previous cablegram, and confirm it as follows: We propose to accept money from residents of this country, to transmit to specified individuals in Austria and Galacia. We shall make no charge for our services or expenses, but shall transmit the entire amount. We shall accept remittances only in dollars, and shall rely upon the local committees to give the payees the full amount in exchange, less, of course, such small unavoidable expenses as must be incurred by the distributing committees.

The distribution committee may be any committee now existing, but you must act as the treasurer. We also expect that the distribution committee will deliver the money to the specified person, or else return it to us so that we may refund to the sender.

We shall open an account with you, supplying you with a bulk sum, against which we shall, from time to time, instruct you to pay specified individuals. These instructions will come to you at regular intervals, by mail, and we should ask you to inform us, regularly, as payments are made, or where payments can not be made.

We should appreciate your adding Mr. Robert Stricker to your committee.[2]

We should receive from you, from time to time, information concerning geographical changes.

We believe that we shall eventually receive large sums in this manner. This will give the two-fold advantage of furnishing relief to the suffering in your country, and add greatly to the prestige of the Zionist organization.

Thanking you and your committee for your cooperation, we beg to remain, with Zion's greetings,[3]

Very truly yours,

1. Johan Kremenetzky (1850–1934), a pioneering Zionist and a friend of Herzl, had been placed in charge of the Jewish National Fund which he organized and developed between 1901 and 1907. He used his background as an electrical engineer to help develop the use of electrical power in Palestine after the war.

2. Robert Stricker (1879–1944) was a young Zionist leader and founder of the Zionist student association. He went on to various positions of importance within the movement, being originally allied with Weizmann but breaking with him in the 1920s to help found the so-called Radical Zionist Party.

Stricker was arrested by the Nazis and then released; but he refused to escape, thinking of it as a desertion of his people. He was retaken and he and his wife died in the gas chambers at Auschwitz.

3. This letter was signed by LDB, Benjamin Perlstein, and E. W. Lewin-Epstein.

To Jehial Tschlenow (Telegram)

May 5, 1915 New York, N.Y. [Brandeis Mss, Z 12-3]

Cable immediately nature of Jabotinskys activities and if working harmoniously with you.[1]

1. Vladimir Yevgenievich Jabotinsky (1880–1940) was an assimilated Russian Jew who converted to Zionism as a result of the pogroms at the turn of the century. A brilliant theoretician and spell-binding orator in seven languages, he was constantly in and out of the Zionist leadership. In 1915 he was trying to organize a Jewish legion, against the wishes of the anti-Zionist British Jewish leadership, and also against the inclinations of some of the English Zionists as well (the difficulties to which LDB alludes in this cable). He ultimately succeeded in establishing the unit, which fought with distinction in the latter stages of the war, especially at Gallipoli. In the early 1930s he broke with the world organization to set up a rival Revisionist Zionist group, which demanded both full compliance by Great Britain with the Balfour Declaration and a Jewish state comprising both sides of the Jordan. He further alienated the General Zionists by advocating illegal immigration to Palestine and a more active policy by the Haganah. He died in the United States in 1940 while trying to organize a Jewish army to fight against the Nazis. For his life, see the two-volume biography by Joseph B. Schechtman, *Rebel and Statesman* (New York, 1956), and *Fighter and Prophet* (New York, 1961); see also Joseph B. Schechtman and Yehuda Benari, *History of the Revisionist Movement* (Tel Aviv, 1970).

To Jehial Tschlenow

May 18, 1915 New York, N.Y. [Copenhagen Office]

FELLOW ZIONISTS: [1] The news that we have been receiving, from confidential sources in Palestine, are reassuring in their nature. Upon instructions from headquarters in Constantinople, the local officials, especially in Jaffa and Jerusalem, have greatly changed their tactics towards the Jewish population. The Commander-in-Chief of the Turkish army in Palestina, Djemal Pascha [*sic*], has visited several Jewish colonies, also the Jewish settlement, Tel-A-

Viv, [sic], and the Hebrew Gymnasium at Jaffa. In every place he praised the work, and has thereby made the Jewish population feel much more at their ease.[2]

All our schools in Jerusalem, Jaffa and Haifa are open and functioning normally; also the schools of the Odessa Committee, namely, the Maedchen-Schule in Jaffa, and the Lehrerin-Seminar, that had been closed previously by the Turkish Government, have been re-opened.

The economic situation in Palestine is far from being satisfactory, but it is hoped that the arrival of the Relief Ship in April with one thousand tons of provisions, will, for a time, alleviate the immediate suffering.

The Loan Fund for Orangeries in Palestine, amounting to six hundred thousand francs, has been perfected, as we have previously informed you.[3] Unfortunately, however, the inability to obtain permission to ship petroleum into Palestine is a source of great concern. We are exerting all our efforts to make it possible to ship petroleum to Palestine, and we still have hopes that we shall succeed in getting the necessary permission from the several Governments.

We have received information confirming our worst fears and suspicions as to the reasons of the first evidences of unfriendliness towards the Zionists on the part of subordinate officials in Palestine. Several Jewish elements in Palestine have helped to instigate the official opposition to Zionism. This is confirmed by confidential reports from Berlin, Constantinople and Palestine, and is one of the saddest phenomena of the Goluth.[4] We are, at present, extremely hesitant about making public the information we have obtained, and we are only awaiting the end of the war to do so. Until then, we must exert supreme efforts for the further strengthening and building up of our organization. We consider it, therefore, as particularly important that the Shekel collection for the current year be pursued with great energy.

We hereby call upon you, worthy comrades, to exert your entire energies, first, for a large increase of the Shekel; second, for the collection of funds for the maintenance of our institutions and schools in Palestine, and, third, most important of all, for a greater strengthening of all local and territorial organizations.

With Zion's greetings,

1. This letter, marked "Report #4," was probably written by Schmarya Levin in German, then translated and signed jointly by LDB and Levin. It was sent to members of the Zionist executive in Europe.

2. See LDB to Benjamin Perlstein, 27 January 1915, n. 1.

3. See "Report #3," LDB to Leo Motzkin, 29 April 1915.

4. There had long been friction in Palestine between the Zionists, who emphasized the secular and cultural aspects of a Jewish settlement in the Holy Land, and the ultra-Orthodox Jews, who saw life in Palestine as strictly a religious obligation. This latter group lived on charity (Halakah) collected among the pious in Europe and America, and believed that any attempt to establish a Jewish homeland in Palestine before the coming of the Messiah was sacrilege. Because their normal source of support, the charitable donations collected in the Diaspora (Goluth) had been cut off, they were now dependent upon Zionist funds; despite this, they continued to undermine Zionist enterprises in any manner they could.

To Benjamin Perlstein (Telegram)

May 20, 1915 Washington, D.C. [Brandeis Mss, Z 3-2]

Carbuncle has developed on my face which compels me to cancel New York appointment leaving here direct for Boston Saturday. Strongly urge that Provisional Committee meeting be held Monday also that meetings arranged by Rosenblatt for Sunday and by Gottheil for Monday and Tuesday be held. Wise, Magnes, and Friedlander [sic] cooperating to make them complete success.

To Bernard Abraham Rosenblatt

May 22, 1915 Boston, Mass. [Brandeis Mss, Z 12-3]

MY DEAR ROSENBLATT: I am very sorry you cancelled meeting for tomorrow. It will not be possible for me to attend the Zionist Association meeting June 5th—but don't postpone that. It would be very bad for our movement if the idea should prevail that I am indispensable to a good propaganda meeting.

I am delighted to hear of the notice on your book.[1]

Very cordially,

1. *The Social Commonwealth: A Plan for Achieving Industrial Democracy,* (New York, 1914).

To Nissim Ezra Benjamin Ezra

May 25, 1915 Boston, Mass. [Brandeis Mss, Z 14-3]

MY DEAR MR. EZRA: [1] Upon my return to the office after a some-what prolonged absence I find your most encouraging letter of March 18th.

The present is indeed a time of trial for all Jews; but it is also a time which offers great opportunities. If we but show ourselves worthy of these opportunities, we shall do much towards solving the ages-long Jewish problem.

It was indeed a great encouragement to receive from far off China such substantial evidence of appreciation and support of our great cause. Nothing has done more to hearten us in our efforts.

Very truly yours,

1. Nissim Ezra Benjamin Ezra (1880–1936) had come to China from India as a merchant, and was an active Zionist in the Shanghai Zionist Association. For a third of a century he published *Israel's Messenger,* a Zionist newspaper which appeared twice each month. He had written to LDB praising his leadership and calling him a second Herzl. Enclosed was a contribution from the Chinese Zionists of $700.

To Frank William Taussig

May 25, 1915 Boston, Mass. [Brandeis Mss, NMF 66-3]

MY DEAR FRANK: Replying to yours of the 15th: [1]

I don't know of any one who has paid enough attention to the working of the important trust dissolutions of recent years to give a satisfactory account of the extent to which there has been a restoration of competition. But I think it not improbable that someone formerly connected with the Bureau of Corporations, and now with the Federal Trade Commission may have made such a study. I should suggest your inquiring of George Rublee, who, as you know, is a member of the Commission.

Very cordially yours,

1. Taussig had asked LDB for the name of someone who might write an article for the *Quarterly Journal of Economics* about the recent trust dissolutions, "particularly the Standard Oil and Tobacco cases." He was interested in exploring to what extent competition in those industries had been restored. In the August issue, Taussig published a note, "The Tobacco Industry Since the Dissolution of the Trust," by H. R. Tosdal.

To Benjamin Perlstein

May 27, 1915 Boston, Mass. [Brandeis Mss, Z 3-2]

MY DEAR MR. PERLSTEIN: Replying to yours of the 26th: [1]

First: As to writing the State Department about Galacia [*sic*]: The Times clipping states that Mr. Marshall is in communication with the Department regarding this matter. I am inclined to think we would better defer writing the State Department until we learn what Mr. Marshall has concluded to do. I presume that Mr. Lewin-Epstein can readily ascertain this.

Second: I should not be inclined to make any tender to Mr. Marshall of our services at present. There are almost certain to be misinterpretations of our attitude.

Third: I am planning to be in New York on Saturday, June 5th. I may have to be absent on Sunday, but should expect to came back for a day or two so as to have opportunity of discussing fully matters to be taken up at Convention, and other pressing subjects. I should suggest for the Provisional Committee meeting either Saturday evening or Monday late afternoon and/or evening.

Very truly yours,

1. Perlstein had enclosed a clipping from the *New York Times* telling of the State Department's appeal to Louis Marshall, urging him to help communicate and send aid to those stranded by the war in Galicia. Perlstein suggested that LDB write to the State Department offering the services of the Zionist organization (see LDB to Johan Kremenetzky, 5 May 1915), and if the State Department was favorable, open collections in America for Galicia. Perlstein also reported that Lewin-Epstein wanted LDB to write to Marshall also, informing him of the willingness of the Zionists to help in this matter.

To Charles Heineman

June 1, 1915 Boston, Mass. [Brandeis Mss, NMF 67-2]

MY DEAR MR. HEINEMAN: [1] It has been impossible for me to be in New York during the past few weeks, and I therefore am not familiar with the details of the break of the protocol; but I feel that so much good was accomplished during the five years which have elapsed since the 1910 strike, by efforts at cooperation between employers and employees in the Cloak and Suit Industry, that some effort should in my opinion be made to arrive at a working agreement.[2]

I should be glad to confer on this subject with you and a few others of those who have been most active in the management of the Association since the 1910 strike, and if it is agreeable to you, could see your Committee here, at my office, either Thursday or Friday of this week at 10:00 o'clock.

You, of course understand that I am writing this entirely on my own responsibility on account of my personal interest in the cause which we have been endeavoring to further in the past.[3]

Very cordially yours,

1. Charles Heineman was the chairman of the Cloak, Suit & Skirt Manufacturers Protective Association.

2. By the end of May 1915, the Protocol of Peace was in desperate, even incurable trouble. Both sides had openly rejected its principles, and with a social instrument like the protocol, the "spirit" of cooperation was all-important. (See LDB to John A. Dyche, 11 February 1915). On 20 May Heineman's association had broken off relations with the Joint Board of Arbitration and had repudiated the protocol.

3. The manufacturers refused LDB's invitation for a conference and LDB, after meetings in New York, agreed that the time was not ripe for one. The protocol hobbled along for another year, but for all practical purposes it was dead (the last meeting of the Board of Arbitration, for example, had been held on 25 April 1915).

To Louis Lipsky

June 1, 1915 Boston, Mass. [Brandeis Mss, Z 1-4]

MY DEAR MR. LIPSKY: I am enclosing my article entitled "The Jewish Problem and the Organization of American Israel", which is a revision of my talk before the Eastern Council of Reform Rabbis on April 25th.[1]

I wish you would read this over carefully, immediately if possible, and return it to me with your suggestions by tomorrow night's mail.

I have already talked with Mr. Perlstein about arranging to have this printed, if possible in all the Jewish publications, both English and Yiddish. With this in view, I purpose to fix the date of release not before June 21st, or possibly the 25th. Mr. DeHaas will have it set up in type this week by the Advocate. Without any expense we can get the copies of the galley to be distributed to the various publications. By sending it out the end of this week, or the beginning of next, everyone of the publications which are to publish it, would have time to arrange to do so.

Can you arrange for the translation in Yiddish?

What date do you suggest for the release? [2]

Very cordially yours,

P.S. I have just read the April and May Maccabaean. They seem to me both in form and matter a great advance over earlier numbers.

1. The address, ultimately entitled, "The Jewish Problem: How to Solve It," went through many editions as a Zionist pamphlet. See LDB to Stephen S. Wise, 2 March 1915.

2. The address was released on 18 June.

To Louis Lipsky

June 1, 1915 Boston, Mass. [Brandeis Mss, Z 1-4]

MY DEAR MR. LIPSKY: If we carry out our plan of having one of our publications go to each enrolled Zionist, I should think that it would be desirable to develop that portion of the Maccabaean which gives current news, so that it may bear more definitely the stamp of a bulletin.

Will you not consider the best form of doing this, and whether it would not be desirable to have classified separately the current news of the several Zionist organizations, so that those specifically interested in the Federation, the Hadassah, Knights of Zion, Sons of Zion, etc. work, could turn readily to their page.

Cordially yours,

To Benjamin Perlstein

June 2, 1915 Boston, Mass. [Brandeis Mss, Z 3-2]

MY DEAR MR. PERLSTEIN: As to the matter of the Budget:

I should be glad to have you and Mr. Lipsky consider, and lay before the Budget committee, this suggestion:

Ultimately all Zionist organizations in America ought to occupy a similar relationship to the Provisional Committee, or a committee of like nature which represents the general authority in Zionist affairs in America; and I have confidence that ultimately the Mizrachi and the Paoli de Zion [sic] can be brought into such relations. It seems, however, practically impossible to effect that result at once, or do more now than to develop a plan of cooperation with those organizations, involving a full exchange of information concerning activities, financial and otherwise, by reports to be made not less frequently than once a month, and to be comprehensive. The Provisional Committee, on the other hand, ought to undertake to aid, so far as it may, the Mizrachi and Paoli de Zion [sic], as well as the other Zionist organizations. And I suggest for consideration the possibility of furthering the general Zionist propaganda, and such a coordination of all Zionist interests, by having the Provisional Committee take over the New England Bureau, and establish, itself, the Bureaus in the other cities. The Provisional Committee would then finance these Bureaus, and would through each of these Bureaus undertake to aid each of the Zionist organizations. In this way, we should be giving to the Federation, and to other societies, in lieu of cash subventions, the services of the Bureaus. And the various organizations would, probably, when so relieved of extra burdens incident to propaganda, have no difficulty in defraying their expenses; and at the same time would lose none of the sense of responsibility for their own expenditures.

I make the above as a suggestion only for full discussion. I should not wish to reach definitely a conclusion on the subject until the matter had been fully discussed by those much more familiar than I with the problems involved. I have talked it over, although not fully, with Mr. deHaas, who is to be in New York on Friday to attend Committee meetings, and will no doubt take it up with you.[1]   Very truly yours,

1. One of the problems that had plagued the P.E.C. since its inception, and which had hindered the growth of the F.A.Z. before that, was a definition of the relationships among the various Zionist groups in the United States. When Gottheil had presided over the fledgling F.A.Z. at the turn of the century, he begged Herzl to designate that group as the official Zionist agency in the United States. But Herzl refused, mainly because the Knights

of Zion and other fraternal groups were just as large as the F.A.Z. and contributed as much in money. To give the F.A.Z. premier status might have alienated other Zionists. By 1914 these other groups had exercised a great deal of independence for over fifteen years, and they were reluctant to accept full leadership by the P.E.C. Mainly because of LDB's leadership, and the growing acknowledgement by the European leaders that centralization was necessary, the various Zionist groups finally did unite in the Zionist Organization of America, under a plan devised primarily by LDB.

To David Rubin

June 7, 1915 Boston, Mass. [Brandeis Mss, Z 2-3]

MY DEAR RUBIN: A reply to yours of the 3rd and 4th was delayed by my absence from the city.[1]

It is desirable that one should not make an important decision while one has any doubt, but it is sometimes impossible to remove doubts altogether. My view was, and is, that you ought to take up the practice of the law as your father and friends advise, unless it is absolutely clear in your own mind that you would not be happy in so doing, and that you must take up the Zionist work.

You have fitted yourself for the practice of the law. Undoubtedly you could earn there a good living, and have reasonable success. That is the simple and natural course before you. To take up the Zionist work is clearly out of the ordinary. It must necessarily involve sacrifices and risks; and you ought not to enter upon a course involving such sacrifices and risks unless you are perfectly clear in your own mind that is what you want to do. Of course if you do take up the practice of the law in Chicago, as you appear to have the opportunity there, you will still have a chance of doing some important work for Zionism; and what you could do there is to throw all of your public work into that one field, excluding the many other calls for public service which will undoubtedly develop. But when you have once decided, whatever that decision is, banish all doubts; and go forward to make a success of that which you have determined to do.[2]

Very cordially yours,

1. Rubin was wrestling with the problem of whether to proceed with his legal studies and take the Massachusetts bar examination on 1 July, or to give up the law and work full time in Zionist activities.
2. Rubin completed his studies and became a practising lawyer.

To Nathan Straus

June 8, 1915 Boston, Mass. [Brandeis Mss, Z 7-1]

MY DEAR MR. STRAUS: The Zionist Bureau for New England has shown me your letter of the 3rd expressing regret at your inability to accept the invitation to attend the Zionist Convention.

It will, I am sure, be a serious disappointment to all Zionists if you are not with us on that occasion, and I therefore venture to ask you to make a special effort to re-arrange your engagements so that you can be with us on the 28th.

Mr. Sands says that you make addresses only "on very rare occasions". I happened to be present on one "very rare occasion" when you did speak, namely, at the annual meeting of the Free Synagogue; and the great success of your address at that time emboldens me to urge upon you the more acceptance of the invitation which our Convention Committee has sent you.[1]

With every good wish,   Very cordially yours,

1. Straus replied two days later, claiming that his heavy schedule simply did not allow him to accede to LDB's wishes.

To Baruch Zuckerman

June 8, 1915 Boston, Mass. [Brandeis Mss, Z 7-1]

DEAR MR. ZUCKERMAN: [1] At a meeting of the Provisional Committee held on Sunday evening, at which the discussion of the budget was completed, it was decided that no step should be taken at this time as to the division of receipts; but that first of all a strong effort should be made to raise what is believed to be the minimum necessity for the Zionist organizations for the ensuing year, to wit: $135,000.

In order to raise this large sum quickly it was unanimously decided that I should address a letter, together with the President of each one of the national organizations, to each individual member of that organization, impressing him with the need that has arisen, and asking him, if possible, to pledge himself to contribute $1.00 a month for the ensuing year towards this budget.

It was further agreed that in making the distribution of such funds as we should collect, there would be taken into consideration the amount of the contributions received from the members of the various organizations.

In pursuance of the action taken by the Committee, as above stated, I gave directions to Mr. Perlstein, as Administrative Secretary, to procure from the various organizations the names and addresses of the several members, and to proceed with the greatest possible expedition in sending out the letters of request.

I understand from Mr. Perlstein that there has been apparently a reluctance on the part of the Poale de Zion [sic] to furnish him with its mailing list,—doubtless owing to the fact that you were not present at our meeting Sunday evening; and that your associates in charge of the Poale de Zion [sic] office do not fully understand the situation.

Will you therefore, take this matter up at once and see that the list is furnished to Mr. Perlstein at as early an hour as possible tomorrow? [2]   Very cordially yours,

1. Baruch Zuckerman (1887–1970) was one of the world's leading labor Zionists. Converted to Zionism at the age of sixteen by hearing Herzl, Zuckerman moved to the United States and helped to found Poale Zion. He was practically spokesman for the organization for nearly a half century. In 1956 he moved to Israel.

2. Zuckerman replied the next day that it was not his absence from the meeting which was responsible for his not sending the list. He was prohibited from giving out the information without the consent of the Central Committee of Poale Zion. He had called a special meeting for that purpose and expected to forward the information soon.

To Horace Meyer Kallen

June 9, 1915 Boston, Mass. [Brandeis Mss, Z 3-1]

MY DEAR KALLEN: [1] *First*:   *Our Financial Needs.*

1. For several weeks our Committee has been considering the budget for the year beginning July 1st; and it appears that to meet the ordinary expenses, of Palestinian needs, and the urgently needed extension of our propaganda work, $135,000 will be required.

2. Of the above amount we estimate that the ordinary income of the several Zionist associations, together with the pledges already made (like that of Julius Rosenwald of $1,000 a month) will give us in the aggregate $75,000. It is necessary, therefore, to raise

otherwise $60,000. I am purposing to pledge personally one-tenth of that amount,—that is $6,000 in monthly instalments of $500. I am to meet Wise in New York on Tuesday, and we ought to get some appreciable contributions there. Wise thinks we may reasonably expect this from at least Nathan Straus and Adolph Lewisohn. Are there not some persons in Cleveland and elsewhere with whom you could take up this matter?

Second: *Recent Progress*.

You have of course seen the report of the action of the I.O.B.A. and the I.O.B.S. Conventions. The declaration at both of these Conventions in favor of Zionism; the recommendation that their members become shekel payers; and the $1,000 contribution voted by the I.O.B.A., seem to me very encouraging. And there are other indications in New York and Boston of widening support.

I had a splendid reception both at the I.O.B.A. and the I.O.B.S. Conventions. The delegates listened with apparent deep interest.

Third: I enclose a copy of my address on the Jewish Problem, which is a revision of my talk before the Eastern Council of Reform Rabbis. Please treat this as confidential until June 18th, on which date it is to be released. Lipsky is arranging for its appearance in both English and Yiddish publications.[2]

Very cordially yours,

1. Very similar letters were sent to Julian W. Mack on this date and to Harry Friedenwald on 11 June.

2. See LDB to Stephen S. Wise, 2 March 1915.

To Joseph L. Cohen

June 11, 1915 Boston, Mass. [Brandeis Mss, Z 10-2]

DEAR MR. COHEN: Referring to your report of June 9th concerning the establishment of Zionist Clubs at the New York settlement houses:

I hereby appoint Miss Sampter, Dr. Pool, Mr. Schneeberg and yourself to a committee to consider the questions which may arise in connection with the introduction in the several New York settlements of Zionist Clubs, and the questions which may arise in connection with the relation of the Zionist organizations to the settlements.

In this connection I request that you consider specifically among other things:

1. What the attitude now is, or is likely to be, of those in control of the respective settlements towards the establishment there now of Zionist Clubs; and in case a friendly attitude does not now exist, how it may be developed.

2. Who of those in New York who have expressed a readiness to do active work for Zionism is now fitted to act as a leader at one of these settlements, or can readily fit himself to do so, and to make inquiries as to others who may be able and willing to undertake that work.

3. What steps should be taken to develop in Zionist leaders the characteristics desired.

I am to be in New York on Wednesday next, and shall be glad to take up any of the questions with you at Zionist headquarters 44 East 23rd Street, at 10:00 o'clock, if you should deem it advisable.   Yours very truly,

To Richard James Horatio Gottheil

June 12, 1915 Boston, Mass. [Brandeis Mss, Z 6-1]

MY DEAR PROFESSOR GOTTHEIL: Replying to yours of the 11th:

I appreciate the suggestion that I should accept the Presidency of the University Society, but I think this would be a great mistake. I think that you want a New Yorker, and the type of man you need would most likely be found among the lawyers or the enlightened business men. It may well be that you cannot find such a man now; but if he cannot be found at the moment, I think with the development of our movement, we shall be able to find him within a few months. For this reason I think it would not be advisable to have Judge Mack as President, but I think it might be proper to select Judge Mack as Honorary President, and as Honorary President, he might temporarily perform certain duties of President, if you cannot get the right man at the present moment.[1]

I look forward to seeing you Tuesday.

Cordially yours,

1. See LDB to Gottheil, 22 June and 28 July 1915.

To Meyer Berlin

June 15, 1915 New York, N.Y. [Brandeis Mss, Z 12-3]

MY DEAR RABBI BERLIN: I greatly regret that it was not possible for you to be present at the meeting of the Provisional Committee today, at which several matters of importance were considered. At this meeting was read your letter to Mr. Perlstein, in which you quote from Rabbi Abramowitz's letter to you concerning remittances to Palestine.[1] We hope that you have already made it clear to Rabbi Abramowitz that the course which he is pursuing in this matter is seriously detrimental to the prestige of the Zionist organization. It is impossible for us to accomplish the great work which we have undertaken unless all those who believe with us in the importance of obtaining Zionist ends are ready and willing to subordinate their own personal views and preferences to the demands of the organization. You, of course, understand this most thoroughly, but I want to urge upon you the importance of making some of your associates appreciate it as well. Will you kindly let me know the result of your further communication with Rabbi Abramowitz?

I am looking forward with pleasure to seeing you in Boston at the Convention.   Cordially yours,

1. Unfortunately, copies of these letters are not to be found in the Brandeis Mss.

To Richard James Horatio Gottheil

June 15, 1915 New York, N.Y. [Gottheil Mss]

DEAR FRIEND: We are making every possible endeavor to secure before our Boston Convention the funds that will be needed in the prosecution of our work during the coming year. We find that we shall need at least $135,000 to maintain our institutions in Palestine, and develop our organizations, in order that they shall be strong enough to meet emergencies that are now, as you know, arising.

We are asking other individual members of the Zionist societies to tax themselves at least $1.00 per month for the maintenance of our Emergency budget during the war period.

I am, however, addressing this personal appeal to you and to about one hundred others, who I hope will together contribute not less than one-quarter or one-fifth of the total estimated budget. The anticipated response would not only make it easier to secure from the rank and file the balance that will be needed, but will offer us considerable encouragement in our undertakings. Both the needs of Palestine and of the organization on which we must, after all, buttress all our work, justifies this appeal. Moreover, I think that you will agree with me that if we are to do effective work in the direction along which most of us are thinking, the Provisional Committee must be free to attend to those problems, instead of having to engage upon the usual time-absorbing plans for raising money.   Faithfully yours,

To Gustave Hartman

June 16, 1915 New York, N.Y. [Brandeis Mss, Z 12-3]

DEAR SIR: [1] I thank you for your courteous invitation to attend your conference on Friday evening, June 18th.

I desire to express the hope that in your deliberations you will consider with great care the problems of the Jewish people arising out of the war. These problems are not so intricate as at first glance they appear to be. In fact, the Jewish problem has two aspects, the one involving the Jew as an individual, and the other involving Jews collectively. Obviously, no individual should be subjected anywhere by reason of the fact that he is a Jew to a denial of any common right or opportunity enjoyed by non-Jews; but the Jews collectively should likewise enjoy the same right and opportunity to live and develop as do other groups of people.

Your committee is being organized as I understand it, to do battle for the emancipation of the individual Jew, and it is to be hoped that your sentiments will be expressed strongly on this point. I would urge you, however, not to be silent on the large phase of the problem, for individual liberty depends for its exercise in large part upon the development of the group of which the individual is a part.

It is this larger phase of the problem which Zionism aims to tackle. Zionism seeks to establish in Palestine, for such Jews as choose to go and remain there and for their descendants, a legally secured home, where they may live together and lead a Jewish life. And in spite of the fact that this movement has seemed to many a dream, it is now on the way to realization. What is needed for the acceleration of this movement is the determination of the Jews themselves to further the aims of Zionism, and that the world at large, the great humanitarian and progressive world, should express itself as sympathetic to these aims, and also help to further them whenever their voices may be heard.

I wish success to your deliberations, and sincerely regret that I shall be unable to attend your conference.[2]

With Zion's greetings

1. Gustave Hartman (1880–1936) was a Hungarian Jewish immigrant who rose from a paper boy in New York City to become a successful lawyer, politician, judge and philanthropist. He served in the New York State Assembly and was elected to the municipal and city courts of New York. He had many interests in Jewish causes, particularly medical, and was the founder of the Israel Orphan Asylum. Hartman was a Zionist and later became a member of the executive committee of the Zionist Organization of America, and a vice president of the American Jewish Congress. He had written LDB inviting him to participate in the formation of a Jewish civil rights organization to be called the American Jewish Emancipation Committee.

2. On 3 July 1915, LDB accepted the chairmanship of the Foreign Affairs Committee of the International Jewish Emancipation Committee.

To Mrs. F. W. Wile

June 19, 1915 Boston, Mass. [Brandeis Mss, NMF 47-3]

DEAR MRS. WILE: [1] Not only the people of New York, but millions throughout the country are anxiously watching the campaign in your State for equal suffrage.[2]

Experience has shown that the American ideal of democracy and social justice requires for its fulfilment that women be granted the suffrage. My own experience in various movements with which I have been connected, and in which I have tried to solve in some small way social, economic and political problems that presented themselves from time to time, converted me.[3] As years have passed, I have become more and more impressed with the difficulty and complexity of those problems and also with the power of society to solve them; but I am convinced that for their solution we must look to the many, not to the few. We need all the people, women as well as the men. In the democracy which is to solve these problems, we must have not a part of society but the whole.

The insight which women have shown into problems that men did not and perhaps could not understand, has convinced me not only that women should have the ballot, but that society demands that they exercise the right.

With best wishes,   Yours very truly,

1. Mrs. F. W. Wile was a suffragette from Rochester, New York, and chairman of the press committee for the Rochester Political Equality Club.

2. New York was in the midst of a hot battle over a women's suffrage amendment. On 2 November the proposition was overwhelmingly defeated, not only in New York, but in Massachusetts (where anti-suffragists carried every single county), and in Pennsylvania as well.

3. For LDB's original view on the question, see LDB to Alfred Brandeis, 30 January 1884, n. 1, or LDB to Amy F. Acton, 1 February 1905.

To Israel Friedlaender

June 22, 1915 Boston, Mass. [Brandeis Mss, Z 11-2]

MY DEAR PROFESSOR FRIEDLANDER [sic]: First: Thank you for your unusually able and luminous statement of the 20th.[1] I shall hope to have the opportunity of discussing this subject fully with you and others in Boston after the Convention. Meanwhile I wish you would supplement your paper by a more definite and detailed statement of that part of it which relates to the method and means of overcoming the hostility to Zionism to which certain prominent members of the American Jewish Committee have given expression.[2]

Second: I presume you have heard from Mr. Perlstein that we are planning to hold, immediately after the convention, a meeting of our Committee, which may possibly last several days, in order that pressing questions may be adequately considered, and plans laid out for the summer's work. I hope that you will be able to arrange to be with us throughout the session.[3]

Third: I am glad that you think my address on the Jewish Problem of value. No, I have not read, or indeed even heard of

the article by Dubnow, to which you refer.[4] I have read nothing
of his except his admirable essay on Jewish History. Have any
other of his writings been translated into English?

Cordially yours,

1. Friedlaender had sent LDB a twenty-three page essay which attempted
to explore the present tensions within the American Jewish community:
"Various occurrences of recent date have revealed a rift in American Jewry
which, if not healed in time, is bound to result in an open conflict. The
agitation centering around the question of a Jewish congress is not the cause
of this rift; it is rather a symptom of the profound difference of opinion and
sentiment which divides the Jews of America. In the realignment of American Jewry which such a struggle will undoubtedly call forth, the American
Jewish Committee, on the one hand, and the Provisional Zionist Committee
on the other, will, of necessity, assume the leadership of the opposing factions." Seeing the problem as a tension between Palestine-Judaism and
Diaspora-Judaism on one hand and between religious Judaism and national-
istic Judaism on the other (aggravated by the social and intellectual differences between German and Russian Jewish immigrants), Friedlaender
pleaded for tolerance and understanding between the leaders of the two
groups. He wrote that each faction must believe that the other faction is
motivated by as high a set of ideals and as noble a purpose as their own.
Only by this tolerance could a workable synthesis be fashioned from the
opposing viewpoints.

2. Friedlaender wrote back suggesting that his analysis be sent to Loius
Marshall and Jacob Schiff for their comments and suggestions. Perhaps this
might be the first step in reaching a better understanding, he thought. LDB,
on 24 June quickly rejected the suggestion: "I do not think it would be wise
for you to submit to anyone outside of the Provisional Committee the statement sent to me under date of June 20th."

3. The convention was scheduled for the last week in June.

4. Friedlaender had called LDB's attention to Dubnow's *Die Grundlagen
des National Judentums*, ["The Theory of Jewish Nationalism"] (Berlin,
1905). The work had been translated into German from the original Russian
by Friedlaender himself—he was the chief translator of Dubnow's works
into German and English. See LDB to Friedlaender, 25 June 1915.

To Richard James Horatio Gottheil

June 22, 1915 New York, N.Y. [Gottheil Mss]

MY DEAR PROFESSOR GOTTHEIL: Replying to yours of the 20th:

First: I am extremely glad to know that you are giving much
thought to the University Zionist Society, as its organization
should mark a very important advance in our movement.

I entirely agree with you that the best way of educating and interesting its members is to begin with the achievements at Palestine and work backwards. For this reason it seems to me that your Publication Committee ought to give immediate, as well as most serious attention to the publication of pamphlets which will make clear to Americans what has been achieved. These pamphlets ought to be works of high order, and we ought to set as our standard of pamphlets a character as high as that established by the Fabian Society. I should be glad to talk this matter over with you when you come to Boston for the Convention.

Second: The election of Mack to the Presidency of the University Society was wise provisionally, but it seems to me that he ought to decline the election, both because he is not a New Yorker, and because he ought to be at the head of a similar society to be formed in Chicago, and covering perhaps the territory subsidiary to it.[1]

We should have some able New Yorker, and I am inclined to think that Eugene Meyer, Jr.[2] is the man we ought to try for, and that it will be possible to get him. Wise writes me that he has pledged $250. a month for the year beginning July 1st, and may give more; and that he is deeply interested. I had never met Meyer until he attended a little dinner some two months ago, which we arranged for the discussion of Zionism with some of the able college men in New York. But all I have seen of him impresses me greatly.

Third: In regard to the Jewish Emancipation Society: I shall be glad to talk with you when you come to the Convention.[3]

Fourth: We are arranging to hold a Provisional Committee meeting immediately after the Convention for the purpose of discussing fully all Zionist problems; and laying out the work for the summer and fall. Such a meeting will require continuously several days of our time, and I hope you will arrange so that you can be with us throughout these conferences.

Very cordially yours,

1. See LDB to Gottheil, 12 June 1915.

2. Eugene Meyer, Jr. (1875–1959) was absorbed, not by Zionism (he eventually joined the Unitarians), but by a long career in public service. He served on a number of wartime boards and was appointed to various federal positions by every President from Wilson through Eisenhower. In 1933, he

began to publish the *Washington Post*. See LDB to Gottheil, 28 July 1915. After a long campaign of persuasion by LDB and others, Meyer accepted the presidency of the University Zionist Society in October.

3. See LDB to Gustave Hartman, 16 June 1915.

To Philippe Belknap Marcou

June 22, 1915 Boston, Mass. [Brandeis Mss, NMF 71-4]

My dear Phil: I am very glad to get your letter of the 29th and to know that you are taking part in the present great struggle in which the French people are acquitting themselves so nobly.

The cause to which you call my attention is one which presents a strong appeal,[1] and I should be very ready to contribute myself to it but for the fact that the fearful suffering of the Jews in Eastern Prussia and Galicia is now making very great demands upon me. They, unfortunately, are subject to all the horrors of war without the support which comes to other nationalities represented by a government which is seeking equal protection for all. I am endeavoring to arouse the American Jews to such action as may afford not only some relief, but also a remedy for their great distress.   Very cordially yours,

1. LDB's friend from Harvard days had been in Paris since the outbreak of the war. He had interested himself in an organization to aid blinded French soldiers in re-establishing their usefulness to society, and wrote asking LDB's financial assistance.

To George Rublee

June 22, 1915 Boston, Mass. [Brandeis Mss, NMF 66-3]

My dear George: Thank you very much for sending me with your letter of the 10th a copy of the decree in the Keystone Watch case.[1] That, and the decision in the Kellogg case show how necessary the agitation for the Stevens Bill is.[2]

I saw Norman last week immediately after his arrival. Both of us were so much occupied that there was not much chance of talking things out with him. English affairs are intensely and distressingly interesting now.

I hope we shall see you soon.   Very cordially yours,

1. The decree grew out of the January decision in *U.S.* v. *Keystone Watch Case Co.* et al., 218 Fed. Rep. 502 (1915). The government brought anti-trust proceedings against the Keystone Watch Case Company, charging that they monopolized the market for watch housings. Among other findings, the Supreme Court held that the attempt of the company to control the price charged for its product violated the anti-trust act.

2. In *U.S.* v. *Kellogg Toasted Corn Flake Co.*, 222 Fed. Rep. 725 (1915) the district court decided that the company could not fix the price that the public paid for the breakfast cereal, despite the fact that the product was trademarked.

To Norman Hapgood

June 23, 1915 Boston, Mass. [Brandeis Mss, NMF 62-1]

MY DEAR NORMAN: I am to deliver the Fourth of July oration at Faneuil Hall this year, and have prepared the enclosed.[1]

The address will doubtless be printed in the local papers on the 5th and 6th, and for this reason, among others, I suppose you will not want this for Harper's; but I don't like to make other disposition of it until I know that you don't care for it. Please wire me tomorrow.[2]   Cordially yours,

1. LDB's Fourth of July oration, entitled "True Americanism," was both a reaffirmation of his beliefs about democracy and industrial liberty and an assertion of the position to which his newly espoused Zionism had led him. He told his audience that true Americanism required a devotion to "our ideals and aspirations" and a willingness to cooperate in their achievement. What were those ideals and aspirations? LDB reiterated the principles he had been advocating for so long: industrial equality, regularity of employment, financial security for everyone, educational opportunity, social insurance, and the control of "capitalistic combination" by such means as labor unions. But, he continued, if there is any characteristic that is "peculiarly American" it is our willingness to extend our opportunities and open our hospitality to widely diverse and differing cultures. "America has believed that each race has something of peculiar value which it can contribute to the attainment of those high ideals for which it is striving." The eighteenth and nineteenth centuries witnessed struggles within many Western societies against aristocracy and the pernicious notion that some men were superior to others; but America went further and applied that principle of equality to cultures as well. Europe's inability to grant the value of other peoples' cultures, LDB concluded, was the central cause of the war of 1914. The oration owes much to the faith in "cultural pluralism," which was being articulated and developed by those opposing immigrant restriction – chief of whom among LDB's

acquaintances were Horace Kallen and Felix Adler. Compare LDB's speech of 1905 before the Century Club (see LDB to Adolph Brandeis, 29 November 1905, n. 1.). "True Americanism" may be found reprinted in *Business — A Profession* (the 1925 edition), 364–74. Also, see next note.

2. Hapgood published LDB's address: *Harper's Weekly*, 61 (10 July 1915): 31.

To Israel Friedlaender

June 25, 1915 Boston, Mass. [Brandeis Mss, Z 11-2]

MY DEAR PROFESSOR FRIEDLANDER [*sic*]: Since writing you yesterday the package has come with Dubnow's "Theory of Jewish Nationalism", the book on Dubnow, and your translation of the Achad Haam.[1]

It may be some little time before I have the opportunity of giving Dubnow the careful reading which I desire, but as soon as that has been accomplished, I will see that they reach you safely.

For the Achad Haam, which you kindly send, I am particularly indebted, as I had already planned to continue my study of his writings during the coming vacation.   Cordially yours,

1. See LDB to Friedlaender, 22 June 1915. Ahad Ha-Am (literally, "a man of the people") was the pseudonym for the great Jewish editor and essayist Asher Zvi Ginsburg (1856–1927). Born in Russia into a Hassidic family, Ahad Ha-Am, largely through teaching himself, came to reject religious faith, espousing instead the firmest possible commitment to Jewish learning and culture. A scholar with a splendid reputation for learning and integrity, Ahad Ha-Am assumed the posture of friendly critic to the principal leadership of the Zionist movement, and was especially close to Chaim Weizmann. The emphasis on rapid settlement and on the economic and political aspects of the creation of a Jewish homeland was, to his mind, naive and misdirected. What was required was not the politics and diplomacy characterized by Herzl; rather Jews needed to cleanse themselves of assimilation, rediscover the magnificence of their spiritual heritage, and prepare themselves intellectually and educationally for their nationalism. True, a spiritual center in Palestine would be a useful weapon in the resurrection and diffusion of Jewish culture, but the emphasis upon political and economic aspects threatened to breed disappointment, frustration, and failure. His challenge to the political Zionists won him many adherents and set the tone and the issues for many important debates within the movement. In 1922, Ahad Ha-Am moved to Palestine himself and remained there until his death. See Leon Simon, *Ahad Ha-Am, Asher Ginzburg: a Biography* (Philadelphia, 1960), although the best sources for his ideas are his four published volumes of essays.

To Henry Morgenthau

June 25, 1915 New York, N.Y. [Morgenthau Mss]

MY DEAR MR. AMBASSADOR: My New York office has sent you under date of June 11th through the Department of State, the sum of $2,500. for the relief of Jewish refugees in Constantinople, and a further sum of $1,000 for Mr. Lichtheim, pursuant to your cablegram.

I write not so much to confirm those remittances as to express to you the very high appreciation of the Zionists, and generally of the Jews in America, for the devoted and efficient aid which you are giving to our bretheren [*sic*] in Palestine. Scarcely a communication, oral or written, comes to us from Palestine, or from Alexandria, which does not express in some form gratitude for the untiring work which you are doing.

With high appreciation,   Very cordially yours,

To Norman Hapgood

June 29, 1915 Boston, Mass. [Brandeis Mss, NMF 62-1]

MY DEAR NORMAN: Replying to yours of the 28th:

First: The Pennsylvania's protest against "Between Bites" is entirely justified.[1] There has been no stock dividend of the Pennsylvania Railroad, at least for a long time. There was stock issued at par, as J.W. Lee states, and the royalties were worth something, but it was not a very large amount. Creel's [2] statement is an instance of inaccurate information. The Pennsylvania Railroad, which has 92,000 stockholders, is the corporation with lines east of Pittsburg and Erie. It owns the stock of many other corporations, including the stock of the Pennsylvania Company. The latter company owns or controls most of the lines west of Pittsburg and Erie. It is this latter Company, the Pennsylvania Company, which issued a stock dividend; but the stockholders of the Pennsylvania Railroad got none of that stock dividend. It all went into the treasury of the Pennsylvania Railroad where it is now. The result is accordingly exactly the same to stockholders of the Pennsylvania Railroad as if the stock dividend had not been made. I do not recall at the moment what the basis was of the stock dividend. It probably represented accumulated surplus.

The impression I have gained of Creel is that he is not accurate.[3]

Second: I think it would be unwise for me to become a director in Harper's; among other reasons, because of the not infrequent appearance of my name in the editorial and other columns.

We are looking forward to your reaching Dedham in time for dinner Friday, July 9th.   Cordially yours,

1. In the 26 June issue, *Harper's Weekly* had published an editorial, "Between Bites," by George Creel (see next note). The editorial was critical of the financing of the Pennsylvania Railroad, and J. W. Lee, a minor official of the company, had written Hapgood complaining about the accuracy of the statement.

2. George Creel (1876–1953) was an unusually prolific editor and free-lance writer who fit into the muckraker mold. He was a regular contributor to *Harper's* but he also wrote for many other magazines. With U.S. entry into World War I, in April 1917, Wilson appointed him chairman of the controversial Committee on Public Information, a committee charged with creating a favorable public opinion about the war through publicity. Soon known as "the Creel committee," the group flooded the country with patriotic and militaristic propaganda, using a variety of media and sometimes coming in for severe criticism by those in America who opposed the war. See his own account, *How We Advertised America* (New York, 1920); for a thorough study see James R. Mock and Cedric Larson, *Words That Won the War: The Story of the Committee on Public Information 1917–1919* (Princeton, 1939).

3. In the 17 July issue of *Harper's Weekly*, Hapgood apologized for the "extraordinarily inaccurate editorial."

To Hamilton Holt

July 6, 1915 Boston, Mass. [Brandeis Mss, Z 7-2]

MY DEAR MR. HOLT: I received just before the Zionist Convention your very kind invitation to write an article for the Independent about the Zionist movement "telling just what is proposed to be done".

I am sending you under separate cover a copy of two addresses of mine "Zionism and Patriotism" and "The Jewish Problem". These will tell you about the movement, and I hope that you will be willing to write some editorial upon it, which I am sure would be more helpful than if I undertook to write an article, which indeed I cannot very well do now. On the other hand if you or one of your editors would care to write more at length on the movement, I should be very glad to talk with you about the matter, and give any information which you desire beyond what you find in my addresses.[1]   Very cordially yours,

1. Holt printed a general editorial, "Spain and Zion," *The Independent*, 83 (12 July 1915): 40, which was probably in print before this letter was written —its shows no influence of LDB's speeches. Extensive treatment of Zionism in the periodical awaited LDB's "Democracy in Palestine," *The Independent*, 84 (22 November 1915): 311.

To Harry Schneiderman

July 6, 1915 Boston, Mass. [Brandeis Mss, Z 11-1]

DEAR MR. SCHNEIDERMAN: [1] I have your letter of the 2nd which formally confirms the invitation that had already come to me through Judge Mack to meet Dr. Cyrus Adler,[2] Chairman of the American Jewish Committee.

As representing the Provisional Executive Committee, I shall be glad to meet Dr. Adler in New York on Monday, July 12th, at any time after 1:00 o'clock, at such place as will be most agreeable to Dr. Adler. Please let me know Dr. Adler's preference.

Following your suggestion, I shall ask Professor Frankfurter to attend the meeting.[3]

As stated when you telephoned me, it is not possible for me to meet Dr. Adler before that date.[4]   Very truly yours,

1. Harry Schneiderman (b. 1885) was a Polish immigrant who entered Jewish organizational life and rose to positions of prominence in a dozen important Jewish groups. Between 1909 and 1949 he worked with the American Jewish Committee, and it was as acting secretary of that body that he had written to arrange a meeting between LDB and Cyrus Adler (see next note), "with a view to deciding whether the two organizations can arrange to cooperate in certain matters."

2. Cyrus Adler (1863–1940) was an Arkansas-born scholar, writer, and archivist, specializing in Hebrew and Middle Eastern studies. He had taught at Johns Hopkins and had worked in the Smithsonian Institution. In 1908 he assumed the presidency of Dropsie College. He worked to found the Jewish Publication Society and the American Jewish Historical Society, and he eventually also became president of the Jewish Theological Seminary. He was to join Louis Marshall as one of the spokesmen for Jewish interests at the Paris Peace Conference, and at Marshall's death in 1929, Adler became president of the American Jewish Committee. While not a Zionist, he was by no means unfriendly to Zionist aspirations, and he advocated programs of unity and cooperation between Jewish factions. He wrote an autobiography,

I Have Considered the Days (Philadelphia, 1941). See also the sympathetic account by Abraham A. Neuman, *Cyrus Adler* (New York, 1942).

3. Schneiderman had suggested that it might be wise to include in the meeting someone who was a member of both the American Jewish Committee and the Provisional Executive Committee. The men who occupied positions in both organizations were, besides Frankfurter and Mack, Joseph Barondess, Harry Friedenwald, Israel Friedlaender, and Judah L. Magnes.

4. The meeting took place on 12 July. Although part of the two-hour meeting was taken up by a discussion of the American Jewish Relief Committee (see LDB to Judah L. Magnes, 18 July 1915), most of the time was spent with the two men fencing over the controversial "congress" issue (see LDB to Louis Lipsky, 18 January 1915, n. 2). Adler presented a list of Jewish organizations that the American Jewish Committee proposed to invite and the number of votes to be given to each. LDB did not care about the number of delegates, but he thought that the means of selecting them was crucial. He therefore proposed that he and Adler select a number of representatives from the list of organizations and invite them to a "preliminary" meeting for the purpose of hammering out the means of selection for the eventual congress. Adler countered that it was no more democratic for him and LDB to pick the "preliminary" committee than it was for the American Jewish Committee to select the delegates for the main "conference." He therefore suggested, incredibly, that there should be a "pre-preliminary" committee who would select the "preliminary" committee, who would in turn deal with the problems of selecting the "conference." The whole controversy, petty and nitpicking as it seems, must be seen as the available issue over which the huge power struggle within the American Jewish community was unfolding. The two men both wished to take the matter up with their respective committees and they adjourned without an agreement. For the next round, see LDB to Adler, 28 July 1915).

To Charles Mills Cabot

July 8, 1915 Boston, Mass. [Brandeis Mss, NMF 71-1]

MY DEAR MR. CABOT: I am glad you approve of my Fourth of July address, and have given instructions to have twenty-five copies sent you.

As to your inquiry about eight hours for steel workers: [1] It seems to me:

First: An effort should be made at the stockholders' meeting to secure a change of practice. There should be presented at that meeting a brief statement of what conditions were found to be by the Federal investigation; the action taken and not taken by the corporation, and an urgent plea be made that something be done. It does not seem probable that the reforms will come through stockholders' action; but publicity will be gained, and the effort, if unsuccessful, will help in securing action elsewhere.

Second: General publicity work should continue. Among other things, it would be desirable to get the Department of Labor to make an investigation to determine to what extent the abuses shown in the Federal Report of 1911 still continue.

Third: A comparison should be made between the business of the independent plants and the steel corporation's. Of course there must be many independent plants where conditions are at least as bad as in the steel corporation's; but there are undoubtedly some where conditions are better.

Fourth: A legislative campaign should be undertaken despite the difficulties of securing legislation. Such a campaign would give the best opportunities for publicity; and after all it is education which the community needs to secure results.[2]

Very cordially yours

1. Cabot, who was a stockholder in U.S. Steel (see LDB to Zechariah Chafee Jr., 5 April 1912), had written: "What are we going to do about 8 hours for steel workers? I say we for I believe you sympathize with my rather feeble attempts to improve the conditions of labor in that industry. . . ." See LDB to Charles H. Jones, 13 February 1912, and to Paul U. Kellogg, 26 July 1912.

2. Within the year Cabot died. The United States Steel Corporation did not grant the eight-hour day until 1923.

To Ezekiel Leavitt

July 8, 1915 Boston, Mass. [Brandeis Mss, Z 7-2]

DEAR MR. LEAVITT: [1] You have asked me how the Boston Jewish Voice,—soon to be converted into a daily,—can best aid the Zionist cause. I answer:

First: Make every reader realize that to be a good American and a good Jew he must be a Zionist; that he must be a Zionist not only in sympathy, but in action; and that he must be prepared to make sacrifices for the cause. Keep constantly before the reader's mind that the first step is that every adult should join some local Zionist society, and that the children should be enrolled as shekel payers.

Second: Give personal assurance to the officers of each of the Zionist organizations in Greater Boston, and elsewhere where the Boston Jewish Voice circulates, that it is your firm purpose to aid each and every one of these organizations at all times to increase their usefulness, and that they may freely call upon your paper for assistance in advancing their work.

Very truly yours,

1. Rabbi Ezekiel Leavitt (1878–1945) was a Russian immigrant who embarked upon many Jewish educational and literary efforts. He had taken over the *Boston Jewish Voice* and would write many books in English and Hebrew on Jewish topics.

To John Purroy Mitchel[1] (Telegram)

July 9, 1915 Boston, Mass. [Brandeis Mss, NMF 67-2]

I accept appointment on Conciliation Council, and will attend Tuesday.[2]

1. John Purroy Mitchel (1879–1918), a graduate of Columbia Law School, had been involved in New York City politics and in 1915 was mayor of the city. In 1918 he enlisted in the Aviation Corps and was killed in an airplane accident in Louisiana.

2. Mayor Mitchel, in a last ditch effort to save the protocol principle and to avoid a strike of fifty thousand workers in the cloak and suit industry (see LDB to Charles Heineman, 1 June 1915), secured an agreement to convene a council of conciliation. The council met under the chairmanship of LDB's brother-in-law, Felix Adler, between 13 July and 23 July. According to Prof. Mason, "Though present at all twenty sessions, Brandeis was conspicuously silent." The council presented a series of recommendations including a wage increase, and when both sides accepted it, the strike was avoided for the present. The results for the protocol itself, however, were negligible and the peace lasted less than a year.

To Judah Leon Magnes

July 18, 1915 New York, N.Y. [Brandeis Mss, Z 10-4]

MY DEAR DR. MAGNES: Among the questions discussed at our Conference of the twelfth, were certain matters connected with the American Jewish Relief Committee, and among them the following:

First: The misrepresentation in the official report issued by the American Jewish Relief Committee, as to the extent or amount of Zionist contributions.

In the report of June 11th, 1915, the Zionist contributions to the "Vulcan Fund" are given as $1,540, whereas, in fact the extent of Zionist contributions, including foodstuffs, were at least $28,000 as appears from the letter of June 19th from Mr. Perlstein to Mr. Bressler, copy of which is enclosed.

You then stated to me that any failure to correctly present the fact was a matter for which Mr. Bressler alone was responsible, as his report was not made upon conference with members of the A.J.R.C. I find, upon looking over our files, the letter of Mr. Bressler to Mr. Perlstein, under date of June 21st, in which Mr. Bressler states that he is presenting the matter to Mr. Warburg for his consideration. Mr. Bressler later informed Mr. Perlstein, on the telephone, that the treasurer refused to take into account the Zionist contributions, in his official reports. I find also, in Mr. Bressler's letter, a paragraph suggesting that you, as Chairman of the Food Ship Committee, give out a formal statement to that effect. Our administrative Secretary wrote you on this subject under date of June 23rd, to which he has received no reply.

You will recall that I first brought the substance of this to your attention in a letter of March 18, 1915, to which I have never had acknowledgment. I repeat what I said in that letter:

"Of course, it is not very material to us whether we have overpaid our pro rata or not, except for the fact that the A.J.R.C., according to the minutes, deems itself apparently free to withdraw the appropriations made and therefore to deny to Palestine the full amount of relief which it, the various local committees and the general public have donated for that specific purpose. The net result would be to reduce materially the Palestinian relief fund, unless the A.J.R.C. should be content, at some future time, to grant additional amounts. It seemed to the Zionist Committee that we had no right to jeopardize Palestine relief by acquiesing [*sic*] in the action of the Executive Committee of the A.J.R.C."

Mr. Bressler, in his letter of June 21st, writes as follows:

"In the final analysis, I know you feel as I do, that the important consideration, and the one which suffices for me, is that the needed money was raised. The source of origin is a matter of only incidental importance."

That is not correct. It may not be of great importance, in one sense, whether Zionists receive credit for work done, but you cannot fail to realize that many Zionists who have exerted themselves greatly to make collections for Palestine, which were entrusted to the A.J.R.C., will inevitably discontinue their efforts in this direction when they find it reported by the A.J.R.C. that their contributions were insignificant, when, as a matter of fact, they were very large. In New England, at least, the failure of the A.J.R.C. to report the facts correctly has already resulted in dampening the ardor of many who had been previously eager to help in the work of the A.J.R.C.

Second: That the American Jewish Relief Committee was not giving Palestine the benefit or credit for all the moneys which had been raised for it. In this connection, I call your attention to the following fact:

The A.J.R.C. has not yet expended on Palestine the full $25,000 which it had pledged for the Relief Ship, while the Zionists have not only made good their pledge of $25,000, but have contributed considerably more than that amount.

From the official report of the A.J.R.C., dated June 11th, it appears that there has been expended, on cash and food, including the Zionist contributions, the sum of approximately $123,000, as follows:

Cash paid by A.J.R.C. for food supplies, travelling expenses and sundries	$58,627.81
Cash with American Consul at Alexandria, for use on behalf of Mr. Levin	10,000,00
Deposited with Gluskin,[1] at Alexandria	16,000.00
Zionist food contributions	29,000.00
Other food contributions, not to exceed	10,000.00
TOTAL	$122,677.81 [2]

Of this total, the Zionist contributions were as follows:

Cash to A.J.R.C. .... $ 1,540.00
Food placed on "Vulcan" 28,000.00
                                          _____
                     TOTAL $29,540.00

leaving a balance of approximately .... $93,000.00 for contributions other than those of the Zionists.

The total funds and food were as follows:

Funds originally pledged and collected $135,000.00
Zionist surplus contribution 4,500.00
Boston A.J.R.C. special appropriation 10,000.00
Collections by A.J.R.C. from general
public 30,784.00
                                          _____
     Total pledges & collections $180,284.00

specifically collected for Palestine.

The expenditure of money and food was 123,000.00
                                          _____
leaving a balance to the credit of Palestine of $57,284.00

Instead of leaving this sum to the credit of Palestine, the treasurer of the A.J.R.C. has requested the return of the $16,000 now on deposit in Alexandria, which, if acted upon, would make a total of funds for Palestine, that had been entrusted to the A.J.R.C., of $73,000, which are being diverted from it.

Third: We learn from the Alexandria Committee that there is a great need of 6,000 Francs a month, for the refugees. In our opinion, an amount sufficient to cover this for the next four months should be turned over to the Alexandria Delegation out of the $16,000, which is now in the hands of Gluskin. The remaining $12,000, in our opinion, should be turned over to Dr. Ruppin for the Palestinian Committee, to be used for relief purposes there. We are informed that there is a great need of cash money in Palestine now. I hope that you will take this matter up with Mr. Felix Warburg, before Mr. Lewin-Epstein sees him.[3]

                                        Very cordially yours,

1. Z'ev Gluskin (1859–1949) was a Russian Jew who, after a period of Zionist activity in Poland, moved to Palestine in 1906 and headed a number of economic and colonizing institutions there.

2. This addition error appears in the original letter.

3. See LDB to Magnes, 8 September 1915.

To Louis Lipsky

July 24, 1915 Boston, Mass. [Brandeis Mss, Z 1-4]

MY DEAR MR. LIPSKY: I note that there is to be a National Conference of Single Taxers in San Francisco August 23rd, 24th and 25th. Undoubtedly Mrs. Joseph Fels will be present. I understand that she is now working her way west. You could get from the office of the Joseph Fels Fund Commission, Cincinnati, or from Philadelphia, Mrs. Fels' itinerary.[1] I think it would be desirable if we could have some Zionist members in the various cities call upon her; and perhaps they could arrange in many instances for small meetings at which Mrs. Fels would be present.

Possibly if Dr. Kallen is to be in San Francisco during the Single Tax Convention, it would be well to have him tell the single taxers about the Jewish National Fund.[2]

Yours very truly,

1. Mary Fels (1863–1953), the widow of Joseph, carried on his philanthropic work as head of the Joseph Fels Foundation, which promoted goodwill between Jews and non-Jews, and assisted Palestinian settlements.
2. See Arthur P. Dudden, "The Single Tax Zionism of Joseph Fels," *Publications of the American Jewish Historical Society* 46 (1956/57): 474–91.

To Benjamin Perlstein

July 27, 1915 Boston, Mass. [Brandeis Mss, Z 8-2]

DEAR MR. PERLSTEIN: Referring to our conversation of last week:
My travelling expenses between March 1st and June 30, 1915 were $299.07.

I wish to bear these expenses myself, but understand that you prefer that this be effected by sending me a check for the amount, as a re-imbursement, and letting me give a check of equal amount as a further contribution to the Emergency Fund.

Yours very truly,

To Cyrus Adler

July 28, 1915 Boston, Mass. [Brandeis Mss, Z 11-1]

MY DEAR DR. ADLER: I have yours of the 21st transmitting the vote of your Executive Committee, which rejects in substance the proposal submitted by me to you on July 12, 1915, for cooperation between the American Jewish Committee, the Zionists and the other national organizations in calling a Congress on a democratic basis to consider the problems of the Jewish people.[1]

The vote of your Executive Committee declares "that the plan, purpose, and scope of the Conference heretofore decided upon by the General Committee at a special meeting on June 20, 1915, be adhered to" except that "instead of the call for the Conference being signed by the American Jewish Committee alone", eight other organizations named by it "be invited to sign the call", and that the Chairman "have power to modify immaterial details". You also state that your "Executive Committee felt that it was without power to change the purpose and scope of the conference", and that "the reason for the limitation of the scope of the conference is that such limitation is representative of the dominant issue before the Jews of America" etc.

The single modification named by your Executive Committee appears to us of no significance. Even though adopted it would leave in full force all the fundamental objections to the Conference plan as originally proposed by your Committee. The Conference would still remain thoroughly undemocratic. It would still not be cooperative. Its scope would still be so limited as to preclude the consideration of certain matters which might be deemed vital to the welfare of the Jews. The fact that your power as Chairman is by the vote expressly limited to the modification of "immaterial details", leads me to urge most earnestly, that before you and I meet again for a further discussion of this subject, the whole matter be referred to your General Committee, in order that the General Committee may take such action as is required to permit your Executive Committee and yourself to deal with the matter broadly in accordance with the widely expressed will of the Jews of America.

When this matter is laid again before your General Committee, I trust you will make clear to them the grounds of objection to your Committee's Conference plan which I set forth at our meeting on July 12th, namely:

First: Your Committee's Conference plan is undemocratic. Democracy demands that those representatives of the Jews of America who are to assemble in Conference to take action con-

cerning the problems of the Jewish People, shall have some voice
in determining the conditions under which the conference shall
convene and the scope of its deliberations. Your Committee has
assumed to determine these matters itself; to determine in advance
not only when and where the Conference shall be held; what the
aggregate number of delegates shall be; which organizations shall
be permitted to send delegates; and what number of representatives of each such organization shall have; but also what its plan
and scope shall be. Obviously the mere formality now proposed
by your Executive Committee of having certain other organizations selected by it sign with the American Jewish Committee
the call to the Conference, would not make the proceeding any
less undemocratic. So fundamental an objection as lack of democratic character can be removed only by a change equally fundamental. All national organizations must be given some voice in
determining the conditions, plan and scope of the Conference or
Congress. It was to this end that I proposed that your Committee
join ours in inviting the leading national organizations, say, 12,
24 or more, to each send one delegate to a preliminary conference
which should determine when, where and how a Congress should
be called, and also the number of delegates; how they should be
selected; and generally the plan of the Congress; and that its
scope to be set forth in the call, be broadly the problems of the
Jewish people; so that the Congress itself might determine, after
full discussion, what particular subjects it shall act upon.

Second: Your committee's Conference plan is not cooperative.
Cooperation demands that those who are to work together shall
all have this opportunity, as well as the responsibility of sharing
in important fundamental determinations. The conditions under
which the Congress (or Conference) shall be held, who should
participate, the extent of participation, how the delegates shall be
selected, and generally the plan and scope, are of the very essence
of the Congress. But your plan vests this grave responsibility in
the American Jewish Committee alone, and precludes others from
participating in the determination of these matters.

Third: Your Committee's Conference plan, according to your
letters, places a limitation upon the scope of the deliberations,
which limitation may greatly impair, if not wholly defeat the
usefulness of the Conference (or Congress). Your Committee un-

dertakes to decide (in advance) for the Jews of America what they shall and what they shall not discuss, and within what limit they may act in Conference (or Congress) assembled. Is it not clear that neither the American Jewish Committee nor the Zionist Committee, acting alone or acting jointly, should arrogate to itself or themselves the function of determining on what subjects the Conference (or Congress) should act. Neither of our Committees acting separately can justly claim to represent all the Jews of America, nor can the two Committees jointly justly take such a claim. Neither of our Committees acting separately, nor the two jointly, has any mandate which entitles it or them, to determine in advance (without even consulting the other national organizations) what measures may best subserve the interest of the Jewish people.

Fourth: The dangers incident to the method adopted by the American Jewish Committee in assuming to determine alone and make itself entirely responsible for all the component elements in such a Conference (or Congress) is exhibited by the "List of organizations to be invited to participate in the Jewish Conference", of which you were good enough to hand me a copy. Taking three of the organizations of kindred type there named, I find your Committee has alloted to their respective memberships the following disproportionate delegate rights: —

To one with 84,000 members,	5 delegates
To one with 4,000 "	2 "
To one with 40,000 "	1 "

In pursuance of your valuable suggestions, Professor Frankfurter (who is a member both of the American Jewish Committee and of the Zionist organization) was invited to be present when you and I were to discuss this matter at Hotel Astor on July 12th. I venture to suggest now, that a special effort be made to insure his attendance at the meeting of your General Committee to be called for the discussion of this subject; because he could aid you most effectively in presenting to your Committee the views which I expressed at our July 12th meeting.[2]

Yours very truly,

1. See LDB to Harry Schneiderman, 6 July 1915, n. 4.
2. See LDB to Adler, 10 August 1915.

To Richard James Horatio Gottheil

July 28, 1915 New York, N.Y. [Gottheil Mss]

MY DEAR PROFESSOR GOTTHEIL: *First:* Thank you for your letter of the 20th enclosing the interesting communication from Sir Cecil Spring-Rice, which I return herewith.[1]

Sir Cecil seems to be more troubled about the possible lack of neutrality after the war than by German sympathies among the Jews now. It certainly ought not to be difficult to convince him that whatever may be the feeling among groups of Jews now, there could be no doubt of the neutrality of the whole people later. Nor can there be much doubt as to the feeling of Palestinians.

Second: I expect to start on my vacation the end of this week, so shall not be in New York August 2nd to 6th. Kallen and Hurwitz will probably be there one or two days. I am very glad that you will endeavor to convene a meeting of the Governing Body of the University Society. There have come to me many communications of interest from men who would, I think, be ready to join the Society, concerning some of which I have written Hurwitz.[2]

When in New York on the 12th I had a long talk with Eugene Meyer, Jr. and broached the subject of his becoming President of the Society. I am strongly convinced, as are Frankfurter, Kallen and Hurwitz, that he would be an excellent choice, and I was much gratified to receive a letter from Felix Frankfurter today in which he says:

> "I have talked with Eugene Meyer and he is very receptive towards the Zion University Men's presidency. He has a fine sense of wanting to "back up Mr. Brandeis", but feels his inadequacy for that leadership. I urged on him the opportunity of fitting himself for leadership. You can land him, I'm sure." [3]

Third: I am enclosing copy of Cyrus Adler's letter to me of the 21st, and of my reply under date of today, of which I am sure you will approve.   Sincerely yours,

1. Sir Cecil Arthur Spring-Rice (1859–1918) enjoyed a long and distinguished career in the British foreign office. In 1912 he was appointed England's ambassador to the United States, serving in that capacity throughout the war. Known for his charm and wit, Spring-Rice was an unusually

popular diplomat. On 9 July he had written to Gottheil that he hoped the war might lead to some solution of the Palestine question, and that he would like to see it go to the Jews as a homeland. He noted that the Jews in England had won by their industry and perseverence a prominent position in British life, and he hinted that the English government would do its best for the Jews. It is difficult to determine whether Spring-Rice was speaking for himself or if he was trying to sound out American Jewish feelings regarding British suzerainty over Palestine, an idea that was already being discussed within the British War Cabinet.

2. In particular, LDB had heard that groups of Jewish musicians, economists, and some who merely wished to study Palestinian conditions without formally joining the Zionist movement had expressed an interest in the University Society.

3. See LDB to Gottheil, 12 and 22 June 1915; Meyer accepted the position after a long period of deliberation.

To Louis Lipsky

July 28, 1915 Boston, Mass. [Brandeis Mss, Z 1-4]

MY DEAR MR. LIPSKY: I have your telegram saying among other things, that Rutenberg's Committee needs $900, and makes it a condition of activity on their part that the Provisional Committee shall guarantee $400 in addition to the $500, which we have agreed to give to the Poale de Zion [*sic*] for special propaganda.[1]

I agree entirely with Mr. Rutenberg and Dr. Levin as to the importance of securing the cooperation of the Jewish workingmen, and if I felt certain that the publication of a weekly from now until the date of the workingmen's convention, would make reasonably certain our gaining the Jewish workingmen to the Zionist cause, I might take the responsibility of committing our organization to this guaranty. With my present knowledge of conditions and prospects I do not feel that I can take this responsibility.

First: I have a grave doubt whether the publication by the Rutenberg Committee of a paper during the next five weeks will be an important factor in securing the Jewish vote; and I can see some dangers incident to their doing so under our auspices, apart from the expense involved. At the present time every Yiddish paper in New York, with the exception of the Vorwaerts, is, I understand practically committed to a Democratic Congress, and is favorable to the Zionist cause. Even the Vorwaerts is ready to take some communications favorable to our contention. The publication of an independent paper by us may antagonize some of the papers which are now friendly, and through that the Zionist cause might lose more than it can gain.

Second: If the publication of some special paper is required, I do not see what conclusive reason there is for assuming that it must be published weekly. If $900. are needed for publishing it once a week, and only $500. are available, it would seem possible to publish it less frequently than once a week.

Third: If a weekly is required as a means of conveying a message to Jewish workingmen concerning the Congress, or the Zionist cause, why should not the Yiddish Folk, and the $500. which we have agreed to contribute to the Poale de Zion [*sic*], be utilized for this purpose? Five hundred dollars would go far towards paying the extra expense of distributing a paper which has to be printed in any event, and even if a part of that $500 should go for articles, enough of it would remain to print a considerable additional number of copies. We should also have this advantage,—of making known the Yiddish Folk to a large number of persons who are at present probably ignorant of its existence. In other words, the Yiddish Folk might be run for the five weeks as a Congress issue; of course in such a way as not to embarrass our organization.

Fourth: Dr. Levin, as well as others, must clearly bear in mind that there is a limit to the expense which we can undertake. Of late we have been devoting ourselves to appropriations, and money is going in every direction.

Your letter in regard to the Mizrachi, received today, indicates very properly the necessity of bearing in mind the financial productivity of all of our expenditures.[2]

Fifth: I feel strongly that Mr. Rutenberg, Dr. Levin and our various friends who are particularly interested in this agitation can do most effective work by the private personal approach to individuals or small groups. This would include discussions not merely with the leaders, but with those who would be deemed part of the rank and file, and yet would be selected as thinking, energetic men. I am sure if Mr. Rutenberg and Dr. Levin will work steadfastly on these, among other lines, they will get tangible results, and the strength of our cause will overcome our opponents.[3]   Very cordially yours,

1. Pinhas Rutenberg (1879–1942), a colorful Russian activist, had fled to Italy because of his involvement in the disturbances of 1905. He later joined Kerensky's government and fought against the Bolshevik coup. After being imprisoned by the Bolsheviks, Rutenberg escaped, fought for a while against them, and finally left Russia for Palestine in 1919. There he used his engineering training and experience to develop Palestinian water and electrical resources, and founded the Palestine Electric Company. During the war years, however, Rutenberg was in the United States. He had come originally to work for a Jewish legion, in co-operation with Jabotinsky's efforts, but while in America he became interested in the Congress movement and wished to publish a paper which would further the Congress idea among Jewish workers. For LDB's evaluation of Rutenberg's appeal and usefulness, see LDB to Julian W. Mack, 26 August and 26 October 1915.

2. While Rabbi Berlin wanted the Provisional Executive Committee to underwrite the entire Mizrachi budget, Mizrachi contributions to the Zionist cause were so minimal as to make even a small investment in the organization a doubtful financial venture. For the tension between LDB and Berlin, see LDB's letter to him of 25 August 1915.

3. See LDB to Jacob deHaas, 8 August 1915.

To William Gibbs McAdoo

July 28, 1915 Boston, Mass. [Brandeis Mss, NMF 68-2]

MY DEAR McADOO: Replying to yours of the 23rd:

I appreciate most highly your offer to appoint me a member of the High Commission.[1] It would give me great satisfaction to join you and the other members of the Commission in the important work prescribed for it; but the obligations which I have assumed for the fall are such that it is impossible for me to enter upon this most promising field of work.

I am extremely sorry to have missed your call. At that time I was in New York, engaged in a task of conciliation in the garment trades. It took a fortnight which I much needed for other things. But the result seems to have justified the effort. It has, however, greatly disarranged my plans, and I fear may make impossible the trip to North Haven, to which I had looked forward.

I am delighted to hear that the baby is much better.

Most cordially yours,

Have you thought of Charles R. Crane in connection with your Commission.[2]

1. The Pan American Financial Conference of 1915 had recommended that each nation's finance minister appoint a high commission of nine men, with himself serving as chairman. When meeting together they would constitute an international high commission to deal with hemispheric financial questions on a semi-official basis. McAdoo had originally asked Henry P. Davison of the J. P. Morgan Co. to serve, but when Davison proved unwilling, McAdoo turned to LDB.

2. Crane was appointed by McAdoo to the chairmanship of the Commission's Committee for Venezuela.

To William Ellsworth Smythe

July 28, 1915 Boston, Mass. [Brandeis Mss, NMF 66-3]

MY DEAR MR. SYMTHE: Upon my return to the city I find your letter about the American Dental Trade Association meeting.[1]

In my opinion the following points can be most effectively developed:

Combinations in unreasonable restraint of trade are a grave evil; but many combinations between competitors are possible which do not stifle competition, and which will greatly advance the common weal. The great line of distinction is this:

Competition should be regulated. That is, we should have combinations which nourish competition instead of combinations that kill competition. Salutary competition is based mainly upon a careful study of the facts relating to particular trades; facts bearing upon demand and supply; upon wholesome methods of conducting business. Associations between competitors which seek to give this information, to be valuable, must come through cooperative endeavor, and the protection against trade abuses ought to be carefully differentiated from the combinations which limit individual initiative and enterprise; and which have for their ultimate purpose some form of monopoly.

Eddy, in his "New Competition",[2] has said a good deal bearing on this subject, and you no doubt have seen some things which I have said in my various talks on trusts.

I wish I might see you again. I think of you often.

Most cordially yours,

1. Smythe had been asked to address the American Dental Trade Association meeting on the subject, "Trade Organizations – Their Value to Members and the Public." As LDB had originally suggested that Smythe be asked to speak, Smythe wrote LDB asking for his opinions on the matter.

2. Arthur Jerome Eddy, *The New Competition: An Examination of the Conditions Underlying the Radical Change that is Taking Place in the Commercial and Industrial World—The Change From a Competitive to a Cooperative Basis* (New York, 1912).[1]

To Thomas Watt Gregory

July 29, 1915 Boston, Mass. [Brandeis Mss, NMF 1-N-3]

MY DEAR GREGORY: I was out of the city when your letter of the 14th reached me, and Anderson's absence delayed our conference until today over the New Haven–Eastern Steamship assignment, referred to in yours of the 14th.[1]

In my opinion it would be unwise for you to assent to the assessment for the reasons which I expressed to you when Mr. Elliott first broached the subject. Furthermore, the proposed investment appears to me to involve clearly a violation of the Massachusetts law, and it would be most unseemly for the Department of Justice to give its assent to an act which is in violation of our law.

Anderson will no doubt write you fully in regard to the matter.

Very truly yours,

1. A New Haven subsidiary company, the New England Navigation Company, owned a large part of the stock of the Eastern Steamship Company. The latter company was in receivership and a plan for re-organization had been presented, which would assess stockholders to get the company back on its feet. At the same time, however, the New England Navigation Company had been ordered to dispose of its interest in the steamship firm by 1917. President Elliott had asked Gregory for permission to pay the requested assessment and save the company.

To Louis Lipsky

July 29, 1915 Boston, Mass. [Brandeis Mss, Z 1-4]

MY DEAR MR. LIPSKY: There is nothing in my present engagements which prevents my making the anniversary celebration of the Austro-Hungarian Zionists, if that proves to be the best use that can be made of the evening (Oct. 2); but in view of the fact that we are looking more than two months ahead, and there may be developments calling for other utilizations of the evening, it would be desirable that any engagement made by you should be upon condition that I could withdraw if the interest of the cause demands.[1]   Very cordially yours,

1. See LDB to Benjamin Perlstein, 8 September 1915.

To Louis Lipsky

July 29, 1915 Boston, Mass. [Brandeis Mss, Z 1-4]

DEAR MR. LIPSKY: Replying to yours of the 28th regarding advances to the Mizrachi: [1]

This application of the Mizrachi and the other demands now being made upon us for propaganda, indicates strongly that the Provisional Committee will be unable to give the assistance which the various organizations require for propaganda work, unless the plan agreed upon sometime ago with and through Dr. Levin,—that the Provisional Committee should receive the shekel money from all English speaking countries, is carried out.

We cannot, of course, determine definitely upon the disposition of this money until we reach an understanding with the Actions Comite; and that necessarily is postponed until Tschlenow and Sokolow come here, as we hope in October. But it is clear that we should insist now upon the payment into the treasury of the Provisional Committee of all shekels collected in the United States, and for this purpose I suggest:

First: That the Federation be requested to pay to the Provisional Committee the balance it now holds on the shekel account.

Second: That the Mizrachi be requested to pay into our treasury the shekel moneys which they have received. There was an oral understanding with Rabbi Berlin at one of our Provisional Committee meetings months ago, that this should be done, and my recollection is that it was understood that the Office Committee would draft a letter to Rabbi Berlin covering relations of the Mizrachi to the Provisional Committee. I do not recall having seen a copy of this letter.

If Rabbi Berlin is willing to pay over to the Provisional Committee the shekel monies collected and to be collected, I think those acting on behalf of the Provisional Committee may properly assume the responsibility of advancing to the Mizrachi $300 recommended by you without awaiting action at a Committee meeting.

Rabbi Berlin stated in his letter to me of the 20th that the Mizrachi now had 7,000 members, and there can be scarcely a doubt that the collections from these, to date, would be least $1250.[2]   Yours very truly,

1. See LDB to Lipsky, 28 July 1915, n. 1.
2. See LDB to Meyer Berlin, 25 August 1915.

To George Washington Kirchwey

July 30, 1915 Boston, Mass. [Brandeis Mss, NMF 67-2]

MY DEAR KIRSHWEY [sic]: I have just had a telegram from Bruere, telling me of the meeting of the Council of Conciliation on Monday, and have now talked with him on the telephone.[1] I explained to him that I had been planning to go off with Mrs. Brandeis on her and my vacation, and that after my many transgressions of the past year, I did not want to postpone Mrs. Brandeis's trip unless it was absolutely necessary. As I said to him, I am perfectly content to agree to anything that you, he, and Dr. Adler concur in, and Bruere told me that he had talked over the matter fully with Hillquit last evening.

I judge that the trouble is wholly from the manufacturers' end, and in view of that, my absence would be quite as helpful as my presence.[2]

Bruere has my address,—South Yarmouth, Mass. The telephone address is care of Charles Brown.   Most cordially,

1. Henry Bruere (see LDB to Bruere, 28 July 1913) had been appointed to Mayor Mitchel's council of conciliation for the garment industry (see LDB to John P. Mitchel, 9 July 1915, n. 2).
2. While the workers had readily accepted the council's proposals, the manufacturers hung back. Finally, in the face of a massive strike threat, the manufacturers signed the agreement for a two-year arrangement on 4 August. By April 1916, however, the agreement was shattered by a manufacturers' lockout.

To Benjamin Perlstein

July 30, 1915 Boston, Mass. [Brandeis Mss, Z 8-2]

DEAR MR. PERLSTEIN: I am enclosing herewith my check for $500. being my contribution for the month of July towards the Emergency Fund.

Prior to July 1st the expenses of the Zionist Bureau for New England were borne, to a limited extent by the Federation, and otherwise by direct contributions made by me. An account of those disbursements was kept in my office under the name Zionist Bureau for New England. Will you therefore kindly send to my office immediately a check to cover the appropriation for the month of July, namely 1/12 of $5000. or $416.66. The check should be to the order of Zionist Bureau for New England.

Yours very truly,

To Benjamin Perlstein

July 30, 1915 Boston, Mass. [Brandeis Mss, Z 8-2]

DEAR MR. PERLSTEIN: Referring to our recent conversation: Please have prepared, so as to send with Mr. Kesselman's [1] report of the expenses of the various Zionist concerns for the month of July, a detailed report giving the budget of the Provisional Committee's expenses in connection with the New York office for the year beginning July 1, 1915: the work performed by each of the employees of the office, and generally the occasion for the various estimated expenses, as appearing in the budget. Also indicate to what extent the expenses are likely to be increased or diminished, as dependent upon the probable operations of the office.

Yours very truly,

1. Robert D. Kesselman (1882–1942) was controller of the Zionist Organization of America. He was born in Russia, emigrating to the United States in 1900. He became a certified public accountant and an active Zionist, making several trips to Palestine shortly after the World War. In 1920 he moved there permanently and established one of the first accounting firms in Palestine. Kesselman and LDB were in the closest of contact regarding Zionist financial affairs during the years before 1920.

To Jacob deHaas

August 6, 1915 Boston, Mass. [Brandeis Mss, Z 12-1]

DEAR MR. DEHAAS: When you and Mr. Lipsky take up the matter of program, I suggest that Herzl's birthday, May 2d, be selected for the Herzl Celebration instead of his deathday. Note the celebration of Washington's birthday and Lincoln's birthday, etc.

Cordially yours,

To Jacob deHaas

August 8, 1915 South Yarmouth, Mass. [Brandeis Mss, Z 12-1]

DEAR DEHAAS: Yours of the 7th recd.

I am not convinced of the wisdom of the course proposed by Mr. Lipsky—doubtless because I am still ignorant in Jewish affairs and particularly in New York Jewish affairs.

1. I have great confidence in your knowledge and wisdom in these matters; and if you and the P.C. office Comt[ee] agree that additional subventions should be made to the Paoli [sic] Zion of $500 for special propaganda, I am willing that it be done.[1]

2. I do not think we should make any statement now showing that A[merican] J[ewish] C[ommittee] negotiations have been broken off;[2] particularly not in view of the proposed action of Kraus in behalf of I.O.B.B. reported by Lipsky. The facts will of course quickly leak out & be commented on—notably the fact that conference sessions are to be secret. Whatever statement the P.C. makes should follow, and precede the statement of the other of the 16 etc. organizations. When the time comes for a statement from us I should like to have a draft submitted by you and Lipsky.

3. I am clear that we ought not at this time guarantee the budget of $10,000 or any amount except as above.[3] If the congress is to be valuable it must be a matter of slow growth. There is no occasion for an early session of the Congress. We need at this time Zionists—not stimmung.[4] There is no very short cut to Zionists. We need patient self-sacrificing work from our men and their associates. If we are to have a Jewish Congress, it should be a congress of free Jews. Little will be gained by changing the source

of subsidies. Before we connect ourselves further let us see what others will do toward raising. What have they done so far?

4. I do not think it wise for me to address the Mass Conference Aug. 19. That would connect the P.C. before we know what support the movement is to have. It is far better that I should remain in the background at this stage.[5]

1. Both Lipsky and deHaas felt that the money requested by Rutenberg (see LDB to Lipsky, 28 July 1915) should be granted.

2. deHaas suggested a formal statement be made indicating the final rupture with the American Jewish Committee. Such a statement "would enable us to ask the sixteen organizations who are against the A.J.C. conference including our own organizations to make public statement either of their non-acceptance of the invitation or their positive acceptance of the Congress attitude."

3. Both Lipsky and deHaas felt that if the Zionists would spend $10,000 "we shall not only carry before us everything in the matter of the Congress, but we shall have succeeded in carrying a large majority of all the pro-congress element into the Zionist camp."

4. "Favorable public sentiment." LDB, according to Professor Shapiro, "meant that the socialists who would support the Congress movement would not join the Zionist Organization, and hence the investment of money would be a waste." *Leadership of the American Zionist Organization*, 86–87.

5. There was to be a mass conference at the Cooper Union on 19 August, and deHaas urged LDB to address it.

To Alfred Brandeis

August 9, 1915 South Yarmouth, Mass. [Brandeis Mss, M 4-1]

DEAR AL: Susan is off suffrage campaigning.[1] Alice, Elizabeth, & I paddled up to the bullrushes this morning & talked much of you as we have the habit of doing at South Yarmouth. We included Mrs. Wilde whom Alice & I called on Sunday evening.

Saturday Susan, some youths & I motored to the Cranes at Woods Hole & saw there Ben and [*] Flexner.[2] The former declared that you looked well when he saw you last (at which I am glad) and that you had become sensible & were not working so hard (which I doubt).

Wilde has bought the Nichols house (where Prescott & his three children live) also the two houses (front & back) adjoining, and all the land at the point. In the lot next to him his friend

Spring has built a house. They are having much dredging done in front & will fill his low land.

Beste Gruesse

1. See LDB to Mrs. F. W. Wile, 19 June 1915, n. 2.

2. Bernard Flexner (1865–1945), a member of the distinguished family of Louisville intellectuals, was trained as a lawyer and practised in Kentucky and Chicago before moving to New York. He was particularly interested in juvenile courts and had already written a book *Juvenile Courts and Probation* (New York, 1914). Convinced in 1917 that Zionism was the only possible solution to the problems of world Jewry, Flexner joined his friends LDB and Julian Mack in active Zionist work. He was present at the Paris Peace Conference and was a founder of the Palestine Economic Corporation, an institution which LDB remembered in his will (see Flexner, "Brandeis and the Palestine Economic Corporation," *The New Palestine*, 32 [14 November 1941]: 15). Flexner never lost his interest in Louisville affairs and particularly his interest in the University of Louisville; in 1938 he wrote a tribute to his friend, *Mr. Justice Brandeis and the University of Louisville* (Louisville, 1938). In 1946, Professor Mason dedicated his biography of LDB to the memory of Bernard Flexner.

To Cyrus Adler

August 10, 1915 Boston, Mass. [Magnes Mss]

MY DEAR DR. ADLER: Absence on a vacation has delayed reply to your letters dated July 28th and August 3rd, which I understand have been duly acknowledged through the Zionist Bureau of New England.[1]

First: As to your complaint that Mr. Lipsky was arranging meetings to urge the holding of a democratic congress while your and my negotiations were pending, you are right in assuming that Mr. Lipsky did this without consulting me, but I am greatly surprised that you should find fault with his action, for he simply followed your example. You cannot have forgotten that although you and I arranged on July 7th for a conference to be held July 12th to work out some plan of cooperation, you proceeded on July 11th to commit the United Synagogue to support the undemocratic conference which the American Jewish Committee had arranged. Mr. Lipsky knew that you had done this and naturally assumed that you would not expect the friends of a democratic congress to remain inactive while you continued your efforts to defeat a democratic consideration of the problems of the Jewish people.

Second: As to your refusal of my request that you call together the full committee to consider my arguments in favor of the American Jewish Committee's cooperating with the other national organizations in a congress to be convened and conducted on a democratic basis; your refusal of my request seems to me most regrettable, for there never was a time when the Jewish people stood in greater need than now of unity and of patient deliberation. I am the more surprised at your decision since at least two members of the American Jewish Committee, Judge Mack, himself a vice-president, and Dr. Harry Friedenwald, supported my request. Your refusal to permit my arguments to be presented to the full committee seems to me strong evidence that there exists in your Executive Committee that absolutistic spirit against which the proposers of a democratic congress have so earnestly protested.

Third: While refusing the request for a hearing of my arguments by your full committee, you courteously renew the invitation to the Zionists to attend the conference at Washington which your committee has called for October 24th. The need of wise counsel in Jewish affairs and of unity is now so great, that I should earnestly urge my associates to yield, where possible, their objections, and attend your conference, if I believed that there was the least likelihood of such a conference serving the Jewish cause. But I am convinced that the conference which you have decided upon will be worse than futile; it will be positively dangerous to Jewish interests. You state: "the conference that we are planning is to meet in executive session, and only the results of its action are to be made known to the public through such definite authorized channels and to the extent which the conference itself shall decide." Secrecy necessarily breeds suspicion and creates misunderstanding. Suspicion and misunderstanding have been among the greatest enemies of the Jews in the past. A conference conducted in secret sessions, as your committee has decided, would, if generally participated in by the Jews of this country, prove a menace both to them and to the Jews of the rest of the world. It is only through a frank and open discussion of the conditions, the sufferings, and hopes of our people, that we may expect to secure the co-operation of non-Jews in our effort to obtain justice and rights. It is only through a congress convened and conducted on a democratic basis that we can expect to secure that thorough cooperation of the Jews for self-help without which they cannot be freed from existing injustice and oppression.

Fourth: You say I err that in assuming that in a matter of this kind "the American Jewish Committee stands upon a footing exactly similar to that of the Federation of American Zionists, or other national bodies." On the contrary, I was fully aware of the powers granted to itself by the American Jewish Committee and set forth in its charter, but the process by which the American Jewish Committee was called into existence was as undemocratic as the steps you have now taken to create a Jewish conference, and I use the term "democratic" in the American sense when I say that an organization in which a system of self-election and perpetuation in office is in vogue, and which meets always in secret session, cannot properly be called democratic.

Fifth: In spite of the publicity which you have given to your refusal, I renew my request that you call a meeting of the full committee, to which my arguments for co-operation in calling a congress to be convened and conducted on a democratic basis may be presented.[2]   Yours very truly,

1. Adler's short letter of 28 July, written before receiving LDB's letter sent that date, complained about a circular letter sent by Louis Lipsky to members of the Federation of American Zionists urging agitation on behalf of a democratically elected congress. Adler felt that such a letter was inappropriate, pending the negotiations he and LDB were conducting. On 3 August, Adler sent an eighteen page reply to LDB's letter of 28 July. In his letter Adler defended the unwillingness of the American Jewish Committee to "reconsider" its plans for a "conference." In addition he attempted to justify both the means of selection of the delegates to the conference and the limitation of the scope of the discussion. Finally, he told LDB that the conference would meet "in executive session" and that only the results of the deliberations would be made public for fear of a careless word uttered in the heat of public debate embarrassing the Jews who were struggling in belligerent countries for their very survival. He closed with the plea that, despite their theoretical differences, LDB would join hands with the American Jewish Committee and give the community the benefit of the advice and aid of the Zionist movement. It is evident that by this stage in the controversy both men were writing for the record and with the notion that the letters would be made public. In August the Jewish Congress Organization Committee, a pro-Zionist, pro-democratic congress organization published *The Jewish Congress versus the American Jewish Committee: A Complete State-*

ment, with the Correspondence Between Louis D. Brandeis and Cyrus Adler (New York, 1915).

2. For Zionist strategy at this point, see LDB to Stephen S. Wise, 25 August 1915.

To Meyer Berlin

August 25, 1915 New York, N.Y. [Brandeis Mss, Z 12-3]

MY DEAR RABBI BERLIN: I have considered with my Zionist associates, the various matters concerning the Mizrachi, which you brought to my attention yesterday afternoon, and I have reached the following conclusion:

First: As I have already stated to you, the Provisional Committee stands, in America, in the same relation to the various Zionist organizations here as does the Actions Committee in Europe. We shall, therefore, in all matters, treat equitably all affiliated organizations, and the Mizrachi or Poale Zion will be treated just as fairly as the Federation of American Zionists and the various organizations subsidiary to it.

Second: In so far as the Zionist Bureau of New England is concerned, you may, as I already wrote you, rely upon the full cooperation of that office in such work as the Mizrachi undertakes in New England territory.

Third: You mentioned that the mere fact that the Federation's office was in the same suite with that of the Provisional Committee created the impression that special favor would be shown the Federation. When the Provisional Committee agreed with the Federation to take the new offices at twenty-third street [*sic*], I suggested to Mr. Perlstein and Mr. Lipsky that it would be desirable to have both the Mizrachi and the Poale Zion arrange for their rooms in connection with the other Zionist bodies. Mr. Perlstein tells me that he and Mr. Lipsky made the suggestion to you, but that you declined to take offices with us, believing that it would be more to the interests of the Mizrachi to have its offices on the East Side.

Fourth: The Provisional Committee recognized the propriety of giving aid to the Mizrachi in its activities but it does not seem to me that we can properly make any further advances to the Mizrachi until the amount due from it for Shkolim, which I understand amounts to about $1,500. is paid over to us or are accounted for, and, in this connection, the stub must be returned, showing the names and addresses of those who paid for Shkolim. When I spoke to you yesterday, you remarked that the Federation had not paid over its Shkolim to the Provisional Committee. I have since inquired, and find that the Shkolim collected by the Federation have been fully accounted for to the Provisional Committee.

Fifth: You stated that the Provisional Committee was represented on the Congress Committee by three Federation members. This was temporary arrangement only, to permit the Federation to elect its own members. These three now represent the Federation and not the Provisional Executive Committee, which I understand is not represented as such in the Congress Committee. I learn, further, that the Mizrachi is also represented by three members selected by you, the Poale Zion being similarly represented. It would appear clear, therefore, that the Mizrachi has full representation on the Congress Committee, equal to that of the Federation, Poale Zion and other bodies.

With Zion's greetings, I am,   Very truly yours,

To Adolf Kraus

August 25, 1915 New York, N.Y. [Brandeis Mss, Z 11-1]

MY DEAR MR. KRAUS: [1] I acknowledged, under date of August 20th, your recent letters, adding that I would reply as soon as I could confer with my associates, with whom, however, a conference was to be obtained with difficulty, owing to the interruptions of the vacation season. We have just met and discussed your proposal, and I hasten to report the result.

First: My associates agree with me that we should accept your invitation to be represented at the conference which you propose to call, understanding that what you propose is strictly a conference, and that no one attending is to bind, in advance, the organization which he represents, to any specific policy which may be submitted or appear to be the prevailing opinion at the conference; in other words, that the meeting is strictly a conference in which we exchange views and endeavor to reach a consensus of opinion as to what it is wisest to do, leaving further action to be determined later.

Second: It would obviously be desirable that such conference should be held at as early a date as possible, consistent with adequate attendance of representatives of such other organizations as should be invited to attend. I suppose it would not be possible for you to arrange for such a conference until after the Jewish Holidays.

Third: We were glad to find in your proposal, substantial agreement with that portion of my proposition made to Dr. Cyrus Adler on July 12th, and subsequently reefrred to in my letter of July 28th: that concerted action on the part of the Jews of this country can be effected only through an understanding reached upon consultation of representatives of those national organizations which actually represent the Jews. Your action, at this time, should bring about a better understanding among all concerned by thus adopting American democratic methods of proceeding in the conduct of Jewish affairs, and I trust you will succeed in securing the assent also of the American Jewish Committee to so reasonable a proposal. If you succeed, you and your organization will have rendered a great service to the Jewish cause.

Will you kindly keep me duly advised of the results of your negotiations?   Most cordially yours,

1. Adolf Kraus (1850–1928) was a Bohemian Jew who settled in Chicago and became a successful lawyer and local political figure. He was head of the Chicago School Board and president of the Civil Service Commission in the mid-1890s. Kraus was the president of the International Order of B'nai Brith from 1905 to 1925 and one of the founders of its famous Anti-Defamation League. He had been urging LDB to give support to his proposal for a "preliminary conference" preparatory to the calling of a Jewish congress after the plan LDB advocated in his discussion of 12 July with Cyrus Adler.

To Stephen Samuel Wise

August 25, 1915 New York, N.Y. [Brandeis Mss, Z 11-1]

MY DEAR DR. WISE: At conferences continued throughout yesterday and today, at which all members of our Zionist organization who were available were present, also leading members of the Congress Organization, the following conclusions were reached as to the course to be pursued:

First: That the policy set forth by me at my conference with Dr. Cyrus Adler on July 12th, and in my letters to him of July

28th and August 10th, is a wise policy to be pursued in the interest of the Zionist Cause, as well as of the general Jewish Cause.

Second: That we should, in every proper way, endeavor to secure a unification of the several factions in Jewry; that following the policy which I pursued in refusing to treat Dr. Adler's letter of August 3rd as a final rejection of a plan for a conference, and urging in my two letters a submission of the matter to the American Jewish Committee, Dr. Friedenwald, Judge Sanders and others should endeavor to secure a special meeting of the American Jewish Committee to re-consider the action taken, and to this end Dr. Friedenwald will enter upon correspondence with several members of the Committee upon his return to Baltimore, tomorrow. (It appeared today from a letter received by Dr. Friedenwald from Judge Mack, that Dr. Adler had acted, in rejecting my proposal, without even calling together a meeting of the Executive Committee). Furthermore, that, in the interest of securing unity of action, we should accept, substantially, the invitation of the I.O.B.B. to participate in a preliminary conference, or consultation, in accordance with my letter to Mr. Kraus, of today, of which a copy is enclosed.[1] As a further effort in the interest of unity, Judge Sanders reported on a letter that he had written Mr. Schiff, asking for an interview with a view to bringing about peace, to which no answer had yet come, and the effort now being made by Judge Sanders in this direction was approved.

Third: That we should pursue, in every proper way, our propaganda for a democratic Congress. At present, fourteen organizations, have affiliated themselves in the Congress Organizations Committee, namely: The Independent Order B'rith Abraham; Ind. Order B'rith Sholem; Federation of Galician and Bukowanian [sic] Jews; Federation of American Zionists; Federation of Rumanian Jews; Order Sons of Zion; Ind. Order Sons of Israel; Union of Orthodox Hebrew Congregations; Mizrachi Federation; Society of Orthodox Rabbis; United Hungarian Societies and other organizations. These organizations, although representing more than three hundred thousand Jews, represent, still, a small part of the Jewry of America. No Congress of American Jews ought to be held until this Committee includes organizations and individuals constituting a much larger part of the Jews of America, representing them not only in number, but also in character, that is, making it representative also of various parts or localities of America and of the several classes and shades of opinion. The work of the Organizations Committee is therefore to be continued vigorously, not only to make the Jews of America understand the need of cooperation, but also the need of cooperation through democratic methods.

Fourth: Since the Organizations Committee is not yet fairly representative of the whole Jewry, it should, in seeking adherents to the Congress plan, confine itself to require a declaration in favor of a Congress, that is, a Congress on a democratic basis, properly representative and public. In other words, those who are asked to join ought not to be formally bound to the Palestinian program, although, of course, our propaganda must necessarily include the Palestinian program, since we see no solution of the Jewish problem, which does not involve that. Furthermore, since the Committee does not yet represent the Jews adequately to be justified in calling a Congress, it obviously does not represent the various classes, localities and interests, sufficiently, to justify the Committee in determining the plan and scope and methods of the Congress. Study should be made of these subjects, but no action should be taken, now, and such action should only be taken when the various organizations who are to participate in a Congress shall have had the opportunity, through their representatives, selected for this specific purpose, of discussing this particular subject in a preliminary conference.

Fifth: Pending the efforts to secure unity of action through

(a) Direct appeal by members of the A.J.C. for reconsideration, and,

(b) The meeting proposed by the I.O.B.B., the effort to interest the Jew in the need of a Congress should continue as above set forth, but we must also use all proper efforts

(1) To prevent the holding of the Conference by the A.J.C., or

(2) If it is held, to reduce its significance by preventing organizations from participating in it, and, furthermore,

(3) If and so far as organizations do participate in it, to make clear that the organizations which do accept do not properly or fully represent the actual membership.

For instance, in discussing this subject, Judge Sanders stated that he was convinced that the I.O.B.A. would, at its Executive Committee meeting, to be held on the 30th, reject the invitation, as the I.O.B.S. had already done; that this fact would be at once made public, and that several others of the national orders would quickly follow suit. Furthermore, that leading lodges of the O.B.A. in various states would set forth their resolutions, directly repudiating the Conference; that others stated that while the Y.M.H.A. Council, in which Mr. Warburg is potent, would probably accept the invitation, local councils and important Y.M.H.A. organizations would decline, in favor of the Democratic Congress, and specifically against participation in the Conference. It is said the Penn. Y.M.H.A.'s have already done so.

Mr. Julius Peyser [2] stated that he believed that the I.O.B.B. would more specifically reject an invitation, and that important I.O.B.B. lodges had already declared their adherence to the democratic Congress program and their protest against a secret conference.[3]

From statements of various members present, there was strong reason to believe that the attendance at the A.J.C. Conference would probably be limited, in the main, to those organizations which were in the control of Messrs. Schiff, Marshall, Adler and Sulzberger, largely subsidized by Mr. Schiff and his associates.

I am sending you, under another cover, a copy of the Congress correspondence, issued by the Committee.

Very truly yours,

1. See preceding letter.
2. Julius I. Peyser (1875–1953) was an important Washington, D.C. lawyer who was also connected in banking. He was involved in a number of civic projects and had an interest in Jewish affairs. He became involved with the Provisional Executive Committee, was a district president of the B'nai Brith, and also worked for the Joint Distribution Committee and other groups involved in Palestine relief.
3. The Zionists' strategy worked, and in October the American Jewish Committee dropped its plans for a conference. See also LDB to Wise, 26 August 1915.

To Julian William Mack

August 26, 1915 New York, N.Y. [Brandeis Mss, Z 11-1]

MY DEAR MACK: In my night letter of August 24th I wired you:

"LETTER TWENTIETH RECEIVED. NEITHER DEHAAS NOR ANY RESPONSIBLE MEMBER OF ORGANIZATION HAS EXPRESSED ANY SUCH VIEW AS YOU REPORT ALL ADHERE TO PROGRAM SET FORTH IN MY JEWISH PROGRAM ADDRESS.   WILL WRITE".[1]

First: Every one connected with the Zionist organization adheres clearly to the program set forth by me in that address and throughout my speeches last year. The Basle Program [2] represents the most that the organized Zionists have ever asked for, and, of course, they have not always insisted upon having all of that. Statements asking for more, such as you inquire about, have been made by some persons who are not organized Zionists, and some of whom have been, in the past, active anti-Zionists. So far as these persons are now friendly with us, we have cautioned them against such utterances as they have made as being damaging to the Cause and to our Palestinian interests, and these persons have expressed themselves as ready to act on our caution. There are, however, some anti-Zionists, American editions of Ephraim Cohen [*sic*], who are endeavoring to use irresponsible and, possibly, mis-quoted statements as a means of bringing Zionists into disrepute, although, in so doing, they are endangering the Jews and Jewish interests in Palestine. A notable instance of this is to be found in the "American Hebrew", in the article in which your participation is stated, contrary to the facts.[3] If there is any way in which you can make clear to your friends on the American Jewish Committee who have been so hostile to Zionism and Zionists, the dangers to which they are thus subjecting our people, you will be performing a very great service.

Second: As to the Congress: I am enclosing your copy of my letter of yesterday to Dr. Wise, setting forth the consensus of opinion of those present. Dr. Friedenwald tells me that he will write you fully in regard to this.

Third: Rutenberg is not an organized Zionist. He is a radical, with great influence among the working people. He has impressed me as being straightforward, forceful and sincerely devoted to the Jewish Cause. From all that I can learn, his propaganda has been helpful in arousing the Jews to the necessity of deep interest and action. He is doing educational work which probably no one directly connected with our organization could do very effectively. There can be no doubt but that through his efforts the Poale Zion will become far more of a factor in developing the Zionist idea in America. Rutenberg is convinced that when he goes to Chicago again, he can, in conjunction with Messrs. Kaplan and Shulman, raise considerable money for the Congress cause. It has not seemed to me probable that your associations were such as to enable you to give any aid in this matter.

Fourth: What I had meant to suggest in regard to your talking to McCormick was to make him realize particularly the importance of the Zionist movement.[4] I think that if you will call to his attention, by letter or otherwise the Hapgood articles,[5] and then talk to him when you go back to Chicago, there probably will be enough to secure the attention which we should have from the "Tribune".

Fifth: As to what action members of our Committee should take, who are also members of the American Jewish Committee, at the proposed A.J.C. Conference, I think it unnecessary to express an opinion now, beyond saying that I think you ought not to commit yourself either way on this proposition. There may not be any Conference, and if there is a Conference, varying conditions may affect the course which should properly be taken. We can cross that bridge if and when we reach it.

I am sending you herewith copy of a letter which was this day sent to Dr. Magnes, also copies of my letters of the 25th to Dr. Wise and Adolph [*sic*] Kraus.   Cordially yours,

1. In his letter of 20 August, Mack had expressed some misgivings about the congress idea and about some recent statements by Zionist spokesmen. Pinhas Rutenberg in particular had advocated in a speech at Chicago not merely the creation of a Jewish homeland in Palestine, but, according to Mack, "some way to make Jews throughout the world members of such a state to be represented by that state, its officials and its ambassadors throughout the world." Mack also said that he had heard rumors attributing similiar sentiments to Jacob deHaas. This position was much further than Mack was prepared to go in espousing a Jewish homeland, and he requested a clarification from LDB. For LDB's position on Rutenberg's address, see LDB to Mack, 26 October 1915.

2. The program adopted at the first Zionist Congress in Basle in 1897 called for the establishment of a Jewish homeland but was notably silent about the relationship of Jewish citizens in other lands to the Jewish state.

3. LDB may have been referring to a series of editorials then running in the *American Hebrew*, a leading Reformed Judaism organ, entitled "The Good and the Ill of Zionism." After noting that Zionism was good for such things as Hebraic studies and the love of religion, the editors then blasted the movement as impractical, leading to divided loyalties and other sins. Without mentioning names, but obviously referring to leaders such as LDB and Mack, the editorials condemned "maturer men" for leading younger, more idealistic Jews down this false path. See *American Hebrew*, 97 (30 July 1915): 314, and subsequent editorials on pp. 340, 364, 388, and 414.

4. In a note of 17 August, LDB had asked Mack to approach the editor of the *Chicago Tribune*, the conservative and influential Robert Rutherford McCormick (1880-1955) about an editorial in support of a democratic Jewish congress. Ironically, by the time of his death few editors in America were as widely distrusted by American Jews as McCormick. Mack had replied that, given his own genuine ambivalence about the congress, he did not think he should be the one to approach McCormick.

5. Undoubtedly at LDB's urging, Hapgood had embarked upon a series of articles on the Jewish problem and Zionism. Beginning in August 1915, the series continued into January 1916. See particularly "The Soul of Zionism," *Harper's Weekly*, 61 (14 August 1915): 150; see also LDB to Hapgood, 24 November 1915.

To Judah Leon Magnes

August 26, 1915 New York, N.Y. [Magnes Mss]

MY DEAR DR. MAGNES: I have heard nothing from you in regard to Congress-Conference matters since our interview on July 12th, after Dr. Cyrus Adler, Prof. Frankfurter and I met at Hotel Astor.

I have just seen Mr. Nathan Straus, and also have a letter from him under date of the 25th, in which he tells me that you expressed the wish to meet me and believe that if we meet it will be possible to reach a mutual understanding that should result in our cooperating for the Jewish Cause. I need not repeat to you what I said at our very pleasant interview on July 12th, that I shall be only too glad to take up this or any other matter relating to Jewish affairs with you at any time.[1] I am very sorry that I did not get this word earlier, as I have been in New York now nearly three days and am obliged to leave this afternoon; but I shall be very glad to see you earlier in Boston, if my next coming here should be somewhat delayed.

I think I ought to frankly state to you that I was deeply disappointed in not receiving even an acknowledgment of my letter of July 28th, in which I urged you to take up my letter of that date with Dr. Cyrus Adler, and to endeavor to bring about some adjustment of the differences of view. It is difficult to understand why Dr. Adler should not have been willing to have this very important matter considered by the full American Jewish Committee, particularly in view of the fact that the circumstances had changed so widely since the subject was originally considered by that Board, and I was the more surprised by Dr. Adler's action (of which I first learned yesterday) that he had not even called together the Executive Committee to consider my request.

The Jewish situation is so serious, that, in my opinion, no stone should be left unturned, in the effort to reach a proper conclusion in this matter, and I therefore, in spite of Dr. Adler's action in making public his refusal of my request, urged again his calling together the full Committee for consideration of the matter.

As soon as I am next here, or get back to my office, where there are some papers to which I wish to refer, I want to take up further with you the matter of the American Jewish Relief Committee, about which I talked to you and wrote you in July.

Very cordially yours,

1. On 30 June Magnes had submitted his resignation as a member of the P.E.C., ostensibly over the question of the congress. He wrote that he did not believe any single organization could speak for all of the Jews of America, and he urged that LDB accept the offer put forward by Louis Marshall (who was Magnes's brother-in-law) for a confederated plan. Actually, there were two unwritten reasons which prompted Magnes's resignation. One was his growing commitment to pacifism and his fear that the Zionists were being pulled into a pro-Allied position through the actions of men like Richard Gottheil. At a time when most members of the American Jewish community felt very strongly about the war, Magnes's pacifism struck a discordant note. The second reason was Magnes's belief that Zionism was moving toward the idea of a state for the Jews in Palestine, while all he wanted was the "spiritual center" advocated by Ahad Ha-Am, with whom Magnes was in close touch. At first LDB refused to accept the resignation, and in several letters he completely ignored it, urging Magnes to continue his role as a mediator between the Zionists and the American Jewish Committee. Upon Magnes's insistence, LDB finally acknowledged the 30 June letter. By this time, Magnes's departure from the P.E.C. was not the loss that it might have been a year earlier. See LDB to Magnes, 5 October 1915.

To Stephen Samuel Wise

August 26, 1915 New York, N.Y. [Brandeis Mss, Z 11-1]

MY DEAR DR. WISE: *First:* Your letters of August 22nd, sent to Boston, and of August 23rd, to New York, were duly received. I was greatly disappointed that you could not make it possible to come to New York for our conference yesterday or today, as matters of great urgency and importance to the Cause required consideration, and we needed your advice and influence. I came here myself for that reason, after a brief and much-interrupted vacation. Fortunately, we had others of the Committee who are in this part of the country who could serve us. Professor Gottheil, coming from Intervale, Dr. Friedenwald, from Baltimore and Mr. Julius Peyser, from Atlantic City, attended, also Mr. Lewin-Epstein and Mr. Louis Robison, from a distance also. Of course, Dr. Levin, Lipsky, Perlstein, Barondess and the various members of the Congress Committee were here.

Second: I wrote you, under date of yesterday, a letter setting forth the course agreed upon at the various conferences held here on the 24th and 25th, extending throughout the day and evening. I am also enclosing you a copy of Adolph [*sic*] Kraus's letter to me of August 17th, and of my three replies, under date of August 20th, 25th and 26th. I am also enclosing you a copy of my letter of today to Judge Mack, and of my letter to Magnes of today.

Third: From my letter to you of the 25th, reporting the course agreed upon, I hope you will agree with me that you must do everything in your power to prevent the Eastern Council from accepting the invitation to attend the October Conference, and that you also should do all in your power to prevent the Jewish Chautauqua from accepting that invitation, and I trust you will take this matter up at once with Mr. Elkus,[1] whom it is impossible for me to see before I leave the city. What your course should be in case, in spite of your efforts, you should fail to prevent the Eastern Council from accepting the American Jewish Committee's Conference invitation, there seems to me no occasion to decide. I think it, however, clear that you ought not to commit yourself, at present, to attend that Conference in any capacity. I am confident that if you and our other friends will actively assist in the course which has been outlined, that we can prevent the holding of any conference, or reduce the conference to such minute proportions as to make it ridiculous, from the standpoint of representing Jewish America, leaving it practically a conference of members of the American Jewish Committee and its subsidiary or subsidized organizations, which do not represent the Jews of America, and a few more organizations in which officers accepted the invitation but whose action does not reflect the opinion of a large part of the membership.

Fourth: I have your several communications about Lichtheim, and we have here also some letters from him. Nothing that the responsible Zionists are doing can imperil Palestine. Certain irresponsible people, who are not Zionists, and some of whom have been anti-Zionistic, have been making statements which are dangerous. Such of these persons as are in any way friendly to us, like Rutenberg, we have cautioned, and we are quite sure that they are ready to act upon our caution and prevent any injury to Palestine. But there are anti-Zionists here who are American editions of Ephraim Cohen, and these persons, as is shown by articles in the American Hebrew, appear to be ready, by their false accusations, to endanger all that has been accomplished in Palestine. If you can, through your eminent informant, or others, induce these gentlemen to refrain from their destructive attacks, you will perform a very great service.[2]

This was one of the matters about which I had hopes to confer with you here yesterday or today. I am uncertain now when I shall next be in New York. I hope that I shall not have to come here until after Labor Day, as practically every day of my supposed vacation has been invaded by Zionist emergencies. I understand that you have agreed to speak at the Y.M.H.A. in Worcester on Sept. 5th, and I hope you will arrange so as to have ample time to confer with me on that day and Labor Day following on the Zionist situation there, in case we do not meet before that time. I am returning today to South Yarmouth.

Fifth: I attended, for a time, a meeting of the Jewish Organizations Committee last evening, for the purpose of laying before them the program set forth in my letter to you of yesterday, and I understand that that program which was supported by Judge Sanders in a long speech, was accepted after I left. I also, at that meeting, declined the invitation to become the president of the

Congress Organizations Committee, telling them that I deemed it would be unwise for me to do so at the present stage of the movement.   Cordially yours,

1. Besides his activities in Democratic politics (see LDB to Eugene N. Foss, 13 August 1912), Abram I. Elkus was also involved in Jewish affairs. A leading member of Wise's congregation (and its president from 1919 to 1927), he and LDB came into frequent contact in Zionist activities.
2. See LDB to Julian W. Mack, 26 August 1915.

To Gilson Gardner

September 7, 1915 Boston, Mass. [Brandeis Mss, NMF 66-3]

DEAR MR. GARDNER: Upon my return to the city I find yours of the 23rd with enclosure.[1]

You are right in assuming that the activities etc., entered upon by the Trade Commission, particularly the recent hearings,—are not what I had contemplated would engage their attention.[2] But the fact that Rublee and Stevens are connected with the Commission leads me to believe that it will still prove a valuable governmental instrument.   Cordially yours,

1. Gardner had sent some clippings critical of the new Federal Trade Commission. One from the 20 August *Memphis Press* read: "The Federal Trade Commission has been in existence six months, without having entered a single order for the correction of any unfair business practice." Gardner challenged: "How about it? This was a creature of your creating. Is this what you intended it to do?"
2. Far from watch-dogging American corporate practices, the early hearings of the Federal Trade Commission were partly a forum for the voicing of complaints by businessmen and partly a means for investigating American trade relations with foreign countries, particularly Latin American nations. Secretary of Commerce William Cox Redfield later put the blame for the failure of the commission on Wilson himself: He hoped to "create . . . a counsellor and friend to the business world. . . . It was no large part of his purpose that the Federal Trade Commission should be primarily a policeman to wield a club over the head of the business community. Rather the reverse was true and the restraining powers of the Commission were thought a necessary adjunct which he hoped and expected to be of minor rather than of major use." Cited in Arthur S. Link, *Woodrow Wilson and the Progressive Era, 1910-1917* (New York, 1954). In time, as was revealed by LDB's conversation with Wilson biographer Ray Stannard Baker, LDB came to agree with Redfield in placing the blame for failure on Wilson's appointments to the commission. See LDB to Edward M. House, 31 December 1914.

To Adolf Kraus

September 7, 1915 Boston, Mass. [Brandeis Mss, Z 11-1]

MY DEAR MR. KRAUS: Upon my return to the city today your letters of August 27th and 31st are before me.

First: I know of nothing to prevent my attendance in New York on October 3rd,—the date you suggest, and I should be glad to have you assume such to be the place and date for our meeting.[1]

Second: I am entirely content that my letter of August 25th to you should be published as you suggest, and in view of your suggestion, have notified my associates that this may be done.

Third: In regard to the details of the conference, and the organizations which we should ask to send representatives: I find it necessary to defer a reply until I shall have an opportunitiy of conferring with my associates. In view of the Jewish holidays it will not be possible for me to do this before Monday, the 13th, when I am to be in New York, and I will let you hear from me then.[2]   Yours very truly,

1. Kraus was attempting to arrange a conference of the presidents of national Jewish organizations to iron out the conference-congress dispute. The meeting, which was held on 3 October, proved futile.
2. See LDB to Kraus, 14 September 1915.

To Judah Leon Magnes

September 8, 1915 Boston, Mass. [Magnes Mss]

DEAR DR. MAGNES: Referring again to your letter of July 29, 1915.[1]

First: Reliable reports which come to us from various sources indicate very great distress in Palestine calling for financial relief far in excess of the $12,000 to be sent to Palestine by the A.J.R.C. and the large additional sums transmitted by the Provisional Committee as general relief funds or on the transfer account.

I therefore deem it necessary to urge that the American Jewish Relief Committee apply to Palestinian relief the additional sums with which Palestine should equitably be credited, as set forth in part Second of my letter to you of July 18th. Your Executive

Committee approved on July 28th the disposition of the $16,000 substantially in accordance with the request contained in paragraph Third of my letter of July 18th: but it appears not to have taken any definite action in regard to the 'balance to the credit of Palestine of $57,284" referred to in Part Second of that letter.

Second: The accounts submitted with your letter of July 29th show that there was transferred from the so-called Vulcan Fund to the general fund, $43, 767.09; and also that the $10,000 sent by the A.J.R.C. of New England was in no part applied to Palestinian purposes. It therefore appears that upon the figures presented by you there is $43, 767.09, which in some way was treated as a part of the general fund, but ought specifically to have been or to be appropriated for Palestinian relief. (According to my figures, as set forth in my letter of July 18th, this amount was $57,284.00

Third: It does not seem necessary to determine at this time whether the balance which should be credited to Palestine is $43,767.09, as your figures would show, or $57,284.00, as my figures indicate, but at least the $43,767.09 indicated by your figures, should be applied to Palestinian relief.

In the original undertaking the pledges were as follows:

Nathan Straus, ...	$50,000
Jacob H. Schiff, ...	25,000
Central Relief Committee, ...	10,000
Provisional Committee, ...	25,000
American Jewish Relief Com.	25,000

making in all
$135,000

According to your account the A.J.R.C. and the Provisional Committee both contributed more than their respective pledges of $25,000, but the total amount contributed by Messrs. Straus, Schiff and the Central Relief Committee, instead of being at least $85,000 was only $35,232.91. (For instance of Mr. Nathan Straus' $50,000. only about $20,000 goes to Palestine and of the $10,000 transmitted by the A.J.R.C. of New England, nothing goes to Palestine).

The result is, therefore, that whereas on your figures the A.J.R.C. contributed to the Vulcan in cash $42,255.76, it took by transfer from the pledges of Messrs. Straus, Schiff, the Central Relief Committee, and the New England contribution $43,767.09. It is this $43,767.09 which on the figures submitted by you should, I submit, be set apart for Palestinian purposes.

I hope you will take up this matter in the Executive Committee as soon as possible.[2]   Cordially yours,

1. For the issues involved, see LDB to Magnes, 18 March and 18 July 1915.
2. See LDB to Magnes, 16 September 1915.

To Benjamin Perlstein

September 8, 1915 Boston, Mass. [Brandeis Mss, Z 8-2]

DEAR MR. PERLSTEIN: I desire to call the following to your and Mr. Lipsky's attention:

First: In a letter from Mr. Julius [sic] Leavitt in which he writes me concerning the matter of organized charity, about which he now has a series of articles in Pearson's Magazine,[1] he adds a paragraph, of which a copy is enclosed, volunteering his services. His address is 4200 Harrison St., N.W., Washington, D.C. I have called Mr. Peyser's attention to Mr. Leavitt and suggested that they meet.

Second: In July I had a letter from Dr. Edward A. Rumely of the Evening Mail,[2] who is a friend of a good friend of mine, Mr. Harrington Emerson, the efficiency engineer, who tells me that he will be glad to carry matter dealing with Zionism, and I think in any effort to secure publicity you will find a friend in him.

Third: The Business Editor, Jacob Nathan, of the Detroit Saturday Night, has expressed himself in a very kind way on my work in connection with Zionism. His paper is one of considerable influence in Detroit, and I think he would be glad to help us so far as he can.

Fourth: David Rubin, who was at Harvard last year, is now at 1440 East 95th Street, Cleveland. He is ready to "obey orders for the cause." He has had some training here under deHaas in addressing assemblies, and I think might be very useful in the work of organizing Cleveland, by persistent effort at small meetings, including the various lodges, etc. I think that he ought to be brought in close touch with our Zionist leaders there, and arrangements made for his utilization in a persistent campaign.

Fifth: I wrote Mr. Lipsky in full concerning Henry Sachs, a prominent citizen of Colorado Springs, a former client of mine, who is very eager for service.[3] He is not a speaker, but would be an influential worker and organizer. He is President of the local I.O.B.B. He has proffered his services, and I think would be thoroughly loyal to me. Did Lipsky write him?

Sixth: I enclose letter from the Austro-Hungarian Zionists of August 27th, which was received during my absence, and acknowledged by the Zionist office rather inadvertently.[4] You will recall that there was some correspondence with you and Mr. Lipsky in regard to my speaking at the October meeting, and that I was then directed to consider the engagement cancelled. I should like to have your and Mr. Lipsky's advice as to what, if anything, should be done in this connection.

Seventh: Enclosed for consideration by our Committee at our next meeting, if possible, is Dr. Melamed's [5] letter to me of August 11th concerning the Hebrew publication.

Eighth: Enclosed for consideration at the next meeting is a letter from Mr. Baron of August 14th, concerning the financial assistance to the St. Louis Hoachooza,[6] and also a letter of August 5th from the Department of State to Mr. Schulman.

Ninth: Monday the 13th during the day will be fully occupied by our consideration of questions to come up before the Committee meeting. I therefore suggest that you set apart Tuesday, at the Aeolian Building for conferences with members of the Congress Committee, or others, relating to Congress matters. Among others, we should have a conference with Judge Sanders, whom I am writing as per copy enclosed.

Tenth: J. L. Barowsky who I understand, with his brother, is in the B & B Paper Supply Co. of Holyoke, Mass., suggested having some paper water-marked as per enclosed, if we and others would be disposed to use it. I told him that I would submit this matter to you, and he doubtless will call upon you. Barowsky was among the Harvard Zionists last year who made a partial translation of Nawratzki book, and Mr. deHaas hopes for some activity from him in the local work.

Eleventh: I have Mr. Segal's memorandum about Raygorodsky

the aviator. It does not seem to me that he can aid us through his flights, but if he is a man of brilliant attainment, he ought to be of value to us otherwise.[7]   Yours very truly,

1. Julian Leavitt (1878-1939), a Russian-born Jew, resigned a position at the Library of Congress in 1911 in order to embark upon independent research and writing. He became interested in Jewish affairs and served as the director of research for both the American Jewish Committee and the Joint Distribution Committee (which he had helped to found). In 1932, he rejoined the Library of Congress and rose to chief of its Catalogue Division. A few months before his death he was appointed as editorial consultant to Franklin D. Roosevelt's Temporary National Economic Commission. The articles referred to here were a four-part expose of organized charities, the theme of which was that organized charity was organized fraud. See *Pearson's Magazine*, 33 (April 1915): 385-96; (May 1915): 581-88; (July 1915): 49-59; and (August 1915): 177-85.

2. Edward A. Rumely (1882-1964) was the publisher of the *New York Evening Mail* between 1915 and 1918. He went on to pioneer in the introduction of vitamins and vitamin-foods in the 1920s.

3. Henry Sachs (1863-1952) had founded the Boston Curb Exchange before moving to Colorado. He was a leading businessman and active in philanthropic work, being particularly connected with the Jewish Hospital in Denver.

4. See LDB to Louis Lipsky, 29 July 1915.

5. Samuel Max Melamed (1885-1938) had come to the United States from Lithuania in 1914. He edited several Jewish periodicals, including the *American Jewish Chronicle* from 1914 to 1928, and *The Reflex* from 1928 to 1936. During the Brandeis-Weizmann struggle, Melamed sided with Weizmann; see his article, "L. D. Brandeis and Chaim Weizmann," *The Reflex*, 2 (May 1928): 1-10. He had written to LDB regarding the creation of a Hebrew Press Association.

6. Maximilian George Baron (b. 1889), a St. Louis lawyer, taught on the faculty of the St. Louis University. He was president of the local Zionist Council and a member of the Provisional Executive Committee.

7. Hyman R. Segal, the managing editor of the *Maccabaean* had called to LDB's attention a young Jewish aviator named Raygorodsky. The young man had been excluded from a Russian air show because of his religion, and this had interested him in Zionism. He proposed a series of air exhibitions and shows which would raise money for Zionist causes.

To Louis Edward Kirstein

September 10, 1915 Boston, Mass. [Brandeis Mss, Z 7-3]

MY DEAR MR. KIRSTEIN: Referring to Rabbi Martin A. Meyer's[1] letter to you of August 20th, which I return herewith.

As I read his letter, Mr. Meyer's only difficulty appears to be this:

If and when a Jewish State is established should a non-Jew be admitted as a citizen? To this I should answer emphatically, yes: because the Jewish State, like every other State, ought to admit to citizenship persons of any nationality. This is what we have done in America. See my Fourth of July oration, of which copy is enclosed. To my mind the ideals which I there set forth for America should prevail likewise in the Jewish State.

Of course the non-Jewish citizen would not become a Jew; but he would become a citizen of the Jewish State.

I trust that Mr. Meyer will, upon further consideration, feel that the obstacle mentioned has been overcome, and that he will join us wholeheartedly.

Mr. Meyer is, I suppose, bearing in mind the fact that the more immediate problem is not the establishment of a political State, but the securing of a publicly recognized and legally secured "homeland" or Jewish centre in Palestine.

You may interested in the enclosed leaflet "Do You Know What Zionism Is?"   Cordially yours,

1. Rabbi Martin Abraham Meyer (1879–1923) was the Reform rabbi of Temple Emanu El in San Francisco.

To Adolf Kraus

September 14, 1915 New York, N.Y. [Brandeis Mss, Z 11-1]

MY DEAR MR. KRAUS:

I have conferred with my associates concerning your recent letter to me, and your letter of August 26th to the Congress Committee.[1]

We are of the opinion:

(1) That the invitation to the meeting to be held October 3rd should be sent out in your name only.

(2) That you should decide yourself whether the number of organizations to be invited to the meeting should be limited to fifteen including yourself, or should be increased to twenty-one, as has been proposed; and also, that you should decide yourself which organizations shall be invited.

As our meeting is to be one for consultation only, it does not seem to us important that there be any attempt made to balance the organizations invited, upon the basis of any opinion held by them respectively in regard to any of the question[s] touching which we are to consult. But since you ask suggestions, we wish to call your attention to the fact that the list of organizations which you named does not include any organizations of Jewish working people, such as the Arbeiter Ring and the Jewish National Labor Alliance.

We also call your attention to the fact that the National Council of Y.M.H.A.'s would be an appropriate organization to invite.

(3) We deem it imperative in order to avoid the possibility of misunderstanding that your invitation should make perfectly clear the fact that this is merely a coming together for exchange of opinion, and that no one attending is to bind in advance the organization which he represents to any specific policy which may be submitted or which may appear to be the prevailing opinion at the conference; in other words, that the meeting is strictly for exchange of views in the endeavor to reach a consensus of opinion as to what it is wisest to do.

My associates and I heartily appreciate the effort which you are making in the interest of Jewish unity.

Very cordially yours,

1. See LDB to Kraus, 7 September 1915.

To Inner Actions Committee

September 15, 1915 New York, N.Y. [Berlin Office]

GENTLEMEN: We report to you, with great regret, the resignation of Dr. Magnes from the Provisional Committee, and that he holds now no office of responsibility in the Zionist Organization.[1] Dr. Levin will write you fully on this subject.

I understand that, in the past, it has been the practice of your Committee to address communications, confidential in character, to various individuals in the United States. It seems to our Committee desirable that all communications should be sent only to the Chairman of this Committee, and any distribution of copies of communications in the United States should be determined by and attended to through this office.

I am asking you, therefore, to have all such matter addressed exclusively to me, at this office. Where it may seem desirable to you to distribute copies, we shall be glad, at any time, to have your suggestion, and would ask that you send us such communications in as many copies appear to you desirable, to facilitate our distribution.

Will you please communicate our wishes in this respect to such officers and officials of the Zionist Organization, such as Dr. Ruppin, Mr. Lichtheim, Dr. Sokolow, Dr. Tschlenow, Dr. Weizmann, Mr. Kahn [*sic*]², and others who have been accustomed, in the past, to send communications of a confidential character to individuals here.   Very cordially yours,

1. See LDB to Judah L. Magnes, 26 August 1915.
2. LDB probably means Jacobus E. Kann. Kann had not been a member of the Inner Actions Committee since 1911, but he still administered several Zionist agencies including the Jewish Colonial Trust.

To Judah Leon Magnes

September 16, 1915 Boston, Mass. [Magnes Mss]

MY DEAR DR. MAGNES: I have your letter of the 13th re Palestinian fund.¹

First: I enclose herewith copy of my letter of September 8th to Mr. Nathan Straus,² to whom I enclosed a copy of my letter of that date to you; and I now enclose a copy of his reply, from which you will see that he is greatly surprised to find that only $20,000 of the $50,000 contributed by him had gone to Palestine.

Furthermore the contribution which the Provisional Committee made to this $135,000 Palestinian fund was on the strength of the pledges made by the other participants, namely: Messrs. Straus, Schiff, the American Jewish Relief Committee and the Central Relief Committee; and no other contributor would have any right to subsequently direct a different appropriation of the money pledged to Palestine.

I therefore renew my request that the A.J.R.C. reappropriate this sum of $33,767.09 to Palestinian relief.

Second: You say that the $10,000 voted by the New England Committee was applied to Palestinian purposes. Will you kindly send me a statement of account showing when and how this was done?   Yours very truly,

1. See LDB to Magnes, 18 March, 18 July, and 8 September 1915.
2. LDB had written Straus, informing him of the failure of Magnes to forward to Palestine the money which Straus had contributed for that purpose.

To Howard Elliott

September 17, 1915 Boston, Mass. [Brandeis Mss, NMF 1-N-3]

MY DEAR MR. ELLIOTT: I am very glad to have your letter of the 10th enclosing data on operations for the twelve months ended June 30th, and the more extensive reports which were received during my vacation.[1]

The community, the stockholders and you yourself are to be congratulated on the results of your two years of service. You are entirely right in what you say about the difficulties of building up after the long illness, and of overcoming the results of mis-education. You have attacked the situation in the way which best promises success; and I have no doubt that with your careful persistent work in matters relating to operation, and by restricting the Company's operations to railroading property, you will in time also overcome the financial obstacles due to past mismanagement.

With best wishes,   Most cordially yours,

1. The New Haven had reported a very successful July with earnings substantially improved over July 1914. For details see the *New York Times*, 10 September 1915.

To Solomon Guedalia Rosenbaum

September 17, 1915 Boston, Mass. [Brandeis Mss, NMF 48-2]

MY DEAR MR. ROSENBAUM: [1] I am taking the liberty of introducing to you Mr. Joseph H. Schiff, whom I have known as valet at the City Club, and who has seemed to me qualified for a position of greater usefulness.

Mr. Schiff cannot run the risk at present of surrendering his position as valet because he must support his father and his father's family. From what he has told me of his father I feel that it ought to be possible to secure work which the father can do, and which would relieve the situation. I hope you will be willing to give Joseph Schiff time to explain the situation to you, and that you may be willing to help in securing a position for his father.

Very truly yours,

1. Solomon Guedalia Rosenbaum (1868–1937) was head of the National Cloak and Suit Company and was also involved in Jewish philanthropic work in New York.

To M. J. Finkelstein

September 21, 1915 Boston, Mass. [Brandeis Mss, Z 11-1]

DEAR SIR: [1] Replying to yours of the 16th:

First: In my opinion you are right in the view that the Jews of Canada should not take any part in the agitation for the Jewish Congress now under way in the United States.

Second: On the other hand, I am of opinion that the Jews of Canada properly should support actively the Zionist propaganda.[2] This is now being done by the Zionists in England; and our general program is wholly in accord with Great Britain's sympathy with the smaller nationalities.

I am sending you under separate cover my address on "The Jewish Problem," in which you will see that I quote freely from English authorities.   Very truly yours,

1. M. J. Finkelstein was from Winnipeg, Manitoba.
2. For the history of Zionism in Canada, see B. Figler, "Canada, Zionism In," in *The Encyclopedia of Zionism and Israel*, 174–79.

To Adolf Kraus (Telegram)

September 22, 1915 Boston, Mass. [Brandeis Mss, Z 11-1]

In inviting me to conference[1] you addressed me as President of Federation of Zionists. Dr. Harry Friedenwald of Baltimore is the President of that body, and should attend as such. I am the Chairman of the Provisional Committee. Please send to Dr. Friedenwald an invitation as President of the Federation, and send to me an invitation as Chairman of the Provisional Committee. Please wire answer.

1. See LDB to Kraus, 25 August, 7 September, and 14 September 1915.

To William Ellsworth Smythe

September 22, 1915 Boston, Mass. [Brandeis Mss, NMF 66-3]

MY DEAR MR. SMYTHE: Thank you for your letter of the 18th with enclosures.

The principle of the Stevens Bill seems to me clearly correct; but it will require a great deal of work to educate Congress and the public to any phase of regulation of competition. Considerable progress has already been made, and the report of the hearings before the House Committee on Interstate and Foreign Commerce, January 30 to February 16, 1914, will prove a valuable text book. I have such confidence in my fellow citizens that I cannot doubt ultimate success in securing this legislation.[1]

From the Federal Trade Commission I should also expect aid in the same direction with Rublee on it, and Stevens as one of its counsel.

I am extremely glad to know that the meeting with the American Dental Trade Association was so successful.[2]

Very cordially yours,

1. For the fate of the principle of the Stevens Bill, see LDB to George Rublee, 18 November 1913, n. 1.
2. See LDB to Smythe, 28 July 1915.

To George Carroll Todd

September 24, 1915 Boston, Mass. [Brandeis Mss, NMF 66-3]

MY DEAR MR. TODD: Your letter of the 22nd enclosing galley proof of the bill in the proposed suit against the United Shoe Machinery Company, in the Eastern District of Missouri,[1] reaches me just as I am leaving the city. I, therefore, have no time to make a careful study of the bill, but some rather fundamental doubts as to the best form of drawing the bill have suggested themselves to me, and I venture to call them to your attention, although you have doubtless already considered carefully the questions involved.

First: The extensive business done in the State of Missouri, and particularly in and about St. Louis, as compared with any other shoe manufacturing centre in the United States, if set out in the petition, would disclose to the Court at once, as is desirable, that this dictated the selection of the Missouri district for this litigation; and would tend to prevent any suspicion arising that the selection was dictated by any other court.

Second: The petition would in my opinion be materially strengthened if the situation in this country as to shoe machinery were set out in further detail. The petition shows inferentially, and perhaps directly, the amount of certain kinds of shoe machinery furnished by the United Shoe Machinery Company, and by all other shoe machinery manufacturers. It does not show how large a part of the entire number of different kinds of machines required is included in this list. It does not show what, if any, other machines could be secured, as a practical matter, from any other shoe machinery manufacturers. It does not show the extent to which other shoe machinery manufacturers have attempted to supply machinery within recent time; or to what extent they are trying now to develop a business; or anything from which a definite confirmation is given of the assertion in the petition that the tying clauses do result in a substantial suppression of competition. It would be well to have it appear on the face of the petition that the natural growth of a shoe machinery business would be by the development of one, or a few machines at a time, and that this development is prevented by a system which prevents the entry of the first machine, not because of the better character of its competitor, but because of the impossibility of getting other machines for other operations pending the natural, gradual development of the competitors' full line.

Third: The petition is silent as to the excess of the charge for shoe machinery over what it would be if the shoe machinery manufacturers were obtaining only a fair manufacturing profit on non-patented machines. The actual injury to the shoe manufacturer and to the ultimate wearer of the shoe, would undoubtedly tend to cause the Court to view the petition with more favor than will be the case if it seems to present only questions of law not of practical importance to the community.

Fourth: It might be desirable to have it appear in more definite terms that the discriminations complained of have been practiced in interstate transactions.

The matters to which I have just referred have more than the usual importance, because if the petition were met by a demurrer, the Court would undoubtedly be called upon to consider the opinions in the Massachusetts District, and would be affected not only by the legal conclusions there reached, but by the narrative of facts therein. So far as these facts did not arrest the attention of the Court, so as to be reflected in these opinions, it is desirable that the Court in the Missouri District should not lose sight of them.

As much of the material covered by the foregoing suggestions is doubtless in the form of affidavits already, I have made these suggestions with the thought that carrying them out would not delay for more than a few days the bringing of the petition. If they did entail any greater delay than this, it may well be that the gain, if any, from the changes in the petition would be much more than offset by the injury caused by any delay at the present time.[2]

I expected to be in Washington for a few hours on Monday, and plan to call at the Department at 9:30 o'clock. I shall hope to see you then. Will you be good enough to say to the Attorney General that I hope also to see him on other matters?

Very truly yours,

1. Todd had sent LDB a copy of the petition against the United Shoe Machinery Company which the Justice Department had prepared, partly as a test of the Clayton Act. For the background of this complex case, and LDB's role in it, see LDB to James A. Lowell, 25 April 1906; to Sidney W. Winslow, 6 December 1906; and, especially, to Moses E. Clapp, 24 February 1912.

2. The petition was filed in October, dismissed by the Federal District Court, and carried to the United States Supreme Court. The Court affirmed the lower court's judgment, with LDB taking no part in the case, on 20 May 1918. For illuminating comment on the decision, see A. D. Neale, *The Anti-trust Laws of the United States of America* (Cambridge, Mass., 1970), 100–103. Finally in 1922, the government brought a successful case against the

United Shoe Machinery Company (258 U.S. 451) declaring the "tying clauses" illegal (see Neale, *The Antitrust Laws*, 326).

To Benjamin Perlstein

September 29, 1915 Boston, Mass. [Brandeis Mss, Z 8-2]

DEAR MR. PERLSTEIN: *First*: I am returning herewith the original letter from Mr. Morganthau [*sic*] of August 21st, together with enclosure, and copy of my letter to him and to Dr. Magnes.[1]

Second: At Sunday's meeting a report should be made showing the number and amount of the pledges classified according to amounts, and also localities, and showing what efforts are being made by the office to secure increases of these pledges. I understood that you had taken some steps in particular localities, sending a list of those who had already given pledges.

Third: It was stated last evening that one hundred committees were formed in Philadelphia for raising war relief, and that most of these were manned with Zionists. We ought to have accurate information in regard to this, both as to Philadelphia and elsewhere. We ought to know accurately to what extent Zionists are participating in war collections; among other things what percentage of those who are really doing active work are organized Zionists, and the names. I wish you would take up this matter first with Philadelphia and get accurate information, and then follow up our inquiries in other cities.

1. The correspondence concerned the need for emergency relief for Jews in Palestine and also in Constantinople. See LDB to Henry Morgenthau, 14 October 1915.

To Zionists (Draft)

September 30, 1915 New York, N.Y. [Brandeis Mss, Z 8-2]

DEAR: [1] At the recent Convention you pledged your city to contribute at least $ to the Emergency Fund. To this date we have received from your city pledges to a total of only $ and only $ in cash has been paid on these. Enclosed is a list of the persons and amount of pledges made by members in your city.

At the time of the Convention we estimated that $135,000 would meet the needs of the Committee for the twelve months ending June 30, 1916. Events which have transpired since the Convention show that at least $200,000 will be required, and a large part of this is required for immediate use.

We therefore urge upon you again, in accordance with the telegram sent you,[2] to set aside the period from October 1st to Chanukah for an energetic and intensive campaign on behalf of the Emergency Fund, and report to us each week the result of your activities. Forward immediately all funds now in hand. Forward every Monday the funds collected during the preceding week.

Your immediate assistance is needed to enable us to proceed with our work.

Awaiting your reply, and with heartfelt Zion's greetings,

Very truly yours,

1. This was a draft of a letter to be sent to Zionists who had attended the Boston convention. It was signed by LDB and E. W. Lewin-Epstein, the treasurer. The amounts for each correspondent were to be entered in the blanks that appear in the text before mailing.

2. On 29 September, LDB and Lewin-Epstein had sent telegrams: "Demands upon Provisional Committee to meet Palestine conditions pressing. Imperative that we have immediately funds to meet situation. Therefore concentrate all efforts beginning October 1st to Chanukah on emergency fund collections securing monthly individual pledges, making house to house canvasses, organizing mass meetings and remit immediately all funds in hand and as collected. Unless you act with energy and efficiency our constructive work must halt for lack of means."

To Gilson Gardner

September 30, 1915 Boston, Mass. [Brandeis Mss, NMF 68-2]

MY DEAR GARDNER: I enclose clipping from this morning's Herald containing Charles S. Bird's letter to McCall.[1] No platform which the Republicans can adopt would reduce the danger incident to the McCall candidacy. The fact of Bird's letter makes it unwise for Richard to do anything himself.[2]

Yours very truly,

1. Charles S. Bird, who had been the Progressive Party's candidate for the governorship in both 1912 and 1913, had written a letter to the regular

Republican gubernatorial candidate, Congressman Samuel W. McCall, promising support if the Republican platform was properly progressive. The
conciliatory move was seen as signalling the end of the Progressive Party in
Massachusetts and the reunification of the Republicans.

2. On the same day LDB sent a similar note to Norman Hapgood, who
wrote a pro-Walsh editorial, "Massachusetts," for the 16 October issue of
Harper's. For the results of the election, see LDB to David I. Walsh, 4
November 1915.

To Agnes E. Ryan

September 30, 1915 Boston, Mass. [Brandeis Mss, NMF 47-3]

MY DEAR MISS RYAN: [1] I find yours of the 23rd upon my return
to the city.

If Miss Jane Addams and Mrs. Catt have accepted as judges, I
shall be glad to accept as a third, if you think it would be helpful
to the cause.[2]   Very truly yours,

1. Agnes E. Ryan was the manager of Alice Stone Blackwell's magazine,
The Woman's Journal. LDB had some close ties to the periodical since
Florence Kelley, Ben Lindsey, and Stephen S. Wise were all contributing
editors. Miss Ryan had written to ask LDB to help judge a contest that
Woman's Journal was running; twenty-five dollars would be awarded to the
person who could design the most effective symbol for the suffrage "ideal."
2. Carrie Chapman Catt (1859-1947) was a tireless, and famous, crusader
for women's suffrage. She joined the crusade in 1887, and within five years
she was a national leader of the National American Woman Suffrage Association. In 1900 she took over the association's presidency from Susan B.
Anthony. She founded the International Woman Suffrage Alliance and
served as its president until 1923. Even before the suffrage amendment became law in 1919, Mrs. Catt confidently organized the National League of
Women Voters and served as its honorary president for over a quarter of a
century. She also involved herself in the peace movement and in the movement to abolish child labor. In the 1930s she organized a petition among non-
Jewish women protesting Hitler's treatment of the Jews.

To Judah Leon Magnes

October 5, 1915 New York, N.Y. [Magnes Mss]

MY DEAR DR. MAGNES: As you requested, I presented to the Committee your letter of resignation.[1]

The conspicuous aid which you had rendered in popularizing
the Zionist ideal in the United States was referred to by many

of the members, and the important services rendered in the past, and which all believed you could render at this critical juncture and in the future, deepened our regret that you should have felt obliged to retire from the Committee. But since your letter of resignation indicates that you are no longer in agreement with the Basle program, the course taken by you appeared to be necessary one, and therefore we accept the resignation, but with regret and with the hope that you may later see your way to return to active work within the organization.

Most cordially yours,

1. See LDB to Magnes, 26 August 1915, n. 1.

To Horace Meyer Kallen

October 6, 1915 Boston, Mass. [Brandeis Mss, Z 3-1]

MY DEAR KALLEN: Upon my return to the city I find yours of the 1st.

First: As to the Pacific Coast conference: I heard Lipsky discussing with Wise the arrangement of such a conference in San Francisco just before or after Thanksgiving.[1] What arrangement he has made I do not know, but I presume he has taken up the matter and doubtless has reported to you before this.

Second: As to making Martin Meier [*sic*] an Associate member of the P.C.[2] Martin Meier, [*sic*] has not yet declared his adherence to the Zionist cause, but Wise was quite sure that he would do so. If he does, it will doubtless be desirable to appoint him first as a member of the Advisory Board.

Third: I entirely agree with you that we do not wish to come into the open with any controversy with Magnes. After much deliberation it was accordingly determined that I should write a very brief reply, a copy of which Perlstein has doubtless sent you. Of course if Magnes undertakes to publish his letter, some regular Zionist will undertake to answer it, but it does not seem to me probable at present that Magnes will care to give the matter further publicity.

Fourth: I agree with you that it would not be desirable that any of our members should go to England at present.[3] As to Weizmann or one of the others coming here,—my own feeling is that we ought to leave that matter wholly to them. They will know better than we whether it is desirable for them to come. By the way, we sent Weizmann $250., as I recall, to be used for travelling expenses. We have never heard what disposition was made of the matter, and indeed so far as I know the Provisional Committee has never received any communication whatsoever from him.

Fifth: As to sending reports to Zimmern[4] and others: It seems to me that it would be unwise to give a general order to send them all reports which go to members of our Provisional Committee. You, of course, get all reports and papers, and I suggest that you let me know from time to time which specific reports or papers should be sent to Zimmern and when sent, what explanation, if any, should be given.

Sixth: I am very glad to know that Zimmern promises to write an article for the round table. I hope it will come soon. When he does write, can't you arrange for its publication simultaneously in the Menorah Journal, or perhaps much better to have it appear in the New Republic.[5]

Seventh: You have probably heard from the New York office about the Kraus-called meeting on the 3rd.[6] The results seem to me eminently satisfactory.

Eighth: I understood from Judge Mack that you were to be in Chicago on the 18th, and I asked him to take up with you, [Nathan D.] Kaplan and [Max] Shulman the various matters relating to the Knights of Zion and the Bureau, on which we are deferring action awaiting your joint report.

Cordially yours,

1. Wise was planning an extended western tour to organize local Zionist groups (see LDB to Otto I. Wise, 22 November 1915).

2. Kallen had written urging the appointment of Rabbi Meyer to the Provisional Committee: "In Jewish affairs," Kallen wrote, "his word is law in San Francisco, and his name would be of inestimable worth." See LDB to Louis E. Kirstein, 10 September 1915.

3. Kallen lamented the lack of proper communication between the English Zionists (who were in closer touch with the European situation) and the Americans. He had received letters suggesting the visit to England by a member of the American organization. Kallen believed, however, that during the war and with American Zionism's need to remain strictly neutral, such a course would be unwise.

4. Sir Alfred Zimmern (1879–1957) was an English student of foreign relations and political science. Not a Zionist himself, he was sympathetic to the movement, and Weizmann occasionally turned to him for advice.

5. Since work published in *The Round Table* was published anonymously, it is hard to know if Zimmern wrote anything on Zionism. He never touched the subject directly for the *New Republic*, but see his comments on "The Meaning of Nationality," *New Republic*, 5 (1 January 1916): 215.

6. See LDB to Adolf Kraus, 7 September and 14 September 1915.

To A. Eichholz

October 7, 1915 Boston, Mass. [Brandeis Mss, Z 7-3]

MY DEAR MR. EICHHOLZ: I have thought much of the picture which you gave me of the Jewish community in Philadelphia when we met on September 26th, and particularly of what you said of the lack of idealism among the young men.

Is it not because they have failed to square themselves with life —that they lack an ideal which would bring out the best that is in them? And is it not possible that Zionism would meet their need?

I venture to enclose a copy of my article on "The Jewish Problem," which I hope you will read.

Very cordially yours,

To Charles Richard Crane

October 9, 1915 Boston, Mass. [Brandeis Mss, NMF 66-3]

MY DEAR CHARLES: You know how general is the disappointment that the Federal Trade Commission is not a stronger body.[1] The effectiveness of the Commission will depend largely upon the selection of the General Counsel. Burling of Chicago is willing to become its counsel, though of course at a great financial sacrifice. Joe Davies is urging Huston Thompson,[2] now Assistant Attorney General in charge of the Court of Claims cases,—a good man for his present job, but in no way qualified for the position as General Counsel of the Trade Commission.

I am told that the selection of the Counsel of the Commission, instead of being made by the Commission itself, will be determined by the President. Also that Cyrus McCormick, if asked for an opinion, would recommend Burling most highly, but that McCormick is unwilling to write the President on the subject.[3] Norman [Hapgood] tells me that he asked you to ask Cyrus McCormick for his opinion of Burling, and after getting it, you should lay it before the President. I agree with Norman that it is highly important that this should be done.

As you know, the Federal Trade Commission has been subjected to considerable criticism, not wholly undeserved, and it will be a great misfortune if the Commission is not rescued from its present position.[4]

With cordial greetings,   Very truly yours,

1. See LDB to Edward M. House, 31 December 1914, and to Gilson Gardner, 7 September 1915.

2. Huston Thompson (1875–1966) was a Colorado lawyer who came to Washington in 1913 and remained there both in public service and private practice. After serving as Assistant Attorney-General, 1913–1918, he became, not counsel for the Federal Trade Commission, but a full commissioner instead. He served in that capacity until the mid-1920s, thereafter accepting many governmental assignments of a legal nature under Presidents Hoover, Roosevelt, and Truman.

3. Cyrus Hall McCormick (1859–1936) was the son of the inventor of the reaper and the inheritor of the International Harvester enterprises begun by his father. President Wilson was to appoint him to the special diplomatic mission to Russia in 1917.

4. The position of Chief Counsel went neither to Burling nor Thompson. Instead, the first occupant of the position (after it was filled on a temporary basis for a number of years) was John Walsh (1872–1941), a Wisconsin lawyer and judge who had served as special counsel to the commission from its inception until his elevation in 1917.

To Stephen Samuel Wise

October 9, 1915 Boston, Mass. [Brandeis Mss, Z 6-2]

MY DEAR DR. WISE: Rabbi H. Pereira Mendes[1] talked with me Tuesday evening about the course of lectures which you were purposing to arrange, in connection with the other Rabbis in New York, on the West side; and that owing to the feeling that exists between the Orthodox and Reform Jews, differences were presenting themselves on the question of cooperation. He suggested that it would be possible to remove all friction if the course were given under the auspices of the Zionist Association, which should then invite the Congregations to cooperate. I entirely agree with you as to the importance of this course, and should be very sorry to lose the cooperation of the several Rabbis. If the plan outlined, and about which Dr. de Sola Pool has written me, could be carried out, would it not be wise to accept the suggestion?

Cordially yours,

1. Henry Pereira Mendes (1852–1937), the leading Sephardic rabbi in New York City, was spiritual head of Congregation Shearith Israel from 1877 to 1920. Mendes had been president of the Union of Orthodox Jewish Congregations.

To Bernard Heller

October 11, 1915 Boston, Mass. [Brandeis Mss, Z 10-2]

MY DEAR MR. HELLER:[1] Upon my return to the office this morning I find your letter of the 8th, and regret that it will not be possible for me to address your meeting.

I am convinced, however, that in Zionist affairs, as in individual matters, Jewish success will come not through others, but through the efforts of the individual. A man of your zeal and determination can, I am sure, if aided by other students of like devotion, develop a strong Zionist organization among your students. When you have done so I shall be glad to take the first opportunity of addressing your organization.   Very truly yours,

1. Bernard Heller (b. 1900) was a young undergraduate at the University of Pennsylvania and secretary of the newly-formed Zionist organization there. He would become a prominent Reform Rabbi, lecturer and author on Jewish and theological topics. He had written LDB asking him to address the opening meeting of the Univeristy of Pennsylvania Zionist society.

To Michael A. O'Leary

October 11, 1915 Boston, Mass. [Brandeis Mss, NMF 68-2]

MY DEAR MR. O'LEARY:[1] I am enclosing check for $250. towards the expenses of the Democratic State Committee.

I deem it particularly important that Governor Walsh shall be reelected; and I am glad to learn through Mr. deHaas that you feel that the Governor is making a fine campaign.[2]

Very cordially yours,

1. Michael A. O'Leary was the chairman of the Democratic State Committee of Massachusetts.
2. See LDB to David I. Walsh, 4 November 1915.

To Julian William Mack

October 13, 1915 Boston, Mass. [Brandeis Mss, Z 11-2]

MY DEAR MACK: I have your note saying that you and Kallen think Alex Aaronsohn would be the man to take charge of the Chicago Bureau work.[1] It would be necessary to consider not only his ability, but also whether he would be in every way satisfactory to Shulman, Kaplan and their associates. The Provisional Committee wants, if possible, to have a man there who will not only meet the multifarious needs of the office, but be entirely agreeable to those with whom he is to work, and I should be glad if you would talk the matter over frankly with Kaplan and Shulman before the question is taken up with the Provisional Committee.   Cordially yours,

1. Alexander Aaronsohn (1888–1948) was a member of the famous Aaronsohn family of Palestinian activists, the brother of Aaron. During the war he, like other members of the family, engaged in anti-Turkish, pro-Ally propaganda (his sister Sarah was captured by the Turks and tortured, and she subsequently killed herself to escape further torture). He had come to America to speak against Turkish rule. He returned to Palestine after the war.

To Office Committee

October 13, 1915 Boston, Mass. [Brandeis Mss, Z 8-2]

DEAR SIRS: In order that the accounts may more nearly represent the actual disbursements incurred, I think it well that there should appear a charge covering not only the Chairman's traveling expenses, but also the necessary clerical services and similar expenses incident to the Chairman's office.

The expenses for the three months ending September 30th are

For travelling expenses, ... $168.65
For telephone and telegrams, ... 25.87
For postage, ... 3.90
For clerical services 72.53

I of course wish to bear all of these expenses myself, but for purposes of accounting you may send me a check for $270.95, and I will send you in return a check for a similar amount as a contribution.   Yours very truly,

To Bernard Gerson Richards

October 13, 1915 Boston, Mass. [Brandeis Mss, Z 11-1]

DEAR MR. RICHARDS: Your two letters of the 11th reach me today.[1]

I learn from Mr. Lipsky that at the meeting of the Committee last night the proposal was rejected.

As I told you when we were last in New York, my conviction is that we should proceed definitely upon the line of organization in which we have been engaged in the various cities,—making a central organization in every city, and taking up also this matter in each of the Lodges in the cities, particularly in New York.

If we proceed definitely upon these lines without any deviation except upon careful conference, I am confident the interest of the Jews will be best subserved.

I hope before long to be in New York, and shall plan then to be able to discuss these matters fully with members of the Congress Organization Committee.   Very truly yours,

1. A new proposal for a conference leading to a Jewish Congress had been developed by representatives of the National Workmen's Committee on Jewish Rights, the Jewish Congress Organization Committee (headed by Richards) and the American Jewish Committee. The proposal was to be considered by the decision-making bodies of each group, and Richards had asked LDB's opinion. The plan called for a conference of 150 representatives chosen by the three organizations, to consider the problems of Jewish rights in belligerent countries, and to elect an executive committee of at least fifteen people for the purpose of organizing a Jewish Congress on a democratic basis.

To Henry Morgenthau

October 14, 1915 New York, N.Y. [Morgenthau Mss]

MY DEAR SIR: I beg to acknowledge receipt of yours of August 30th, suggesting to our Committee to make another appropriation to the Jewish Committee at Constantinople.

The funds that our Committee received are designed specifically for Palestine and we are powerless to change their destination, even were there sufficient funds to meet the specific purposes. I have, however, forwarded your communication to the American Jewish Relief Committee, of which I am a member, and was very glad that an allowance was secured of $5,000. for the relief of Jews in Turkey, outside of Palestine, of which you have already been advised.

With deep appreciation of the services you are rendering, and kindest personal regards, I am   Sincerely yours,

To Arthur Menahem Hantke

October 15, 1915 New York, N.Y. [Berlin Office]

FELLOW ZIONIST: [1] During the last few months we have devoted our utmost attention to the inner development and perfection of our organization in the United States. We became convinced that only by so doing could we meet the requirements imposed by the new conditions developing throughout the world. The new problems in Palestine cannot be met simply through gathering funds. The Zionist tendencies must be developed into effective organization so that the masses of our Jewish population may become a real power.

THE GROWTH OF ZIONIST SENTIMENT IN AMERICA.

The Convention of American Zionists held in Boston from June 25th to July 2nd was a success in every respect. The American press gave great attention to its proceedings and devoted much space to the Zionist cause otherwise. The official meetings which took place during the Convention shaped themselves into imposing and dignified demonstrations for the Jewish cause to a degree as never before witnessed in America. The gatherings were attended by many thousands by people. The Jewish population was roused to a degree of enthusiasm yet unprecedented. And even non-Jews showed an understanding of our ideas. They made efforts to show their good will towards us and their moral support and encouragement. The full particulars of the work of the Convention were reported in the Maccabaean of July and August, 1915.

The fact that three large Jewish organizations, the Independent Order Brith Abraham, the Order Brith Sholom, and the Galician Verband, were represented at the Convention through their Grand Masters, and there expressed themselves in favour of the Zionist Program, is of great importance. This was the best proof that the Zionist thought has already implanted itself in the life of the Jewish Community in this country to a considerable extent. This, however, does not signify that the members of the above mentioned orders may already be regarded as Zionists. The declaration of the leaders, however, has given us access to all the lodges and has thus offered us the opportunity of widening the sphere of our organizing activity as well as that of our propaganda, for these said orders number approximately 300,000 members. To have opened this door may rightly be considered a gigantic step forward; for it indicates that American soil is hereafter to be open for fruitful Zionist work.

Apart from this series of successes, the fruits of which will be reaped only gradually, the Federation of American Zionists is already enjoying the advantage of an increase in the number of the shekel payers. These have doubled since last year; and we hope for further large growth.

NECESSITY FOR STRONGER ORGANIZATION.

While this development is very gratifying, we must caution you not to assume that we can carry, without extensive help from you and others, the burdens assumed on behalf of the Actions Committee. In order to support us in the task of carrying out our great problems, of maintaining the organization and to maintain our institutions in Palestine, we must have your aid.

In all our work we must always keep before us the necessity of maintaining and strengthing [sic] our organization. While there is a proper understanding, on the part of some of us, of the importance of the institutions already existing in Palestine, others fail to comprehend the importance of the organization as such. We therefore repeat that in all our activities we attribute as much importance to the organization as to the institutions created by the organization. Only in strengthening our organization and maintaining it in its full activity until the war is over, shall we be in a position to carry on our work without interruption after peace is established. Every organized Zionist must bear this fact in mind.

THE SITUATION IN PALESTINE.

Mr. Louis Levin and Dr. Samue Lewin-Epstein, the representatives of the Provisional Committee as well as of the American Jewish Relief Committee, have returned from their trip to Palestine and have reported on the Vulcan Relief Work. It was ascertained that Palestine does not suffer from lack of foodstuffs and despite the grasshopper plague that has destroyed a considerable part of the harvest this year, it is nevertheless possible to purchase food for gold. However, the Jewish population has been deprived of its means of subsistence on account of the war which has brought trade and industry to a standstill and, without outside assistance, the Jewish population will hardly be able to maintain even a miserable existence. The population of the colonies is in a somewhat better condition, but the colonists are also in urgent need of energetic assistance in the form of loans, so as to be enabled to carry on the agricultural work in the vineyards, orangeries, and fields. This population had, in the course of the last few years, experienced an economic uplift. It suffers now because through the war it is cut off from the markets of the world—and because of the locust pest. We were successful in our efforts to secure a 400,000 francs loan for the orange plantations, which loan was made possible by the energetic support of generous lovers of Palestine. It will be necessary to help other planters in the same way.

Our schools in Palestine are open and carry on their work regularly. Although some of the directors have left Palestine, the teachers have remained at their posts and devote themselves as usual to the performance of their duties of educating the young, though at largely reduced salaries.

THE JEWISH CONGRESS MOVEMENT.

American Jewry as a whole considers it to be its sacred duty at this historic moment to unite in order to discuss ways and means of meeting Jewish needs and for the inaugurating of important measures involving the future of our people. No doubt, it is extremely difficult to lay down a program upon which all the Jewish groups may agree. One thing is clear to us, namely, there must be a free discussion of our national Jewish needs; and to this end we must educate the Jewish masses. We are working hand in hand with other organizations standing on the same basis with us in regard to the question of Jewish Nationalism. and we shall inform you as soon as a plan for the realization of a Jewish Congress will be formulated.

We deem it appropriate to enter into some particulars of this point. A Jewish Congress in America is not primarily a Zionist plan. It originated simultaneously in different groups in the Jewish communities; and many organizations which can by no means be characterized as Zionistic, have adopted this idea. Only the enemies of Jewish Nationalism, those who oppose any national organization that exceeds the narrow sphere of philanthropy—in order to discredit the idea of a Jewish Congress, have spread the rumour that this idea has been created by the Zionists who are thus carrying on an exclusively party policy. This superficial opinion is wholly unfounded in fact.

The main object of the entire congress idea does not lie in the intermediary party which the Jewish representative body is to play in the peace conference of the belligerent nations. The congress is to satisfy an inner need, and its chief purpose will be the development of the organization of the Jewish forces of America —a utilization of strength that has not in the past been used for the welfare of our people. Primarily we want to organize not merely for the sake of presenting our position to the world at large, but to be in a position to mitigate the tremendous suffering of the Jews in some of the lands involved in the war. We must develop our ability to help ourselves.

Every thinking Jew must grieve to think how little has been done until now to save portions of our people from annihilation; and it has become apparent in many large Jewish circles, that are in touch with the people, that the main trouble, is not the lack of will to help, but the utter weakness of Jewish organization or even lack of any organization.

The movement on behalf of the congress has made great progress. It has been joined by organizations representing all classes in the community—and the working classes recognize fully the need of a Congress. We cannot expect the whole world to become Zionists at once, but we believe that as soon as the Jews begin to organize on a national basis, the Zionist idea will steadily gain ground.

OUR BUDGET.

Our original budget for the current year called for an expenditure of approximately $135,000. It has become clear that a much larger sum will be required. We shall exert all our efforts to meet the enlarged demands and we rely upon your lending us all the support in your power. Above all else we ask you to carry on the shekel activity this year with special energy and to remit your collections promptly. It is also necessary for us to take up collections among the loyal and well-to-do Zionists for the maintenance of the organization. The collections should be made in either the form of single donations or of yearly self-taxation.

With Zion's greetings, we beg to remain,

Faithfully yours,

1. This letter, marked "Not for Publication," was sent to a number of Jewish leaders all over the world. Schmarya Levin cosigned it with LDB, and probably had drafted portions of the letter.

To Stephen Samuel Wise

October 15, 1915 Boston, Mass. [Brandeis Mss, Z 6-2]

MY DEAR DR. WISE: *First:* In response to the postscript of yours of the 14th, I wired you as follows:

"I agree with Lewin-Epstein that your speaking at Armenian meeting would be dangerous." [1]

Second: As to yours of the 13th about San Francisco: A. L. Filene has written to Mrs. Koschland. and also to Martin Meyer about Mrs. Koschland. I have written Mack as per enclosed copy.[2]

Third: As to Ruppin: I have given this matter careful consideration, and have reason to doubt whether it would be desirable to ask our Government to take any action except this:

To inquire whether there is any truth in the rumor that Ruppin is liable to be expelled.[3] I should be glad if you would arrange to have such an inquiry made by the State Department. You will know best whether it is necessary for this purpose for you to see Lansing [4] or [William] Phillips. Of course it would be desirable to obtain in answer to such an inquiry, a clear picture of the situation, if that is possible.   Cordially yours,

1. Wise had written: "I have consented to speak at the meeting to secure funds for the Armenian sufferers and to protest against the atrocities of which the Armenians have been the victims. Lewin-Epstein thinks it may be unwise and even dangerous for me to speak at the meeting because of my relation to the Provisional Committee. Do you agree with him? If so, I would ask to be excused. . . ."

2. Wise's brother had advised making contact with Mrs. Marcus Koschland (1867–1953), whom he described as "very influential and very wealthy," to help insure the success of Wise's forthcoming western tour. Cora Koschland was a San Francisco philanthropist and patron of the arts.

3. Turkish officials had periodically threatened to expel Ruppin because of his Zionist work but had deferred doing so because of pressure from German officials who in turn were acting at the behest of the Zionists. Ruppin was finally expelled from Palestine in 1917, and he spent the rest of the war in Constantinople.

4. Robert Lansing (1864–1928) had been elevated to Secretary of State on 23 June 1915, in the wake of Bryan's resignation over the *Lusitania* crisis. A graduate of Amherst, Lansing was a practicing lawyer until his marriage to the daughter of a former Secretary of State, John W. Foster. From 1892, Lansing's career became the conduct of foreign policy. Even before Bryan's resignation, Lansing had assumed many of the duties of the secretaryship and was therefore well prepared to handle the arduous tasks of wartime diplomacy, including the difficult job of working with two unofficial "secretaries," President Wilson and Colonel House. Friction between Wilson and Lansing grew over differences about the peace negotiations and culminated in Wilson's request for his resignation on 12 February 1920. For a study of Lansing's problems during these years, see Daniel M. Smith, *Robert Lansing and American Neutrality, 1914–17* (Berkeley, 1958).

To Julius Levy

October 16, 1915 Boston, Mass. [Brandeis Mss, Z 7-3]

MY DEAR MR. LEVY: [1] You have been in the past so good a friend to our Palestinian cause that I venture to call to your attention more specifically the great need of assistance there.

The cessation, as a result of the war, of practically all contributions from Europe, threw upon America the burden of maintaining Palestinian institutions, and supplying relief to the needy there.

And these needs have been greatly augmented by the practical stoppage of all imports and exports, and more recently by the locust pest, which has inflicted upon the colonists a loss estimated at 3,000,000 francs.

Fortunately the damage done by the locusts appears to be limited to the year's crop, and as the plantations are recovering, our colonists are reported as full of hope; and are carrying forward not only their work, but also their schools with old time vigor.

The conduct of the Palestinian Jews throughout the trying year just past has given new proof of the significance of this Jewish Renaissance; and I hope we may count upon you for additional aid to our Emergency Fund. We find that we must raise this year at least $200,000.   Very cordially yours,

1. Julius Levy was a Baltimore businessman.

To Benjamin Perlstein

October 16, 1915 Boston, Mass. [Brandeis Mss, Z 8-2]

MY DEAR MR. PERLSTEIN: I was extremely sorry to learn that you have not been well, and I hope you will take very good care of yourself. Be sure to consult a physician; and do not hesitate to take some time off if you find that you need it.

Most cordially yours,

To The Editor

October 18, 1915 Boston, Mass. [Brandeis Mss, NMF 68-2]

To THE EDITOR: It is not my practice to take part in political campaigns. Such public work as I have done has been directed towards policies and measures, not to securing party victory or the success of particular men. But this year active participation in support of Governor Walsh seems to be demanded. His defeat would imperil the maintenance of policies and measures for which forward looking men have been striving for a decade. His defeat would help pave the way for the restoration of the regime of Cannon, Penrose and Barnes.[1]

The end for which forward-looking men have striven is this:

That the power of Government shall rest in men, not money; in the many not the few; and that the power of government shall be exercised for the benefit of all and not of the few.

Forward-looking men have sought to accomplish this:

First: By improving the condition of the working people.

Second: By curbing the power of wealth and of privilege.

Forward-looking men—with statesmanlike progressiveness— which is farseeing conservatism—have sought to avert a war of classes by removing just causes or discontent. Like the great Mazzini,[2] they have by their acts declared that there shall be "no hostility to existing wealth, no wanton or unjust violation of the right of property, but a constant disposition to ameliorate the material condition of the classes less favored by fortune."

To that program Governor Walsh has proved himself true. He has shown his adhesion not by words but by deeds; not by single acts merely, but a constant attitude. He probably has made mistakes in detail—who would not? But his administration has been consistent with determined striving for true democracy and social justice.

Let me speak of his accomplishments in some fields of public service with which I have reason to be familiar.

Every person who has in a practical way attempted to relieve hardships and misery among working people, recognizes social insurance as a pressing need, and Governor Walsh has devoted himself to its development. The workmen's compensation law to provide against industrial accidents has been greatly strengthened through Governor Walsh's active aid. The weekly compensation for disabled workingmen was increased from one-half to two-thirds of the weekly wage. The payment of compensation was extended from 300 weeks to 500 weeks. The maximum payment receivable was increased from $3,000 to $4,000. All this without increased burdens upon employers; but with the result that the percentage of the insurance premium paid which now goes to the disabled employees, has been doubled. In a single year these changes have put nearly $900,000 more into the pockets of injured working people or their dependents than would have been paid in the same period if Governor Walsh had not secured the changes in the law for which he worked.

Equally far seeing has been his attitude towards the public service corporations, whose administration so vitally affects the whole public. His veto secured the elimination of dangerous provisions from an otherwise desirable act in aid of the financial reorganization of the New Haven Railroad. He gave active support to a proper bill to facilitate the effective reorganization of the Boston & Maine. He sought to secure an investigation of telephone charges, to which the people of Massachusetts were fairly entitled; and perhaps the best evidence of his intelligent appreciation of the needs of the community was furnished by placing upon the Public Service Commission Mr. Joseph B. Eastman, who, during long years of service as Secretary of the Public Franchise League, had become specially qualified and had proved himself an able, devoted and courageous servant of the people.

No Governor of Massachusetts, be he Republican or Democrat, has been freer from the subtle influence of wealth, or has striven more conscientiously to serve all the people.

To progressive minded men such a record gives more assurance of performance than the belated and inconclusive platform declarations of the last Republican Convention.[3]

1. Former Speaker of the House, arch-conservative Joseph G. Cannon; Boies Penrose (1860–1921), the high-tariff spokesman from Pennsylvania in the United States Senate; and William Barnes, Jr., (1866–1930), the influential Albany editor and old-guard spokesman, recently retired from the chairmanship of the New York Republican Committee.

2. Giuseppe Mazzini (1805–1872) was a famous Italian patriot and a lifelong crusader for Italian independence and the establishment of a republican form of government.

3. This letter was published in all the leading Boston newspapers. For the results of the election, see LDB to David I. Walsh, 4 November 1915.

To Julian William Mack

October 19, 1915 Boston, Mass. [Brandeis Mss, Z 11-1]

MY DEAR MACK: I have yours of the 18th.

Alexander Aaronsohn's great success at the Y.M.H.A. talk is just what I should have expected from my private talk with him and from what Felix F. had told me about his talk in Washington.

Your report on Cincinnati is most encouraging.[1] Among other things I am delighted to know that Dr. Kaplan is so able and tactful a man. You probably heard while in Cincinnati that Fechheimer had called upon me, and that after a full discussion I had agreed that I would go there at the request of his group of thirty and talk at a small meeting, provided you would join me.[2] I had postponed writing you until the formal invitation, which Fechheimer said he would send, should arrive. In a few days I will try to suggest a date.   Very cordially yours,

1. Mack and Nathan Kaplan had conducted a Zionist meeting in Cincinnati on 17 October, and Mack reported very good results: "[M]any hostile and indifferent converted."

2. For the background of the tension between LDB and the Reform community of Cincinnati, see LDB to Louis Lipsky, 5 October 1914.

To Nathan D. Kaplan

October 20, 1915 Boston, Mass. [Brandeis Mss, Z 3-1]

MY DEAR MR. KAPLAN: Replying to yours of the 16th:

First: Dr. Kallen reported on the agreement reached by you and your associates to hold the Knights of Zion local Convention in January, with the understanding that the organization would be properly represented also at our general Convention.[1] I understand that this is a provisional arrangement, which shall look to later modifications, and result in an ultimate consolidation of the Knights of Zion convention with the Conventions of the other organizations. This provisional arrangement will, I believe, be satisfactory to the P.C.

Second: As to attendance at the Convention: It seems to me proper that Dr. Levin should attend. I deem it clear that *both* Dr. Wise and I should not attend. I also deem it clear that a grave mistake will be made if the mass meeting, which you purpose holding, is to be treated as a "stellar aggregation". In the first place you must have fresh in your mind from our St. Louis experience, the inherent difficulties. Several Knights of Zion men must appear as speakers. If you add to them several easterners, you will create an embarrassment which will result as unsatisfactorily as at St. Louis. Wholly aside from that, you will necessarily have a mass meeting at which no one speaker has time to add anything material to the knowledge and understanding of those present; and knowledge and understanding are essential to a proper development of the Zionist organizations. Every effort must be made to make our members clearly understand what the P.C. is attempting to do, and what individual members of the Zionist organizations can do to fit themselves for our great work. I presume that you will deem that a so-called mass meeting is an essential; but I am convinced that it should take on the character, so far as possible, of an informing meeting, and in the next place that it will be of practically no value unless it is so treated as to become the basis for action thereafter in securing new members, and intensifying the knowledge and interest of the old ones.

Third: So far as concerns Dr. Levin:

If he attends the Convention it should be in connection with carefully worked out arrangements by which for, say, the next fortnight after the Convention he shall undertake intensive work in Chicago and suburbs. This program should be carefully arranged so that Dr. Levin has his time fully occupied, so far as regular meetings are concerned and also has the opportunity of meeting privately such persons through whom he can advance the cause.

Fourth: I am willing to arrange to attend the Convention; but it will not be with an idea mainly of speaking at the mass meeting. Indeed I should be happy to be relieved of that, if that were possible. My purpose in attending the Convention would be with a view to taking up first with leaders and then with the members, some plan of rendering the Knights of Zion more effective,—not merely for making our much needed collections, but through intensifying the organizations both by additions to membership, and by thorough educational organization, and a development of active organizations in each of the states. It would therefore seem to me desirable, if I am to attend the Convention at all, to arrive on Saturday morning, so as to have the whole of Saturday for conferences with you and other leaders, including some men from cities other than Chicago,—like [Maximilian G.] Baron of St. Louis, and Dr. Lehman of Kansas City. I should hope also to have the proceedings at the Convention so arranged as to give ample opportunity for a discussion of these problems at the Convention, in order that appropriate action might be taken with the sanction of the delegates.

Fourth: It is my opinion that matters should be conducted in such a way as to get for the Zionist cause the great aid which Judge Mack's adherence to it renders possible. For this reason I should be extremely glad if Judge Mack should take a very prominent part in our deliberations so that not only the members of the organizations may become acquainted with him, but the public realize how greatly we rely upon his judgment and cooperation.

Fifth: Alexander Kanter of Minneapolis has expressed to me from time to time the greatest interest in the Zionist cause, and a readiness to take an active part. I presume he has little Zionistic knowledge, but he is well grounded in one fundamental of Zionism—democracy; and he has an enthusiasm and working power which has been manifested in American political work, which we ought to fully utilize. When I was in Chicago I had a letter from him offering to come down to see me to talk matters over. My stay there was so short I could not arrange it, but I believe we shall lose the benefit of a very valuable asset if Mr. Kanter's enthusiasm is not fully utilized. I wish you would let me know whether you have been in touch with him. and if so, with what results.

Sixth: The date, Sunday, January 2nd, which you name for the mass meeting, would be satisfactory to me. I should like to know definitely what the plans are for the other days of the Convention. It will be necessary for me to make some other engagements in Chicago and elsewhere at the earliest possible day.

Seventh: I find that I have not on hand a photograph which I can send you, but am today ordering some additional photographs from the photographer, and will send you one as soon as they are received. It should have gone to you sooner.

Cordially yours,

P.S. As to the mass meeting:

I think it would be much better to have only Mr. Levin and myself as the speakers, and have Judge Mack act as presiding officer. Then let Judge Pam, yourself, Mr. Shulman, Mr. Zolokopf and others speak at the banquet.[2] As you see, I am anxious to make the mass meeting an "informing meeting", and at the same time limit the length of the session.[3]

1. See LDB to Kaplan, 7 September 1915.

2. Judge Hugo Pam (1870–1930), the brother of Max Pam, had been judge of the Illinois Superior Court since 1912. Probably LDB refers to Leon Zolotkoff (1885–1938), a Russian-born Zionist leader who settled in Chicago where he founded the *Chicago Jewish Courier*. He was Grand Master of the Order of the Sons of Zion. Zolotkoff was most famous for his work on the *Jewish Daily News*, which he began upon moving to New York City.

3. See also, LDB to Kaplan, 22 November 1915.

To Louis Lipsky

October 20, 1915 Boston, Mass. [Brandeis Mss, Z 1-4]

DEAR SIRS: You will find in the October–November 1915 number of the Intercollegiate Socialism a brief article on "Nationalism and Socialism" by Professor Herbert Adolphus Miller,[1] which you may care to reprint in the Maccabaen [Sic], to the effect that socialism must yield precedence to Nationalism; in which he says:

> "The Jews who have contributed more to socialism than any other single group from Marx to Hillquit, are likely to be diverted for the same reason. Zionism is a movement to hang together until genuine national self-respect is created, and the Jew is free. In other words group consciousness will dominate until discrimination disappears." [2]

Yours very truly,

1. Herbert Adolphus Miller (1875–1951) was a sociologist at Oberlin College. His particular interest was in Czechoslovakian society and Czech immigration.

2. The article was reprinted, "Nationalism and Socialism," *The Maccabaean*, 27 (December 1915): 146.

To Alfred Brandeis

October 22, 1915 New York, N.Y. [Brandeis Mss, M 4-1]

DEAR AL: Was glad to have a glimpse of Jean last week & am promised more soon.

Met Walter Child Wednesday. He bids me to express to you

his distinguished consideration & included in his greeting the several members of your family including the grandson.[1]

Have been supplementing Jewish activities by woman suffrage, gubernatorial, garment workers arbitration and public franchise excursions. Am today going to Philadelphia for Frederic Winsor [sic] Taylor Memorial Meeting.[2] Thus is the honest practice of a profession interfered with. Still as the world is topsy-turvey there is no good reason for expecting peace on earth since there is no good will among men.

1. Alfred's daughter, Amy Brandeis McCreary, had given birth to her first son, Alfred, on 24 August 1914.

2. LDB's address at the Taylor memorial meeting was entitled "Efficiency by Consent." In his speech, LDB lamented the unwillingness of the labor movement to enlist themselves fully in the pursuit of scientific management and industrial efficiency. The primary task of those interested in the efficiency movement, he said, was to recruit support among the laboring elements of the population. This would only be possible by educating workers to the benefits of increased efficiency and dispelling their fears that scientific management was an essentially anti-labor device. Hapgood published the speech in *Harper's Weekly* 61 (11 December 1915): 568. It can also be found in the 1925 edition of *Business—A Profession*, 51–56.

To Angus McSween

October 26, 1915 Boston, Mass. [Brandeis Mss, NMF 66-3]

MY DEAR MCSWEEN: [1] Absence from the city has delayed a reply to yours of the 19th. I am thoroughly in accord with Mr. Van Valkenburg on the subject of prohibiting gift coupons. That prohibition, together with the stopping of illegitimate price cutting, through the sanctioning of price maintenance, as provided in the Stevens bill, would go a long way towards eliminating unfair competitive methods, and the establishment of equal opportunity in business.

The coupon device and the illegal cutthroat competition are twin evils through which the small and medium-sized retailer is being sacrificed.

If the provisions of the Stevens bill in the interest of fair trade were understood, the bill would no doubt secure overwhelming support, and be soon enacted into law. What could be more effective in the interest of fair trade, and the small merchant, than its publicity provisions as to prices to jobbers or retailer, and the prohibition of quantity or discriminating discounts. It is these quantity, secret, discriminating discounts which enabled the chain stores, and, at times, the great department stores, to drive out the smaller dealers. In no branch of business has the coupon system brought more disaster to the small trader than in connection with the tobacco monopoly; and it is natural that from those who had been associated with the tobacco trust should come the proposal to extend the leech-coupon system into every branch of the retail trade.   Yours very cordially,

1. Angus McSween, of the *Philadelphia North American,* had written at the request of editor Edwin A. VanValkenburg to request LDB's opinion of so-called "gift-coupons" in tobacco packages.

To Julian William Mack

October 26, 1915 Boston, Mass. [R. Szold Mss]

MY DEAR MACK: *First:* Immediately after our telephone talk on Sunday morning, I telegraphed Secretaries Houston [1] and Lansing, and Richard T. Crane [2] who you know, is Secretary to Lansing, to arrange for an interview with you for early Monday morning, and to do what they could to aid you. Late Sunday afternoon I got your telegram to the effect that you would not go, but that Alex [Aaronsohn] would go to Philadelphia to see [Cyrus] Adler. I had at the same time arranged for a conference with Louis Marshall, which he had asked for; and in discussing the matter with him, it was agreed that he would talk further with Cyrus Adler, and would let me know what he and Adler thought I could best do. Later I received a letter from Louis Marshall; and thereupon telegraphed Secretary Houston and Richard Crane that in your stead Cyrus Adler or Louis Marshall would call with Alex on Tuesday or Wednesday. I urged upon Marshall strenuously not to let Alex go alone.[3]

Second: Replying to your letter of the 22nd: I have not yet received the formal invitation from Cincinnati,[4] nor have I heard definitely from Nathan Kaplan about the Knights of Zion Convention dates.[5] My thought was to take in Cincinnati on the same trip with the Convention the beginning of January; and I had hoped that if that were done, you could come down to Cincinnati for some day, say, Thursday, January 6th. Please let me know about this immediately so that I may be able to act promptly when I hear from Nathan Kaplan and Fechheimer. Saturday or Sunday would interfere with other plans for that trip.

Third: I note what you say about Aaronsohn, and have also a letter from Kallen on the subject. It seems to me important that Aaronsohn should now become an organized Zionist, joining preferably a Chicago society; [6] and I wish you would take up with Kaplan, Shulman and Kallen arrangements for some intensive educational work for him. He ought to be employed at least every evening in talking at meetings large or small. We had heard from Kaplan that it would be undesirable to open the [Chicago Zionist] Bureau before January in any event. If Alex Aaronsohn could get to work now, he ought within two months to have so won over the various factions in the Knights of Zion territory as to secure their adhesion; and if he could be given some prominence at the Knights of Zion Convention, the way ought to be open for a salaried position. Kallen states in his letter that Alex felt very reluctant about accepting the salary.

He ought by two months of intensive work to gain the position with those in Knights of Zion territory so that he would appear to be the inevitable man.

Fourth: Alex Aaronsohn promised when I last saw him to get to work writing the story of Sichron Jacob [*sic*].[7] I wish you would ask him whether he has finished this, and if so, to send me the paper.

Fifth: Re Ruttenberg [*sic*]: I am glad to know that Ruttenberg [*sic*] impresses you and Kallen so favorably. He has made a similar impression upon Levin, Lipsky, deHaas and me.

There is no mystery about Ruttenberg's [*sic*] position. The Jewish working men were, as a whole, until within the last few months, strongly opposed to a movement which would bind all the Jews together regardless of classes, and thus tend to undermine the socialist strength. They also objected to the movement, because, even if it did not undermine the socialist strength, it would divide the activity and emotion of their members. Ruttenberg [*sic*], who is an extreme radical, was practically the first one to give them a jolt. The fact that he, without being an organized Zionist, came out for Zionist aims, made a tremendous impression upon the radical forces. He has deemed it important to keep up definitely the fight against the old line socialist workingmen's organization, and his paper "The Congress" is one of the instruments with which he is working. The Congress Organization Committee would doubtless be glad to subvention the paper if they had the money to do so; but it requires a considerable amount of money, and it was therefore deemed advisable to let Ruttenberg [sic] attempt to raise money through his independent efforts. It was also deemed by Ruttenberg [sic] desirable not to use the Zionist Order "The Yiddish Folk", his instrument of attack of the workingmen's body, because he felt that by so doing, he would be far less effective than if he stood independently.

We all believe that Ruttenberg [sic] is of great service to the Zionist movement.

Sixth: I had a very friendly conference with Louis Marshall on Sunday concerning the Congress and related matters, and am to have a further talk as soon as possible.

I also had some talk with Magnes yesterday on Zionism.

I attended the American Jewish Relief Committee yesterday. There was a very friendly tone throughout, Mr. Schiff accepting unreservedly Mr. Lewin-Epstein's proposal, and every other person present proved to be in accord.

Seventh: I had a meeting yesterday with Dr. Rosenblatt and some of the representatives of the National Jewish Trade Council, with reference to the Congress; and it is probable that some subcommittee of that body, of the American Jewish Committee, and of the Congress Organization Committee will meet together to consider the possibility of working out a harmonious plan for the Congress.   Cordially yours,

1. David Franklin Houston (1866–1940) was Wilson's Secretary of Agriculture. The former president of the University of Texas and chancellor of Washington University in St. Louis, Houston was named to the cabinet largely on the strength of his friendship with Col. House. He proved himself to be one of the most conservative members of Wilson's official family and what Arthur Link calls "something of a misfit in a progressive administration." See Link, *Wilson: The New Freedom,* 137–39. For his own version, see Houston's *Eight Years with Wilson's Cabinet, 1913–1920,* 2 vols. (Garden City, 1926).

2. Richard Teller Crane (1882–1938) was the son of LDB's friend Charles R. Crane. After some years in business, he entered public service. For a short time he was Lansing's private secretary, and he was later named minister to Czechoslovakia.

3. Probably the conference was intended to inquire if the United States could help in the shipping of petroleum, desperately needed by Palestinian orange growers.

4. See LDB to Mack, 19 October 1915. The meeting was eventually set for 6 January 1916.

5. See LDB to Nathan D. Kaplan, 20 October 1915.

6. Aaronsohn had surprised many by announcing publicly that he was not a Zionist. Upon questioning, it was discovered that he meant simply that he had not joined an organized Zionist group. Mack wrote: "[I]t's a foolish statement for A. to make as it leads to just such misunderstandings." Nevertheless, Aaronsohn refused to formally join a Zionist organization.

7. Zikhron Ya'akov was a village near Mount Carmel founded in 1882 by Aaronsohn's father and a group of Rumanian settlers with the aid of Edmond de Rothschild.

To Stephen Samuel Wise

October 26, 1915 Boston, Mass. [Brandeis Mss, Z 6-2]

MY DEAR DR. WISE: *First*: Upon my return I find much enthusiasm about your meetings here. You apparently were in error in supposing that there were few of the Temple members at the Sunday morning meeting. I am told that about one-fourth of all present were from the Temple, and that of these quite a number have already announced membership in either the Zion Association of Greater Boston or the Hadassah.

Second: A. Lincoln Filene has had a reply to his letter to Mrs. Koschland, who is apparently endeavoring to arrange with your brother to have you at her house on at least one occasion.[1] Mack also reports that he has written to his friends there.

Third: Eugene Meyer and I were at Daniel Guggenheim's yesterday. B. M. Baruch was also present.[2] Guggenheim said at the close of our interview that he would give us some money, but wanted to consider over night how much. I told Meyer that he must endeavor to get $10,000 from him. Baruch has got somewhat interested, but I do not know whether he will do anything. Meyer is also to follow that up.[3]   Very cordially yours,

Thank you for yours of the 26th.

I am glad that you are postponing the Sunday luncheon arrangement. It would be better to talk with Miss Lewisohn, on
another occasion when we shall have ample time.

1. See LDB to Wise, 15 October 1915, n. 2.
2. In 1915, Bernard Mannes Baruch (1870–1965) was best known as an
unusually astute expert on the stock market. He had joined the Wall Street
firm of Arthur A. Houseman in 1889, and thirteen years later he had accumulated over three million dollars. Because of his intimate knowledge of
the American economy, particularly with regard to raw material supply,
President Wilson engaged him in public service in 1916. During American
participation in the war, Baruch, as chairman of the War Industries Board,
had unprecedented power over the national economy. (See, however,
Robert D. Cuff, "Bernard Baruch: Symbol and Myth in Industrial Mobilization," *Business History Review*, 43 [Summer 1969]: 115–33.) His reputation
for administrative ability and judiciousness made him, thereafter, the intimate
adviser of nearly every American president. He was involved particularly
with President Franklin Roosevelt's wartime administration and the development of American atomic policy under President Truman. Baruch was never
a Zionist and he opposed the establishment of any state on the basis of
religion. At one time he favored a Jewish refuge in Africa. He wrote a two-
volume autobiography, *Baruch* (New York, 1957–1960). See also, Margaret
L. Coit, *Mr. Baruch* (Boston, 1957).
3. Meyer was able to get only $2,500 from Guggenheim.

To Arthur Menahem Hantke

October 29, 1915 New York, N.Y. [Berlin Office]

GENTLEMEN: [1] In view of the outstanding neutrality of the United
States, it is assumed that at the end of the war, the Jews of the
United States will be able to exert specific influence on behalf of
Jews in other countries.

Believing this assumption to be well founded, two efforts were
made to coordinate Jewish public opinion and action in the
United States. One, the limited and circumscribed conference,
having provoked much opposition, appears to have been abandoned, or indefinitely postponed. The other, the Congress, based
on democratic principles, has already won the support of a
majority of the Jews in this country. Agitation will, we hope,
bring the balance into the agreement.

It is therefore desirable that you make known (a) through the press and (b) through such organizations as are concerned in the general problems of the Jews:

First: An American Jewish Congress will be held.

Second: Its democratic basis will assure the responsibility for its decisions.

Third: The time for holding the Congress has not yet been fixed.

Fourth: Until the Congress is convened, no organization or committee is authorized to speak for or on behalf of the American Jews.

Fifth: The Jewish Congress Organization Committee has been formed, representing fourteen national Jewish organizations, with a membership of 650,000, among them being the Independent Order B'rith Abraham, the Independent Order B'rith Sholom, the Federation of American Zionists, the Union of Orthodox Congregations, the Federation of Russian Polish Jews, the Federation of Bessarabian Jews, the Union of Orthodox Rabbis, the Mizrachi and others. There has also been formed a national workingmen's committee, with a membership of 350,000, to further the organization of the Congress. The Jewish Congress Organization Committee has offices established at 1 Madison Avenue, New York. This committee maintains a strict neutrality towards the nations now at war, as is demanded by Jewish interests.

Sixth: The Jewish Congress Organization Committee will, in due course, establish a permanent organization committee for the Congress, under authority from the leading Jewish bodies of national scope. It seems desirable that any organization in Europe or elsewhere, seeking to associate itself in the solution of the problems arising out of the war, should place itself in communication with the temporary Jewish Congress Organization Committee. As soon as the permanent committee is organized, it will put itself in communication with organizations in Europe and elsewhere which are interested in the proper solution of the Jewish problems arising out of the war.

Seventh: Because of the fundamental democratic issue raised, the Zionist Organization is in accord with and will support the convening of the Congress; but the Zionist Organization is not identical with the Congress Organization Committee, nor is the Congress Organization Committee composed only of Zionists.

The Zionist Organization has stood for democracy, publicity and an open platform, thereby assuring a hearing for all primary issues now concerning the Jewish people.

Eighth: The Provisional Zionist Committee makes this statement to you for transmission to all who are concerned.

Cordially yours,

P.S.   We are sending you, under separate cover, three pamphlets that have been published, bearing on the Jewish Congress situation; and also twenty copies of this letter, for further transmission, as you may see fit.

1. This letter, which is in the nature of a report on the congress situation, was sent to a large number of world Zionist leaders, many of them receiving additional copies to distribute. LDB and deHaas had been considering such a report, and they were moved to action by the rumors that the American Jewish Committee had entered into negotiations with the Anglo-Jewish Association. For background on the congress question, see LDB to Louis Lipsky, 18 January 1915.

To Office Committee

November 2, 1915 Boston, Mass. [Brandeis Mss, Z 8-2]

DEAR SIRS: Referring to B[enjamin]. P[erlstein].'s letter of Nov. 1st, concerning the letter prepared for foreign Federations concerning the Congress: [1] I have discussed this matter with Mr. Lipsky and Mr. deHaas, and we are all of opinion that this letter should not be circulated in America at present.

1. See preceding letter.

To *The Wahrheit*[1]

November 2, 1915 Boston, Mass. [Brandeis Mss, Z 8-1]

I desire to express my appreciation of the services rendered the Jewish cause by the Warheit [*sic*] during its ten years of vigorous development.

There is need of clear thinking and discussion to clarify Jewish public opinion if the interests of our people are to be wisely protected. Not all of us may be of the same opinion, but we should be able to arrive at decisions requiring such action as should have the unanimous support of all loyal Jews.

The outstanding problem which confronts the Jews of America is one of organization. Unless we are efficiently organized, reaching down into the ranks of indifference and apathy, and drawing strength from every element, class or party in Israel, we cannot hope successfully to cope with the great and pressing difficulties of the Jewish problem.

Organization not for its own sake, but for the purpose of creating a bulwark of strength behind propositions tending to solve the Jewish problem, is essential. The Jewish people, suffering on every frontier, will soon be called upon to decide its future. No one has the moral right to decide for them. Whatever may be decided must express not only the best judgment and the maturest experience of the few, but also of that large and hitherto inarticulate mass of Jews who have to date refrained from expressing themselves. Only when we secure from them direct participation in Jewish affairs have we attained a point in our development which may bring tangible and permanent results.

In addition to the need for organization among Jews, there is also demanded at this time clarity of thinking on the problems of the international Jewish position. Our brethren abroad are divided in antagonistic camps, and they have amply demonstrated their loyalty to those interests they are defending together with their fellow citizens.

But in this country, which is neutral and not involved in the conflict, the sense of responsibility of all Jews should be aroused to the need of guarding the interest of the Jewish people so that we may reap the benefit of their great sacrifices. Our position is strong if we consider duly the interests of the entire Jewish people. The lot of our brethren is difficult. They look to us to speak for them when the time comes. We should so act that we shall then be unhampered in our speech and free to defend the interests of our people.

This is the time for preparing with a keen vision for what tomorrow may bring forth of value to Jewish life. Our present duty is that of saving the remnants of our brethren, relieving distress wherever relief is possible, and preparing for the day when rehabilitation of our waste places may also be possible. In the lands where the war still rages, only elementary aid is possible. In Palestine, we may by generous cooperation, maintain all our Jewish possessions, for there the opportunity remains open to protect and strengthen those citadels of Jewish life established by the pioneers who went there to create something that would be of lasting benefit to future generations.

Wishing you success in your efforts to build up a responsible American Jewry, I am

With Zion's greetings,   Yours cordially,

1. *The Wahrheit* had requested a letter for its tenth anniversary number. It is probable that Lipsky wrote this letter for LDB's signature.

To Inner Actions Committee

November 4, 1915 Boston, Mass. [Berlin Office]

FELLOW-ZIONISTS: We beg to acknowledge receipt of yours of August 27th, in which you inform us that you have collected the sum of 49,3000 Mk. for Palestinian relief, of which you have transmitted 30,800 Mk., leaving a balance of 18,500 Mk., which you desire to withhold for your current expenses, and request that we forward this sum to Palestine for relief, in accordance with the proposal of Dr. Levin.

In order to make matters clear, we desire to inform you that we have undertaken to meet the following budget:

For the Palestinian schools hitherto supported by the Actions
Committee and the Palestina Amt, annually,— $40,000.00
For special Palestine work and special contributions
to Palestinian institutions, annually,—   10,000.00
                                                     ─────────
Making a total of,— $50,000.00

that we shall endeavor to raise annually for Palestinian work.

We are not yet certain of being able to procure this sum, but it is quite certain that we shall be unable to assume any obligations beyond this account.

For the work of the Bureau in Berlin, or Copenhagen, we cannot undertake to furnish you any sums beyond the net remaining from the Shekel collections, and there seems no likelihood that there will be any balance available until after October 31, 1916.

We are enclosing attached herewith a statement of the account of the receipts and disbursements on account of the Shekel collections. You will note that we have, until now, expended $12,450.60 in excess of our receipts for Shkolim.

However, in view of your great need of funds, we are this day forwarding to Dr. Ruppin the equivalent of 18,500 Mk., with the information that it comes from the Actions Committee for relief work, and we are charging your account against Shkolim with the equivalent.

Mr. Lewin-Epstein sails for Europe this week, and we hope that it will be possible for you to meet him somewhere on neutral soil. He will also take up with you, at that time, the question of Mossinsohn's coming to America.[1]

With Zion's greetings,   Very cordially yours,

1. See next letter.

To Benzion Mossinsohn

November 4, 1915 Boston, Mass. [Copenhagen Office]

MY DEAR DR. MOSSINSOHN: [1] We have, on several occasions, considered the advisability of your coming to America at this time for special propaganda work, and also to help us in the collection of funds for the schools of Palestine. There have been certain matters which made your coming at this time inadvisable, which reasons have been difficult to convey to you by letter.

Mr. Lewin-Epstein sails for Europe this week, and will communicate with you, possibly from Paris. It is our hope that a meeting between you two can be arranged, and Mr. Lewin-Epstein will discuss the matter of your coming to this country with you.[2]

With Zion's greetings,   Very truly yours,

1. Benzion Mossinsohn (1878–1942) was a Ukrainian Jew who had been a teacher and a Zionist since his early twenties. He moved to Palestine in 1907 and continued his educational work, becoming the principal of the first Hebrew high school in the country. Mossinsohn was active in Zionist organizations and a member of the Actions Committee.

2. Mossinsohn had been expelled from Palestine by the Turks. He arrived in America early in 1916 where he undertook extensive propaganda work for the Zionist movement. In 1919 he returned to Palestine.

To Cushing Stetson

November 4, 1915 Boston, Mass. [Brandeis Mss, NMF 73-4]

MY DEAR MR. STETSON: [1] I regret the delay in replying to your telegram of October 27th and letter of November 2nd.

With the general purposes of your Society I sympathize, but in important matters bearing upon methods and means I have not as yet found myself in accord; and I therefore think it would not be proper for me to associate myself, either as officer or member, with your Society.[2]

With high appreciation,   Very truly yours,

1. Cushing Stetson was secretary to the Board of Trustees of the American Defense Society.

2. The American Defense Society was founded, according to Stetson, "to offset the pernicious influence of upwards of sixty anti-armament, anti-enlistment, and peace-at-any-price societies in this country." The society advocated extensive propaganda for the purposes of expanding officer training, military training for boys in public schools and colleges, the formation of rifle clubs, and the preparation of military displays for exhibition around the country.

To David Ignatius Walsh

November 4, 1915 Boston, Mass. [Brandeis Mss, NMF 68-2]

MY DEAR GOVERNOR: Of course I deeply regret that you were not elected; but you made a campaign admirable in every way. It has greatly strengthened your own position in the Commonwealth, and that of progressive democracy. Despite your defeat, you and we are to be congratulated.[1]   Cordially yours,

1. The Republicans made a clean sweep in Massachusetts, sending Walsh to defeat (along with the woman suffrage proposition which he favored) by a plurality of over 6,000 votes. (The election also saw the young Republican Calvin Coolidge elected Lieutenant Governor.) Seen as a blow to the Wilson administration's program, since Walsh was a strong supporter of the Wilson measures, the election gave the signal that the Republican Party was once more united and the breach between the regulars and the Bull Moosers had been practically healed. The Progressive Party received less than three per cent of the vote. See LDB to Gilson Gardner, 20 September 1915.

To Zionist Bureau (Copenhagen)

November 4, 1915 Boston, Mass. [Copenhagen Office]

GENTLEMEN: We beg to acknowledge receipt of your letter of October 13th, regarding Jabotinsky and his activities. We have circulated this among the members of our Committee for their information, as a confidential document.[1]

We feel that it would be extremely inadvisable, on our part, at this time, to make any public statement or any disavowal of Jabotinsky's responsibility. His agitation has gained no publicity, as yet, in America.

Should he come to America, or should there be any endeavor to make propaganda of his idea, it would then be time to take such action as may be necessary.

With Zion's greetings, we are   Very truly yours

1. Unfortunately there is no copy of the 13 October letter in the Brandeis Mss, but it undoubtedly concerned Jabotinsky's increasingly energetic and vocal campaign to establish a Jewish Legion. See LDB to Jehial Tschlenow, 5 May 1915, n. 1.

To The Editor, *Jewish Daily News*

November 5, 1915 Boston, Mass. [Brandeis Mss, Z 8-1]

In the building up of Jewish life in America, the Yiddish press has played an important part. It has served the interests of Jewish solidarity by providing a medium of communication which has given expression to the ideals and the aspirations of the Jewish people. Especially in the smaller communities, living their own provincial life, the Yiddish newspaper has fostered a consciousness of kinship with the rest of the Jewish world. In the larger centers, it has functioned as the forum for the discussion of vital Jewish issues. For those who came to these shores equipped with only their mother tongue, strangers in a strange land, the Yiddish press has been a necessity and an inestimable comfort.

The Jewish Daily News was the pioneer in the field of Yiddish journalism, and deserves great credit for having maintained, throughout its long life, a clear-cut position on most of the issues of Jewish life.

You have been a persistent advocate of the Zionist cause. Especially since the outbreak of the European war, you have driven home the needs of the Jewish people as a whole by insisting that at this time more particularly Zionism is the only practical solution of the pressing Jewish problem. Nothing has revealed the great and urgent need for the realization of the Zionist program than what is now transpiring in Europe, where our brethren are fighting on every frontier, and yet lack any assurance that they will derive any advantage from their great sacrifices.

The Jewish Daily News was one of the first to recognize, and to advocate effectively, the idea that unless the Jewish people living in this free land are organized to speak on behalf of their brethren, there will be no possibility for us to have any one to advance our claims when peace is negotiated. The Congress movement is intended to create for the Jews of America a responsible organ to speak for them and to give expression to our claims in the light of the facts revealed by the war. To render effective any utterance of this responsible organ speaking for the Jews of America, we must be organized, and our people must be made to appreciate the fact that it is they who must make effective whatever demands may issue from the Jewish Congress. Without this democratic responsibility no Congress will be effective. The Congress is to create a widespread cooperation in Jewish affairs. It is to arouse the dormant and the indifferent, and to make them feel that they have a distinctive part to play in the realization of any plans that may be formulated.

The Jewish Daily News will render valuable service to the Jewish cause if it lends the weight of its influence to the instruction of the American Jewish people on this point: for unless they are made to feel that the responsibility rests not upon the few but upon the mass of Jews of this country, we cannot hope to cope with the situation that has arisen.

Great crises bring forth adequate leadership. If we grapple with the situation that confronts us with energy and persistence, patience and farsightedness, employing the utmost of our sagacity and our experience to the fullest measure, we may be privileged to witness, blossoming out of the welter of blood in which the world is now submerged, a self-reliant and self-emancipated Jewish people.

In this labor I trust the Daily News will be found as hitherto fighting side by side with the progressive, democratic forces in Jewish life.[1]

1. This letter was published as part of the thirtieth anniversary issue of the *Jewish Daily News*.

To Office Committee

November 5, 1915 Boston, Mass. [Brandeis Mss, Z 8-2]

DEAR SIRS 1. I enclose copy of my letter to Mr. Perlstein in Washington.

2. I have two letters of B[enjamin]. P[erlstein].'s of November 4th relating to the proposed agreement between the A.J.R.C. and the C.R.C. It is not clear to me which of these two letters was written earlier. The one beginning: "Herewith is a memorandum of agreement between the two sub-committees, which will be presented to the American Jewish Relief Committee and our Committee at their next meetings" would seem to have been written later in the day.

As reported, this agreement is entirely unsatisfactory, and is directly contrary to the recommendations stated in the vote at our last meeting, and various letters which have passed between us. It makes no special provision for a percentage of all relief to go to Palestine. For us to adopt any such agreement would be suicidal.   Yours very truly,

To George Sutherland

November 6, 1915 Boston, Mass. [Brandeis Mss, NMF 69-3]

MY DEAR SENATOR: A somewhat detailed report has been made to me concerning the proceedings in the Hillstrom trial.[1] If this report is substantially correct, it would seem that there had been a grave miscarriage of justice, and that Hillstrom ought to have a new trial.

I know nothing about Hillstrom's merits or demerits, but as a lawyer I feel special concern over the growing tendency to discredit the integrity of proceedings in our Courts.

The occurrences in the [Leo] Frank case subjected the reputation of the Courts to severe strain; [2] and if Hillstrom should be sentenced without having had a fair trial, that which we must regard as the foundation of law and order will be seriously undermined.

I am venturing to write you of my apprehensions because of your high position as a lawyer, coupled with your influence in Utah.[3]   Most cordially yours,

1. Joseph Hillstrom, originally named Joel Emmanuel Haaglund, was best known by a third name, Joe Hill (1872–1915). An obscure Swedish immigrant who arrived in America around the turn of the century, Hill won renown as a radical and spokesman for the International Workers of the World. His essays and letters, but particularly his songs were published regularly in I.W.W. material (it was Hill who coined the phrase "pie in the sky" in his song "The Preacher and the Slave"). In January 1914, he was arrested in Salt Lake City and charged with murder. His trial, in June, was based on what many people felt was circumstantial evidence; Hill maintained his innocence and charged that he was being framed in order simply to eliminate him. By October 1915 there had grown a great outcry for a new trial—even Samuel Gompers and President Wilson tried to intercede in the case. See Gibbs M. Smith, *Joe Hill* (Salt Lake City, 1969).

2. For the Frank case, see LDB to Roscoe Pound, 27 November 1914.

3. On 19 November, Joe Hill was executed by a firing squad. The evening before, he had telegraphed to "Big Bill" Haywood, leader of the I.W.W.: "Don't waste any time in mourning. Organize." Hill became the subject of many songs and stories (the most famous being the ballad by Alfred Hayes beginning, "I dreamed I saw Joe Hill last night"), and he emerged in radical literature and folklore as the symbol of the downtrodden American worker, betrayed and murdered by American injustice.

To Israel Benjamin Brodie

November 11, 1915 New York, N.Y. [Brandeis Mss, Z 12-3]

MY DEAR MR. BRODIE: [1] I assume that you are proposing to have your membership committee meet frequently, at least as often as once a week, in their aggressive campaign to build up the Baltimore organization. I should like to keep in close touch with the growth of membership in Baltimore, and I should be grateful if you would send me, to Boston, a weekly report of the additions in members.[2]   Cordially yours,

1. Israel Benjamin Brodie (1884–1965) was, in 1915, a young lawyer and Zionist from Baltimore. By the 1930s, he became a prominent business executive and one of the leading American Zionists. He was one of the founders and, later, director of the Palestine Economic Corporation and was involved in a number of projects directed toward the economic development of the region.

2. This letter is similar to others sent to various local membership chairmen.

To Bernard Gerson Richards

November 16, 1915 Boston, Mass. [Brandeis Mss, Z 11-1]

MY DEAR MR. RICHARDS: I received yesterday your telegram at Montreal and today your letter. I have also seen a copy of the formal report of the meeting of the American Jewish Committee which was sent to the Jewish Advocate.[1]

First: Our friends and the press must (without of course quoting me) be made to see that the A.J.C. have put themselves in an absurd position. They tie their hands so as to make a Congress a sham. A congress after the termination of hostilities may mean a congress after the time has passed when Jews could accomplish something by participating in a conference. It is perfectly clear that there might be peace conferences while hostilities were still under way.[2]

Second: The A.J.C. now takes the position that even a conference cannot be trusted. Now a conference is conclusively presumed to lack discretion to properly determine whether a Congress ought to be called. You will remember that it was claimed,—I am told it was by Dr. Magnes,—and possibly in print, that under the original Adler plan the conference was to have power to determine whether a Congress should be called, and if so when. Now, after all of this discussion, the A.J.C., while pretending to yield, have even abridged the right of the Conference.

Third: The A.J.C. has further weakened itself by now repudiating their advisor, Dr. Magnes.[3]

Fourth: This alleged compromise which they offer is on the same basis as the original offer of the Conference in June. As a compromise between those who wanted a Congress and those who wanted no gathering of any kind, this action is as futile as was their action in June.[4]

Fifth: The course for our C[ongress]. O[rganizing]. C[ommittee]. is clear. We ought to press forward in every possible way the Congress agitation, getting in many cities and more organizations.[5] I am delighted to hear of the success in Philadelphia.

Sixth: I expect to reach New York on Friday morning, November 26th, and to be in New York for several days. I shall be glad to arrange for a meeting with members of our sub-committee, to discuss the situation on, say, Friday afternoon, at 3:00 o'clock. If that time will not be agreeable, please arrange with Mr. Perlstein for some other time.   Very truly yours,

1. On 14 November 1915, the American Jewish Committee, now under severe pressure because of the growing momentum of the "democratic congress" movement, held its annual meeting at the Astor Hotel in New York City. Their deliberations over the congress question marked another step in their retreat before the position of LDB and the Zionists. Now they expressed themselves as willing to call a preliminary conference to discuss the question of the congress, but, they stipulated, the congress could not meet until the war in Europe had been concluded. The American Jewish Committee was also still reluctant about the democratic election of representatives (see Shapiro, *Leadership of the American Zionist Organization*, ch. 4). The combination of the A.J.C.'s acknowledgement of defeat and LDB's appointment to the Supreme Court eventually made possible a compromise for a congress, to be democratically elected, but which would not convene until after the war. See LDB to Louis Lipsky, 2 December 1915.

2. See next letter.

3. Interestingly, while turning their backs on his advice, the American Jewish Committee chose Magnes (together with Judge Mack) as three-year members of their Executive Committee.

4. See LDB to Harry Schneiderman, 6 July 1915.

5. LDB felt ready to call formally for a congress at a preliminary conference in March 1916 in Philadelphia.

To Harry Friedenwald

November 17, 1915 Boston, Mass. [Brandeis Mss, Z 11-2]

MY DEAR DR. FRIEDENWALD: *First*: I am glad to have your report of the November 15th meeting.[1] It is true that in appearance the A.J.C. have yielded much. In fact, the A.J.C. have not yielded; and I am convinced that if I had the opportunity of discussing the matter with you, I could make it clear that the Congressists would stultify themselves if they accepted the arrangement on the lines which the A.J.C. voted on the 14th. What the A.J.C. have done, and are asking us to assent to, is not to express an opinion on the advisability of holding a Congress, but to prophesy. We may all be agreed that it is undesirable to hold a Congress now, or in the near future; but to bind ourselves by agreement not to hold a Congress until after hostilities cease, is to prophesy that conditions in the future will be relatively the same as they are at present.

The difficulties of the situation are such that no man who exercises judgment, even as of today, can feel certain that his judgment is sound. But it seems to me clear that we cannot exercise a sound judgment now on an unknown situation which may arise in the future.

I am enclosing a copy of my letter of yesterday to Mr. Richards. These communications are of course to be treated as confidential.

Second: I have a letter from Mrs. Friedenwald about Rabbi Lazaron's invitation, and also a letter from him. I am enclosing a copy of my reply to him.[2]

Third: I hope that active work is being done with a view to increasing the Baltimore membership. The situation there seems to me to be very promising.   Cordially yours,

1. See preceding letter.
2. Printed below.

To Maximilian Heller

November 17, 1915 Boston, Mass. [Brandeis Mss, Z 8-1]

MY DEAR MR. HELLER: I am extremely sorry to learn from your letter of the 12th how far from well you have been.

By all means take the advice of Mrs. Heller and your friends for a two or three months' winter vacation. Shift upon others the responsibility for the war sufferers collections. The Jewish cause will gain most by having you restored to full health and strength at the earliest possible moment.

Nothing needs your help more than the Zionist cause, but the Zionist cause too must get along as best it can while you are getting the needed rest.

You are fortunate that while you are resting your son here can be relied upon to do good work for the cause.[1] Dr. S. Levin, who attended with him at one of the recent meetings spoke with enthusiasm of his spirit and accomplishment.

    With every good wish,   Most cordially yours,

    1. Rabbi Heller's son was James Gutheim Heller (b. 1892), who himself became a rabbi in 1916. After serving a number of congregations, he became head of Cincinnati's Isaac M. Wise Temple in 1920 and remained there, teaching musicology at the Hebrew Union College, until 1952. In the 1940s Heller headed a number of important Zionist organizations.

To Morris Samuel Lazaron

November 17, 1915 Boston, Mass. [Brandeis Mss, Z 8-1]

MY DEAR RABBI LAZARON: [1] Upon my return to the city I find your letter of the 11th. You are entirely too modest in assuming that you require identification.

    I was much impressed with what you said to me after the meeting as to the effect of Zionism in deepening Jewish consciousness; and was particularly glad to have your letter expressing confirmation of that view. You are entirely right as to the importance of taking up this work with the younger men, and particularly with students and University graduates. It is from those still young to whom we must look in Jewish affairs, as in others, for progressive work; and I should be glad of the opportunity of joining with you in rousing the young people of Baltimore, if my time permitted. Unfortunately the other calls upon me are too great to allow me to consider going to Baltimore again in the near future. I hope, however, that you will be willing to take up this work with the young people.

    I am venturing to send you under separate cover copies of three addresses of mine:

    "Zionism and Patriotism"
    "A Call to the Educated Jew"
    "The Jewish Problem"

which I hope you will care to read.

Most cordially yours,

    1. Morris Samuel Lazaron (b. 1888) was the rabbi of the Baltimore Hebrew Congregation from 1915 until 1949. He became a notorious anti-

Zionist and one of the founders and vice-presidents of the anti-Zionist American Council for Judaism in the 1940s.

To Benjamin F. Levy

November 17, 1915 Boston, Mass. [Brandeis Mss, Z 8-1]

MY DEAR MR. LEVY: [1] Absence from the city has delayed a reply to yours of November 8th, for which I thank you.

It does not seem possible at this late day to bring before the National Bureau and our Committee the question which you so properly present. In my own opinion, however, our case is so different from that which Colonel Roosevelt and President Wilson had in mind, that there ought not to be any chance of confusion.

The editorial in the Boston Herald, of which a part is quoted in the October number of the Menorah Journal on page 236, seems to me to state the Zionist situation most clearly.[2]

I trust you will find it possible now to take an active part again in Zionist affairs.   Very truly yours,

1. Benjamin F. Levy (1874-19[?]) was an attorney from Elmira, New York. He had been active in Jewish affairs, but was disturbed by recent Zionist emphasis upon Jewish nationalism. In view of recent condemnations of so-called hyphenated Americans by men like Roosevelt and Wilson, Levy wondered if the posture of Zionists was appropriate.

2. The editorial said in part: "Hebrews willingly neglectful of their own inheritance cannot hope to be of much value as Americans. Nor is the republic interested in suppressing this or any other valuable legacy from the past. . . . Our civilization is enriched, not impoverished, by these diverse race traits."

To Samuel S. Fels

November 18, 1915 Boston, Mass. [Brandeis Mss, Z 8-1]

MY DEAR MR. FELS: *First*: Referring to our discussion on Zionism on Saturday: I am sending you under separate cover three addresses which I hope will remove the doubt which you expressed to me:

"Zionism and Patriotism"
"A Call to the Educated Jew"
"The Jewish Problem".

Second: You asked me to let you know the ways in which relief could be given in Palestine, so that you might the better select the course most in accord with your views. There are three funds for which we are raising money:

(a) An Emergency Fund of $200,000 (last year we undertook to raise for this purpose $100,000, but the need this year is much greater than last.) This fund is used primarily for the schools and other institutions in Palestine, and also for the necessary maintenance of the Zionist organization abroad and here. It was to this fund that you sent me a check for $1,000 on Jan. 13, 1915.

(b) The olive and almond planters' loan fund: We are endeavoring to raise a special fund to lend to planters who suffered from the locusts last year, and who are unable to get loans in Palestine now because of the shutting down of the Anglo Palestine Company, of which you will recall I sent you the ten year report last year. We hope to raise for this fund $80,000; and unless things go very ill in Palestine, we expect this loan to be repaid in instalments with interest. This fund is similar to the Orange Loan Fund, to which you contributed last year at the request of Judge Mack.

(c) The Palestine General Relief Funds. These are funds for the general relief of the poor Jews in Palestine, who are of course in great need.

Of these funds my own preference in way of your contribution would be the first or second. The Palestine Relief is of course very worthy, but there are many people who recognize the appeals for charity, who do not appreciate the importance of the work of construction and conservation, which is more directly represented by the first and second funds.

The leaflet "Help Save Palestine", which I enclose, will give you some further idea of Palestinian needs.

Very cordially yours,

To Moses O. Ades

November 19, 1915 Boston, Mass. [Brandeis Mss, Z 2-4]

MY DEAR MR. ADES: [1] Upon my return to the city I find yours of the 12th.

I have also today a letter of the 17th from my brother. You

speak of the auditorium in the Y.M.H.A. as accommodating 450 people. My brother speaks of the "large hall" which would seat about 700.

I think that a hall seating 450 would probably be too small, but one seating 700 would be about right. I shall be glad to have you talk with my brother in regard to this.

It is my purpose to make this meeting productive both in membership in the Zion Society, and in the raising of an Emergency Fund, so far as that is possible. And of course the success of such a project would depend almost entirely upon the work which was done by way of preparation before the meeting, the seeing of men, and getting of pledges.   Very cordially yours,

1. Ades was writing about arrangements for LDB's projected Zionist speech in Louisville in early January 1916. See LDB to Alfred Brandeis, 8 December 1915.

To Judah Leon Magnes

November 19, 1915 Boston, Mass. [Brandeis Mss, Z 11-1]

DEAR DR. MAGNES: Referring again to your letter of the 17th in relation to a Congress: [1]

It may be of some service in discussing this matter with the Sub-committee of the Congress Organization Committee, if you will let me know:

First: Which are the "about sixteen national Jewish organizations (that) have accepted the invitation of the American Jewish Committee to attend a Conference which was to have been held on October 24, but which was postponed pending the Annual Meeting of the American Jewish Committee."

Second: What you had in mind in saying: "It was also understood that in convening the Conference provided for in the foregoing resolution due account is to be taken of (that) fact".[2]

Awaiting your reply,   Very truly yours,

1. See LDB to Bernard G. Richards, 16 November 1915. Magnes asked that a sub-committee of the Congress Organizing Committee meet with a sub-committee of other interested organizations in order to discuss the resolution.

2. In his reply of 22 November, Magnes listed the sixteen organizations. He thought it proper that no future plan for a conference should reduce the

representation of any of these sixteen groups as "the American Jewish Committee has natural obligations towards these organizations." See LDB to Louis Lipsky, 2 December 1915.

To Felix Moritz Warburg

November 19, 1915 Boston, Mass. [Magnes Mss]

MY DEAR MR. WARBURG: There was a general meeting of our Committees last evening, as the result of which I am asking you to send me at the earliest possible moment reports covering the following:

First: A detailed report, classified according to states and cities, of all remittances received from individuals or societies resident or located in either Massachusetts, New Hampshire, Maine, Vermont or Rhode Island, which were remitted direct to your office from the date of the formation of our Committee up to the date of your report—otherwise than through our local treasurer.

I am writing Mr. Bressler to endeavor to secure from the Central Relief Committee a similar report covering collections from New England.

You will recall that at a meeting of our Committee held last month, I called attention to the embarrassment and dissatisfaction that had arisen in our territory through the request which had unfortunately been issued from the New York Committees to those resident in our territory, to collect funds and make remittances direct to New York. At a meeting of our New England Committee last evening, this matter was commented upon with considerable feeling, and in response to demands for greater activity it was insisted (with reason) that the report of our Treasurer failed to show the actual contributions of this territory. I promised that at our next meeting I would submit a comprehensive report, and I should be greatly obliged if you would lend all the aid you can to securing at as early a date as possible the data for such a report.

Second: A comprehensive report on the distribution of the funds abroad: stating, among other things, the methods and composition of the Committee. I realize the difficulty in securing the data for such a report, and am, of course, mindful of such information already given by our Committee, particularly in No. 10 of the Monthly Bulletin. But it seems to me imperative that we should get sufficient data as as to meet in a comprehensive way the natural demand for this information.

You will remember that I called attention last spring to the fact that in our territory the zeal for collections had been greatly dampened by the doubt in the minds of many as to the character or efficiency of our distributions abroad. The only way to meet that situation is to prepare a report which shall be so comprehensive and detailed as to leave no room for doubt. Particular inquiry was made in regard to the distribution through our German connections.[1]   Very cordially yours,

1. On 22 November, Warburg promised the information would soon be gathered and forwarded.

To Nathan D. Kaplan

November 22, 1915 Boston, Mass. [Brandeis Mss, Z 3-1]

DEAR MR. KAPLAN: *First*: As to the raising of money: I feel quite sure from our past experience that we cannot rely upon the enthusiasm of the banquet to raise money.[1] The work of preparation for that, and the securing of written pledges in advance, which can be made public at the banquet, is the work which will tell. You should appoint an active, efficient committee, which will undertake to commence immediately the work of securing such pledges. With a good start so made you would probably succeed in doubling the amount otherwise obtained.

Second: You are entirely right that you must secure a definite agreement from Dr. Levin covering the dates and character of the engagements. I feel certain, however, that in view of what he has been willing to do in New England, and what he has already told me, he will be willing to give several additional weeks' time to Chicago; that he will be entirely content to speak at small meetings, as well as large; that he will be willing to speak in the Synagogue at meetings either Friday evening or Saturday. I advise your writing him at once to New York, securing his definite and categorical assent.

Third: My idea was not for an all day conference, but for a series of conferences, in which the various matters could be discussed—with those who are active workers, or who you believe will become such. I hope that in arranging for the Saturday meeting, it will be possible for you and Mr. Shulman to keep yourselves reasonably free, as both of you and Mr. Bernstein ought preferably to be present at substantially all of the conferences with me.

Fourth: As to the character of the changes in your organization, which I have in mind, I will write you later.[2]

Fifth: Our thought had been that Dr. Levin would add so much to the development of your local societies by his presence, that you would be very ready to defray the relatively small daily expenses attendant upon his long visit; but we shall be glad to consider your definite suggestions on this subject.

Yours, very truly,

1. See LDB to Kaplan, 20 October 1915.
2. See LDB to Kaplan, 29 November 1915.

To Otto Irving Wise[1] (Telegram)

November 22, 1915 Boston, Mass. [Brandeis Mss, Z 8-1]

Delighted with your telegram. Congratulations to you and your brother.

1. Otto Irving Wise (1871–1919) was the brother of Stephen S. Wise. He was a San Francisco lawyer and had been instrumental in arranging for his brother's western tour on behalf of Zionism (see LDB to Horace M. Kallen, 6 October 1915 and to Stephen S. Wise, 15 October 1915). Otto Wise had wired: "It will interest you to learn that as a result of mass meeting addressed by my brother last night twenty two thousand dollars was secured and I am confident that at least five thousand dollars more will be received for Palestine relief today."

To Norman Hapgood

November 24, 1915 Boston, Mass. [Brandeis Mss, Z 8-1]

DEAR NORMAN: *First*: I have a copy of your letter of the 23rd to Felix F[rankfurter]., and he tells me he has written you and will write you further on the subject.[1] I have discussed this matter also with deHaas, who thinks that you can get valuable information particularly with reference to the attitude of the Universities towards Jews as professors or instructors from:

Dr. Richard Gottheil
Dr. Spingarn
Dr. Judah Joffe.[2]

And as to the attitude of the Universities towards students from Dr. J. Selwyn Shapiro [*sic*] of the New York City College—the attitude of Columbia, Barnard and his own college.[3]

Charles McCarthy spoke to me recently of the difficulties in this connection at the University of Wisconsin. There were a number of articles on this subject in the Jewish Weekly, which was published last year in New York as a part of Herman Bernstein's paper The Day. The Jewish Weekly had a short life, and these articles, as I recall it, appeared within the last month or two before the publication was discontinued.

Second: I am glad to know that you are hearing much from your articles on the Jews. The one in this week's issue seems to me particularly helpful.[4] I am afraid that the office did not do very effective work in calling these articles to the attention of the Jewish papers, because deHaas had not known that they were appearing.

Third: The question has also come up in connection with boarding schools,—particularly the girls' boarding schools,—on which there was considerable published in the way of correspondence and comments. It might be well for you to address a letter to each of the following Jewish Weeklies:

The Jewish Independent of Cleveland
The American Hebrew, New York City
Jewish Comment, Baltimore
Jewish Exponent, Philadelphia
Jewish Ledger, New Orleans
Jewish Sentinel, Chicago
Immanuel, San Francisco
American Israelite, Cincinnati
Jewish Criterian, Pittsburg
Jewish Advocate, Boston.

It would also be worth while for you to write to Dr. Emil G. Hirsch of Chicago, who, I am informed was interested in a case in the University of Chicago involving appointment in the teachers' staff.

Fourth: The further disclosures connecting the German Government with deliberate violations of American law are making the situation almost unbearable. Although we must practice forebearance, I hope you will make clear how serious Germany's affront is.[5]   Very truly,

1. Hapgood was gathering material for his series of articles on Jews in America (see LDB to Julian W. Mack, 26 August 1915, n. 5). Currently, he was working on a piece about discrimination against Jews in colleges and universities; it was published in two parts as "Jews and College Life," *Harper's Weekly*, 62 (15 January 1916): 53, and "Schools, Colleges and Jews," *ibid.* (22 January 1916): 77.

2. Joel Elias Spingarn (1875–1939) had taught comparative literature at Columbia until 1911. After serving in the army he went into private publishing. Spingarn is best remembered for his pioneering work in Negro civil rights. He was one of the founders of the National Association for the Advancement of Colored People and served in official capacities in that organization for nearly thirty years. Judah Achilles Joffe (1873–1966) was a musicologist and an expert on Slavic languages, but he was best known as an authority on Yiddish linguistics.

3. Jacob Salwyn Schapiro (b. 1879) is an intellectual historian of modern Europe. He taught at City College from 1909 until his retirement in 1947.

4. Hapgood's article, "The Future of the Jews in America," *Harper's Weekly*, 61 (27 November 1915): 511, was an attack on Jacob Schiff as "a court Jew," and an advocacy of democracy and Zionism to preserve the identity of the Jews in America.

5. There was no need to spur Hapgood on. *Harper's* had been growing increasingly anti-German since the start of the war.

To Edgar Bar Friedenwald

November 29, 1915 Boston, Mass. [Brandeis Mss, Z 8-1]

DEAR DR. FRIEDENWALD: [1] Upon my return to the city I find yours of the 25th.

The matter to which you refer was considered at a meeting of the officers of the Congress Organization Committee on the 26th. The Congress Organization Committee believes it to be improper at this time for any of the local organizations to take part, as an organization, in mass meetings to protest against Russian atrocities. What is to be done by local Congress committees should be determined in advance of the Congress by the Congress Organization Committee, or the conference which precedes the Congress.

Of course, as individuals, members who are affiliated with the Congress movement are free to participate in such mass meetings, but they should be careful to prevent the public being misled into the belief that they are acting in any official capacity.

Yours very truly,

1. Edgar Bar Friedenwald, (1879–19[?]), the brother of Harry Friedenwald, was a Baltimore pediatrician and professor at the University of Maryland Medical School. He was the chairman of Baltimore's Congress Committee, and had written LDB to ask advice about participating in a mass meeting to protest Russian atrocities against the Jews which was being organized by the National Jewish Workmen's Committee.

To Horace Meyer Kallen

November 29, 1915 Boston, Mass. [Brandeis Mss, Z 3-1]

MY DEAR DR. KALLEN: Upon my return to the city I find yours of the 23rd.

There is no question but that the Congress movement ought to be pressed vigorously. The difficulty is in securing men to undertake the work. The lack of officers is the greatest obstacle to more rapid Zionist development, as I have written you from time to time, and the Congress movement is tending rather to accentuate that difficulty. It is casting a new burden upon Zionists, there being but few non-Zionists who are taking any appreciable part in the Zionist movement.

If you know of any men who can be intrusted with and will really work for the Congress movement, and who can be put in the positions of officers, we can press it forward with great rapidity.

The group of men whom you got together in April in New York for Zionist work have, in the main, been rather disappointing in performance. I am glad you are coming east soon, and I trust that you will be able to impress them with the sanctity of a promise, and secure performance.   Very truly yours,

To Nathan D. Kaplan

November 29, 1915 Boston, Mass. [Brandeis Mss, Z 3-1]

MY DEAR MR. KAPLAN: You have asked me what changes in organization I had in mind so that you and your associates might consider my suggestions in advance of our meeting in Chicago.[1] I submit the following for consideration:

First: The Knights of Zion, as at present organized, must necessarily fail to get the effective results which your rich territory makes possible, because the intensive work necessary cannot be carried on consistently with the present organization. The territory covered is geographically so large that there cannot be such close working together with the different communities, as is essential. This conclusion we have reached after practically a year's experience in Massachusetts and Northern New England. We cover a territory of nominally 58,030 square miles. There is no occasion for us to reach nearly half of that, as there are no Jewish communities in central and northern Maine, and in a large part of Vermont and New Hampshire. Yet the New England States have an area about equal to Illinois, with its 56,650 square miles. When we undertook to establish the New England Bureau, we concluded that it was not wise to include the State of Connecticut with its 4,990 square miles; because we felt that we had work enough for ourselves in the other States, and would lose, rather than gain, in efficiency by adding Connecticut at the start. Experience confirms that decision.

The Jewish population of the five New England States, in which the Boston Bureau operates, is little more than one-half of the Jewish population of the State of Illinois alone.

In my opinion the State of Illinois should be made a unit (and I hope may become the banner unit) for Zionist work. You men of Illinois, who have been the leaders in the Knights of Zion movement, ought to organize yourselves into a State organization, and undertake to so intensify the work as to secure in the State of Illinois alone, within a relatively short time, at least four times as many members as there are now in the societies of the Knights of Zion in all of the ten States.

It was with a view to carrying out that idea that I deemed it important that you should arrange in the wake of the Zionist

Convention for at least several weeks of meetings in Chicago alone in which Dr. Levin could participate. I have in other movements quite remote from Zionism had the same experience which we Zionists are having in New England. It is only the intensive work which is effective—both in securing members and in retaining them. Individual efforts, not intensive, are like drops of rain,—the benefit of which is lost by early evaporation.

It seems to me that if you men of Chicago would organize a modest Bureau for Illinois work alone, and make such an arrangement with Mr. Zolotkoff as would secure a part of his time each day, and with him organize for such intensive work, you could do the best possible that could be done for the cause.

Second: What is proposed above for Illinois we should look forward to doing ultimately (of course in a smaller way) for each of the other nine States. We ought to establish in some way an office in each State. Undoubtedly it would not be possible for us to incur at the outset any material expense in perhaps any of the other nine States. But we could doubtless make an arrangement for headquarters in each of the States, to be in charge of some person who would become the organized leader for that State supported by a State Committee. We could have stationery printed for the various headquarters. This would doubtless add to the gravitation of State work in the State headquarters. As to who the men are in each of these other nine States who could most effectively develop the work, I should be glad to have your, Mr. Shulman's, Mr. Zolotkoff's and Mr. Bernstein's [advice].

Specific work which has already undertaken in conjunction with the P.C. in Ohio and in Michigan, may prove the first step to such State organization. We have in Cleveland a Committee with Rabbi Margolies [2] at the head, who is undertaking to organize Northern Ohio, more particularly with a view of raising contributions for the Emergency Fund; but also to develop membership and general Zionist interest. A similar committee has been formed in Detroit, for the State of Michigan, with Rabbi Hirschman as Chairman. We suppose that in Missouri with such strong men as Baron and Dr. Wolf [3] in St. Louis, and Dr. Lehman in Kansas City, it ought to be possible to develop an effective organization. In Indiana we think you could count on the active cooperation of Abrahams of Fort Wayne. There is an excellent group both in St. Paul and Minneapolis. The very fact that State leaders are created, and responsibility placed upon them, will tend to develop men and activity. In each of these States when the preliminary organizations are established, we may well look forward to the discovery of much new interest on the part of men who in the past have not shown their heads in Zionist matters.

Third: It will undoubtedly be desirable for the Provisional Committee to establish an office in Chicago, in addition to your own Illinois Bureau, and doubtless in connection with it. Of course if the work is to be intensively pursued in each of the ten States, it will greatly facilitate the work to have within the territory, and in its several cities, an office to which these leaders would naturally come, and where they may from time to time meet for conference and information, and develop a Middle West District Council.

Fourth: In order to enable the Knights of Zion Societies to properly perform their functions, it is, in my opinion, necessary to raise the membership dues to not less than $3.00 a year. In the most successful of the New England societies,—the Zionist Society for Great Boston,—(which has a membership of about 425), the dues are $5.00 a year. To be effective a Zionist Society must offer something to its members. It must in the first place offer to each member the means of informing himself in regard to current Zionist affairs. For this purpose every Zionist member ought to have a copy of the Federation Bulletin, and either the Yiddish Volk or the Maccabaean. It should also be possible for each society in the large cities to hold meetings at least once a month, and to have at those meetings speakers who can contribute something material to the knowledge of and interest in Zionist affairs. To do this a reasonable membership fee is absolutely necessary. Practically every organization outside of the Zionist body finds that a very small membership fee presents insurmountable obstacles to success.

Fifth: As indicating the work which a Provisional committee Bureau can perform, it may be valuable for you to know just what the Boston Bureau is doing for Zionist organizations in New England territory. I am enclosing you a memorandum which describes its work.

Sixth: I laid before the P.C. at its meeting on the 27th the above views in regard to the middle west situation, and the Committee deemed it wise for that reason, and because of our very depleted Emergency and Propaganda fund, to make only a temporary subvention of $500. to the Knights of Zion, and to await the result of my conference with your leaders in January. I hope you will have an opportunity to take this matter up fully with the leaders in the middle west.

Seventh: I saw Dr. Levin on the 27th, and he tells me that he has written you that he will remain in Chicago until January 16th. I think that if you can arrange a profitable program, he might be induced to remain there somewhat longer, and I am sure that he will be prepared to give you and Mr. Shulman and Mr. Zolotkoff all possible aid.

Eighth: I enclose editorial clipping from the American Jewish World of Minneapolis of November 5th. This periodical has shown marked friendliness to the Zionist cause, and I should think that you with our Minneapolis friends might obtain through it considerable aid.   Yours very truly,

1. See LDB to Kaplan, 20 October and 22 November 1915.
2. Rabbi Samuel Margolies (d. 1918) was a Cleveland rabbi and the son of the foremost orthodox rabbi in the United States, Moses S. Margolies of New York City.
3. Alexander S. Wolf (1870–19[?]) was a St. Louis physician and authority on venereal diseases. He had known Herzl in his youth and was an active Zionist. He served as president of the St. Louis council, and in 1917, a St. Louis's representative to the American Jewish Congress.

To Henry Moskowitz

November 30, 1915 Boston, Mass. [Brandeis Mss, NMF 67-2]

MY DEAR HENRY: I have talked with Lincoln Filene about your letter of the 26th, and we are both of [the] opinion that it is advisable for you to resign as you suggest from the clerkship of the Board.[1]

It is too bad that this should have become necessary; because the work which we have done in the last five and a half years seems to me really important. But I hope that in an unofficial capacity we may work together until the end of our time.

I know Rosensohn and have a very high opinion of him, and shall be glad in due time to take up the matter of your successor with my associates.[2]

With keen regret, Most cordially yours,

1. Belle Moskowitz had accepted a position as clerk of the Manufacturers' Association. In view of that fact, Moskowitz thought it best that he resign as clerk of the Board of Arbitration for the garment industry. Moskowitz wrote: "It breaks my heart to disassociate myself from the Board officially, yet, under the circumstances, it seems to me the wisest thing to do."

2. Moskowitz had recommended as his successor Samuel Julian Rosensohn (1880–1939). Rosensohn had been Felix Frankfurter's roommate at Harvard. After practicing law in New York City, he was appointed Assistant Corporation Counsel by Mayor Mitchel and during the war worked for Newton Baker (as did Frankfurter) as a labor adviser. In 1925, he participated in the defense of Scopes in the famous "monkey trial" in Dayton, Tennessee. In the late 1920s, Rosensohn became an active Zionist, holding several positions of leadership within the movement. At the close of World War I, he became Chairman of the Board of Conciliation for the garment industry.

To Louis Lipsky

December 2, 1915 Boston, Mass. [Brandeis Mss, Z 1-4]

MY DEAR MR. LIPSKY: Replying to yours of the 1st concerning the Congress: [1]

First: At the joint conference on November 12th of the sub-committees of the C[ongress]. O[rganizing]. C[ommittee]., the N[ational]. W[orkmen's]. C[ommittee]., and the A[merican]. J[ewish]. C[ommittee]. at which representatives of the Kellilah, Mr. Nathan Straus and Mr. Richards were present, Colonel Cutler[2] proposed at the close of the meeting that we should not take any vote upon the Magnes resolution, to which you, Dr. Bluestone[3] and I had assented on behalf of the C.O.C.; but that that resolution should be submitted by the three sub-committees to their respective committees for consideration, after which action our sub-committees should hold a further conference.

Second: On November 14th the American Jewish Committee refused to accept the Magnes resolution, substituting in place thereof a resolution which postponed the holding of a Congress necessarily until after the close of hostilities. On November 26th there was a joint meeting for the consideration of the matter by the sub-committee and administrative committee of the C.O.C., at which Mr. Carlinger,[4] among others, was present. It appeared to be the unanimous opinion of all present that it would be fatal to the Congress movement to accept the A.J.C. amendment; and also that it was imperative that no time be lost before issuing notice of the holding of a conference to consider the preliminary problems incident to a Congress.

At the opening of the meeting Judge Sanders's letter, advising acceptance of the A.J.C.'s resolution, was read. Judge Levy also stated that he attended that meeting at the request of Judge Sanders to present that as Judge Sanders' view—Judge Sanders personally being unable to attend; but that he felt obliged, since he was a member of the Administrative Committee, to state that he was diametrically opposed to Judge Sanders in this respect; and believed that it would kill the Congress movement to accept the amendment.

Third: In view of this opinion of the members of the Administrative Committee and of the C.O.C. Sub-committee, I concluded that there would be no impropriety in the sub-committee meeting with the sub-committee of the N.W.C. and the A.J.C. preparatory to the general meeting of the C.O.C., which was to be held during the present week. I accordingly re-arranged my plans so as to remain in New York over Sunday for the holding of a meeting of the three sub-committees on the evening of the 27th. The holding of this meeting, which had been arranged by Mr. Richards, with Dr. Rosenblatt and Dr. Magnes, was cancelled because Col. Cutler was unable to attend, and desired to be present.

Fourth: In view of the fact that the Administrative Committee had represented it as imperative that prompt action should be taken for the calling of a preliminary conference, it seemed to me that there should be laid before the Committee of the C.O.C., at its meeting this week, a draft for calling of such a Congress. After my consultation with you this draft was prepared, and the revised draft prepared by me was sent to you on the 29th. Both your draft and mine proposed to make as the first business of the preliminary conference, at which all organizations and local committees affiliated with the C.O.C. should be represented, the question whether or not the conditions prescribed by the A.J.C.

prohibiting the holding of a Congress before the close of hostilities, should be accepted.

Fifth: Your letter of the 1st following Mr. Richards' letter of
November 30th discloses that not only Mr. Carlinger, who was
present at the joint conference with the Sub-committee and the
Administrative Committee of the C.O.C. on November 26th, but
also Dr. Weiss [5] of the Administrative Committee favor acceptance of the conditions imposed by the A.J.C., as does Judge
Sanders.[6]

In view of the facts above set forth, I do not see that anything
could be gained by a meeting now of the three sub-committees;
and I greatly doubt even the propriety of holding such a meeting.
I, personally, as a member of the C.O.C. sub-committee, should
feel the gravest doubt as to what my power was. The doubt which
has been raised by Judge Sanders, Mr. Carlinger and Dr. Weiss
presents a question which should be decided by the Congress
Organization Committee itself, if it deems that it has the power to
do so, or by such a conference as is sketched in the draft of notice
which you and I prepared. I am, therefore, of opinion that a
meeting of the Congress Organization Committee should be held;
that the draft of notice sent you on the 29th should be submitted
to that meeting for consideration; and that the Committee upon
full discussion should determine what action should be taken.

Sixth: The full committee, in considering this matter will of
course realize that the decision it makes must be definitive in its
character; and it must be made clear what the effect of a decision
either one way or the other is.

Yours, very truly,

1. For the background of this letter, see LDB to Bernard G. Richards, 16
November and Judah L. Magnes, 19 November 1915.

2. Harry Cutler (1875–1920), a colonel in the National Guard and an
aide to General Pershing in the 1916 Mexican campaign, was active in manufacturing, politics, and Jewish philanthropy. He was one of the nine delegates whom the American Jewish Congress sent to Versailles to represent
Jewish interests in 1919. He served on the executive committees of both the
American Jewish Committee and the Zionist Organization of America.

3. Joseph Isaac Bluestone (1860–1934) was a New York physician who had
long been active in Zionist affairs. Portions of his diary dealing with early
American Zionist activities have been published; see Hyman B. Grinstein,
"The Memoirs and Scrapbooks of the Late Dr. Joseph Isaac Bluestone of

New York," *Publications of the American Jewish Historical Society*, 35 (1939): 53-64.

4. Jacob Carlinger (1881-1946), a New York hospital official soon to become superintendent of the Jewish Memorial Hospital, was an organizer of the Congress movement.

5. Julius Weiss (1876-1939) was a Rumanian immigrant who became a Bronx physician. He was president of the Rumanian Jewish Federation and a delegate to the early Jewish congresses.

6. Sanders and the others had suddenly decided that the Magnes proposal (see LDB to Bernard G. Richards, 16 November 1915) marked a "complete surrender" on the part of the American Jewish Committee. The clause about awaiting the cessation of hostlities was merely inserted, they thought, to save face; it could easily be ignored once the preliminary conference had convened. They therefore favored accepting the proposal without delay.

To Judah Leon Magnes

December 3, 1915 Boston, Mass. [Brandeis Mss, NMF 71-6]

MY DEAR DR. MAGNES: Rumor reaches our office here that the Central Relief Committee is about to send widespread through New England a request for remittances direct to it of funds being collected.

In New England there had been no such division of forces as existed in New York between the Central Relief Committee and the American Jewish Relief Committee. The circular which was sent out by the American Jewish Relief Committee a few months ago greatly embarrassed our workers here, and the effect of a similar circular emanating from the Central Relief Committee intensified the result.

We have been working of late to overcome the partial paralysis which resulted from these conflicting directions. If the Central Relief Committee now sends out new notices, our workers will become entirely confused, and the confusion will inevitably result in serious damage to the cause.

The situation in New England was probably different from that existing in many other places, as we had succeeded in securing cooperation of all the diverging forces on a basis apparently satisfactory to all.

I shall be glad if you will take this matter up with members of the Central Relief Committee.

Awaiting your reply,   Very truly yours,

To Louis Lipsky

December 4, 1915 Boston, Mass. [Brandeis Mss, Z 1-4]

MY DEAR MR. LIPSKY: Replying to yours of the 3rd:

First: It does not seem to me wise to attend the meeting of the C.O.C. on December 8th.[1] I think it probable that if I attend, I could, with the support of our Zionist forces, Judge Levy and others who attended our meeting on the 26th, induce the C.O.C. to adopt the program set forth in the draft of notice sent you November 29th; but I gravely doubt the wisdom of exercising our united influence to overcome such opposition as exists. If we, as Zionists, had a large number of men competent to fill officer's [*sic*] positions as leaders of the Congress movement, we could undoubtedly through that movement greatly enhance the Zionist forces, and I think that the policy which you and I agreed upon is so clearly the true policy for the American Jew, that resistance to our policy would serve only to advance the cause, because the contest would serve as a great campaign of education. We are, however, unfortunately in the position that we are seriously lacking in the number of officers required for strictly Zionist work, and if we compel our Zionist leaders to assume the burden of the Congress fight, we shall seriously cripple the Zionist movement, while still having inadequate forces to carry the Congress movement to a successful issue.

Second: My position has been throughout of making the Congress movement truly what it purported to be,—a democratic movement. My hope and expectation was that the Congress movement would develop among non-Zionist adherents men competent and willing to be leaders, with whom we might effectively cooperate, and gain for our general Zionists democratic views through the strength of our cause. I have not yet given up the hope of accomplishing this; but I feel that the only way in which it can be accomplished is to leave with those who are primarily responsible for the Congress movement the responsibility for meeting the emergencies which arise—the struggle over important issues, as well as the financial demands.

I feel, therefore, that the question ought to be put squarely to the C.O.C.; that it ought to be put particularly squarely to that great factor of the C.O.C.,— the I.O.B.A. If, as Judge Levy says, the great majority of their Board is opposed to Sanders, and that

Sanders has only one vote, they ought to fight it out together, and the I.O.B.A. ought to defeat Sanders,—not the outside organization. Let us have the contest go forward, if there is to be one, in each of the organizations which are represented on the Congress Organization Committee. There is certainly nothing in the situation which required [sic] immediate action, and whatever time is necessary for the various organizations to take to understand this situation, and to reach a conclusion in regard to it, should be taken. What we are doing is undertaking to educate the Jews in these problems. If we carry through successfully our views now, by force, largely, of personality, we certainly will have done little in the way of education, and will have to meet the same situation again and again. I should personally also be confronted probably with this embarrassing position: A new appeal would be made to me, and possibly again by Sanders, to accept the Chairmanship or Presidency of the C.O.C. Committee. To refuse it would be at least ungracious. To accept it would be injurious to the Zionist cause.

Third: At the meeting of the C.O.C. called for December 8th it seems to me you should present the draft of notice as embodying our proposal. You should supplement it by a calm explanation of the reasons from the Congress standpoint which support the measure. But no attempt should be made to override the natural inclination or will of the other members. And they should be made to realize fully what both the acceptance and the rejection of the A.J.C. condition imposes. They should be also made to realize the advantages and disadvantages to the C.O.C. of calling into conference upon the question whether the A.J.C. condition should be accepted, representatives from all of the national organizations and local city committees.

Very cordially yours,

1. See LDB to Lipsky, 2 December 1915.

To Alvin Theodore Sapinsky

December 4, 1915 Boston, Mass. [Brandeis Mss, Z 10-2]

MY DEAR MR. SAPINSKY: [1] Replying to yours of the 3rd:

In assenting to your suggestion that I write certain letters, I supposed that your committee had very definitely in mind certain individuals, and the things that you wanted said to them, and merely wanted them to come from me, among other things, because of my official position in the Zionist movement.

So far as my own inclination goes, I should not consider it profitable to approach men on this subject through correspondence, unless such correspondence has been elicited by previous interviews with them. My belief is that the way to secure new members for the University Society is for the present members to undertake, each individually, to interest men with whom they come in contact in the Zionist movement, and in this particular organization. Education is necessary; and nothing except that personal discussion, involving, in many instances, a campaign with a particular individual covering months, will secure the men we ought to have, equipped as we ought to have them.

Very cordially yours,

1. Alvin Theodore Sapinsky was a young New York City lawyer who was a leader in the University Zionist Society and chairman of its membership committee. On 30 November he had requested a letter from LDB which might be sent to prospective members of the society. LDB had asked Sapinsky to prepare a suggested draft for him to consider; but on 3 December Sapinsky wrote asking LDB to write himself "as I want the letter to have your own spirit."

To Lawrence Fraser Abbott

December 6, 1915 Boston, Mass. [Brandeis Mss, Z 8-1]

MY DEAR MR. ABBOTT: I am glad to know that the Outlook is interested in the question of Zionism.[1] It will not be possible for me to prepare at this time a thousand word statement of my reasons for advocating the movement; and indeed I doubt whether to an uninformed public one thousand words would suffice to adequately state the situation. I have, however, prepared recently an article entitled "Palestine and the Jewish Democracy," which I enclose herewith. Possibly you may care to publish that.

The Jewish press has contained a considerable discussion of Zionism, and the Jewish public is reasonably familiar with the opinions of American Jews on this subject. What I think would interest them most would be the opinion of non-Jews. Perhaps the Outlook may care to secure opinions from such on that subject.[2]

Yours very truly,

1. Abbott, noting the rise of interest in Zionism, asked LDB for a thousand-word article explaining why he approved of the movement. The article was to be published along with one by an opponent of Zionism.

2. *The Outlook* ran the symposium on 5 January 1916. It began with LDB's article, "Palestine and the Jewish Democracy." Similar to his article "Democracy in Palestine," which appeared in *The Independent*, 84 (22 November 1915): 311, the *Outlook* article attempted to compare the early Zionists with the Pilgrim fathers. LDB tried to dispel some of the myths concerning Zionism and painted the movement as one rich in democratic potential, educational and cultural advance, and increased freedom for the Jews of the world. The article is reprinted in *The Curse of Bigness*, 238-45. LDB's article was followed by "Why American Jews Consider Zionism Undesirable," by Rabbi Samuel Schulman (1864-1955), the Reformed leader of Temple Beth-El of New York City and a prolific author on Jewish topics. Schulman (who, significantly, may have been the first to use the expression "the melting pot" in describing America) argued that Jewish nationalism deprived Jews of their traditional mission to all the peoples of the earth and threatened the purity of the Jewish religion. Finally, Abbott himself closed the discussion with a short paragraph in support of Rabbi Schulman's position.

To Nathan D. Kaplan

December 6, 1915 Boston, Mass. [Brandeis Mss, Z 3-1]

MY DEAR MR. KAPLAN: *First:* I will endeavor to let you have in detail sometime during the month a report on the various matters as to which you seek information.[1] I write now merely to say that you and your associates are entirely in error in supposing that the views which I had expressed are due to the effort on the part of any of us in the east to minimize the work which has been done by you and your associates. I am personally responsible for the views expressed in my letter. They originated with me and are the result of my own study of the situation. You and your associates will I trust understand that they are not criticisms of individuals, but efforts to secure an improvement of the system, such as I have been hoping to secure also in other parts of the country. It should be noted, however, that the Knights of Zion success is confined practically to what you and Mr. Shulman, and a few others, have been able to do in Chicago itself. It is there where you raise large amounts of money and develop enthusiasm. The situation in St. Louis, and in other large cities within your territory, is certainly far from satisfactory. What I have hoped would be done is to get in Illinois the full benefit of the work of such men as Mr. Shulman, Mr. Zolotkoff, and yourself, and not lose the benefit of a large part of it through an attempt to cover too much ground. As I said before, it is intensive work that counts.

Second: I am enclosing for the Sentinel an address entitled "Palestine and the Jewish Democracy", which I prepared recently, and which I should suppose would be appropriate for the Convention number.   Very truly yours,

1. Kaplan had written a lengthy reply to LDB's letter of 29 November. He first requested more information about the actual performance of other Zionist groups, arguing that the number of square miles in a district was not a sufficient guide to organizational effectiveness. In addition, he went on to defend vigorously the record of the Knights of Zion under its present organization: "However, I don't want to be understood as being satisfied with our status, nor do I mean to convey the impression that I do not believe there is much room for improvement along the lines that you suggest; but I do mean to emphasize this; that it appears to us here, that there seems to be some influence in the East that is persistently underestimating the efficiency of the Knights of Zion."

To Jessie F. Attwater

December 7, 1915 Boston, Mass. [Brandeis Mss, NMF 69-3]

DEAR MRS. ATTWATER: [1] Thank you for your courteous invitation to contribute to the series of Futurist Articles.

I am so much engaged at present that I do not feel able to engage in prophecy.   Yours very truly,

1. Mrs. Jessie F. Attwater, president of the National News Company of Boston, was putting together a series of articles for the magazine *Femina*. Each article was to deal with some aspect or element of American society as it was likely to appear in the future. Mrs. Attwater had asked: "Kindly let me know if we may include you among the prophets."

To Max Roseman

December 7, 1915 Boston, Mass. [Brandeis Mss, Z 8-1]

MY DEAR MR. ROSEMAN: [1] I am glad to know from yours of the 4th that the Zionist Society of the University of Wisconsin has called a conference of the Zionist Societies of the State of Wisconsin to be held at Milwaukee on December 12th.

I venture to suggest the following:

The formation of a State organization in Wisconsin presents a unique opportunity to the workers who have undertaken the task to group together the Zionists under a local leadership in a State in which the Jewish community is not too large and in which, moreover, the Jewish centers are scattered and rather wide apart. This geographical point ought to be well borne in mind in the effort that is made. By aiming too high the failure in fulfillment is bound to prove discouraging.

In the State of Wisconsin the problem of organization may be divided as follows:

(a) How to reach the Jews in order to induce them to join Zionist Societies.

(b) How to maintain the interest of members in Zionist societies.

(c) How to regulate the activity of Zionist societies.

(d) What is the maximum due that the members can afford as against the minimum demand that is needed to keep up a society.

(e) Proper arrangement of a budget which can cover the rather heavy expenses involved in travelling propaganda.

(f) Is it practical to carry on propaganda by correspondence.

I believe a committee on organization should sit down with a State map in front of it, making a mark on every spot at which there is known to be no more than even two or three Jewish families, and devise its operations on the principle that it is determined to link up even these twos and threes.

Probably, for financial and other reasons, it will not be possible to call many regular gatherings of such leaders. Therefore, the effort of the conference should not be wasted in the outline of some intricate constitution which no one will be able to operate.

For the present it seems expedient to suggest, as far as the organization is concerned, that each society be entitled to elect one or more deputies to an annual or semi-annual conference, and that these deputies elect a state leader and that through him the affiliation be completed with other state organizations in the middle west. These conferences should not be miniature copies of any of the national conventions, but should be gatherings held for the purpose of discussing and working out in detail problems that effect the efficient organization of Zionists within their territory. If they confine themselves to these problems they will not only be helping themselves, but they may be able to place on record ideas and methods from which others in other parts of the country can gain.

The whole problem of organization is a huge one. It never has been and never can be worked out satisfactorily at national conventions. The question of Zionist policies come to the forefront at the National gatherings, and so constitutional changes are effected in such a rush that the majority of these changes are meaningless to the delegates. The state organization being much closer to the society and the individual, can work out this problem, and the more it devoted itself to that, the bigger its success and our success.   Very truly yours,

1. Max Roseman of the University of Wisconsin Intercollegiate Zionist Association wrote to LDB asking advice on organizational matters to be discussed at a statewide meeting in Milwaukee on 12 December.

To Alfred Brandeis

December 8, 1915 Boston, Mass. [Brandeis Mss, M 4-1]

MY DEAR AL: *First:* I wrote Mr. Cooper; but yesterday had a letter from him saying that his trip is deferred until next summer.

Second: I return you Grier's letter. I have also had another letter from him, but I do not see how I can agree now to go out there in February, and am writing him to that effect.

Third: I have heard nothing further from the Louisville Zionists about the hall in which the meeting is to be held.[1] I, of course, am not obdurate upon its being a very small hall, but I feel very strongly that a reasonably small one is apt to bring better results than a large one, with the so-called mass meeting. I presume that they would arrange for tickets with reserved seats, which would be held until a time mentioned on the tickets, when all seats not then claimed would be released to the public. In that way they could be sure of having seats for Zionist members and for such of the German Jews as you and they wanted to have present.

Fourth: I am glad you are reading Herzl. I assume you will remember that it is not the Jewish State, but the short articles and addresses that I was particularly anxious to have you read to get an idea of the man.

It was good to see Jean the other day.

1. See LDB to Moses O. Ades, 19 November 1915.

To Alice Lillie Seligsberg

December 8, 1915 Boston, Mass. [Brandeis Mss, Z 8-1]

MY DEAR MISS SELIGSBERG: I have the letter of the 6th signed by yourself, Mrs. [Ida] Guggenheimer, Mrs. [Ida S.] Danziger and the Misses [Lotta] Levensohn, [Nellie] Straus, [Jessie] Sampter, [Henrietta] Szold and [Sophia] Berger.[1]

First: I entirely agree with the proposition that before "any purpose of the masses becomes articulate" the two conditions which you state must have paved the way.[2] To a certain extent both of these conditions have existed. There is no difficulty in accepting the general principle. The difficulty is in the obstacles which prevent that principle being acted upon in the way which you suggest.

Second: If we had men and women with the ability, equipment, time and devotion which are required to do the things which it is desirable to do in order to advance the Zionist movement, and generally to work towards the solution of the Jewish problem, undoubtedly the sending of some men, properly equipped, to Europe at this time, to get in touch with the Jews there,—to learn exactly what they are doing, and to make them fully understand what we are doing, would be highly desirable. But we have no such persons available. Indeed we are utterly lacking at this moment in the requisite forces to conduct in America the most necessary work of our Zionist organizations; not to mention the demands of the Congress movement.

There is no part of our work, and no part of our country for which we are adequately equipped. Every day convinces me more fully of this truth. And every day convinces me also more fully of the need of patient, individual work, not only to convert men and women to the Zionist cause, but to keep them interested, and make them active in the cause, even after they admit the correctness of our fundamental proposition.

Third: You have mentioned as men whom it is probably desirable to send abroad, Judge Mack, Dr. Pool and Mr. Leon Kohn.[3] I am confident that Judge Mack's official work would not permit him to go even if he desired to do so. I do not know what the possibility would be for Dr. Pool; but I am certain that all the time that he can possibly give to the Zionist cause in New York is demanded, specifically by Young Judaea. Neither do I know whether Mr. Leon Kohn could leave and go to Europe; but I am sure from my recent visit in Newark that our cause demands of him all the time that he can properly give to it.

Mr. Lewin-Epstein, one of the ablest men connected with our movement, and perhaps the best equipped of all because of his Palestinian experience, is in Europe, and is developing under particularly favorable circumstances the kind of thing which it seems to me is the most necessary in connection with the European situation.

Third [*sic*]: I have spoken only of our need in workers. We have also great need of money for our Emergency Fund. Our ability to help Palestine, and to carry on our own organization work is seriously imperilled by the failure to raise for this fund the amounts which we need. The expedition to Europe which you propose would not only deprive us of a worker here, but involve material expense.

Fourth: You say "We ought not to let the fate of the Jewish Congress idea depend wholly upon America; we ought to send an emissary or emissaries abroad to spread the idea of organization."

This proposition may be sound; but it is perfectly clear that we should in any event be ineffective abroad if we are not effective at home, and our lack of force and of money has prevented us—in the development of the Congress movement here—from doing that which it is necessary to do in order to make that movement the success which we hope.

If you or any of your associates can give me any suggestions as to where I can find ably equipped, enthusiastic workers willing to give the time either to the Zionist movement or to the Congress movement—not only men and women whom we would like to have, but whom we can get—I am sure that we can do far more to advance our cause by setting them to work here, for the Jewish cause, on tasks which can be definitely laid out for them, than to send them abroad. You say that "an emissary would not only carry inspiration abroad, but might bring even greater inspiration back". This is of course possible, but we cannot afford to make the experiment.

Fifth: You say: "We as Jews ought to be articulate wherever the cry of the people for peace with justice makes itself heard. We ought to send an envoy to the central receiving station, to the Hague, to arrange that representatives of the Jewish people be invited to participate in any permanent international body that may form."

I cannot believe that any such action would be desirable at the present time.   Cordially yours,

1. The women urged that the Jewish community of America send to the Hague "an envoy" who might "arrange that representatives of the Jewish people be invited to participate in any permanent international body that may form" as a result of the war.

2. The letter contended that "there must previously have been numberless independent attempts to speak out, that failed, and there must later have been evolved an instrument that voiced the purpose of the masses and at the same time continued to receive and distribute the sound."

3. Leon A. Kohn (1884-1956) was a New York insurance executive, active in Jewish philanthropy and in the Zionist organization in America.

To Chaim Weizmann

December 8, 1915 Boston, Mass. [Weizmann Mss]

MY DEAR PROFESSOR WEIZMANN: I am very glad indeed to have your letter of the 24th of November, and to know of your constant thought of the cause.[1]

I appreciate fully the circumstances which you call to my attention.

We are hard at work here, and I trust the results will be satisfactory.   Very cordially yours,

1. Weizmann had written in response to some remarks made by Horace Kallen in a letter to Leon Simon, in which Kallen had complained about the lack of communication between the English Zionists and the Provisional Committee. Weizmann wrote that he prayed for better cooperation in the

future, but that at the present he was engaged in negotiations that he could not talk about. "It is my duty as a Zionist and as a member of this community. I am sure that you will fully understand the position. My work is on record and certainly will be known to you when the time arrives." The negotiations, of course, ultimately led to the Balfour Declaration in November 1917; for details of Weizmann's role, see Leonard Stein, *The Balfour Declaration* (London, 1961). On 15 December Kallen wrote to Weizmann and partially apologized for his comments, saying that perhaps a greater effort at communication should have been made by the P.E.C. He went on, however, to point out lapses on Weizmann's part completely separate from the secret negotiations, such as failure to acknowledge receipt of money.

To Stephen Samuel Wise

December 8, 1915 Boston, Mass. [Brandeis Mss, Z 6-2]

MY DEAR DR. WISE: Thank you for your letter of the 6th.

First: I hope that you will be able to give more than a few hours to the discussion on the 18th. There are many things of great moment which should be considered very carefully,—particularly in the light of what you can tell us as the result of your trip west.

Second: The large funds which you have raised will make our Palestinian relief problem much simpler.[1] It is fine that you should have been able to move the people on the coast so deeply. Our Emergency Fund problem, however, has become increasingly serious since you left, and we shall have to do much hard thinking and hard work to meet its demands. I wish you would give this matter careful consideration before we meet on the 18th.

Third: As to the remittances for Palestinian relief: I think it would be well for us to send $10,000 of that money now, which would be practically accompanying the $10,000 sent by the A.J.R.C., and the $10,000 by the C.R.C. What should be done in later months must depend in part upon what the A.J.R.C. and the C.R.C. bind themselves to do. I suggested to Mack that together the A.J.R.C. and C.R.C. ought to send at least $10,000 a month, and Mack will doubtless take the matter up at the meeting today of A.J.R.C.

Fourth: I am glad to know that Martin A. Meyer would be willing to become a member of our Advisory Committee. I feel sure that it would be helpful to have him. This matter should be taken up on the morning of the 18th. I should be glad to learn from you, Lipsky and Perlstein what the effect is likely to be on other Zionists on the coast. On the 18th also we can discuss with Lipsky and Perlstein the Pacific Coast situation, and I shall endeavor to get deHaas to be there at the same time.

Fifth: I trust you have seen Eugene Meyer. You will learn from him that there is trouble with Untermyer, as well as with Nathan Straus.[2] Eugene Meyer sent me Untermyer's letter, and I simply wrote Untermyer that as there appeared to be some misunderstanding I thought the matter had better await your return. I had hoped that by this time we should have had something definite from Lewin-Epstein relating to the loan. Possibly a letter will come within a few days.

I judge from a recent report from Berlin that the planters would accomplish much without the full $80,000 which we had planned. The A[ctions]. C[omite]. speaks of a loan of 300,000 francs, which would mean only about $50,000. Would it not be possible to bring up the loan to that amount?

I spoke to Eugene Meyer some weeks ago of the possibility of his getting together a group of men to whom we could talk in the hope of raising perhaps $1,000 or $2,000 from each. I have heard nothing from him, and hope that he will take up this matter also with you.

My plan now is to be in New York only on the 18th and 19th, but I can probably come one day earlier, or stay a day later, if our cause requires it.

Sixth: Mack and I are to speak for the Fechheimer—Senior crowd on January 6th. I am to speak for Dr. Kaplan on the 7th.

Very cordially yours,

1. Wise had been able to raise $55,000 on his trip to the West Coast.
2. There was some mixup about the amount of and the purposes for a large contribution from Samuel Untermyer. Regarding Straus, Julian Mack had written LDB on 6 December: "I found him in a nervous and excited condition. He seems to feel that people want to direct him what to do with his money and he resents it. Under all the circumstances, I think he should be humored if he attaches new conditions. . . ."

To Robert D. Kesselman

December 14, 1915 Boston, Mass. [Brandeis Mss, Z 14-2]

MY DEAR MR. KESSELMAN: *First:* I am enclosing herewith copy of letter to the Office Committee concerning statements which I hope can be completed by the 17th, or at all events be available in the early morning of the 18th. I hope you will give the office such assistance as may be possible so as to complete the statements by that time.

Second: In the monthly reports which you have submitted it appears that the statement of receipts and disbursements for the Provisional Committee, the Yiddish Folk, the Maccabaean, the Federation, and Young Judaean, are drawn off from the face of the books without audit.

This is not what I had expected would be done. My intention was to have a current audit of the accounts reported on monthly and I had supposed that that was what we were getting. Possibly I do not understand fully what you mean by "drawn off from the face of the books without audit". I trust that in presenting the report for the month of November, which I am glad to note we may expect before the close of this month, we may expect a complete audit of the accounts, at least of the various organizations whose offices are at 44 East 23rd Street.

In making up the report for November and subsequent months, I assume that the matter of rent, light, heat and telephone, referred to in yours of December 3rd, will be adjusted.

Third: I also assume that in your November report you will include the figures of the Jewish National Fund Bureau. Your statement for September and earlier months refers also to this statement as "drawn off from the face of the books without audit", and what I have said in regard to the audit of the other organizations applies also to this, and to the Hadassah Central Committee.

Fourth: Your report even for October contains no reference to Mizrachi or Poale Zion. I understood from your letter regarding the Poale Zion that you were told that you could not get the information until the latter part of this month. I assume that then you will give us a report of the Poale Zion covering the six months ending November 30th. I had not understood from you that the difficulty continued as to a report of the Mizrachi. I trust that you will also be able to give us the six months' report to November 30th of this organization.   Yours very truly,

To Office Committee

December 15, 1915 Boston, Mass. [Brandeis Mss, Z 8-2]

DEAR SIRS: *First:* I am enclosing check for $250 for the Emergency Fund from Mr. Louis E. Kirstein, 416 Washington St., Boston.

Second: I do not find in the Kesselman reports any indication that we are covered by fire insurance. If we are not, action to this end should be taken promptly.

Third: I do not find in the reports any indication that we have bonded any of those directly connected with the handling of money. As our accounts are now being regularly audited, the bonding company would undoubtedly be ready to give the Committee such protection, and in view of the large amounts which are being handled, the Committee should be protected in this manner. If this matter has not already been taken up by you, it should be done immediately.

Fourth: I did not discover in the Kesselman reports any payments from the Order Sons of Zion to the Provisional Committee or the Federation. Have any such payments been made during the last six months; and if so, what amounts?

Fifth: On the face of the reports the mail order business of the Yiddishe Folk appears to be operated at a loss. I should like to have presented at our conference on Friday or Saturday statements showing the facts in this respect. I had supposed that when we were discussing this matter in May and June last it was deemed undesirable for the Yiddishe Folk to continue the mail order business.

Sixth: We should arrange to have Dr. Wise join Dr. Levin at the Toronto meeting.

To A. Rosenberg

December 15, 1915 Boston, Mass. [Brandeis Mss, NMF 67-2]

MY DEAR MR. ROSENBERG: [1] I congratulate the Jewish wage earners of New England, and their employers, on the decision of your Board to publish a paper in Yiddish which shall make clear to your members the rights and duties of the trade unionists, and the great opportunities which the protocols afford of promoting the welfare of both employer and employee.

The advantages of the protocol can be appreciated only by those who fully understand its workings. The protocol can be fully appreciated only by those who know the difficulties which are inherent in any plan approximating industrial democracy. There cannot be liberty without self-discipline. There cannot be self-discipline without knowledge and understanding of the system under which the union and the employers are operating. And in order that the knowledge may be adequate, men must be kept informed of the difficulties from time to time as they arise, and the manner in which they have been solved.

With the high standard of intelligence of your members, and the devotion to the cause, you should find it possible to contribute much to the prosperity of the whole trade in Boston— employers as well as employees.   With best wishes,

1. A. Rosenberg was the manager of the Joint Board of the Cloak, Skirt and Waist Makers Union of Boston. He wrote to tell LDB that a Yiddish semi-monthly was about to begin, "to propagate real unionism amongst our fellow workers in Boston and also to enlighten them of their rights and privileges under the existing Protocols, and at the same time their obligations to their employers as well as to the unions." He asked LDB for an article and this letter was sent to the paper for publication.

To Rose Schneiderman

December 15, 1915 Boston, Mass. [Brandeis Mss, NMF 67-2]

DEAR MISS SCHNEIDERMAN: [1] As you have already been advised, it will not be possible for me to attend your meeting on the 29th.

The great advantages which the adoption of the protocol has brought should make clear to both employers and employees in the waist and dress industry that thorough organization is desirable. And this task in Boston ought to be greatly lightened by the success which the Unions have already attained under their able manager, Mr. Rosenberg.

Trade unionism in the Jewish trades has passed out of the stage of experiment. It has been made a pronounced success; and every Jewish worker, man or woman, ought now to give it unqualified support when it is proposed to extend further the operation of the protocol.   Very truly yours,

1. Rose Schneiderman (b. 1882) was at the beginning of her long and distinguished career as a social worker and labor organizer. A Polish immigrant, she went to work in the New York garment industry and became an organizer and strike leader. From 1918 to 1949 she served as president of the New York Women's Trade Union League, and attended the Paris Peace Conference in 1919. During the New Deal, she served as labor advisor to the National Recovery Administration. Miss Schneiderman was planning a mass organizational meeting for the International Ladies Garment Workers Union in Boston for 29 December. She asked LDB for a fifteen-minute address to the group, but he informed her by telephone that he was unable to be present. Doubtless this letter was written to be read to the meeting.

To Office Committee

December 16, 1915 Boston, Mass. [Brandeis Mss, Z 8-2]

DEAR SIRS: *First:* I have just received a telegram dated December 15th from Robert Lansing as follows:

"From Constantinope quote: —Please send two thousand dollars for end 1915 Quarter 1916 Lichtheim. End quote."

In my opinion the P.C. cannot properly send any money on Emergency account to Lichtheim or even to Palestine, until the deficiency in the Emergency Fund shall have been made good, and sums accumulated on Emergency account sufficient to meet the remittances as well as current operating expenses.[1]

Second: As per your telegram I am holding Sunday evening, January 9th for Buffalo. Obviously your letter to Lisitzky[2] did not make clear that I am engaged in Rochester that day during the forenoon and early afternoon, and shall not reach Buffalo until evening.

Third: Other matters referred to in your letters of December 14th will be taken up with you on Friday morning at the Aeolian Building. No letter of December 15th has yet arrived.

1. See LDB to Richard Lichtheim, 20 December 1915.
2. Ephraim E. Lisitzky (1885-1962) was head of the Hebrew schools of Buffalo; he later held the same position in New Orleans. A Russian immigrant who arrived in 1900, he is best known as a poet, editor, and translator. His poetry, mostly on Jewish topics (especially after World War II), also includes pieces on the American Indian and the Negro. Lisitzky translated some of Shakespeare's plays into Hebrew.

To Moses O. Ades

December 20, 1915 Boston, Mass. [Brandeis Mss, Z 2-4]

MY DEAR MR. ADES: I have your letter of the 16th setting forth tentative plans for the noon and evening meetings on January 5th. The arrangements which you have made are entirely satisfactory.

To avoid the possibility of misunderstanding I ought to add that I shall wish to breakfast and spend the forenoon with my brother, and shall also wish to spend the afternoon, after our luncheon, until the evening meeting with him.

I am enclosing a copy of my letter to Dr. Bloom.

Very truly yours,

To Henry Bruere

December 20, 1915 Boston, Mass. [Brandeis Mss, NMF 47-2]

MY DEAR MR. BRUERE: Thank you for your letter of the 13th, and for the report on centralized purchasing, which shows another great advance for Mayor Mitchell's [*sic*] administration.[1]

I hope that some comprehensive statement similar to Mayor Mitchell's [*sic*] admirable April address will be published soon, covering the achievements of his administration.[2] I am confident that if ways are devised of making known these achievements to the people of New York, Mayor Mitchell's [*sic*] re-election would be certain. The task of making them known is of course an extremely difficult one. It needs writers and talkers, but it ought to be possible in the great city of New York to find one thousand men who would be willing to enlist for the cause,—men competent to understand, willing to study, and able to express the results of their study. The immediate gain would be to New York, but an inestimable service would be rendered to the whole country.[3]   Very truly yours,

1. Bruere was the chairman of a special Central Purchasing Committee which had just completed a year's experiment in city finance. Twenty-eight departments under the jurisdiction of the mayor made purchases through a central board. The report of the committee indicated considerable savings to the city, increasing efficiency, and greater competition among suppliers. It recommended expanding the program to more city departments.
2. For Mayor Mitchel's report on his first fourteen months in office, see *New York Times*, 13 April 1915.
3. In 1917, despite his record of reform and honest administration, Mayor Mitchel, who had antagonized many New Yorkers, was soundly defeated for reelection by the Tammany Hall ticket.

To Richard Lichtheim

December 20, 1915 Boston, Mass. [Berlin Office]

DEAR MR. LICHTHEIM: We are in receipt, through the Department of State, of a cablegram from you reading: "Please send two thousand dollars to end nineteenhundredfifteen quarter nineteenhundredsixteen".[1]

We are sorry that we are unable to make any remittance at this time. Contributions made in America to the Zionist organization of late have been definitely given for relief in Palestine or for National Fund purposes, so that demands upon our Emergency Fund have completely exhausted that fund, and left a deficit of $10,000. Until that deficit has been met, and additional funds raised to meet our administrative expenses, we are unable to make remittances.

We are engaged in special efforts now to raise funds for the Emergency work, and trust it will not be long before we are able to resume remittances. Meanwhile we are also notifying the Copenhagen office, and trust that it will be able to arrange for the present to satisfy your immediate needs.

Very truly yours,

1. See LDB to Office Committee, 16 December 1915.

To Frances Crane Lillie

December 21, 1915 Boston, Mass. [Brandeis Mss, Z 8-1]

MY DEAR MRS. LILLIE: [1] I find upon my return to the city your letter of the 15th (and also the one of the 13th of November enclosed) in which you ask my advice as to the advisability of presenting a protest "to the President as the Mayor and Governor have done nothing." [2]

In my opinion this is not a matter which should be presented to the President. It will not do to center all our responsibilities on the President of the United States. Difficult as conditions may be, we must attempt to make those nearer home feel the responsibility; primarily your Mayor, and then your Governor. I venture to suggest as a first step that you have a calm experienced investigator like John A. Fitch of the Survey, make a thorough investigation, and a judicial report. Such a document would be the best basis for a protest. When that is done not only the Mayor and Governor can be properly approached, but if necessary some proper way could doubtless be found of presenting the situation to Congress and others.   Very cordially yours,

1. Frances Crane Lillie (1870–1958) was the sister of LDB's friend Charles R. Crane and the wife of the well-known University of Chicago zoologist, Frank Rattray Lillie (1870–1947). Mrs. Lillie was a social worker and philanthropist with wide interests in Chicago charities and labor organizations. She had worked at Hull House and associated with John Dewey in educational reform. In 1919 she received national attention by supporting a strike of the workers of the Crane Company, the business started by her father and headed by her brother. She had written LDB to ask whether, in view of the inaction of the mayor of Chicago and the governor of Illinois, aid ought not to be requested from President Wilson in the Chicago garment workers strike.

2. The mayor of Chicago was the flamboyant and controversial William ("Big Bill") Hale Thompson (1869–1944), the former cowboy and real estate dealer who was one of the city's most colorful mayors. See Lloyd Wendt and Herman Kogan, *Big Bill of Chicago* (Indianapolis, 1953). The governor of Illinois was Edward Fitzsimons Dunne (1853–1937), himself a former mayor of Chicago.

To Julian William Mack

December 22, 1915 Boston, Mass. [Brandeis Mss, Z 11-1]

MY DEAR MACK: I have yours of yesterday referring to Philipson's editorial, which has just been called to my attention.[1] In my opinion the answer to that editorial had better be made by you both by an article now, and when we speak in Cincinnati; and I hope you will take this up at once. I was particularly impressed with your presentation of this subject at the Boston meeting.

Very truly yours,

1. Mack had suggested that LDB answer the editorial by Rabbi Philipson in the 16 December issue of the *American Israelite*. The editorial was critical of American Zionism, and suggested that Americanism and Zionism were not compatible.

To Henry Morgenthau

December 22, 1915 Boston, Mass. [Brandeis Mss, Z 14-3]

MY DEAR MR. MORGANTHAU [*sic*]: The Administrative Secretary of our Committee has shown me the letter addressed to you under date of December 8th, requesting you to act as the first intermediary for the transmission of funds to Palestine in connection with our work in transmitting to individuals and institutions in Palestine funds sent by their relatives in this country.

It is highly desirable, for the purposes of record and confirmation, as well as to assure the public that the funds are being promptly and safely delivered, that the Local Distributing Agents be asked to send in as of the end of each month, a report giving the following information:

(a) Payments made during the month, giving the number of our advice, the amount paid in Francs and whether the money was paid to the individual mentioned in our advice or whether to an authorized agent.

(b) A record of all payments not made and reasons for non-payment.

(c) Balance in the hands of the Committee.

We will thank you to forward a copy of this request to all Consuls, Committees or Local Representatives.

We would suggest that these reports should not be held back until several months accumulate, but that they be mailed as soon as complete to us, and that in any event an account be sent us once a month.

At this end we make absolutely no charge to the remitter. It has been customary, however, previously for the local Paying Committees to charge such a rate of exchange that will cover their minor expenses for clerical services. We believe that this should be continued, but that in the monthly reports the distributor shall indicate the rate of exchange and also the expenses incurred, showing the accrued balance, if any. The rate of exchange to be adopted can then be determined from the cost of distribution.

In any event it will make only a small fractional difference.

Very truly yours,

To Otto Irving Wise

December 22, 1915 Boston, Mass. [Brandeis Mss, Z 8-1]

MY DEAR MR. WISE: I am extremely glad to learn of the meeting called for January 10th to perfect the Congress organization in San Francisco, and that you and Dr. Martin A. Meyer are taking so active a part.

The discussion of these subjects in San Francisco will do much to bring to our people an understanding of the fundamental problems involved. We are confronted with a stupendous work of educating, and can accomplish our task only by intensive effort along the lines which you are entering upon.

I endeavored to set forth succinctly my views on the general question of the Congress and Jewish Unity in the enclosed article, which you and Dr. Meyer may have already seen.[1]

Yours very truly,

1. LDB's address, "Jewish Unity and the Congress," was delivered in Baltimore on 27 September 1915. It was printed by the Jewish Congress Organization Committee and reprinted in *The Curse of Bigness*, 233–37. The address was a plea for a Jewish congress that would assure, not unity of opinion, but unity of action. The congress must be democratic and open, LDB insisted, and must avoid every appearance of secrecy. He praised the attempt of Adolf Kraus to begin the process with the meeting of 3 October

(see LDB to Kraus, 7 September 1915) and condemned the American Jewish Committee meeting, still scheduled for 24 October.

To Frances A. Kellor

December 27, 1915 Boston, Mass. [Brandeis Mss, NMF 73-4]

MY DEAR MISS KELLOR:[1] I extremely regret that I found myself obliged to telegraph that I could not adjust my plans so as to speak at your January meeting, which Colonel Roosevelt's address will surely make memorable.[2]

The material which you sent me deepened that regret. The facts therein stated show more clearly than any argument the fundamental importance and urgency of the work in which your Committee is engaged. I am returning you herewith these very intelligent special reports which you sent me, and which I presume you require for your files. I should, however, be glad if you would let me have about the 25th of January such material of this nature as may be available, as I should like to take the best occasion that may present after that time for laying these facts and their lessons before the public. I look forward to the opportunity of discussing these matters quite fully with you and Colonel Roosevelt.

I am enclosing check for $100. to your Committee as a contribution towards its expenses.   Very truly yours,

1. Frances A. Kellor (1873-1952) was a social worker particularly interested in the problems of immigration and the immigrant. She held a number of important positions both in immigrant associations and in the federal government's immigration endeavors. She was a member of the Executive Committee of the National Americanization Committee; she had invited LDB to share the platform with Theodore Roosevelt for an address on 20 January 1916.

2. Under the heading "Fear God and Take Your Own Part," Roosevelt made a rambling address to the mass meeting of the National Americanization Committee. Speaking on both domestic policy (railroad regulation, trust control and the role of government) and the foreign situation, the speech was most notable for its condemnation of "hyphenated" Americans. Asserting that dual loyalties were incompatible with patriotism and that a man who loved other countries as well as his own was on a par with the man who loved other women as well as his own wife, Roosevelt called for the undivided loyalty and allegiance of newly-arrived Americans. For an

account of the speech, see *The New York Times*, 21 January 1916. The speech was widely reprinted and gave its name to a collection of Roosevelt's militarist speeches and writings, *Fear God and Take Your Own Part* (New York, 1916).

To Henry Pereira Mendes

December 27, 1915 Boston, Mass. [Brandeis Mss, Z 8-1]

MY DEAR DR. MENDES: Your letter of the 23rd concerning the establishment of a congregational center of the students at Cornell has just reached me.[1] The appeal ought by all means to go forward, but I think it would not be wise for me to join in signing the appeal, among other reasons, because I have recently declined to join in several requests for similar appeals, and my joining in this might be misinterpreted. There is, however, a further reason, in my opinion, why I ought not sign. Here is work specifically for Jewish students at Cornell. There must be among the graduates of Cornell a large number of Jews who could themselves contribute, or whose fathers could contribute to this fund. I suggest that a careful study be made of the alumni of Cornell with a view to determining which of those men might become interested and be willing and able to contribute. Probably every graduate could contribute something. Make it specifically a Cornell College matter, and appeal to the loyalty of Cornell College men, and pride of their parents. Professor Gottheil could be of great assistance to you in this connection.

With best wishes,   Very cordially yours,

1. Mendes had asked LDB to join him in a mailed appeal for the establishment of a Jewish center at Cornell.

To Stephen Samuel Wise

December 27, 1915 Boston, Mass. [Brandeis Mss, Z 6-2]

MY DEAR DR. WISE: Replying to your letter of the 25th about Gluskin's coming:

First: In view of the fact that you "have not been encouraged over much" as to your ability to raise the loan fund, I suppose we ought to cable Lewin-Epstein immediately to have Gluskin come, if he deems it advisable. On the whole it seems to me clear that we ought not, in view of Lewin-Epstein's opinion, take a position which would be deemed a refusal of our assent to Gluskin's coming. If you agree with this, please cable Lewin-Epstein at once.

I have by this morning's mail a letter from Joseph Cowen concerning raising funds for the bank, and enclose you a copy, also a copy of my letter to R. Lewin-Epstein. I do not know that we can at present accomplish much, but if anything can be done for the bank, Gluskin would undoubtedly be helpful in that connection also.

Second: The 300,000 francs voted by the A.J.R.C. for Palestine, taken together with the $10,000 of our own, and the $24,000 additional recently transmitted through the A.J.R.C., will doubtless take care of the immediate strictly relief matters of Palestine; but I am not sure that we can rely upon the A.J.R.C. sending any such sum as $55,000 to Palestine quarterly or even semi-annually. Indeed I think that all of their recent contributions have been due, in large measure, to the attitude of insistence by the Provisional Committee, and particularly to the funds which you have raised on the coast. It is a striking coincidence that they should have fixed upon $55,000 for relief now—the exact sum which you are reported to have raised on the coast.

You inquire whether $25,000 of the money raised by you on the coast could not be used as a loan fund.

I agree with your suggestion that probably it is largely relief, just as schools are relief, and that, too, relief of the best kind; but I do not feel that I know enough about the conditions under which this money was raised to determine whether your contributors on the coast would so regard it. And if there were any doubt on this subject, the appropriation of the money to the Loan Fund might subject our Committee to criticism, particularly as the loan is being made to the colonies as distinguished from other Jews in Palestine. If you think that your contributors would be satisfied to apply it to the loan Fund, I suggest your writing your brother to make inquiry of the largest contributors, and if you got specific consent of the contributors to that disposition of the money, all doubt would be removed.   Very cordially yours,

To Stephen Samuel Wise

December 27, 1915 Boston, Mass. [Brandeis Mss, Z 6-2]

MY DEAR DR. WISE: Referring to yours of the 25th re Montefiore's[1] request for the Evelina de Rothschild School:[2] I think it is clear that nothing ought to be done for the Evelina de Rothschild School unless it be on a specific application by Montefiore to the Provisional Committee. There would be an advantage in having him request the P.C. to maintain the school, and an advantage in the Committee's complying with his request. No outsider could properly object that Palestine relief money applied to the Evelina de Rothschild School was improperly so applied, at least if the contributors assented. The American Jewish Relief [Committee], at its meeting on December 23rd, applied 100,000 Rouble for the Schools of the 'Mifitze Haskala' in Russia, and $100,000 for similar schools in German Poland.

If Montefiore should make a specific request to the Provisional Committee to maintain this school for a year, and you could secure the approval of the contributors on the coast, I should be inclined to think the Provisional Committee would act wisely in taking from the coast relief fund as much as was necessary to maintain that school for a year. As you suggest, it might be possible to get consideration [considerable?] additional money outside so that the demands upon our relief funds would probably be much less than the sum named.

I am returning herewith Montefiore's two letters.

Cordially yours,

P.S. I note from the report of the minutes of the A.J.R.C. meeting on Dec. 23rd the following:

"Regarding the appropriation for Palestine, Dr. Magnes called attention to a suggestion from Mr. Nathan Straus, that he would be pleased if out of the $100,000 contributed by him to the fund of the American Jewish Relief Committee, $25,000 would be appropriated as follows:
$15,000 to go to the Health Bureau in Palestine
$10,000 for the orange growers, whose groves have been destroyed by the locusts

Mr. Straus' suggestion met with unanimous consent, and it was ordered that $25,000 out of the 300,000 fr. appropriated for Palestine, be applied as requested."

I assume that the words "for the orange growers" was by error, and that what was intended was Vineyard and almond growers.

1. Sir Francis Abraham Montefiore (1860–1935) was a grandnephew of the leading Jewish financier and philanthropist Moses Montefiore. Sir Francis was a close associate of Herzl's and a leader in the English Zionist movement. He was particularly close to the English Rothschilds and Herzl hoped, through Montefiore, to win over the Rothschilds to Zionism. Montefiore left the World Zionist Organization during World War I because he felt it to be too closely tied to Germany and German war allies.

2. Evelina Rothschild (1839–1866) had been the wife of Ferdinand James Rothschild, a member of the British branch of the family. Her death in childbirth was commemorated by the establishment of a school in Jerusalem.

To Edward Nash Hurley

December 28, 1915 Boston, Mass. [Brandeis Mss, NMF 66-3]

My dear Mr. Hurley: I regret the unavoidable delay in replying definitely to your letter of the 11th asking my opinion on the powers of the Federal Trade Commission regarding approving standard forms of accounting on the part of individuals, corporations, and trade associations.

The Act to create a Federal Trade Commission provides, Section 6, that the Commission shall also have power:

(a) To gather and compile information concerning business, conduct, practices and management of any corporation engaged in commerce.

(b) to require, by general or special orders, corporations engaged in commerce or any class of them, or any of them, respectively to file with the Commission in such form as the Commission may prescribe, annual or special, or both annual and special reports, etc.

Proper forms of accounting are practically essential to reliable information concerning any business corporation; and uniform systems of accounting in particular lines of business are practically essential to proper comparison of the reports of different corporations. The Commission would probably be held, therefore, to possess the power to require such uniform reports of corporations from whom reports are required, relating to subjects of information as to which reports are required; and would as an incident of that power have authority to examine into and itself recommend the proper form of accounting.

There is grave doubt (particularly in view of the refusal of Congress to grant the Commission power to require uniform accounting) that there exists in the Commission any general power to promote uniform accounting. But it is quite possible that such power, if exercised by the Trade Commission, would be generally acquiesced in, as similar exercise of power by other Departments of the Government have been.

With best wishes for the New Year for yourself and the Commission,   Very cordially yours,

P.S. I thank you for your letter of the 17th with enclosure.

To Louis Lipsky

December 28, 1915 Boston, Mass. [Brandeis Mss, Z 1-4]

MY DEAR LIPSKY: I have from Richards a copy of the C.O.C. resolution of December 23rd, and your draft of letter to the N.W.C. and A.J.C. based thereon; and have written him as per enclosed copy.

In my opinion the Committee has taken a step which is likely to prove disastrous to the Congress movement.[1] The course which you, deHaas and I agreed upon, embodied in the draft of resolution submitted by the Sub-committee, and approved by the Administrative Committee, presents a courageous and hopeful line of attack. It involves dangers, but only such as are inherent in the present situation. On the other hand it offers opportunities for great gain to the cause. We talked the matter over so fully that I am sure argument is unnecessary with you. You will know whether there is any possibility of securing a favorable re-consideration. The resolution of December 23rd seems to me to be subject to a number of objections. Among others, it resorts to an ultimatum of January 15th, with its obvious dangers and provocations of criticism. The resolution of December 23rd is not even a hopeful instrument on which to base negotiations. Its only effect can be to throw onus of the break on us, and the onus of a Congress on us, under conditions which we are not able to bear.

Very cordially yours,

1. On 23 December the Congress Organization Committee had passed a resolution which had the effect of an ultimatum to both the American Jewish Committee and the National Workmen's Committee. The resolution decreed that a pre-congress "conference" would be held and that the conference would decide all matters relating to the Jewish Congress. The resolution demanded replies by 15 January, and, if no replies were received, the Congress Organization Committee would proceed to call the meetings independently.

To George Rublee

December 28, 1915 Boston, Mass. [Brandeis Mss, NMF 66-3]

MY DEAR GEORGE: I thank you for your letter of the 20th.

Your doubts as to the legal power seem to me well founded, and you will note from the enclosed carbon of letter to Mr. Hurley that I agree with your views. All the papers which you enclosed are returned herewith.

I endeavored to get from Norman some further light as to what you and the Commission were doing, but could get little. I hope you are really making progress. Send me a copy of your report to Congress as soon as it appears.

I am going to talk before the Chicago Bar Association next week on "The Living Law".[1] I wish I might be able to tell them that the Supreme Court had sustained the Oregon Minimum Wage law.[2]

With best wishes for the New Year,

Most cordially yours,

1. Not since his 1905 address, "The Opportunity in the Law," (see LDB to Leonard A. Jones, 8 May 1905) had LDB spoken so comprehensively about the law and the legal profession. Noting the recent dissatisfaction with the law, a dissatisfaction as pervasive among laboring men as among businessmen, LDB argued that discontent would continue so long as law remained abstract and unrelated to the needs and conditions of modern life. The last fifty years were years of immense change and dislocation, involving such obvious injustice and such clear threats to human liberty that nearly

everyone except the judiciary noticed it. The law, instead of conforming itself to changing conditions, steadfastly continued to reach decisions by a set of eighteenth-century assumptions of individual autonomy. Law must be harmonized to life to avoid the just criticism of the people, LDB said; and although he could cite some recent hopeful court decisions (including several in which he had played a part as attorney), nevertheless the courts were still too often captivated by their preconceptions. The speech was delivered on 3 January. Three weeks later, on 28 January, President Wilson electrified the nation by nominating LDB to the Supreme Court. The interest created by the appointment made requests for LDB's speech numerous and it is probably the most often reprinted of any of his addresses. It may be found in 10 *Illinois Law Review* 461 (1916), 48 *Chicago Legal News* 246 (1916), *Harper's Weekly*, 62 (19 and 26 February 1916): 173, 27 *American Legal News* 25 (1916), *Business—A Profession*, 344–63, and *The Curse of Bigness*, 316–26. See also, David W. Levy, "The Lawyer as Judge: Brandeis' View of the Legal Profession," 22 *Oklahoma Law Review* 374 (1969) and Melvin I. Urofsky, *A Mind of One Piece*, ch. 2.

2. The irony, of course, was that when the Supreme Court finally ruled (*Stettler* vs. *O'Hara*. 243 U.S. 629 [1917]), LDB was a member of that body. Naturally he disqualified himself and the other eight justices divided four to four thereby sustaining the constitutionality of the Oregon law.

Index

Numbers in italics indicate letters addressed to the person named.
Asterisks (*) indicate page on which note identifies the person named.

Aaronsohn, Aaron 117, 128, 155, *157*, 434, 473
Aaronsohn, Alexander 603*, 613, 619
Aaronsohn, Sarah 603
Abbott, Lawrence F. 393, *657*
Abrahams, I. A. *433*, 434*, 648
Abramowitz, Rabbi 533
Abrams, Mr. 246
Abelson, Paul 429, 430
Achoosa Movement 469, 475
Actions Comite 291, 322-27, 426, 449, 461, 470, 472, 510, 561, 569, 606, 628, 666
Adair vs. United States 63
Adams, Charles F. 342
Adams Express Co. 24
Adams, Henry Carter *5*
Addams, Jane 432, 597
Ades, Moses W. 353, 354*, *639*, *671*
Adkins, Jesse C. 211*, 227, 245
Adler, Cyrus 409, 544*, *551*, 555, *566*, 571, 572, 574, 577, 578, 619, 634; see also American Jewish Committee and Jewish Congress Movement
Adler, Felix 242, 307, 503, 547, 562
Adler, Helen G. 272, 503
Adler, Margaret 503*
Adler, Ruth 272*
Adler, Simon 509*
Advanced Rate Cases 47, 49, 78-80, 142-43, 162-65, 192, 202-203, 210-11, 245, 288-89, 295, 330-31, 334, 337, 345-46, 373, 383, 385-86, 399-400, 410-11, 484, 502-503
Agricultural Experiment Stations 26, 469
Albee, George H. *12*
Altman, Benjamin 199*
American Advance 83

American Defense Society 629
American Express Co. 23
American Fair Trade League 94
American Federation of Labor 88
American Hebrew 577
American Jewish Committee 294, 309, 315, 324, 387, 434, 438, 483, 536, 544-45, 551-54, 564, 566, 570-72, 575-76, 578-80, 604, 621, 625, 634-35, 640, 561-54, 656, 675-76, 681
American Jewish Congress 294, 314, 408, 653; see also Jewish Congress Movement, American Jewish Committee, and Adler, Cyrus
American Jewish Emancipation Committee 535, 538
American Jewish Relief Committee, 352, 359, 362, 367, 382, 387, 397, 403, 408, 414, 421, 424, 436-37, 461, 472-74, 481-84, 504, 547-50, 578, 582, 589, 604, 607, 621, 632, 641-42, 654, 665, 678-79
American Judicature Society 167
American League to Limit Armaments 419
American Palestine Company 159, 186, 226; see also Palestine
American Society of Jurisprudence 10
American Tobacco Co. 35, 39, 523
Ames, James B. 86
Anderson, George W. *109*, 129, 150, 172-73, *177*, 191, 195, *218*, 244, *245*, *264*, *276*, 277, 297, 392, 560
Angel, Walter F. 43
Anglo-Jewish Association 404
Anglo-Palestine Bank 431; see also Palestine

Anglo-Palestine Company 356, 413, 416; see also Palestine
Anti-Semitism 38, 348-49, 373-74, 534-35, 643-45
Antitrust Movement 11-12, 35, 39, 41, 48-49, 100-103, 116-17, 171, 187-88, 195, 218-21, 234-37, 247-60, 290, 440, 523, 592-95
Artaud, Mr. 384
Ashinsky, Aaron M. 328*
Ashley, H. W. 229, 239
Associated Advertising Clubs 111
Association of National Advertising Managers 94
Associated Press 225
Atlanta Constitution 174
Atlantic Coast Line 9
Atlantic National Bank of Providence 161
Attwater, Mrs. Jessie F. 659*
Atwood, Albert W. 268*, 271
Austro-Hungarian Zionists 560, 585
Avery, Susan L. 280*

Baer, Boris 403
Bahkmeteff, George 375
Baker, Newton D. 350*, 651
Baker, Ray S. 394, 581
Balfour Declaration 23, 296, 317, 327, 520, 665
Ballard, Samuel T. 89*, 237, 244
Ballinger, Richard A. 33; see also Pinchot-Ballinger conservation controversy
Baltimore & Ohio Railroad 266
Bancroft, Edgar A. 232*
"Banker-Management; Why It Has Failed: A Lesson from the New Haven" 147, 168
Bankhead, John H. 411*
Bank Insurance League 263
Barfod, Einar 445
Barnes, William, Jr. 613*
Barnet, Philip 332*, 484
Barnett, Maurice 97
Baron, Maximilian G. 586*, 615, 648

Barondess, Joseph 314*, 323, 488, 545, 579
Barowsky, J. L. 585
Barret, Alexander G. 240*
Barrett, John C. 442, 443*
Baruch, Bernard M. 623*
Bass, Robert 224, 246
Batchelder, Wallace 440*
Bates, Henry M. 288*
Bauer vs. O'Donnell 100, 103, 105, 113, 121, 127, 170, 196
Bawden, William T. 402
Beale, Joseph H. 13*, 18
Beatson, J. W. 260, 281
Beckham, Mr. 383
Belnap, Hiram W. 109, 110*, 122, 124, 141; see also New York, New Haven & Hartford Railroad: lack of safety on
Bemis, Mr. 211
Ben Jehuda, Eliezar 355
Berger, Julius 328*, 423
Berger, Sophia 662
Berlin, Meyer 505*, 510, 533, 558, 561, 569
Berman, William 428*, 484
Bernheim, Isaac W. 354*, 454
Bernstein, Herman 401*, 431, 642, 644, 648
Bigelow, Herbert S. 375, 376*
Billard, John L. 167, 175, 266, 284
Billikopf, Jacob 412, 413*
Billings, Edmund 170
Bingham, George H. 54*
Bird, Charles S. 79, 125, 596
Bird, George E. 440*
Bishop, George W. 192
Biskind, Israel J. 359, 350*, 375
Bismarck, Otto 404
Blackwell, Alice Stone 319*, 597
Blaine, John J. 383
Blankenburg, Rudolph 179*
Bliss, Elmer J. 223-24
Bloch Publishing Co. 386
Bloom, Dr. 671
Bluestone, Joseph I. 653*

B'nai Brith 365, 369, 373
Bobbs Merrill Co. vs. Straus 121
Bohn, Frank 88*, 98, 104
Bohn, William E. 98*
Bond, Frederic D. 266
Borglum, Gutzon 272*
Bosley vs. McLaughlin 364, 381, 392, 400, 444
Boston American 3, 53, 72, 80, 181, 509
Boston Chamber of Commerce 79, 194, 223-24
Boston Common 80, 104
Boston Consolidated Gas Company 166; see also Sliding Scale principle
Boston Elevated Railroad 163
Boston Evening Traveller 61
Boston Finance Commission 162, 200
Boston Fruit and Produce Exchange 66, 70-73
Boston garment workers 669-71
Boston Globe 83, 110
Boston Herald 127-29, 392, 638
Boston Jewish Advocate 526, 634
Boston Journal 110, 127-29, 181-82, 191, 225, 229
Boston & Maine Railroad: see New York, New Haven & Hartford Railroad
Boston News Bureau 181, 191
Boston Post 83, 90-93, 124
Boston Transcript 110, 464
Bradley, William M. 440*
Brady, James B. 130*, 133
Brandeis, Adele 37, 165
Brandeis, Albert, 400
Brandeis, Alfred *3, 42, 58, 85, 110, 127, 143, 164, 165, 229, 231, 236, 244, 246, 262, 264, 271, 280, 310, 330, 331, 334, 339, 340, 345, 353, 368, 381, 383, 387, 399, 420, 443, 444, 465, 484, 488, 503, 508, 513, 565, 617, 629, 661, 671*
Brandeis, Alice G. 40, *207, 221, 222, 223, 224, 227, 228, 229, 231, 234, 236, 237, 238, 244, 259, 262, 263, 271, 339, 340, 344, 345, 378, 380,*

387, 420, 444, 503, 513, 562, 565
Brandeis, Amy: see McCreary, Amy B.
Brandeis, Elizabeth 231, 235, 244, 246, 259, 271, 420, 503, 513, 565
Brandeis, Fannie 443
Brandeis, Jean 617
Brandeis, Jennie 354, 381, 444, 484
Brandeis, Louis D: and rumors of a cabinet position 32, 35-41, 44-45, 129-30 and the New York, New Haven & Hartford Railroad, the Boston & Maine Railroad, and subsidiary companies 3, 12-16, 20-21, 23-25, 49-50, 53-55, 58, 66-68, 70-73, 106-109, 123-24, 127-30, 132-35, 141, 143, 145-46, 148-50, 153-54, 164, 171-73, 175, 177-81, 186, 188, 190-95, 204, 244-45, 264-66, 268-71, 274-77, 282-87, 306-307, 560, 590 see also New York, New Haven & Hartford Railroad; and general railroad affairs 5-6, 8-9, 17-18, 45, 49, 58-59, 67-68, 90-93, 109, 142-43, 156-57, 182, 263, 266-68, 281-82, 339, 342-44, 372, 542-43 see also Advanced Rate cases and individual railroads; and savings bank life insurance 8, 411, 457-58; and the garment workers' arbitration and Protocol 6, 9, 27-28, 57, 73-74, 81-82, 104-105, 208-209, 211-15, 401-402, 428-30, 524-25, 547, 562, 650-51, 669-71, 673; and price maintenance of trademarked goods and trade associations 31-32, 89-90, 93-97, 99-103, 105, 111-13, 118-22, 125-27, 131-34, 138-39, 146-47, 152, 169-70, 173-74, 216-18, 225-27, 434, 446-48, 539-40, 559-60, 592, 618-19; and the antitrust movement 11-12, 35, 39, 41, 48-49, 100-103, 116-17, 171, 187-88, 195, 218-21, 234-37, 247-60, 290, 440, 523, 592-95; and the Advanced Rate cases 49, 78-80, 142-43, 162-65, 192, 202-203, 210-11,

Brandeis, Louis D. *(continued)*
245, 288-89, 295, 330-31, 334, 337,
345-46, 372, 383, 385-86, 399-400,
410-11, 484, 502-503; and Zionism
and Jewish affairs 22-23, 64-66, 77-
78, 141, 147-48, 158-59, 174-75, 192-
93, 226, 291-96, 298-303, 305-306,
308-20, 322-30, 332-36, 338-41, 344,
349-63, 365-69, 371-83, 386-89, 393-
95, 397-410, 412-19, 421-28, 430-
39, 441-46, 448-88, 490-508, 510-39,
541-58, 560-92, 595-611, 613-17, 619-
28, 630-68, 670-72, 674-82; and
Palestine 117, 155-59, 186, 206, 226,
235-36, 312-13, 317-18, 336-37, 354-
56, 372-73, 416-18, 421-25, 427-28,
452-53, 468-77, 492, 495-501, 513-17,
520-22, 580, 607, 609-11, 638-39,
674-75, 678-80; and the Jewish
Congress movement 408-409, 544-
45, 551-58, 564-82, 587-88, 591-92,
604, 607-609, 619-25, 631, 634-36,
640-41, 645-46, 651-56, 681-82; consulted on various federal patronage positions 40, 42-44, 47, 53-54,
56, 61-62, 85-86, 88-89, 95-96, 104,
130, 138, 140, 148, 154, 161-62, 180,
190, 194-97, 200-201, 206-207, 218,
297, 311, 321, 347, 371, 393, 439-40,
467-68, 600-601
—opinions on: legal profession and
judiciary 62, 82, 109, 166-68, 176,
181, 242, 281, 378-79, 632-33, 682-
83; the legislative process 19-20;
conversation and land policy 23,
31, 59-60, 146, 217; immigration
restriction 4, 52, 389, 506-507, 676;
tariff 34, 83-84, 169; welfare 34-35;
minimum wages 56, 442-43 see also
Stettler vs. O'Hare; children 36-
37; the woman's movement 26, 32-
33, 48, 319, 535-36, 597, 618; teachers' pensions 28; the "single tax"
151, 489-90, 551; water rights 6-7,
146; agricultural conditions 151-
52, 272-73; the co-operative movement 139, 215, 272-73, 451; socialism 209-210; the preferential union shop as opposed to the closed
or open shop 9, 10-11, 52, 55, 57,
73, 260-61; labor unions and labor
conditions 9-11, 29, 52, 55, 60-61,
86-87, 97, 107-108, 209-210, 215-16,
230, 260-61, 363-64, 390, 407, 428-
30, 489-90, 545-46, 669-71 see New
York garment workers; arbitration
of labor disputes 25, 55, 60-61,
107-108, 184-85; profit sharing 97;
municipal finance 132, 152-53, 159-
60, 179, 261-62; gas and the sliding
scale principle 69, 166, 276-80, 375-
76, 509-10; rate making 45-46, 273,
345-46, 383, 396 see also Advanced
Rate cases; the efficiency movement 11, 17-18, 19-20, 47-49, 127-
28, 133-34, 142-43, 151, 240-41, 281,
618, 671-72; the "New Freedom"
219-21, 234-37; Negro rights 297-
98, 305; bankers 49, 168-69, 171,
179, 202, 207, 219-21, 259-60, 266-
67, 282, 339, 342-43; interlocking
directorates 20-21, 49, 76, 78, 80,
85, 187-88, 211, 220, 243, 247-60,
310-11; anti-semitism 348-49, 373-
74, 534-35, 643-45; Russia 155, 303-
304, 360, 374-75, 490-93, 645-46;
China 57-58, 523; Poland 369, 381,
431-42, 436, 456-57, 486
—writings and speeches: "Banker-
Management; Why It Has Failed:
A Lesson from the New Haven"
147, 168; "Big Men and Little
Business" 89; *Business—A Profession* 199, 230, 233, 238, 260, 263,
283, 390, 451, 489; "A Call to the
Educated Jew" 413, 637, 638; "The
Constitution and the Minimum
Wage" 364, 443; "Cutthroat Prices:
The Competition that Kills" 125,
128, 137, 170, 196; "Democracy in
Palestine" 658; "Efficiency by Con-
sent" 618; "Efficiency and the One-
Price Article" 125; "An Essential
of Lasting Peace" 436; "Financial
Condition of the New York, New
Haven & Hartford Railroad

Company and of the Boston and Maine Railroad" 106; "How Boston Solved the Gas Problem" 69, 166, 375; "How Europe Deals with the One-Price Goods" 125; "The Jewish Problem: How to Solve It" 455, 526, 543, 591, 600, 637-38; "Jewish Unity and the Congress" 675; "The Living Law" 682; "The Massachusetts Substitute for Old Age Pensions" 216; "The New Haven—An Unregulated Monopoly" 129; "On Maintaining Makers' Prices" 89, 94, 101; "Opportunity in the Law" 682; *Other People's Money and How the Bankers Use It* 49, 60, 146-47, 165, 168, 171, 179, 183, 187, 188-90, 195, 204-205, 207, 211, 216, 219-21, 232, 238, 272-73, 280, 284, 344, 440, 451; "Our Financial Oligarchy" 169, 187; "Palestine and the Jewish Democracy" 657, 659; "Patriotism and Zionism" 371; "Price Fixing and Monopoly" 101; "The Road to Social Efficiency" 390, 489; "Serve One Master Only" 247; "The Solution of the Trust Problem: A Program" 102, 195, 219; Testimony in the U.S. Steel Investigation 25; Testimony before House Committee on Interstate and Foreign Commerce 217; Testimony before House Committee on Patents 89, 99, 101, 103, 170; Testimony before Senate Committee on Interstate Commerce 12, 27; "True Americanism" 540; "The Twin Evils of the Literacy Test" 506; "Where the Banker is Superfluous" 261; "Why I am a Zionist" 308; "Zionism and Patriotism" 356, 358, 412, 416, 492, 543, 637, 638

"Brandeis Substitute" 284
Brandeis, Susan 246, 339, 354, 380, 387, 420, 503, 513, 565
Bressler, David M. *414**, 548, 641
Brett, George P. 89*

Briggs, Alton E. *70*, 71-73
Brinsmade, Chapin *305**
Brodie, Israel B. *633*, *634**
Brody, Joseph I. *359*, *360**
Bromberg, Edward J. *485*, *486**
Brooklyn Rapid Transit Company 32
Brooks, John G. 87, 98, 104
Brown, Arthur L. *43**, 53
Brown, David F. 167
Brown, George N. 55
Brown, Herman L. *85*, 175, 222, 223, 287
Brown, William C. *5*
Bruce, Helm 384*
Bruere, Henry *152*, *153**, *562*, *671*
Bryan, William J. 38, 42, 44, 48, 56, 57, 65, 115, 239, 304, *330*, *354*, 418, 455, 465, 495, 610
Bulkeley, Robert J. 273, 289
Buell, Katharine *281*, *282**, *283*
Bullock, Harry A. *32*
Burleson, Albert S. *9**, 338
Burlingham, Charles C. *68*, *150*
Burling, Edward D. 601
Burnett, John T. 138
Business—A Profession 199, 230, 233, 238, 260, 263, 283, 390, 451, 489

Cabot, Charles M. *545*
California Eight Hour Cases: see *Bosley vs. McLaughlin*
Calkins, Grosvenor *132**
Call, Joseph H. 31
Callahan, Lee 271
"A Call to the Educated Jew" 413, 637-38
Campbell, Ben *337*, 338*
Cannon, Joseph G. 611
Cardozo, Benjamin N. 145
Carlinger, Jacob 654*
Carmalt, James W. *210*, *211**, *305*, *330*
Carr, John F. *4**
Carr, Wilbur J. *495*, *496**
Carroll, Francis M. *201**
Carton, Sidney 306
Catherine II of Russia 158
Catt, Carrie Chapman 597*

Celebration of the One Hundredth Anniversary of Peace Among English Speaking Peoples 17
Central Jewish Relief Committee for War Sufferers 359
Central Zionist Bureau 309, 320
Chamberlin, Frederick 95, 96*
Chantland, William T. 169, 170*
Chazenovitch, Leon 330*
Chesapeake & Ohio Railroad 5
Chibbath Zion 156
Chicago & Alton 22
Chicago garment workers' strike 673
Chicago Great Western Railroad 50
Chicago Tribune 368, 371
Child, Richard W. 125
Child, Walter 111, 617
Choate, Charles F. 72, 79, 382
Churchill, Thomas William 391*
Cincinnati, Hamilton & Dayton Railroad 264, 266
Cincinnati Zionists Controversy: see Philipson, David & Fechheimer, Samuel M.
Clapp, Moses Edwin 39, 224
Clark, Walter E. 69*
Clarke, James P. 434*, 446, 467
Clayton Anti-trust Act 25-26, 84, 100-103, 188, 247-259, 290, 310, 592-95
Clayton, Henry DeLamar 196*, 260
Clements, Judson C. 140*, 143
Cleveland, Grover, 42
Cleveland Municipal Court 181
Cleveland, Treadwell Jr. 60, 80, 119-20, 370, 467
Cloak, Suit & Skirt Industry 9
Codman, Edmund D. 22*
Cohen, Abraham B. 430*
Cohen, Edward J. 465, 485
Cohen, Ephraim: see Cohn-Reiss, Ephraim
Cohen, Israel 358*
Cohen, Joseph L. 516, 517*, 531
Cohen, Julius Henry 6
Cohn-Reiss, Ephraim 398*, 434, 496, 575, 580
Collier's Magazine 33, 176, 199, 243

Collins, Frederick L. 31*, 47, 128, 138, 176
Colston, William A. 281*, 381
Commerce Court 126, 180
Commercial Travellers Association 340
Common Counsel Club 239
Commons, John Rogers 88, 99, 100*, 227
"Competition That Kills" 170
Connelly, Christopher P. 44, 199
Conrad, Sidney S. 501*
"Constitution & the Minimum Wage" 364, 443
Congress Organizing Committee 409
Cooke, Morris L. 142, 179, 349, 376, 393, 396
Coolidge, Calvin 350, 458, 629
Coolidge, J. Randolph 221
Co-operative British Wholesale Society 151
Cooperative League of America 139
Cotton, J. P. Jr. 393, 496
Cotton Garment Manufacturers' Association 86
Cowan, Charles 426*
Cowen, Joseph 329*, 418, 678
Cox, Charles M. 268, 277
Cox, Roland 448*
Crane, Charles R. 8, 18, 20, 31, 38, 51, 75, 110, 176, 238, 306, 375, 378, 383, 503, 565, 600, 622, 673
Crane, Richard T. 622*
Creel, George 433, 543*
Croly, Herbert 208-209, 222, 402
Crozier, General William 244*
Curtis, James Freeman 86*
Curtis, Rennselaer 161*
Cutler, Harry 653*
"Cutthroat Prices: the Competition that Kills" 125, 128, 137, 196

Daniel, Josephus 421, 465
Dannenbaum, Harry 365, 367*, 369
Danziger, Ida S. 662
Darnay, Charles 306
Das Volk, 313

Davies, Joseph E. *116*, 117*, 174, 210, 394, 447, 600
Davis, D. D. *425*
Davis, James *376**, 377
Davis, Oscar K. 4*
Davison, Charles Stewart 36*
Davison, Henry P. *559**
DeHaas, Jacob 64, 65, 155, 186, 206, 226, 292, 308, 314, *319*, *335*, *338*, *355*, 356, 358, 382, 388, 406, *414*, 417, 462-63, 472, 474, 504, 525, 527, *564*, 575-76, 584-85, 603, 620, 625, 644, 666, 681
Delano, Frederic Adrian 89*, 194, 282, 343
DeMille, Cecil B. 200
"Democracy in Palestine" 658
Denison, Winfred T. 126, *134*, 262
Dennison, Henry S. 228*
Der Tag 401, 429, 432, 644
Dewey, Davis R. 203*
Dewey, John 673
Dewey, Judd 458
Dewey, Mary H. 203*
Dickens, Charles 306
Diggs, Annie LePorte *28*, 29*
Dodge, Cleveland H. 51*
Dodge, Frederic 161*
Dodge, James M. 241*
Donaldson, William T. *184*, 185*
Dorf, Samuel 438*
"Do": see Goldmark, Josephine
Doten, Carroll W. 228*
Doubleday, Page & Co. 30
Dreyfus Affair 156
Dreyfus, Alfred 374*
Dr. Miles Medical Company vs. Park & Sons Co. 121
Droppers, Garrett *56*
Drury, Horace B. *240*, 241*
Dubnow, Simon M. 308, 537, 541
Dunne, Edward F. 673*
Dyche, John A. 81, *428*

Easley, Ralph M. 228
Eastman, Joseph B. 21, *54*, 75, 133, *162*, 222, 276, 287, 392, 396, 613

Eddy, Arthur J. 560
Edelman, Samuel 456*
Edison, Thomas A. 200
Edwards, Seeber *42*, 43*
Edwards, Stephen O. 489*
"Efficiency by Consent" 618
Efficiency Society of New York 20
"Efficiency and the One-Price Article" 125
Ehrlich, Eugen 288*, 382
Eichholz, A. 600
Eisenhower, Dwight D. 538
Eliot, Charles W. 52, 77, 332
Elkus, Abraham I. 579
Elliott, Howard 143*, 153, 221, 223, 231, 265, *346*, 385, 560, *590*
Emerson, Harrington 142, 241, 584
Engineering Magazine 78
Epstein, Benjamin 318*, 326, 476
"An Essential of Lasting Peace" 436
Estabrook, Arthur F. 179*
Evans, Elizabeth G. 119, 259
Evans, G. 231
Evelina deRothschild School 405, 679
Everybody's Magazine 199
Ewing, Thomas 127*
Ezra, Nissim Ezra B. 523*

Fabian Society 538
Fahey, John A. 61
"Fanny Brandeis" Steamship 85
Farrand, George E. 320*
Fechheimer, Samuel Marcus 405*, 415, *438*, 442, 444, 454, 465-66, 614, 620, 666
Federal Reserve Act 25, 40-41, 48, 113–16, 187, 190, 221
Federal Trade Commission 84, 101, 219, 237, 310, 320, 345, 347, 370, 380, 393, 440, 447, 468, 496, 502, 523, 581, 592, 600, 680
Federal Trade Commission Act 259
Federation of American Zionists 141, 147, 193, 313, 322, 324-26, 356, 406, 417, 426, 438, 450, 460, 462, 470-71, 476, 485, 488, 526-27, 561, 568-69, 591, 606, 624, 667-68

Feiker, Frederick M. 392*
Fels, Joseph 236*
Fels, Mary 551*
Fels, Samuel S. 406*, 514, 638
Filene, Abraham L. 52, 428, 609, 622, 650
Filene Company 137
Filene, Edward A. 61, 382
"Financial Condition of the New York, New Haven & Hartford Railroad Co. and of the Boston & Maine Railroad" 106
Findley, Oscar 271
Finkelstein, M. J. 591*
First Universal Races Congress 307
Fischel, Harry 363*
Fisher, Boyd 30*, 98
Fisher-Ellis Act 275-77, 282-83, 285
Fisher, Robert C. 161*
Fisher, Walter L. 8, 23, 44
Fitch, John A. 673
Fitzgerald, John F. 162, 200
Fleishner, Otto 37
Flexner, Abraham 508
Flexner, Bernard 566*
Foerster, Robert F. 34, 35*
Forbes, Frederick F. 78*
Ford, Henry 230*, 294
Forward 81
Foss, Eugene N. 58, 67, 86, 172, 182, 191, 195, 245
Foster, John W. 610
Fram, Harry 426*
Frank, Leo M. 373*, 383, 633
Frankel, Lee K. 228
Frankfurter, Felix 18-19, 38, 88, 134-35, 144, 146, 203, 209, 236, 242, 262, 288, 296, 373, 428, 454, 460, 467, 487, 516, 544-45, 555, 577, 613, 643, 651
Friedenwald, Edgar B. 645, 646*
Friedenwald, Harry 302, 303*, 323, 356, 472, 531, 545, 567, 572, 574, 579, 591, 635, 646
Friedlaender, Israel 445, 446*, 517, 522, 536, 541, 545
Freeport (Illinois) Daily Standard 36

Friess, Horace L. 272
Fritch, L. C. 50
Fromenson, Abraham H. 353*
Fuller, Frederick T. 80*
Furuseth, Andrew 464

Galena Signal Oil Co. 210
Gallinger, Jacob H. 320*, 440
Galsworthy, John 307
Gantt, Henry L. 241
Gardner, Gilson 39, 467, 581, 596
Garrett, Garet 202*
Garrett, Robert 268*
Garrison, Lindley M. 144, 147*
Gary, Elbert H. 310
Gay, Edwin F. 122*
Geiger, Abraham 386
General Electric Co. 205
George, Henry 133, 490
Gibbons, James C. 203*
Gilbreth, Frank B. 241
Ginsburg, Asher Zvi: see Ha-Am, Ahad
Glass, Carter 115*
Glavis, Louis R. 33, 239
Glazebrook, Otis A. 496*
Gluskin, Z'ev 550*, 677
Goldmark, Josephine 63, 154, 168, 227, 235-37, 383, 513
Goldstein, Dora 353
Gompers, Samuel 228, 464, 633
Going, Charles B. 241*
Goldfogle, Henry M. 348*
Goldman, Julius 516*
Gordon, Harry A. 27*
Gottheil, Richard J. H. 155*, 296, 299, 302, 309, 312, 314, 339, 341, 344, 360, 374, 378, 400, 403-404, 428, 446, 456, 460, 471, 490, 517, 527, 532-33, 537, 555, 578-79, 644, 677
Grady, Alice H. 223, 232, 238, 259, 263, 362
Graham, George F. 295*
Graham, Howard S. 342, 343*
Graham, Mr. 112, 119

Green, Bernie F. *419**
Gregory, Thomas W. *105*, 106**, 150,
    167, *175*, *182*, *188*, *190*, *204*, 221,
    223-24, 228, 245, 276, 285, *290*, *297*,
    321, 338, *439*, *560*
Griffin, F. A. *440**
Grossman, Louis 442**, 465
Guggenheim, Daniel 5*16**, 622
Guggenheimer, Ida 662
Grozier, Edwin A. 140
Gurion, David Ben 328

Ha-Am, Ahad 303, 446, 541**, 578
Hadassah 300, 463, 470, 488, 495, 526,
    622, 667
Haines, Lynn *43**, *81*
Hale, Cushman & Flint 233
Hale, Matthew 229
Hale, Ralph T. *233**
Hale, William B. *30**
Hall, Charles P. 245
Hall, Henry C. 195, *264**, 444
Hall, Prescott F. *506*, *507**
Halvosa, Philip J. *356**
Hamlin, Charles S. 47, 140, 148, 227,
    241
Hand, Learned 467
Hannan, John J. 237
Hansen, Elisha 468**
Hantke, Arthur M. 328**, *421*, *486*,
    605, *623*
Hapgood, Norman 4, *20*, 31-2, 38, *43*,
    47, 75, *104*, 110, *117*, *125*, *128*, *137*,
    144, *146*, 176, *183*, *191*, *195*, *199*, *205*,
    211, 215, 223, *224*, 232, 243, *266*,
    303, *305-306*, *310*, *384*, *392*, 393,
    436, *440*, *451*, *457*, *493*, *540*, *542*,
    576, 597, 601, 618, *643*, 682
Hard, William *217*
Harding, Warren G. 99
Harlan, James S. *107**, 140, *163*, 164,
    165, *192*, 201, 237, 305, 331, 339,
    383, *385*, *484*, *502*
Harley, Herbert L. *166*, *167**
Harper, Samuel N. 491**
Harper's Weekly 4, 21, 31, 47, 49, 51,

75, 104, 117, 138, 144-47, 160, 165,
    168, 176, 183-84, 189, 211, 216, 224,
    230-31, 234, 239-40, 242, 272, 280,
    285, 306, 393, 436, 458, 493, 540,
    542-53, 577, 618, 643-45
Harriman, Edward H. 207, 220,
    267
Harriman, Florence J. H. 30**, *51*
Harriman, Mrs. J. Borden 88, 119,
    222, 236-37, 239
Harris, Albert H. *5**
Harris, Robert Orr 161**
Harrison, Benjamin 304, 439
Harrison, Leon 405**
Hartman, Gustave *534*, *535**
Harvard Law Review 13
Harvard Law School 13, 18, 134-36,
    209, 240, 288
Harvard Menorah Society 340
Harvard [Zionist] Society 332, 381,
    427, 460
Hashomar 513
Haskins, Henry S. 419**
Hastings, Paul 383
Hawley vs. Walker 237
Hay, John 304
Hayes, William P. *154**
Hayesod, Keren 327
Haynes, Frederick *49*
Hayward, William 518**
Haywood, William 633
Hearst, William R. *3**, 53, 222
Heineman, Charles *524*, *525**
Heller, Bernard 602**
Heller, James G. 637**
Heller, Maximilian 314**, 359, 430,
    636
Hely-Hutchinson, Maurice R. *343*,
    344**
Heney, Francis J. 33, 222
Henry, Alice *26**
Hermann, Mr. 332
Herzl, Theodore 156**, 293, 296, 303,
    327, 329, 374, 404, 519, 523, 527,
    530, 541, 564, 650, 662, 680
Hibbard, Caroline I. *48**
Higgins, William E. *167**

Higginson, Henry L. 38, 144
Hill, James J. 50
Hill, Joe 633*
Hines, Walker D. 502*
Hirsch, Emil G. 315*, 368, 405, 439, 645
Hirschman, Rabbi 648
Hobbs, William J. 177*
Hodges, Henry G. 390, 391*
Hoffman, Frederick 228
Hollis, Allan F. 246
Hollis, Henry F. 124*, 130, 206, 273, 345
Holmes, Oliver W. Jr. 64, 121, 176, 209, 223, 262, 373
Holt, Hamilton 393, 402, 543
Homans, Robert 78
Home Building & Loan Association vs. Blaisdell 36
Homestead Policy 31
Hoover, Herbert 368, 401, 601
Hourvitch, Samuel H. 458
Hourwich, Isaac A. 81*, 105, 228
House Committee on Interstate & Foreign Commerce 217
House Committee on Patents 89, 99, 101, 103
House, Edward Mandel 38, 77, 106*, 154, 338, 393, 610, 621
House of Truth 261
Houseman, Arthur A. 623
Houston, David F. 621*
Houston, Herbert Sherman 89*, 490
Hovey, Carl 199
Howard, Jeremiah 443*
"How Boston Solved the Gas Problem" 69, 166, 375
Howells, William D. 229
"How Europe Deals with the One-Price Goods" 125
Hull, G. G. 229
Hull, Roger B. 242*
Hurley, Edward N. 394*, 680, 682
Hurwitz, Henry 193, 297*, 299, 314, 332, 460, 505, 555
Hustis, James H. 386*
Hutchins, F. Lincoln 143*, 202

Independent Magazine 543
Independent Order of Brith Abraham 435-38, 531, 572, 574, 606, 624, 655
Ingersoll, Charles H. 489, 490*
Ingersoll, Ruth 111
Ingersoll Watch Co. 120-21, 126, 196
Ingersoll, William H. 26, 27*, 96, 105, 118, 121, 138, 144, 173, 217, 225, 434, 446, 467, 490
Inner Actions Committee 588, 627
Intercollegiate Menorah 193
Intercollegiate Zionist Association 357, 460, 659-660
Interlocking Directorates 76, 78, 79-80, 85
International Harvester Corporation 51, 171, 232, 601
International Ladies' Garment Workers Union 81
International Socialist Review 98
International Workers of the World 87-88, 98, 104, 632-33
Interstate Commerce Commission 21-22, 23-25, 38, 40, 42, 47, 50, 54-55, 66, 70-73, 76, 78, 82-83, 96, 107, 110, 111, 124, 130, 134, 136, 140-41, 143, 149, 162-65, 177, 179, 181, 188, 192, 194, 196, 207, 218, 223, 228, 235, 236, 241, 244-46, 263, 266, 280, 284, 287, 295, 305, 320-21, 330-31, 334, 342-43, 346, 380, 383-84, 387, 400, 444, 502
Israel Alliance Universalle 404
Ives, David O. 21, 194, 196, 201, 207, 218, 223, 237, 245, 287

Jabotinsky, Vladimir Y. 520*, 558, 630
Jacobson, Jeanette 406
Jacobson, Victor 353*, 423, 425, 496
James, William 226, 413*
Japanese Relations 96
Jewish Advocate 155
Jewish Agency for Palestine 23
Jewish Agricultural Experiment Station 155

Jewish Colonial Trust 313, 329, 356, 589

Jewish Colonization Association 499

Jewish Congress Movement 408-409, 544-45, 551-58, 564-82, 587-88, 591-92, 604, 607-609, 619-25, 631, 634-36, 640-41, 645-46, 651-56, 681-82

Jewish Congress Organization Committee 568, 570-74, 581, 604, 621, 624, 635, 640, 645, 651-56, 681

Jewish Daily News 630

Jewish National Fund 317, 325-26, 356, 452, 461, 476-77, 501, 515, 517, 519, 551, 667, 672

"Jewish Problem: How to Solve It" 455, 526, 543, 591, 600, 637-38

"Jewish Unity and the Congress" 675

Jewish Weekly 644

Joffe, Judah Achilles 645*

Johnson, Alvin 208

Johnson, Hiram 222

Johnson, J. F. 119*

Johnston, Harry H. 306*

Joint Board of Sanitary Control 9, 73-74

Joint Distribution Committee 316

Jones, Charles H. *132*, 246

Jones, Thomas Davies 51*

Jose, Ernest Parlin *6, 7*

Joseph, Samuel 304

Joy, Henry B. *93*, 94*, *111*, 112, 119, *131, 188, 197, 243*

Jusserand, Jean J. 340, 341*, *360*

Kadima 456

Kallen, Horace M. 226*, 296, 314, *405, 415, 426*, 427, 439, *441, 459, 530*, 541, 551, 555, *598*, 603, 620, *646, 664*

Kann, Jacobus H. 329*, 356, 589

Kanter, Alexander *357*, 358*, 616

Kaplan, Nathan D. *313, 314*, 323, *371, 376, 407, 461*, 474, 576, 599, 603, *614*, 619, *642, 647, 658*, 666, 667

Kaplan, Walter 332

Kaplansky, Shelomoh 329*, 356, 452, 476

Katzenelsohn, Nissan 356*

Kazman, Boris 457*

Keely, James 200

Kelley, Florence 228

Kellogg Corn Flakes Co. 96

Kellogg, Paul U. 407, *432-33*

Kelley, Florence 597

Kellor, Frances A. 676*

Kent, William *8*, 21, 32, 222, 308

Kesselman, Robert D. 563*, *667*, 668

Kidder, Peabody & Co. 269

Kiefer, Daniel *132*

Kirchwey, George W. 288, *562*

Kirstein, Louis E. 363*, 365, 501, 668

Knapp, Ella A. *32*

Knights of Zion 314, 462, 526-28, 599, 614, 619, 647, 658

Knoeppel, Charles E. *107*, 108*

Kohler, Kaufmann 415*, 439

Kohn, Leon A. 664*

Kolinsky, Abraham *378*, 379*

Koomer, Manuel *424*, 425*

Koschland, Mrs. Cora 622

Koschland, Mrs. Marcus 610*

Kraus, Adolf 564, *570*, 571*, 572, 576, *579, 582, 587, 591*, 599, 675

Krauskopf, Joseph 388*

Kremenetzky, Johan *518*, 519*

Kriegshaber, V. H. *174*

Kuhn, Loeb & Co. 207, 229, 267, 340

LaFollette, Belle 227, 236

LaFollette, Fola 45

LaFollette, Marion 236

LaFollette, Philip F. 169*

LaFollette, Robert M. 29, 38, *40*, 45-46, 75, *100*, 111, *119, 129, 133, 145*, 150, *153, 169*, 227, 235-37, 244, 255, 274, 301, 383, 420, 440, *464, 506*

LaFollette, Robert M. Jr. 506

LaFollette's Weekly Magazine 9, 76, 101, 104, 129, 153, 274, 302, 506

Lamont, Thomas R. 4, 21, 31, 47, 75, 221, 230

Lane, Franklin K. *23*, 38, *40*, 42-44, 127, 195-*96*, 201, *218*, 331

Lansing, Robert 330, 431, 610*, 619, 670

Lauck, William J. 215*

Lazaron, Morris S. 636, 637*

Leavitt, Ezekiel *546*, 547*

Leavitt, Julian 586*

Ledyard, Henry B. 25*

Lee, J. W. 543*

Legal Protection Federation 73

Lehman, Dr. 615, 648

Leiserson, William M. 365*

Lennon, John B. 381*

Lenroot, Irvine 255, 274

Leon, Eva 155, 378, 462-63

Leon, Maurice *35*

Levenson, Henry H. 437*

Levenson, Joseph 295

Levensohn, Lotta 662

Levin, Louis H. 467*, *468*, 474, 482, 607

Levin, Schmarya 293*, 299, 313, 315, 317, 322, 324, 326, 345, 353, 356, 358, 369, 376, 405, 415, 417, 421-27, *448*, 472, 477, 487, 495, 499, 500, 516, 556, 561, 579, 588, 609, 614, 620, 627, 636, 642, 648, 650, 668

Levine, Manuel *181*

Levy, Benjamin F. *638*

Levy, Julius *610*, 611*

Levy, Judge 655

Levy, Leonard 439

Levy, Samuel J. 353

Lewin-Epstein, Elias W. 328*, 338, 354, 365, 418, 424, 472, 480, 514, 524, 550, 579, 596, 609, 621, 628, 663, 678

Lewin-Epstein, Samuel 477*, 607, 678

Lewis, James H. 6*

Lewisohn, Adolf 361*, *491*, 514, 531

Lewisohn, Leonard 361*

Lichtheim, Richard 499*, 542, 580, 589, 670, 672

Life and Labor Magazine 26, 55

Lillie, Frances Crane 673*

Lillie, Frank Rattray 673*

Lindsey, Benjamin B. 38, 88*, 597

Lippmann, Walter 98, 402

Lipsky, Louis *64*, 65*, *141*, *147*, 206, 306, *311*, 313, *316*, 319, 322-23, 335, 351, 355, 358, *387*, *394*, *405*, *408*, *416*, 417, *425*, 449, 466, 470, 471, 478, 494, 517, *525*, *526*, 531, *551*, 556, *560*, *561*, 564, 566, 569, 579, 585, 598, 604, *617*, 620, 625, *651*, *655*, 666, *681*

Lisitzky, Ephraim E. 671*

Little, Arthur Dehon *135*

Littman, Lydia *379*, 380*

"Living Law" 682

Lochner vs. New York 64

Lodge, Henry C. 420

London, Meyer *348*, 363

Louisville & Nashville Railroad 15-16, 280, 383, 400

Lovett, Robert Scott 207*

Lowell, A. Lawrence 287

Lowell, James A. 228*

Lowell, Percival 331

Lowry, Edward G. *66*

Lubin, David *272*, 273*

Lucking, Alfred 434*

Lutz, Charles A. *13*, 16*, 22

Lyons, Joseph T. 321

Maccabaean 416, 495, *526*, 586, 606, 617, 649, 667

Mack, Julian W. 19, 180, 288, 296, 340, 363, 389, 415, 428, 454, 460, *487*, 514, 531, 532, 538, 545, 566-67, 572, *575*, 579, 599, *603*, *613*, 616, *619*, 622, 635, 663, 665, 666

Mackenzie, Frederick W. *9*

Macmillan Company 11

Macnair, William M. *171*, 172*

Madie: see Brandeis, Adele

McAdoo, William G. *40*, 44, 47, *61*, *85*, *95*, 106, 115, *138*, *140*, 148, *154*, *160*, *167*, *170*, *189*, *558*

Magnes, Judah Leon *192*, 193*, 296, 298-99, 323, 330, 338-39, 341, *351*, *359*, 362, 365, 400, 421, 454, 466, 471-72, 474, *481*, 494, 507, 522, 545,

547, 576, 577, 582, 588, 589, 595, 597, 598, 621, 634-35, 640, 651-52, 654, 679
Malloch, E. Louise 22, 263
Malone, Dudley F. 162
Maltbie, Milo Roy 384, 517
Manley, Basil 215*
Mannheimer, Leo 429, 430*
Marble, John Hobart 38, 39*, 40, 142, 331
Marble, Joseph R. 145
Marcou, Philippe Belknap 539
Margolies, Moses S. 650
Margolies, Samuel 650*
Margolis, Max L. 334*
Marks, E. Homer 73*
Marks, Marcus M. 57*
Marshall, Louis 193, 293, 294*, 311, 341, 366, 409, 435, 437, 491, 524, 537, 544, 574, 578, 619, 621
Martin, Selden O. 122*
Marx, Karl 617
Masliansky, Zvi H. 311*
Massachusetts Board of Railroad Commissioners 90-93, 148
Massachusetts Commission on Unemployment 396
Massachusetts Labor Commission 203
Massachusetts Peace Society 419
Massachusetts Public Service Commission 149, 172-73, 175, 177, 180, 182, 190-91, 195, 231, 287, 392, 613
Massachusetts Minimum Wage Commission 56
Massachusetts Railroad Commission 59, 68
"Massachusetts Substitute for Old Age Pensions" 216
Massachusetts Teachers Association 28
Mazzini, Giuseppe 613*
McCall, Samuel W. 596
McCarthy, Charles 4, 29, 288, 363, 380, 409, 644
McChord, Charles C. 106, 107*, 110, 122, 124, 133, 141, 186
McClure's Magazine 31, 51

McClure's Publishing Company 31, 137
McCormick, Cyrus H. 232, 601*
McCormick, Robert R. 577*
McCreary, Amy B. 37, 618
McCreary, William H. 37*
MacDonald, William J. 228*
Meeker, Royal 402*
Meier, Ed. 384
Melamed, Samuel Max 586*
Mellen, Charles S. 3, 13, 72, 123, 127-29, 133, 140-41, 143-46, 149, 178, 180, 190, 204, 224, 284
McElwain Company 137
McElwain, William H. 230
Mendes, Henry P. 602*, 677
Menominee Indians Reservation 23
Menorah Journal 193, 297, 398, 412, 416, 460, 599, 638
Menorah Movement 193, 297, 332, 357, 368, 370, 395, 398, 401, 460, 505
Meriwether, Walter 32*
Merrill, John F. A. 440*
Metropolitan Magazine 200
Meyer, Balthasar H. 244*
Meyer, Eugene Jr. 538*, 555, 622, 666
Meyer, Julius 65, 66*, 335, 466
Meyer, Martin A. 587*, 598, 609, 665, 675
Meyer, Walter E. 19*
MacFarland, Grenville S. 3, 53, 62, 172, 274, 277, 321
McGinty, George B. 331*
McGovern 383
Michigan Central Railroad 25
Middleton, George 45
Miller, Adolph C. 244*
Miller, Dickinson S. 57
Miller, Herbert A. 617*
Miller, L. C. 266*
Miller, S. F. 5
Miller-Tydings Act 217
Missouri, Kansas & Texas Railway Co. 5
Mitchel, John P. 547*, 651, 671
Mitchell-Inness, Alfred 261, 262*

Mitchell, Max 362*, 365, 366, 403
Mizrachi 323, 505, 510-13, 527, 557, 561, 569-70, 572, 624
MacLeod, Frederick J. 67, 90, 192
Montefiore, Francis Abraham 680*
Montefiore, Moses 680
Morawetz, Victor 236
Morgan, Anne 228*
Morgan, J. P. 3, 9, 25, 48, 50, 168, 171, 204, 228-30, 266, 267, 269, 310
Morgenthau, Henry Sr. 4, 302, 325, 336, 418, 425, 431, 434, 473, 496-97, 504, 542, 595, 605, 674
Morley, John 260
Morningstar, Joseph 272*
Morningstar, Joseph Jr. 272*
Morrison, Stuart D. B. 167, 168*
Morse, Charles W. 13
Moskowitz, Belle 651
Moskowitz, Henry 9, 27, 55, 81, 104, 168, 241, 307, 402, 650
Mossinsohn, Benzion 628*
Motzkin, Leo 487*, 513
Moyer, Charles H. 227*
McReynolds, James C. 35*, 39, 41, 42, 44, 53, 106, 112, 161, 180, 200, 221, 223-24, 231, 247, 259, 283, 288, 290
McSween, Angus 467, 618, 619*
Muller vs. Oregon 237, 364
Mumford, Charles Carney 43*
Murchie, Guy 321
Murdock, Victor 237*
Murray, William F. 170
MacVeagh, I. Wayne 21, 57
Myers, George H. 239*

Nagel, Charles 42, 263, 334, 389
Nathan, Jacob 584
Nathan, Paul 235*, 398
National Association of Clothiers 57
National City Bank of New York 167
National Civic Federation 88
National Conference of Jewish Charities 340
National Conference of Mayors 348

National Conservation Association 7, 59-60, 67, 77
National Consumers' League 168, 364, 443
National Economic Association 109
National Economic League 281
National Jewish Relief Committee 362
National Municipal League 12
National Relief Committee 351, 365-66
National Single Tax League 133
National Voters' League 43, 81
Neall, Frank L. 193
Nebbia vs. New York 36
Negro Rights 297-98, 305
Neill, Charles P. 52
Nelson, Knute 29
Nerney, May Childs 297, 298*, 305
Newark (New Jersey) Evening News 60, 119
Newell, Frederick H. 50*
New England Association of Railroad Veterans 198
"New England Transportation Monopoly" 283
"New Haven—An Unregulated Monopoly" 129, 283
Newman, Oliver P. 130*
New Republic 208, 222, 599
Newspaper Enterprise Association 121, 157
Newton, Byron R. 44*, 62
New York Bureau of Municipal Research 153
New York Central Railroad 5
New York City Bank 267
New York City Board of Education 391
New York Evening Post 7, 66
New York Garment Workers Arbitration and Protocol 6, 9, 27-28, 57, 73-74, 81-82, 104-105, 208-209, 211-15, 401-402, 428-30, 524-25, 547, 562, 650-51
New York Kehillah 193
New York, New Haven & Hartford

Railroad, Boston & Maine Railroad, and subsidiary companies: LDB's fight against 3, 12-16, 20-21, 23-25, 49-50, 58, 66-68, 70-73, 106-109, 123-24, 127-30, 132-35, 141, 143, 145-46, 148-50, 153-54, 164, 171-73, 175, 177-81, 186, 188, 190-95, 204, 244-45, 264-66, 268-71, 274-77, 282-87, 306-307, 560, 590; financial affairs of 12-16, 21-25, 49-50, 54-55, 58-59, 66-67, 70-72, 78-79, 91-93, 107, 108, 149-49, 153-54, 164, 167, 172-73, 175, 177-79, 188, 191, 218, 267, 268-71, 282-83, 343-44, 346, 385-86, 560, 590; expenses for secret publicity 180-81, 182, 191, 225, 240; lack of safety on 3, 9, 106-107, 109-10, 122-23, 141, 186

New York Public Service Commission 384, 518

New York State Division of Industrial Relations 11

New York Stock Exchange 385

New York Times 32, 372

New York Times Annalist 202, *230*, 385

Nichols 565

Nicholson, Mrs. R. C. 369

Nims, Harry Dwight 119*

Nordau, Max 303*, 336, 341

Noyes, John H. 448

Noyes, Pierrepont B. 139, 448*

O'Donnell, William J. *10**

Office Committee *603*, *625*, *632*, *668*, *670*

Ogilby, Charles F. R. 444*

Ogilby, Remsen B. 444

O'Keefe 42

Old Dominion Copper Mining and Smelting Company 360

Oldfield, William A. 99, 111, 112, *126*

O'Leary, Michael A. 603*

Olsho, Sidney L. 389*

"On Maintaining Makers' Prices" 89

Oppenheim, Wilfred A. 350

Oppenheimer, Franz 193*, 517

"Opportunity in the Law" 682

Order of Brith Abraham 435-38, 574

Oregon Minimum Wage Case: see *Stettler vs. O'Hara*

O'Reilly, John B. 155*, 157

O'Reilly, Mary B. *155**, 157, 235

Osborn, William H. 190*

Oshkenaniew, Mitchell *23**

Other People's Money and How the Banker's Use It 49, 60, 146-47, 165, 168, 171, 179, 183, 187, 188-90, 195, 204-205, 207, 211, 216, 219-21, 232, 238, 272-73, 280, 284, 344, 440, 451

"Our Financial Oligarchy" 169, 187

Outlook 657

Owen, Robert Latham 115, 202*

Pacific & Eastern Railroad 16

Page, Thomas Nelson 17*

Paine, Horace W. *234**

Painter, Roy *55*, 56*

Pale of Settlement 157

Palestina Amt 452, 461, 472, 627

Palestine 117, 155-59, 186, 206, 226, 235-36, 312-13, 317-18, 336-37, 354-56, 372-73, 416-18, 421-25, 427-28, 452-53, 468-77, 492, 495-501, 513-17, 520-22, 580, 607, 609-11, 638-39, 674-75, 678-80

Palestine Agricultural Experiment Station 117

Palestine Economic Corporation 352

"Palestine & the Jewish Democracy" 657, 659

Palfrey, John G. 223

Palmer, A. Mitchell 347

Pam, Hugo 617*

Pam, Max *211**

Pan American Financial Conference 559

Parlin, Charles C. 116, 139

Pasha, Jemal 418, 431, 520

"Patriotism & Zionism" 371

Patten, Simon 208

Pennsylvania Railroad 15-16, 542

Penrose, Boies 347, 613*

People's League 29, 50-51
People's Lobby 29
People's Municipal-Ownership League 133
Percy, Eustace S. C. 20, 262, 344*
Perkins, George 4
Perlstein, Benjamin 295*, 298, 306, 350, 361, 365, 372, 374, 406, 410, 417, 426, 445, 449, 461, 466, 470-71, 477, 478-79, 494, 503, 522, 524, 525, 526, 530, 533, 536, 548, 551, 563, 569, 579, 584, 595, 598, 611, 625, 632, 635, 666
Peters, Andrew J. 218*
Pewsner, Samuel J. 477*, 514
Peyser, Julius 574*, 579, 584
Phagan, Mary 373
Philadelphia North American 78, 113, 119, 444
Philipp, Emanuel Lorenz 409*
Philipson, David 310, 317*, 334, 370, 405, 415, 426, 430, 438, 441, 444, 464, 466, 674
Phillips, William 382*, 492, 610
Pierce, Dante M. 301*
Pinanski, Nathan 301, 302*
Pinchot-Ballinger Conservation Controversy 246, 394, 464
Pinchot, Gifford 7, 8, 18, 33, 59, 66, 77, 345, 467
Pinsker, Leo 156
Poale Zion 323, 330, 527, 529-30, 557, 564, 569, 667
Poland 369, 381, 431-32, 436, 456-57, 486
Pool, David deSola 450, 451*, 531, 602, 663
Poole, Ernest 233
Portenar, Abraham J. 10, 11*
Porter, George F. 75*
Pound, Roscoe 13, 18, 50, 109, 134, 135, 209, 281, 287, 373, 382
Prescott 565
"Price Fixing and Monopoly" 101
Price, George M. 74
Price Maintenance of Trademarked Goods and Trade Associations 31-

32, 89-90, 93-97, 99-103, 105, 111-13, 118-22, 125-27, 131-34, 138-39, 146-47, 152, 169-70, 173-74, 216-18, 225-27, 434, 446-48, 539-40, 559-60, 592, 618-19
Proctor, Charles W. 172, 173*
Progressive Party 4, 33
Promboin, Jacob 485
Protocol: see New York Garment Workers Arbitration and Protocol
Prouty, Charles A. 21, 47, 66*, 70, 76, 108, 123-24, 133, 136, 164, 177, 181, 194, 218, 223, 245, 287, 410, 439
Prouty, W. 76*
Provisional Executive Committee for General Zionist Affairs 291, 293, 295-96, 298, 302-303, 313, 317, 320, 322-29, 332, 351-54, 356, 359, 365, 367, 372, 376, 394, 400, 408, 416, 421-25, 433, 445, 448-49, 452, 461-62, 468-84, 486-88, 490, 496-501, 507-508, 510-13, 517, 521-22, 526-34, 537, 544-45, 547-50, 551-54, 556-58, 561-75, 579-90, 595-600, 603-10, 614, 623-25, 649, 667-68, 670, 678-80
Prussian, Aaron 338*
Public, The 104
Public Franchise League 75, 129, 133, 191, 276, 278, 287, 613
Public Service Commission of New Hampshire 24, 49
Public Service Commission of Wisconsin 46
Pujo, Arsene P. 49*
Pujo Committee 48, 165, 169, 184, 187
Pujo Investigation 84
Pullman, George M. 25*
Pullman, Raymond W. 45, 80

Radical Zionist Party 519
Raffalowich, S. 496
Railroad Conference Commission 156
Railroad Securities Bill 284
Railroad Securities Commission 26
Railway Age Gazette 50
Railway Business Association 224

Randall, Samuel *348**
Ratshesky, Abraham C. 368*
Raushenbush, Elizabeth B. 100, 111
Reading Railroad 182
Ream, Norman B. 268*
Redfield, William Cox *41*, 42, 44, *73*, *94, 102, 112, 211*, 581
Remick, James W. *156*
Ressler, Roy E. *109**
Retail Dealers' Association 96
Review of Reviews 139
Richard, Livy S. *79*, 121
Richards, Bernard G. *22*, 358, 409, *604, 634*, 636, 651-52, 681
Richards, James L. 166, 204, 245, 265, 276, *277, 282, 285*
Ricker, E. P. 179*
Riggs National Bank of Washington 509
Right Relationship League, Inc. 214
Riley, Thomas P. 321*
"Road to Social Efficiency" 390, 489
Robbins, Edward Denmore *175**
Robison, Louis 579
Rockefeller, John D. 30, 48, 433
Roe, Gilbert E. 145*, 150, 154, *301*
Rogers, Walter S. 21*, 184
Roosevelt, Franklin D. 30, 84, 106, 117, 119, 296, 382, 586, 601, 623
Roosevelt, Theodore 96, 107, 209, 222, 440, 638, 676
Root, Elihu 420, 493
Roseman, Max *659*, 661*
Rosenbaum, Solomon G. *590*, 591*
Rosenberg, A. *669**, 670
Rosenblatt, Bernard A. *150, 186*, 377, 454, *522*, 621
Rosenblatt, Gertrude G. 463*
Rosenbush, Al. A. 403
Rosensohn, Samuel J. 651*
Rosenwald, J. 368, 376, 421, 514, 530
Ross, Edward A. 331, 507
Rothschild, Baron 477
Rothschild, Edmond 499*, 622
Rothschild, Evelina 680*
Rothschild, Ferdinand J. 680
Rothschild, Jerome J. 389*

Rubin, David 358*, *381, 395, 427*, 459-60, *528*, 584
Rubinoff, Jacob 389*
Rublee, George 183, *216*, 217, *226*, 236, *260, 320*, 383, 394, 434, 440, 464, *467, 496, 502*, 523, *539*, 581, 592, *682*
Rudy, Jacob M. *62, 63**, *82*
Rumely, Edward A. *586**
Ruppin, Arthur *303**, 312, 314, *317*, 324-26, 336, 425, 434, *452*, 461, 466, 468-69, *470*, 473-74, 476, 497, 508, 514, 550, 589, 609, 628
Russell, Joseph B. 171*, 245
Rutenberg, Pinhas 558*, 565, 575, 580, 620-21
Ryan, Agnes E. *597**

Sachs, Alexander 351*, *459*, 517
Sachs, Henry 585, 586*
Saffro, Joseph *375**
Sale, Samuel 370*
Salzberger 574
Sampter, Jessie 463*, 531, 662
Sanders, Fielder *181**
Sanders, Leon *389**, 438, 572-73, 580, 585, 652, 655
Sanders, Thomas 205*
"Santogen": see *Bauer vs. O'Donnell*
Sapinsky, Alvin T. *656*, 657*
Saturday Evening Post 243
Savings Bank Life Insurance 8, 411, 457-58
Schaff, Charles E. *5**
Schapiro, Jacob S. 645*
Schatz, Boris 513
Schechter, Solomon 22
Schiff, Jacob H. *207*, 325, 340, 477, 481, 514, 537, 572, 574, 583, 621
Schiff, Joseph 590
Schiff, Nathan 421
Schneeberg, Mr. 531
Schneiderman, Harry *544**
Schneiderman, Rose *669*, 670*
Schulman, Samuel 658*
Schurman, Jacob G. 457*
Schwab, Charles M. 310

Scott, Frank 222
Scripps, Edward W. 307
Scripps-McRea Newspapers 119, 157
S. D. Warren & Co. 289
Seamen's Bill 464
Segal, Hyman R. 586*
Seligman, E. R. A. 209
Seligsberg, Alice L. 463*, 662
Senate Committee on Interstate Commerce: Louis D. Brandeis' Testimony Before 12, 27
Senior, Max 439*, 444, 464, 466, 666
"Serve One Master Only" 247
Shaw, Arch W. 133, 134*
Shaw, George Bernard 200
Shekel Collection 461
Shekel Payment 147, 515, 521, 546, 569-70, 606, 627
Shekels 325, 498
Sherman Antitrust Law 41, 93, 97, 220, 290
Shohan, Joseph 77*
Shulman, Max 352*, 377, 407, 462, 474, 576, 585, 599, 603, 620, 643, 648, 658,
Sicher, Dudley E. 86, 87*
Sidney, Frederic H. 198*
Siegel, Henry 121*
Simons, Leon 517, 664
Sims, Thetus W. 229*
Skeffington, Henry J. 129
Slaton, John M. 373*
Sliding Scale Principle 166, 276-80, 375-76, 509-10
Small, Maynard & Co. 232, 259, 263
Smith, Dix H. 209, 210*
Smith Immigration Bill 389
Smith, Joseph R. 243*
Smythe, William E. 31, 559, 592
Sokolow, Nahum 22*, 65, 158, 324, 353, 494, 497, 561, 589
Solis-Cohen, Emily 389*, 395, 416
Solis-Cohen, Solomon 65*
"The Solution of the Trust Problem: a Program" 102, 195, 219
Sonnichsen, Albert 139*
Sons of Zion 526

Southern Pacific Railroad 182, 207
Spreckels, Rudolph 44, 489
Speed, James 231
Speyer, James 268*
Spingarn, Joel E. 645*
Spring-Rice, Cecil A. 555*
Squires, Fred D. L. 82, 83*
Stalin, Joseph 117
Standard Company 523
Standard Oil Co. 103, 120, 210, 373
Stanley, Augustus O. 25, 311
Steed, R. E. 166*
Steffens, Lincoln 87-88, 98, 104
Stern, David 45, 46*
Stetson, Cushing 629*
Stettler vs. O'Hara 364, 381, 392, 444, 683
Stevens, Earnest R. 396*
Stevens, John F. 16*
Stevens, Raymond B. 84*, 123, 217, 224, 227, 246, 320, 340, 345, 347, 434, 441, 447, 467-68, 496, 539, 581, 592, 618
Stevens, William H. S. 11, 12*
Stewart, John Appleton 16, 17*
Stillman, James 268*
Stimson, Henry L. 134-35, 209, 286
St. John, Vincent 98, 99*, 104
St. Louis & Southwestern Railroad 19
Stokes, Frederick 233, 238
Stone, Edward E. 172, 192
Stone, Galen L. 204*
Storey, Moorfield 63
Straight, Willard D. 47, 222*
Straus, Nathan 299*, 300, 302, 313, 361, 421, 424, 426, 473-74, 481, 504, 529, 531, 577, 583, 589, 651, 666, 679
Straus, Nellie 662
Straus, Oscar S. 313*, 341, 362
Strauss Magazine 48
Strecker, Charles B. 62* 402, 406
Stricker, Robert 519*
Strull, Charles 353
Sughrue, Michael J. 162, 201
Sullivan Gas Bill 276-77, 509
Sullivan, John A. 190, 200

Sullivan, Lewis R. 280*
Sullivan, Mark *33*, *83*, *176*, 222, 243
Sulzberger, Cyrus L. 340*
Sulzberger, Hays 340
Survey 433
Sutherland, George *632*
Swan, Mary A. *36**
Sweney, Fred W. 107*
Swift, Henry W. 86*
Syrkin, Nachman 329*, 330
System 134, 392
Szold, Henrietta 300*, 323, 344, 361, 365, *463*, 467, 470-71, 480, *495*, 662

Taft, William H. 30, 42-43, 183, 389, 464, 491
Taussig, Charles W. 509*
Taussig, Frank W. 110, *523*
Taussig, William 127, 509
Taylor, Frederick W. 240, 618
Taylor, William 140*, 154
Thayer, James B. 209, 240
Thompson, Huston 601*
Thompson, William H. 673*
Thomson, Elihu *204*, 205*
Thomson-Houston Electrical Company 205
Thorne, Clifford 164, 202*, 518
Thornton, Jesse E. *56**
Todd, George C. *171**, *592*
Torrey, Mr. 223
Tosdal, H. R. 523
Tousley, E. M. *215**
Towne, Henry R. *152**
Trade Associations: see Price Maintenance of Trademarked Goods and Trade Associations
Trauerman, M. R. *273**
Treaty of Berlin 304, 404
"True Americanism" 540
Truman, Harry 601, 623
Trumbull, Frank *5**
Tschlenow, Jehial 353*, 494, 497, *520*, 561, 589
Tucker, William A. 38
Tumulty, Joseph P. 77*, 420
Tupper, Frederic A. *28**

Turkish Empire 156, 158-59, 312, 336, 345, 356, 404, 417-18, 431-32, 470, 495-501, 513-14, 517, 520, 603-604
"Twin Evils of Literacy Test" 506
Twombly, E. J. 73*
Typographical Union 10

Uganda 329
Underwood, Charles 196
Underwood, Oscar W. *34**, *83*
Underwood-Simmons tariff 169, 196, 221, 263
Union Pacific Railroad 182, 207
United Press 76
United Shoe Machinery Company 42, 224, 369, 592-95
United States Attorney General 41; see also McReynolds, James C., Gregory, Thomas W., and United States Department of Justice
United States Bureau of Corporations 94, 210, 259, 523
United States Bureau of Labor 9, 55, 208, 213
United States Bureau of Labor Statistics *136*, 402
United States Bureau of Standards 219
United States Commission on Industrial Relations 30, 74, 76, 87, 89, 95, 97, 104, 214, 228, 237, 239, 282, 407, 433
United States Department of Agriculture 137
United States Department of Commerce 41, 103, 210, 211; see also Redfield, William C.
United States Department of Interior 7, 9, 40
United States Department of Justice 41, 84, 97, 111-12, 131, 133, 145, 154, 188, 210, 268, 277, 282, 286, 290, 560, 592-95
United States Department of Labor 73, 214
United States Department of the Navy 465, 492

United States Department of State 382, 465, 492, 524, 585, 609, 672

United States Department of the Treasury 40, 161, 162, 509; see also McAdoo, William G.

United States vs. Kellogg Toasted Corn Flake Company et al. 97, 112, 539-40

United States vs. Keystone Watch Case Company 539-40

United States vs. Louisville and Nashville Railroad Company 444

United States Steel Corporation 25, 310, 311, 545-46

United States Supreme Court 36, 42, 63, 99, 103, 111, 113, 120, 126, 182, 231, 288, 364, 381, 384, 392, 400, 420, 444, 539-40, 635, 683

United States Tariff Commission 84

U.S.S. Vulcan 421, 424, 431, 454, 467, 468-70, 474, 481-84, 487, 511, 514, 548, 583, 607

Unity Life Insurance Company 8

University Zionist Society 532, 537, 538, 555

Untermyer, Samuel *48**, *84*, 115, *168*, 184, *187*, *416*, 666

U'ren, William S. 223*

Valentine, Robert G. 203, 262, *396*

Van Camp, W. J. *74**

Van Hise, Charles R. 87, 95, 119

Van Valkenburg, Edwin A. *112*, 237, 618

Vick, Walker W. *17**

Vrooman, Carl 3, *410*

Vulcan: see *U.S.S. Vulcan*

Wahrheit 625

Wald, Lillian D. *407*, 432

Walpole Tire and Rubber Company 161

Walsh, David I. 80, 265, 392, *397*, 457, 597, 603, 611-13, *629*

Walsh, Frank P. 30*, 88, 95, 97, 380, 433

Walsh, John 601

Walton, John M. *159*, 160*, 179

Warburg, Felix M. 340*, 341, *397*, 504, 550, 574, *641*

Warburg, Otto 329*, *421*

Warburg, Paul M. 268*

War Labor Board 30

Warren, Charles *63**, *190*

Warren, John E. *289*

Washburn Bill 90-93

Washburn, Robert M. 59

Washington Herald 21

Washington Post 385

Watson, Mr. 222, 229, 234, 237

Watterson, Henry 334

Webb, A. L. 485

Weed, Charles F. *75*

Wehle, Harry 444

Wehle, Louis B. 42, 264, 354, **444**

Wehle, Oscar 369

Wehle, Otto 334, 444, 484

Weinstock, Harris 89*

Weiss, Julius 654*

Weissberg, Nat W. 353

Weizmann, Chaim 22, 303, *322*, 327*, *353*, *500*, *519*, 541, 586, 589, 600, **664**

Welliver, Judson C. 467

Wells, Henry G. 276-77, *278*, 280*

Wells, Herbert G. 304*

Wells, Philip P. 7, *146*

Wertheim, Maurice 367*, 393, **395**, 413, 416, 434, 473, 514

Werdenbach, Ed. 272

Western Federation of Miners **227**

Weyl, Walter E. *208**, *401*

Wheeler, Harry A. 89*

Wheelwright, John T. 154*

"Where the Banker is Superfluous" 261

White, Clinton 192

White, Edward Douglass 42*, 399

White Goods Manufacturers **27**

White, Herbert 37, 271

White, Howard *25**, *242*

White, Norman 232, 263

Whitlock, Brand 229

Whitman, Charles S. 385*, 518

Whitman, William 34

Whitney, Dorothy 222
Whitridge, Frederick W. 261*
Whittier, C. A. 289*
Whittier, Edmund A. 434, 447
"Why I Am A Zionist" 308
Wickersham, George W. 39, 182
Wilcox, Delos F. 384*
Wilde 565
Wile, Mrs. F. W. 535, 536*
Wilensky, Max H. 348, 349*
Willard, Daniel 17, 264, 334
Willcox, Mary A. 52*
Williams, Arthur 215, 216*, 228
Williams, S. M. 85
Willis, Henry P. 115*
Wilson, James B. 209
Wilson, William B. 239*
Wilson, Woodrow 4, 8-9, 17-18, 27,
30-31, 36-38, 40-42, 44, 51, 56-58,
65, 67, 76, 77, 84, 87, 95-97, 103,
104, 106, 113, 116-17, 127, 130, 144,
147, 170, 173, 187, 190, 194, 196,
201, 206, 218-21, 223, 234-38, 286,
288, 290, 311, 317, 320, 338, 347,
350, 363, 371, 389, 394, 402, 420,
429, 464, 465, 467, 468, 506, 538,
581, 601, 610, 621, 623, 629, 633,
673, 683
Winchester Arms Company 132
Winslow, Charles H. 52, 55, 209*,
213, 261, 401
Winsor, Robert 259
Wise, Isaac M. 317
Wise, Otto I. 610, 622, 643*, 675
Wise, Stephen S. 296*, 298, 300, 308,
309, 314, 323, 351, 360, 362, 365,
374, 389, 401, 403, 415, 418, 426,
430, 439, 446, 454, 465, 471, 504,
508, 522, 531, 538, 571, 575, 576,
579, 597, 598, 601, 609, 614, 622,
643, 665, 668, 677, 679

Wolcott, Roger 264, 274
Wolffsohn, David 22, 328*
Wolfson, Harry A. 460*
Woman's Journal 597
Women's Trade Union League 55
Wood, L. Hollingsworth 419*
Woodruff, Clinton Rogers 12, 153
Woolley, Robert W. 312*
World Zionist Congress 147, 156
World Zionist Organization 23
Wyman, Bruce 225*, 240

Yahuda, Abraham S. E. 341*
Yellin, David 367*

Zimmern, Alfred 600*
Zion Association of Greater Boston
66, 77
Zionism & Jewish Affairs 22-23, 64-
65, 77-78, 141, 147-48, 158-59, 174-
75, 192-93, 226, 291-96, 298-303,
305-306, 308-320, 322-30, 332-36,
338-41, 344, 349-63, 365-69, 371-83,
386-89, 393-95, 397-410, 412-19,
421-28, 430-39, 441-46, 448-88, 490-
508, 510-39, 541-58, 560-92, 595-611,
613-17, 619-28, 630-68, 670-72, 674-
82
"Zionism & Patriotism" 356, 358, 412,
416, 492, 543, 637-38
Zionists 595
Zionists of America 291
Zionist Central Bureau 291, 630
Zionist Congress 158
Zionist Organization of America 528
Zionists of Philadelphia 333
Zola, Emile 374*
Zollschan, Ignatz 386
Zolotkoff, Leon 617*, 648, 650, 659
Zuckerman, Baruch 529, 530*